A History of Danish Literature

A History of Scandinavian Literatures

Sven H. Rossel, General Editor

VOLUME I

A History of Danish Literature

Edited by Sven H. Rossel

Published by
the University of
Nebraska Press,
Lincoln & London,
in cooperation
with The American-
Scandinavian
Foundation

Manufactured in the United
States of America
The paper in this book
meets the minimum
requirements of American
National Standard for
Information Sciences –
Permanence of Paper for
Printed Library Materials,
ANSI Z 39.48 – 1984
Library of Congress
Cataloging-in-
Publication Data
A History of Danish
literature / edited by Sven
H. Rossel. p.   cm. –
(A History of Scandinavian
literatures: v. 1) Includes
bibliographical references
and index.
ISBN 0-8032-3886-X (cl.:
alk. paper) 1. Danish
literature – History and
criticism. I. Rossel, Sven
Hakon. II. American-
Scandinavian Foundation.
III. Series.
PT7663.H57   1992
839.8'109 – dc20
91-46729 CIP

Contents

Preface

This book is part of a five-volume work on the histories of the Scandinavian literatures. Its first objective is to satisfy a deep need in Anglo-American scholarship. Various studies dealing with individual Scandinavian literatures have been published in English. Most of them, however, are outdated, out of print, or cover only limited chronological periods, and only few match contemporary expectations of stringent research; furthermore, most of these works have viewed their subject in isolation.

The five volumes of the present work attempt to view Danish, Faroese, Finnish, Icelandic, Norwegian, and Swedish literature as part of both a continuous interrelationship and world literature at large. For the first time, women's and children's literature have been included, and in addition to a comparatist approach, it has been a major editorial wish to incorporate social and cultural history in the discussion.

Almost fifty internationally recognized scholars from the United States, England, and Scandinavia have contributed to the project. It is aimed at students, comparatists, and a general readership interested in familiarizing themselves with a literary tradition that has produced fifteen Nobel laureates. Since the Middle Ages Scandinavian writers and works have been immensely influential in the development of world literature. They are being introduced and discussed here with the hope that an even larger public will find them attractive, exciting, and entertaining.

Acknowledgments

I would like to extend my thanks to the contributors to the volume, all of them outstanding, internationally recognized scholars from the United States, England, and Denmark; their cooperation and patience have been extraordinary. Special thanks go to Gabriele Bodenmüller (University of Washington) for providing computer expertise and to my colleagues and friends Niels Ingwersen (University of Wisconsin), Alan Bower (Thisted, Denmark), and David W. Colbert (Seattle) for editorial assistance. David also translated Chapters 2 and 10. The following colleagues have contributed invaluable assistance: Patricia L. Conroy (University of Washington) with a discussion of Faroese balladry in Chapter 8, Susan Brantly (University of Wisconsin) with the pages on Karen Blixen in Chapter 6, and Malan Marnsdóttir Simonsen (Tórshavn) with information about Faroese women writers in Chapter 9. A note of deep-felt appreciation to the various evaluators of the manuscript is also in order: Patricia L. Conroy, Bo Elbrønd-Bek (University of Wisconsin), Niels Ingwersen, James Massengale (University of California at Los Angeles), Harald S. Naess (University of Wisconsin), Maria Nikolajeva (University of Stockholm), Bertil Nolin (University of Gothenburg), and Mary Kay Norseng (University of California at Los Angeles).

As the general editor I would like to extend my appreciation to the cooperative efforts of the other volume editors: Patricia L. Conroy (Iceland), George C. Schoolfield (Finland), Harald S. Naess (Norway), and Lars G. Warme (Sweden).

It is with gratitude that I acknowledge the financial support received from the National Endowment for the Humanities.

Finally, without the wonderful support and patience of my wife, Dominika, and my daughter, Eva Maria, this volume would not have been possible.

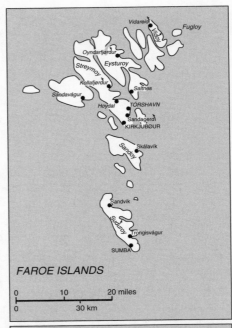

FAROE ISLANDS

```
0          10         20 miles
0              30 km
```

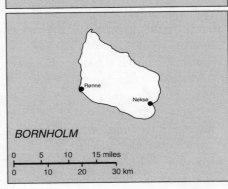

BORNHOLM

```
0     5     10    15 miles
0     10    20    30 km
```

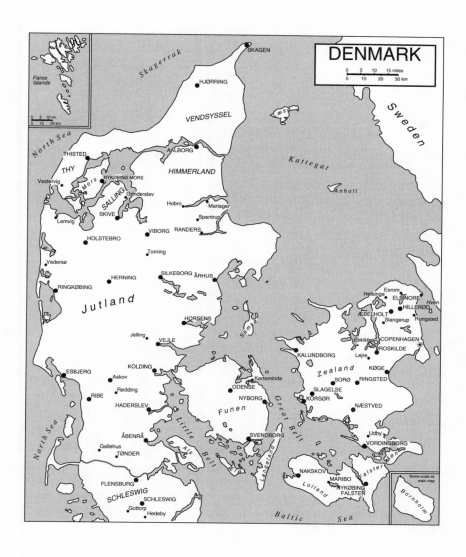

DENMARK

0   5   10   15 miles
0   10   20   30 km

Faroe
Islands

0   5   10 mi.
0   10   20 km

North Sea

Skagerrak

SKAGEN

HJØRRING

VENDSYSSEL

Sweden

ÆbS

Kattegat

Anholt

THISTED
THY
Vestervig
NYKØBING MORS
Mors
SALLING
Grinderslev
SKIVE
Lemvig

AALBORG

HIMMERLAND

Hobro
Mariager
Spentrup

VIBORG   RANDERS

HOLSTEBRO

Vedersø

Torning

Jutland

HERNING

RINGKØBING

SILKEBORG ÅRHUS

Samsø

Helsinge   Esrom
ÆBELHOLT   ELSINORE   Hven
HILLERØD
Slangerup   Rungsted
Eskildsø   COPENHAGEN
Lejre   ROSKILDE

HORSENS

Jelling
VEJLE

ESBJERG
Askov
Rødding
RIBE

KOLDING

HADERSLEV

Funen

ODENSE
NYBORG

Kerteminde

KALUNDBORG

Zealand   KØGE
SORØ   RINGSTED
SLAGELSE
KORSØR
NÆSTVED

Great Belt

ÅBENRÅ
Gallehus
TØNDER

Als

Little Belt

SVENDBORG

Langeland

Udby
VORDINGBORG

FLENSBURG
SCHLESWIG
SCHLESWIG
Gottorp   Hedeby

NAKSKOV
MARIBO
NYKØBING
FALSTER

Lolland

Falster

Baltic   Sea

Same scale as
main map

Bornholm

Introduction

Previous treatments of Danish literature in a foreign language have mainly consisted of brief, often rather superficial introductions that exclude women's and children's literature. Frequently, only certain periods were covered and rarely were attempts made to discuss the literary works in their social and historical context or to view them in a wider international perspective.

The present volume is unique in that it covers Danish literature from its beginnings to 1990), allowing ample space for each literary period and presenting the literary works in their interdependence with various cultural and ideological currents. As an innovation, separate and extensive discussions have been included on Faroese literature, children's literature, and women's literature. The reason for treating children's and women's literature in separate chapters is not based on any theory of exclusivity—many of the writers discussed here are also dealt with in other parts of the volume—but a desire to let the critical methods developed within these two areas come to the fore.

The theoretical diversity of Danish literary criticism is maintained in the present volume. Extrinsic as well as intrinsic approaches are incorporated (often within the very same chapter), ranging from philological scrutiny to essayistic discourse. In some chapters a sociological method dominates, in others that of intellectual history. Some contributors focus on the development of the genres, others on ideological changes. The inclusion of quotations varies from chapter to chapter (all translations were made by the contributors unless otherwise noted). I have not attempted to achieve stylistic homogeneity beyond providing general guidelines for format and the overall periodization, which for the sake of clarity and for pedagogical reasons remains traditional. It is my conviction, even at the risk of some unevenness, that methodological pluralism as well as free reign of the individual contributor's personal taste and style are virtues that not only enhance the general readability of the volume but also increase its scholarly value. This editorial policy both explains the different methods of interpretation and justifies the occasional discussion of the same author in different chapters.

Any one-volume treatment of a national literature as rich as Denmark's implies a strict, and often painful, process of selection. Again, it has been the task of the individual contributors to decide which authors and titles to include as well as how to structure their chapters. Although it has been general editorial policy not to succumb to a mere listing of names and titles, a volume of the present size will by its nature contain an abundance of names and titles. An exhaustive index, which also includes concepts and factual references, facilitates the use of the volume and enhances it as a reference work. With this aim a selected bibliography has been compiled which focuses on secondary literature in English. A map of Denmark including the most frequently mentioned place-names completes the volume.

The Middle Ages

David W. Colbert

1

The first four centuries A.D. are known in the North as the Roman Iron Age because of Roman influences in the archaeological record. Especially in the Danish islands the dead are found laid out before a rich otherworldly banquet, often served up in costly vessels of Roman bronze, silver, or glass, which have sometimes been signed by the artisan or original owner. A similar import of this period was the art of writing runes. The origin of the runic alphabet, called the *futhark* from its first six runes, is variously claimed as Greek, Latin, or Alpine. No single hypothesis can explain every detail; perhaps it made use of several alphabets (as did Gothic) or developed in several stages. But Classical or pre-Classical Latin is clearly the main source of the earliest futhark of twenty-four runes, which were given a new order and new names and augmented so as to complete the phonemic inventory of the Germanic language. The earliest inscriptions are from the third century A.D., suggesting the origin of the older futhark in the first two centuries A.D., probably in Denmark among those merchant chieftains whose grave goods attest to their Mediterranean connections.

This alphabet is found scratched or worked into weapons, jewelry, or everyday objects, usually simply the name of an artisan or owner, as on the imported Roman wares. The figures on the two golden drinking horns from Gallehus in South Jutland remain enigmatic, but around the lip of the smaller horn found in 1734 is clearly inscribed in runes: *ek hlewagastiR : holtijaR : horna : tawido* ("I Lee-Guest Holti's [offspring] made the horn"). Dating from about A.D. 400, the inscription is runologically and linguistically Nordic, but only barely so. It represents the Northwest Germanic dialect spoken by either Jutes or Angles, who at this very time were beginning to emigrate to the British island. If its alliteration is accidental, then the Tjurkö bracteate (a kind of coinlike pendant) is the earliest example, from around 500, of the alliterative long-line of Germanic poetry: *wurte runoR an walhakurne* ("[for Kunimundur Heldur] carved the runes on Celtic corn [=gold]"). Accent on the root syllable made alliteration the natural rhyme for Germanic languages, and accent rather than syllable count the natural metrical unit. Although end rhyme had replaced alliteration by the fourteenth century, accentual meter was to hold its own in Danish until the metrical reforms of the seventeenth century.

The Germanic Iron Age (400–750) remains a legendary era, in which for the first time we hear not only of Nordic tribes but of their kings. Danish legend relates how the Swedish king Ypper sent his son Dan to govern Zealand and the islands to its south, "which were all with one name called Withesleth [Wide Plain]." Here Dan founded the town of Lejre and ruled as petty king; here in the sixth century ruled the Skioldung dynasty of Danish "folk-kings" whose glory is recalled in the Old English epic *Beowulf*. As yet there was no Denmark. But according to the legend, the Jutes requested Dan's assistance in defending their southern border, thereupon acclaiming him their king and giving the kingdom his name. This legend may well contain a long mythic memory of the expansion of the kingdom of the Danes, most likely accomplished by the time of Godfred, King of the Danes (slain 810). In 808 he sought to strengthen the Danevirke earthworks in South Jutland, begun in 737, and founded the market town of Hedeby at its eastern end where the trade route across the isthmus between the North Sea and the Baltic intersected the Army Road to Viborg. The king was now the protector of trade, for the Viking Age (750–1050) brought with it a trade boom and the first market towns in Ribe and Hedeby. It is from the presence of "South-Danes" in the border marches of South Jutland that their kingdom got its name. According to the Englishman Wulfstan, sailing out of Hedeby in the 890s, Skåne, and what is probably Halland, also "belong to Denemearc." The addition of Bornholm and Blekinge by about 1050 established the borders of Denmark until 1658, although this kingdom was not always united under a single monarch. Thereafter, Skåne, Halland, and Blekinge came under Swedish rule.

Runic Literature
Their angular forms without horizontal strokes made the runic letters suitable for scratching into wood, which has rarely survived. Runic sticks were certainly used for accounts and correspondence in the Viking Age; many have been uncovered from medieval Bergen (in Norway), and one at least

from ninth-century Hedeby, though it remains inscrutable. Probably as a result of greatly increased mobility and trade, the Viking Age erected memorial runestones, or to put it differently, placed runic inscriptions on monoliths, often as part of a larger monument (*kumbl*) that might include a mound or "ship-setting." These stones could be the home or vessel of the dead but more commonly were memorials prominently placed along the highways. The two hundred Danish runestones from the Viking Age had their heyday in the period 950–1025. They use a short futhark of only sixteen runes, which seems to have originated in Denmark and given rise to more "shorthand" forms of the same alphabet in Sweden and Norway. The younger futhark is not always easy to decipher, since many of the runes represent several sounds each. But it was decidedly easier to use and to remember, especially with the aid of a runic verse such as the "Abecedarium Nordmannicum." Behind its hybrid Old Saxon text lies a (presumably Danish) verse that served as a mnemonic device:

Fe [wealth] is first, *ur* [aurochs] after,
  thurs [giant] the third letter,
as [god] is above it, *red* [riding] at last written,
  kaun [boil] thereupon clings.

The names of the runes seem to represent, however unsystematically, the sacral universe of the Germanic peoples. Two Swedish stones call the runes *raginaku[n]do,* "derived from the Powers," alluding to the mythological origin of the runes in the god Odin's sacrifice to himself on the gallows. This descent into shamanistic practice, a parallel to the myth of the origin of poetry as the mead of Odin, does not make the runes magical in themselves. It is rather in the spoken word that their true power lies. Thus every reference in Nordic literature to runic magic is matched by an identical function of verbal magic.

In a preliterate culture the power of the word derives from the experienced unity within acoustic space of the spoken word with its sense, the innate essence of the thing denoted. Thus language made of spirit-breath has the power to call things into being. This awesome power is evident in various ways among the runic inscriptions. The Bronze Age pictographs presumably functioned as "demonic doubles" of their models, and where the runes serve as ideograms for their names, they seem to recapture some of that simple mythic force. The power of the name over an evil spirit is demonstrated in a runic exorcism for bloodletting from an eleventh-century Canterbury manuscript, commanding "Gyril wound-spear" to depart once his name has been discovered and invoked. Several stones enjoin the dead to "make good use of the monument," apparently implying that he will find rest in his stone home and should not go spooking about.

Alphabetic writing can be comprehended in a fundamentally oral culture only by being referred back to sound, by reading aloud. "Whispering" seems to be the etymology of *rune*, and the inscriptions indeed state that the stone "lives" and the runes "speak." In this manner objects "speak" their names or that of their owner or fabricator in the older futhark, while the monoliths in the younger futhark "name" the deceased with the endurance of stone:

> the stone states here it long will stand,
> it will name Waltoki's cairn.

The deceased are named according to the following formula: *A* (and *B*) carved these runes (raised this monument) for *C*. If the inscription goes beyond the formulaic praise of "a very noble fellow," the dead are endowed with ideal virtues: courage, loyalty, and generosity. On occasion they are praised in true lapidary fashion and even in verse form. Æsbiorn Tofi's son

> did not run off at Uppsala,
> but fought the while he held a weapon.

This is a half-stanza in regular epic meter (*fornyrðislag*), the common Germanic verse form with its half-lines of two accentual feet each, joined in pairs by alliteration. In one instance the runes "live" in regular chant meter (*ljóðaháttr*), in which a long-line in (often shortened) epic meter is followed by a three-stress line with interior alliteration:

> these rune-staves for Thorgunn
> will live very long.

Regular verse forms are, however, relatively rare: the aforementioned half-stanza in chant meter plus nineteen long-lines in epic meter on Danish stones of the Viking Age. More frequently, rhythm and alliteration, combined with rhetorical figures like the litotes of "He died the most unchary of men," were used in loose, nonformalized patterns best characterized as folk poetry, composed for the immediate purpose. Thus although the runic literature (publ. 1941–42*)[1] is only marginally poetic, it employed elements of poetic style for its own artistic ends, and many memorial stones have a quiet dignity about them. At the same time, poetry itself (including what we think of as fiction) remained oral, without the least need of letters.

---

1. An asterisk refers to an anthologized source listed in the bibliography.

At his homestead in Jelling the founder of a new Jutland dynasty of kings, Gorm the Old (died ca. 940), raised a burial mound and runestone: "King Gorm made these monuments for Thyre his wife—Denmark's boot [remedy]." His son Harald Bluetooth (ca. 940–ca. 986) raised an even larger mound and stone opposite those of his parents and built extensions to the Danevirke, walls around Hedeby and Århus, the four circular fortresses now thought to have helped subdue the countryside, and the first cathedral at Roskilde. These royal works display a vigorous organizational ability of which Harald justly boasted on his stone at Jelling: "King Harald had these monuments made for Gorm his father and for Thyre his mother; that Harald who won for himself all Denmark, and Norway, and made the Danes Christian." Its three sides are splendidly carved in relief; above the mention of Norway a great beast is entwined in combat with a serpent, and above Denmark's baptismal certificate stands Christ with arms outspread among interlacing ribbons. Crown and Church here stood side by side in quelling the forces of chaos.

CHRISTIANIZATION AND THE LATIN MIDDLE AGES: 1100–1300

Saint Ansgar, who had followed the newly baptized King Harald Klak to Denmark in 826, stayed little longer than this imperially backed pretender to the Danish throne. But he did succeed in establishing churches at Hedeby and Ribe, no doubt mostly for foreign merchants, and in getting all of Scandinavia incorporated under the archbishopric of Hamburg-Bremen. When the monk Poppo a century later impressed King Harald Bluetooth with the power of the Christian god by undergoing ordeal by fire and the country was "made Christian" around 960, churches were still confined to market towns. The spread of churches and their new cult into the countryside was both gradual and peaceful. A century after the conversion Sven Estridsen (1047–74) had established regular bishoprics, and Adam of Bremen claims in *Gesta Hammaburgensis Ecclesiae Pontificum* (ca. 1070; publ. 1917; Eng. tr. *History of the Archbishops of Hamburg-Bremen,* 1959) that Skåne, Zealand, and Funen together boasted 550 churches. In spite of the organization from Hamburg-Bremen chronicled by Adam, even he had to admit that much of the actual missionary work was done by Englishmen. That was especially true after the conquest of England in 1013 by King Sven Forkbeard (ca. 986–1014), and during the reign of Knud the Great in both England (1016–35) and Denmark (1018–35). The earliest lives of the saints were thus written by English Benedictines in Odense and Ringsted, respectively, and the earliest annals were compiled in Lund from Anglo-Norman annals. Surely the new religion was more palatable when it came without ties to the Holy Roman Empire, and in 1104 the request of Erik the Good (1095–1103) for an independent Nordic church directly under Rome was granted when Lund was raised to an archbishopric.

Three of its early archbishops, Eskil (1137–77), Absalon (1177–1201), and Anders Sunesen (1201–22), were to have enormous influence on Danish life and letters. Eskil had studied under Saint Bernard of Clairvaux; some of their later correspondence has survived, and two chapters in the Cistercian *Exordium magnum* (publ. 1917–22*; Complete Foundations) are devoted to Eskil. This new order stressed a renewed ascetic intimacy with God through his mother Mary. Eskil brought Cistercians from Citeaux to Herrevad in Skåne, and from Clairvaux to Esrom on Zealand, from which eight additional foundations were made. One of them is related at greater length in the *Exordium monasterii Carae Insulae* (publ. 1917–22*; Foundation of Øm Monastery). Absalon had studied in Paris, and as bishop of Roskilde (1158–77) he summoned Saint Willelm from Paris to reform the Augustinian house on Eskilsø on Zealand, later moved to Æbelholt. These contemplative orders brought pen and parchment as well as horticulture to the country. In the 1220s the mendicant orders arrived in the market towns to beg and to preach. The Dominicans have left us their history (publ. 1917–22*), and as we shall see, the Franciscans were to become particularly active with literature in the vernacular.

Unlike the case in England and Iceland, there is a centuries-long lapse between the Latin and vernacular literatures of medieval Denmark, which makes a crude division between the Latin and vernacular Middle Ages around the year 1300 possible. In the earlier period there was generally no need to write in Danish, for what existed in oral form did not need to be written down, any more than a literate person needs to memorize reference works. What did require script also required a schooled scrivener, who had been trained in Latin composition but not in Danish, for the cathedral grammar schools taught letters and Latin together. Denmark's close proximity to cultural currents on the Continent long preserved the use of Latin as the natural medium for *literatura*, and as a result a vibrant oral tradition was long left intact for oral poetry and narrative. The notion of transcribing oral material was first applied when it was a question of the "letter" of the law; in the case of verse, ballads were first recorded purposefully after 1550, and the transcription, as opposed to the retelling of oral narrative was not practiced until a little over a century ago. From the Middle Ages comes merely a collection of proverbs, created only as a tool for Latin instruction. Thus in the twelfth and thirteenth centuries there is a Latin literature occasionally reflecting Danish oral poetry and narrative that would otherwise be lost. After 1300 these traditions, oral and literate, begin to merge to become Danish literature.

Legends of Danish Saints

Perhaps the earliest work penned in the North is the *Passio sancti Kanuti* (ca. 1095; Saint Knud's Passion), by an English monk at Odense. Saint Knud (1080–86) was as much a king as a martyr, and his legend combines the historical chronicle with the traditional legendary material: the life, passion, and posthumous miracles of the saint. This pattern has a precedent in England's legends of its martyr-kings, and it was another Englishman, Ælnoth from Canterbury, who elaborated on the *Passio* in 1122. Robert of Ely's legend of Knud Lavard, duke of Schleswig (ca. 1096–1131), written shortly after his murder, exists only as excerpts. In 1170, however, his son Valdemar the Great (1157–82) had Archbishop Eskil anoint and crown, for the first time in Denmark, his young son and successor, Knud IV (1182–1202). At the same time, Knud Lavard's canonization was celebrated by translating (i.e., transferring) his relics to the high altar in Ringsted Church, for which occasion offices for the saint's days of passion (i.e., death) and translation were compiled. The hymns, responses, antiphons, and a sequence of the office, in various accentuated meters, form a traditional legend, while the prose lessons comprise a continuing chronicle. Together with Ælnoth's legend of the earlier Knud, it confirms through the two Knuds the sacral role of the royal dynasty from Sven Estridsen to Valdemar the Great.

With the help of these legends (publ. 1908–12*) of martyred royalty, the monarchy now had an unassailable argument for its primacy which rested on the dualistic ideal mindset of literate Christian philosophy, evident in even the earliest of the Danish legends. The primitive Church had allegorically interpreted the passion of Christ in terms of the Old Testament, and King Knud's *Passio* remarks that his exile was like Joseph's, and his death, from a lance wound in the side, like Christ's. To this construal had been added a morally edifying or tropological interpretation adopted from classical philosophy: like Joseph, Knud "took council with Rebecca, that is, reasonable patience." The symbol here stands for an ideal abstraction that transcends ephemeral actuality, just as the word exists before and after it is written or read. Thus the saint is said to have valued this transitory world's fame as fluff, desiring to reach through martyrdom a certain and lasting kingdom. This interpretation is as un-Nordic as it is unhistorical, and outside the literate culture of the monasteries it is uncertain how widely such sentiments were accepted, in early medieval times at least. For the legends also show how much popular piety resided in the cult of relics, an expression of the preliterate, mythic mindset. As the monk Adam of Bremen noted, "'It is the way of barbarians to seek after a sign," a *jærtegn*, or "pure token," of divine power in return for loyal service. This power was made accessible through God's saints, who were bodily present in the relics as they spiritually stood before the holy throne, just as there is a spiritual power in the spoken word.

It is in the hagiography of the local saints that the emphasis lies on the miraculous. The murder of Saint Margareta of Roskilde was proved by fire coming from heaven, and her legend deals only with the translation of her relics. Those of Knud and of the missionary Saint Theodgar (Thøger) of Vestervig proved their sanctity through a standard trial by fire, while those of Abbot Willelm (Vilhelm) of Æbelholt and Blessed Nicolaus (Nils) of Århus were attended by miraculous lights. The miracles attributed to holy relics are principally faith healings, often well documented, particularly in the case of King Erik Plowpenny; for King Knud they were put into verse by the monk Arnfast, probably in the thirteenth century. They give ample witness to the popularity of pilgrimages to the holy shrines. Especially in the lives of the local saints we sense the effect of a popular audience on their legends, which often border on the fairy tale. Blessed Andreas (Anders) of Slagelse was best known for his miraculous sky-ride home from Jerusalem in a single day, probably a common pilgrim's tale, skin to the ride provided by mound folk in recent folk legends. And the skull of Pope Lucius I, on its way from Funen to Roskilde, is said to have rebuked a demon of the deep that was holding the ship and demanding sacrifice.

We therefore find already in the hagiography a variety of responses, from lay piety's native Germanic belief in miracles as hierophanies or immanent presence of divinity, through the homilist's dramatized dualism, to monastic piety's abstracted idealist presentation in terms of universal concepts like vices and virtues. This range corresponds to a change from an oral, through a rhetorical, toward a literate culture. Thus it was that Christianity, and the philosophical and literary heritage of classical antiquity with it, gained entrance into the traditional Germanic culture in Denmark.

Annals and Chronicles

Annals have their origin in short notices added to the appropriate year in the Easter tables governing the liturgical year. The earliest Danish example, the *Annales Colbazenses* (compiled 1130–70; publ. 1980*; Kolbatz Annals), has just this character, prefaced by a general world history from the Creation in

5154 B.C. The *Annales Valdemarii* (1185–1219; publ. 1980*; Annals of the Valdemars) is a set of dated historical notes independent of an Easter table, while in the *Annales Lundenses* (ca. 1250–1307; publ. 1980*; Lund Annals) the notices have become small articles taken from diverse sources. These early annals from chapter and chancelry were succeeded by monastic annals, from the Benedictines at Skovkloster near Næstved and at Essenbæk near Randers; from the Cistercians at Sorø and at Ryd near Flensburg came the *Chronica Sialandie* (1282–1307; publ. 1917–22*; Zealand Chronicles) and the *Annales Ryenses* (1260s–1288; publ. 1980*; Ryd Annals), respectively.

Also of simple origin are several lists of Danish monarchs, the earliest in the *Necrologium Lundensi* (1103–71; publ. 1917–22*; Lund Necrology), which was extended back to King Harald Klak (ca. 812–ca. 826), mentioned in Frankish annals under the date 826. It is this date, of the first Danish king to be baptized, that begins the *Chronicon Roskildense* (ca. 1138; publ. 1917–22*; Roskilde Chronicle). Between 826 and the next date mentioned (the death of Sven Estridsen in 1074) is a confused compilation of history taken from written sources including Adam of Bremen; without chronological benchmarks, persons and events from one source have become doublets of those from another. For the last two generations—that is, for the span of living memory—it is a more detailed chronicle, especially of the bishops of Roskilde. Though it was a church history, it tended toward a national chronicle, ending with an impassioned account of the civil war of the 1130s viewed from the losing side (that of King Niels [1104–34], Gregorian church reform, and the see of Roskilde, which had been passed over in favor of Lund as archbishopric). The chronicle was later continued during the reign of Valdemar II (1202–41), then from the viewpoint of the victorious monarchy.

The *Chronicon Lethrense* (publ. 1917–22*; Lejre Chronicle), which survives as an interpolation before the first Danish king to be mentioned (under the date 768) in the *Annales Lundenses*, could have been intended as a prologue to the *Chronicon Roskildense*, in that it relates the history of the kings at Lejre, referred to above, in prehistoric or legendary times. In doing so the author has had recourse to oral legends, "*antiquorum memoria*," accepted as history and presented in a brief and unadorned Latin. Many no doubt represent brief local legends from the Roskilde-Lejre vicinity. Narrated at greater length are the migratory legends of the dog-king Rakki and his successor Snio, the truthsayer who must announce Rakki's death in riddles and begins with a proverb, "Without a leader the bees get lost."

The Age of the Valdemars

Denmark was frequently without a leader in the first half of the twelfth century. Saint Knud Lavard's death in 1131 had been one of several among the many pretenders to the throne. After the Battle of Grathe Heath in 1157 his son Valdemar the Great emerged as sole survivor and began rebuilding the nation. He saw to it that his foster-father's son Absalon, newly returned from Paris, remained his chief counselor and was elected bishop of Roskilde the following year. After Archbishop Eskil, who favored an independent church on Gregorian lines, had gone into exile and retired to Clairvaux, the king also ensured Absalon's election as archbishop. Where Eskil had built the monasteries, Absalon and Valdemar jointly rebuilt the Danish fleet and fortresses to protect against the raids of the heathen Wends. In 1169 this Slavic people was defeated at Arkona on Rügen. This conquest, followed by those of Pomerania and Mecklenburg, began Denmark's Baltic empire and put it in direct competition with the Holy Roman Empire. The rivalry carried over into literature. Regard for favorable opinion abroad prompted Danish historians to continue to write in Latin, as hagiographers and annalists had done before them. They differ in this respect from learned Icelanders, who wrote in the vernacular for domestic consumption.

Sven Aggesen

The first of these historians is Sven Aggesen (ca. 1185), a royal retainer from a distinguished family and nephew of Archbishop Eskil. Sometime after 1185 he combined historical legends and more recent oral narratives in *Brevis historia regum Dacie* (publ. 1917–22*; Short History of the Kingdom of Denmark). His style is unpretentious, though with a commonplace of affected modesty he calls it "inelegant." His treatment is episodic, focusing among the legendary material on two legends of defense of the southern border. Offa the Angle has by this time become the Danish prince Uffi. Although hitherto mute for shame because two Danes had once slain a single Swede, he becomes both eloquent and overpowering against two champions for the (Holy) Roman Empire. This exemplum is followed by the glowing novella of Queen Thyre, "Denmark's adornment" (the *Danmarkar bot* of King Gorm's stone at Jelling). By means of her ingenuity and resourcefulness, the Danevirke is built in the face of the German threat. Sven also dwells on Saint Knud the King, passing over the other sons of Sven Estridsen with the excuse that "according to the illustrious Archbishop Absalon, my fellow [*contubernalis*] Saxo was then laboriously writing a comprehensive history of all those in an elegant style" (tr. Karsten Friis-Jensen).

Saxo Grammaticus

Saxo (ca. 1150–ca. 1220) was of noble family, a secretary (*clericus*) in the archepiscopal court; these terms do not clarify whether as a "tent-mate" he was ever a housecarl or whether as "clerk" he took holy orders. He must already have started his life's work, *Gesta Danorum* (publ. 1931; The Deeds of the Danes; Eng. tr. *The History of the Danes*, 1979–80; and *Danorum regum heroumque historia, books x–xvi*, 1980–81), when Sven Aggesen was writing about 1190, and finished it sometime after 1208. He benefited from the close cooperation of Church and Crown, and he shared Absalon's zeal to glorify Denmark's history as an incitement to and justification for its role as a Baltic power. As one who had studied in France during the twelfth-century renaissance of Classical Latin poets such as Virgil and Ovid, Saxo wished to show that Denmark could equal any accomplishment of the Roman Empire, ancient or modern. Thus, for instance, Frothi is made to rule over a northern empire rivaling that of Augustus when all the world was at peace at the birth of Christ.

The *Chronica Sialandie* refers to "Saxo, surnamed Longus, a clerk of astonishing and polished eloquence," and a later compendium calls him "an excellent Latinist [*grammaticus*]." It is thus that Saxo has been remembered by posterity, as much a stylist as a historian. By a remarkable stroke of luck, four leaves of his draft manuscript survived in a late medieval binding in the library in Angers, France, and here we see Saxo refining his text by what often seem to be immaterial corrections aimed, for instance, at improving the form of prose rhythm known as *cursus*. His vocabulary is huge and shuns standard medieval Latin words like *episcopus* (bishop) in favor of antique models like *pontifex* (pontiff) or *antistes* (presiding priest). His stylistic refinement has not endeared him to posterity, and even fourteenth-century readers were baffled by his huge vocabulary and use of *prosimetrum* (alternating prose and verse). But an elevated subject demanded an elevated style, and Saxo certainly set out to speak well on behalf of his country. Judged by his own standards, he is a sterling exemplar of the twelfth-century renaissance, admired for the variety of his style by the great humanist Erasmus of Rotterdam.

This variety extends beyond vocabulary into passages that subordinate many predicates to a single period, frequently expressing stylistic variations of the same idea. They often seek out the significance of his narrative as a kind of commentary, in contrast to traditional oral narrative, which is both anonymous and objective not only in content but also in attitude. A passage from the story of Amleth—the source of Shakespeare's *Hamlet*—serves to illustrate:

> Fengi was inflamed with jealousy at his successes and determined to set a trap for his brother. A man of true worth is not safe even from his near relatives. Once given an opportunity to dispatch him, Fengi dyed his hand in blood to satisfy his black desires. Besides butchering his brother he added incest to fratricide by taking possession of his wife. Whoever commits himself to one crime soon finds himself sliding downhill toward the next; the first speeds on the second.
>
> (Tr. Peter Fischer)

A Danish compendium captures the literal meaning of this passage: "Afterward Feng killed Ørwendel out of jealousy and took his wife as his bride." Saxo has amplified an unadorned narrative of this sort first in terms of the abstract universals *incestus* and *parracidium* and then as a moral lesson in the form of several maxims. These variations of a single theme are akin to the historical, allegorical, and tropological levels of meaning as practiced in medieval allegoresis. Because Saxo's ideal mindset takes its departure not from concrete images but from abstract universals and refashions the narrative accordingly, those ideals insinuate themselves into the narration with all the craft of classical rhetoric. On a larger scale it has been held that Saxo ordered his material into sixteen books that illustrate these various ideals: Amleth, for instance, stands for the union of two of the cardinal virtues, *fortitudo* and *prudentia*.

Saxo's work is generally read today for the "fiction" in especially the first nine books, which cover legendary history before the conversion to Christianity. But for his contemporaries both history and story were called *historia*, in Danish *sagn* and *sage* ("statement, report"). The modern empirical historian prefers primary data to oral tradition with its lack of perspective, which is a product of continuous reinterpretation in the light of contemporary experience. For oral tradition the narrative has virtually the only available data, which to be handed on at all must be recreated afresh. Saxo simply reflects a mindset conditioned by countless generations of reliance on oral tradition when he gives greatest credence to oral sources, in particular to Absalon's "wondrous account as if it were some tuition from heaven."

The legendary origin of the Danes can serve as an example of how Saxo's generation has reinterpreted oral traditions in its own light. According to *De profectione Danorum in Hierosolymam* (publ. 1917–22*; The Journey of the Danes to Jerusalem), written by a Norwegian about 1200, Absalon's brother Esbern Snare urged Danish nobles to participate in the Third Crusade by citing the heroic conquests of former "Danes," the Lombards and the Normans. Saxo cites the Venerable Bede on the Angles and Paul the Deacon on the Lombards, but counters the Norman historian Dudo of Saint Quentin's derivation of the Danes from the Danaans (Greeks) and passes over in silence King Dan's descent from the Swedish king Ypper as recounted in the *Chronicon Lethrense*. The Danes were thus an indigenous population that had conquered and settled abroad and by implication ought to continue to do so—for instance, in their Baltic conquests under Absalon and the Valdemars. Saxo made full use of written sources but did not rely on them. He thus reversed the political allegiances of the *Chronicon Roskildense* so that Erik the Good is praised for his just administration. The long paragraph on Skiold's justice and generosity added into the margin of the Angers fragment is surely Saxo's own attempt at completing the portrait of the *rex justus* from whom the Danish kings (and kingship itself in skaldic verse, as Sven Aggesen had already noted) took the name of Skioldungs.

If antiquity did differ at all from contemporary times, it was in being exemplary. Today we view this feature as fictional, but it was a self-evident truth in an age that believed in the cosmic entropy of "this aging world," as mentioned in Sven Aggesen's preface. What nonverbal data there were only served to reinforce this notion of the gradual decline in things, for who but giants or men of preternatural strength could have constructed the megalithic dolmens and "giant's chambers" (*jættestuer*) that dot the Danish landscape? Saxo knew enough to distinguish truth from fable, of the sort that Norway's King Sverre is said to have called "lying sagas." So, too, recent oral tradition is able to distinguish the folktale from the legend (*sagn*), which is associated with known persons and is believed to be the truth. Saxo rejects only its more mythic aspects, including of course the heathen gods themselves, which are reduced from myth to legend according to the euhemeristic theory also propounded by the Icelandic historian Snorri Sturluson, who equated the Æsir with men from Asia, that is, Troy. Thus Saxo's heroes Høther and Hadding perform deeds attributed to the (false) gods Höð and Njörð in Snorri Sturluson's *Prose Edda*.

Oral legend is also located in historical time, measured not by the abstract dates of the annals, but by the rulers of the earth and the generations of men. Saxo, too, gives not a single date even in the historical portion but places events within the royal line of succession going back to Dan. In spite of his vastly different style, Saxo also preserves the form of oral narratives, with its adherence to the so-called epic laws; the plot is often made up of independent episodes each with its own ethos, so that heroic, marvelous, and romantic elements may occur in quick succession. Saxo also shows great relish in proverbs, riddles, and verbal contests, as in the tale of Amleth.

Saxo does differ from oral tradition in his lack of anonymity. Although he does not name himself, he puts in frequent first-person appearances, and tradition has remembered his name. The value judgments implicit in his ideal approach to his material are especially far removed from the traditional narrative objectivity of the *Chronicon Lethrense*, for instance. But this conscious authorship is focused primarily on Latin and exegesis, the stylistic achievement for which he was known to posterity as *grammaticus*; and his sense of authorship cannot be shown to extend beyond compiling the hitherto unparalleled "sequence of Denmark's history." His attitude toward the subject matter itself accorded, as mentioned, with that of the oral tradition from which he gathered so much. Where he added substantive detail, he was no doubt conscious only of recreating the *historia* as he supposed it ought to be related.

Saxo specifically claims to have followed epic verse assiduously, rendering one meter by another. Like Snorri Sturluson, he recognized the greater stability of verse in oral tradition and accorded it greater trustworthiness. Ulike Snorri, however, he uses the verse not as witness to his narrative, but only as dialogue within it, as in the Norse sagas of skalds and of ancient times. Saxo and these sagas probably represent independent elaborations of the brief stage directions and short legendary notices that must have accompanied the verse in oral tradition, rather than a narrative elaboration from the verse itself. Saxo also assimilated the verse to a tradition of Latin *prosimetrum*, except that his verse was the "utterance of antiquity" rather than the voice of the author. As a consequence he translated verse in popular rather than skaldic meters, supposedly recited by his Danish poet-heroes from the period before the first Christian mission.

Of the fifty poems in twenty-four quantitative Latin meters, only four stanzas correspond closely with verses found in the vernacular. Comparison shows that Saxo amplifies, generally at a ratio of two (usually longer) lines for one, as in his hexameter version of the "Lay of Biarki," where only the italicized words correspond to the fragment of the "Bjarkemál" that survives in Old Norse:

> *I do not* ask <*wake*> *you* to learn *to sport with* young
> *girls* and stroke their tender cheeks, *or* give
> a bride sweet kisses and squeeze her delicate breasts,

*drink*ing bright *wine* as you rub your hand on her smooth
thigh and cast your glance at her snow-white shoulders.
No, I rouse you to the bitter contests of Mars *<Hild>*.
We need to fight, not frolic in love. No part here
for nerveless languor. This moment calls us to conflict.
(Tr. Peter Fisher)

As with his prose, the verse is here amplified by rhetorical variation based on the epic parallel (the six variations on "converse with women") and epithet ("bright" wine) and is followed by abstract restatement and a hortative moral. Yet he does represent the content, if not the style, of the original. No translation can equal its original, and Saxo more than equals his. For his aim was not only to guarantee that his story was "a faithful image of the past," but in particular to demonstrate that the ancient Danes could vie with Rome in poetics as well as warfare by making Latin poesy out of the Danish. Seen from abroad, Saxo ranks among the great writers of the twelfth-century renaissance, and with him Denmark could take a place of honor in Latin Europe. At home he applied Latin culture and an ideal mindset to native traditions and values and indeed played no small part in bringing his country intellectually into the European community.

When Saxo refers to verses as "Danish," he means no more than that the poets composed them in what was still called the "Danish tongue." In his preface he acknowledges "the diligence of the men of Iceland" for "their store of historical treasures." Judging from such criteria as name forms and localizations, we may conclude that well over half of the legendary material is from West Nordic, probably Icelandic, sources. This material predominates not least because it is generally narrated at greater length, on its way to becoming what were known as sagas, whereas the Danish material (with notable exceptions) is largely derived from less artistic folk legends. Concerning Icelandic saga men, Saxo mentions a certain Arnold Icelander in Bishop Absalon's retinue in 1167, who excelled at narrating stories that the king asked to hear; and an Icelandic list indeed includes Arnhall Thorvaldsson as one of King Valdemar's skalds. But it is the material from Danish oral tradition which interests us here. It is important to remember that we possess creative literary versions of an oral tradition that we can know only by inference. No amount of skullduggery can recreate lost oral versions, even of the relatively stable verse. It is nevertheless possible to gather certain impressions of the "utterance of antiquity" from the pages of twelfth-century histories and chronicles.

Saxo makes brothers of Dan and Angul, and Old English poetry recalls the valorous deeds of its brother people. As early as the seventh century *Widsith* mentions Hrothgar and Hrothwulf and the war with Ingeld, as well as Offa the Angle. The great epic *Beowulf,* probably from the eighth century, is a more recent fabulation on what is obviously a well-established legendary cycle of the Skioldung dynasty of Danish kings, alluded to in several digressions: the eponymous King Skiold's origin and funeral, the feud with Ingeld, the feud between Hrothulf and Hrethric, and the fall of Heorot. Where *Beowulf* hints at an interfamily feud among the Skioldungs, the "Lay of Biarki" such as we have it in Saxo's Latin is formed instead as an exhortation by two champions to fight and fall faithfully beside their lord Rolf Kraki (=Hrothulf), greatest of the Skioldungs. As the impetuous Hialti and the staid Biarki taunt each other, they boast about prior exploits. Rolf's munificence and their scorn of death reinforce the retainers' faith: "Sweet it is to repay the gifts of our master." Even as Rolf is slain they fight to avenge his death, but after Biarki is wounded he asks to see Odin through the curved arm of Ruta, Biarki's second-sighted wife, vowing that if he sets eyes on the warrior god, Odin will not go unscathed from Lejre; the king's retainers thus prove to be more faithful than the god of victory.

The mutual duties of generosity and fidelity between lord and retainer were the heart of the code of the comitatus (retainer), mentioned as early as A.D. 98 by Tacitus in *Germania*. The *Vederlov* (ca. 1182; Law of the Housecarls) is cited by Saxo in connection with Knud the Great, to whom it is attributed. Saxo found its ideal of ancient simplicity and severity of discipline embodied in the poet-hero Starkather. This hero is of uncertain, even mythic, origin, and the kings he served were originally foes of the Skioldungs, the Heatho-Bards; the *Chronicon Lethrense* makes them into another dynasty of Danish kings and with Saxo records a Scanian localization for Starkather's duel with Angantir. This is strong circumstantial evidence that the poems and associated legends known to Saxo dealing with Starkather and Ingell are Danish. The first of them, the "Lay of Helga," upbraids the king's sister for an "ignoble passion" for a base goldsmith, who receives a shameful wound worse than death itself as his just desert. Against indulgence in love and finery, the poet commends to the girl a proper respect for her noble bloodline: "Let your flesh and blood keep its glory." This ethic, applied to the matrimonial sphere, is probably in imitation of the broader ethic applied to the duty of revenge in the next poem, the far grander "Lay of Ingell." Both poems are attributed to Starkather, express aristo-cratic kin ideals, are found only in Saxo, and clearly touched a central nerve with him in their reverence for the Spartan simplicity of the ancient heroes:

As furious pleasure catapults you along,
my distressed thoughts recall the shape
of a former time and tell me here is much
matter for grief. (Tr. Peter Fisher)

Ingell has accepted the daughter of his father's killer as a peace offering, as perhaps alluded to on the ninth-century Swedish Rök stone, and as related in *Beowulf*, how an old warrior would one day "with bitter words" incite In-gell to revenge. The "Lay of Ingell" has expanded its theme from the re-venge itself to the ancient virtues in general, quite possibly Saxo's own con-tribution, as he makes of it a Horatian ode in Sapphic strophes condemning the sort of introduction of Saxon luxuries in his own lifetime which he chronicles at the court of Sven Grathe (co-regent 1146–57).

Whereas love figures as a dissipation in the lays of Biarki and Helga, it be-comes an integral part of the heroic ethic in the "Lay of Hagbarth," a *pros-imetrum* courtship tale. Here love comes into conflict with the code of re-venge: Signe secretly promises herself to Hagbarth, who has killed two of her brothers in revenge. Signe's love is "heroic" first of all in that she prefers the accomplished hero to a handsome atheling. When Hagbarth comes to her disguised as a shield-maiden, they seal their pact as an act of heroic will that is stronger than death. When Hagbarth is betrayed and seized by Signe's father, King Sigar, the hero proves it by having his cape hung in the gallows and watching in joy as Signe burns herself in her bower; he is now ready for death, knowing that both his revenge and his love have preceded him into the netherworld. Norwegian and Icelandic skalds have used Hag-barth's and Signe's names in kennings for gallows or noose, so the story must have been a familiar one as early as the ninth century. But like most of the "Lay of Biarki" it survives only because of Saxo, who localized it to the vicinity of Sigersted on Zealand.

The Jutland tale of Amleth presents a different sort of hero altogether, one who wreaks his long-planned revenge through cunning disguised as folly, with none of the tragic indecision of Shakespeare's Hamlet. Even folly follows a heroic code and must always speak a metaphorical truth, hidden sometimes in puns, sometimes in riddles. To the fatuous suggestion of those trying to test his wits that an oar is a knife and sand dunes are flour, Amleth replies that the "knife" has a large ham to cut and that the "flour" was milled and bleached by the waves. The first of these wordplays is based on a pun on Old Danish *lar* (thigh, shoal waters), which Saxo does not try to translate; the latter became a skaldic kenning (Amleth's flour = sand), which confirms that this story was known in the early eleventh century. A Jutland localization (Ammelhede) proves that it was current in Danish, where it seems to have developed in a more fantastic and romantic direction since then. The hero's role as truthsayer has attracted elements of a fairy tale concerning his marvelous sensitivity at the British court, for which he is rewarded with the hand of the princess, and he changes character again to the true fairy-tale hero, the child of fortune, as he is sent to woo the dangerous queen of Scotland. This episode in particular is yet another courtship tale that seems to have attracted fairy-tale motifs into the sterner tales of ancient heroes—without, however, adopting the freely fabulating fantasy of the folktales or "lying sagas" that must have existed in oral tradition by Saxo's time.

Anders Sunesen

The acknowledged Danish master of Latin verse is Anders Sunesen (1167–1228), cousin once removed of Absalon, and his successor in 1201 as archbishop of Lund. His poem on the seven sacraments is lost, but not the *Hexaëmeron* (publ. 1985; The Six-Day Work). Its 8,040 hexameters in twelve books were intended for the advanced student and an international audience, both to teach the correct classical pronunciation of Latin through the quantitative verse form and to sum up Scholastic dogmatic theology and thus obviate the danger of learning falsehood from classical poets. The work is formed as an allegorical interpretation of the biblical stories of the Creation (the six days of the title), Fall, and Redemption. This sort of allegoresis presents the mystery for the intellect to contemplate: just as Adam is a *typos* for Christ (Rom. 5:15), so Eve was a type for the Church, taken from Adam's side to be neither lord nor slave but helpmeet. The poetry of Anders Sunesen shows just how thoroughly Danish intellectuals had assimilated the leading currents of European culture by the end of the twelfth century.

The literature of the Latin Middle Ages was begun in Denmark about 1095 by hagiographers and analists of English extraction and was continued by native chroniclers recording native traditions in Latin letters. They were completely overshadowed after 1180 by the monumental works of Saxo and Anders Sunesen, spokesmen for an international European culture, including the twelfth-century renaissance of the culture of classical antiquity. In its spirit Saxo went so far as to refashion native traditions in the likeness of antiquity. But Denmark proved no rival to the Roman Empire, ancient or modern.

Political Poetry

After Saxo and Anders Sunesen, Latin is, as it were, penned in order to demonstrate Denmark's eclipse as a European power by the mercantile might of the Hansa and by feudal dissolution at the hands of the German princes. Valdemar II (1202–41) had extended Denmark's Baltic empire into much of northern Germany and in 1219 undertook a crusade to Estonia, carrying a crusaders' banner that was to become Denmark's flag; according to legend, it floated down from heaven at the Danish victory at Lydanis. But at the very height of his power the king and his son Valdemar were taken prisoner by Count Henrik of Schwerin while on a hunt on the island of Lyø in 1223. The "Planctus de captivitate regum Danorum" (publ. 1917–22*; Plaint on the Danish King's Capture) from the same year reflects this sudden shock and recalls Denmark's former greatness. The king and his son were eventually ransomed for a large sum, but his charismatic invincibility was gone, and his power was soon challenged south of the border. "At his death," says the *Annales Ryenses*, "the crown truly fell from the head of the Danes," as the kingdom's might was sapped by internal strife. Rivalry among pretenders to the throne resulted in the murder of Erik Plowpenny (1241–50). Friction between the king and nobles was allayed only briefly by the royal charter (*håndfæstning*) of 1282, Denmark's Magna Carta. Four years later King Erik Klipping (1259–86) was murdered while out hunting, for which deed Chamberlain Rane Jonsen, Lord Marshal Stig Andersen, and other nobles were banished. Friction between bishop and abbot in the 1260s is documented in the continuation of the *Exordium monasterii Carae Insulae*. Renewal of the Gregorian claim for an independent Church had led to Archbishop Jacob Erlandsen's imprisonment by King Christoffer I (1252–59), and in 1294 King Erik Menved (1286–1319) imprisoned Archbishop Jens Grand, who was moreover a close relative of Stig Andersen. *Jens Grands fængselskrønike* (The Chronicle of Jens Grand's Imprisonment) survives only in the Danish translation of Arild Huitfeldt's sixteenth-century chronicle. A worthy precursor to Leonora Christina, the author relates with indignation the calculated cruelty of the twenty months of the archbishop's captivity in Søborg Castle and his hair-raising escape with the aid of the cook.

By the end of Erik Menved's reign much of the country had been mortgaged abroad in return for currency, with which the king had sought to improve public relations through lavish chivalric festivals in northern Germany. As a consequence, a major mortgagee, Count Gert of Holstein, ruled as regent for eight years (1332–40) with little regard for traditional Danish privileges. The "Planctus de statu regni Danie" (1329; publ. 1917–22*; Plaint on the State of the Danish Kingdom) bewails the state of discord and violence, advocating penitence instead. But in the following year Count Gert was assassinated by Niels Ebbesen, as celebrated in a popular ballad, and King Valdemar Atterdag (1340–75) began the work of reconstruction.

THE VERNACULAR MIDDLE AGES: 1300–1530

Saxo excuses the Danes for not writing their history down because they previously knew no Latin. Recognizing the vast difference between runic inscriptions and *historia*, he and his contemporaries would no more have dreamed of writing their history in Danish than runemasters could have "used the very stones as their books" in any but the most figurative sense. The runes were still in use, once again largely on sundry objects such as church bells and baptismal fonts, but occasionally in manuscripts, where there was a short-lived attempt to introduce the runes for the vernacular, just as after the introduction of printing, gothic type was retained for Danish and roman type for Latin. To illustrate a section on runes in his grammatical treatise, the Icelander Ólaf Thórdarson, who had visited the court of Valdemar II around 1240, quoted a short phrase "compiled" by the king. It is an all-letter sentence containing the twenty-five runes of the medieval Danish futhark: "Burst man's hawk fled twin lair." This sounds like a riddle for "speech": the thought leaving the breast and mouth of a man with split lips. This riddle demonstrates once more the power of the spoken word behind the written, and the existence of various forms of oral traditional poetry in medieval Denmark, still a fundamentally oral society. Danish letters arose from purely practical rather than poetic ambitions and for a lay public that simply did not comprehend Latin.

Law

The earliest work penned in Danish of the medieval body of laws (publ. 1933–61*) was the *Sjællandske Kirkelov* (Church Law for Zealand), laid down in 1171 "because the law between bishop and yeoman was too harsh before" and revised a few years later as the *Skånske Kirkelov* (Church Law for Skåne). It was in the interest of laymen to keep this compromise between ancient custom and canon law intact in a language they could comprehend and verify, "so that yeomen could lawfully defend themselves and not have to tolerate injustice" (appendix to the *Skånske Kirkelov* from 1257). In contrast, the ancient *Vederlov*, revived by Archbishop Absalon and King Knud IV, was first codified in Latin by Sven Aggesen about 1182 (publ. 1917–22*), although it was eventually translated into Danish. Shortly before 1200, laymen began codifying the conventional laws of the three Danish "provinces," beginning with Zealand's *Arvebog og Orbodemål* (Hereditary and Criminal Law), set down by a provincial parliamentary commission. This work was in turn incorporated into the *Skånske Lov* (Law of Skåne) and into the so-called *Valdemars sjællandske Lov* (Valdemar's Law of Zealand) and *Eriks sjællandske Lov* (Erik's Law of Zealand). Only the *Jyske Lov* (Law of Jutland) ever gained royal assent, by Valdemar II in 1241. Its prologue especially is heavily influenced by canon law; according to the *Vita Gunneri* (publ. 1917–22*; Gunner's Life), it was written with the aid of Viborg's Bishop Gunner (1222–51), who had studied in Paris. Despite its Latin origins and use of abstract and borrowed words, it had achieved a remarkably pithy and elegant literary expression epitomized by its proverbial opening sentence: "A land shall be built on law." The laws themselves are considerably closer to the spoken language, in particular to an oral delivery relying on loose rhyme, alliteration, and rhythm, in the form of precedents generalized as a case ("If a man . . . ") followed by the rule of law (" . . . then he shall . . . "); addition of the grounds for a ruling is presumably a result of its literary codification. City and guild bylaws had their origin in the 1300s, with *Flensborg Stadsret* (Flensburg City Law), the first to be translated from Latin. Among Danish names in administrative records, the several lists in *Kong Valdemars Jordebog* (ca. 1231; publ. 1926–43; King Valdemar's Cadaster) are of particular interest for their place-names.

Popular Science

After law and administration, lay interest in medicinal herbs, gemstones, and cuisine demanded translations (1908–20*). Henrik Harpestreng (died 1244) was King Erik Plowpenny's personal physician and a canon at Roskilde, and is probably identical to Henricus Dacus, author of a Latin treatise on laxatives and a *Liber Herbarum* (publ. 1936; Book on Herbs). He is certainly the author of two *Urtebøger* (Herbals), which introduced medicine according to the school of Salerno. This school explained illness as an imbalance in the four cardinal humors: blood, phlegm, and yellow and black bile. In a manuscript penned about 1300 by the Sorø monk Knud Juul, the *Urtebøger* are followed by a *Stenbog* (Book on Gemstones) and a *Kogebog* (Cookbook), the latter containing the earliest recipes of French cuisine to be found anywhere. A *Lægebog* (Medical Treatise) attributed in part to Harpestreng and arranged from head to toe lies behind the heavily redacted texts in five manuscripts. Another manual of medicine from the early fifteenth century, from an unknown Latin source, is characterized by much folk medicine including the use of charms.

In the fourteenth century the monasteries began preparing works of more general interest to the laity. *Lucidarius* (publ. 1933*) is a translation of the German adaptation of several works of Honorius of Autun, perhaps at the Augustinian monastery at Vestervig in northern Jutland, sometime after the middle of the fourteenth century. The versified prologue begs divine aid for the author's tongue, that he might "write and teach" to the glory of God. This beginning seems to imply a reading before a popular audience. Its "fair knowledge" deals with the triune God, the symbolic meaning of the office of the mass, the Creation and Fall, and finally Doomsday. Despite some natural geography and astronomy in the third part, the book presents more popular theology than science, rather more so than its original. In doing so it also includes the earliest Danish versions of the Lord's Prayer, Credo, and Te Deum, as well as the earliest sermon, masterpieces of free Danish prose with a fine sense of beauty. Its author mentions the fair sound of the fiddle and the music of the spheres, and he certainly had both an ear for his mother tongue and a sound rhetorical training from the pulpit. Likewise in form of a dialogue, *Sydrak* (publ. 1921–32), from a Low German version of the *Livre de Sidrac*, is a later and inferior encyclopedia of especially social and moral questions. The popular geography of Asia that appears in *Lucidarius* is explored at greater length in *Mandevilles Rejse* (publ. 1882; Mandeville's Travels), as the imaginary English author continues his pilgrimage into the fabled realms of India and Cathay, in imitation of travelogues by thirteenth-century missionaries but with a rich admixture of wonders concocted from Pliny's *Naturalis historia* and fabulous bestiaries like the second-century Greek *Physiologus*. This medieval best seller from Liège was translated from Latin in 1434 or 1444 by Peter Hare and copied by Brother Olavus Jacobi (Ole Jacobsen) in 1459 at the behest of his Franciscan prior at Næstved. Mandeville was supposed to have returned by way of the kingdom of Prester John, and his satirically fabulous letter was eventually translated from Latin and printed in 1510 as *Historien om Jon Præst* (The Story of Prester John).

Religious Translations

The earliest surviving religious translation is a (late) thirteenth-century fragment of Saint Benedict's *Regula monachorum* (publ. 1931–37*; Monastic Rule). In the two surviving leaves the rule stipulates how it is to be read to the novice, who apparently could not yet be trusted to comprehend Latin. While the rule is thus in the vernacular, citations from Scripture are characteristically in Latin followed by a paraphrase. Latin remained a second language acquired by the clergy, by males only, and only gradually by those following secular careers. It was therefore natural that the first translations should be for the benefit not only of the layman or novice, but especially of women religious. In a manuscript from about 1300 Harpestreng's *Urtebøger* originally followed a collection of legends (publ. 1931–37*) that was probably identical to *Hellige Kvinder* (publ. 1859; Holy Women), a complete collection of fourteen legends in a later manuscript. Three of the four legendary fragments that may be traced to the fourteenth century are also about women.

Saint Birgitta of Vadstena, who gained universal fame with her *Revelationes* (Revelations), founded her order in 1370, three years before her death. Here monks and nuns were cloistered in the same houses, which became fertile soil for devotional literature in the vernacular. Fragments have survived of an independent Danish translation of her *Revelationes* and of instructions for a Brigittine convent (publ. 1931–37*). The *Mariager Legendehåndskrift* (publ. 1917–30; Mariager Legendary), compiled in 1488 by Brother Nicolai Magni for Sister Elizabeth Hermanni, contains lives of Saint Jerome and Catherine of Sienna, a confessor for each sex. Several other works betray their Brigittine origins by frequent Swedisms (the so-called Brigittine Danish). The first of these is *Sjælens Trøst* (ca. 1425; publ. 1937–52; The Soul's Comfort), derived through Swedish from a Low German tract; the Ten Commandments are here a doctrinal frame around a large collection of exempla. A dialogue between father and daughter concerning the cloistered life is a fragment of a similar frame, probably of Brigittine origin. Two collections of sermons also have a Swedish source.

Hellige Kvinder included a translation from Scripture, the passion according to Matthew with a few redactional changes. The earliest Bible translation proper, however, from the Vulgate as far as the Second Book of Kings, is from the late fifteenth century and probably from the Brigittine house at Mariager. Translations of the seven penitential psalms are found in another late fifteenth-century miscellany (publ. 1933*). *Hellige Kvinder* also included apocryphal legends, "Of Joachim and Anna and Mary," "The Birth of Our Lord," the Assumption of Mary, and a "Vision of Paul." The first derives from a translation that was also used for the chapbook *Jesu Barndoms Bog* (1508; The Childhood of Jesus), based on the apocryphal gospel known as Pseudo-Matthew and other sources. Besides the "Vision of Paul," visionary literature is represented by several fifteenth-century fragments, notably one leaf of a legend of Saint John and the Bridegroom (publ. 1931–37*) on the theme of a moment spent in heaven being equal to 250 years on earth.

Its rustic locale and naive style (the local priest looks up parish records in a "missal") seem to indicate that rather than being a translation of a Latin legend it is an oral variant of the folktale "Friends in Life and Death," adapted as a miracle for a legend of Saint John the Evangelist from some lost legendary.

In addition to Saint Birgitta's *Revelationes*, the category of mystical visions includes a work attributed to Saint Bernard of Clairvaux and translated in *Mariaklagen* (publ. 1929; The Lamentation of Mary). It survives in six leaves written in runic characters, apparently from a text in Latin letters. Written in the early fourteenth century in Skåne, this manuscript, together with the runic manuscript of the *Skånske Lov*, experimented with using runes for the vernacular, illustrating the mental gulf that still stood between Latin letters and vernacular speech. That a monk has nevertheless bridged this gap so well was probably made easier by the metaphorical aspects of mystic devotion, which gives flexibility to a concrete language unused to abstract concepts. Mystical literature is represented in the fifteenth century by a manuscript from the Augustinian monastery at Grinderslev in Salling (ca. 1500). Here are bound together translations of the dominican mystic Heinrich Suso's *Horologium Sapientiae* (ca. 1333; Little Book of External Wisdom), Thomas à Kempis's *De Imitatione Christi* (1441; Imitation of Christ), and two shorter works attributed to the Seraphic Doctor, the thirteenth-century Franciscan Bonaventura. Mystical devotion, which from the time of Saint Bernard had sought ever closer personal identification with Christ, in particular through the humble love of his mother, attained its most natural expression in the mother tongue among the dozen prayer books and six books of hours compiled from 1474 into the 1520s, mostly for ladies of the nobility, both religious and lay (publ. 1946–82*). Mystical metaphors have here been incorporated as a poetic element in the literary prose that, although translated (usually from Latin, occasionally from German or Swedish), nevertheless came from the heart.

Medieval translation practice varied extensively from overly literal imitation to broad paraphrase. Danish translations in particular disclose a culture groping, at times uncertainly, at times happily, from oral to literary means of expression. The biblical translations have a scrupulous slavishness, for instance toward Latin gerunds and ablative absolutes and in the still-current practice of using Latin inflectional endings for biblical names. For hymnody the few verse translations have chosen free paraphrase out of necessity, while the literal style of the prose is content to let the compound images of poetry stand, as in the prose translation of "Ave maris stella" from Karen Ludvigsdatter Rosenkrantz's book of hours (ca. 1500):

Ave maris stella,	Hail, star of the sea,
Dei mater alma	holy God's mother
Atque semper virgo,	and ever virgin,
Felix caeli porta.	blessed gate of heaven.

By contrast, Christian Pedersen's analytic and interpretive version (printed in 1514) is much closer to modern literary prose style:

> Hail Maria, Jesu Christi mild mother, who is called star of the sea, thou art a pure virgin forevermore and a gate by means of which sinful people shall enter into the heavenly paradise.

Here a humanist is at once thinking in linear, literary logic and in Danish, as few medieval writers were capable of doing, and none at any length. When the Latin did not come out right in Danish, the medieval author might opt for a freer paraphrase "as best befits our speech and is most pleasant to hear" (*Lucidarius*)—in other words, adapt it to oral usage. Thus the legends of the saints often achieve a more oral narration by substituting an additive style for a subordinating one. They frequently shorten their "readings" (*legendae*) to less than half of the original, even at the cost of coherence, retaining only the more memorable passages. In a manuscript culture each scribe is potentially his own editor, compiler, and translator. And as long as story was accepted as history, few authors of what we call fiction aspired to any more than that.

Proverbs

To all who spoke it, medieval Latin was a second language, and yet it came first as the written language. Latin and letters were taught together at the schools, where a favorite pedagogic device was the use of Latin proverbs, usually in leonine hexameters, for teaching two-thirds of the trivium—grammar and rhetoric—while rewarding the pupil with something sentious. Collections of such proverbs go back to the eleventh century and are coupled with vernacular glosses in a thirteenth-century French collection and in Danish. *Peder Låles ordsprog* (publ. 1979; Peder Låle's Proverbs), printed in 1506, had been associated since about 1440 with the name Petrus Laale, and a Swedish version from the first half of the fifteenth century seems to date the original Danish collection to the previous century. If Peder Nielsen Låle, subdeacon in the Odense diocese and messenger to the curia at Avignon in 1331–32, is its compiler, then the original four-fifths of the 1,204 proverbs in the printed edition date back to about 1340.

Its pedagogical purpose is explicit in the proverb "He scoops water with a sieve who learns without a book" (#454, also in a thirteenth-century Latin collection). In such cases the Danish is clearly a translation; in others the Latin is a translation, at times one of repeated translations, from the Danish, as in the proverb cited earlier translated in the *Chronicon Lethrense*: "When the leader is abroad, the bees get lost" (#146); in yet other instances a Latin proverb has been paired with a native Danish cognate. The collection in its several redactions follows an oral tradition and a learned tradition that were forever reformulating themselves and influencing each other, so that oral and literary origins are not sharply distinguished. All the same, it is possible to gauge the general effect of oral tradition on a proverb's style, evident in perhaps three-fourths of the 1,036 Danish proverbs. A spontaneous alliteration tends to predominate over the more contrived end rhyme, although this pattern is not necessarily a sign of antiquity. The subtle rhymes and loose meter border on folk verse, for formal patterns do not precede the proverb but are hit on in use. Unlike many of the Latin hexameters, the oral proverbs are full of pith, simple in syntax, and chary with words. Where they are not simple statements, they make much use of contrasts and parallels. Special types are the epigrammatic priamel and the Wellerism. The latter places a proverb or sentence within a dramatic and ironic context: "Sorrow ever comes and slakes another; yesterday my husband died, today I lost my needle" (#595).

The ironic distance in the Wellerism between proverb and context bears out the importance of the context for a proverb's meaning. Proverbial apothegms are in the minority, and many of them seem to have a legal context ("Better is mercy than right," #526) or are special types such as weather proverbs. The majority are metaphorical, that is, simple or even categorical statements ("It is silly drowning on dry land," #887) that are accorded truth value in some other context. The padded hexameters of Peder Låle and especially the annotations in Christian Pedersen's edition (Paris, 1515) often show a literary tendency toward abstractions. Metaphorical proverbs illustrate how truth is situational rather than abstract for the preliterate mind, however. Wellerisms, much more common in later tradition, seem to apply abstract truth within a situational context and chuckle at the discrepancy between the two. In the best of the proverbs we still feel the power of the metaphor to generalize on primal experience rather than to abstract from it, for "Sight is the mightiest saw" (#140) and "Experience is a good servant" (#582). Peder Låle thus epitomizes the strength of the oral bedrock under Danish men of letters, and perhaps in part because of the attention paid to them in the schools, proverbs were to prove an important source of inspiration for Danish medieval poets.

Didactic Verse

Three fragments in rhymed accentual four-stress couplets have survived from the first half of the fourteenth century. There are parts of two leaves of *Et gammeldansk Digt om Christi Opstandelse* (publ. 1955; An Old Danish Poem on Christ's Resurrection), a rhymed translation of the apocryphal Gospel of Nicodemus. Composed in Skåne shortly after 1300, and thus contemporary with the Swedish Euphemia romances, it shares some of their poetic diction even as prosaic style and simple rhymes predominate. Also from Skåne are a dozen lines of *Sjælens og Kroppens Trætte* (publ. 1931–37*; Dispute of Body and Soul), a translation of the *Visio Philiberti*. It begins like the "Vision of Paul" as the dreamer sees a soul departing from its body, but develops as a dispute in which soul and body berate each other for their common damnation, which, in the complete version printed in 1510, is described in dolorous detail. Forty-four lines of "Kvindelig Kyskhed" (publ. 1931–37*; Female Chastity) appear to have been translated after a lost German original.

Popular verse of a gnomic character first appears around 1300 as a nonce couplet that paraphrases several passages from the *Skånske Kirkelov* to the effect that the inhabitants of Skåne were not wont to tolerate injustice; similar verses are not uncommon in Swedish law codices. Gnomic verses of popular origin form just one of the ingredients in the curious menagerie that is *De gamle danske Dyrerim* (publ. 1908; The Old Danish Rhymed Bestiary). The surviving copy is apparently in the same hand as the preceding copies of *Mandevilles Rejse* and the *Sagnkrønike* (Legendary Chronicle). It was therefore copied, and perhaps compiled or composed, shortly after 1460 by Ole Jacobsen, a Franciscan friar at Næstved. At the core of this flock of verses are some in which each animal narrates its own nature and habits. Much of this is sheer booklore complete with Latin notes excerpted from two thirteenth-century encyclopedists, the German Dominican Albertus Magnus and the English Franciscan Bartholomeus Anglicus. The first sixty-three animals are birds and other winged creatures, followed by beasts until an even hundred is reached. The collection is prefaced by a dialogue between a youth and a young girl. The youth, disappointed in love, recommends the chaste life and learning about the nature of birds instead of patting some bitch on the thigh. The girl would like to dally a little first and wonders why God created her so, with a body so often at war with the soul. Echoing *Sjælens og Kroppens Trætte*, she wishes she were like the birds of the air and free of such cares, a sentiment that gives the youth the opportunity to introduce his aviary in order to demonstrate that nature also suffers affliction. The introduction is thus a theory of nature in popular form, demonstrating that nature is common to man and animal. It is this theme that binds the apparently disparate verses that follow.

For each bird there are sixteen or eighteen lines of verse, with fewer for the beasts. This is no parliament of fowls, for they do not meet as in Chaucer's *Parlement of Foules* to discuss love, or act out a political allegory as in the ballad "Ørnevisen" (Ballad of the Eagle). Here each bird and beast describes its own nature, as in the sixteenth-century Low German bird poems. Rather than theological lessons in the tradition of *Physiologus*, these animals impart an ethical wisdom; thus the heron:

> Fish in the water I can snare
> by wading in, though my legs be bare:
> upon my word I tell you plain,
> you will get nothing without pain.

A verse like this one has the form of the gnomic commonplaces that crop up in both ballads and lyrics. The birds are by no means restricted to lessons of affliction. The lark praises God with all its might, and so should all—though not in the same way as those hypocrites who will hear no laughter but bellow in church like oxen and must have fat cabbage and roast chicken for their sour stomachs. Satirical attacks, jests, and epigrams of this sort are not infrequently aimed at the clergy.

The section on the beasts, in Latin alphabetical order, resembles collections of oracular verses in the second person gathered under animal devices, in Danish in *Lycke-Bogen* (1562; Book of Fortune). Some attempt was made to preface these verses with the beast's first-person monologue and to annotate them in Latin, but this effort was soon abandoned. Conversely, some oracular and epigrammatic verses have made their way into the aviary; thus the heron continues with portents for a young gentleman:

> Without good counsel, marry not:
> with the white throw in your lot,
> she is as black as any troll,
> take her not into your control,
> with fifteen men she is not content,
> her love for you will soon be spent.

The connection between the natural and ethic halves of the gnomic commonplaces varies considerably, perhaps in a reflection of the free interplay between nature and aphorism in the work as a whole, despite the logic of the introduction. It is well that the author allowed himself this liberty, for it is a piebald collection of unexpected insight, sudden fancy, and irreverent wit that is not restrained by moral systems. No other Danish medieval work gets so close to the daily lives and language, the follies and foibles, the hopes and ambitions of ordinary people such as the pert young girl of the introduction.

Annals and Chronicles

The decline in Latin learning in the fourteenth century is frankly admitted by the author of the *Compendium Saxonis* (publ. 1917–22*; Saxo Compendium), who sought to put Saxo's work "in plain words," continuing it to 1342 in the co-called *Chronica Jutensis* (publ. 1917–22*; Jutland Chronicles). The continuation of the *Chronica Sialandie* to 1363 (publ. 1980*) has this same broad narrative form, and in the *Annales Scanici* (1316–89; publ. 1980*; Annals of Skåne) keeping annals in Latin died out altogether with a quote from Psalm 149: "Glory to God forever, who has given unexpected victory into a woman's hand, to wit 'kings in fetters and their nobles in manacles of iron.'" This woman was Margrete I (1387–97, regent 1375–1412), who was proclaimed the "empowered lady and master of the house" in Norway and Denmark on the death of her young son Oluf III (1375–87), who had inherited Norway from his father in 1380. Queen Margrete gained Sweden in 1389 through revolt and civil war, and from this victory arose the Kalmar Union, sealed in 1397 when Margrete's young great-nephew Erik of Pomerania (1396–1439) was elected king in all three realms. Sweden had its difficulties with the Union and left for good in 1523, but the dual monarchy Denmark-Norway, which included Iceland, the Faroe Islands, and Greenland, was to last until 1814. With the Union the Crown finally abandoned, as the last nation in western Europe, the practice of using Latin even for domestic documents.

Danish translations and compilations of historical interest frequently turn up in law codices and are clearly a product of a similar interest in public affairs among the aristocracy and affluent townspeople. The earliest is a list of succession from King Dan to Erik Menved in three redactions, one in the runic manuscript from about 1300 of the *Skånske Lov*. The same codex includes *Runekrøniken* (publ. 1887–1913*; Runic Chronicle), a list of monarchs in which some deed, taken from the *Annales Ryenses*, is mentioned for each. Of the *Annales Ryenses* themselves there are no fewer than three different translations (publ. 1887–1913*): a fourteenth-century version carried down to 1314 and two fifteenth-century versions. The first two follow the Latin in combining a numbered list of monarchs with dated annal entries from the emigration of the Lombards in 687 on, while the third has attempted a continuous narrative with only occasional dates and omission of all material not directly bearing on the history of the kingdom. Annals covering 1074 to 1255 are a translation from about 1400 of a lost Latin original; the little *Jysk årbog* (1410–72; publ. 1980*; Jutland Annals) is the first to have been kept in Danish.

There is little space in *Runekrøniken* or even in the continuous narrative of the third translation of the *Annales Ryenses* for anything more than brief objective narration. Localizations for Kings Rakke and Snio in the little *Kongetalskrønike* (publ. 1887–1913*; Succession Chronicle) nevertheless suggest at least the remains of heroic legends in fifteenth-century Jutland. The scenic structure of oral legend, with its dramatic encounters and direct speech, was used in the earliest translation of the *Annales Ryenses* for retelling the history of kings Rakke, Snio, Vermund, and Uffe from the *Chronicon Lethrense* and Sven Aggesen's *Brevis historia*. The second translation introduces an involved and well-told tale about the feud between Knud the Great and Earl Ulf, transferred to King Hardeknud as part of a religious legend that is connected with a holy spring struck at his death by Bishop Vilhelm of Roskilde. Two fifteenth-century prose chronicles were the first attempts to compile rather than to translate history in Danish, and yet they rarely go beyond a brief objective summary of their Latin sources. The rubric *Gesta Danorum pa dansk* (publ. 1887–1913*; The Deeds of the Danes in Danish) refers in the medieval manner to the subject matter, and not to Saxo's work, for it is based largely on the *Annales Lundenses* (including the *Chronicon Lethrense*), and translates its legends of Rakke and Snio and of Rød's visit to the giant Læ in his "mountain" on Læsø. These same legends are narrated vividly, with many additional scenes and better epic motivation, in the *Sagnkrønike*, originally sandwiched between *Mandevilles Rejse* and *De gamle danske Dyrerim* in Ole Jacobsen's manuscript. These short passages retold in dramatic narration, apparently inspired by various kinds of oral legends, represent Danish prose narrative literature in "saga" style. They may also have been inspired in part by exposure to the saga literature of Norway after the two kingdoms were united in 1380. In the course of the fifteenth century the highly developed vernacular literatures of Norway and Sweden were adapted and imitated for Danish use, introducing new genres into Danish literature: the rhymed chronicle, the romance, and perhaps also the troubadour lyric.

The Rhymed Chronicle

Like other annals and chronicles, *Den danske rimkrønike* (publ. 1958–61; The Danish Rhymed Chronicle) is a product of the monasteries. Its main sources are the *Compendium Saxonis* and its continuation, the *Chronica Jutensis*, as far as they go (1342), supplemented by various annals, especially the *Annales Ryenses* for the early portion and the continuation of the *Chronica Sialandie* until 1363. It accepts the succession according to Saxo from the *Compendium*, likewise without numbering the monarchs as in the lists of succession. But to this well-established chronicle form it adds narration in verse, a genre begun in French with Robert Wace's *Brut* (1155) as a historical parallel to the versified romance and introduced in Swedish with *Erikskrönikan* (1320s; Erik's Chronicle). The Danish chronicle is to some degree involved in a propaganda war with the continuation of *Erikskrönikan*, *Karlskrönikan* (Karl's Chronicle), and Swedish political songs, notably Bishop Thomas's "Frihetsvisan" (1439: Ballad of Freedom), which were directed against Danish monarchs. The tail rhyme (rime couée) sestet that appears in the last third of the Danish chronicle and in its preface was probably patterned after these songs, while the monologue form that is also found in *De gamle danske Dyrerim* was adopted by the Swedes for *Lilla rimkrönikan* (ca. 1450; Little Rhymed Chronicle). As one result of this war of words, the *Chronicon Lethrense*'s tale of the dog-king Rakke sent by Sweden to humiliate the Danes is labeled a Swedish fabrication. The chronicle's political tendency, pro-Union and anti-German, reflects a cooperation between monastery and monarchy similar to Saxo's, and its nine editions (1495–1613) demonstrate the coalition between king and commoner which was the strength of the new kingdoms in the sixteenth century. The Kalmar Union is eloquently defended in Queen Margrete's rhyme, beginning with a proverb from both Ecclesiastes (4:12) and Peder Låle (#890):

> The cord that has been twined from three,
> > so says the wise man truly,
> it will not break so readily
> > if it has been fashioned duly.

With Saxo the emigration of Danes to Lombardy, as mentioned by Paul the Deacon, is placed in Snio's reign and serves as a precedent for Denmark's colonial ventures.

Den danske rimkrønike is the only incunabulum in a Nordic tongue, printed in 1495. Two shorter and three longer manuscript fragments survive, covering almost the entire work, together with a complete Low German translation, which ends with Crown Prince Hans's betrothal in 1477. The last-mentioned translates a dedicatory preface, dating from 1460–74, to King Christian I (1448–81) and was presumably presented to him in his native Low German before the marriage in 1478, or at least before the king's death in 1481, both mentioned in the printed edition. Scholarship has concerned itself with the question of authorship much more than did the Cistercian monks at Sorø, who according to the preface had taken up the project of writing "the chronicle," much as Saxo had done in the same monastery several centuries earlier. A certain Danish manuscript preface makes "a brother in Sorø" its author, and the Low German gives his name as Nigels (Niels). What part he had in writing any or all of the 116 royal monologues remains uncertain. There is evidence in pleonastic and rhyme words for five different sections, but the corresponding differences in narrative style could just as well be due to different oral narrative models. Related to the problem of authorship is that of date. In view of its scope, the work could easily have taken a generation to complete. The "Danish chronicle" adduced by King Erik of Pomerania in 1439 could well be this work, in which case the last three monologues are later additions, just as the last was revised in 1477–78, again together with the preface in 1495, and augmented by King Hans's Chronicle for the 1533 edition. The various revisers all use the first person for the authorial commonplaces of their prefaces, and as long as the concept of authorship is this undifferentiated, we know only that the work issued from Sorø Monastery in 1477–78, perhaps written, perhaps only compiled, by a certain Brother Niels. In any case, it is more than we know for most medieval literature.

Each monarch steps forth and relates the events of his own reign, usually introducing them with a moral sentence, often quite out of character, by means of which the chronicle takes on the aspect of a mirror for kings, with examples for imitation or admonition. The events themselves are generally narrated in a stereotype "chronicle style," with formulas in a balladesque manner for royal election, legislation, taxation, armament, victory or defeat, natural death, and so on, and in the latter half exact dates in annal and (German) minstrel ballad style.

This chronicle style is used for narrating isolated events and predominates in the historical half of the chronicle, where the sources are more annalistic. In the earlier legendary portion, stories predominate over history, and so the style becomes more fluid, with three sections in particular standing out. The first is the legend of Amleth, which is prominent even in the *Compendium Saxonis*. The chronicle follows the tale closely, but with use of direct speech and a rapid prose narrative style, as in Amleth's test of wits:

> As we then came down to the strand
> we found a rudder on the sand.
> They said it was the largest knife
> that they had seen in all their life.
> I gave them right reply withal,

"The ham it goes with is hardly small."
Then we walked right down to the strand
and I took up some of the sand.
I asked my companions what it might be.
"Just flour," was what they answered me.
I thereupon answered them again,
"I think a windmill has ground this grain."

The first change of meter, from *knittel* couplets to septenary quatrains with crossed rhyme, occurs in a group of monologues that includes Saxo's series of courtship tales. This change could have been prompted by the metrically similar long couplet of the medieval ballads, which are often versified courtship tales, too. This portion of the chronicle also employs ballad diction and ballad commonplaces. The name Signild for Signe is balladesque and possibly shows acquaintance with the ballad of "Hagbard og Signe" (Hagbard and Signe). In particular, the tale of Oder and Syreth, who would not raise her eyes, is narrated very much in the style of a courtship ballad. Oder has repeatedly been repulsed by Syreth's modesty:

But late in the evening, darkness spread,
and Oder wished to go to bed.
He had her hold a lighted brand
that was burning down onto her hand.
She remained seated just as still
as if she had lost both sense and will.
He pitied her and said withal,
"Damsel, spare your fingers small
and look upon them graciously
if you will nowise look on me."
It was then she raised her eye,
her mood began to mollify,
she followed him to bed with speed,
of friends and family she gave no heed.

These tales of princesses also show an influence from the folktales that are suspected behind Saxo's rendition; here we can hear them in Danish, as when Syreth's father "has proclaimed across all lands" that whoever makes his daughter look at him shall have her in marriage. The tale of Torkil's visit to the realm of giants is perhaps the most successful narrative in the chronicle. There are ballad elements here, too, although its narrative quality is especially indebted to the sort of troll tale that was retold in prose in the

Sagnkrønike, which also includes the hero's escape by saying three truths to the giant:

> Then Torkil answered and spoke this saw,
>   "I will tell you on the level:
> a nastier nose I never saw
>   on either man or devil.
> I have never been any place a guest
>   of which I have not been fonder,
> and thus I hold that foot is best
>   that first can bear me yonder."

Here, too, the narrator has improved the epic structure of the tale by rearranging details.

Thus the best narrative portions of the *Den danske rimkrønike* are those in which the poet has drawn on the resources of oral poetry: ballad, legend, folktale, proverb, and possibly gnomic commonplace. The Low German preface includes a sestet in which the author regrets not being acquainted with foreign literatures:

> I have not drunk of France's wine,
> nor of that which grows by the Rhine,
>   and I regret it rather.
> But I must now put my mind at rest
> and rhyme and write in the tongue I know best,
>   as I learned from my mother and father.

It is characteristic for the Danish Middle Ages that the author does not even miss a deep draft from the cellars of classical antiquity.

Romances

Translations of French romances appear in Norway in 1226 and in Sweden in 1303, by which time every nation of western Christendom had its romances—except Denmark. Romance heroes were no doubt known by reputation, and the *Annales Lundenses* noted about King Godfred that he was the father of Ogier the Dane (Holger the Dane). An abridgment of the story of Alexander the Great, ultimately derived from a second-century Greek romance, forms a final admonitory exemplum in *Sjælens Trøst*. But the earliest trace of romances in Danish is a copy of *Ivan Løveridder* (publ. 1869–77*; Ivan, Knight of the Lion, after Chrétien de Troyes's *Yvain, ou Le Chevalier au lion*), a close translation of the Swedish verse romance, at the end of a manuscript from about 1450 containing the second translation of the *An-*

nales Ryenses, a book on gemstones, and *Hellige Kvinder.* Before this time Danish texts were essentially functional translations that were kept segregated in the manuscripts: history with provincial laws, and natural philosophy with theology and religion. This manuscript and Ole Jacobsen's attest to an eclectic literary interest presumably due to increased readership, especially among the aristocracy, as literary use of the vernacular grew after the Kalmar Union. Ballads had no doubt previously functioned to confirm chivalric ideals; now they were both supplemented and augmented by acquaintance with the romance literature of the other Nordic dialects.

By 1500 there was an entire romance manuscript (publ. 1869–77*). The first two and the last of its six romances are much freer translations from Swedish of all three Euphemia romances (named after Norway's Queen Euphemia): *Ivan Løveridder, Hertug Frederik af Normandi* (Duke Frederik of Normandy), and *Flores og Blanseflor* (the French *Floire et Blanseflor*). Not only has the translator used an idiomatic (Jutland) Danish, but agreements with the French originals against all other versions prove that he—or she— used a less abridged Swedish manuscript than those that survive. The closing verses of *Frederik* and *Flores* imply that the scribe, or else the translator (authorial, editorial, and scribal roles are not particularly distinct in a manuscript culture), is a woman.

Dværgekongen Lavrin (The Dwarf-King Laurin) is an abridged translation of the earlier, shorter version of the German *Laurin.* King Diderik and his champions tilt with the dwarf-king whose marvelous rose garden they have despoiled and then rescue the sister of one of those champions after Laurin has broken the truce by recourse to magic. The translator has left these two threads of Celtic faery even more loosely entwined, and the foreshortened conclusion is anticlimactic. *Persenober og Konstantianobis* (1484; Persenober and Constantianobis) retells in verse the same version of the French *Partonope de Blois* as does the Icelandic *Partalopa saga* (Eng. tr. 1983). The name forms seem especially to imply that its author has composed these verses from memory: the heroine (Marmoria in Icelandic) has assumed the name of her capital city, which in turn has become Constancia. The plot has a certain resemblance to the folktale "The Search for the Lost Husband," except that sexual roles are reversed in a courtly manner: the hero must not look on her for two years, and when he does so must win her love again by excelling in a tournament. A certain Jep Jensen "put in rhyme" the novella *Den kyske Dronning* (The Chaste Queen) in 1483. While the king is on a pilgrimage, the queen of Poland is falsely accused of adultery by the wicked steward Scares. When the king returns and repudiates her, her former foster son, now king of Bohemia, first tests her in monkish disguise as her confessor and then rescues her as her unknown champion by mortally wounding Scares in the joust. When the king later dies, the hero returns and is recognized by the queen's chemise, with which he had bound his jousting wound, and the two are married. The historical material seems to come from Kasimir the Great's Poland, much distorted by assimilation to a widespread tale type. Closest at hand is the novelistic ballad "Ravengaard og Memering" (Ravengaard and Memering), closest in details perhaps the English metrical romance *The Earl of Toulouse*, but the oedipal aspect like the Slavic locale are without parallel, and there is a suspicious lack of names in general. It would appear that Jep Jensen has written this original Danish romance freely from his own resources for an audience of listeners at a single sitting whom he addresses in the opening lines. The romance is accordingly punctuated by minstrel addresses, including the rhetorical question of the German sort: What did he do next? The narration is generally fluid, slowed only by frequent use of pleonastic half-line fillers of the type: that noble man, the maiden good. Despite these oral features, ballad style is wholly absent except where it is patterned after the Euphemia romances. Jep Jensen's romance is not oral poetry, but craft literacy, written for oral delivery from the page. In all this it is similar to *Persenober*, "composed in rhyme" the following year, perhaps by Jep Jensen as well.

The six romances in the manuscript are closely interrelated; all are in a pronounced Jutland dialect, and all but *Lavrin* are courtship tales in one form or another. *Lavrin* is a German marvel-tale of dwarf-kings like *Hertug Frederik*, just as *Persenober*, like *Flores*, is a French roman d'aventure set in the Levant. From the Arthurian *Ivan Løveridder*, a despoiled magic garden reappears in *Lavrin*; a broken taboo, exile, and rehabilitation in *Persenober*; and various forms of invisibility in *Frederik*, *Lavrin*, and *Persenober*.

Karl Magnus' Krønike (publ. 1960; The Chronicle of Charlemagne) is found together with various Low German works in a manuscript from Børglum Monastery dated 1480 (apparently from an original in the dialect of Skåne) and in a printed edition of 1509. Of special interest for a Danish public was the story of Holger the Dane, derived ultimately from the first song of *La Chevalerie Ogier* by Raimbert of Paris. Like its source, the Norwegian *Karlamagnús saga* (Eng. tr. *The Saga of Charlemagne*, 1975–80), the chronicle is in prose, containing all eight parts of the earlier redaction of the saga (which now lacks the eighth), but abridged to less than a third its length. The story line is intact, but descriptive and expository passages have been expunged; there is a blow-by-blow description of the battle scenes, while taunts and tirades are reduced to one-liners. This mode of translation much resembles that employed in the saints' legends, except that the adapter has maintained coherence throughout, even improving on those inconsistencies in his source stemming from the diverse French works, mostly chansons de geste, of which it is compiled. In removing all traces of the retarding elements of these oral epics, the Danish prose falls in line with oral prose narration, as when the dispute between the paladins at Roncesvals (corresponding to stanza 86 of the Old French *Chanson de Roland* [Song of Roland]) is captured in a few proverbial phrases: "Oliver answered, 'A man is not afraid because he scans the lumber pile [the revision of 1534: looks to his advantage]. I saw so many heathens that all the mountains were covered and all the valleys were filled, and you will now see grief come on our people because we are all too few against so large an army.' Roland answered, 'Woe worth a timid heart in a man's breast.'" This Danish Malory for the Matter of France is a chivalric thriller that was beloved both by the aristocratic churchman (Bishop Jakob Friis or Dean Niels Stygge) responsible for the Børglum manuscript and by the "common man" to whom Christian Pedersen recommended his edition of 1534, for whom it became a favorite chapbook, reprinted eighteen times (1572–1862).

Folk Songs and Lyrics
On the last leaf of the runic manuscript of the *Skånske Lov* (before 1309), after delineating the Dano-Swedish border and uttering a short prayer, the scribe Tuli has noted a melody and the words of its first half: "I dreamed me a dream last night, of silk and illustrious pall." This is most probably the opening long-line of a folk song. Its on-verse is a formula that recurs in about 1500 both in parody and as a ballad refrain. Two other medieval pentests present a dancing scene. Taken together, these medieval fragments in first-person narrative seem to give their accidental witness to an oral tradition of narrative lyrics that lived on in the Renaissance, for instance in "Ungersvends Drøm" (The Young Man's Dream). A short couplet has been used as a line filler in a decretal codex: "In the world I know a wife / I shall honor this lady's life." Some argue that it demonstrates the origin of troubadour lyric in Danish as far back as 1225–50. Its blatant Germanism implies a literary background in the *Minnesang*, but it is unlikely that the literary aspects of *Minnesang* could have made their way into oral tradition at this time. *De gamle danske Dyrerim* from ca. 1460 is familiar with the concept of the love song (*elskovsvise*) and with its formulaic diction; the rook even quotes four lines of a love song. Like both the gnomic commonplaces and the lyrical formulas common to romance, lyric, and ballad refrains, these lyrical fragments give accidental witness to an unpretentious love lyric that could have served as lyrical passages in narrative lyrics, as refrains for the bal-

lads, or as a genre in its own right. Whatever the case, this oral love lyric was a far cry from the full-fledged troubadour lyric that first appears after 1450 in whole texts, four of them Swedish and one Danish. Sweden already had literary songs like the "Frihetsvisan" (Ballad of Freedom) in more elaborate meters, a tradition that can be traced back to the late fourteenth century. Together the troubadour lyrics agree in their more elaborate stanzaic forms and rhyme patterns, in their minstrel address ("I will sing you a song . . . "), and in their use of acrostics or references thereto. The last-named makes it especially clear that they originated in written form, and later evidence suggests an epistolary function, quite like the German songs that they imitated.

Although of literary origin, troubadour lyrics have also become traditional songs, and three of the five stanzas of the Danish song, together with half of one of the Swedish lyrics, crop up eighty years later in a Renaissance manuscript, in company with a host of similar lyrics of presumably later origin. Very few love lyrics have survived in oral tradition much longer than this, however, in part because of their popular style, as in "Jeg ved så dejlig en urtegård" (I Know Where So Lovely a Garden Grows); in part aided by the broadside press, as in "Nonnens Klage" (The Nun's Complaint). The troubadour lyric was conceived and passed on through written form and consequently survives in whole texts and in great numbers in the ballad manuscripts from the Renaissance.

The lone medieval Danish troubadour lyric, "Ret Elskovens Dyd" (True Love's Virtue), is a literary masterpiece with all the refinements of its kind:

> The virtue of an upright love
>   I will praise with song and delight.
> A flower, the same I will not name,
>   is honored in this my dite [song].
> She is all virtuous, fair, and feat [elegant],
> wise and clever without deceit,
>   and true without any gall.
> As the sun before so many a star,
> so is that maiden both near and far
>   among ladies and maidens all.
> Eya, eya, would she would send me her call.

The poet desires only to see her who has caused him such sorrow that he resembles a corpse. Although he fears she may not be true to him, he wishes her success in finding her equal. He is powerless except to renounce hope and keep her in his heart forever, always ready to come crawling if she should send for him. The poem indeed proves the virtue of true love, a devotion in all things even as all hopes for possession are as far off as the social distance between them. Although an exponent of courtly love, the poet commands a popular style with formulaic diction and direct syntax that was presumably learned from the oral love lyric.

The two leaves containing "Ret Elskovens Dyd" were glued into the first gathering of what was to become a monastic, probably Franciscan, miscellany (publ. 1933*). Besides *Lucidarius* and Latin texts, the manuscript includes some Marian hymns. Some have interpreted "Ret Elskovens Dyd" as Marian as well, in spite of the text and of the presence of other worldly songs, such as a Goliard lyric against slanderers, in the first gathering. All the same, four of the Marian hymns have striking stylistic similarities to the troubadour lyric. One is formed as an acrostic on the name Maria, beginning with a minstrel address and ending with an envoy in which the poet gives his name as Per Ræv Lille, which he will not "turn," that is, disguise in an acrostic.

Scholarship has generally ascribed all five poems to Per Ræv, which like medieval attributions should be accepted only with reservation; this style in particular is highly formulaic, unacquainted with modern standards for originality. The hymns from this "school of Per Ræv" make full use of troubadour conventions in describing Mary from top to toe, yet with a metaphorical raiment stitched out of bestiary and Bible, especially the Song of Songs and the Apocalypse. This gives them a metaphorical density that like skaldic poetry requires familiarity with the mythology. All four hymns open with an invocation to the Godhead to overcome the poet's inadequate tongue, agreeing with the mystics—and with the sermon from *Lucidarius*—that humans can only grope at divinity and saintliness with metaphors. Despite these distancing traits, however, the hymns remain warmly human, perhaps one of the best reasons for ascribing them to a single author.

Of the seven other Marian hymns, Marine Jespersdatter's prayer book contains a fervently lyrical translation of the "Stabat mater" (At the Cross Her Station Keeping). It has a nearly syllabic meter that seems to have been composed in song, while its rising rhythm and interior rhyme show how Danish poets had found their own voice in the two centuries since *Mariaklagen*:

By cross's tree so dolefully
Christ's mother stood with tears in flood,
on the cross her son was hanging.
. . . .
O maiden mild, go to your child

with motherly prayer when death is near
and save my soul from peril.

The monastic miscellany includes a translated Latin hymn, "Christe, du est
både lys og dag" (Christ, Thou Art Both Light and Day), a stately Marian
liturgy, and two most unchivalrous monkish songs directed against faithless
womankind:

A woman's love I'll never
    praise nor give it honor,
because it goes no further
    than he can spend upon her.

With an echo of the satirist of *De gamle danske Dyrerim*, it is a vast distance
from the song at the beginning of the manuscript, "Ret Elskovens Dyd."

Latin Verse

After the 1329 "Planctus" and Peder Låle's humble hexameters, Latin poetry became, as it were, expatriated in the fourteenth century. A Marian rosary of 150 stanzas, the "Salutacio Beate Marie Virginis" (Greeting to the
Blessed Virgin Mary), was written by a scholar from Roskilde, undoubtedly
the same Jacobus Nicholai de Dacia who in 1363 dedicated his hexametrical
Liber de Distinccione Metrorum (publ. 1967; Book on Metrical Distinctions)
to the Countess of Pembroke (Mary de Sainte Paul) and who studied at
Pembroke College, Cambridge, and later at the Sorbonne in Paris.

Having at last obtained papal permission, the University of Copenhagen
opened in 1479. Here an older peasant student, Morten Børup (1446–1526),
received his master's degree, and in a poem he celebrates the city as a center
for commerce, art, and learning at the expense of the other cathedral towns.
Written after 1501, it marks the long silence in Danish poetry in Latin by
borrowing the meter and one line from the 1329 "Planctus." Having become rector of the cathedral school at Århus, Børup wrote "Veris adventus"
(The Arrival of Spring) for his pupils to sing as sprigs of spring were
brought into town on May Day. According to the Renaissance poet
Erasmus Lætus, it was these same pupils who were to carry a rebirth of Classical Latin and a new humanism throughout the land, and it is from them
that we have Børup's two songs.

The Medieval Drama

The drama appears later than do the lyric and epic genres; instead of an adaptation of oral techniques to literature, it is an application of craft literacy

to oral performance. There is some evidence for a Latin liturgical drama in Denmark in the form of props (and a text from Sweden) for the Easter *Sepulcrum* rite representing the deposti on of Christ's body in the sepulcher, and in later survivals of the procession of the Magi as once practiced by the pupils at the Latin schools. As part of a ritual such liturgical dramas mime a mythic re-presentation of an eternal return, as in the Eucharist itself. The earliest dramas in Denmark represent a further development to the hagiographic miracle play, which presents the saint's life as a (tropological) exemplum of an abstract moral truth. They were first written a generation after Jep Jensen's minstrel romance(s) and are likewise in rhyme.

The *Ludus de Sancto Canuto duce* (publ. 1868; Play of Saint Knud Lavard) was written after 1500 and survives among documents from the 1570s relating to the royal burials at Ringsted. The play is a faithful presentation of the readings from the office for this saint's day of passion (Jan. 7), which end with his assassination. Unless there was another play drawn from the readings for the day of translation (June 25), the miracles that are typical of the miracle plays are absent. It was presumably performed before pilgrims to the shrine.

Because the play is an exemplum, the actors portray roles that are more ideal than historical. In his righteousness and piety, Knud fails even to comprehend the false wiles of his foil, Prince Magnus. The original legend was a royalist document, and the play also voices general political views on the role of the just king which are not necessarily a protest from the final years under Christian II (reigned 1513–23). Its moral is voiced by the herald Tyrne, who tries to warn Knud not with a song of kin treachery as in the legend, but with lyrical verses:

> The whole world is full of guile and fraud,
> happy the man who keeps his guard.
> There is peril outside every man's door,
> as well as ever there was before.

The Latin stage directions indicate the use of the simultaneous stage with separate locales about which the audience is free to cluster. Thus Knud is able to mount a real horse and ride in seconds from Roskilde to his "palatium" in Schleswig, and Magnus can plot in a "grove" while Knud and King Niels silently continue their Yuletide feast before the audience. This stagecraft required naturalism in costume and props for depicting the role and the action, whereas for an exemplum historical accuracy and unity of time and place are of little consequence. Only the presence of Tyrne as prologue, player, and epilogue, apparently a stock figure absent in the sources, binds together the events of 1102–31 into a single performance.

Similar staging is also indicated for *Dorothea Komedie* (publ. 1972; The Comedy of Saint Dorothy), a verse translation from 1531 of Chilian Reuther's Latin closet drama of 1507. A colophon attributes the translation to Christiernus Joannis (Hansen or Jensen), a teacher at Our Lady Latin School in Odense. Whether or not the play was ever produced by his pupils, it gives a good measure of the kinds of stage effects, including gruesome torture scenes and a regular heaven and hell, of which early sixteenth-century drama was capable. The staging was surely more effective than the poetry, which only in the saint's description of heaven (with parallels in several ballads) rises above doggerel. Its homiletic epilogue makes the play an exemplum of the proper balance between works and faith, in concordance with the Catholic reform movement.

Christiernus Joannis's manuscript contains three gatherings, presumably three promptbooks representing the dramatic repertory of the pupils in Odense. The first two plays are farces in the tradition of German Shrovetide plays, performed from house to house especially during Shrovetide by students in hopes of gratuities. Their slapstick tone is at once apparent:

> Whoever will not now keep mum
>> and hearken to our farce,
> I will hit him across his bum
>> and give him a pain in the arse.

Later in this same play, *Den utro Hustru* (publ. 1874*; The Unfaithful Wife), a peasant gets just this sort of treatment from his wife, a monk from a courtier, and a devil from an old crone, for each has failed to seduce a goodwife whose husband has gone on a pilgrimage. After failing with the devil, the crone succeeds on behalf of the courtier with a weeping dog she claims to have been her daughter before she refused a courtier's advances. This folly gives the farce the topsy-turvy moral proper to Shrovetide, that to succeed one should seek help from an old crone.

Humanist learning had rediscovered classical mythology, which suggested the elopement ballad "Paris og Dronning Ellen" (Paris and Queen Helen) and the farcical morality play *Paris' Dom* (publ. 1874*; The Judgment of Paris). The play's epilogue cites the Italian humanist Publio Andrelini (1462–1518) to the effect that many fables contain a germ of truth; and Juno, Pallas, and Venus, besides being bickering bitches in a farce, are allegorical figures for power, knowledge, and earthly love in a morality. True to the farce, Paris chooses the last-named, while the morality ends with an ode urging peaceableness. Although Shrovetide frivolity was prohibited in 1521 and the miracle play was doomed to extinction by the Reformation, the dramatic traditions of the farce lived on in the more respectable Renaissance school drama.

Poetry in Print

The art of printing from movable type was brought to Denmark only after it was well established on the Continent. Its earliest patrons were prelates, who commissioned migrant German printers to provide relatively inexpensive copies of works widely used in the Church liturgy. Johan Snell printed a breviary in Odense in 1482, and Stephan Arndes a missal in Schleswig in 1486. The first resident printer was the Dutchman Gotfred of Ghemen, who published twenty-five titles in Copenhagen between 1489 and 1510, including some established Danish works: *Den danske rimkrønike* (1495), *Flores og Blanseflor* (1504), the *Sjællandske Lov* (1505), the *Skånske Lov* (1505), *Peder Låles ordsprog* (1506), the *Jyske Lov* (1508), *Jesu Barndoms Bog* (1508), the *Karl Magnus' Krønike* (1509), *Lucidarius* (1510), *Sjælens og Kroppens Trætte* (1510), and *Historien om Jon Præst* (1510). With the printed book came such novel notions as title page and title, edition and authorship, originality and plagiarism, concepts that were rudimentary at best in a manuscript culture.

Matthæus Brandis had printed the *Jyske Lov* both in Low German (Lübeck, 1486) and in Danish (Ribe, 1504). After his death in Copenhagen his material was taken over by the canon Poul Ræff, who printed thirteen Catholic titles between 1513 and 1533. This first native-born printer published three works of the first Danish poet to have written for the printing press, Father Michael Nicolai, a priest in Odense. From his poem *Om Jomfru Mariæ Rosenkrans* (1515; On the Rosary of the Virgin Mary), it appears that he wrote at least this work for the printing press, at the behest of Queen Christine in 1496, but seems to have died before it was published. He is clearly aware of reaching a new audience of devout laymen through the mass production of the word, an extension of his work as cofounder of the Rosary Guild at Odense in 1492. The poem is an interpretation of the prayers of the rosary, freely taken from the works of the chief apologist for this psalter for the illiterate, the French Dominican monk Alanus de Rupe (ca. 1428–75). Like all of Fr. Michael's works, it is almost entirely in the tail-rhyme sestet that had been used in *Den danske rimkrønike*, *De gamle danske Dyrerim*, and several Marian lyrics. Like all medieval authors, he does not fear the familiar motif or the cliché but makes no use of longer formulas. His stanzas are always homespun, more prosaic than lyrical, yet logically organized and ably wrought.

Om Skabelsen (1514; On the Creation) is an epic treatment of the Creation for the sake of man, the creation of man, his Fall and expulsion from Paradise, with running comments interrupting the epic narration to point out the moral dimension, in the manner of the homily. Both *Om Skabelsen* and *Om Jomfru Mariæ Rosenkrans* contain the reproach of Nature for the Fall: fire once warmed, now it will burn, and so on. The inexorable logic of such oppositions carries the poet well into a patent dualism that is clearest of all in *Om Menneskets Levned* (1514; On the Life of Man). In expounding on twenty Latin couplets by an unknown author, it follows everyman from birth through death and so on to Doomsday. Its Memento Mori theme is tolled with the onset of death:

> Life in this world may be likened so
> to one who builds upon a floe,
> > thinking it long will abide:
> a windstorm breaks the ice in twain,
> the building can no more remain,
> > so then it starts to slide.

This poor soul's progress is viewed form the vantage point of Judgment Day, which puts into focus the afflictions and vanity of human life and the anguish of facing divine retribution. As in *Sjælens og Kroppens Trætte*, the world is beset by demons, who are closer at hand throughout the poem than is Mary. We miss especially any final appeal to her intercession at the hour of death, as expressed in the rosary prayer. One of the Latin couplets in *Om Menneskets Levned* holds that Judgment Day will be hard when Christ judges according to merit, and this is ironically just what Fr. Michael depicts, at least for the unrepentant sinner. The linear logic of written language with its resultant dualism is here furthermore enclosed within the inalterable printed page, which helps to establish a point of view for the individual, isolated work. Whereas the manuscript *De gamle danske Dyrerim* is intertextual and encyclopedic in nature, freely quoting matter in Latin that is irrelevant to the Danish verse and its lesson of affliction, the anguish suffered by fallen man is pursued with unflagging energy from cradle to Doomsday in *Om Menneskets Levned*.

In the next generation, which was educated by means of printed books, the closure and point of view fostered by the mass production of the word were to aid in reformulating the very foundations of faith. Yet all the elements of the Reformation were already in place in Fr. Michael's works, including marginal references back to the Bible, the one form of intertextuality the Reformation would perpetuate. All that was required to make a Reformation was a certain expurgation of the nonessential marginal elements of which medieval life, like medieval manuscripts, were so full. This Protestant approach to its Christian heritage is illustrated in the use of Catholic hymns in the new printed songbooks now in everyone's hands. Hans Thomesen's hymnal of 1569 includes seventeen hymns used "under the papacy." Half are derived from Latin hymns, and in some instances Thomesen's text is a new one. But use and adaptation of medieval Danish hymns range from "Christ stod op af døde" (Christ the Lord is Risen Again), in the first hymnal of 1529, to such "papist" songs as "Jeg vil mig Herren love" (I Will Praise the Lord) and "Maria hun var en jomfru ren" (Mary Was a Virgin Pure), which even in their "corrected" Lutheran form still present the vestige of a Marian lyric in troubadour style, as it were, in palimpsest. The medieval morning song "Den signede dag" (The Blessed Day) contains several gnomic commonplaces:

> The wild birds they fly so high,
>   the wind blows under their wing;
> it is so hard with little might
>   over tall mountains to spring;
> the streams they run so merrily
>   under the hills so green
> Mary mother, gentle rose,
>   keep us from dread and teen [affliction].

The last two lines are missing in Thomesen's version. The reformers stripped more than Mary's name from the hymns; their songs no longer flower merrily under her motherly protection, but in effect concentrate their efforts on the graced leap of faith to impossible heights. Where the medieval morning hymn sang the arrival of day and its gentle graces, Thomesen's version added three stanzas recalling the onset of night and our pilgrimage away from this wretched life, a pilgrimage away from the spiritual immanence characteristic of preliterate thought toward a sovereign transcendence fostered by the closure and isolation of the inalterable printed page.

Danish literature was begun as early as 1171, during the high tide of the Latin Middle Ages, but remained what we could call nonfiction until the first attempts at didactic verse shortly after 1300. Only after the Kalmar Union (1397) did closer contact with the literature of Norway and Sweden give rise to entirely new genres in Danish poetry and narrative: five translated and one original romance, *Den danske rimkrønike*, and possibly also a troubadour lyric. In this period (1440–90) the prose chronicles have traces of "saga" style, and *De gamle danske Dyrerim* and *Den danske rimkrønike* show elements of oral style, which may be inspired from abroad but make use of native oral traditions. With the exception of *Peder Låles ordsprog* and a handful of fragments, these traditions remained unrecorded until the Renaissance. After 1500 the drama made its first appearance with two miracle plays, a farcical morality play, and a farce, while the printing press inaugurated poetic authorship with the works of Fr. Michael. Literature thereupon began to relate author and title to individual, original works; at the same time, oral traditions continued through their own period of manuscript semiliteracy until they too were made superfluous by print.

THE MEDIEVAL BALLAD

The term *medieval ballad* is used to refer to the genre, which dates from the Middle Ages. Unlike the timeless simple forms of folk poetry such as proverbs and legends, the ballad has a medieval origin as well. Being oral poetry, the genre—the combination of stylistic features that make it possible to recreate a narrative in song—precedes the text and can thus be treated under the medieval period, though virtually every text was recorded later. When we finally meet with what might paradoxically be called "oral literature" (i.e., documents of oral performance), it is generally the result of an effort to get the ballads onto paper, not to formulate them there. They have none of the marks of good literary style, such as pure rhymes or a normal orthography, and the ballads have lost none of their orality in the process.

The Tradition

Although coming after the close of the Middle Ages, abundant documentation occurred relatively early in Denmark, originally the result of a songbook fashion imported from the Continent. Begun in 1553, the aptly shaped Heart Book is the first of four spontaneous garlands, into which young noblemen (and one woman) at the Danish court gathered their favorite songs, mostly troubadour lyrics together with some ballads. By the 1580s the royal historian Anders Sørensen Vedel was collecting, for antiquarian purposes, mostly medieval ballads from both aristocratic and peasant traditions. From his four manuscripts he published *Et Hundrede udvalgte Danske Viser* (1591; One Hundred Choice Danish Ballads). As early as 1583 he seems to have inspired somebody, probably Margrete Lange, to compile the great volume of two hundred ballads called Karen Brahe's Folio after a later owner. Through the period of aristocratic hegemony, other ladies of the landed gentry, especially in Jutland, were inspired by Vedel's example to a kind of spontaneous antiquarianism, from which stem about twenty major manuscripts and the posthumous edition of further Vedel texts, *Tragica* (1657) by Mette Gjøe. The vigor and variability in this tradition attest that the ballads thrived among the aristocratic folk. In spite of a gradually increasing literacy, this group remained like most of us musically illiterate, and only five or six melodies accompany the 2,338 texts recorded before 1700.

After 1660 the aristocratic manuscripts began losing their originality, and they died out altogether around 1750, the victim of changed tastes. In the meanwhile Peder Syv had augmented Vedel's edition with another hundred ballads in 1695. The authority of the Vedel-Syv edition tended to hamper further collecting by the educated, even after the preromantic revival sparked by Thomas Percy in England and Johan Gottfried Herder in Germany, although an augmented reissue in 1814 occasioned the first collection of ballad tunes. This same period also saw a spontaneous revival in peasant songbooks and especially broadside prints as tradition was reinforced—and standardized—by printed texts. When Svend Grundtvig began to plan his monumental edition of *Danmarks gamle Folkeviser* (1853–1976; Ancient Folk Songs of Denmark; hereafter abbreviated DGF), he put out a call in 1843 for fresh versions that would prove the survival of the ancient ballads into recent times. The richest harvest, often in versions reflecting the oral tradition of the Renaissance rather than printed texts, was gleaned from 1867 on by Evald Tang Kristensen among the rural proletariat of central Jutland.

Ballad Style

Despite the relatively rich and early Danish documentation, only three fragments survive from the Middle Ages, and one might ask by what right the rest may be called medieval ballads. An earlier generation felt certain it could reconstruct each ballad in its "genuine" medieval form from the surviving oral detritus. But as Grundtvig insisted, the only genuine texts are those from a living oral tradition, that is, within the repertoire of a singer in a specific community or "folk," who has improvised new versions of old ballads or new ballads in the old style. Despite their formulaic nature, there is no evidence that ballads were ever improvised during performance like the Yugoslav epics, for they seem always to have been memorized. Yet there is a continual proliferation of variant passages and entire versions, due not only to lapses in perception or memory, but especially to imaginative and associative recreation reflecting the singer's active engagement with the song she or he has chosen to remember and rehearse. This is sometimes nonsensical or silly; the mother returning form the grave in "Moderen under Mulde" (The Buried Mother) nourished the imagination of one little girl with a touching blend of reality and fantasy:

The one she gave sandwiches, the other hasty pudding,
on the third she set a golden crown. (DGF 89V*3)

But good balladeers such as Sidsel Jensdatter (1793–1871) revivify the ballad by bestowing renewed pith on the issue of their fertile imagination:

The babe she suckled at her tit,
there was a robust strength to it. (DGF 89øa13)

Nevertheless, the ballads are not at the mercy of endlessly individualizing variation, for they are held together by stylistic features that, taken together, define the genre. The precious fragments from the Middle Ages are enough to demonstrate that the genre itself is indeed medieval. Pen-tests in a theological manuscript written in 1454–62 are the refrain of the royalist "Marsk Stig" ballad—or at least a lyrical commonplace that, when combined with its proper melody, is the lyrical mold into which a ballad narrative has been poured. The Greenland place-names in Claudius Clavus's second Ptolomaic map of northern lands (after 1424) are the words of a garbled but still recognizable opening stanza with its proper refrain, so that this bizarre cartographic dodge is certain witness to the Swedish subtype of "Angelfyr og Helmer Kamp" (Angelfyr and Helmer Kamp) in the fifteenth century. Since this is also a derivative subtype of a heroic ballad based on *Hervarar saga ok Heiðreks konungs* (Eng. tr. *The Saga of King Heidrek*, 1960), the genre itself is no doubt substantially older.

The ballad's formulaic diction is archaic but not easily dated. Morphemes that are archaic in Danish (ma*r*, i grøne*n* lund, ung*er*svend) long survived in the more conservative Nordic dialects. The saga ballad reported by the Dane Clavus and seven stanzas of "Ridderen i Hjorteham" (The Knight in Hart Disguise), added in about 1500 in Danish to a back page of a Swedish collection of sermons from Norway, are graphic evidence of a Kalmar Union in the world of balladry, at a time when songs readily and no doubt frequently passed from one dialect to another across Scandinavia. An artificial ballad language was thus concocted out of various unassimilated dialectical features, retained for purely poetic reasons.

These seven stanzas from "Ridderen i Hjorteham" are nevertheless enough to demonstrate both the orality of the Renaissance manuscripts and the generic features of the ballad. A rhymed or assonating couplet with narrative content, objective point of view, and formulaic diction is accompanied by one or more (usually) lyrical refrains.

It was then Sir Peder,
he spoke to his squires two:

Could ye for me proud Ose-li'l
with pleasant speeches woo?
—*I've dreamed of the maiden every night.*

The ornamental formulas of improvised epic (stichic) poetry are also found as one-liners in the ballads, of the type "he stood in scarlet so red." The ballad formulas, however, do more than ornament the action; they present it, normally with a kind of formulaic posturing that segments a plot into scenes, each articulated by a scheme of situation, confrontation, alarm or action, and reaction. Thus following the aforementioned situation formula, we find:

Confrontation:
   Away then went the armigers
   to where proud Ose maun be:
Alarm:
   My lord he awaits aboard his ship,
   with you he would wish to speak.
Reaction:
   Then answered them proud Ose-li'l,
   she answered this with a word:
   It is not a maiden's wont
   on ships to go aboard.
Incremental repetition:
   It is not a maiden's wont
   on ships to go aboard:
   both disgrace and shame will follow her home,
   so many a scornful word.

The return of the messengers is related with an identical scheme and very much the same words, what one may call local repetition:

Confrontation:
   Back then came the armigers,
Alarm:
   They told their lord the news:
   We could not proud Ose-li'l
   with pleasant speeches woo.
Reaction:
   Could ye not proud Ose-li'l
   with pleasant speeches woo,
   then I shall put on the shape of a hart,
   her I will surely woo. (DGS67AI–6)

The balladesque narrative technique, including local and incremental repetition, is remarkably well articulated in this comparatively early text. Moreover, Nordic tradition is unique in possessing at so early a date an entire battery of stanzaic commonplaces, such as the first stanza above.

The Origin of Ballad Style

The stanzaic commonplaces, of which there are more than a hundred, are such a ubiquitous feature of the medieval ballad that they are easily recognized in totally different contexts. This is the most likely explanation for certain passages in *Herr Ivan* (1303; Sir Ivan), the Swedish source for the romance *Ivan Løveridder*. When Ivan has rescued a wounded lion from a dragon, for instance, he places it on his shield and carries it off; but an elopement formula seems to have intruded itself into the Swedish adaptation, with curious consequences:

> He went off to where the lion lay
> and lifted her onto his shield straightway,
> *and lifted her then upon his horse,*
> *as best he could he led her forth.*
> He sometimes carried her himself.

It is in France that we find, recorded in every century from the twelfth to the twentieth, the only song genre that is formally close to the Nordic ballads: the short dance song called the *ronde*, from which the more elaborate *rondeau* developed. Like the ballads, rondes have one or more lyrical refrains contrasting with (but not necessarily irrelevant to) the objective text; the latter is normally a suite of assonating long or short lines, a couplet in each stanza. Formally identical to the Nordic ballad stanzas are these two thirteenth-century rondes:

> Renaud and his sweetheart were riding through the lea,
> all the night went riding till day grew clear.
> *—I shall ne'er be happy from loving thee.*

> It's down among the leafy trees
> *—I've a love—*
> Marion there takes her ease.
> *—I've a truelove who is pleasing.*

Both ronde and ballad refrains frequently refer to an actual dance situation ("So lightly the dance goes under the greenwood"), and the ronde seems to have been imported as the result of a dance craze that swept Denmark off its feet sometime in the thirteenth century. The Faroese still dance to their ballads with the same *branle* steps used by sixteenth-century Normans when dancing to the rondes. The first unequivocal, native Danish reference to the dance, dating from the 1260s, is an (anachronistic) mention in the *Annales Ryenses* of dancing at the royal court in 1156. In the Swedish *Erikskrönikan* (1320s), Round Table festivities of jousting and dancing are depicted as exercises of chivalric "virtue and good custom." We see nine gentlefolk dancing across the wall of Ørslev Church on Zealand (ca. 1350), perhaps toward perdition. For the dance is a perilous place, where love is casually bandied about. The six text lines of one thirteenth-century ronde, which would have been concatenated as five stanzas, tell the same story as the opening scene of "Stolt Signild og Dronning Sofie" (Proud Signild and Queen Sofie):

> Proud Signild asked her mother outright:
> —*there may he wake that will*—
> May I go to the wake-feast tonight?
> —*Where she wakes, the proud Signild, under the greenwood.*
>
> O, what will ye at the wake-house do
> without sister or brother to go with you?
>
> And neither brother nor bridegroom
> ye shall not go to the wake-house alone.
>
> . . . .
>
> The king and all his men will come,
> so mark my words and stay at home.
> (DGF 129.2–7; Tr. after Robert Jamieson)

Although the ronde can have more than one stanza, its medieval texts at least are limited to these little type-scenes, which have just the same connotative dimension and use of commonplace we find in ballad formulas. If a maiden goes down to the water, it is to meet her lover; but if to her garden to pluck flowers, she is picking her first love, or perhaps her marriage partner, and she will likely consult with the nightingale or have him carry her message, as in "Ravn fører Runer" (The Raven Rune-Bearer) and several other ballads. Similarly, if a ballad hero prepares for an audience by "shouldering" his cape and thus exposing his sword, he expresses frankness; but not so if he cloaks his head, for then the audience can expect the worst. Or if a man bids his horse be saddled, we know that he will soon be requesting a woman's hand and that we can expect some complication in the affair.

In the medieval ronde, however, these expectations usually went unspoken. Perhaps the narrative development of the Nordic ballads came as the naive response to these symbolic scenes: whatever did become of the girl at the dance? There is one Old French genre that may better have satisfied some of this curiosity, the *chanson de toile* (or *d'histoire*). Its opening scene, a woman at her needlework (*à toile*), unfolds from repose to conflict according to the epic "Law of Opening." This scene recurs fairly regularly among Nordic ballads, as in "Jomfruens Harpeslæt" (The Maiden Strikes her Harp), but not in the ballad literature of other nations:

Little Kirsten and her mother,
—*from the trees who breaks the leaves?*—
their silken caps they broidered.
—*From the earth the dew she treads.*

Her mother sewed so fine a seam,
her daughter's tears ran like a stream.

Hear ye, little Kirsten, my daughter dear:
why blanches your cheek, why fades your hair?

No wonder I'm sickly and wan of hue,
as much as I've to shape and sew.

Here's maidens enough in town I know
that better can shape and better can sew.

I can no longer keep it form thee
that our young king has lured me.
(DGF 265A1–6; Tr. after Robert Jamieson)

Of the ten anonymous Old French texts that narrate beyond this point, two are, as it were, resung in ronde form in the Danish tongue. Individually, such ballads may or may not be medieval; together they are concocted of the most common ballad motifs, which are more or less the same as those witnessed by *Herr Ivan* in 1303, just when the chansons de toile disappear from the record.

Other theories of origin have been proposed for the Nordic ballads, but only their genesis as chansons de toile resung as rondes can account for both the medieval evidence and the stylistic features of the genre. The Breton lays are a lost genre, German heroic songs are stylistically different, and British ballads became stylistically similar only in the eighteenth century. Moreover, the basic theme of the chanson de toile—true love, kin opposition, rendezvous, elopement, and marriage—recur in the knightly ballads.

Knightly Ballads

Many ballads begin by saddling up for a betrothal journey. The visit is to the guardian, not to the intended, for marriage in an agrarian kin society was not an affair between two individuals, but a contract between two kin groups affecting the inheritance of landed property, with contractual forms not unlike those for the exchange of allodial lands or for family reconciliation after slayings. Other ballads begin with a father's return from his business at the local assembly, where he has betrothed his daughter to one whom she does not love. This scene lays open the fundamental theme of the kin ballads, often merely implied by an introductory betrothal situation: an inevitable tension between individual love and the kin institution of marriage.

In this light a kin's outright disregard for the consent and will enjoined by the Church and conceded by the law is more a poetic theme than a mirror of society. It has a functional parallel in the adulterous relationship assumed in the troubadour *canso*, which served to raise the ideal of love above the marriage of convenience. Of the many varieties of medieval song on the Continent, the chanson de toile alone assigns the kin group a genuine part, not merely a lurking in the wings like the "slanderers" in troubadour lyric. The latter is more abstract and man's poetry; the former more earthy and woman's song.

For all their romantic idealism, the ballads require two ingredients for a happy ending: the woman should be wearing fine clothes and furs, and she should lie each night in the arms of her truelove—and husband. A relationship between two isolated individuals is viewed with fascinated but genuine horror in "Rane Jonsens Giftermaal" (Rane Jonsen's Marriage):

> Fields have eyes and woods have ears:
> —*I have heard it all before*—
> my lass, we are driven away from here,
> —For we're both of us *outlawed*
> *from all our own kith and kin.*
>
> (DGF 148B12)

Most kin ballads do end happily: indeed, the loving couple thwarted by family designs but eventually incorporated into a renewed society is, as in the eighteenth-century plays of Holberg, the archetypal narrative of comedy. Here, as in Shakespearean romantic comedy, the emphasis is not on the follies of family but on the means of reconciliation. The kin ballads thus accept the ideology of traditional kin society, at the same time exposing its human cost and seeking somehow to comprehend within its framework that broader ideology of medieval Europe, true love.

The lovers may convert kin opposition by perseverance or pluck, by force of love or arms; the means vary from a well-timed swoon to a general slaughter of all opposition. But they may also seek to circumvent it by eloping together, apparently to his own patrimony beyond the reach of the woman's (or rival's) kin. Elopements occur especially as the hero arrives just in time to rescue the woman from a forced marriage, in "Svend Dyrings Bruderov" (Svend Dyring's Abduction) and a dozen other ballads.

> Now thanks to Sir Svend Dyring,
> he kept his faith so well:
> he's taken her to his own castle,
> and there his wedding is held.
> —*Today the swain takes his leave from his lord.*
>
> And now the Mistress Ellinsborg
> has lived down all her harms:
> now she sleeps so happily
> within Sir Svend Dyring's arms.
>
> (DGF 394A32–33)

This is in fact a courtship tale of a type frequently attested in Nordic sources, thrice by Saxo. In the ballads, however, it is usually recast in a more mimetic mode, signaled by the everyday atmosphere of the various introductory scenes. It is this (idealized) mimetic portrayal of medieval rural aristocracy that has given us the term *knightly ballad* (*riddervise*) for the majority of ballads. In them the hero succeeds more by pluck than by prodigious feats of arms, which displays faithfulness more than fortitude.

The ballads also know the legendary hero, who may enter the lady's bower as a lover but leaves it as a berserk. Such are "Samson" from *Þiðriks saga* (Theodoric's Saga) or the ill-starred hero of "Ribold og Guldborg" (Riborg and Guldborg). Ribold possesses all the heroic virtues, including an implicit faith in love's unending paradise, where only the cuckoo sings and streams run with wine. For him the kin group is little more than an adversary to be overcome; but Guldborg looks back over her shoulder at the kinfolk who still tug at her loyalties. At the crucial moment in their elopement she is torn asunder by divided allegiances and breaks his superhuman power and his inordinate love by calling out his name, thereby bringing his mortal and social nature into being and making him vulnerable to a death blow from her last surviving brother. The kin ballads can dream of a reckless love that conquers all, and yet they are bound to a traditional kin society by more than convention. The story of Guldborg has been resung in "Hildebrand og Hilde" (Hildebrand and Hilde) as the tragic monologue of a woman sitting at her needlework, thereby bringing the kin ballad, as it were, full circle to its probable origin.

In the ballads of rivalry the hero is opposed more by a rival than by a kin group, often in combat. These ballads may have a happy ending, which in "Lave og Jon" (Lave and Jon) is given a humorous twist through the hero's running comments formed like Wellerisms in the variable signal verse (a ronde feature), as when he hops into bed with his rival's bride:

Sir Jon he locked the bower-door tight:
—*ye are well bound*—
Ye bid Sir Lave have a good night.
—I'm sleeping! *said Jon.*
—*Ye bind up your helmet of gold, and follow Sir Jon.*
   (DGF 390A14; Tr. after Robert Jamieson).

Where women are rivals, the ballad sides with the mistress (*slegfred*) against the betrothed, usually with tragic results. In "Stolt Signild" the jealous Queen Sofie poisons the dancing maiden, and in "Valdemar og Tove" (Valdemar and Tove) she roasts the king's concubine in a sauna. When the rival is the hero's brother, the conflict becomes too entangled for anything but tragedy. The woman sides with kin and rival brother in "Ebbe Skammelsøn":

Hear ye Mistress Lucy-li'l,
come flee the land with me:
I will slay Peder my brother,
and bear this grief for thee.
—*And thus treads Ebbe Skammelsøn so many wild ways.*

If you kill Peder your brother,
then you shall also lose me,
and you will pine yourself to death,
like a lone bird in a tree.
   (DGF 354A28–29)

Thus rebuffed, Ebbe vents his alienated passion through violence on both love and kin.

Where kin and rival remain in the background, the lovers themselves become more or less antagonists in the courtship ballads, which are closely related to Continental folk-song themes. Ballads bordering on narrative lyrics and singing games (*sanglege*) develop the dance, orchard, well, and night-visit type-scenes, as well as the widespread pastourellle theme in which a knight out hunting meets a maiden in the greenwood and courts her with or without success, with honorable or dishonorable intentions. In "Den dyre Kaabe" (The Dear Robe), a pastourelle ballad of German origin, the wooer disdains to make love on his precious cloak and so loses the girl. The converse of gaining a love through courtship is to lose one in death, and the truelove's death is a tragic variety of the courtship ballad, to which belong most ballads about death. Its most poignant expression is "Fæstemanden i Graven" (The Buried Fiancé), in which a man returns to his truelove from the grave to ask that she weep for him no more, whereupon she dies of sorrow. The ballad echoes "The Second Lay of Helgi Hunding's Bane" from the *Elder Edda*. Where true love is elsewhere pitted against kin or rivals, in the courtship ballads it is thus contrasted with shallow forms of love that lack the indelible mark of perennial fidelity in marriage or, failing that, in celibacy or death. Although they differ according to their character structure, all three kinds of ballads—kin, rival, and courtship—usually have a common theme: the fidelity that is the moral imperative of all these true-love ballads.

Without a promise of marriage, a seduced woman like the heroine of "Jomfruens Harpeslæt" has lost her honor. Where honor is subordinated to love, the true-love ballads seek to regain it in marriage or go to perdition in mutual suicide. But where honor has become the dominant theme, its loss must be avenged. The two violated sisters of "Herr Ebbes Døtre" (Sir Ebbe's Daughters) wreak revenge when their father demurs, and two sisters avenge their father's death in "Døtre hævner Fader" (Daughters Avenge Father). In addition to chastity and kinship, honor takes the form of fealty, as when a faithful squire saves his lord in combat in "Danneved og Svend Trøst" (Danneved and Swain Trusty). Some of these ethical ballads are dominated more by a sense of justice as in "Bønderne dræber Herr Tidemand" (Yeomen Slay Sir Tidemand), in which exorbitant taxes provoke a killing. "Jomfruen paa Tinge" (The Maiden at the Assembly) presents her allodial lands to the king in order to keep them from her profligate relatives, and receives them again in fief together with a lord and husband: a happy romantic judgment that reinstates both her honor and that of her rural lifestyle far from court.

In certain ballads the twin themes of love and honor collide. "Torbens Datter" (Torben's Daughter) is, as it were, a rejoinder to the punishment for abduction in "Herr Erlands Vold og Straf" (Sir Erland's Violence and Punishment) and seems by contrast to suggest that love can ameliorate the stern code of blood revenge:

> Had I but known you had been so good,
> —*under hillside*—
> I would never have seen your father's life-blood.
> —*Now the day it dawns, and the dew it drifts far and wide.*
>
> (DGF 288.11)

Torben's murderer then takes the slain man's daughter into his care. But the marriage of reconciliation ends tragically in "Nilus og Hillelille" (Nilus and Hillelille), as in the "Lay of Ingell" before it, when the bride trusts her uncle's forebearance of a blood feud for her sake; nor is her sister-in-law willing to care for the widowed bride:

> How could I to proud Hilleli'l,
> ever be kind or good?
> It's all her fault I have lost two sons
> and my brother lies in his blood.
> —*They played out the play, and the play was all of anger.*
>
> (DGF 325A29)

True-love and ethical ballads comprise the central mass in Danish tradition, with the former in a clear majority. This preponderance is also evident from the frequency with which extraneous narrative material has been assimilated to these thematic patterns. From the folktale come, besides the courtship tales mentioned above, the "unknown paramour" motif in a group of ballads such as "Brud ikke Mø" (The Bride Not a Maiden), in which a woman must reveal having been raped and her bridegroom turns out to be the violator. We find also the lowly hero or heroine who marries a princess or prince, a motif at variance with the aristocratic ethic of equal matches. In "Møens Morgendrømme" (The Maiden's Morning Dreams) it results from a dream of future greatness; in "Tærningspillet" (The Dice Game), from a girl's loss of honor in a game of dice to a prince in humble disguise. The game of dice itself is a fitting symbol for the reversal of fortune that tends to replace love as the theme of such folktale ballads. It is seen from a different, tragic viewpoint in the gnomic introductory stanza to "Aslag Tordsøn og skøn Valborg" (Aslag Tordsen and Fair Valborg):

> The dice so often turn about,
> from great to small they go:

and so does unstable Fortune,
the wheel turns to and fro.
—*She turns about so often.*
(DGF 475A2)

Historical Ballads

Historical events and legends have also been assimilated to traditional ballad
themes. Four major cycles, centered on Sofie, Dagmar, Marsk Stig, and
Folke Algotsson, dominate the historical ballads. The first cycle features
Valdemar the Great's queen Sofie, the jealous villain of six ballads of rivalry;
the names in this group of ballads could place the origin of the cycle as far
back as the thirteenth century. The first two ballads about Valdemar II's
queen Dagmar generated several other royal wedding ballads, a historicized
variety of the courtship ballad. In "Dronning Dagmars Død" (Queen Dagmar's Death) the king's grief at her death is, as in most ballads about death, a
tragedy of true love; her final testament is that of a virtual saint, comple-
menting the morning-gift request from the royal wedding ballad "Dronning Dagmar i Danmark" (Queen Dagmar in Denmark). Of the four ballads about Lord Marshal Stig Andersen's part in the murder of King Erik
Klipping, the royalist ballad "Kongemordet" (The King's Murder) is formed as a true-love tragedy, although its interests are political. The other
three ballads side with the party of the nobles and are also more genuine
knightly ballads. "Marsk Stig og hans Hustru" (Marsk Stig and His Wife) is
an ethical ballad with a happy ending, motivating the murder as just revenge, with loyal aid of a kinsman, for rape. "Landsforvisningen" (The Banishment) accuses the queen of adultery and, together with "De Fredløse"
(The Outlaws), has the more typical anticentralist stance of the knightly ballads. All four ballads were combined and elaborated into "Den lange Marsk
Stig-Vise" (The Long Ballad of Marsk Stig) during the Renaissance.

Connected to the Marsk Stig cycle are the abduction ballad "Rane Jonsens Giftermaal" (Rane Jonsen's Marriage) and the lover's death ballad
"Rane Jonsens Endeligt" (Rane Jonsen's Death), one of which was probably that referred to by the Swede Ericus Olai about 1470. From Sweden
comes a cycle of three abduction ballads developed on the elopement motif;
the earliest is probably based on fourteenth-century memorates about Folke
Algotsson's abduction in 1288. In Danish this figure gradually reverted
from that of an abductor in "Magnus Algotsøn" and "Herr Mattis og Stolt
Ingefred" (Sir Mattis and Proud Ingefred), to a queen's lover in "Folke Lov-
mandsøn og Dronning Helvig" (Folke Lawman's Son and Queen Helvig),
and finally to the familiar eloper in "Albret bortfører Bruden" (Albret

Elopes with the Bride) and in "Lovmand og Tord" the rescuer of a truelove from a forced marriage. Yet another epic of political assassination is "Niels Ebbesen," which upholds traditional Nordic freedoms against Continental feudalism:

> There is none that's joined together,
> as a monk is to his hood:
> a knight may come a knight may go,
> where he finds the service good.
>
> (DGF 156A23)

Its lack of refrain perhaps reflects a literary origin. The pen is certainly implicated in the minstrel address, precise historical detail, and freedom from ballad formulas and themes that mark the style of a few chronicle ballads such as "Christian II i Sverige" (Christian II in Sweden) which border on broadside balladry. It is the only kind of historical ballad to escape the attraction of the central themes of the knightly ballad.

Faery and Religious Ballads

The objective behavioristic ballad style is capable of depicting the emotional dimension of life and love only to the extent that it results in action within the ethical dimension; all true-love ballads are in this sense ethical. Of the psychological and physiological analysis of emotions found in Chrétien de Troyes's romances or in troubadour lyric, the ballads mention only the visible symptoms. A face turns red and white from love or black from sorrow; distraction interrupts the sewing scene; and in normal ballad style the few lyrical expressions of emotion occur only in dialogue. The mysterious power of love has instead been expressed through an image of magic, as seen above in Ribold's invincibility as long as he remains unnamed. "Ridderen i Hjorteham" is thus a fairly obvious symbol for the seductive power of the male beast. The knight who tries to cut down the forest to catch the title character of "Jomfruen i Fugleham" (The Maiden in Bird Shape) disenchants her only by offering her the flesh from his breast. Even Vedel suggested that such transformations were symbolic in nature, implying something like "Love is won through love." Although ancient as motifs, playing harp or horn and casting runes function, like the love philtre in the Tristan legend, as (interchangeable) images of seduction rather than as genuine folk belief, the same image that is present when we speak of love's "enchantment" or "charm." Music and runes arouse a compulsion that the will cannot resist. In spite of their magical imagery, these works are courtship ballads that situate erotic powers within the ethical dimension. The frivolous seduction undertaken for a bet in "Ridderens Runeslag" (The Knight's Casting of Runes) ends in humiliation and suicide, while "Ridder Stigs Runer" (Sir Stig's Runes) leads through unflinching chastity on the part of the practitioner to marriage.

Seduction also appears as a sinister supernatural being. A merman in "Nøkkens Svig" (The Water Sprite's Treachery) and a gnome in "Jomfruen og Dværgekongen" (The Lady and the Dwarf King) carry maidens away, while an elf in "Elvehøj" (Elf Hill) and "Elveskud" (Elf-Shot) tries to bewitch the hapless hero. The elf-shot of this ballad, the beast in "Varulven" (The Werewolf), the merman in "Harpens Kraft" (The Power of the Harp), and the raven in "Germand Gladensvend" (Germand Gladenswain) are bloodthirsty elements that bring about the truelove's death, even if the merman is subsequently conquered through the power of music. The folklore on the disenchantment of werewolves (perhaps too of "corpse ravens") is here ignored in favor of an elemental image for death in its many guises. "Ridderen i Fugleham" (The Knight in Bird Shape) and "Ravn fører Runer" are images for love-longing, as in love lyrics. In all these faery ballads (trylleviser) the element of faery has been borrowed from folklore but is taken out of context to serve as a concrete image for the mysterious powers at work below the objective surface of the true-love ballad. The symbolic implications of faery imagery reach deeper into the unconscious than does the ethical portrayal of true love as will, and from romanticism on this imagery has continued to cast its spell on ballad scholars and readers alike.

Yet other ballads do not merely use faery images, but are in effect folktales or legends resung as ballads. Thus whereas "Germand Gladensvend" and his truelove don their feather shapes of love and do battle with a chimera of death that is sometimes sea monster, sometimes wild raven, the beast of "Valravnen" (The Corpse Raven) is a transformed human who finds disenchantment by drinking a child's blood, in accordance with the folktales of transformation. So, too, people are rescued from the gnomes, monsters are bound by runic spells, the dead return to see that justice is done, a mermaid foretells the future, a pregnancy is magically prolonged: this is the stuff of folktale and legend. It has been thought that the earliest ballads were those closest to living folk belief and the "heathen fear of nature." But this view implies that at some time a prose narrative spontaneously broke into song, which would have been an even more wondrous transformation. Rather, this kind of faery ballad represents folklore resung in an existing ballad genre, presumably prompted by an existing faery imagery.

The Christian beliefs that are only marginally present in the ballads at large come to the fore in the legendary or religious ballads (legendeviser), a small group even rarer in early sources. A few seem to have originated as one form of *legenda* (reading) in an oral culture, the religious equivalent of re-sung legends of the supernatural. A medieval legend of Saint Olav tells that when he was in dire straits the land opened up into a sound before his ship, and in "Hellig-Olavs Væddefart" (Saint Olav's Race) this miraculous journey was continued right across country, along with the ballad itself, leaving in its wake a version of the legend localized to stations along the pilgrim routes to the saint's grave in Trondheim. In contrast, certain ballads like "St. Jørgen og Dragen" (Saint George and the Dragon) were no doubt penned by clerks in church or school and are thus the religious equivalent of the chronicle ballad. It was probably this ballad of Saint George that was sung, according to the Swedish *Sturekrönikan* (The Sture Chronicle), before the battle of Brunkeberg in 1471, a victory over the Danes about which the Swedes also wrote a chronicle ballad. The pen is certainly implicated in the eleven religious ballads that first appeared in eighteenth-century broadside prints.

Jocular Ballads

The jocular ballads (publ. 1927–28*) (*skæmteviser*) parody the style and the themes of the knightly ballad, shifted from the high mimetic into the ironic mode. The scene is accordingly among lower social classes and species of animals, and all norms have been turned bottoms up. Love is reduced to sex as the seduction of "Elvehøj" and the compulsion of "Ridder Stigs Runer" are parodied in three ballads dealing with men raped by women; in "Bispens Datter og den frygtsomme Ungersvend" (The Bishop's Daughter and the Timid Lad) chastity and justice become a laughingstock when the chaste youth is laughed out of court. Courtship is parodied by the cheap price of honor in "Her bliver vel bedre Køb" (A Better Bargain) and marriage by "Fluens Bryllup" (The Wedding of the Fly). Rivalry becomes adultery, whether the laugh is on the cuckold as in "Bondens Kone besøger Hovmand" (Peasant's Wife Visits Courtier), or on the would-be seducer as in "Munken i Vaande" (The Monk in Agony). Beyond the general parody of the knightly ballad, the jocular ballads can directly satirize the aristocracy, as in "Kællingen til Skrifte" (The Crone's Confession), which assigns a light penance for having murdered a courtier. Another source of humor comes from exaggerating the familiar out of all proportion in lying songs such as "Den store Krage" (The Big Crow).

Heroic Ballads

The heroic ballads (*kæmpeviser*) display prodigies of courage and endurance in the miraculous mode in far-flung scenes among the kings, berserks, and vikings of antiquity. Relatively rare in Denmark, they are found in great numbers in Faroese tradition. There they are stylistically distinct form East Nordic balladry, approaching the Icelandic ballads in refrain forms and the rhymed narratives (*rímur*) in their minstrel formulas, skaldic diction, and especially their multiepisodic narratives. These narratives are frequently derived from the legendary, romantic, and marvel sagas. The long Faroese heroic ballads (*kvæðir*) are probably best characterized as saga narratives resung, within a wholly oral culture, with the (minstrel) narrative structure of the *rímur,* but with the form, style, and particularly the (oral) narrative technique of the knightly ballads in Icelandic tradition. With the last-named came the love theme with its courtship, kin, and rivalry structures; but in the heroic ballads this theme always leads to some kind of conflict whereby the hero tests his mettle as a champion. This particular combination of themes was already present, for example, in *Hervarar saga ok Heiðreks Konungs* (the source for "Angelfyr og Helmer Kamp"), in which the rivalry between Hjálmar and Angantýr leads to the mighty duel on the island of Samsø. It was no doubt resung as a (heroic) ballad because the balladeer was already familiar with knightly ballads of rivalry. Once love had been subordinated to heroic fortitude, other saga narratives could be adapted without reference to a love affair. Their theme became heroic honor, as in some Diderik ballads derived from *Þiðriks saga.*

> King Diderik stands upon a hill,
> and he looks out so wide:
> Would God I knew a hero so free,
> durst meet me in the field!
> —*There stands a fortress named bern, and therein dwells King Diderik.*
> (DGF 7BI; Tr. after Robert Jamieson)

One version of "Kong Diderik og hans Kæmper" (King Theodoric and His Champions) is like a multiepisodic *kvæði.* Its first fit, "Vidrik Verlandsøns Kamp" (Vidrik Verlandsøn's Fight), is a troll ballad in which Vidrik sallies forth to slay a giant. Its second fit, "Kampen mellem Sivard og Humelum" (The Fight between Sivard and Humelum), is a ballad of champions in which King Isak's champion Sivard does battle with Diderik's champion Humelum, a battle waged not for patriotism or power but solely for heroic honor. When they discover they are kinsmen, the victor Sivard allows Humelum to tie him to an oak, until he spies Vidrik approaching:

> And it was Sivord Snarensvend,
> he dared not meet him bound:

he pulled the oak up by the root,
he readied himself to go.
—It thunders under the gallant courtiers, as out they sally.
There is a dance at Brattingsborg,
the champions dance so bold:
there dances Sivord Snarensvend,
and at his side the oak.

(DGF 7E35–36)

With heroic honor reestablished all around, the swordplay thus ends in gargantuan merriment.

The relatively few heroic ballads in Danish tradition have been further assimilated to the dominant knightly style and themes. Apart from a single version, they are always a single fit and usually shortened as well. From *Vǫlsunga saga* (Eng. tr. *The Saga of the Volsungs*, 1965) comes the Faroese "Brynhildar táttur" (The Ballad of Brynhild); its average 195 stanzas may be compared with the average 25 stanzas of "Sivard og Brynild" (Sivard and Brynild), stripped of every epic circumstance down to the bare essentials of a stark tragedy of slighted love, revenge, and regret. Whereas the Faroese "Arngríms synir" (Arngrim's Sons) is a tragic ballad of champions, and the Swedish "Kung Speleman" (King Speleman, from whence came Clavus's Greenland stanza) is a happy ballad of fealty, the Danish ecotype "Angelfyr og Helmer Kamp" is a tragic ballad of (fraternal) rivalry in which a father slays one son for slaying another. The many adventures in "Svend Vonved," in which the hero sets out to avenge his father's death, tend to come unraveled, and recent versions have kept only the riddling scene. A dissatisfaction with the revenge theme is voiced through "Hævnersværdet" (The Avenging Sword), in which the sword, being able to speak, takes over the avenger's mind in order to make it "as hard as my point is quick," with gory results until the avenger proves that the word is mightier than the sword by naming it back to its proper nature. In penance he goes about in chains until they fall off when he crosses the slain man's grave (as in some versions of "Ebbe Skammelsøn"). Contrition, penance (including wergeld), and forgiveness have replaced the implacable duty of revenge that was urged by Starkather of old and by West Nordic sagas, *rímur*, and ballads. Danish ballads took kinship seriously when it came to marriage but sometimes sang the fantastic heroic ballads tongue in cheek as good parodies of themselves. Not only "Tord af Havsgaard" (Thor of Asgard) from the *Elder Edda*'s rollicking "Lay of Thrym," but also "Greve Genselin" (Count Genselin) include the monstrous meal motif of certain jocular ballads.

Chronicle and Romance Ballads

Danish ballads were sometimes, like the Faroese saga ballads, derived from literary sources. Historical and religious chronicle ballads have already been mentioned. Out of *Karlamagnús saga* comes Holger the Dane, the figure of chivalry incarnate in "Holger Danske og Burmand" (Holger the Dane and Burmand); its refrain captions a Swedish fresco from about 1480. In "Kong Diderik og Holger Danske" (King Diderik and Holger the Dane) he also figures as Denmark's protector in time of crisis, as in popular legend. Another tale from the Matter of France is the story of the master thief "Allegast," taken from a Middle Dutch romance; that this Dutch name was used in *Karl Magnus' Krønike* is probably due to the ballad, which thus must have existed before 1480. Of the Arthurian matter, "Tistram og Isold" (Tristan and Isolde) seems to depend on either the Norwegian saga or the German chapbook (1484). One of the German versions of the romance of Appolonius of Tyre was probably the source for "Kong Apollon" (King Apollon). "Langobarderne" (The Lombards), reproducing the very rhymes of *Den danske rimkrønike*, derives ultimately from Saxo's interpretation of Paul the Deacon in favor of Danish origins for the Great Migrations. A jocular use of the chronicles appears in "Dansk Kongetal" (The Danish Royal Line), in which an old crone names eleven of the twenty-four kings under whom she has lived, beginning with Dan. Probably deriving directly from Saxo, "Hagbard og Signe" (Hagbard and Signe) may be compared with his rendition of the "Lay of Hagbarth." When reduced to the love story itself, it is a courtship tale that fits well into the basic stock of kin ballads; the internecine feud between Hagbard and King Sigar is alluded to only in the opening long-line and then as the result of the love affair rather than its obstacle. The lay's dialogue is transformed into a scenic structure in which, for instance, the lovers' mutual death pact is portrayed rather than declaimed. Hagbard proves as fanatical in chivalry as he is prodigious in strength by letting himself be bound only with one of Signe's hairs. After their double deaths Sigar regrets not having realized that their love was so strong and has the spying handmaid buried alive, again proving how completely the kin ballad with its love and justice themes and chivalric overtones has been isolated from its original context within a story of revenge. The earlier alliterative treatment died out with Saxo, but the ballad became exceedingly popular, giving birth to numerous local legends in Denmark, Sweden, and Norway.

Danish heroic ballads retain the heroic theme but shorten the narrative content of the West Nordic *kvæðir;* conversely, some ballad romances (*romanviser*) have the multiepisodic narratives of the saga ballad with the mimetic style and romantic themes of the knightly ballad. These could well have been composed by Danish noblemen in royal service in Norway after the Union with Denmark in 1380, and several take place there, most notably "Aslag Tordsøn og skøn Valborg."

Thematic and Historical Development

A survey of balladry which employs the usual classification based on special content (heroic, faery, religious, and historical) or lack thereof ("knightly"), in conjunction with a theory of modes (miraculous, mimetic, and ironic), of aesthetic attitude (happy vs. tragic, ethical vs. comical), of theme (love, honor, justice, fortitude), and of character structure (kin, rival, courtship) is less useful for filing ballads into cubbyholes than for approaching them in all their diversity. That their history can be presented as above, as a single coherent development—one might say accumulation—of themes from a probable origin in Old French folk song to the welter of Renaissance texts is due in part to a kind of poetic decorum (for instance, in the use of modes) and in part to a reliance on thematic commonplaces for the creation of new ballads in an oral tradition.

Each piece of the meager evidence coming to us from the Middle Ages has its own degree of uncertainty. Yet when taken as a terminus ante quem for the theme that each attests, they corroborate in aggregate the thematic development of the genre. Beginning with the early thirteenth-century Old French folk songs as a terminus post quem, basic themes of the true-love ballad are attested by 1303 (*Herr Ivan*); perhaps, too, the simplest form of historicization, of giving historical names to stock figures (the Queen Sofie cycle). Historical events appear to have been capable of reshaping ballad themes by the fourteenth century (Folke Algotsson's abduction). A ballad of champions, already resung as a ballad of fealty, was parodied by the second quarter of the fifteenth century (the Greenland stanza). By 1460–80 we meet with probable traces of a troll ballad ("Holger Danske"), a chronicle ballad ("Allegast"), a literary religious ballad ("St. Jørgen"), and a politicized ballad of a lover's death ("Marsk Stig"). By about 1500 faery imagery appears in "Ridderen i Hjorteham" and possibilities for the jocular in a fragment of a bawdy song.

The International Ballad

Of course, the genre did not cease to develop with the Renaissance. One source of change was the folk song of non-Nordic nations, which beyond providing the material for individual ballads has in many instances occasioned stylistic innovations. French folk song seems to have inspired not only the genre itself, but also a certain variety of form within it. Besides the normal short and long couplets (four and seven measures per line, respectively), which are usual Germanic accentual interpretations of a variety of syllabic meters, there occur both the so-called Stolt Elin verse of six measures (e.g., in "Fæstemanden i Graven") and the Liden Karen meter, the Nordic version of the lyrical alexandrine (e.g., in "Tærningspillet"). Both meters are unstable in tradition. Concatenation of a suite of lines with unchanging rhyme was imitated directly in "Kærestens Død" (The Lover's Death). But this effect of enchainment is coupled to changing rhyme by the repetition stanzas, which appear to be a Nordic adaptation of French stanzaic forms, including the lyrical alexandrine. Judging from their optional use in tradition, they were probably adopted, like the usable metrical forms, after the dominant forms were already well established. That implies a persistent influence from medieval French folk song, which is also evident in the occasional appearance of ballads in dialogue form. Behind the earliest version of "Elveskud" (1583) can be discerned the tragic dialogue of the spouse's death in the French folk song "Jean Renaud," which has been prefaced with a tale of fairy enticement and avenging death. Later dialogue ballads of international currency are "Den forgivne Datter" (The Poisoned Daughter) and "Søster beder Broder" (Sister Woos Brother), a metaphorical pursuit reversed in Danish through using the incest theme.

Whereas French folk song has been marginally assimilated to medieval ballad style, German folk songs have often been directly translated in their own rather different style, which has created a neighboring genre that we might call the volkslied ballad. Such ballads have no refrains, use longer stanzaic forms like the *Hildebrandston*, employ local repetition rather than commonplaces, and contain frequent addresses in minstrel tone. The scene is usually generalized as much as possible without the mimetic quality of the medieval ballads, the action is often more symbolic than realistic, and the characters are often nameless fair knights and maidens, huntsmen, soldiers, and so on. It is possible that a couplet in the Swedish "Frihetsvisan" (1439) was taken from the German ballad "Der Bremberger"; in any case, the volkslied ballad is well represented in sixteenth-century sources and derives largely from German broadsides and songbooks, such as "Danyser" (Tannhäuser), "De to Kongebørn" (The Two Royal Children), "Skomager og Edelmand" (Cobbler and Nobleman). In other instances a volkslied has been resung in medieval ballad style, as in "Den dyre Kaabe" and "Kvindemorderen" (The Lady-Killer). A volkslied ballad "Tro som Guld" (True as Gold) soon became "medievalized" as "Troskabsprøven" (Proved Fidelity). Conversely, its faery theme and Nordic refrain type indicate the origin of

"Wassermanns Frau" in the late ballad "Agnete og Havmanden" (Agnete and the Merman). In spite of their proximity in tradition, the "medieval" ballad and the volkslied ballad remained stylistically distinct narrative techniques. The broadside and market-song features of the latter no doubt had their origin in city life and in the age of printing, so it is presumably of later origin than the rural "medieval" ballad style.

The stylistic similarity of British and Nordic balladry has long been recognized; yet it is greater in later (Scottish) than in earlier (English) tradition, and greatest in versions collected in Aberdeenshire in the 1820s by the printer Peter Buchan. This pattern suggests assimilation of British balladry to Nordic style and themes in eighteenth-century Scotland, in part from the Vedel-Syv edition and occasional Danish broadsides. Thus "The Child of Ell" (ca. 1650) bears a thematic resemblance to the elopement ballads and "The Douglas Tragedy" (Broadside 1792) recounts the outline of the story of "Ribold," while "Earl Brand" (after 1829) reproduces the stanzaic form and a good many stanzas of the "Ribold" ballad. Only in the late seventeenth century were ballads clearly borrowed between Britain and Scandinavia, even if the direction is not always clear. Both "Herr Peders Slegfred" (Sir Peder's Mistress) and "Lord Thomas and Fair Annet" first appear in seventeenth-century broadsides, as does "The Twa Sisters," together with an Icelandic manuscript version of "Den talende Strengeleg" (The Talking Harp). From the eighteenth century come "Edward" and "Svend i Rosengaard" (Svend in the Rose Garden); "Sir Patrick Spens," perhaps inspired by "Jon Remordsøns Død paa Havet" (Jon Remordsøn's Death at Sea); "Sweet William's Ghost," perhaps from "Fæstemanden i Graven"; and conversely, "Jesusbarnet, Stefan og Herodes" (The Infant Jesus, Stephen and Herod), apparently from an early version of the ballad carol "The Carnal and the Crane." Stylistically, British ballads with genuine refrains and true commonplace stanzas first appear in eighteenth-century tradition. The extent of their debt to Nordic tradition has, however, never been studied in detail.

Borrowed ballads have done more to influence an established style than to create it, and differences in national style seem to reflect the different and independent origins of the "ballad" from folk-song material within each language area. In France it is scarcely distinct from the lyric; in Germany and Britain it was shaped by minstrel and market-song—that is, commercial—forces. In Scandinavia, among the closely related Nordic dialects, the medieval ballad is unusually well delineated, created and recreated orally by amateurs by means of its distinctive style. Only in recent tradition with its heavy dependence on broadside texts and verbal-memorial recreation has the medieval ballad assimilated itself to European ballad tradition.

Social Milieu

Attempts at placing the ballads more precisely within medieval times and the social milieu are often enlightening but never definitive. According to Vedel, heroic ballads were prevalent among commoners, while there is a marked preference for knightly ballads in the aristocratic manuscripts. There is no reason to deny any level of Danish society a share in ballad production before 1650; after that, cultured society retained at best a literary relationship to oral folk songs. The operative definition of a "folk" must be relative to orality and literacy. In ballad commonplaces, for instance, the nobility sends messages either by having a letter written (by a scribe) or by sending a servant with a "clever tongue." Medieval sources like the *Annales Ryenses* place dancing at the court, which during this period was held throughout the kingdom. The ballads themselves often speak of paying the minstrel well at weddings, but it is the aristocratic folk who do the singing, often at the dance, where a lead singer could make quite a social splash. The marginally literate aristocracy of the Middle Ages and at least the ladies of the Renaissance shared in an oral community that can justly be called the "aristocratic folk," even as ballads were exchanged—that is, taught and learned—by means of scribal intermediaries. Aristocratic balladeers were anything but possessive about their folk songs, which they must have considered the property of anybody who was anybody.

In the thirteenth century, at a time when Anglo-Norman chivalric romances were being translated at the court of Norway's King Hákon Hákonarson, the Danish court was still disporting itself with a runic riddle—and the latest dance. The few works penned in Danish during this century were all, like the dance itself, naturalized products of French culture. French recipes were invaluable in the kitchen, but out in the great hall the dance songs were being concocted from oral ingredients. The Nordic ballads are more likely to have begun as an oral import than as sunken literature—as knightly rather than as saga ballads. Whether or not that occurred in Denmark, the history of Danish medieval literature time and again bears out both the persistence of oral traditions in proverbs, riddles, rhymes, legends, and folktales, and the comparatively late date at which oral traditions were adapted into literary forms. Until 1440 or so, literary culture was Latinate, foreign to both aristocratic and common folk, who shared a fundamentally oral secular culture. The 574 Danish ballad types give some measure of the creative possibilities of an oral tradition inherited from the Middle Ages, a tradition that has functioned best without literary interference. In particular, Danish indifference to the romance genre until 1450 is better understood if we allow that both its narrative and its ideological function were fulfilled by the knightly ballads.

The sharply delineated picture of medieval rural aristocracy is best explained as a product of the aristocratic folk, but here too there are stylistic differences within the genre. The more mimetic portrayal of the daily life and concerns of the rural gentry, including the lesser squirearchy, has created a domestic-realistic style, represented by "Ebbe Skammelsøn" or "Herr Ebbes Døtre," which is particularly concerned with the importance of kin and the independence of women, championing freedom of action for both. For this style the long couplet permits greater detail, including patronymics and place-names that suggest a closer attachment to local and family traditions. A courtly-romantic style, represented by "Ridder Stigs Bryllup" (Sir Stig's Wedding), the royal wedding ballads, many national-historical ballads, and perhaps the symbolical faery ballads such as "Ridder Stigs Runer," shows a love for finery and refinement, chivalry and fealty, and a respect for royal power. It is a commonplace that those who serve at the royal court are "dight in scarlet, clad in martin," and much of ballad finery, mentioned as early as about 1300 in "Drømte mig en Drøm i Nat" (I Dreamed Me a Dream Last Night), could have originated within this style. The lyrical-generic style, as in "Jomfruens Harpeslæt" and in international folktale ballads, is a more generalized common denominator in which the knightly setting has been accepted as stereotyping that is proper to the genre. Here the nuclear family replaces kin, and women are frequently the passive victims of violence.

We can only speculate about which of these styles was the earliest. If the Nordic ballad began as *chansons de toile* resung as *rondes*, perhaps among students returning from Paris, then it started in the generic style and developed characteristic differences in both theme and style at court and at manor, for instance in the Marsk Stig cycle, in which royalists and nobles sang different kinds of ballads. So, too, "Jomfruen paa Tinge" develops its courtship theme in a realistic style and demonstrates the role that women and the rural gentry had in ballad tradition, as they did for the ballad manuscripts. At the manor houses an archaic ideology, for instance regarding the social position of the common-law wife, was nourished by resident copies of the provincial laws. The dynamic tension between dynastic marriage and true love which is the artistic power behind the knightly ballads must have been felt especially strong here. And it is doubtless the loss of this tension that occasioned thematic elaboration within the generic style, as the common folk fetched down folk songs, at whatever date, in the manner depicted for the sixteenth century by "Visesangeren" (The Song Carrier):

Once I served a gentleman
for a summer and a fall;
he gave me ale and mead and meat,
and full reward withal
—He taught me *so many ballads*.

It is presumably the common people who are largely responsible for folktale motifs among the knightly ballads, for fairy tales resung as faery ballads, and legends resung as religious ballads. And commoners have proven receptive both to international ballads with their universal human themes in an even more abstract generic style and to heroic ballads in a heroic-fantastic style of West Nordic origin.

If these assumptions are correct—and they are at least coherent and consistent with medieval evidence—the origin and elaboration of the medieval ballad genre parallel the later development of Danish manuscript sources: a foreign fashion that was imitated at court, apparently in the thirteenth century, then domesticated by the manor folk, and finally appropriated by the common people.

From the Reformation to the Baroque

F. J. Billeskov Jansen

2

At the threshold of the sixteenth century, Denmark, Norway, and Sweden were three kingdoms united under the Danish king. The Kalmar Union, created in 1397 and later broken, was reestablished in 1497. But by 1500 the dominance of the Danish king and nobility had already weakened. A campaign that was meant to force the little north German province of the Ditmarshes into submission under the Danish Crown ended catastrophically. During a battle in the marshes facing the North Sea, the inhabitants opened the floodgates so that the sea rushed in. The charging cavalry in heavy armor became easy prey for the Ditmarshers, who used their spears as poles to vault over the muddy dikes. Rumor of the defeat induced Sweden to secede, and although this country was subject to the Danish king for a short period in 1520–21, the separation was in reality completed and a national antagonism established as well. Thus in the following centuries Sweden received its cultural impulses from other sources, avoiding Denmark, while Denmark and Norway, which remained united until 1814, essentially shared destinies, not least in the relation between religion and politics.

Despite periods of profound setback, caused especially by the military ambitions of the Crown, the double monarchy Denmark-Norway, together with the partly German-speaking regions of Schleswig, Holstein, Oldenburg, and others, was a highly respected monarchy; its prestige even survived the painful loss of the rich provinces of Skåne, Halland, and Blekinge, which Sweden conquered in 1658.

The Reformation in Denmark in 1536 was a revolution, an upheaval of values of all sorts. The new faith evoked a storm of exultation in the minds of many, coinciding with shifts among the social classes. It was a time of unrest in which powerful personalities put their mark on political history as well as in the literary manifestations of the movement.

The loser in the disastrous campaign in the Ditmarshes was King Hans (1481–1513). His son and successor, Christian II (1513–23), had his father's erratic mind, which was to have grievous consequences for the country. To check the nobility, he relied on the new enterprising middle class, which prospered through growing trade. But in Jutland nobleman and peasant rose against him, and when the king wished to ferry across the narrow Little Belt from Funen to Jutland one night in February 1523, he sailed back and forth twenty times, and the game was lost; Christian went to the Netherlands to get help, while his uncle Frederik I (1523–33) was crowned king, though only after having besieged and taken Copenhagen. When Christian failed to gain support, he spent a year, 1523–24, in Germany. He sought out Luther and Melanchthon, whose instruction made a Protestant of him, while in Wittenberg he lived in the painter Lucas Cranach's house. Everything was new. In 1517 Luther had posted his provocative Ninety-five Theses against Catholicism on the door of the chapel of Wittenberg Castle; in 1520 he publicly burned the papal bull that had excommunicated him; in 1521 he was sentenced to outlawry by the Diet of Worms; in 1522 in the security of Wartburg he translated the New Testament to German. Here for Christian II, too, was the weapon against the Catholic Church in Denmark. The king got some Danes in his retinue started on a hasty translation, which was printed in Leipzig in 1524 and was sent to Denmark as political propaganda. In an introductory epistle one of the king's men, Hans Mikkelsen, defended Christian II, whom the new faith had taught to repent old sins. At the same time, the Catholic Church was attacked for unchristian opinions and acts. It is the cantankerous tone of ecclesiastical controversy that is adopted here. It is used in the polemics that are taken up in the political ballads from these years, with gripping poetry in the allegorical "Ørnevisen" (Ballad of the Eagle). It begins like a traditional medieval "parliament of fowls." The birds elect the eagle (Christian II) as their king, so that he can protect them from the proud hawk (Frederik I). But the latter summons his fellows, and because of the hawk's supremacy the eagle has to "fly the woodland"; the crow therefore goes hungry and the owl hides uneasily in the thicket.

In the struggle for the crown, Frederik I was unrelenting. When Christian II went ashore in Norway with an army of recruits in 1531 and sailed to Copenhagen with a pledge of safe conduct to negotiate with his uncle, the latter broke his promise, and Christian remained a prisoner in Danish castles until his death in 1559.

Religious Polemics

Frederik I refused to take sides in the religious struggle, which was therefore essentially verbal in nature until his death in 1533. It had two eloquent combatants: the Carmelite monk Poul Helgesen, or Paulus Helie (ca. 1485–ca. 1535), and Hans Tausen (1494–1561), the Johannite monk who after a stay in Wittenberg in 1523–24 preached Lutheranism in Viborg and was expelled from the order. Helgesen was a reform Catholic, but as theological lector at the university he turned against Luther's claim that we are saved by grace alone: we are saved by the grace of God, but only if our free will accepts it and if we become true Christians in faith and works. And only within the Catholic Church is there salvation. Tausen had attended Helgesen's lectures in 1521–22 and perhaps lived at the Carmelite monastery, where Helgesen was prior. They had, said Tausen later, "consumed much bread" together. Around 1530 they clashed over the interpretation of the Mass. In a pamphlet on this subject Tausen's theological anger expands into ironic insults against Helgesen's "spirit and high heavenly intellect" and into direct resentment of this ungodly and shameful liar.

Helgesen left at his death an anonymous Latin chronicle of Denmark from 1046 to 1534, which was discovered in 1650 walled up behind the altar of Skibby church on Zealand. In this *Skibbykrøniken* (publ. 1773; Skibby Chronicle), as it is called, contemporary monarchs are judged with irate passion. Christian II is a Nero, Frederik I a church robber. Helgesen was an idealist who became a fanatic when he had to take sides. He translated Erasmus of Rotterdam's appeal for reconciliation between Catholics and Protestants in 1534, but in *Skibbykrøniken* he writes that when Tausen arrived in Copenhagen in 1529, the capital "became the most criminal haunt of all sorts of ungodliness and desecration."

In these disputes the theater gained a modest place as an anti-Catholic institution. A *Dialogus* (1533) on the new mass was transmitted from Switzerland—in which Poul Helgesen gets a role with the derisive name of Dirick Turncoat. *Peder Smed og Adser Bonde* (1559; Peder Smith and Adser Farmer) is a localization of a German exposé of a Catholic priest who makes the image of the Madonna weep. Death, which asks all ranks to dance, was represented since the High Middle Ages in the danse macabre, which in its Danish production from the 1530s, *Dødedansen* (publ. ca. 1555; The Dance of Death), took on a clear Protestant tendency. *Broder Rus' Historie* (1555; Brother Carouse's History) unfolds outside the theater, a Catholic satire on monks which in Danish took on an unequivocal anti-Catholic emphasis.

The Civil War

In about 1530 the evangelical movement took Copenhagen by storm, and it remained the Lutheran bastion of the middle class. Two days after Christmas 1530 an iconoclastic riot took place in Our Lady Church. When Frederik I died in April 1533 at Gottorp Castle in Schleswig, conflicting dynastic, religious, and class policy interests created a reign of terror for Denmark: the Count's War (*Grevens Fejde*). Closest to the crown was the king's eldest son, Christian; he was Lutheran and undesirable for the majority of the great nobles who administered the country as the National Council. At the head of an army from Lübeck, which was Lutheran, Count Christoffer of Oldenburg came to regain the crown for Christian II. But in August 1534 Prince Christian was proclaimed king in Horsens; now as Christian III (1534–59) he had to wrest the country from Christian II's supporters. In bloody battles he defeated the peasant army in North Jutland and the Lübeckers in Funen. After a year's merciless siege he captured a starved Copenhagen in June 1536.

In contrast, the establishment of the new Lutheran Church was essentially bloodless. The Catholic clergy was unfrocked; monks and nuns were only gradually turned out. According to Luther's doctrine, the king was lord over the Church, replacing the pope as authority. The Crown confiscated the monastic lands, thereby rescuing the country's miserable economy. The nobility retained its riches and gained greater power over the peasants; the influence of the middle class was checked.

Translations

It was a Lutheran principle that the people should read the Bible in their own language. In a Protestant country Bible translations are mileposts in the history of the national language. In Catholic Europe the norm was the authorized Latin translation, the Vulgate, established in about 400. The great humanist Erasmus of Rotterdam had in 1516–19 published the original Greek text of the New Testament, accompanied by a Latin translation. This work was important for Luther's understanding of the Testament when he translated it to German, and also for Christian II's people when a first Danish translation was sent home from Germany in 1524; it was criticized for having by turns conformed to Luther's German and Erasmus's Latin interpretation.

A greater linguist was Christian Pedersen; in his translation of *Det ny Testamente* (1529; The New Testament) he followed the Vulgate in all essentials but held to Luther's principle that a translation must first and foremost be understood: one should think of what the angel would have said to Mary if he had spoken German. Pedersen says in his preface that no one should "be surprised that the Danish does not everywhere follow word for word with the Latin. . . . Had I written word for word what is in the Latin, then no Dane would have understood the Danish properly." In the same place he says, "If God will grant me his grace, then I shall render the Old Testament in Danish in the future." In 1531 he gave a new rendition from the Vulgate of *Davids Psaltere* (The Psalms of David), "which the Holy Ghost himself made through David's mouth." Pedersen is fully aware of the poetic character of the psalms; he translates in free, rhythmic style and in the postscript writes the prophetic words: "The psalms ought rightly to be rendered in verse and rhyme, if it is possible; for they were so first in the Hebraic tongue, which is most subtle, but our tongue is too coarse for this." Pedersen apparently did complete his translation of the entire Old Testament in 1543, and the text became the foundation for the work of the commission that led to the monumental so-called *Christian III's Bible* of 1550. It was according to the king's wishes that the commission came as close as possible to Luther's Bible translation of 1534 and even included Luther's later corrections from 1541 and 1545.

No single person has had greater importance for Danish usage than Christian Pedersen (ca. 1480–1554), a former canon in Lund and author of a Catholic family devotional book, *Jærtegnspostil* (1515; Homilies on Legends), for which he later apologized when he became Christian II's retainer. He was the translator of the Bible and in 1534 of the highly popular *Kong Olger Danskes Krønike* (King Holger the Dane's Chronicle). In Paris he apparently heard of a prose romance, *Ogier le Dannoys*, and received the king's request to translate it for "good wages" to Danish. But since he could not understand the French tongue, he had the chronicle translated "for gold and fee" into Latin and "wrote it in Danish after the Latin with much toil." The orthography of Pedersen's works became normative for the written language for centuries.

Peder Palladius's Visitations

The new church constitution, *Kirkeordinansen*, was written in 1537 and revised in 1539. The Catholic bishops disappeared, but the new superintendents were commonly called by the old designation. The Reformation's combatants were gradually succeeded by the new kingdom's victorious generation, whose leading and most vigorous figure was Peder Palladius (1503–60), doctor of theology from Wittenberg, in 1537 both bishop of the diocese of Zealand and professor of theology at the university. Palladius became a restless organizer of the religious life in his large diocese, where from

1537 to 1543 he visited its 390 churches. En route he composed, as a hand-book for himself, what he recited for the parishioners. It became a unique work, *En Visitats Bog* (A Book of Visitation), which we know from a copy made in the seventeenth century, published for the first time in 1867. It was the bishop's duty to expel the Catholic leaven from the parishioners' minds and impress on them the evangelical insight that Luther had brought.

According to Palladius's directions, first the local pastor reads aloud the letter in which the king appoints the bishop and charges him with superin-tending all his parishes. The bishop does not go immediately into the pulpit. With a sense of situation he employs rhetorical effects in action and words, and he constantly uses a clear and natural style. The bishop begins by sitting down on a chair near the church wardens and charging them with taking care of the church building and churchyard. He appeals to their own condi-tions, with homely ad hominem arguments: "Keep this church under a dry roof, as you would have it at home. Just as the churchyard's graves should stand clean and cleared, keep the cattle away from them. The grave is now your parents' bed and will be yours: who would have his bed at home in his house filthy and sullied?" Next the bishop cautions the congregation from the pulpit that everyone should go to church, even small children, whom Jesus let come to him: "A good woman and true can always retreat a little into the nave with her child when it will not keep still, long enough until it falls asleep or is quiet again." When the preacher exhorts young maidens and youths, he presents critical situations tangibly. The girls are told not only that they should defend themselves, but also how: "If a rogue comes to you and wants to violate you . . . then all your nails should sooner be seen upon such a rogue's forehead, that he might say that he has been there, before he should be able to have his way with you."

It is curious that the *Visitats Bog*, with its wealth of down-to-earth detail, has to this day been translated only into French, by a Swiss Reformed minis-ter, Jean Sauter, who married a Dane and in 1963 brought the book out un-der the title *Paroisses vivantes* (Living Parishes).

Hymnals
Together with the Bible in the mother tongue, a Danish hymnal was a major goal for the reformers. In 1528 small hymn pamphlets began to turn up, in-creasing in number until Hans Tausen's *En ny Salmebog* (1553; A New Hymnal), in which hymns from the Catholic repertory were introduced with the remark: "We have put down these old songs that everyone may see that there have been pious Christians amid the blindness and error which we were in." A schoolmaster and pastor, Hans Thomesen (1532–73), created

Den danske Salmebog (The Danish Hymnal), which was authorized in 1569. It was an unusually well made book and included many melodies: of its 268 hymns, about 200 are accompanied by musical notation. The nucleus in the treasury of Danish hymns was, from the very beginning, Martin Luther's hymns; then renditions of the Psalms of David; and finally, hymns by various Danes such as Peder Palladius, Hans Thomesen, the historian Anders Sørensen Vedel, and the nobleman Herluf Trolle. When a Catholic hymn was included in Latin, a Danish translation was set line for line:

Puer natus in Bethlehem
It barn er fød i Bethlehem   A child is born in Bethlehem
unde gaudet Ierusalem
thi glæder sig Jerusalem.   wherefore exults Jerusalem.

This hymn is still sung every Christmas when the Danish family dances around the Christmas tree on Christmas Eve. *Den danske Salmebog* was not replaced until 1699, by Kingo's hymnal. Before the Reformation century finished, Denmark had its first original hymn writer, Hans Christensen Sthen (1544–1610), rector and later pastor in Elsinore. It is within the framework of the poetic prayer book that we find Sthen's simple and delicate "En Morgen Sang" (A Morning Song), in which the soul calls to mind both that Easter morn when the Lord rose from the dead and the six days of Creation when everything first appeared. In his evening prayer, "En Aften- eller Natsang" (An Evening or Night Song), he prays for a good night free from devilry and sin—and not to wake up in sorrow.

Philipp Melanchthon and Niels Hemmingsen

Under Christian III, the "priest-king" as he was called, Luther's words and message were dominant. When Frederik II (1559–88) succeeded his father as king in 1559, Philipp Melanchthon gained steadily increasing influence in Denmark. While Luther was expatiating in violent polemical tracts, Melanchthon edited the manifestos of the new movement such as the Augsburg Confession (1530), which became the Lutheran constitution. Melanchthon attributed greater ability to human reason and will than did Luther. He maintained that every young person has, like Hercules at the parting of the ways, the freedom to choose between vice and virtue. While Luther liberated the mother tongue with his Bible translation and his hymns, Melanchthon became the founder of the new pedagogy. He was early on a keen supporter of raising the level of humanist education. He authored schoolbooks in dialectics and rhetoric, as well as Greek and Latin Grammars. We have a copy of his *Elementa latinæ grammatices recognita ab autore* (1542; Elements of Latin Grammar Examined by the Author) preserved with autograph signature and notes by the later Frederik II. When the University of Copenhagen, following the disturbances of the civil war, was reestablished in 1537 and was given a new charter in 1539 that remained in force until 1732, it was patterned this time on Wittenberg and therefore in the spirit of Melanchthon. In the struggle for pure doctrine there was a need to know not only Latin well, but also Greek and Hebrew, as well as how to reason clearly and convincingly; grammar and rhetoric became important subjects.

We can throw light on Melanchthon's role in Danish intellectual life by reading a funeral sermon delivered in 1565 by his most brilliant disciple, Niels Hemmingsen (1513–1600), who in 1537–42 had stayed in Wittenberg and had later become professor at the University of Copenhagen. With his teacher he shares a faith in human reason, and in his work *De lege naturæ* (1562; On Natural Law) he establishes, with greater consistency than Melanchthon, that purely human reason can arrive at a doctrine of justice and morality coinciding in all essentials with the Ten Commandments of the Mosaic Law. Hemmingsen therefore stands as an important forerunner for more recent founders of natural law.

At Wittenberg, Hemmingsen had become acquainted with a young nobleman, Herluf Trolle (1516–65), who in 1536–37 had studied with Melanchthon. Contact had been maintained, for in 1559 Melanchthon dedicated a book interpreting the Epistle to the Colossians to Trolle; the dedication stressed how crucial it was just then to stand firm against the many enemies of the true faith: atheists, unbelievers, Jews, and Catholics. Trolle held high positions in the service of the Crown. Frederik II wished to reestablish the Nordic Union; during the Seven Years' War with the Swedes (1563–70) Trolle was high admiral in the naval action against the Swedish fleet and died of his wounds June 26, 1565. Hemmingsen's eulogy of him was printed in 1572. The biography is a typical picture of the rich and pious nobleman who in his Lutheranism combined obedience to royal power with faith in doctrine. Trolle had, Hemmingsen says, at an early age placed money at the disposal of the grammar schools in Elsinore, Næstved, and Roskilde: "For he well knew that as long as schools endure, there are also sure to be people who can serve the congregation of Christ." Hemmingsen could have cited Melanchthon's words of warning: "To neglect youth in school is the same as taking spring out of the year, for without schools religion cannot be upheld." We know that Trolle and his wife had attended a princely wedding in Saxony in 1548. It was probably then that he had heard about what Hemmingsen calls "certain free elementary schools in Germany" where great care was taken with the disciples. These were the famous "princely schools," two learned boarding schools that the Elector Moritz of Saxony had established in Pforta and Meissen, entirely according to Melanchthon's school plan and under his supervision. It was with these prototypes in mind that, by charter of May 23, 1565, shortly before the final and fatal naval action, Herluf Trolle and Birgitte Gøye established a boarding school at Herlufsholm, near Næstved on Zealand, where it still functions.

Hemmingsen continues by speaking about Trolle's loyalty to authority: "He well knew that he who is not loyal to his king and ancestral kingdom would not be faithful to our God either. . . . And I often heard these words from him that Saint Peter says: Fear God; honor the king." When Trolle was wounded in battle, he did not want to be bandaged before others, recounts the preacher. He came ashore very weak. When Hemmingsen as confessor spoke to him about the matter of his salvation "and wished to comfort him, I found greater comfort from him than I could give him. But so that Lady Birgitte should not observe that he was preparing himself to journey to his dear Savior Jesus Christ, he asked me to speak Latin." The injured man fortified himself with passages from the gospel and from the Psalms of David. If he should live on, it was "that I might be of benefit for our new school; but I will commend it to almighty God, he will surely find a way according to his holy will."

As in all the numerous printed funeral sermons we have from the sixteenth to the eighteenth century, Hemmingsen dwells on the dying man's last communion, his parting with relatives and domestics. The genre offers us copious reports of encounters with death. Trolle had himself dressed, and expired sitting up in his chair.

Hemmingsen's funeral sermon has yet another dimension. In the introduction to Lady Birgitte it comes as a comfort to her that her good husband "is with Jesus, among angels and pious ancestors, expecting daily with all God's children that God should soon put an end to this world." If the destruction of the world was to take place in 1588 as expected, then Hemmingsen was to find the deadline had been postponed. He became the greatest builder of systems in his generation.

As a brilliant author of textbooks he elaborated Melanchthon's theological standpoint in the handbook *Enchiridion theologicum* (1557; Handbook of Theology) and the entire Christian philosophical system in *Syntagma institutionum christianarum* (1574; Presentation of Christian Principles). But this crowning work of Hemmingsen's life became the ground for his dismissal from the university. In Saxony the Elector August, whose wedding with Anna, the sister of Frederik II, Herluf Trolle had attended, had begun to take a stricter course with theologians who inclined toward the Calvinist interpretation of eucharistic dogmas. Contrary to Catholics and Lutherans, who with certain nuances regarded the eucharistic bread and wine as Christ's body and blood, Calvin celebrated in the Eucharist his memory and fellowship. Melanchthon and Hemmingsen with him distanced themselves from Luther. In the *Syntagma* Hemmingsen had taught that the eucharistic guest receives the body of Christ not with his mouth but with his faith. Thus he could be regarded as a secret supporter of Calvin, a crypto-Calvinist. The Elector, who considered himself the head of the Protestant princes in Germany, forced Frederik II to transfer Hemmingsen, even though he recanted his interpretation. He was given a canonicate in Roskilde and continued to enjoy an international reputation. When King James VI of Scotland was in Denmark in 1590, he visited Niels Hemmingsen in Roskilde and Tycho Brahe on Hven.

When we combine these two stars in Danish learning of the period, we can perceive in their conjunction what science meant in Frederik II's epoch. The key word was coherence, the comprehensive view. Faith in God, in his Creation and gifts of grace, was a focus for all knowledge, but within it everything in nature and in human life should be contained. A profound coherence exists among all that is, has been, and will be.

THE PHILOSOPHY OF NATURE AND THE STUDY OF HISTORY

Europe's master in speculative natural science was the Swiss Paracelsus (1493–1541). God had created the first uniform substance, *materia prima*. In it a spiritual primordial force, *astrum*, acts, unfolding in both the macrocosm of the universe and the microcosm of the human body. Astrology can consequently read a person's fate in the position and movements of the heavenly bodies. Nature has three basic substances: salt, mercury, and sulfur. From them are compounded the four elements: earth, air, fire, and water. It is from these four that the elemental corporeal, earthly world is sustained; but this world has a hidden interaction with the astral world of the heavens, and both have connections with the divine world that nourishes and strengthens our immortal spirit in its faith in Christ. No wonder that the best heads in the North were fascinated by a system that saw an inner kinship among the natural sciences, astrology, and theology.

Curiously enough, Paracelsus, who supported himself as an itinerant physician, was with the Danish army in Stockholm in 1519–20. His Danish pupil, court physician Peder Sørensen, latinized as Petrus Severinus (ca. 1540–1602), gathered the master's ideas in *Idea medicinæ philosophicæ* (1571; Outline of Philosophical Medicine), which undoubtedly appealed to the most important Nordic admirer of Paracelsus, Tycho Brahe. It is only from Paracelsus's comprehensive view that one can grasp Brahe's scientific achievement.

Tycho Brahe

Tycho Brahe (1546–1601) was a child prodigy; Latin became a second tongue for him from the age of six and was his language as author of both prose and verse. He entered the university at the age of twelve; a solar eclipse on August 21, 1560, awakened him to astronomy: he saw something literally divine in the confidence with which the astronomers had predicted this heavenly phenomenon. The learned youth spent his early years, 1562–71, mostly abroad studying astronomy and astrology as well as chemistry, which he pursued after Paracelsus's model for the sake of medicine. Once home again, he established a chemical laboratory, but then the heavens themselves gave him a sign: on November 11, 1572, Brahe saw a new star in the constellation Cassiopeia and the following May he published, despite pressure from friends—for a nobleman really ought not to occupy himself with publishing books—*De nova stella* (On the New Star). In an accompanying Latin poem, "Elegia in Uraniam" (Elegy to Urania), he promises the firmament eternal faith, and in *De disciplinis mathematicis oratio* (publ. 1610; Oration on the Mathematical Sciences) he praises astronomy for providing profound insight into the Creation.

In 1576 Frederik II granted Brahe the island of Hven so he could there construct Uranienborg, an imposing building in three stories: an observatory at the top, living quarters in the middle, and a chemical laboratory in the basement. With his collaborators Brahe performed countless observations of the heavenly bodies, not only in order to know God's marvelous work more accurately, but also better to calculate in advance life on earth. He brought out annual forecasts, *Prognostica*, of the course of nature in the coming year. He drew up horoscopes for the king's sons, including the later Christian IV (1596–1648)—and his determination of this king's character and destiny proved remarkably correct. The foundation of a horoscope was the position of the heavenly bodies at the moment of a person's birth. Yet it must be borne in mind that a person's life is not completely foreordained, for as is said in Prince Christian's nativity: "There is in every person something divine that is raised above the orbits of the stars and that, if the person understands how to put it to use, makes him dependent upon the destiny of the stars to the least degree." Paracelsus's theory of humans' triune nature is wholly Brahe's: We belong to the elements but have as well a share in the wisdom of the lofty heavenly bodies, and via our immortal spirit we have access to God himself. In his chemical laboratory medicines were prepared, which Brahe dispensed free to his peasants.

For twenty years Hven was an international research center, especially for astronomical work. Frederik II died in 1588, and in 1596 Christian IV came of age and acceded to the throne. He reduced Brahe's income, and in 1597 the proud and famous astronomer left Hven to seek support from another prince. In his living, passionate Latin he complains of the affront in a grand poem to Denmark, "Ad Daniam," beginning "Dania, quid merui?" (Denmark, what is my offense?). With justified self-esteem he asserts that he has raised his country's reputation to the stars. He accuses not the king but those few who were the cause of his fall. He now seeks a country where the holy heavens are held in veneration. He found it with Emperor Rudolf II of Austria, but exile brought Brahe many bitter hours until his death in 1601. He lies buried in the Tein Church in Prague. Although Brahe worked without a telescope—which was first invented after his death—his observations were amazingly precise, accurate to less than a minute of an arc. When the German astronomer Johannes Kepler obtained Brahe's permission to use his planetary observations, they enabled the younger astronomer to establish his theory of the elliptical form of planetary orbits.

History

As in the universe, there was order and coherence in history, both national and international. Everyone knew that as the world was created in six days, and as one day is with the Lord as a thousand years (2 Peter 3:8), the world would last for six millennia, divided into three periods of two thousand years each. The first, from Adam to Abraham, was without law and government; with Abraham's introduction of circumcision the law, God's Law, was put into force; and after Christ's appearance the age of the Messiah commences; but as evil and ungodly as the world is, its destruction could very well occur before the two millennia are concluded. After the Judgment follows the seventh day of Creation, the Lord's Day, the eternal sabbath.

It was a triumph for the Danes when in 1514 Christian Pedersen had Saxo's chronicle printed in Paris. Here the antiquity of the kingdom was documented: upward of a hundred kings going back to Dan! To outdo Saxo, Swedish historian Johannes Magnus in 1554 constructed a Swedish succession going back to Noah's son Japhet; as in the medieval *Gesta Danorum pa danske*, Humble was a Swedish king who installed his son Dan as viceroy over the islands west of Sweden. This fruitless rivalry in the historiography of the fantastic continued for the rest of the century. But the work of historian Anders Sørensen Vedel (1542–1616) did bear fruit in his translation of Saxo's Latin into a vigorous, plain Danish, *Den danske Krønike* (1575; The Danish Chronicle); Vedel was subsequently invited by Frederik II's queen, whom he met at Tycho Brahe's, to publish the medieval ballads. *Et Hundrede udvalgte Danske Viser* (1591; One Hundred Choice Danish Ballads) turned out to be a collection of ballads without equal in any other nation at this time. Although Vedel was the royal historiographer, the laborious collection, redaction, and annotation of these ballads from the Middle Ages and later were not really a digression. They were for him historical sources. But they were also a source of joy, because of their tunes, "when otherwise chanted with a woman's pure tone or a man's robust voice," as he writes. The *Et Hundrede Viser* became a treasury of song for centuries, reprinted many times, augmented in 1695 to two hundred ballads by Peder Syv. As a textual basis for the ballad dance it still lives on in the Faroe Islands.

When Frederik II died in 1588, Vedel gave a funeral sermon for him, printed the same year in a stately edition. It is arranged in the generic pattern, including a careful account of the last days of the deceased. With outspokenness the preacher discusses the king's death. He says that if the king had abstained "from the commonly harmful drinking that is now all too widespread through all the world among princes and nobles and the common man, then it would seem to human eyes and thoughts that His Grace could have lived many a good day longer. But it is now futile to argue about this. Death will have its cause."

As a Renaissance prince, Frederik II wished to build grandly. Krogen, an ancient stronghold near Elsinore, was transformed into the huge fortress Kronborg Castle, a plausible scene for Shakespeare's *Hamlet*. Frederik exchanged Skovkloster near Næstved (brought under the Crown by the Reformation) for Hillerødsholm, owned by Herluf Trolle. The latter established Herlufsholm School in Skovkloster in 1565, and the king established a grammar school at Hillerødsholm after the same pattern; it was moved to Sorø, where it still exists as an academy. As a scholarship foundation for students at the University of Copenhagen, Frederik II established in 1569 the Community, with a large number of tenant farms as its financial base. He promoted research as well as education. He thus provided an honorable retreat for Niels Hemmingsen. As long as Frederik reigned, Tycho Brahe resided in his Uranienborg and his friend Anders Sørensen Vedel in his large house "Liljebjerg" in Ribe. Not until 1594 did Vedel lose his post as historiographer, because he had made no progress with the necessary history of Denmark.

This history was an urgent task of state, and it was accomplished by a nobleman and trained administrator with a high literary education. Arild

Huitfeldt (1546–1609) was a member of the National Council and as the chancellor of the realm was responsible for the judicial system, in addition to being a landowner and lord lieutenant. As a public official he had access to government archives and for many years had documents copied, which he eventually fused into *Danmarks Riges Krønike* (1595–1603; Chronicle of the Kingdom of Denmark). He started with the history of Christian III and worked backward in six parts to King Dan. Huitfeldt wrote history as an experienced politician. His prototype was the French statesman Philippe de Commines's *Memoires* (1524–28), in which people and events are judged according to their political success. Huitfeldt gives earnest instruction in his preface to the young Christian IV, who had personally assumed power in 1596. Huitfeldt's ideal was a religious balance between Lutherans and the Reformed Church, and a political one between king and nobility. He therefore praises Frederik I but castigates Christian II, whom he finds suspicious even as an unborn child:

> It is said of Prince Christian that he is supposed to have wept in the womb so that one could hear him loud and clear. And in the hour of his birth to have appeared with one hand open, the other clenched. Which being opened by the midwife was found to be full of blood and slime. Signifying that he was to be a bloodthirsty man, and a lamentable time under him impending, which was later made manifest. . . . Christian II was very shaggy and hairy on his body and in his face, which is indicative of a hot nature.
> (Tr. David Colbert)

Christian was now and then troubled by a kind of depression. About this man branded by nature Huitfeldt even says that the National Council had sufficient cause to oppose his "violence, power, and tyranny. For he has not reigned like a lord and king with discretion, law, and justice, but as a tyrant and abuser." With Huitfeldt's character sketch we catch a glimpse of how his age inferred inner spiritual conditions from a person's outer bodily ones.

And so the chronicle was produced in Danish, down to 1559. Regard for the opinion of foreign powers concerning the Danish kingdom demanded in addition an account in flawless Latin. Competition with Sweden was still intense. Learned men could be hired in the Netherlands, and in 1618 the Swedish king Gustav II Adolf appointed the Dutch classical philologist Daniël Heinsius (1580–1655) as Swedish royal historiographer, the same year, his compatriot Johannes Isacius Pontanus (1571–1639) was commissioned as royal Danish historiographer, supplemented in 1625 by another Dutchman, Johannes Meursius (1579–1639). The two historians produced a complete history of Denmark in Latin, of which the latter parts, however, were not printed until 1740–46.

LITERATURE IN LATIN AND DANISH

From the Middle Ages Denmark's literature was bilingual. Over against ballads and legal texts stood Saxo's history and Sunesen's *Hexaëmeron*. During the two centuries following the Middle Ages Saxo's elegant prose became the prototype for Danish historians writing in Latin, just as his brilliant treatment of Roman verse forms aroused a spirit of emulation in the new poets. It is in Latin that generations of Danish poets in the sixteenth century exercised their sense of verse form, until in the seventeenth century a regular Danish prosody and an equally artful stylistics made their mark. The metrical reforms begun around 1625 cannot be understood without knowledge of the philological preparatory school that practically all poets attended. As a rule they graduated from grammar school with Latin, Greek, and Hebrew, and from the university as well, the majority with a degree in theology. In the same period, and even in the same poets, two stylistic norms could exist: a cultivation of form in learned Latin versification and a popular formlessness in the accentual meters (*knittelvers*) adopted from the Middle Ages. In addition, Latin poetry in Denmark is not a uniform quantity; it has periods with changing stylistic ideals, periods that poetry in the Danish language follows with a delay of one or two generations.

Latin Poetry

Before the Reformation finally succeeded, the Church had its first prominent Latin poet since Saxo. Olaus Chrysostomos (died 1553), whose name is a hellenization of Gyldenmund, held a great oration in hexameters as a teacher at the university on the occasion of a new rector. In this work, *Lamentatio ecclesiæ* (1529; Lament of the Church), the Church laments its decline, the rejection of the veneration of the saints and celibacy by the new sects, and ecclesiastical ignorance. The oration was printed the next year, and almost simultaneously Chrysostomos joined the Lutherans. He later became a professor at the reestablished university and died as a bishop in North Jutland. There is a classical eloquence in his poem. His imagery borrows its comparisons from classical mythology, and when he sees the ungodly aspiring after hell and depicts the tortures awaiting them, they are the torments of such as Tantalus and Sisyphus.

Danes who were journeymen in Wittenberg met not only Luther's faith but also Melanchthon's scholarship. The latter's *Grammatica latina* (1526;

Latin Grammar) closed with a poem about the art of composing poetry, "De arte versificandi." After a stay in Wittenberg, Peder Lille, latinized as Petrus Parvus (died 1559), became the university's professor in Latin rhetoric. The widely traveled Hans Frandsen, latinized as Johannes Franciscus (1532–84) composed two Latin poems, *De natali domini ac salvatoris nostri Jesu Christi* (1553; About the Nativity of Our Lord and Savior Jesus Christ) and *De oculorum fabricatione et coloribus* (1556; About the Structure and Color of Eyes). In Heidelberg he was crowned poet laureate. But when he wished to pay homage to Vedel in Danish for his translation of Saxo, he used stanzas with alternating rhyme that turned out extremely clumsy.

A renowned traveling Latin poet was Rasmus Glad, latinized as Erasmus Lætus (1526–82), who also worked as a professor at the university from time to time. His journeywork was a collection of pastoral colloquies in hexameters, *Bucolica* (1560), which praise idyllic nature in Frederik II's Denmark. He went abroad in 1572, no doubt in order to get a series of large Latin poems that he had completed or planned into print. In Basel his *Colloquia moralia* (1573; Moral Colloquies) was published, in which plants, animals, rivers, and so on debate philosophical subjects; in the last colloquy the Tiber River and the Jutland Gudenå converse about the thesis that "great men live by virtue of their spirit." *De re nautica* (1573; On Navigation) was dedicated to the Republic of Venice, just as *De republica Noribergensium* (1574; On the Republic of Nuremberg) was offered to that city's senate. *Margareticorum libri decem* (1573; Ten Cantos on Margrete), an epic poem on Scandinavia's queen, was with clear intentions submitted to Queen Elizabeth of England. A chronicle, *Romanorum Cæsares Italici* (1574; The Roman Emperors), was presented to the reigning Holy Roman Emperor, Maximilian II. Unlike the previous poems, which were in hexameters, the latter was written in distichs, that is, in stanzas each consisting of a hexameter and a pentameter. There is a joy in Lætus's massive presentation of historical and geographical material. These six poems comprise 27,200 lines of verse. Yet his major work, *Res Danicæ* (1573; Danish Events), contains 16,300 hexameters. The poet unrolls, as it were, a tapestry as far as Frederik II's wedding, illustrating the time since Noah left the ark after the Flood and his son Japhet began his migration northward, where his posterity founded the kingdom of the Danes, an epic half again as long as Virgil's *Aeneid*, which leads to the foundation of Rome. His style is always elegant but without pomp. Lætus wants poetry to preserve the memory of great and noble deeds, rendering them in precise and graceful form. He fancied himself a descendant of the Roman Golden Age.

Latin and Danish verse meet in the prolific historian and pastor Claus

Christoffersen Lyschander (1558–1624). As a young, ambitious theologian, he depicted in Latin verse the history of the noble family Krabbe (1581) and the introduction of the Christian faith into Scandinavia, *Propagatio fidei* (1582; Propagation of the Faith). But when in about 1597 he wished to regale one of the Bille family with his genealogy, he shifted to Danish accentual verse for the sake of the noble lady. In *Billeslægtens Rimkrønike* (publ. 1722; Chronicle of the Bille Family) fifteen mothers step forth and relate their own histories, with a simple joy in life and confidence in death. Lyschander quickly found himself at home in the art of rhyming in Danish, and sometime into the new century he transferred the ambition of the Latin poets—the large, detailed poem—into composition in the mother tongue. For these long narrative and descriptive poems he used primarily a six-lined stanza with fixed rhyme pattern. *Den grønlandske Chronica* (1608; The Greenland Chronicle) narrates with fine epic energy voyages to Greenland through the ages; *Den calmarnske Triumf* (1611; The Calmar Triumph) describes Christian IV's capture of the city of Kalmar on the Swedish coast. Christian IV's eldest son was in 1608 chosen as his successor; the subject of the poem *Christian den Femtes Udvælgelses og Hyldings Historie* (1623; History of the Election and Homage of Christian V). The prince never became king, for he died in 1647, a year before his father. Learned poetry had with Lyschander acquired an original Danish expression.

Around 1600, just as the poets in the mother tongue wished to weigh their poems down with learning as in the admired scientific works of the New Latin poets such as Lætus, Latin poetry was about to slip off its learned harness to move freely in brief, pointed poesy. Sixteenth-century taste in Latin preferred the serious, heavy-gaited poems, but the seventeenth century cherished the small, light, and sprightly ones, and the epigram became the best-loved genre. It is the Holsteiner Willich Westhovius (1577–1646) who marks the turn of the tide. He rendered in Latin hexameters a skillful oration by the Greek rhetorician Isocrates, *De legitimo regis officio* (1610; On the King's Legitimate Office), expatiating in the many nuances of the epigram. Westhovius cultivated the emblem, a symbolic picture (in woodcut or engraving) explained in prose and in a poem. This subtle relation between picture and word flourished in the sixteenth and seventeenth centuries. Westhovius descended literarily from the Italian Andrea Alciati, whose emblem book appeared in 1531, through the Englishman Geoffrey Whitney, who published *A Choice of Emblemes* in 1548. Westhovius published *Emblemata* (1613), dedicated to the Holy Roman Emperor Matthias, and a second collection (1640) inscribed to Christian IV.

If Erasmus Lætus was the Golden Age poet, Bertel Knudsen Aquilonius

(1588–1650) became the typical Silver Age virtuoso. In his books of Latin verse from 1609 he cultivated style for the sake of style, with a partiality for the most artificial meters. The only original epigrammatic poet was the diplomat Henrik Harder (1642–83), whose approximately four hundred *Epigrammata* came out in 1679. Like his mentor, the Englishman John Owen, Harder used his clever wit for philosophical, humorous, and edifying epigrams. One of the last-named category builds on the polysemantic nature of the words "life" and "death." It is entitled "Til Christi Grav. Gravskrift over Døden" (To Christ's Sepulchre: Epitaph to Death): "In this grave no dead man lies, but Death itself, whose conquerer was Life that sacrificed itself." The spiritually refined style lasted the rest of the century, as shown by a two-volume anthology that a young scholar, Frederik Rostgaard (1671–1745), published in Leiden, *Deliciæ quorundam Poëtarum Danorum* (1693; Delights of Certain Danish Poets).

In the sixteenth and seventeenth centuries Danish poetry in Latin passed through three phases, which can no doubt be found in other European countries. At the onset of humanism around 1530 a passionate rhetorical style was dominant, with classical mythology and legendary history as poetic lever, as exemplified by Chrysostomos. The latter half of the century and first part of the next was characterized by a poetry heavy with content, an entire school with the Virgilian Lætus at its midpoint (1560–74). The rest of the seventeenth century was the great age of delicate Latin poesy, with Aquilonius its most prominent figure but the epigrammatist Harder its most significant poet.

The School Drama

Danish drama had a short heyday in the years around 1600. Luther had recommended that grammar school pupils put on classical and new comedies, to train themselves in Latin, and he saw the Bible as material both for tragedies (plays with princely persons, an example being the Book of Judith) and for comedies, common subjects with happy endings (like the Book of Tobias). Melanchthon was fond of staging and playing a part. With his slight frame and high-pitched voice he was a success in women's roles.

The drama was bilingual, like much of Danish literature. In the Netherlands, Germany, and Switzerland plays appeared in both Latin and the national languages. Danish pedagogues learned readily, and so many plays were translated and written that some are still not published. There were four dramaturgical centers for the original school comedy: Elsinore, Ribe, Viborg, and Randers.

We know that in Elsinore the rector of the grammar school between 1570 and 1574, the hymn writer Hans Christensen Sthen, had his pupils put on plays in the town hall. One of them was presumably his morality play, *Kort Vending* (Turnabout), in which Fortune lets rich, haughty, and lazy people exchange fate with the poor, humble, and diligent. The play's epilogue declares that we indeed cannot be saved without faith, but "good deeds should adorn faith." There was another theater in Elsinore. In 1585 an English troupe played in the town hall courtyard. Kronborg Castle stood almost finished before the eyes of the English actors and appeared some years later in Shakespeare's *Hamlet*.

One of the most zealous theatrical pedagogues was Peder Jensen Hegelund (1542–1614). After studying in Wittenberg, he came to Ribe in 1569, where he became a teacher, a parish pastor at the cathedral in 1588, and bishop in 1595. He had Terence's *Andria* and modern Latin plays staged, as well as translations from Latin and German. He himself rendered into Danish the Swiss Sixt Birck's Latin *Susanna*, performed in 1576. It is the story of the chaste Susanna, condemned to death by lascivious old men but saved by the prophet Daniel. Calumnia (Slander) appears in an interlude. In the text and in an accompanying woodcut she is provided with "two large ears, two tongues in one mouth, double heart [after Psalm 12:13], wings from both her arms and feet, and she is everywhere trimmed with feathers and down." Perhaps such a figure stood on the scene when Shakespeare's *Henry IV* (Part 2) was begun: "Enter Rumour, painted full of tongues."

Hegelund was an eloquent intermediary and the Ribe school was fertile soil for dramatic art, but it was in Viborg that the genre culminated, for this Jutland town possessed a dramatist of great caliber, Hieronymus Justesen Ranch (1539–1607). He had studied in Wittenberg, was called in 1572 to minister to the parish of Grayfriars Church in Viborg, and in 1591 became dean. He created his first play on an order from the court, to pay homage to Prince Christian, the later Christian IV, when he became heir to the throne at the age of seven. The work was staged in the marketplace in Viborg in June 1584. Ranch based his play about homage to an heir on the First Book of Kings, where it is told that when King David had grown very old, his son Adonai set himself up as king; therefore David, who had promised Bathsheba that her son Solomon would succeed his father, had to have Solomon anointed as king. Since there was no struggle for the crown in Denmark, Frederik II, Queen Sofie, and their court could attend *Kong Salomons Hylding* (Allegiance to King Solomon) to watch the abortive rebellion, the anointing of the rightful successor, the penitence of the rebel, and the elected king offering him peace and reconciliation. The festival play makes no mention of Solomon's finding an excuse soon after for having his brother killed: it concludes with the old king's long blessing on them all. The stirring plot is accompanied by buffoonery.

There is also a fool in Ranch's musical play *Samsons Fængsel* (ca. 1599; Samson's Captivity). In the Book of Judges the relations of Samson with the Philistine women, one of whom he marries, are an inspiration "of the Lord; that he sought an occasion against the Philistines" (14:4), but in Ranch's Lutheran play the motive is a moral one: because Samson "yielded to promiscuity / His God was angered mightily." But this "lamentable tragedy," as the subtitle calls it, is enlivened by songs and entertaining scenes: when Samson falls asleep, the barber comes and cuts off his long hair. The stage mechanics even saw to it that the pillars could collapse and crush both Samson and the Philistines.

Entertainment and edification, merriment and moralism were joined again by Ranch in his masterpiece, *Karrig Niding* (Nithing the Niggard). This comedy probably existed in 1598, but the first known production was in Randers in 1606. It was composed as a Danish counterpart to Plautus's comedy about the skinflint, *Aulularia*, without thematic borrowing but with Roman technique in casting and plot design. The story about the miser who, in order to save household expenses, locks up the house's pantry and leaves his wife, children, and servants to starve is familiar from Walter Map, a twelfth-century English author, and also from German and Danish folk songs. The characters are built up with dramatic skill, including the handsome beggar, Jep Skald, who arrives with his apprentice; feeds the household from his well-stocked scrip; charms the wife, Jutta; and shares the night with her. Meanwhile, a dream about what has actually happened disquiets Nithing's mind, but on returning home he is recognized by no one, all the locks having been changed. In another comedy by Plautus, *Amphitruo*, the title figure comes home and doubts his own identity because Jupiter has been with his wife in her husband's form. Similarly, Nithing is persuaded that he has dreamed his earlier condition as master of this house and that he is really an itinerant beggar. Now that he has had food and drink he becomes quite wanton and fancies that Jutta, in whom he sees Jep Skald's wife, is making eyes at him, the vagabond:

> I dreamt the strangest dream last night,
> A beggar held my good wife tight,
> Let's hope it does not indicate,
> That Jep Skald's wife will meet that fate:
> See how her eyes now take my measure,
> As though she'd buy me for her pleasure.

And if perchance it came to pass,
I'd laugh until I burst, alas!
But to her love I don't aspire,
Neither is it my desire,
To sleep in Jep Skald's woman's bed,
I hope to find my own instead.
(Tr. Frederick Marker)

With Ranch's *Karrig Niding*, Danish humanist theater left an enduring mark, performed with success in recent times. The school drama's final flower occurred in Randers; its repertoire is known from the voluminous Randers Manuscript. Its best piece is perhaps by Ranch. The Book of Tobias, which Luther had recommended for dramatization, has in *Tobiæ Komedie* (ca. 1600; The Comedy of Tobias) acquired a tinge of moral fairy tale. Devils come for the ungodly bridegrooms, who do not deserve the beautiful and virtuous Sara. She is released only by the young Tobias, who charmingly kneels with her beside the bridal bed to witness before God that he has entered wedlock to beget children for the glory of God.

When looking back over the sixteenth century, we see quite distinct periods. An era of upheaval, when literature in Danish and Latin was characterized by religious-political crisis, existed until 1533. With Christian III's complete rule, the framing of the Lutheran-monarchical state began; Peder Palladius gave the finest proof of it in his *En Visitats Bog*. Frederik II culturally reaped the fruits of a new age. Humanistic scholarship was consolidated; national self-assertion promoted the study of the kingdom's ancient history with Anders Sørensen Vedel as its leading figure. Large-scale Latin poetry flourished with Erasmus Lætus. Simultaneously, Tycho Brahe engaged in both the conquest of the sky and the deciphering of the course of an individual's life as expressed in the planets. The years 1584, when Frederik II in Viborg had the later Christian IV honored as heir to the throne, and 1596, when the latter was crowned in Copenhagen, form the boundary between humanism and Renaissance. The royally organized festivities on these occasions point forward to the Crown Prince Christian's high nuptials in 1634. In all these areas the growing influence of a dynamic, politically and culturally self-assured working sovereign was felt.

RENAISSANCE AND HUMANISM

With the Randers theater, as with Lyschander's poem on Christian IV's deeds, *Den calmarnske Triumf*, we have crossed over into the seventeenth century. The new king had in 1625–29 unwisely intervened in the Thirty Years' War (1618–48); he suffered defeat and was forced to make peace with the Holy Roman Emperor. Afterward he wished to gain prestige as a mediator in the great central European war. In his primer for a modern prince, *Il principe* (1532), Machiavelli had maintained that the political prestige of a country could be measured by its cultural level. When Christian IV was to celebrate Crown Prince Christian's wedding with Magdalena Sibylle of Saxony, he made the occasion into a sumptuous manifestation of the cultural capacity of the Dano-Norwegian Crown. Ambassadors from many countries were present, and without regard for expense the huge party was entertained with elaborate pageants and splendid fireworks, combined with mythological and allegorical masques and an opera ballet in large, modern style. An English troupe also performed, no doubt Robert Archer's, whose actors had as court players in Poland memorized their repertoire in German.

Unfortunately, Christian IV again intervened in the war in 1643–45 in order to constrain Sweden. The upshot was a humiliating peace. The old king died in 1648, and his younger son ascended the throne as Frederik III.

Humanism laid great stress on thorough knowledge of the three sacred languages: Hebrew, Greek, and Latin. To aid in the closer study of the Bible, the clergy wanted a translation that philologically reflected the original texts. A new one (1607) was prepared by the later bishop Hans Poulsen Resen from the original languages, in tortuous Danish, a painfully precise translation half incomprehensible for the common reader. It became the scholar's Bible, a reference book for pastors. Professor of Hebrew Hans Svane undertook a slight revision (1647), supplying it with many new philological marginal notes. Thus Denmark had two types of Bible translations, for Christian III's Bible (1550), republished as Frederik II's Bible (1589) and Christian IV's Bible (1633), remained the church Bible, in folio, opened during church services; Resen's and Svane's Bibles were in a smaller format. Seventeenth-century theologians were well versed in the Scriptures. The poet Thomas Kingo used about a thousand biblical citations in a funeral sermon in 1691, of which many were freely rendered from memory. Virtually all the books and epistles of the Old and New Testaments are represented, and the citations demonstrate by their wording that Kingo was acquainted with all five translations. He, like many of his contemporaries, knew the Bible by heart. Behind almost all the texts in this century, including those in natural science, we can sense the Bible.

The French and Italian Renaissance

Late in the seventeenth century a literary movement reached Denmark from Italy and France. It aimed at an artistic refinement of the mother tongue. Inspired by Italian aestheticians, the French poet Joachim du Bellay, who lived a long time in Rome, published a little polemical book, *Défense et illustration de la langue française* (1549; Defense and Embellishment of the French Language). He urged poets to revive old French words and to fashion new ones after Greek and Latin words. At the same time, the earlier genres of French poetry were rejected and those of antiquity recommended, such as the solemn ode and "that delightful invention of the Italians: the sonnet." Comedy and tragedy should be established in their ancient dignity, and, du Bellay proclaims, let us see reborn an admirable *Iliad* and an artistic *Aeneid*. Seven poetic stars, Le Pléiade, formed a group to realize this artistic program, especially in the lyrical genres. A Calvinist votary of this school, Guillaume du Bartas, let the world be recreated in his vast poem about the week of Creation, *La Semaine* (1579; The Week), which for a century was for Europe the admired prototype for the universal Renaissance poem, the great epic that could stand alongside the Renaissance ideal: Virgil's *Aeneid*. It was this poem that mediated the French poetic Renaissance to Denmark.

Metrical Reform and Anders Arrebo

Before the arrival of the Renaissance a reform of the metrical system in Denmark took place. Danish verse from the Middle Ages and the sixteenth century, from ballad to school drama, was based on a common number of stressed syllables in the rhyming lines, filled out at random with the aid of unstressed syllables. This syllabic system, widespread in Italian and French poetics, was used by the pastor Jacob J. Wolf (1554–1635) in his long *Jødekrønike* (1603; Chronicle of the Jews). In Germany, Martin Opitz established in his epoch-making *Buch von der deutschen Poeterey* (1624; Book on German Poetics) a regular alternation between stressed and unstressed syllables as the principle for versification in German. This system was carried through in Danish by Anders Arrebo (1587–1637), whose entire achievement opened a new era in Danish poetry. His destiny illustrates the relations of poets among themselves and to the powerful in the country. The young theologian Arrebo gained Christian IV's favor, becoming court chaplain at Copenhagen Castle, a position he repaid with occasional poems for the monarch. In 1618 he was named bishop of Trondheim in Norway. Here a catastrophe occurred. The young and lighthearted bishop took an unconstrained part in Norwegian parties; a satirical ballad of his injured the district judge, Peder Lauridsen, who took revenge by reporting the bishop for unsuitable conduct one morning during a prolonged feast. A lawsuit developed, and in June 1622 the bishop was removed from his episcopal calling. The king presided at the proceedings but did not intervene.

During the subsequent years of adversity Arrebo translated the entire Book of Psalms, *Kong Davids Psalter* (1623; The Psalms of King David). In a revised edition of 1627, many corrections were aimed at respecting the relative stress of the syllables. The 1627 edition of *Kong Davids Psalter* is the first larger work of Danish poetry in which modern versification is sustained virtually throughout.

Arrebo had a patron in one of the highest public servants in the realm: the king's chancellor, Christian Friis. The dismissed bishop had his offense pardoned in August 1625, and from January 1626 until his death was the incumbent of the humble calling of Vordingborg on southern Zealand. Friis urged him to translate du Bartas's great work, and procured a copy for him and other books useful for the purpose, no doubt the German and Dutch translations of *La Semaine*. It was the chancellor's idea, as appears from the preface to Arrebo's work, that as Italians, Frenchmen, Germans, and Dutchmen had "begun with particular correctness in their language in the trochaic and iambic manner . . . to rhyme and compose harmonious poems," so too should Arrebo "give proof in our Danish language, that it alone should not forfeit and lack its praise."

When du Bartas portrays God's progressive Creation day by day in artistic style, he satisfied a Renaissance need for viewing and grasping the things that God has made as one great work of art. Throughout a century Europe labored with du Bartas's work from 1579; it was translated into Latin (twice: 1579, 1583), Italian (1593), English (1604), Dutch (three times: 1609, 1620, 1621), Spanish (1610), German (1609–31), Polish (1629), Danish (1661), and Swedish (1685). Most of the translations followed the original with small variations, but Arrebo undertook a radical adaptation, used in 1685 as a model by the Swede Haquin Spegel in *Guds Werk och Hwila* (God's Work and Rest).

Du Bartas's poem was in alexandrines, twelve-syllable lines with caesura, in couplets with alternating masculine and feminine rhyme. Every translation into a living language had used alexandrines; those in Latin were in hexameters. Arrebo wished to combine classical and newer prosody and invented the double-rhymed hexameter by pairing hexameters with masculine internal rhyme before the caesura and feminine end rhyme. This pattern gives a festive upbeat to both "Fortalen til Skaberen" (Foreword to the Creator) and the canto on the First Day. In the latter Arrebo departed from his French original and tied in to Luther's commentary on Genesis, *Enarra-*

tiones (1521; Interpretation). Where the Calvinist du Bartas showed how God drives the inveterate sinner to eternal damnation, Arrebo asserted, in part guided by Zacharias Heins's Dutch translation and with reference to Job's story, that God allows Satan to tempt both the pious and the impious, so that all may be tested in their faith and gain grace.

After the First Day, Arrebo abandoned his hexameters and employed alexandrines, unlike the French with regular feminine rhymes. On the Third Day he made himself a contemporary of Noah's: "For I am in your ark, the waves with us are drifting." With the Fourth Day he followed du Bartas more closely by letting the vault of heaven with its stars and planets entice the Earth to love and fertility. The Fifth and Sixth Days share the animal kingdom between them, together with the creation of man. During the long journey Arrebo had gradually pushed the French original aside. He had only a few traces of the German translation but seemed steadily to follow the Dutch. Du Bartas described how magnificent a body man has received. The Calvinist gave himself away in his verses about the mouth, which secures us contact with heaven: for with it we can by prayer temper the wrath of God. The German followed this text closely; but the Dutchman, like Arrebo, wrote that with the mouth we can gain the grace of God. As Arrebo used geographical and zoological literature as supplements, his poem took on an even more encyclopedic character than its French prototype. Nevertheless, he never reached Creation's weekend. He closed the Sixth Day with:

> Break off, turn out the light, the sabbath craves its rest;
> tomorrow early up, the house of God to guest.

Arrebo's version is therefore called *Hexaëmeron* (The Six-Day Work). It was published in 1661 by his son, who wrote a preface for it.

The Inspiration from Arrebo

Hexaëmeron arrived early enough to make an impression on the greatest Danish poet of the century, Thomas Kingo; but its new signals were picked up beforehand by less talented poets. The earliest printed Danish alexandrines are the work of a young theologian, Bertel Wichman (1617–65), who had studied in Germany and had become a sworn follower of Martin Opitz. Wichman was a poet at second hand. Opitz had composed a topographic poem, *Zlatna, oder von der Ruhe des Gemüts* (1623; Zlatna, or Concerning Mental Composure). In honor of the lord of a Zealand manor, Otto Brahe, Wichman used Opitz's words, but with them he depicts *Nesbyholm* (1644). The German poem and the Danish expound in Horace's spirit the joys of country life and therefore have traits in common with another poem by Opitz, *Lob des Feldtlebens* (1623; In Praise of Rural Life), which Wichman rendered in Danish as *Agerlevneds Lov* (1644; Praise of Life Afield) and Søren Terkelsen as *Det rolige Bonde-Levned* (1656; The Quiet Farm Life).

It was Søren Terkelsen (died 1656 or 1657) who mediated a renewed pastoral poetry to Denmark. The huge French pastoral prose epic, *L'Astrée* (1607–27; Astrea), by Honoré d'Urfé, became a lawbook for lovers across Europe: fidelity is demanded above all. Through a German intermediary the epic's first part was translated to Danish as *Den Hyrdinde Astrea* (1645–48; The Shepherdess Astrea). This work was done in Glückstadt, a fortified town founded by Christian IV at the mouth of the Elbe. Its translator, Terkelsen, was a customs official in Glückstadt and had connections with the vibrant poetic milieu in the Hamburg area. Such German-speaking poets as Johann Rist and Gabriel Voigtländer wrote popular erotic pastoral songs, and from these collections Terkelsen borrowed texts and melodies to songs that appeared in Danish as *Astreæ Sjunge-Kor* (1648, 1653, 1654; Astrea's Song-Choir). These three little books of twenty songs each were rightly a great success. Terkelsen was no great poet; many of his verses limp and hobble. But here tuneful and accessible melodies were offered to lyrical themes, merry and mournful, of the loves of shepherds and shepherdesses. A happy song, "Engang alt om en Morgen" (Once in a Morning), is about the shepherd Corydon and the shepherdess Phyllis, who in the early morning go looking for their sweethearts but come home as a loving couple. And Corydon's sorrow-stricken song "Med Graad min Vænneste" (With Tears, My Fairest) is about the envy and hatred that have forced him away from the noble Delia. These are the two finest pastoral songs before Kingo's "Chrysillis" and are likewise its precursors.

Theology and Witchcraft
Scientific life under Christian IV bears the stamp of the king's temperament and broad interests. His robust Christianity was opposed to all devilry. The bishop of Zealand, Jesper Brochmand (1585–1652), praised Christian IV in his dogmatic monument *Universæ theologiæ systema* (1633; System of General Theology) because he had seen to it that all his subjects should think and speak alike about God and everything concerning God. A clergyman was dismissed if he attempted to have the exorcism of the devil removed from the baptismal rite. Brochmand had with certainty enumerated the signs of demonic possession and the measures against it (*Systema* I, 8, 2–3). It was Satan's purpose with witches and warlocks to spoil Christ's work of salvation. To wipe them out was to frustrate these designs.

Under Christian IV, witches were briskly burned. In the years just after 1600 the market town Køge on Zealand was the locale for an epidemic of witch-hunting that culminated in 1607–15 among a merchant family. The housewife set down a graphic account that was reproduced in the rector Johan Brunsmand's (1637–1707) work *Køge Hus-Kors* (1674; The Køge Hellcat), reprinted several times, published in Leipzig in Latin (1693) and in German (1696). Here are all the symptoms experts could wish for: the shaking bed, the gaping eyes of the possessed person, doors flung open, and bodies raised in levitation. But when the Dutch pastor Balthasar Bekker published from 1691 on his rationalistic refutation of the theology of the devil and the persecution of witches in *De betoverde Weereld* (Eng. tr. *The World Bewitched*, 1695), he reduced Brunsmand's book ad absurdum in the fourth part of his work (1693). The last woman sentenced for witchcraft was put to death in 1693, and when a witch trial was opened in Thisted in northern Jutland in 1696, reason gained a victory: the accusers were harshly sentenced, and in an official publication of 1698 a sober and ironic "report" was given of the Thisted possession. It was in Thisted that Holberg was to locate his comedy *Hexerie eller Blind Allarm* (1723; Witchcraft, or False Alarm).

The School in Sorø

During Frederik II's reign, establishing Latin schools was the most vital concern within higher education. The king imitated Herluf Trolle and in 1568 founded a grammar school in Hillerød, which in 1586 he moved into the empty Cistercian monastery in Sorø. At the same time, a new demand arose in Germany for higher schools for public servants. They had existed since 1589 in Würtemberg and since 1599 in Kassel. Besides the grammar school in Sorø, Christian IV established in 1623 a costly academy for young noblemen educating themselves for public office in domestic or foreign service. The academicians, as they were called, generally matriculated at the age of sixteen to eighteen. The instruction was comprehensive. In addition to the ancient languages, French and Italian were practiced with native teachers. Theology, law, mathematics, history, and geography, as well as chivalric accomplishments such as riding, fencing, dance, music, and painting (including architectural drawing) were also taught. In 1643 the academy attained the rank of a university. It functioned in Sorø until 1665 and had about three hundred alumni in all.

Among the teachers were two of importance for literature. The many-sided north German Hans Lauremberg (1590–1658), professor of mathematics, wrote two German masques full of symbolism for the wedding festivities of 1634, the so-called high nuptials; they were printed in 1675. In a

Latin *Satyra* (1636; Satire) the professor complained that the high-born students would rather practice the art of fencing in preparation for duels according to a bad French habit than participate in intellectual exercises. In his native Low German, Lauremberg wrote *Veer Schertz Gedichte* (1652; Four Mocking Poems), published the same year in an anonymous Danish translation as *Fire Skæmte-Digte* (Four Mocking Poems). The meter in both languages is correct alexandrines; snobbery for foreign, especially French, fashions is criticized with coarse wit.

The other teacher was the historian Stephanus Stephanius (1599–1650), who passionately studied Saxo's Latin chronicle and in 1644 published a text-critical edition with copious commentary, *Historia Danica* (A History of Denmark). We can follow his progress in his correspondence with his colleague Ole Worm. Almost two thousand letters are preserved from and to Worm, who corresponded with all of Europe. The learned men wrote to one another in Latin, even when they were two Danes living in Sorø and Copenhagen.

Ole Worm and the Runes

Ole Worm (1588–1654) was a friend across all national borders, and his correspondence (translated to Danish in 1965–68) gives an absorbing picture of everyday life in Europe's learned republic. Worm was an international type, an astonishing product of the century of polyhistors. He was born in Århus, where his father was an alderman and later mayor. The family hailed from the Rhineland, and the boy entered a German grammar school at thirteen and continued his studies abroad, first in theology and later in medicine, botany, anatomy, surgery, and chemistry. In 1611 he received the degree of doctor of medicine in Basel. Returning home, he was attached to the University of Copenhagen in 1613, first as a professor of elementary subjects such as logic and grammar, then Greek, physics, and finally (in 1624) medicine. Professor Worm was a conscientious teacher and physician who always based himself on practical experience. He wrote medical treatises and practiced among all classes. He did not leave the capital during perilous epidemics; the plague of 1654 killed him.

When Worm became a professor of physics, he held a Latin inaugural lecture in which he declared that the scholar distinguishes himself by scrupulously observing God's Creation, "by which coherence and causes, that is to say God's designs, are explained. The uneducated man is not much better than an animal who looks agape at the exterior of things, but does not make coherent observations." Worm wished to demonstrate the phenomena of nature for his students and began to collect varieties of stones, plants, and animals. He had a catalog of the collection printed in 1642, with a new edition in 1645. On his death the complete, systematically arranged description of 1,663 objects from the mineral world and the plant and animal kingdoms, in addition to objects made from natural products, was ready for publication; the folio work, *Museum Wormianum* (1655; The Worm Museum), was published in Amsterdam and holds a distinguished position among European descriptions of collections. It is a curiosity that Worm is probably the earliest Dane documented to have seen a coffee bean. But it is of importance to note that Worm was the first to be able to determine with scientific stringency and detailed knowledge that what had been called unicorn horns were narwhal tusks.

Worm was not content with an interest in things in the world at large. He was ardently engaged as well with his country's ancient culture, such as it emerged in the oldest Scandinavian alphabet, the runes. With the support of Christian IV's chancellor, Christian Friis, Worm had a royal edict dispatched in 1622 to the Danish and Norwegian bishops to see to it that all relics and documents of antiquity were forwarded to the chancellery. The edict was passed on to the clergy, and in this way the populace was, more than in most countries, aware at an early stage of the importance of objects found in the earth and of old manuscripts, a circumstance that still does its share in maintaining the connection of Danes and Norwegians to their distant past. Among the objects submitted was a runic calendar that began with 1328. It became the pont of departure for Worm's first antiquarian work, *Fasti Danici* (1626; The Danish Calendar). The runic alphabet long remained in use as signs in almanacs for the weekdays, lunar cycles, and holy days. Worm later published a book on the nature and origin of the runic alphabet, *Runir seu Danica litteratura antiquissima* (1636; Runes, or the Oldest Danish Literature). As Hebrew was regarded as the first language, Worm derived the runes from the Hebraic characters. This interpretation was incorrect, but the riddle of the origin of the individual runes has still not been solved.

In 1639 a golden horn was found in South Jutland. Christian IV asked Worm to interpret it, which he did in *De aureo cornu* (1641; On the Golden Horn). He incorporated this work into his folio volume *Monumenta Danica* (1643; Danish Monuments), which described Danish burial customs in antiquity and reported all 144 of the then-known Danish runic inscriptions. They were depicted, transcribed, and translated into Latin. With this monumental work, which went all over Europe, Danish archaeology and runology were established.

Christian IV died in 1648 and was succeeded by his son, Frederik III (1648–70), who was to live through the dismemberment of Denmark and the elevation of the royal house. With this development the spiritual climate was decided for the rest of the century, including the reign of Frederik III's son and successor, Christian V, in the years 1670–99.

Christian IV's unsuccessful campaigns had weakened Denmark, and his son wished to strengthen the country as well as the Crown. In June 1657 he declared war on Sweden, which was engaged in a campaign in Poland. But the Swedish king, Karl X Gustav, hastily led his army up into Jutland, and when the Danish belts froze over, he led his troops with unheard-of daring over to the islands and threatened Copenhagen. To avoid capitulation, the Danish negotiators at the Peace of Roskilde in February 1658 had to surrender the fertile provinces east of the sound: Skåne, Halland, and Blekinge. The Swedes marched home, but unsatisfied with the triumph, Karl Gustav wished to annihilate Denmark's independence completely and landed on Zealand in August 1658. Copenhagen was now better prepared and withstood a severe winter siege. King Frederik won the admiration of the populace by his courage; he remained in the capital with a text from the Book of Job (29:18): "I shall die in my nest." On the eve of February 11, 1659, Karl Gustav undertook a major assault, which was completely repulsed, just as his army was suffering setbacks elsewhere. Suddenly, the Swedish king died in February 1660, and a peace could be concluded in Copenhagen that determined Denmark's borders with Sweden for all time. By holding both shores of the sound, Denmark could have shut Sweden out from the open sea, the Kattegat, and moreover could have demanded unlimited tolls when ships of all nations passed Elsinore. Holland and other maritime nations were therefore opposed to letting Denmark regain the Scanian provinces. The painful outcome of the 1658–60 war was the condition for establishing peace in Scandinavia, even though it was not secured immediately.

The war had a profound effect on the country's domestic situation. At an assembly of the Estates of the Realm in Copenhagen in September 1660 the rights of the nobility were abolished; all citizens were made equal under Frederik III as absolute hereditary monarch. By this coup d'état, achieved by the king in conjunction with the middle classes and the clergy, absolutism became the Danish form of government until 1849.

The Renaissance kings, Frederik II and Christian IV, had a predilection for spectacular trappings. Frederik III was a more introverted, meditative type of person, a learned man who collected a library of books and manuscripts, called in French bookbinders, and in 1665 had his master builder begin the construction of a library close to where the Royal Library stands today. At the king's death in 1670 the collection included about twenty thousand volumes.

Ole Borch

The creative spirits of Frederik III's reign mastered even more fields than in earlier times. Ole Borch (1626–90) obtained public support for a six-year study trip abroad in 1660–66. He kept a Latin travel diary, *Itinerarium* (publ. 1983; Itinerary), which provides detailed information about scientific activities in Holland, England, France, and Italy. Borch was also engrossed by life and manners, nature, and art, enjoying Rembrandt's paintings in Amsterdam and visiting miniaturist Gerard Dau in Leiden. Borch had practiced medicine before his journey, and he took the doctoral degree in medicine en route in Angers in 1664; in Copenhagen he became the king's family physician and earned a fortune from his practice. But it was chemistry that obsessed him. In Rome, Swedish Queen Christina often summoned him so that they could converse about the secrets of chemistry. He was impressed by the Italian physician and alchemist Francesco Borri, whom he met again in Copenhagen, where he had been called by Frederik III. In Copenhagen a building was fitted out for the Italian's experiments in 1667–69 in making gold. Borch wrote thick volumes, *De ortu et progressu chemiæ* (1668; The Origin and Progress of Chemistry) and *Hermetis, Ægyptiorum et chemicorum sapientia vindicata* (1674; In Defense of the Wisdom of Hermes, the Egyptians, and the Chemics). He implored the Danes not to neglect chemistry, "that noble science, purest delight of Nature and all lofty souls, which from Tubal Cain (Gen. 4:22) and across Egypt (whose god Thot was taken for the Greeks' Hermes) has migrated around the world right up to our North." In this finale we can hear the Latinist Olaus Borrichius's emphatic rhetoric. As a youth he had composed a guide to writing Latin verse, *Parnassus in nuce* (1654; Parnassus in a Nutshell). No doubt the learned republic could exist without poetry, he wrote, but it would then be like a sky without stars, like a body without a soul. Borch was himself a refined devotee of learned poetry. His Latin poems fill out much of Frederik Rostgaard's anthology *Deliciæ quorundam Poëtarum Danorum* (Delights of Certain Danish Poets) from 1693. He later produced seven monographs called *De poëtis* (1676–81; On the Poets), a short history of world literature, in which Shakespeare is nevertheless missing, down to contemporary Denmark: "Danish verse previously stammered; from the time of Arrebo the luster of Danish rhythms has developed so high that they dare to vie with any in Europe in pleasantness and grace."

Ole Borch was an alchemist with the same genuine conviction that made Tycho Brahe an astrologer. Faith in the mysteries of chemistry did not prevent him from performing practical chemical experiments, and in a treatise from 1680 he reported the detection of oxygen almost a century before Karl Wilhelm Scheele and Joseph Priestley.

Niels Stensen

For humanists theology was usually the basic academic subject; for natural scientists medicine was the normal foundation. It included botany for the sake of medicinal plants, chemistry, and—especially after Paracelsus had established medicinal chemistry—chemiatrics. Late in the seventeenth century anatomy and physiology made tremendous advances, to which Danish physicians contributed with important discoveries. A nephew of Ole Worm, Thomas Bartholin (1616–80), assumed a professorship in anatomy in 1645; he did physiological experiments on dogs and discovered the lymphatic vessels, which he also found in man (*Vasa lymphatica*, 1653). In Sweden Olaf Rudbeck had made the same discovery, and for some years these two scholars squabbled in noisy Latin pamphlets over their rights of discovery. For many years Bartholin was a skillful and self-opinionated organizer of Danish medicine with widespread contacts abroad, partly by virtue of a textbook in anatomy which he took over from his father, Caspar Bartholin (1585–1629), in 1641 and published in numerous updated editions, and partly through his periodical *Acta medica*, which he edited from 1673 until his death. Bartholin made Copenhagen one of Europe's centers of medical research.

The success of the medical profession attracted those with talent, and among them was the greatest scientific genius that Denmark has fostered, Niels Stensen, latinized as Nicolaus Steno (1638–86), who was to achieve a destiny and status in European intellectual history on a par with the Frenchman Blaise Pascal. He was the son of a Copenhagen goldsmith, and from the domestic workshop he became familiar with metals and their treatment by using acids. He would later display a brilliant knack for contriving instruments for experiments. In Our Lady Grammar School he had a superb Latin teacher in the young Ole Borch, and in mathematics, which was to become a much-cherished discipline for him, the school's rector, Jørgen Eilersen. At the university he matriculated in 1656 with medicine as his major subject and chose Thomas Bartholin as his private preceptor, the professor who supervised the students' work and conduct.

The siege of Copenhagen (1658–59) broke off Stensen's studies; he served in the students' regiment. Yet despite the press of events, the spirit was willing, as we know from a large Latin manuscript he called *Chaos* (publ. 1986; Eng. tr. *Niels Stensen: A Danish Student in his Chaos-Manuscript*, 1987). It is a detailed study diary running from March 8 to July 3, 1659, the months after the unsuccessful Swedish assault on the eve of February 11. The twenty-one-year-old student was well advanced in the study of medicine. He made many excerpts from scientific literature, but at the same time he was tempted by digressions into other matters and could not keep to the medical handbooks. He made excursions into special scientific studies and performed his own experiments. And on March 30 he knew what his future would be: "From now on I shall spend my time, not on musings, but solely in investigation, experience, and the recording of natural objects and the reports of the ancients on the observation of such things, as well as in testing out these reports, if that be possible." Here is a research scientist in embryo. He warns against false analogies, such as that "the fetus is fixed by the umbilical cord in the womb just as plants are by their roots in the soil" (April 15). The scientist must begin with the things themselves: "In the natural sciences it is better not to be bound by any knowledge, but to refer everything that can be observed to certain titles and then, by one's own exertions, to elicit something from it, if nothing else at least some kind of certain conception" (March 20). But in judging the interpretations of others, one should be loyal: "In examining the teaching of others, one must not proceed from one's own foundations but from those of the author. . . . Thus the words to be interpreted ought not, either, be treated differently from the author" (April 16) (Tr. David Stoner).

Thus equipped, Stensen went out on the traditional study trip, during which he had a chance to make and publish brilliant scientific observations. In April 1660 in Amsterdam he dissected a calf's head and found the path of discharge of the parotid gland in the oral cavity; it still bears his name, *ductus Stenonianus*. In Leiden in 1662 he demonstrated by examining a sheep's head that tears had the simple function of keeping the eye damp. Finally, in 1664 he established that the heart is not the seat of occult powers but simply a muscle. In 1664, his fame having gone before him, Stensen arrived in Paris. At once he entered a scientific circle much resembling the one in which Pascal, who had died two years before, had moved. Its soul was Melchisedech Thévenot, and the circle was constituted by Cardinal de Richelieu in 1666 as the Académie des Sciences. For this forum Stensen held, in 1665, a lecture that was printed in 1669 as the *Discours sur l'anatomie du cerveau* (Discourse on the Anatomy of the Brain), today regarded as the proper point of departure for modern studies of the brain. The lecture began with this declaration: "Gentlemen! Instead of promising that I shall satisfy your curiosity in what relates to the anatomy of the brain, I begin by publicly and frankly owning that I know nothing of the matter" (Tr. G. Douglas).

In the summer of 1665 Stensen continued south to Italy, where in strange ways his destiny, both scientific and human, was to be fulfilled. In Florence in April 1666 he was granted splendid working conditions by the Grand Duke Ferdinand II of Tuscany, who gave him financial support and quarters in the Palazzo Vecchio.

When Stensen was given the task of examining a giant shark, he employed mathematics to explain muscular effort. In his book on the subject from 1667, *Elementorum myologiae specimen* (The Elements of Muscular Knowledge), he shows as a supplement that certain objects of stone found on Malta were shark's teeth that had been petrified; he deduces that this must have occurred in the sea, arriving at the further conclusion that Malta was thus once covered by the sea. During excursions in the vicinity of Florence he collected a huge material for study, the results of which he embodied in a work founding three new sciences: geology, paleontology, and crystallography: *De solido intra solidum naturaliter contento dissertationis prodromus* (1669; Eng. tr. *The Prodromus of Nicolaus Steno's Dissertation Concerning a Solid Body Enclosed by Process of Nature Within a Solid*, 1916). It was earlier thought that this Latin work was overlooked at the time, but that is not the case. Members of the Royal Society in London eagerly participated in the discussion of Stensen's geological and paleontological discoveries, and his pioneer work was translated into English for the first time in 1671.

Coinciding with Stensen's passionate occupation with the natural sciences, another passionate movement took place, curiously enough, in his soul, in the direction of a religious breakthrough. Perhaps in the concept of experience we can see a common denominator for Stensen's scientific conclusions and religious development. As early as *Chaos* the student had declared that one sins "against the majesty of God by being unwilling to look into nature's own works and contenting oneself with reading the works of others" (March 30). In a late theological work Stensen says that as he had heard people openly speak about anatomy without any knowledge of it, so he had witnessed that Protestants condemn the piety of Catholics while knowing nothing about it. In Florence two noblewomen put their entire souls into persuading him of the truth of Catholicism; one of them declared that she would give her life for his salvation. Shortly thereafter, on November 1, 1667, he experienced in a quiet moment the truth of Catholicism. The experience of faith apparently had for Stensen the same character of evidence, which according to Descartes was the criterion for truth within the scientific sphere.

The new convert was burning to convert former fellow sectarians. When the philosopher Spinoza, whom Stensen had known in Leiden, published his Bible criticism *Tractatus theologico-politicus* (1670; Theological-Political Tract), Stensen sent him a large epistle (printed in 1675) in which he wished to demonstrate the truth of the Catholic religion. The core of this demonstration is once again experience: it is the conduct of the faithful that proves or invalidates the truth of their faith. "Holiness of life demonstrates truth of doctrine," he wrote to Spinoza. Only the Catholic Church, he adds, has produced such exemplars in every century. Stensen would soon try to become one himself. But first he was called by the Danish king, Christian V, through his powerful minister Peder Griffenfeld, to Copenhagen, where in 1672–74 he lectured as the royal anatomist. In his inaugural lecture, preceding the public dissection of a corpse, he praises man as God's creation. He employs a three-stage series that has often been quoted (for instance, by Goethe) but also often misunderstood: "Pulchra sunt quae videntur, pulchriora quae sciuntur, longe pulcherrima quae ignorantur." This statement must be interpreted as follows: Beautiful are the parts of the body that we see; more beautiful the whole arrangement of the body as a work of art that we (through investigation) understand; most beautiful of all the connection, incomprehensible to us, between us (body and soul) and our divine origin.

Although Stensen was assured of the free practice of religion, he returned to Florence, where he allowed himself to be ordained in 1675 and was persuaded in 1677 to become the bishop of Hanover and at the same time apostolic vicar to the apostate Scandinavian countries; in 1680 he moved to Münster and in 1685 to Schwerin, where he died in 1686. Before his conversion Stensen was a dapper man of the world. As a Catholic he wished by his example, and yet in deepest humility, to be a witness to the truth of his faith, a martyr. He lived as a hollow-cheeked ascetic and, although bishop, under the poorest conditions. Since 1938 work has been underway within the Catholic Church to canonize him. He was declared venerable in January 1984 and blessed in January 1988. He can thus be invoked in northern Germany and Denmark. New and exhaustive investigations of his activities could lead to his elevation from beatification to canonization, to becoming a saint who may be invoked everywhere within the Catholic Church.

The Rise and Fall of Peder Griffenfeld
When Niels Stensen lectured in Denmark, the country was ruled by Christian V (1670–99). The young king did not have his father's intelligence and

refinement. He was convinced of his God-given dignity, of his and the king-dom's high prestige, but dependent on his counselors. His prime minister, Peder Griffenfeld (1635–99), was originally named Schumacher. The son of a wine merchant, from his childhood he had shown an exceptional intel-ligence and maturity; he matriculated at the age of thirteen, and after his studies at the university he pursued extensive linguistic and constitutional studies in Germany, the Netherlands, England, and France. In 1663 he be-came Frederik III's librarian and won the king over with his scholarship and shrewdness.

Under early absolutism members of the middle class could make careers in government. The librarian became the king's secretary and framed the new constitution, *Kongeloven* (1665; Royal Law), in Latin and Danish. His influence grew and he became a landowner, the count of Griffenfeld. He governed Denmark-Norway's domestic and foreign policy until an aristo-cratic rival party brought charges against him and had him overthrown. The charge of corruption was just, but not so the charge of high treason, which in May 1676 brought Griffenfeld the death sentence. He was reprieved at the place of execution and spent the rest of his life in prisons. Griffenfeld, whose rise and fall became important themes in Danish poetry, was an ob-ject lesson for the firm seventeenth-century belief in fortune's capricious-ness, most especially under an absolutist government. In a religious song of 1681 by Thomas Kingo which might well have been inspired by Griffen-feld's fall, the poet calls honor and favor inanity and vanity: what high favor puffs up is dispelled like fog when the sun appears.

Ole Rømer

The absolute monarchy showed favor to science, for the sake of both fame and utility. Quite near the heart of the monarchy was Ole Rømer (1644–1710), a scholar with Stensen's ability to see and solve scientific problems and a sublime sense for making scientific reason the basis of practical de-vices. As a young man he got the chance of his life when a member of the newly founded French Académie des Sciences, Abbot Jean Picard, came to Copenhagen in 1671 to make a precise determination of Uranienborg's geo-graphical position. To use Tycho Brahe's unique observations performed on Hven, one had to know the difference in longitude between Paris and Ura-nienborg. This task was to be done by fixing in both places the point in time when the middle of Jupiter's moon was eclipsed. The young Rømer was designated Picard's assistant, and when the Frenchman became ill, Rømer performed the observations alone. He thereby embarked on a study of the moons of Jupiter, and when on Picard's invitation he went to Paris, where he was appointed to the academy, he continued his astronomical observations. This work led him to the discovery of the speed of light. Descartes had claimed that light traveled with infinite speed, consequently without using up time. But Rømer demonstrated, in a clear and concise paper in the periodical *Journal des Savants* for December 7, 1676, that light "requires time." In a later Latin report the misleading expression *mora luminis* was used, and historians of physics often still speak of the "delay of light."

The French had discovered Rømer's technical genius, and thus he came to assist in laying out the fountains at Versailles. After he returned home in 1681, he not only attended to his position as astronomical professor and observer, but also acted as the government's technical handyman. In his note and record book, *Adversaria* (publ. 1910; Notebook), we can follow how he solved problems according to clear, rational principles. One of the strengths of absolute government is its ability to decree order and uniformity. Under Rømer's direction the same weights and measurements were introduced in 1683 for the whole country. Here weight was determined, a century before the origin of the metric system, by means of length: "The proper weight of a Danish pound shall be determined by a cubic foot of fresh water, which shall weigh sixty-two pounds." Rømer instituted a permanent night-watch corps for Copenhagen and established a complete land registry, an inventory of all holdings with specification of their estimated productivity. He also had the first milestones placed along the highways, which impressed foreign travelers. In a special triumph Rømer cautiously persuaded Christian V to introduce the Gregorian calendar, although the reform had originated from a pope. In the year 1700, February 18 was followed by March 1, so that Denmark had the same calendar as most of Europe.

Jurisprudence

The government's largest achievement in the literature of practical life was of juridical character. Since the Middle Ages the Danish provinces had had separate legel complexes. Through the long and painstaking labor of a commission the government now had a common legislation drafted for all the provinces. Its primary author was the professor and judge in the Supreme Court that was created in 1661, Rasmus Vinding (1615–84). *Christian V's Danske Lov* (1683; Christian V's Danish Law) was remarkable for its well-arranged composition and the clarity of its language. Some years after the law had gone into effect, it was described by an English ambassador, Robert Molesworth, who in his book *An Account of Denmark, as it was in the year 1692* (1694) was very critical of absolutist Denmark. But, he says, being now to speak of the Danish Laws, I must needs begin with this good Character of them in general; that for Justice, Brevity, and Perspicuity, they exceed all that I know in the World. They are grounded upon Equity, and are all contained in one Quarto Volume, written in the Language of the Country, with so much plainness, that no Man, who can write and read, is so ignorant, but he may presently understand his own Case, and plead it too if he pleases, without the Assistance of Counsel or Attorney.

POETS OF THE BAROQUE
Anders Bording

Poetry could also be practical when it entered government service. At midcentury devotees of the lyric enjoyed the work of an industrious poet, Anders Bording (1619–77), who wrote poems for weddings, christenings, and burials but also knew how to form a long poem in defense of women's access to studies. Bording was an entertaining guest at manor houses. He acquired a master's degree but did not do well as a teacher or pastor. He was satisfied to be a literary bohemian who could compose both drinking songs and hymns, as well as verses tragicomically lamenting the free student's empty pockets. But beginning on July 1, 1666, Frederik III put him in a position to bring out a four-page monthly newspaper in verse, *Den danske Mercurius* (The Danish Mercury). Until April 1, 1677, Bording informed the public in his fluent alexandrines about events at home and abroad; he had successors up to 1691. The Danish news was especially about the court; the king's travels took up much space. From other countries came primarily political and military news.

Thus began the Danish press—with a newspaper in verse. In 1672 ordinary Danish newspapers began to appear. The driving force behind them was an enterprising bookseller and printer, Daniel Paulli (1640–84), who from 1672 on, besides a weekly paper in German, *Extraordinaire Relationes* (1672–76), published a monthly paper in Danish, *Extraordinaires Maanedlige Relationer* (1672–84; Extraordinary Monthly Reports), and the weekly *Dansk Advis* (1675–80; Danish Notices).

Thomas Kingo

A far greater poet than Bording was Thomas Kingo (1634–1703), son of a linen and damask weaver in Slangerup. He became a bachelor of divinity in 1658 and returned to northern Zealand, where as private tutor and later as chaplain he displayed a lighthearted humor and erotic outspokenness in jocular poems intended for his friends in the large manors.

When a serious passion took hold of Kingo, he used the pastoral style to give form to his feelings. His inspiration was Cecilie, called Sille, widow of the newly deceased deacon Peder Worm, whom Kingo had served as chaplain. It was presumably within the long year of mourning that Kingo wrote his song, "Chrysillis," in which the lover promises to wait precisely "the heaven-ordained time." He refers to himself by the heroic name Myrtillo from Terkelsen's *Astræ Sjunge-Kor*, and here too he found "Krisillis" (after the German original's Crysillis), discovering "Sille" concealed within. Cecilie Balkenborg and Thomas Kingo were married in July 1669; she died in July 1670.

Frederik III heard Kingo preach and secured a good town calling for him. When Christian V, the first hereditary absolute monarch, was anointed and crowned in Frederiksborg Castle on June 7, 1671, Kingo wrote a congratulatory poem for the event, *Hosianna*, which was the inauguration or consecration of the new hyperbolic style; a true poet can make flattery into art. Kingo was inspired by an image from the term for Louis XIV, *le Roi-Soleil*, the Sun King, which occurs as early as 1663 on a French medal. The sun is the Danish king, whose power is warmth, a life-giving strength for the wet and cold earth. The moon is his heavenly queen. The royal pair were wed in 1667 and at the time of the anointing had not yet had any children. With an ingenious touch, taken from Revelation 22:1–2, the poet asks God to let the river of life flood the queen. His prayer was heard before it was put forward. On October 11, 1671, a successor was born, the later Frederik IV.

It was in conformity with the endeavors of absolutism that a public official, Peder Hansen Resen (1625–88), professor of law and mayor of Copenhagen, was kept busy by a comprehensive Latin description of Denmark, *Atlas Danicus* (Danish Atlas). The enormous material was never printed; the bulk of it burned in 1728, and only in the twentieth century have portions come out in Danish translation. But Kingo profited from Resen's industry. Erasmus Lætus had cultivated the large topographical poem in Latin, and Arrebo had sharpened the delight in tangible, material reality. Kingo took from Resen the material for a long poem, *Kroneborgs korte Beskrivelse* (1672; Short Description of Kronborg), dedicated to the king, and for *Samsøes korte Beskrivelse* (1675; Short Description of Samsø), brought as a tribute to Griffenfeld when he bought this lovely island. It is the poet's triumph with this last large poem that it is still reprinted in our day and praised for its lifelike delineation in spite of the fact that Kingo had never been to Samsø.

As one can see topography becoming poetry in these poems, so we can follow in Kingo's martial poetry how journalism is put into verse. Denmark would not resign itself to the catastrophic loss of the provinces of Skåne, and Christian V's government thus waged war with Sweden in 1675–79. Newspapers gained a new impetus, and Kingo followed the king's expedition of 1676–77 in *Ledings-Tog* (War Expedition) in alexandrine verses; eventually, after Anders Bording's death, it became a monthly report. When Admiral Niels Juel in April 1676 conquered the island of Gotland off the east coast of Sweden, which remained Danish until 1679, Kingo took the opportunity to frame after Erasmus Lætus's example in *Res Danicæ* a national epic with perspective back to Noah: Gotland was discovered and populated by the progeny of the Cimbrians, who descended from Noah's son Japhet!

Although the Danes triumphed at sea, the war did not change national boundaries. But Juel's capture of Swedish warships, which were exchanged by the king for prize money, made the great admiral very rich. He died in 1697 and was buried in a separate chapel in the naval Holmens Church in Copenhagen. For eight marble reliefs representing naval battles in which Juel had participated, Kingo wrote a series of inscriptions in verse. Under the centrally placed half-length portrait of the admiral, Kingo placed ten lines of verse, all iambic hexameter with masculine endings. The poet chose short, pithy words. He wished to chisel his words as the sculptor his marble:

> Halt, wanderer! Gaze upon a sea-king's bust,
> and, if thyself not stone, salute his dust.
> For this is Juel, who marrow and blood did bring,
> and fiery heart, to vindicate his king;
> whose sturdy feats in many a battle stand
> bruited in honour over sea and land.
> A man of ancient worth, a simple Dane
> of yes and no and what is fair and plain.
> Here rest his bones; his soul's with God on high;
> His name will live until the sea runs dry.
>
> (Tr. R. P. Keigwin)

The age was musical. Singing was an important subject in the schools. With his fashionable lovely song about Chrysillis, Kingo had shown that he knew how to whistle the latest tune, which had been used in *Astreæ Sjunge-Kor* and its sources. To make the "melodious and pleasant tunes so much more heavenly," Kingo used this store of secular melodies for religious songs that are gathered in the two parts of his *Aandelige Sjunge-Kor* (Spiritual Song Choir), published in 1674 and 1681, respectively. The two collections were intended for devotions in the home. In the first part a melody is chosen for each day of the week; a morning song, an evening song, and a versification of one of the seven penitential Psalms of David are composed for each melody. The morning songs have a fixed series of themes, just as the evening songs have theirs, merging nature with piety. The point of departure is usually a description of nature:

> The sun is coming up
>> in orient glory,
> it gilds the mountaintop
>> and promontory.

Nature forms part of the images with which Kingo makes powerfully graphic the sum of grace that is poured over him, as well as all Christians, in the morning hour:

> As countless as the sand,
>> and past all knowing
> as deep as seas may stand
>> the grace is flowing
> with which the Lord my head does daily cover:
> each morning in my cup
> a grace keeps filling up
>> and pouring over.
> (Tr. David Colbert)

Through the following stanzas thanks are given for protection in the everperilous night. God will help you through the day, free you from sickness and sin, provide bread for you and yours. God will defend his church, the king, and country. He will give you your part, until with thanks you can climb down into the valley of death and the grave's dungeon. The thought of death is relinquished neither morning nor evening. Death is not a nap we know from our sleep, but sleep is on the contrary a portent of death.

The second part of the *Aandelige Sjunge-Kor* has twenty songs. They are concerned with people primarily in special circumstances: before and after Communion, on journeys, or at sea. Only one of the melodies is from the first part. Kingo otherwise refers to melodies that seem to have had predominantly religious application.

Two important exceptions are nevertheless the volume's masterpieces. "Far, Verden, far vel" (Fare, World, Farewell) and "Sorrig og Glæde de vandre til Hobe" (Sorrow and Joy They Wander Together), composed to melodies that seem to be of secular origin, relate to the human condition as a whole. Both build on the contrast between this world and the other. "Fare, World" is sung by a soul who is "sick of the world and devoted to heaven."

The first stanzas have a refrain from Ecclesiastes: "Vanity, vanity." The final stanzas offer in vivid contrast to life on earth the delights of heaven, which are enjoyed according to the refrain "In Abraham's Bosom." In the second poem the contrasts are built into each of the first five stanzas. Each line or couplet advances contradictory concepts but in such a way that these spare abstractions stand out from the page and become figures in flesh and blood: Sorrow and Joy "wander" together, Fortune and Misfortune "walk" abreast, Vigor and Youth "carry their heads" high above others. The varying refrains of these stanzas proclaim the immutability of heaven, which is also the subject of the last three stanzas, where Poverty "is adorned," Weakness "is raised up," Envy "stands imprisoned." The fifth stanza has always evoked the greatest admiration:

> Loveliest roses are stiffest of thorn,
>   fairest of flowers with blight may corrode,
> withering heart under rose-cheek is worn,
>   for yet is Fortune so strangely bestowed!
>   Here our land rides
>   on peril-tides,
> Blissfulness only in heaven abides.
>   (Tr. David Colbert)

The absolute monarchy understood the importance of a man with Kingo's political loyalty and artistic quality. In 1677 he was made bishop of the diocese of Funen. In 1683 he was entrusted with editing a new hymnal; the existing one was a reprint of *Den danske Salmebog* from 1569. Kingo saw to it that, according to instructions, each Sunday had its own hymns in which the scriptural text of the day was versified. He thereby created a treasury of narrative, historical hymns such as "Over Kedron Jesus træder, / Vader med sin bare Fod" (Jesus steps across the Cedron, / wading in with unshod foot), "Sover I? Hvor kan I sove" (Sleep ye now, how can ye slumber?) and "Gak under Jesu Kors at staa" (Go and stand beneath his Cross). Like the songs for domestic devotion in the *Aandelige Sjunge-Kor*, Kingo's new texts have as a common characteristic a profound sense of the religious situation. It is his poetic genius that Kingo enters into the spirit of and gives expression to the devotional hours and the stages in the life of Jesus. With this breadth of feeling, he single-handedly renewed both the private devotional lyric and the church hymn.

The genesis of the new hymnal had a turbulent course. When Kingo wished to have the first half authorized for all the churches as *Vinter-Parten* (1689; The Winter Part), he met resistance from the king, among others, who rejected the work. Another clergyman was given the assignment, but his proposal was also turned down. Then a commission was established, and finally in 1699 *Den forordnede ny Kirke-Salme-Bog* (The Ordained New Church Hymnal), which came to be called Kingo's hymnal, was published. Out of 297 hymns, 86 were by Kingo, and he has always held a large field in the varying hymnals, except in the rationalistic *Evangelisk-christelig Psalmebog* (1798; Evangelical Christian Hymnal), which had only 17 of his hymns. The present hymnal, like the first called *Den danske Salmebog* (1953), has 92 out of 754. Thomas Kingo was the earliest of the four greatest Danish hymnists. H. A. Brorson followed in the eighteenth century and N. F. S. Grundtvig and B. S. Ingemann in the nineteenth.

Among the most gripping of Kingo's poems are his elegies on death, whose themes he merges into the statement, "We are born to die." Even in the womb death threatens us; and fire, air, water, and earth, which should aid us, are ready to fail us. Illness attacks us as hounds do a stag. Often enough the best are stricken in the flower of life, letting depraved people live to be old crows. In this score of poems Kingo interprets Chapters 5 and 6 of the Epistle to the Romans: Adam brought sin into the world and with sin death, which strikes us all because we all sin. The wages of sin are thus death, but the gift of God's grace is eternal life in Christ. Death is interpreted as a person, the enemy of humankind, who with God's permission strikes people down for the sake of their sins. In a grandiose poem from 1690, "Medlidigste Tanker" (Pitiful Thoughts), about a shipwreck on the Norwegian coast that cost the lives of the prefect Laurits Lindenov, his wife, and his sister-in-law, Kingo has depicted the work of death in a tremendous storm. Here he uses a poetry of concreteness, whose maritime terminology he explains in extensive footnotes. At the same time, he fashions a dialogue between Lindenov and his pregnant wife. The husband thinks with sorrow about the child who will never see the light of day but who will still be found among the blessed. His wife replies that as they came together in the joy of the bridal bed, they share sorrow and distress in the ship. Joy and sorrow, wedding and child, death and resurrection are linked in this long and deliberately ponderous poem.

After his first wife's early death, Kingo married a fifty-three-year-old widow, Johanne Lund, in 1671. During the later years of this marriage the bishop fell in love with the young daughter of a physician from Odense, Birgitte Balslev, and she with him. In May 1694 Kingo's second wife died. As he had done twenty-five years before, Kingo experienced the anguish of the period of waiting, as voiced in his poem "Candida" (1694), again expressing the love-longing that in pastoral poetry amorously permeates nature. Kingo gives free reign to his yearning, letting his tears flow over his pale cheeks. For every creature in air and water has his own love, and the hart has the doe, but "I alone, Candida, am left behind." Seven months after his wife's death, Bishop Thomas Kingo, aged sixty, and Birgitte Balslev, aged twenty-nine, were married and remained inseparable for the nearly nine years they had together until Kingo's death in 1703.

The Satirist Jacob Worm

In various ways Kingo's career was linked to the ambitious and sharp-tongued poet Jacob Worm (1642–ca. 1693), a stepson of Kingo's first wife. During a conflict of authority in Slangerup, Worm had exposed the parson to ridicule. Worm served Christian V and Griffenfeld with flattering poems in 1672, but when they did not yield a profit he began in 1673 to spew satires in verse at Griffenfeld. Worm triumphed at Griffenfeld's fall in 1676, but he also suggested to the king that he show mercy. Worm received a humble parish calling in Viborg, where he soon quarreled with his ecclesiastical superiors.

As early as 1675 Worm had in his poems, in his own name or anonymously, set about guiding the absolute monarch, warning him especially against evil counselors. Worm regarded himself as God's servant, entitled to criticize the mistakes of absolute monarchs. He rashly censured the king directly toward the end of 1679 in a prose satire formed as an academic thesis, in which King Jeroboam from the First Book of Kings 12–14 must hear that the golden calves he has set up and enjoined Israel to worship are comparable to theft from the church and the old aristocracy. In this light, the introduction of absolutism into Denmark becomes a crime. Moreover, Christian V's relations with his official concubine (Sofie Amalie Moth) is called an abominable stain that can arouse God to anger against the entire country.

That was the limit. Worm was sentenced to loss of honor, life, and property. Kingo interceded, asking the king not to bend so low as to become angry with a flippant mouth that has been mocking him. Worm was furious at this assistance, saying "I have never cursed the king." He was reprieved with deportation to Tanquebar, the Danish dependency in India. He sailed in April 1681; in 1685 he was instructed to function as the local pastor; he probably died around New Year 1693.

Jacob Worm had the gift of indignation and bore its yoke. His often well-deserved criticism had mostly quite private origins. Worm will stand in history as an early critic of the weaknesses of the new absolutism; despite his proficiency in poetic formulation, however, he has not gained a very high position as a satirist in the history of Danish literature.

The School of Kingo

Few poets in Denmark and Norway, after the two *Aandelige Sjunge-Kor* appeared, escaped Kingo's influence in versification and style, at the same time as the latest development within German baroque poetry left its trace. Thus Elias Naur's (1650–1728) passion epic of more than fifty-six hundred lines of alexandrines is modeled after a declamatory and musical play of 1645 from Nuremberg, by Johann Klaj. *Golgotha paa Parnasso* (1689; Golgotha upon Parnassus) falls into five acts, bewailing the agonies of Jesus and at the same time promising revenge on those who whipped him and predicting the ruin of Jerusalem in A.D. 70 as punishment for his death. To the pathos of the grand genre is added the emphasis of the little epigram, for instance with four lines of verse whose pious play with words outdoes the related Latin epigram by Henrik Harder, "Til Christi Grav." When Jesus is interred, Life lies dead, Naur writes; Death has murdered Life. With the death of Jesus an even greater murder has occurred, of Death itself, which thereby lost its sting.

When Naur's *Golgotha paa Parnasso* was published, it was accompanied by a laudatory poem by Jens Steen Sehested (1635–98), son of the statesman Hannibal Sehested and an accomplished poet, mostly of cheerful moral doggerel. One of his poems is about the stages of womanhood: *Pigernes Dyd- og Laster-Spejl* (ca. 1671; Mirror of Virtues and Vices for Girls). The style, in accord with the age depicted, speaks nursery words over the baby, alternates in its description of the teenager between speech touched by impertinence and eroticism, and becomes matronly stiff when the woman is solidly anchored in wedlock. In his various poems, in part unpublished, Sehested plays a German-influenced baroque against a popular tone.

Something of a bohemian himself, Sehested was sympathetic toward the quite lawless Poul Pedersen, whose dates of birth and death are unknown. For part of the 1680s Pedersen lived with Sehested at his manor "Sellebjerg" on Funen. The intensified Danish baroque style became humorous with Poul Pedersen. He retold in alexandrines a novella by the Frenchman Paul Scarron, *La précaution inutile* (1655; Measure of Precaution in Vain). Pedersen's version, *Don Pedro af Granada* (publ. 1724; Don Pedro of Granada), deals with the tragicomical amorous adventures of Don Pedro, whose theme is that "beauty and reason cannot dwell with virtue." The idolized women are pretty but too gifted, which is why they play the fool with him. So he marries a pretty and stupid girl, but she is also unfaithful to him, precisely because she is foolish, and Don Pedro dies of a broken heart. Pedersen not only translates Scarron's simple classical prose to the impressive rhetoric of the baroque, but at the same time parodies a series of love poems from the collection *Deutsche Übersetzungen und Getichte* (1673; German Translations and Poems) by another of his sources, the fashionable German poet Christian Hoffmannswaldau.

Leonora Christina

In Pedersen's preface to *Don Pedro*, Kingo is called the Danish Homer, no doubt by virtue of his lofty, figurative, stylistic art. To Kingo's diocese belonged not only Funen but also the island of Lolland, and during a journey the bishop paid a visit to Leonora Christina. On that occasion the century's two great masters of the Danish language met. Leonora Christina (1621–98) was a daughter of Christian IV from his marriage with the noblewoman Kirstine Munk. She was quick-witted and gifted with languages. At the age of fifteen, in 1636, she married the courtier Corfitz Ulfeldt, who was soon to make a brilliant career in the king's service. In 1643 he was royal steward, the highest office of state. Numerous childbirths did not prevent Leonora Christina from leading a princely life with her husband in the capital city, out hunting, or on diplomatic journeys, in 1646–47 to Holland and France. Her beauty and intelligence attracted attention at the court of Louis XIII.

Leonora Christina was her father's favorite, but with his death in 1648 the couple's glory came to an end. Frederik III found Ulfeldt too high-handed, and Queen Sophie Amalie looked with jealousy and hatred on Leonora Christina's self-assured behavior. Ulfeldt's influence was curtailed, and in 1651 the king demanded a probe of his conduct of office. Ulfeldt had apparently enriched himself along with government contractors. He did not dare attend the audit; he fled with his family to Stockholm. When his attempt at making peace with Frederik failed, Ulfeldt was considered an enemy of the state. He became an open traitor when he supported the Swedish king during his campaign against Denmark in 1657–58, although Karl X Gustav repaid his services with a death sentence. Ulfeldt fled to Copenhagen; Frederik had both husband and wife arrested and put in the fortress of Hammershus on Bornholm. They tried in vain to escape; they were released on condition of surrendering nearly everything. Ulfeldt's ambitions gave him no peace. While pretending to take the baths in France, he offered the throne of Denmark to the Elector of Brandenburg. In July 1663 in Copenhagen the Supreme Court sentenced Ulfeldt to forfeit life, title, and property. Leonora Christina, who under all circumstances had followed her husband with loyalty, tried in England to get a sum paid back that Charles II had borrowed from the couple. By stratagem and force she was brought on board a ship that took her to Denmark. She remained in confinement in Copenhagen Castle from August 8, 1663, until May 19, 1685.

"My days of imprisonment have been twenty-one years, nine months, and eleven days." Thus the captive countess was to assert at the conclusion of her detailed memoirs, *Jammers Minde* (publ. 1869; Memory of Woe; Eng. tr. *Memoirs of Leonora Christina*, 1929). Their commitment to paper began well into her captivity, as the first years were very harsh, without book or pen to occupy her. Only after Christian V's accession to the throne in 1670 were her conditions alleviated. A German-Danish historian, Otto Sperling the younger, got the captive royal daughter to write an autobiography in French. Here she relates with humor her adolescence under a strict governess and with suspense Ulfeldt's and her unsuccessful attempt to escape from Hammershus down Bornholm's cliffs. She tells how her jailer, the palace steward, craftily tries to get her to express an opinion about Frederik III's queen, Sophie Amalie, who hates her. She adroitly avoids disclosing her sentiments; but although in these same days she wished she were dead, she did not forget a comical misunderstanding. The steward's nonsense makes her pray in French that God punish this coarse fellow: "Dieu vous punisse." The man says in German: "Aha, she would piss," and he summons a maidservant!

Like Job, Leonora Christina upbraided God, but on August 31, 1673, she awoke with words from Scripture in German, burst into a fit of tears, and could then with the same Job unconditionally turn to the grace of God. With inconceivable strength she retained her identity and self-respect for nearly twenty-two years. Large portions of her narrative of this period were produced after Sophie Amalie was dead and Christian V could grant his aunt her freedom, which she came to enjoy in Maribo Convent. She idiomatically reproduces scenes from her coarse daily life; conversations in Low German are rendered with a reality reminiscent of contemporary Dutch painting. It is part of the picture of Leonora Christina's life in captivity that she got good food, including wine, and a succession of peasant women to wait on her.

At the conclusion of *Jammers Minde* Leonora Christina expresses her gratitude toward Christian V and others who had shown her kindness, and her satisfaction that eleven named persons who had treated her badly had died a painful death. It was part of her Christian conviction that God settles his score with an individual already in this life.

She had an unusual character, possessed by passion like a tragic heroine. Her love for Corfitz Ulfeldt, deserved or not, was unconditional and lifelong. To her desperation he was executed in effigy outside the castle: a wooden figure was decapitated and quartered by the executioner on November 16, 1663. Ulfeldt's death as a free man three months later was in contrast a comfort to her.

She was fully aware of her noble descent but in her degradation knew how to command respect by the inner strength of her own personality. We now can also see this high-born woman as an author in the spirit and style of the Renaissance. Other noble ladies were learned as well, such as Birgitte Thott (1610–62), who in 1658 published *Seneca Skrifter* (Seneca's Works), a monumental translation of the Roman philosopher Seneca. In its preface she asserted that women ought to have access to studies: for ignorance leads to moral depravity. In a posthumous work about meritorius women, *Hæltinders pryd* (publ. 1977; Heroines' Adornment), Leonora Christina stated, "The soul is no regarder of sex and remains unchanged by outward aspect and form." She understood some Latin and spoke German, Dutch, French, Italian, Spanish, and even English. Her autobiography equals in quality many contemporary books of memoirs. Like Palladius before her, she broke the pattern of her age. She wrote without literary pretensions and let her style shape itself to her material. Thereby she exposed and touched reality. By virtue of her mastery of her native tongue and other spoken languages, Leonora Christina depicted herself and her surroundings in timeless vignettes.

Back to the sources, *ad fontes*, is the common watchword for humanism and Reformation, Erasmus of Rotterdam and Martin Luther, Christian Pedersen and Peder Palladius. The beacons of the Danish Renaissance were Anders Sørensen Vedel and Hieronymus Justesen Ranch. The phases of the poetic baroque were marked by Anders Arrebo and Thomas Kingo. What was to follow?

Renewal in Sight

In 1671 Christian V established a new nobility, whose counts and barons ranked above the old nobility. A man of the latter, Mogens Skeel (1650–94), wrote a prose comedy in the style of Molière. Throughout five short acts, *Grevens og Friherrens Komedie* (publ. 1871; The Comedy of Count and Baron) pokes crude fun at the newly dubbed nobility. It is the servants, Peder and Mette, who drive the plot. The daughter of a count is not allowed to marry her sweetheart because he is not distinguished enough. It does not help that she asserts the moral of the comedy before her mother, that "honor and dishonor come from our selves." She must marry a newly named baron, but after the pattern of Molière's *Tartuffe*, the young girl gets to know the villain's true nature. When Peder brings a false rumor that the king has exposed the baron, the count's family reverses itself, and before the false rumor is invalidated, the maiden is married to her cavalier.

In 1684 Ludvig Holberg was born in Norway, and in 1702 he came to Denmark. Skeel's comedy gives us a taste of the modern western European spirit that Holberg will bestow on Danish letters.

The Age of Enlightenment

P. M. Mitchell

3

SECULARISM CHALLENGES THEOLOGY

Every distinguishable age can be looked on as an era of transition. To a certain extent this is a truism. Nevertheless, some points in history in retrospect seem to be more marked and more significant than others. One such identifiable transitional period of consequence is the passage from the late seventeenth to the early eighteenth century. By generally accepted terminology, this transition is from the era of the baroque to the era of Enlightenment. These two periods had many elements in common in Denmark (and, less obviously, in its co-kingdom of Norway) as well as in the rest of Europe, for there was a higher social culture that was international in orientation and neoclassical in style at the same time as there was a vernacular culture—separate from and at first disregarded by the intelligentsia. The classical orientation remained dominant in the eighteenth century as the vernacular slowly came into its own. Latin poetry continued to be produced, but that poetry is forgotten today, for it was gradually superseded by the vernacular culture that we now tacitly assume to be the norm.

To speak of the eighteenth century as a recognizable literary epoch and entity is neither arbitrary nor idle. For Denmark the early part of the century marks the establishment of a secular imaginative literature in the vernacular, while the end of the century is punctuated by enthusiastic works engendered in part by a rejuvenation of indigenous tradition and in part by an awareness of a new literature to the south: German classicism. The eighteenth century also saw the proliferation of literary and critical genres as the numbers of readers grew.

When we use the term *literature* today we most often think only of belles lettres, whereas at the beginning of the eighteenth century belletristic works constituted but a fraction of the printed matter that emanated from European presses. The literature of the day was overwhelmingly theological or religious in nature. Political tensions also generated a considerable amount of printed matter. To be sure, the mere number of titles published in a certain genre is not in direct relation to their effect and importance; nevertheless, in the seventeenth century imaginative literature did not make up more than one percent of the books and pamphlets issued in Denmark. There was a slow but steady increase in the number of belletristic works, but even at the end of the eighteenth century such works issuing from Danish presses did not exceed twenty percent of all publications.

To discuss the literary history of the eighteenth century and to confine one's view to the belles lettres—as we indeed tend to do—is to create a false impression of the culture of that time. Our excuse and reason is, however, neither arbitrary nor irrational if we wish to determine the early role of imaginative literature and be able to recognize the forerunners of the kind of literature written for a larger public which seems important to us today.

If we wish to understand the role of the book in the eighteenth century insofar as it is possible, we need knowledge of the conditions under which imaginative literature was produced and familiarity with the social, political, and religious conditions of the times. We must bear in mind, however, that a knowledge of such conditions does not fully explain a human phenomenon that is of a spiritual and aesthetic origin and nature. Accumulating the details about daily life in a past age, as interesting as that may be per se, does not produce an equivalent understanding of the efforts of the imaginative writer, the poetic traditions with which the writer is working and to some extent altering, or the formal demands of genre. Nongeneric writing—memoirs in the first instance—can be of historical value and fascinating reading in itself without, however, being capable of classification with poetry, imaginative prose, or drama. Moreover, as far as the eighteenth century is concerned, even memoirs shed light only on limited facets of life—and of relatively few, educated urban dwellers. There is little documentation about the life of the ordinary person in eighteenth-century Danish literature, although Ludvig Holberg's comedies do provide some humorous insights into the activities of the servant class.

In considering the literature of the eighteenth century or of any other century, we must be aware of the fact that belletristic endeavor, although it mirrors the culture in which it is produced, cannot simply be equated with that culture. In recent years literary critics have paid considerable attention to aspects of human existence in the past which were disregarded in earlier literary history. In Denmark as elsewhere the lives of the poor, the efforts of workers to better themselves, the struggle to change a class system derived from earlier centuries, and the emancipation of women have attracted critical interest. The literary evidence for such depiction is slight for the eighteenth and earlier centuries. For a variety of reasons there was little self-depiction of a proletarian nature. In the first place, the education required to write convincingly was difficult to come by, and so, too, was the free time of the rural as well as the urban worker, for whom the concept of leisure as we know it today scarcely existed. Moreover, the influence of the Christian faith permeated the lives of all classes and to some extent contributed to making the uneducated accept their lot as providential.

History and Society

Unlike the literary situation in England or Germany, that of Denmark during the eighteenth century suffered under the repression that was a corollary of the absolute monarchy. The relative freedom of the press obtained in England and in several German states was not shared by Denmark until the end of the century, when there was a sudden and temporary total freeing of the press in 1770–71 under the enlightened dictatorship of the German-born Johann Friedrich Struensee (1737–72), who pushed through a long series of liberal reforms. As the physician of the demented King Christian VII (1766–1808), he had taken the reins of government into his own hands in 1771 by issuing decrees signed by the king. One year later Struensee was overthrown and executed because of his disdain for what was Danish and his seduction of no less a person than the queen. The palace revolution was led by the king's stepmother, Juliane Marie (1729–96), who for the next twelve years maintained a strict, conservative rule. The mood of the times became one of great caution as far as the expression of original or radical ideas was concerned, despite the fact that intellectual Denmark accepted the philosophy of the Enlightenment. Whoever uttered an opinion that could be construed as negative criticism of the royal house might pay dearly for it.

The traditional history of Denmark-Norway in the early eighteenth century comprises a description of political tensions and military and naval battles. It should be borne in mind that in the eighteenth century Denmark was still a European power with what at that time could be considered a world empire. This position carried political obligations. The war with Sweden from 1675 to 1679 meant a great loss of territory for Denmark. There were repeated conflicts regarding the duchies of Schleswig-Holstein, disputes that would continue into the second half of the nineteenth century and not find a final solution until 1920. The Great Nordic War (1700–20) dominated the first two decades of the century, with Sweden, Denmark-Norway,

Russia, Saxony, Poland, and Hanover the major participants. As important as the series of wars must have been politically and economically, they directly affected the lives of the ordinary inhabitants of Denmark-Norway very little. In part this may be ascribed to the fact that the battles in question were not fought on Danish soil. It is nevertheless surprising to examine the imaginative and critical literature of the time and find a lack of reference to events that in retrospect and from a modern political point of view would seem to have been significant—and unavoidable as a subject of contemporary conversation and discussion.

Internally, Denmark also had its problems. As elsewhere, the absolute monarchy grew less and less satisfactory. A large percentage of the population was in virtual servitude, with limited freedom of movement for tillers of the soil and tenant farmers. Gradually, such restrictions were eased, and by the end of the 1780s far-reaching reforms had been promoted which meant that Denmark avoided the drastic movements and violence of other European countries, particularly France. That is, there was no need for a radical social revolution of the Gallic variety.

A particular misfortune was Copenhagen's lot in 1728, when for several days a fire raged through a large part of the city and destroyed among other things the university library, including a large number of Icelandic manuscripts and many other cultural artifacts.

If the number of imaginative writers was not large, neither was the reading public. It is indisputable that the growth of imaginative literature is intimately associated with centers of population. Few writers have arisen in the past from a rural background—with the notable exception of Iceland, which preserved its own literary tradition even though academically educated Icelanders were oriented on the Danish capital. Within the complex Danish monarchy in the eighteenth century—a union that comprised Norway, Iceland, and Schleswig-Holstein as well as the kingdom of Denmark—Copenhagen was the center of literary activity.

To be sure, even what could be termed belletristic at the beginning of the century was permeated by theology, whereas by the end of the century and the first years of the nineteenth century the situation had radically changed. The middle-class novel, the secular drama, the "Spectator"- type essay (modeled after the English periodical *The Spectator*), and personal lyric poetry, all of which were divorced from the ecclesiastical tradition, had won the day. It is, however, easier to observe and record these changes than it is fully to account for them. Within a comparative context it is evident that the changes that took place in Denmark reflected new currents of critical thought emanating from France, England, and the Netherlands as well as the conglomeration of petty states that was Germany, currents that reached Denmark directly or indirectly and altered the literary scene dramatically. At the same time, Denmark was beginning to generate a literature unlike the literature produced in the seventeenth century and not merely a part of a predominantly Latinate European literature. Writers in Denmark began to bring forth a literature that at once reflected other nascent national literatures and was itself emancipated.

Judged from a retrospective standpoint, little original literature in Danish carried over from the seventeenth into the eighteenth century except for hymns and folk ballads. These genres should not be dismissed lightly, however, even though there was no Danish equivalent of Shakespeare or Vondel, Molière or Pope, Cervantes, Opitz, or Grimmelshausen.

THE PRIMORDIAL IMAGINATION

If we consider Danish society in the eighteenth century, we realize that sophisticated belles lettres were confined to a minority even within the Danish capital. Intellectual activity that was based on some familiarity with the classics and with French literature was a matter for the tiny percentage of the population that made up the well educated and the well-to-do. Denmark was nevertheless a literate nation, as is demonstrable by the quantity of printed matter that issued from the Danish presses. The single kind of printed imaginative literature with which the general public was regularly confronted was the hymn. That is to say, the average Dane was exposed to poetry—in the form of hymns—every Sunday and, willy-nilly, absorbed some sense of rhythm and poetic language from them.

Numerous hymns from the seventeenth century were durable for three reasons: first, Thomas Kingo in particular was a poet of stature, despite the limitations of subject matter that the hymn imposed on him; second, all Danes knew his (and other) hymns by virtue of the commanding position of a state church; and third, the hymns were often set to secular melodies, a fact that enhanced their appeal and served as a mnemonic aid.

At the same time, another poetic tradition was alive primarily orally: the popular ballads that were often of a historical nature, albeit dramatic in content, and several of which date from the Middle Ages. There is, however, no denying that an oral tradition was present and that hundreds of ballads were alive among the urban as well as the rural population. Just what the role of the ballad was in the eighteenth century is not possible to determine. Quite a number got into print as broadsides, but we are uncertain who knew or transmitted most ballads at any given time. They were transmitted nevertheless, as demonstrated by the work of the folklorists of the nineteenth century who, with the rise of interest in the indigenous cultural past, started to collect and write about the ballads. In the interim the Danish ballads have come to be looked on as a great treasure—indeed, they comprise the largest collection of popular ballads in Europe—but as far as the eighteenth century is concerned, we can say little more than that they continued to live.

In addition to the hymn, the popular ballad, and the folktale (rarely considered dignified enough to make its way into print), there was a fourth kind of popular literature: the chapbook, a European and not merely a Danish phenomenon. The chapbooks used tales known in more than one country, but the Danish chapbooks had been mediated by Germany. The story of *Griseldis* (1528; Griselda) from Boccaccio (and in the English-speaking world, Chaucer) is best known. Though the first twenty chapbooks date from the sixteenth century and the later eight chapbooks from the seventeenth, they all enjoyed a wide circulation during the eighteenth century as the number of Danish presses increased. Several of the early chapbooks drew on biblical material, as, for example, *Jesu Barndoms Bog* (Book of Jesus' Childhood). This particular volume was first printed in Copenhagen in 1508, but the next half-dozen issues that are preserved all date from the years 1760–61; and editions continued to appear in the late eighteenth century and into the nineteenth. The forty-fourth known edition was published in Århus in 1884.

The growing amount of popular reading material being published in the eighteenth century speaks for an increasingly literate Danish public. Although such reading matter was unsophisticated, was rejected by the literary arbiters as a waste of time, and has historical rather than aesthetic or philosophical value today, it did serve the valuable purpose of getting people to read and to seek relaxation and vicarious experience through the printed word that did not need the guardianship of the hymnal to keep it alive. In some other European countries in the eighteenth century reading beyond the catechism was limited, but in Denmark the reading of chapbooks, love stories, and tales of adventure helped create a fluency that encouraged the literate person to proceed to more demanding and intellectually satisfying texts.

THE PREDOMINANCE OF LUDVIG HOLBERG

While the awakening of interest in the indigenous past and the use of the vernacular are notable characteristics of eighteenth-century Denmark—as of various other European countries—educated Danes of the century still felt themselves primarily to be members of the republic of letters. Preferences were determined aesthetically and philosophically rather than nationally. The continuance of this attitude was aided by the fact that Denmark was still an international power and was a multilingual country. Nevertheless, Danish literature was not developing on a par with the major European literatures, even though the spirit of the Enlightenment was present and, philosophically and theologically, the conservative traditionalism of the seventeenth century as well as the literary excesses identified as baroque had been overcome.

As far as Danish literature is concerned, the one figure that exemplifies the early triumph of the vernacular and a socially aware literature that could appeal to a broader audience is the Norwegian-born historian, dramatist, and essayist Ludvig Holberg (1684–1754). When we think of eighteenth-century Danish literature, his is the one name that readily comes to mind. He seems to stand as the sole representative of the Enlightenment in Denmark, although that is a false impression, for he was one of many contemporaries who took up ideas from beyond the borders of Denmark-Norway and molded them to suit the time and the place.

Among Holberg's contemporaries, Christian Falster (1690–1752) deserves some attention as a successful satirist. In a series of satires (1720–30) and moral essays, *Amoenitates philologicæ* (1729–32; The Pleasance of Learning), he attacks the same human follies as Holberg: authoritarianism, vanity, and superficiality. Hans Adolph Brorson was an important religious poet of the time—something Holberg was not—decisively influenced by German pietism. Jørgen Riis has a niche on the Danish Parnassus as the author of the first Danish journal, inspired by the English *Spectator,* from 1744, the same year as Holberg's own, not dissimilar, collection of *Moralske Tanker*.

Holberg was scarcely a man of the people. Born in Bergen, he belonged to that small group of Dano-Norwegians who were privileged to attend a university, able to travel and to study abroad, and could live from their intellectual pursuits. From his thirtieth year Holberg was a professor at the University of Copenhagen. Although he did not break with the Latinate culture, he did transcend it. He remained an international as well as a national figure, as is evident from these three facts: first, he continued to write some works in Latin for a larger, European audience; second, he encouraged the publication of some of his own works abroad in Latin or in translation; and third, he synthesized ideas and experiences gained in the Netherlands, England, France, Italy, and to a lesser extent Germany, to create a Danish literature—one might even say, a fortunate literary amalgam—that had not existed before. Not until after Holberg's death in 1754, however, does Danish literature really assume a radically different physiognomy, notably with the debuts of the Norwegian writers who make themselves known in the 1750s and 1760s and, ten years after Holberg's death, with the advent of a poetic genius, Johannes Ewald.

In retrospect it is surprising that Holberg should enjoy such a singular reputation while his contemporaries are overshadowed, although the training, interests, and publication of several of them were similar—similar, but not identical. By accident or a happy constellation of events, Holberg was in the right place at the right time. The explanation of his unique success lies not only in his genius but also in his use of the vernacular and in an approach to the human situation that was immediately comprehensible to his Danish and Norwegian contemporaries and to later generations as well. He was not the only satirist in Denmark, nor was he even the only writer of comedy; not the only historian of Denmark, nor the only essayist. But in all these genres he won a more appreciative audience than did his contemporaries. Others had written satire with their point of origin in Juvenal, as did Holberg—but they wrote in Latin, whereas Holberg wrote in Danish. Christian Falster's Danish as well as Latin essays are a parallel to Holberg's *Epistler*, but they did not have the wit or poignancy of Holberg's essays and consequently could not compete with them in popularity. Joachim Richard Paulli (1691–1759) also wrote comedies in Danish, but with neither the vigor nor the humor that made Holberg's works a theatrical success. There were other histories of Denmark, but they did not share the organization and effective presentation of the material that attracted readers to Holberg and consequently made new editions of his books necessary. Holberg's success is to be explained not by his originality, for he made assiduous use of the works of his predecessors, but rather in his international orientation and his easy Danish style.

Although a literary (and musical) bent could be perceived in Holberg's early years as a student and scholar, he became the titan of eighteenth-century Danish literature during his lifetime by fortuitous circumstance. We are not well informed on the origin of his activity as a playwright, but literary historians accept the hypothesis that he was approached in 1722 by René de Montaigu, the French director of a new Danish theater, which was obliged to present plays in Danish, and that he acquiesced and wrote some twenty plays in the course of two years. That Holberg was approached at all is easily explicable, for he had already made a name for himself as a satirist, first and foremost as the author of the mock heroic epic *Peder Paars* (1719–20; Eng. tr. 1962), which had become a best seller of the day.

Norwegian-born Holberg had necessarily come to Copenhagen for a university education, for it was not until 1811 that a Norwegian university was established. After rather spasmodic study in the Danish capital he traveled abroad extensively, first to the Netherlands (1704), then to England, where he spent nearly two years (1706–8), mostly at Oxford, and subsequently to France and Italy (1712–16). He left an entertaining description of his peregrinations in his memoirs (1728–43; Eng. tr. *The Memoirs of Lewis Holberg*, 1827). The experiences and observations of young Holberg, who had next to no funds, provided a basis and background for his later comedies, in which he was to depict common human foibles in a humorous fashion.

The works for which Holberg is primarily known today constitute a sideline to his serious and prolific academic activity. He had published his first scholarly work, of little originality, *Introduction til de fornemste europæiske Rigers Historie* (Introduction to the History of the Principal Kingdoms of Europe), in 1711. Three years later he became "professor designatus," an appointment that secured his future at the University of Copenhagen, without, however, providing him any salary.

Satirical Works

Holberg's early satires, *Fire Skiemte-Digte* (1722; Four Satires), though no longer read today, made it clear that he was a young man of wit and genius who could appeal to a broader audience than the academic community of which he was a member. Like every other learned man of the time, he was at home with the Latin classics and of these he was particularly attracted to the Roman satirist Juvenal. The early satires are in the spirit of Juvenal, but since they were in the vernacular, they could have a more widespread effect than the Latin works of any variety that he and his contemporaries continued to produce.

Peder Paars, a parody in Danish on Virgil's *Aeneid*, although published under the pseudonym Hans Mickelsen, "brewer and poet in Kalundborg," immediately made Holberg a public figure. He was to remain so until his death in 1754 as a respected historian, the benefactor of Sorø Academy (reestablished in 1747 as an institution for providing the absolute monarchy with well-educated administrators and diplomats), a wealthy baron, and an imaginative writer. Whereas Virgil had made use of elevated persons from the realm of the Homeric epic, Holberg, who doubtless was impatient with Virgil's dramatic pathos, chose to hold such pathos up to ridicule by transferring it into the world of the everyday by means of a homely tale. In the same way, Nicolas Boileau-Despréaux in his parody *Le Lutrin* (1672–83;

The Lectern) depicted in high-flown language the "battle of the books," and somewhat later Holberg's older contemporary Alexander Pope used the technique in *The Rape of the Lock* (1714).

Peder Paars, a miller, wishes to visit his beloved Dorothea, who lives in Århus on the east coast of Jutland. He sets out from the harbor of Kalundborg on the west coast of the island of Zealand and meets the same complications of fate as the classical Aeneas. He is shipwrecked on the island of Anholt and is beset by both natural and supernatural catastrophe. In the place of Dido, who was abandoned by Aeneas, a local maiden of Anholt, who has become enamored of Peder, is abandoned by him after helping him escape from the island. Because of unfavorable winds and a sleeping pilot, Peder is driven to the northern tip of Jutland, where he has a series of new misfortunes before he finally can proceed to Århus. The success of the epic derives not so much from the depiction of Peder's grotesque misfortunes as from the satirical presentation of the ridiculous petty authorities on Anholt, who merely exemplify foibles in everyday Denmark, in the same spirit as in many of Holberg's comedies. The owner of Anholt, a prominent statesman and professor at the University of Copenhagen, started a suit against Holberg because of the mocking epic, but the authorities found Holberg's work simply to be amusing and the suit was dropped. Parenthetically, it is worth noting that when Holberg began publishing *Peder Paars,* he was professor of metaphysics, a subject in which he did not feel at home, whereas by the time the work was finished, in 1721, he had been promoted to professor of Latin literature, an appointment that not only was more agreeable to him but reflected the Latin origins of his satirical vein. Holberg's academic goal was, however, a professorship in history.

The literary genre most abundantly represented in eighteenth-century Denmark was the drama, which, until the end of the century, was almost exclusively comedy. The orientation was entirely foreign: French and German. Although there were some dramatic efforts in Denmark earlier, Danish drama really began with the establishment of the theater for which Holberg wrote in 1722. Not only had plays been given in French and German in Copenhagen by visiting companies, but numerous plays continued to be printed in French or German in the Danish capital—evidence of familiarity with those languages on the part of a large segment of the city's population. In 1749–50 an eight-volume set of plays in French was issued, and twenty years later several additional sets were published in Copenhagen. Individual plays were still being published in French or in German in the early nineteenth century. The number of translations issued—not an indicator of the number of foreign plays staged in translation—was small until the 1770s.

A translation of Molière's *L'Étourdi* (The Blunderer) appeared in 1723, and eight or nine of Pietro Metastasio's plays were issued in translation from the Italian between 1748 and Holberg's death in 1754. Between 1722 and about 1770 the number of Danish plays other than Holberg's was small and their intrinsic significance slight. Holberg's sole competitor was Johann Richard Paulli, who in 1724 had the poor judgment to try to improve on Holberg's *Den politiske Kandestøber* with his own version (using the same title).

The one name that stands out in respect to the theoretical development of a theater in Denmark is the German Johann Elias Schlegel (1719–49), who had studied in Leipzig with the reformer of the German theater, Johann Christoph Gottsched, and who a few years later was able to win Holberg's confidence. The young Schlegel, who had come to Denmark in Saxon diplomatic service, soon familiarized himself with Danish conditions and learned Danish. In his journal, *Der Fremde* (1745–46; The Stranger), he touched on dramatic matters and even included one of his own plays. More important was his active interest in the establishment of a Danish national theater, an idea that found expression in the essay "Gedanken zur Aufnahme des dänischen Theaters" (1747; Thoughts about the Establishment of the Danish Theater). It is noteworthy that Schlegel also wrote a historical tragedy, *Canut*—in German, but for the Danish stage—in 1746; a Danish translation was issued the following year. Schlegel was made a professor at the Sorø Academy in 1748 but died the next year. The stage, so to speak, was set for the further development of a national Danish drama after Holberg, but as we shall see, the dominant theater continued to be French and German not only until the end of the eighteenth century, but right on into the nineteenth.

The Poetic "Raptus"

Holberg's new academic assignment coincided with the beginning of his productivity as a dramatist. Holberg himself speaks of a poetic "raptus," and one can indeed use the term to describe his venture into imaginative literature. Starting in the autumn of 1722, within three years' time he had written some two dozen comedies, among them his best-known: *Den politiske Kandestøber, Den Vægelsindede, Jean de France*, and *Jeppe paa Bjerget*. These plays and the comedy *Erasmus Montanus* are among Holberg's most frequently performed.

The new Danish theater opened in September 1722 with a Danish version of Molière's *L'Avare* (The Miser). The next performance was of Holberg's first comedy, *Den politiske Kandestøber*, a play that is representative, if not typical, of all of the comedies. Though the comedies are original dramatic works, they show the inspiration and influence of Molière, Plautus, and the Italian commedia dell'arte. Holberg had read both the French and the Latin dramatists, although we are uncertain which plays he may have seen on the French—or Danish—stage before he started to write his own comedies. From his autobiography, however, we do know that he familiarized himself with the Italian farce firsthand while he was in Rome.

Den politiske Kandestøber (1723; Eng. tr. *The Political Tinker,* 1990), like several of the other plays, is a mixture of the comedy of character with that of situation. Herman von Bremen is a tinker in Hamburg who has vague and naive political ambitions and, with a group of his peers, meets to discuss—in a pompous and foolish manner—European matters of state to the detriment of his own work, which he quite neglects. His *Besserwisserei* (loosely translated as "know-it-all attitude") and his boasting lead to his being taught a lesson by his betters: he is made to believe that he has been appointed mayor of the city with the result, first, that he and his wife assume roles for which they are quite unfitted and cut ridiculous figures and, second, that he is unable to cope with all the imaginary problems—invented for the occasion—confronting him. Woven into the situation is a secondary intrigue that involves his daughter and her would-be suitor. Faced by dilemmas and multiple, insoluble problems presented nominally by a delegation of hatters and other supplicants, Herman recognizes his inability to solve these difficulties and cries out in despair that he would remain a tinker and nothing but a tinker the rest of his life.

There is a parallel between this first comedy and Holberg's most successful play, *Erasmus Montanus* (1731; Eng. tr. 1885, 1990). Here the young Rasmus Berg, after a year at the University of Copenhagen, is barely able to communicate with the inhabitants of his native town, since they know no Latin, and is in danger of losing his fiancée because of his unacceptable claim that the world is round. Defeated in the eyes of the public through a comic Latin disputation with the ignorant but sly local deacon, and apparently about to be drafted into the army, Erasmus is brought to admit that the world is flat, "flat as a pancake"; all his superficial book learning does him no good. A similar series of events is in the comedy *Jean de France* (1723; Eng. tr. 1990), in which the title character's francophile bubble is burst through his being manipulated by the clever maid, Pernille—one of many cases in which the servants (generally named Henrik and Pernille) actually are the moving forces in the action of the play.

The substance of *Jeppe paa Bjerget* (1723; Eng. tr. *Jeppe of the Hill,* 1906, 1990), the transformed peasant, is a motif widespread in world literature, although according to his own testimony Holberg used the German Jesuit playwright Jakob Bidermann's *Utopia* (1644) as his source. This particular comedy is, however, unlike the others, for there is a recognizable tragic moment in Jeppe's situation—something that is sensed in the complaint, "They say Jeppe drinks, but they do not say why Jeppe drinks." Jeppe, found drunk on a manure pile by the local baron and his retainers, is brought senseless to the baron's castle and awakes in the baron's bed. At first believing he is in heaven, he is gradually convinced that he is indeed the baron, and he quickly assumes an autocratic role while retaining the proletarian's knowledge of skulduggery on the part of some of the baron's employees. Enjoying the sudden sense of power, he is ruthless and coarse to those about him who seem to curry his favor. When the joke has gone far enough, he is made drunk again, only to awaken on a manure pile. Condemned to death in a mock trial for having imitated the baron, he takes touching leave of his family and the animals who have been faithful to him. After overcoming the effect of a sleeping potion, he wakens, at first in the belief that he has died, only gradually to discover that he has been hoodwinked and that all is the same and nothing better than before. Despite the laughter the play provokes, an unmistakable undercurrent of pity is educed for the misused Jeppe.

Among the perennially successful comedies of the Danish stage are also Holberg's *Den Stundesløse* (1731; Eng. tr. *The Fussy Man*, 1912, 1946) and, to a lesser degree, *Den Vægelsindede* (1723; Eng. tr. *The Weathercock*, 1946), both caricatures related to Molière's *Le Malade imaginaire* (The Imaginary Invalid) of a half-century earlier. While "the weathercock," Lucretia, is a psychological study of a woman who overexercises her privilege to change her mind, "the fussy man," Vielgeschrey, imagines himself so involved with business and other matters that he gets nothing done. The role can be very effective on the stage, as indeed can be the complementary roles in the same comedy. Vielgeschrey wants to marry his daughter to the dull son of a bookkeeper, but the daughter, Leonora, is in love with Leander. Through an amusing intrigue devised by the ubiquitous and clever maid, Pernille, the family's aging housekeeper is foisted off on the bookkeeper's son, while Leonora is given to Leander by her father through a series of misunderstandings, also invented by Pernille. There is thus a triple plot, whose strands are interwoven. At one point in the comedy, in good comic tradition, the bookkeepers, the lover, the maid, and the housekeeper all seem to be something other than they are. Holberg thus uses familiar elements of the comic theater, but his genius lies in the witty permutations of those elements and his command of language both in characterizing individuals and in achieving grotesque situations that constitute the complications of the plot and the denouement of the play.

Several other comedies hold stock characters up to ridicule in situations that depend on intrigue for resolution, as, for example, *Jacob von Tyboe* (1725), which portrays the boastful soldier of Latin comedy. Other comedies make fun of certain social customs, notably *Barselstuen* (1724; The Lying-In Room), which nominally depicts a series of visitors to the mother and her newborn while revealing suspect relationships and the characters' own shortcomings, but not without the employment of some slapstick. In still other comedies Holberg is primarily entertaining an audience, as in the story of the indentured farmer's son, *Den pantsatte Bonde-Dreng* (1731; Eng. tr. *The Peasant in Pawn,* 1950), or of Pernille's role as a young lady of the nobility, *Pernilles korte Frøkenstand* (1731; Eng. tr. *Pernille's Brief Experience as a Lady,* 1990). As has been pointed out to excess by some recent critics, Holberg is clearly questioning some aspects of the social order of his day but always in a humorous way without the intent of destroying the underpinnings of the social and political life of the time. On one point Holberg used extreme caution: there is no mention of religious or ecclesiastical matters in his plays; they did not lend themselves to comic presentation if one accepted the status quo. This fact is noteworthy in view of the domination of Danish literature by theological publications in Holberg's day.

One further comedy deserves special mention by virtue of its having been given new life as an opera in the twentieth century, *Mascarade* (1724; Eng. tr. *Masquerades,* 1782, 1946). The play, with its traditional intrigue and usual oblique criticism of foolish social mores, was successful per se, but the nestor of Danish literary history in the early twentieth century, Vilhelm Andersen, recognized the possibilities that the piece offered and produced a libretto that Denmark's greatest composer, Carl Nielsen, set to music in 1906. The combination of Holberg, Andersen, and Nielsen proved a success. The opera is played frequently at the Royal Theater in Copenhagen.

Holberg's early comedies depicted human folly—ridiculous social beliefs and prejudices, the frequent arrogance of the dim-witted but well-to-do person toward the clever and witty servant—and did so humorously; the humor was not unpleasantly satirical or cutting. To be sure, Holberg customarily added a superfluous moral lesson at the end of a comedy, but there was no reason for anyone to be offended by his criticism. When he once again turned to satire, however, his narrative was something more than merely humorous. *Nicolai Klimii iter subterraneum* (1741; Eng. tr. *The Journey of Niels Klim to the World Underground,* 1742, 1960) was in a different vein than the plays. It was quite simply a Danish *Gulliver's Travels* and, like Swift's work, was sly and trenchant in its satire on social conditions and the governmental establishment. It was, moreover, directed not merely toward a Danish public but toward the international, sophisticated reading public, for it was written in Latin. The Danish publisher was aware of the reaction such a book might provoke among the powers that be and arranged to have it issued beyond the pale of Danish censorship, in Leipzig. The book was an immediate success and was translated at once into German, Dutch, and French. The first Danish translation appeared in 1742, entitled *Niels Klims Reise Under Jorden*. A Swedish translation followed in 1746, a Russian in 1766, and a Hungarian in 1786. The work had clearly touched a sensitive nerve in the European conscience and at the same time acquired the status of a modern classic. Polish and Finnish translations were published in the nineteenth century. Despite the implied and evident negative criticism of conditions that obtained in various European states, the book was nowhere suppressed. The narrative is akin both to Swift's *Gulliver's Travels* (1726), which it resembles in concept and structure, and to the popular imaginary voyage, the most famous of which was Montesquieu's *Lettres persanes* (1721; Persian Letters). With assumed naiveté the traveler describes the conditions with which he is confronted, leaving the most severe but inevitable judgments to the reader.

Holberg's Niels Klim explores a cave in Norway and falls into a shaft that deposits him in the world underground. He arrives first in the land of Potu—the name is presumably part of Thomas More's term "Utopia" spelled backward. Here the inhabitants, all trees, are wise and deliberate. Niels reveals many flaws of the modern society that he represents, for Potu is ruled strictly by reason. When Niels proposes that women be kept from public office, he is put on trial and narrowly escapes being hanged by virtue of his foreign birth. He is exiled to an upper realm that is ruled by apes. Here he is taken to be a savior sent from the sun but after introducing modern warfare and making himself ruler not only of Martinia, the land of the apes, but of the lands of various other animals, he loses his judgment and becomes an arrogant and autocratic ruler. As a result, he is toppled from his high position and escapes to a cave from which he falls back to the very spot in Norway where his voyage had begun. Addressing his curious countrymen in the language of the underworld, he is first taken to be the Wandering Jew, but ultimately he is accepted back into everyday Norwegian existence and ends his days as a sexton.

The many situations described in the underworld are grotesque and hilarious and may be said to turn the world upside down, but with satirical intent. When a doctoral thesis is defended, for example, a pail of cold water is poured over the hand of the candidate and he is given a laxative, symbols of spiritual purification. Like Swift and Montesquieu, Holberg can still be read and enjoyed today. As in the case of his English and French contemporaries, his satire and social criticism have retained validity and humorous effect. Satire permeated by humor could accomplish what direct criticism could not—and without the critic's subjecting himself to dangers similar to those that befell Niels in the netherworld.

Essays

Holberg was not a philosopher; he was a historian, dramatist, critic, and essayist. In all his work he was nevertheless guided by a philosophical principle: reason. Directly or indirectly, reason was the criterion he applied in all his evaluations and judgments. Nowhere is this clearer and more pointed than in the imaginary voyage of Niels Klim, which makes the reader conclude that humankind's arbitrary and unreasonable rules for social organization and behavior are often absurd and ludicrous. Here Holberg depends on the irony of the situation to make his point, whereas in the later essays he is less circumspect and less devious—while he remains witty. There are even connecting links between the imaginary voyage and the essays. The essay "Quislimiri," contained in the first volume of *Epistler* (no. 79), purports to be a section that was omitted from *Niels Klim*. Tongue in cheek, Holberg here argues for discrepancies in wages for persons performing the same task and purports to be convinced that only such discrepancies will encourage competition.

The *Moralske Tanker* (1744; Moral Thoughts) and the five volumes of *Epistler* (1748–54; selected Eng. tr. *Selected Essays*, 1955; *Moral Reflections and Epistles,* 1991) constitute Holberg's contribution to the genre that is identified with the so-called moral weekly known as "Spectator" literature. This form spread like wildfire from England after the appearance of Richard Steele's *Tatler* in 1709–11 and of Steele's and Joseph Addison's *Spectator* (1711–12, 1714). The *Moralske Tanker* are the earlier—and the more sober—of Holberg's essays. They are nominally the exegeses of some of Holberg's own Latin epigrams, *Epigrammata,* which he had published in 1737. In many ways they are in the tradition of the "Spectator" literature; for example, they begin with a quotation, although we may assume that most of Holberg's readers gave the Latin epigrams (which often were only loosely associated with the essay itself) short shrift, in order to read and enjoy what really was on Holberg's mind in regard to a multitude of moral, practical, and even philosophical subjects. More than any other work, the *Moralske Tanker* expresses the sexagenarian Holberg's personal philosophy. Although the essays of the *Epistler* are closely related to *Moralske Tanker,* they are more of a catchall and are more given to humor. These later essays cannot be classified under only a few categories, for they range widely. The largest single group pertains to religious or ecclesiastical matters, but the reader senses Holberg's plea for tolerance rather than any advocacy of dogma or a certain belief. The second largest category embraces history and biography as befits their author, a professor of history. Further division into categories is idle, since Holberg felt free to write, entertainingly, on a wide range of subjects, from tea and coffee to marriage, from friendship to geography. One must remember that he lived and wrote in an age of so-called universal learning. His most important source of inspiration for the essay was Pierre Bayle's encyclopedia, *Dictionaire historique et critique* (1695–97; Historical and Critical Dictionary), of which Holberg had acquired the third edition from 1720.

Holberg's dependence on Bayle reminds us that the culture of eighteenth-century Copenhagen was not an indigenous one. The impulses that informed literary, philosophical, social, and political thought came from outside—from France and the Netherlands, from England and to a somewhat lesser extent politically fragmented Germany, often firsthand and regularly through the printed word. Once again Holberg is an exemplar par excellence, for he acquired some familiarity with the same centers of learning and culture whose impulses and influence were to amalgamate in the northern capitals. He was by no means the only Dano-Norwegian to use the Bodleian Library at Oxford, to sojourn in Paris, or to visit Rome, but he did all these things at a propitious time that permitted him, unlike those countrymen who had preceded him, to fulfill the unspoken demand for an indigenous literature. Ideas that emanated from the Netherlands, France, and England he synthesized and expressed in his native tongue as a creative writer, a historian, and an essayist.

Several parallels may be drawn between Holberg and some of his Dano-Norwegian contemporaries, but only on one count or the other, not as a whole: the multifaceted Frederik Rostgaard (1671–1745), at one time Holberg's adversary but soon thereafter a supporter of the recently established theater; Andreas Hojer (1690–1739), who was Holberg's equal as a historian writing in a vernacular—but in German, not in Danish; Jørgen Friis (1684–1740), a neoclassical poet who wrote in Danish; and Hans Gram (1685–1748), philologist, librarian of the Royal Library, royal historiographer, and a founder of the Royal Academy of Sciences. These figures and others were important in their time and deserve honorable mention in any assessment of eighteenth-century Denmark, although they no longer engage our imagination or command our awareness. Holberg does.

The gradual rise of a nationally oriented belletristic literature during Holberg's lifetime can be observed by leafing through thirty years of Denmark's first learned periodical, *Nye Tidender Om lærde Sager* (News of Learned Matters), which started publication in January 1720, issued by the enterprising printer-publisher Joachim Wielandt (1690–1730). Essentially, the periodical is a Danish version of the several learned journals published in German-speaking areas. There are reports on and sometimes résumés of books issued in France, England, Germany, and the Netherlands. At the end of each number is a list of recently published items—in Latin, German, Dutch, and French—but at first next to nothing issued in Denmark or in the Danish language. By September 1720, however, there is a printer's advertisement for seven books, six of which are in Danish; none is, however, belletristic. As early as November of the first year there is a summary of Defoe's *Robinson Crusoe* (1719) in a German translation, issued in Hamburg. (The book is treated as being historically reliable.) In December, finally, there is a review of a Danish book, about the origin of the nobility. By 1723 several learned books published in Danish are mentioned, as well as *Idea historiæ litterariæ Danorum* (1723; The Form of Danish Literary History) by Albert Thura (1700–1740), the first part of which treated the Danish language. This book, incidentally published not in Denmark itself but in Hamburg, can be seen as laying a foundation for the acceptance and serious consideration of a Danish national literature. Aesop's fables in Danish as well as Latin and Danish epigrams are mentioned by 1724. That same year the existence of the new Danish theater is recognized, notably by mention of Molière's *L'Avare*, "translated for the use of the Danish theater." On page 574 in the journal of that year are found verses in English—not insignificantly, with a plethora of errors in spelling that suggest the inclusion of any English to be a tour de force.

Occasional Poetry

Only five years after the journal had begun, there is clearly a greater awareness of imaginative literature, although the contents of the periodical are still predominantly scholarly. By 1730 one finds mention of Holberg's Danish plays, a German poem by Johan Ulrich König, and a list of books available at His Majesty's and the university's press in Copenhagen. They include Boileau's satires, Philipp von Zesen's novel *Assenat* (1670), several plays, and ten chapbooks, all in Danish translation. There is also a certain amount of poetry in French for the edification of "those who can read

French." There must then have been readers of the journal who could not read French; that would scarcely have been the case a decade before. Later in the 1730s more attention is paid to publications that appear in Denmark, and Denmark acquires an equal standing with the oldest European nations' publications reported on in the *Nye Tidender*. German poetry begins to supersede French. There is Danish verse by Thomas Clitau (ca. 1695–1754), later to become editor of the journal, and Christian Frederik Wadskiær (1713–79), who for two years before Clitau also was editor of the journal. While these two authors of occasional poetry used chiefly Danish as their medium, they also wrote in both German and Latin.

To judge on the basis of *Nye Tidender*, Thomas Clitau was the leading Danish poet of his time. In 1740 the periodical was still printing some of Clitau's poetry, both in Danish and Latin, with additional occasional poetry by Wadskiær in Danish, German, and Latin. The linguistically gifted Clitau, whose poetry was published as *Poetisk Tids-Fordriv* (1738; Poetic Pastime), evokes no nod of recognition today. Wadskiær, on the other hand, who later held a professorship of poetry at the University of Copenhagen, is at least a known entity in the annals of literary history, because of the wit that informed even his occasional poetry, such as his *Poetiske Reflexioner* (Poetic Reflections), written on the occasion of the anointing of King Frederik V (1746–66) in 1747.

Mention of Wadskiær is indicative of the fact that the age of Holberg also produced its share of occasional poetry. Baptisms, weddings, birthdays, appointments, and funerals gave opportunity to express sentiments in verse. This part of the baroque tradition lived on, but little of the verse written at the time has a claim on the attention of the modern reader; much is formulaic and without substance or originality, as ever has been the case with occasional verse. Nevertheless, a sense for the appropriateness of poetic expression was felt on notable occasions, indeed enough so that he who could not compose verses himself hired another to produce appropriate public sentiment. Wadskiær was a prolific writer of verse, some of which leads a fragile existence in anthologies. There have been some attempts at a positive reevaluation of his work but with limited results.

Also prominent in his own time was the clergyman Jørgen Sorterup (1662–1723), who early in the century wrote some material verse, notably about a victory at sea over Sweden in 1715. His lengthy poem *Nye Helte-Sange* (1716; New Heroic Ballads) begins with an appeal for the recognition of the medieval "Kiempe-Viiser" (Songs of Heroes), or heroic ballads. Merely metrically, the verse stands out in contrast to the usual occasional poetry produced by Sorterup's compatriots. At another, higher level of recognition is the Norwegian Christian Braunmann Tullin (1728–65), whose *En Maji-Dag* (A May Day) on the occasion of a wedding in Christiania (now Oslo) was first printed in Copenhagen in 1758, reprinted in Trondheim the next year, and issued three times more in the 1760s in Copenhagen. Most of Tullin's other works also went through more than one edition in Copenhagen, and an unauthorized collection of his works was issued in three volumes in 1770–73, a remarkable testimony of his position on the Danish literary scene, although he lived in Christiania from 1748 until the end of his life. Some of his poetry was translated into Swedish, German, and, later, English. Tullin, who has been praised as the first Dano-Norwegian poet of nature, has his place in literary history.

Hans Adolph Brorson and Ambrosius Stub

Two Danish contemporaries not to be categorized as occasional poets are, however, part of Danish literary consciousness, the one for religious, the other for worldly, poetry: Hans Adolph Brorson, pietistic clergyman and for many years bishop of Ribe, and Ambrosius Stub, who, unrecognized in his own time, was at the end of his life a schoolteacher in Ribe. Brorson (1694–1764) made a major contribution to Danish hymnology with the publication of *Troens Rare Klenodie* (1739; Faith's Rare Jewel), which contained not only many of Brorson's own hymns, several of which are known to every Dane today, but a large number of hymns translated chiefly from German. No hymn by Brorson is more often sung than "Op, al den Ting, som Gud har gjort" (Rise, All Those Things That God Has Made). The essence of Brorson's religious fervor is captured with sublime simplicity in these lines from "Den yndigste Rose er funden" (Now Found Is the Fairest of Roses):

My rose is my gem, my delight
My rose is my bliss and my light;
The poisonous lusts he crushes.
The Cross then sweetness gushes.

For his poems Brorson frequently adapted the meters of the secular aria and cantata. His poetry's high level of stylistic accomplishment is also displayed in his sophisticated, often bold use of imagery from the Bible and the mystical tradition, aesthetic experiments that he continued in the posthumous collection *Svane-Sang* (1765; Swan Song). Several editions of *Troens Rare Klenodie* appeared in his lifetime, but the collection gradually fell out of use. Individual hymns were revived in the next century so that

Brorson is now named with Thomas Kingo of the seventeenth century and B. S. Ingemann and N. F. S. Grundtvig of the nineteenth century as one of the four greatest Danish authors of hymns.

Brorson is evidence of the existence of more than one strong cultural current in eighteenth-century Denmark. His work represents the fundamentalist pietistical theology that came from Germany via the duchies of Schleswig and Holstein and, during the reign of Christian VI (1730–46), became the unofficial, very restrictive state religion of Denmark. The pietists not only devoted themselves to religious activities but spearheaded some social reforms, such as the opening of modern orphanages, poor-houses, and hospitals. The contrast in basic values is demonstrated by viewing Holberg and Brorson as contemporaries. Where Holberg was the thoroughgoing rationalist and great secular writer of his time, who addressed himself not only to belles lettres but also to history, ethics, and philosophical matters, Brorson was the most gifted religious poet of the same era. Holberg's world was anthropocentric; Brorson's was theocentric. Holberg acquainted himself with the thought and mores of other countries. Brorson stayed within the perimeter of received theological thinking and inflexible ecclesiastical convictions.

Ambrosius Stub's (1705–58) fame was posthumous. His unaffected and humorous style—he was a master of playful improvisation—and his appreciation of nature, although discussed favorably in Jacob Baden's *Kritisk Journal* (Critical Journal) of 1771, was comprehended really only in the nineteenth century, when he became an animated figure in the popular mind by virtue of being the subject of a play in 1877, *Ambrosius,* by C. K. F. Molbech (1821–88).

Most of Stub's poems, including his two masterpieces "Du deylig Rosen-Knop" (Thou Beautiful Rosebud) and "Den kiedsom Vinter gik sin Gang" (The Tedious Winter's Gone Its Way), are, like many of Brorson's hymns, modeled on the contemporary rococo aria and distinguish themselves through their exquisite musicality. In the first, female beauty is compared with that of the perishable rose; in the second, Danish nature receives one of its first and finest realistic descriptions. The scenery, however, is personalized and the poem turns into a glorification of the Creator, who guides everything for the best. Here, but particularly in a series of penitential hymns, it becomes evident to what extent Stub—under the direct influence of Brorson—was affected by the intense devotional if not ascetic aspects of pietism.

Tøger Reenberg

A curious piece of evidence attesting the beginning of the Danish aesthetic evaluation of belles lettres was written the very first year of the eighteenth century. The *Ars poetica* (1701) by Tøger Reenberg (1656–1742) is a work in verse that demonstrates both the literary orientation of the late seventeenth century and the new literature of the early eighteenth. Merely the title advises of a familiarity with Horace and at the same time an effort to produce a new literary standard for the times. Reenberg possesses none of Horace's sophistication; his was homely iambic verse and his goal was to encourage the production of Danish poetry.

In view of the fact that the seventeenth century was dominated by Latin, Reenberg's advocacy of Danish is noteworthy. His attitude was not parochial, to be sure. To the south, efforts were being made to give more prestige to the vernacular. Some instruction had already been given in German rather than Latin at a German university, and critics were beginning to assess seriously some works written in the vernacular. It is a curious parallel that the leading critic of the early eighteenth century in Germany, J. C. Gottsched, prefaced his poetics, *Versuch einer Critischen Dichtkunst* (1730; Essay on a Critical Poetic Theory), with a German translation of Horace's *Ars poetica*, and in 1674 the late seventeenth-century Boileau had produced his own French *Art poétique*, which was to set the tone on the literary scene for decades. Succinctly put, Reenberg was moving with the spirit of the times.

Reenberg's orientation was synthetic: on the one hand, he was working with the elements of classical antiquity in the *Ars poetica*, but on the other, he was also aware of Old Norse literature and mythology. He mentions such disparate phenomena as the Edda, Milton, and even Isaac Voss. The international awareness is not surprising, for Reenberg, much like Ludvig Holberg two decades earlier, had traveled widely, had spent considerable time at Oxford, and had visited France and Italy—that is to say, had taken a kind of student's grand tour. The fact that young Danes of an academic persuasion were able to travel abroad and visit centers of learning and culture contributed to making Danish literature a part of European literature and not an isolated occurrence. Although it is notable that Reenberg wrote his *Ars poetica* at the beginning of the century, it does not follow that the work had any effect on the contemporary literary scene, for three decades passed until the poem was printed. Nevertheless, it may be viewed as a small historical monument if not as an achievement that affected Reenberg's contemporaries. That is, Reenberg is of importance only in retrospect.

Poetry

The state of Danish poetry around 1725 is explicitly demonstrated by a series of fourteen fascicles published that year by Joachim Wielandt and entitled *Til en Samling udaf smukke og udvalgde Danske Vers og Miscellanea Nationen til Ære og Sproget til Ziir* (Toward a Collection of Pretty and Choice Danish Verse and Miscellanea to the Nation's Honor and the Language's Elegance)—in all, more than nine hundred pages. Despite the fact that Denmark's great baroque poet Thomas Kingo is well represented, there is little that is outstanding and almost nothing that is lyrical in the entire collection. The poetry consists overwhelmingly of occasional verse, often in an elevated and elegiac style with commendable use of rhythm and rhyme. There is also a suggestion of the pastoral, notably in the poetry of Anders Bording. Incidentally, a plaintive note is struck about the deportment of the younger generation.

There was, then, an awareness of the role and importance of poetry in the vernacular and a pride in the existence of such poetry, without, however, such Danish verse making any claim to a place on the European Parnassus. The anthology was necessarily retrospective, and the extravagant metaphor dominates. That is to say, its mood is baroque, a persuasion soon to be brushed aside by a new, strong current of rationalism. Nevertheless, the fact that such a series of fascicles could be sold is indicative of the existence of an audience and an appreciation of literary creativity, even if it was but the ornamentation of the everyday. In academic circles some poetry continued to be a by-product of the philological or historical activity of scholars, the best known of whom was Frederik Rostgaard, whose poetry (chiefly in Latin), however, was rather insignificant.

Influences from Abroad

Throughout the century collections of anecdotes and humorous tales were also printed. Most of the literature of entertainment, which increased as the century progressed, was of foreign origin or at least inspiration. Such books, notably love stories, appeared only in single editions. Most of the 120-odd satires printed in the eighteenth century appeared in the 1770s and later, that is, during and after the years of Struensee's rule (1770–72), which temporarily brought freedom of the press.

If we view the eighteenth century as a whole, we see in addition to the new awareness of the indigenous past an identifiable English influx in Continental literature, including that of Denmark: "Spectator" literature, Milton, Shakespeare, Richardson—all were to make themselves felt across the English Channel. In Denmark they arrived not directly but generally through the medium of the Netherlands and Germany. For the first half of the century the neoclassical spirit was predominant and French influence pervasive even though different models, notably English, informed the German belles lettres to the south. Early in the century Molière and Fénelon were the brightest lights on Parnassus: in 1727–28 a four-volume translation of Fénelon's *Télémaque* appeared in Danish, and in 1728 the first of three different translations of a French "Robinsonade" by Eustache Le Noble, *Zulima, ou l'Amour pure* (1695; Zulima, or Pure Love), was published. These "Robinsonades" were issued even before Defoe's work was translated into Danish. Incidentally, two editions of *Der Beyerische Robinson* (The Bavarian Robinson) were issued in Copenhagen, in 1729 and 1749. In comparison with the English literature of the early eighteenth century, Danish literature seems bleak. There is no imaginative writer of the stature of Fielding or Defoe, Richardson or Sterne, although, after a time, these very writers found an audience in Denmark. Thus Defoe's incomparable, successful, and widely imitated *Robinson Crusoe* from 1719 did not appear in Danish until 1744–45, although Samuel Richardson's *Pamela* (1740) was published in Danish between 1743 and 1746.

Henry Fielding's novel *Joseph Andrews* (1742) appeared in Danish as early as 1749, whereas his *Tom Jones* (1749) was not translated until 1781. Jonathan Swift's *Gulliver's Travels* had to wait an inexplicably long time to be made available in Danish. Originally issued in 1726, it appeared in Danish forty years later. Laurence Sterne's *Tristram Shandy* (1759–67) and *A Sentimental Journey* (1768) were translated in 1794 and 1775, respectively. Denmark moved slowly toward the forefront of the new prose literature. The Danish translations cannot be taken as the full measurement of the position and influence of the new bourgeois novel, for German translations of such works were accessible in Denmark even if firsthand acquaintance with English texts was minimal.

It is scarcely possible to establish with precision the role of a foreign literature in translation, whether with regard to its immediate popularity or in terms of its effect on the domestic literature. Foreign authors who are referred to or quoted repeatedly and who have appeared in more than one edition in Danish translation may be considered to be of importance for the time. Such writers as Alexander Pope, Voltaire, and C. F. Gellert and such publications as *The Spectator* are visible as models in a Danish context. The apparent dominance of English literature is actually misleading, for Danish acquaintance with English writers in the eighteenth century was often through the medium of translation, and particularly in the case of the "Spectator"-type publications that had proliferated in Germany.

The state of literature in eighteenth-century Denmark was affected from without by the arrival, in 1751, of Germany's young and yet most renowned poet: Friedrich Klopstock (1724–1803), author of *Der Messias* (1748–73; The Messiah). Although, at that time only the first few cantos of the epic poem had been written, it had immediately won him fame and had brought him an invitation from the Danish Crown to come to Denmark on a stipend that would continue until the epic was completed.

Klopstock resided in Denmark for nineteen years but never really became one with Danish culture. On the contrary, we recognize a German circle in Copenhagen. Not a few other Germans came to the Danish capital in Klopstock's wake, a condition that would last until the fall of Struensee. While Danish writers were not actually disciples of the German poetic genius, he did have an impact on Danish literature. The odes of Denmark's most promising young poet, Johannes Ewald, owe their inspiration in part to Klopstock's odes.

The "Spectator" Literature and Other Journals

By 1745 the major concern of the *Nye Tidender* is with various other journals of the "Spectator" genre. Although a Danish translation of *The Spectator* did not appear until 1742–43, Danish imitations were published as early as 1726 and a Danish translation of the leading Swedish journal, *Den svenska Argus* (The Swedish Argus) by Olof von Dalin, was issued in 1740. Many moral weeklies were published from the 1750s onward. Toward the end of the century the weekly and monthly journals of the *Spectator* variety had multiplied; most of them were short-lived, but the demand for such publications was apparent. They were removed from the unsophisticated popular literature discussed previously and can justifiably be mentioned with Holberg, whose essays, both the *Moralske Tanker* and *Epistler* have a spiritual affinity with *The Spectator*. In fact, the Dutch translation of Holberg's *Moralske Tanker* is entitled *Den deensche Spectator* (The Danish Spectator).

A forerunner of the Danish "Spectator" literature which was to have an effect on the contents of the *Nye Tidender* and of later Danish weeklies was the *Hamburg Patriot*, which had appeared in 1724. Danish orientation on the German literary scene is explicit in the publication in 1728 of selections from that German periodical as *Den fordanskede Patriot* (The Danicized Patriot), but the pieces were all anecdotal or didactic in tone, lacking the wit and sophistication of the original English *Spectator*. Despite the English inspiration and the German model, the tone of the Danish publication is set by the motto *Salus Patriae suprema lex* (The welfare of the fatherland is the supreme law), a quotation from Cicero that reinforces the impression of the continued classical orientation of the time. The first step had nevertheless been taken in the direction of the triumphant *Spectator*, which generated hundreds of imitations in German but also a variety of "Spectators" in Denmark in no fewer than three languages within three years' time. A complex start was made by Jørgen Riis (1717–49), who began the publication of *Den Danske Spectator* (1744–45; The Danish Spectator) very much in the style of its English forebears but, in its second number (May 23, 1744), with a clear reference to the earlier *Hamburg Patriot*. Riis attracted public attention to his undertaking by issuing a kind of counterpublication, in verse, between July 1744 and March 1745, *Den Danske Anti-Spectator* (The Danish Anti-Spectator). While he won attention from the reading public, he also met with negative criticism. Still a third journal that was his work was *Den Danske Spectators Philosophiske Spectator* (1744–45; The Philosophical Spectator of the Danish Spectator).

Riis's German-born contemporary Johann Elias Schlegel, who absorbed the critical acumen of Leipzig and Zürich, that is, of J. C. Gottsched as well as of J. J. Bodmer and J. J. Breitinger, before coming to Copenhagen in 1743, started the publication of *Der Fremde* in April 1745. Although written in German, it was directed to a Copenhagen audience and altered the Danish literary scene by infusing the spirit of the English *Spectator,* albeit by way of German imitations. *Der Fremde* appeared for only one year but enjoys a respected place in the history of Danish literature, for Schlegel rapidly familiarized himself with Danish conditions and contributed much to the development of Scandinavian literature by his theoretical essay dealing with the Danish stage.

La Spectatrice Danoise (1748–50; The Danish Spectator) by Laurent Angliviel de la Beaumelle (1726–73) suggests the French orientation of the Copenhagen intelligentsia. Although critical and caustic in tone, his journal was without the philosophical substance of Schlegel's *Der Fremde*. Schlegel's role on the Danish literary scene was cut short by his early death; de la Beaumelle departed Copenhagen after a sojourn of less than five years and faded into obscurity as far as the development of Danish literature is concerned.

A French-language parallel to the Danish *Nye Tidender* was the *Mercure Danois* (1753–60; Danish Mercury). Despite the use of French, it was more concerned with Danish affairs and cultural matters than its Danish predecessor the *Nye Tidender* or contemporary *Lærde Nyheder* (Learned News), for it brought lengthy résumés of books issued in Denmark, in addition to letters and news from Paris, London, Stockholm, and other centers of culture. Notable, for example, is a lengthy extract from a book about Iceland, *Tilfældige Efterretninger om Island* (Incidental Reports about Iceland), as well as reviews of works by Holberg. *Mercure Danois* was initiated by the Swiss historian of Denmark, Paul-Henri Mallet (1730–1807), who spent some eight years in Copenhagen, taught at the university, and published two histories of Denmark that reached a European audience. The journal must be said to have served Danish literature well abroad, for it had agents in Stockholm, Hamburg, The Hague, Amsterdam, London, and Paris. The interest in Iceland is particularly noteworthy, for between April 1753 and December 1755 there are no fewer than 17 entries, sometimes of many pages, pertaining to Iceland and two concerning the *Edda*. Though the journal did not have a long life, it let Denmark speak with a clear voice throughout the contemporary republic of letters.

By mid-century there is extravagant editorial praise in *Nye Tidender* of France as the true home of the arts, which the French are said to have brought to "perfection." Nevertheless, the very next year is characterized by a discussion of Holberg's *Moralske Fabler* (1751; Moral Fables), of Klopstock's *Messias,* of Gellert's poems, and, unexpectedly, of Icelandic poetry that is given in Latin translation.

Jens Schielderup Sneedorff (1724–64) was a new bright light, if not a meteoric figure, on the Danish literary landscape of the 1750s and 1760s. After several years of study abroad, chiefly in Göttingen, and the intensive study of French to the extent of his being able to publish in French, Sneedorff received an appointment as professor of history in the newly resurrected Sorø Academy. In addition to books in what we now would call political science and translations into Danish of Voltaire, he wrote and published the uncensored moral weekly *Den patriotiske Tilskuer* (1761–63; The Patriotic Spectator), discussing economic, political, pedagogical, and aesthetic problems of the time. His liberal ideas as well as his lucid and elegant style attracted a large body of readers and enabled him to command the esteem of his contemporaries. It was Sneedorff—and not Holberg—who became the father of modern Danish prose. He was the leading spirit in the establishment of a society for the advancement of the arts and the encouragement of good taste in 1759 and was sufficiently respected as a judge of literature that the young Johannes Ewald—later to be looked on as Denmark's greatest poet of the century—submitted his first poetic work to Sneedorff for assessment.

Danish weekly and monthly journals had proliferated during the years 1771–72 under the freedom of press declared by Struensee. Twenty-seven began publication in those years. To be sure, most did not last a twelve-month, but even after Struensee's fall there was a gradual rise in the number of new Danish periodicals, although, again, only a very few became established. Some thirty journals began publication between 1773 and 1800. Their mere number demonstrates a bourgeois desire to acquire knowledge and to orient oneself on the new currents of thought at home and abroad, as well as to be entertained and stimulated through the printed word.

The necessary selection process of literary history often makes it appear that very few authors were writing at any given time, as authors of stature tend to obscure lesser figures when judged by the aesthetic standards of succeeding generations. Other writers were not necessarily insignificant in their own time. So, too, in eighteenth-century Denmark.

LITERARY SOCIABILITY

To peruse the lexicographer Jens Worm's (1716–90) ambitious retrospective three volume biobibliography of Danish writers, *Forsøg til et Lexicon* (1771–84; Attempts at an Encyclopedia) is to become superficially acquainted with a large number of prolific but forgotten authors, translators, and editors of the Danish monarchy, which of course embraced Iceland, Norway, and the duchies of Schleswig and Holstein, as well as the Kingdom of Denmark proper. And it could be assumed that users of Worm's book could read Latin and German as well as Danish, for there are many items listed in the three languages. We are in the first instance struck today by the preponderance of theological, devotional, and moralizing works, items that may have had a limited appeal in their own time but are significant by virtue merely of their total mass. True to his time, Worm makes no effort clearly to distinguish between imaginative literature and other sorts of writing, a fact that should remind us of the very recent dominance of imaginative works under the general heading of "literature." If one reads through Worm's hundreds of titles, however, the gradual rise of imaginative literature in the course of the eighteenth century becomes apparent as well as the extensive role that translations from the major languages played, especially plays translated from the French. Certain names appear repeatedly in translation, notably Gellert from the German, Young and Pope from the English, and a large number of French playwrights without a single playwright dominating.

The role of the translator in the transmission of literature is generally given little heed, and the Danish translators of the eighteenth century were a mixed lot who came from various walks of life. Frederik Løvenørn (1715–79), a translator of plays by Destouches and Legrand, for example, was a naval officer, whereas Barthold Johan Lodde (1706–88), among the most active and influential translators of the century, was a clergyman without a parish. It was Lodde's Danish version (1743–46) of Richardson's *Pamela* (1740–41) that marks the advent of the modern bourgeois novel on the Danish literary scene. He translated Gellert's *Fabeln und Erzählungen* (1746–48; Fables and Tales) in 1751 and Voltaire's *Zaïre* (1732) in 1757; and between 1754 and 1761 he edited a multivolume journal of translated pieces entitled *Bie-Kuben eller Andres Tanker* (The Beehive, or Others' Thoughts). It contained material mainly from the English but also from the French, notably Voltaire and Fontenelle, and from the German, chiefly poems by Gellert, who must be recognized as Germany's most widely read and imitated author of the day. In an apologia for his periodical Lodde explained that, since the death of Holberg a few months before, there were "few original texts that could be reading for everyone." *Bie-Kuben* was sufficiently successful to be republished in 1778, incidentally at the same time that a new periodical appeared, *Det almindelige danske Bibliothek* (The General Danish Library), a title that echoes Friedrich Nicolai's successful *Allgemeine Deutsche Bibliothek* (1765–92; The General German Library). In all, Lodde rewrote more than thirty plays, chiefly taken from the French, for the Danish stage. His favorite author was, however, the Calvinistic evangelist James Hervey (1714–58), several of whose books he issued in Danish between 1761 and 1785. Late in life (1787) he translated works by Edward Young.

Drama after the Midcentury

The most prolific of the Danish publicists in the second half of the eighteenth century was Martin Hallager (1740–1803), who was active as a printer, translator, editor, and author of books on a spectrum of subjects. His only lasting contributions were, however, schoolbooks—both readers and grammars. His French ABC from 1797 was many times reprinted in augmented form, the last time in 1869, while his German reader from 1799 was reprinted in 1879, and his Danish reader from 1800 went through its forty-seventh printing in 1891. His own imaginative efforts, such as the play *August og Cecilia eller de tvende ulykkelige Elskere* (1771; August and Cecilia, or the Two Unhappy Lovers), were mostly anonymous and did not enjoy any similar popularity. Several of his translations from German and French were more successful. Hallager's example alone suffices to demonstrate that there was a market for moralizing publications in several genres. He was not alone as an author of such publications but was for a time the most prolific Danish author of his kind.

Because of their intrinsic lack of substance and a shifting critical evaluation coupled with the unawareness of the conditions that engendered momentary popularity, such works are unknown today to all but the historical scholar. Once a name has been dropped from standard literary histories, for better or for worse, there is slight hope ever of rehabilitation. Nevertheless, there was widespread literary achievement in eighteenth-century Denmark. There were writers of drama besides Holberg in the first half of the century, and some of their works went through more than one printing and were played successfully on the Danish stage. Even Holberg's one-time publisher Joachim Wielandt tried his hand at tragedy in 1725, with *Achilles og Polixena* (Achilles and Polixene). Of course, many plays given on the Danish stage never were printed. There were, moreover, numerous translations from the German plays by C. F. Gellert, C. Gärtner, and even Friedrich Klopstock, whose tragedy *Der Tod Adams* (The Death of Adam) was translated in its year of publication, 1757. In the 1760s the young Charlotte Dorothea Biehl (1731–88), who was later to win lasting renown as the translator of Cervantes' *Don Quijote* (1605–15) into Danish (1776–77), wrote several comedies in the manner of Destouches (some of whose plays she also translated from the French) and enjoyed fleeting success as a playwright. Of her several well-received plays, *Den kierlige Mand* (1764; The Loving Husband) was the most notable. Her plays have, however, been too sentimental for the taste of later generations, as is also the case with a still earlier original Danish comedy, *Mariane* (1757) by Anna Catharina von Passow (1731–57). Works of both women dramatists were translated into German and von Passow's into French as well—clearly a demonstration that their efforts were suited to the taste of the times. In addition to her plays and translations, Charlotte Dorothea Biehl wrote a series of moralizing stories published as *Moralske Fortællinger* (1781–82; Moral Tales).

There was a strong theatrical if not dramatic tradition from the middle of the century. The stage was reestablished in 1748 after the death of the pietistic Christian VI in 1746. It offered an accessible and vigorous means of entertainment. Ludvig Holberg once more came to the fore as a playwright. Six of his plays appeared after 1748: *Plutus* (1753), *Den forvandlede Brudgom* (The Changed Bridegroom, 1753), *Huus-Spøgelse eller Abracadabra* (1753; House Ghost, or Abracadabra), *Sganarels Reise* (1754; Sganarel's Journey), *Philosophus udi egen Indbilding* (1754; Philosopher in his Own Imagination), and *Republiqven eller det gemeene Beste* (1754; The Republic, or the Common Good). According to Holberg's own testimony, *Plutus* was the most successful of all his plays, but its success was not long-lived; it has not appealed to later regisseurs. It was different from the plays that had preceded it, for it was, as Holberg stated, "as much for the eye as for the ear" and incorporated music and dancing. *Plutus* and *Den forvandlede Brudgom* have a classical orientation, in that the story is laid in antiquity. *Den forvandlede Brudgom* is noteworthy as having all parts written for women, contrasting with *Huus-Spøgelse*, in which all the actors are male. Moreover, *Den forvandlede Brudgom* is the only later play that has been given frequently, chiefly in the twentieth century. Both *Philosophus* and *Sganarels Reise* deal with two of Holberg's favorite targets: pedantry and idle philosophizing.

Of signal importance in the history of the Danish stage was the appearance of Denmark's first theatrical journal in the Struensee era: *Den dramatiske Journal* (1771–73; The Dramatic Journal). It was written by a student, Peder Rosenstand-Goiske (1752–1803). His criticism of a play by the Norwegian Niels Krog Bredal (1732–78), who was later to become the director of the theater, and Bredal's countercriticism in dramatic form led to violence in the Royal Theater in 1771. It was Bredal who, in 1756, had introduced the singspiel on the Danish stage, with *Gram og Signe* (Gram and Signe). This musical drama with an Old Norse topic as well as several others from Bredal's hand were enthusiastically received at a time when Bredal still lived in Norway. After assuming the directorship of the Royal Theater in Copenhagen, however, he staged his own *Tronfølgen i Sidon* (1771; Royal Succession in Sidon), about which public opinion soon was much divided after Rosenstand-Goiske severely criticized the weakness of the play in his journal. Bredal replied right away with a sharp dramatic satire on Rosenstand-Goiske, entitled *Den dramatiske Journal* (The Dramatic Journal), which gave rise to bitter partisanship in the theatergoing public and pitted military men against students in the audience on November 25.

Johan Herman Wessel

Den dramatiske Journal was not given again, and Bredal ceased writing for the theater he headed and instead offered a prize for the best Danish tragedy. The prize was awarded to another Norwegian, Johan Nordahl Brun (1745–1816), for his tragedy *Zarine* (1772), which was very much in the French pathetic manner. Although well received, Brun's play was the subject of a witty parody, *Kierlighed uden Strømper* (1772; Love without Stockings), by still a third Norwegian, Johan Herman Wessel (1742–85). Wessel's play, in alexandrines, evoked laughter because of the ridiculous motif of a young couple's being unable to marry on the only day that the young woman had dreamed must be her wedding day simply because the bridegroom cannot obtain the proper white stockings for the wedding. Although Wessel's success signaled the ultimate demise of French tragedy on the Danish stage, both Brun's and Wessel's plays continued to be given, but that season (1772–73) must be considered a turning point in the history of the theater in Denmark.

Wessel was not only a masterly writer of satirical comedy; he also achieved popularity with his versified "comic tales." On the one hand, they resemble the *Comische Erzählungen* (1765; Comic Tales) of the leading German writer of the day, Christoph Martin Wieland, and, on the other, suggest the later German humorist Wilhelm Busch. In an easy, lighthearted, and witty manner that freely employed hyperbole, Wessel poked fun at human weakness and affectation, including literary absurdities in imitations of both French and older classical style. Many of Wessel's tales have been reprinted since his early death, and some, for example, "Smeden og Bageren" (The Smith and the Baker) and "Gaffelen" (The Fork), regularly make their way into Danish and Norwegian anthologies and readers. Notable is Wessel's poem to the young Jens Baggesen, "Til Hr. Jens Baggesen" (To Mr. Jens Baggesen), written in the year of Wessel's death. Wessel looked—correctly—on the young Baggesen as the most promising writer on the Danish Parnassus. Indeed, Baggesen's own immensely successful *Comiske Fortællinger* appeared that same year and projected his name to the forefront of Danish imaginative literature.

REDISCOVERING THE INDIGENOUS PAST

Peter Frederik Suhm

The changes in literary orientation, the dominance of certain genres, the choice of subject matter, and the general political awareness in eighteenth-century Denmark are reflected in the work of a single man, who is now all but unknown and is at best remembered as a book collector: Peter Frederik Suhm (1728–98). He was in fact *seriatim* a dramatist, a translator, a journalist and critic, a political commentator, and, finally, a historian. Toward the end of his life he was appointed royal historiographer. He may be considered a central figure without per se being a writer of lasting importance. After his marriage in Norway to a wealthy woman, he became an avid book collector. His private library ultimately grew to one hundred thousand books and manuscripts, most of which are now to be found in the Royal Library of Copenhagen.

In 1775 Suhm opened his private library to the Copenhagen public at a time when there were no public libraries and when accessibility to scholarly libraries was limited. That is to say, Suhm was infused with the democratic spirit of the Enlightenment and the conviction that a well-read public was important for the common good.

As a young man Suhm aspired to be a playwright and sent two of his plays to Holberg for criticism. Holberg dismissed Suhm's own plays but urged him to translate plays from the French. Suhm took his mentor's advice, and some of his translations of, for instance, Molière became texts used at the theater in Copenhagen; they were, however, not printed. His years in Norway, when he edited a critical periodical, *Tronhiemske Samlinger* (1761–65; Trondheim Collections), show a broad European cultural orientation in the hundreds of reviews that Suhm himself wrote, even then with an emphasis on Scandinavian history. A few years after he returned to Denmark he reacted patriotically against the cultural and political dominance of the Germans as favored by the court in Copenhagen, a situation that eventually led to the enlightened despotism of Struensee. In 1772, the year of Struensee's execution, Suhm issued his most forceful and widely read pamphlet, *Til Kongen* (To the King). Suhm looked with skepticism at the advancement of foreigners in Denmark to the detriment of native sons, and his pamphlet was in part an attempt to set things right by a restitution of monarchy. While *Til Kongen* was popular in its appeal and without equal for its effect, Suhm's actual advocacy of the establishment of a constitutional monarchy remained concealed. His appeal was interpreted only as a patriotic and conservative reaction against the excesses of Struensee's rule.

An interest in the indigenous Scandinavian past as well as his patriotic persuasion led Suhm to write several novellas that drew on early Danish history for their subject matter. The first one, *Sigrid*, which used material from Saxo, was also issued in the momentous year 1772. Suhm had already given evidence of his command of factual material and his exacting use of documentary evidence as a historian, but the appearance of *Sigrid* indicated that he was intimately associated with the cultural movement that in retrospect is identified as the "Germanic renaissance."

The Germanic Renaissance

Interest in the Scandinavian past had been aroused in the second half of the seventeenth century, and particularly in Sweden, for patriotic reasons. There was a desire to establish a native heritage that could be substituted for or equated with the classical achievements of Greece and Rome. For lack of an older Swedish literature, Swedish scholars looked to medieval Icelandic literature just as the Danes also were to do in the mid–eighteenth century and the Germans starting from the late eighteenth century onward. One important publication of Old Norse-Icelandic literature in Denmark had appeared as early as 1660: Peder Resen's edition of Snorri Sturluson's *Prose Edda* with some translations into Latin and Danish. About eighty years later, in 1746, there was a similar, Swedish edition by Johann Göransson. There had likewise been editions of Snorri Sturluson's *Heimskringla* in

Sweden in 1697 and in Copenhagen in 1633 and again in 1757. That is to say, some of the most important literary-historical documents of West Scandinavia were accessible for the diffusion of historical knowledge and for critical assessment. The Icelandic *Íslendingabók* (Book of Icelanders) had been issued with Latin translation in 1733, and a Danish translation (from the Latin) was published in 1738. Oddly enough, the most influential work in calling attention to the Scandinavian past and in particular to the poems of the so-called *Elder Edda* was written by Paul-Henri Mallet. The book was originally issued in French in Copenhagen in 1756 entitled *Monumens de la mythologie et de la poésie des Celtes et particulièrement des anciens Scandinaves* (Monuments of the Mythology and Poetry of the Celts and Particularly of the Ancient Scandinavians); a new edition appeared with the imprint "Genève et Paris" in 1787 and again in Geneva in 1790. Of the English translations there were no fewer than nine editions between 1770 and 1902; such was the authority assumed by the work, even though Mallet had written on the basis of knowledge of only three poems from the *Edda* available in seventeenth-century Latin translation.

All this provided a basis for Suhm's burst of activity in the field of Old Icelandic starting in the 1770s. The attempt consciously or unconsciously to foster an awareness of the nation's past and a literary heritage that might rival that of classical antiquity was well underway. There was now considerably more flattering evidence than the work of Saxo, whose twelfth-century Latin chronicle *Gesta Danorum* (The Deeds of the Danes) had hitherto stood alone as a monument of the Danish past, notably in the translation into Danish by Anders Sørensen Vedel from 1575 (a new edition of which had been made available in 1752). For want of an older literature, the Danes now embraced Old Icelandic literature as their own. One could argue that, after all, Iceland was a part of Denmark. Moreover, the mass of Icelandic manuscripts that were preserved were to be found in Copenhagen, in the foundation established by the will of Árni Magnússon in 1730, albeit not chartered until 1760 and not a publisher until 1772, when it issued the text of *Kristni saga* (Saga of Christianity). Suhm acted in the spirit of Árni Magnússon by providing the subventions necessary for the publication of four important Icelandic texts between 1780 and 1787. That a sumptuous, trilingual (Icelandic, Danish, Latin) edition of Snorri Sturluson's *Heimskringla* was begun in 1777 and funded by the Danish Crown is telling evidence of the critical acceptance of Old Icelandic literature as being significant for the history and fame of Denmark.

Suhm had progressed from an orientation on French comedy to an orientation on national history. Indeed, his major work was *Historie af Dan-*

mark (1782–1828; A History of Denmark) in fourteen volumes (half of which were issued posthumously) that reached only to the end of the fourteenth century. Suhm's national awareness at a time when Klopstock and the German circle were identified with Copenhagen was soon reflected in two other kinds of literary production in Copenhagen: the writings of Norwegians living in Copenhagen—among them Bredal, Brun, and Wessel—all members of the so-called Norske Selskab (Norwegian Society), established in 1772, and the works of the most gifted poet of the Danish eighteenth century, Johannes Ewald. It is noteworthy that Wessel's effective parody of the French *tragédie larmoyante* also dates from the year of the coup against Struensee, 1772.

Johannes Ewald
There is no question but that the young Johannes Ewald (1743–81) admired Klopstock. Like the German poet, Ewald reworked a biblical motif, the Fall of Man, in the neoclassical tragedy *Adam og Ewa* (1769; Adam and Eve). It was Klopstock who recommended the publication of Ewald's tragedy in prose, *Rolf Krage* (1770), analogous to Klopstock's own efforts to dramatize the Germanic past by using the Arminius motif in several plays. *Rolf Krage* is a Shakespearean drama of action. Its Nordic motif is taken from Saxo's chronicle but is used to illustrate contemporary ideas of humanity and patriotism. In 1774 Ewald wrote a tragedy (performed as a singspiel in 1778) on the death of the Old Norse god Baldr, in fact a drama about the all-consuming power of erotic passion, *Balders Død* (1774; Eng. tr. *The Death of Balder,* 1889). It became a milestone in the revival of Old Icelandic literature, and because of its happy transmutation of Old Norse mythology into imaginative, dramatic form, it served as an inspiration to several later poets, notably Adam Oehlenschläger, at the beginning of the nineteenth century.

Another singspiel by Ewald lives today in the consciousness of his countrymen, *Fiskerne* (1779; The Fishermen), not because of his historically significant use of the common man as a dramatic hero in the tragedy of a shipwreck on the Danish coast, but because it contains what became the royal anthem, the magnificent poem "Kong Christian" (King Christian).

Ewald was not limited in his orientation or the selection of subject matter. Not only Klopstock but also Shakespeare and Ossian attracted his attention. At one time he even planned to travel to Scotland to collect folk songs, but his health did not permit it. Major events of his life are recreated in his fragmentary autobiography *Levnet og Meeninger* (1773–77; publ. 1804–8; Life and Opinions), in which Ewald approaches the topics of adventure, women, and wine with imaginative flight reminiscent of Laurence Sterne's novels. From his early adult years Ewald had to combat what was to become crippling arthritis as well as alcoholism. It is the more wonder that he was able to write creatively, as he indeed did, in part through the aid of his mother and in part through the assistance of various friends and patrons who recognized his genius despite his improvident way of life. His cantata on the death of King Frederik V in 1766, beginning

> Cease, tears, to flow
> And zither, play thou low!
> Now to his grave is borne
> The king

evoked admiration on all sides. It subsequently gave Ewald the chance to write many occasional poems that provided him with a small income at a time, 1773–75, when he was able to lead a regulated life under the care of thoughtful friends in the village of Rungsted.

Like Klopstock, Ewald was solely a poet and was in fact the first professional Danish writer. And the poet Ewald is known to every Dane as the author of a few poems exuding a pathos that still touches readers' hearts, notably the hymn to the natural surroundings of Rungsted (which almost two centuries later was to become the residence of Karen Blixen), "Rungsteds Lyksaligheder" (1775; The Joys of Rungsted), which rises to an enthusiastic glorification of God. After the years in Rungsted, Ewald's production diminished, but he nevertheless wrote some of his best-known verse, including an ode to his benefactor, the young Count Frederik Moltke, "Til min Moltke" (1780; To My Moltke). Here, in unrhymed, antique meters, Ewald indirectly praises his own poetic genius and the purpose of his writings: to glorify God and the loftiest of human virtues. Ewald's last poetry is predominantly religious confession. "Til Sielen. En Ode" (1780; Ode to the Soul) is a grandiose description of man's condition until he has placed his destiny in God's hands. The story of the fallen soul is symbolized in the disobedient young eagle that has fallen from its nest and helplessly strives toward the light until its mother comes to its rescue:

> Tell me, thou fallen, enfeebled powerless kin
> Of angels! Tell me why thou spreadest forth
> Featherless wings!—Alas, in vain
> Flutt'ring up towards thy first abode!
> (Tr. John Dussinger)

Toward the end of his short life Ewald was regarded as the leading poet of

Denmark, and a new literary group sprang up about him as symbolic patrons of a new literature. He had suddenly become a celebrated figure and at his death all of Copenhagen mourned. Such was the power of his poetic diction, his mastery of form, and in part the sentimentalism engendered by the tragedy of his personal situation.

Ewald's poetic gift is indisputable, but part of his immediate success can be ascribed to the musical settings of several of his early occasional poems by the expatriate German composer Johann Adolph Scheibe. The Copenhagen public appreciated both operatic and concert music, and the musical life in the Danish capital received impetus in the 1740s. In the 1760s and again in the 1770s under Guiseppe Sarti and Paolo Scalabrini the Italian opera—of which the Leipzig-born Scheibe, like his literary master Gottsched, was an outspoken opponent—enjoyed both royal patronage and popular acclaim.

Transitional Figures

After Ewald's death one senses something of a generation gap, a pause before a new star is to rise on the horizon. To be sure, there were some contemporary writers who were of passing importance, among them Edvard Storm (1749–94), still another Norwegian who lived in the Danish capital and, foremost, the author of patriotic poems and drinking songs. The physician Johan Clemens Tode (1736–1806) was active as a publicist, translator (for instance, of the novels of Tobias Smollett), and dramatist, incorporating the period's penchant for sentimental moralizing in his writings. Thomas Thaarup (1749–1821) is known as the author of several singspiels, of which the most acclaimed is *Høst-Gildet* (1790; Harvest Celebration), fusing idyll and melodrama with royalist sentiment. It was Thaarup who, with remarkable intuition, prophesied that the young Jens Baggesen would soon be at the forefront of Danish poets.

A pivotal figure in the struggle between German and indigenous Danish cultural-political dominance in the second half of the eighteenth century was Werner H. F. Abrahamson (1744–1812), who, although born in Schleswig into a German-speaking family, became the champion of the practical and literary use of Danish in the Kingdom of Denmark. When he entered the military cadet school and later the artillery school in Copenhagen, German was the language of instruction and the cadets were not permitted to use Danish. Abrahamson nevertheless acquired a complete command of Danish in a short time and was writing Danish verse within two years. Moreover, when he started to teach at the cadet school, he used Danish as the language of instruction, and when he later became the head of the artillery school, Danish was established as the language of the school.

Abrahamson was not only a military officer and a teacher, but a poet of considerable ability and an antiquarian enthusiastic about Danish folk ballads and the saga literature of Iceland. Just before his death he was, with Rasmus Nyerup and Knud Lyne Rahbek, to publish the first volume of a collection of ballads.

Unlike Abrahamson, Heinrich Wilhelm Gerstenberg (1737–1823), a native of Tønder, wrote solely in German, despite being the coeditor of an anthology pertaining to Danish imaginative literature published in 1765. His *Briefe über Merkwürdigkeiten der Litteratur* (Letters about the Peculiarities of Literature), which appeared in Schleswig in 1766–70, called attention to the value of Old Norse mythology, and especially with his poem *Gedicht eines Skalden* (1766; Poem of an Old Norse Skald), he was to mark the beginnings of the Germanic renaissance in both Germany and Scandinavia with its renewal of interest in Old Norse mythology, history, and poetry. Without notable success, Gerstenberg also tried his hand at writing plays, the name of only one of which, the tragedy *Ugolino* (1768), its motif taken from a sanguinary episode in Dante's *La divina commedia* (ca. 1307–20) and its atmosphere from Shakespeare's *Macbeth,* has any claim to being mentioned today. Gerstenberg was one of many German-speaking officials serving under Struensee, but unlike most others associated with him, Gerstenberg subsequently suffered no harm as a result. An admirer of Shakespeare, he was instrumental in the revival of the English bard.

CURRENTS OF SOCIAL CHANGE

Toward the end of the eighteenth century a new, small group of writers put their stamp on Danish literature without themselves being distinguished poets, dramatists, or editors of lasting import. They should, however, not be underestimated, for they were influential in their own time and modified the direction of Danish belles lettres well into the nineteenth century.

Although Denmark was physically removed from the cataclysmic changes that took place in France in the wake of the revolution in 1789, the new doctrines of republicanism and egalitarianism did penetrate the Danish border by word of mouth and particularly by the printed word, doctrines that ultimately were to effect social and political changes in the Scandinavian countries. Not surprisingly, some of the advocates of a new political philosophy were writers, both critical and imaginative. They were only few, but they must be separated into two distinct categories. The first comprised those individuals who were outspoken in their allegiance to a radically different social and political philosophy and who volubly rejected the established order of Danish monarchical government and of the conservative majority. The second, less voluble, group comprised those who harbored republican sympathies but who were cautious enough in their modes of expression to avoid a loggerhead confrontation with authority. As might be expected, the ideas of the more radical thinkers ultimately came to be accepted, but only after several decades. Denmark did not become a constitutional monarchy until 1849.

Peter Andreas Heiberg and Malthe Conrad Bruun

The two names identified with the fearless advocacy of egalitarianism and republicanism are those of Peter Andreas Heiberg and the much younger Malthe Conrad Bruun, both of whom paid for their espousal of concepts inimical to the established order by being exiled and spent the rest of their lives in France. Peter Andreas Heiberg (1758–1841) is remembered today primarily as being the father of Johan Ludvig Heiberg, the prominent critic and dramatist of the first half of the nineteenth century, secondarily as the first husband of the Countess Gyllembourg-Ehrensvärd, Johan Ludvig's mother and later in life herself an important Danish novelist. In his own time Heiberg was active as a dramatist and publicist. After several irregular youthful years spent partly in Sweden and Norway, he published some translations of Moses Mendelssohn and Jean de Laveaux which attracted public attention. He then wrote several satirical plays, the most remarkable and best received of which was *De Vonner og de Vanner* (1792; The Von's and the Van's), which was highly critical of government officials—and soon was banned. It was only a matter of time before Heiberg would be in greater difficulty with the authorities, and Christmas Eve, 1799, he was exiled from Denmark.

Beginning in 1787 Heiberg had also made a name for himself with a kind of novel that appeared in fascicles and took half a dozen years to complete, *Rigsdalersedlens Hændelser* (1787–89; The Adventures of a Banknote), an analogue to the earlier *Chrysal; or, The Adventure of a Guinea* (1760) by Irish author Charles Johnstone. Both authors used the device of a banknote's passing through various hands to draw attention to the conditions of life at various levels of society, but Heiberg was more moralistic in creating a situation that contrasted ambition and virtue in the selection of a marriage partner. Although Heiberg was not a skilled writer or a particularly clever utilizer of literary devices, his book was widely read and his satirical vein was appreciated by the public in general, a public that later felt he had been ill-treated by being driven into exile.

Although Malthe Conrad Bruun (1775–1826) shared many of Heiberg's political beliefs, he was contentious and, as often is the case among liberal thinkers, was soon at cross-purposes with Heiberg despite the similarity of their goals. Bruun managed nevertheless to gain popular admiration for some of his poetry, but his authorship of *Aristokraternes Catechismus* (1796; The Aristocrats' Catechism) and his pamphlets that were critical of the government—if indeed not also of Christian belief— brought him into court and led to his banishment just a year after Heiberg's. Subsequently, Bruun, known outside Denmark as Malte-Brun, began a new career and became one of Europe's leading geographers.

Knud Lyne Rahbek

Knud Lyne Rahbek (1760–1830), in contrast to Heiberg and Bruun, kept his low-keyed republicanism on an intellectual level, although his admiration for the American Revolution is indicated by a stone bearing the name of George Washington in the garden of his home. Rahbek was much given to social life. He was notably active in Drejer's Club in the 1780s. The club was one of the earliest of such associations and for a decade or more the most influential bourgeois club in the Danish capital, a gathering spot for witty heads of a rationalist persuasion and men who would exchange ideas with their peers, enjoy refreshments, and make use of the club's library.

A glance at its holdings in 1792 (when a book list was printed) gives us an idea of the taste of the times and the interests of the club members. One notes at once the occurrence of the English *Spectator* in Danish translation, of several Danish journals, and of Wieland's *Der Teutsche Merkur* (1773– 1810; The German Mercury). Overall there were more titles in German than in Danish; the ratio was 327 to 232. Sixty books were in French, including Diderot's *Encyclopédie* in thirty-six volumes; ten were in English, one of which was a thirteen-volume edition of Shakespeare. The library tended toward contemporary literature: of 1,839 titles, some five hundred had been published in the foregoing twenty years.

Although much of what Rahbek published dates from the first third of the nineteenth century, his orientation as well as his major contributions to Danish intellectual life belong to the late eighteenth century, when he was most enterprising and possessed with the most initiative among his contemporaries. His inspiration was derived in part from the last decades of the German Enlightenment and the beginning of German Classicism, and in part from English models. His own contributions were, above all, three: the foundation of aesthetic criticism on the Danish literary scene; the publication of a journal of general interest, *Minerva*, which maintained a high level of criticism and interlocution and at the same time encouraged promising young writers; and evocation of interest in specifically Danish literary tradition. Without being an imaginative writer of particular note himself, Rahbek was at the center of literary development between 1780 and 1810 in the Danish capital. It would not be accurate to call him a transitional figure. Although his work helped lay a foundation for the new literature of the first decade of the next century—a selection of his poetry was issued as *Poetiske Forsøg* (1794–1802; Poetic Attempts)—he continued to pursue the ideas and methods to which he had become dedicated from about 1785 onward.

Rahbek had gained attention by the publication of the first volume of his own *Prosaiske Forsøg* (Prose Attempts) in 1785, but that year also saw the publication of the first volume of his journal *Minerva* (1785–1808), which was to be the leading organ for serious contributions from a variety of disciplines. *Minerva* was important also as a periodical of the middle class which maintained a high standard by virtue of a judicious choice of contributors and articles. It mirrored the times and reached a wide, appreciative audience, especially in the earlier years of publication. Indeed, it was the standard against which other journals could be measured; none was to surpass *Minerva* for two decades. As a critical and moralistic journal it combined the tradition of the moral weekly with newer ideas and contemporary subject matter. The ninety-one volumes of *Minerva* bespeak the importance of the journal.

Rahbek also edited several other, very different periodicals; one is notable, *Den danske Tilskuer* (1791–1806; The Danish Spectator), which carried on the tradition of "Spectator" literature going back for Denmark to the first quarter of the century. The many facets of these two journals alone suggest Rahbek's several interests and multiple abilities. He was not only himself a poet but also an (unsuccessful) dramatist; a prolific (successful) translator, especially of plays; a literary historian; a sometime university professor; and a clubman. Early in his career Rahbek was a republican sympathizer, but he was more cautious than his friends P. A. Heiberg and Malthe Conrad Bruun. In his later life he was, with his wife Karen Margarete ("Kamma") Rahbek, to provide a center of literary activity in their home, "Bakkehuset."

Rahbek, although not himself an independent and liberal thinker, was for a time purveyor of a new philosophical aesthetic at the University of Copenhagen. With Rasmus Nyerup (1759–1829), Rahbek enjoys a reputation as the progenitor of the first critical history of Danish literature, *Bidrag til den danske Digtekunsts Historie* (1800–1828; Contributions to the History of Danish Poetry). The two professors jointly held lectures on poetry at the university for several semesters. They thus followed a different course from that of the historians of "literature," for whom poetry was part and parcel of the entire body of literature (a tradition that dominated Danish literary history into the twentieth century through the standard works of N. M. Petersen, Peter Hansen, and Vilhelm Andersen and Carl S. Petersen). Nyerup and Rahbek stressed poetry as it existed in Danish from the end of the Middle Ages until their own times and were champions of a national, imaginative, poetic literature. The national literature was being judged aesthetically for the first time, a condition that derived from the appointment in 1790 of Rahbek as the first professor of aesthetics at the University of Copenhagen. Aesthetics was no longer to be merely an adjunct of rhetoric or eloquence.

It is a curious turn of events that, when Rahbek resigned his professorship in 1799, the position was allowed to lapse for a decade, and when the next professor of aesthetics was appointed, he was the great new hope of the Danish Parnassus, Adam Oehlenschläger, champion of the new poetry. Oehlenschläger drew on indigenous tradition for much of his subject matter and, in part following and in part superseding Ewald, realized the dream of a Germanic renaissance that had inspired Suhm and later Rahbek and Nyerup.

Jens Baggesen

Before the restless background of the end of the century—a time that might be called *fin de siècle,* with the connotations engendered by that term—there appeared on the Danish literary scene a young writer who attracted the attention and applause of his contemporaries: Jens Baggesen (1764–1826). Baggesen had begun writing poetry early in life and some of his verse, printed in a New Year's publication of 1783, had caught the eye of Johannes Ewald, who recognized Baggesen's promise and was optimistic about his future.

With such approbation Baggesen's ability seemed so certain that when his Copenhagen publisher announced for prenumeration a forthcoming collection of comic tales in verse, the *Comiske Fortællinger* (1785; Comic Tales), the volume had twelve hundred subscribers, an enormous number for the time and impressive in a city with fewer than one hundred thousand inhabitants. The book was well received and suggested a brilliant literary career for its twenty-year-old author. The versified tales were reminiscent in particular of Wieland's *Comische Erzählungen* but also of the comic tales in verse that had been published in Danish somewhat earlier by Johan Herman Wessel. After the fashion of Wieland and Wessel, Baggesen's humorous poems comprise witty and sophisticated anecdotes that are both fanciful and sly. One reads them to be amused, and not to be instructed or enlightened. Lighthearted and worldly, they depend on an unexpected arrangement of the familiar and a grotesque interpretation of the commonplace.

In 1789 Baggesen produced a well-wrought translation into Danish (from the original Latin) of Holberg's *Niels Klim*. The surge of interest in the new poet gave him an entrée to high society and access to the pages of *Minerva* and other journals. Baggesen's popularity continued and allowed him to publish the libretto of an opera, *Holger Danske* (1789; Holger the Dane), with a motif from Wieland's epic *Oberon* (1780) and, in 1791, a two-volume edition of his early writings, *Ungdomsarbeider* (1791; Youthful Works). In some ways Baggesen's many poems, another volume of which, *Nye blandede Digte* (New Miscellaneous Poems), was published in 1807, can be viewed as documentary for the times. The mass of occasional poetry and letters in verse do not appeal to today's reader, however; nor do the Gothic features of his ballads or the sentimentality that permeates his numerous elegiac love poems.

Oddly enough, the fact that Baggesen's opera libretto was at once translated into German and recommended by the translator with extravagant—some thought fulsome—praise was the cause of dissension and some questioning of Baggesen's position vis-à-vis his German-speaking admirers and within Danish literature. This episode called forth a spate of publications both supporting and attacking the opera. That 1789 marked in public consciousness the beginning of the French Revolution may also have played some role in a revaluation of the young poet who shared the fairly widespread sympathies with the first years of the upheaval in France, a condition that might seem to contradict his close association with the German-Danish nobility. Nevertheless, it did not deter his noble patrons from providing him with the financial support needed to undertake a journey southward as far as Switzerland. In the same momentous year, 1789, Baggesen started the journey that three years later was to result in the publication of the first substantial, literary Danish travel account, *Labyrinten* (1792–93; The Labyrinth).

Labyrinten may be compared with the travel accounts of Heinrich Heine written nearly half a century later, although Baggesen's humor is more pronounced and less sophisticated and understandably less mature than Heine's. The journey is essentially a trip through Germany, and there are many lengthy and anecdotal descriptions of Baggesen's experiences and observations, in such places as Hamburg, the Lüneburg Heath, Bad Pyrmont, Göttingen, and Frankfurt am Main. Even though he states that one should not write à la Laurence Sterne, there can be no question about his—and his times'—awareness of Sterne's *Sentimental Journey*; Baggesen often quotes from Sterne.

In Bad Pyrmont, Baggesen devised a set of commandments for the traveler which begins, "Travel constantly as far south as you can." The twelfth and final commandment is, "Try to feel at home everywhere, be a German in Germany, a Swiss in Switzerland, a Frenchman in France, Lutheran with the Lutherans, Catholic with Catholics, a heathen with heathens; sorrowful with the sorrowful, happy with the happy—a human being everywhere and respecting humanity everywhere." Among supplemental rules to his twelve commandments he gives the example, "Every day read a passage in Tacitus, Horace or Rousseau," a comment that reveals something of the author's orientation, reading, and taste.

When Baggesen writes, "To be truthful I am really a friend of extremes," he allows some insight into his psyche. His tendency to extremes and notably his inability to settle anywhere was to diminish the promise of his early writing and explain his failure personally to achieve a well-balanced and stable existence. Baggesen remained an emotional individual, easily moved, restless, ever seeking some perfect solution that escaped his grasp. After his visit to Switzerland in 1790 he married Sophie von Haller, a granddaughter of the famous Swiss naturalist and poet Albrecht von Haller.

Jens Baggesen's departure from Denmark in 1800 is a fixed point in Danish literary history: at a soiree in his honor in Drejer's Club before leaving the country, Baggesen declared that he was willing his lyre to the young Adam Oehlenschläger. It was almost a laying on of hands: Ewald had looked on Baggesen as a worthy successor; now Baggesen saw Oehlenschläger as the most promising member of a new generation of Danish poets—which indeed he was. Nevertheless, Baggesen continued to write and, in an attempt to establish himself as a writer in Germany, to an increasing extent in German. He was overshadowed by a younger generation of Danish writers without winning wide acceptance in the German-speaking lands.

A CENTURY IN RETROSPECT

We have focused primarily on the literature that has had some lasting claim on critical attention because of its intrinsic character and individual nature or the fact that several generations of critics and historians have judged it aesthetically worth preserving. But a much larger body of literature that was influential in its own times has been mentioned only spasmodically: dramatic texts. Just as most people today devote more time to watching television or attending motion pictures than to reading books, similarly in the eighteenth century the theater was of more widespread interest than the printed word. The plays given in the past must, however, have existed in printed form if we are to pass any analytical judgments about them today, and indeed most of the plays performed in eighteenth-century Denmark do exist in print. If we examine *Bibliotheca Danica,* the Danish national bibliography covering the years up to 1830, we are able quickly to draw some conclusions about the quantity, nature, and origins of plays given in Denmark in the eighteenth century. It is at once apparent that the dramatic works outnumber narrative or poetic works, with a concentration of published plays from the last quarter of the century.

Between 1775 and 1800 there were issued twenty-nine volumes of plays translated into Danish from other languages, chiefly French and German. In addition, there were fifteen volumes of collected Danish plays as well as four volumes of Danish plays translated into German. There were no fewer than 230 individual plays by Danish authors as well as 25 anonymous Danish plays published in the eighteenth century after Holberg—and several hundred plays translated from the German, French, English, and Italian. The authors of the plays in question vary from such well-known names as the Germans Goethe, Lessing, and Kotzebue, the French Corneille, Racine, Molière, Voltaire, Marmontel, and Regnard, the English Shakespeare and George Lillo, and the Italians Goldoni and Metastasio, to scores of lesser lights that do not ordinarily find mention in standard literary histories. Molière and Kotzebue were the most widely played French and German dramatists, respectively (with each about fifteen published plays), but as far as quantity is concerned, they do not compete with the Italian Pietro Metastasio, of whom thirty separate editions of single plays appeared (not counting reprintings). These statistics do not include the texts of ballets and pantomimes.

We are thus confronted with an impressive mass of dramatic literature that can only reinforce our thesis of the singular importance of the theater in the eighteenth century after the moral strictures of pietism, which had inhibited theatrical performances, were loosened following the death of Christian VI in 1746. Most of the plays published and given in Copenhagen during the last half of the eighteenth century have faded into obscurity, save for the titles by certain playwrights that are still known to us today and a few plays, such as Wessel's *Kierlighed uden Strømper*, that possibly for extraneous reasons enjoy a special place in literary history. The large body of ephemeral plays contributed a larger purpose than merely entertaining audiences; these plays were responsible for the development of a strong commitment to the theater as an institution and thus were a supporting base for a new drama in the nineteenth century.

There is a curious bit of evidence about the Danish literature of the eighteenth century viewed from abroad in retrospect which we may draw on to ascertain what seemed most important in that literature just fifteen years into the next century. In 1816 one Nicolai Fürst (ca. 1779–1857), a Danish journalist who was employed in Vienna, published *Briefe über die dänische Literatur* (Letters about Danish Literature) to acquaint foreign readers (in any case, readers of German) with what seemed to be the outstanding literary works produced in Denmark during the previous century. One is not surprised to find that more than half the book is devoted to Ludvig Holberg, with emphasis on the comedies, the mock epic *Peder Paars,* and the imaginary voyage *Niels Klim.* Notable is the fact that these are still today the works on which Holberg's reputation abroad rests—and that Fürst dealt only with imaginative literature rather than literature in the broader sense. That is, the mass of Holberg's work is not analyzed, since he is not presented as a historian or an essayist.

Only two other authors receive close scrutiny: Johan Herman Wessel and Johannes Ewald. Wessel's farcical comedy *Kierlighed uden Strømper* commands a great deal of space in Fürst's exposition, although not primarily because of its historical significance in overcoming the dominance of the versified, sentimental, French tragedy, but rather because of the humor that informs the play itself. Both Brun's serious effort with *Zarine* and Wessel's parody of it continued to be given on the Danish stage for some months, a fact that suggests the shift from the French classical tradition to bourgeois drama was not as sudden as otherwise might be intimated. Neither of these two plays commands the attention of sophisticated audiences today.

Agreeing with the assessment of Johannes Ewald in Denmark, Fürst sees Ewald as Denmark's one great poet, even at a time when Adam Oehlenschläger had begun to command admiration in German translation. Nor does Fürst seem to comprehend that to some extent Ewald was a forerunner of Oehlenschläger in employing indigenous themes that drew on sources from Danish antiquity. He is aware of Ewald's debt to Friedrich Klopstock, both as a master of the ode and as an early champion of what is identified as the Germanic renaissance. Fürst even makes an effort to acquaint his readers with some of Ewald's poetry in translation.

The eighteenth century ended on a much different note than it had begun. The dominance of Latinate theology had given way to indigenously inspired imaginative and critical literature. German and English models had to a large extent superseded French models. The ideas of rationalism and democracy had infiltrated Danish thought while the reading public expanded and the conviction grew that the common people should be encouraged to read books of imaginative as well as practical and didactic content.

From Romanticism to Realism

Sven H. Rossel

4

When the controversial writer Jens Baggesen decided in 1800 to leave Denmark in order to pursue an international career, the young poet Adam Oehlenschläger arranged a farewell party at the venerable Drejer's Club against the wishes of its members. Consequently, most of them stayed away, but the evening became memorable nevertheless. Baggesen repaid the homage by symbolically bequeathing Oehlenschläger his Danish lyre.

Even though this spontaneous gesture and the celebration itself had no immediate impact on the literary scene—the two writers hardly knew one another and later never reached a level of mutual understanding—the event can be interpreted as a new century's rebellion against the past. Baggesen and Oehlenschläger shared a strong opposition to the conservative, petty-bourgeois views of the club members and their nostalgic, sentimental adherence to eighteenth-century rationalism and utilitarianism. In the final analysis both were revolutionaries: Baggesen, the outsider with a split, almost modernistic philosophical and psychological concept of life, and Oehlenschläger, the first Danish writer to embrace romanticism with cogency and genius and to create a new poetic language. The two were united in their boundless worship of the self and the poetic genius unrestrained by societal chains and guided not by tradition but solely by divine inspiration.

There had been other indications that a new age in Danish literature was coming to the fore, characterized precisely by this new concept of the supremacy of the creative artist. At a memorial ceremony in 1791 for the German writer Friedrich Schiller (who was wrongly thought to have just died), Baggesen himself had enthused his audience by reciting the poem "Die Künstler" (1789; The Artists). In this attempt to aestheticize and sublimate the political message of the French Revolution of 1789, Schiller declares the artist to be the herald of final truth and the source of all progress.

As early as 1759 the British poet Edward Young, in his treatise *Conjectures on Original Composition*, had favored artistic intuition over adherence to academic rules and recommended that the modern poet rely on his own creative talent and reject the strict poetics of classicism. The impact of these suggestions was immense. In his *Briefe über Merkwürdigkeiten der Litteratur* (1766–70; Letters about the Peculiarities of Literature) Heinrich Wilhelm Gerstenberg not only praised Shakespeare as just such a "modern" poetic genius, but also drew attention to the Danish medieval ballads as a hitherto overlooked treasure. To the writers of Danish romanticism, both Shakespeare and the ballads became popular sources of inspiration. The German poet Friedrich Klopstock had also been influenced by Young's essay. He spent nineteen years in Denmark and became the primary model for the preromantic poet Johannes Ewald, as Ewald shaped his high-flown poetic diction and placed his self-reliant and sensitive self at the center of his writing.

The natural focal point of Drejer's Club was Knud Lyne Rahbek, an amiable and flexible poet and critic, whose home, "Bakkehuset," paradoxically enough, became the rallying ground around 1800 for the next generation of writers. In particular, Rahbek's wife, Karen Margarete, called Kamma, was successful in gathering the young romantics around her—Adam Oehlenschläger, B. S. Ingemann, and Poul Martin Møller, for instance—and Baggesen was also a guest at the frequent dinner parties at which all sorts of aesthetic topics were discussed late into the night. "Bakkehuset" was no literary salon in the French style. Rather, it functioned both as a connecting link between two centuries and as a hothouse for young talents. It has thus contributed to the somewhat distorted picture of Danish romanticism in its early phase as a Copenhagen movement centered on its genius, Oehlenschläger, who in the summer of 1800 met Kamma's sister, Christiane. They were married ten years later at "Bakkehuset."

Danish romanticism had, in fact, an earlier and much less local point of departure in the writings of the German-born Schack von Staffeldt; and its theoretical foundation, developed in Germany, was introduced by another foreigner, the Norwegian-born Henrich Steffens.

THE THEORY OF ROMANTICISM

Romanticism grew from the rejection of the eighteenth-century doctrines of objectivity, rational thought, and adherence to the fixed genres of classicism. Instead, it favored intuition, imagination, and formal experimentation. A major philosophical base can be found in Immanuel Kant's proposition that man can neither apprehend scientifically the Absolute (i.e., God) nor perceive the innermost substance of things, *"das Ding an sich,"* but only their external appearance. This distinction, derived from Plato, inspired Johann Gottlieb Fichte to his theory of the outer world as simply a product of man's self. Thus, the individual is raised above the world in absolute freedom, and only through his imagination, through art, is it possible to approach the Absolute. Since art, then, is a creation of the self, the illusion of art can be disrupted by the artist any time, thus evoking what has been labeled "romantic irony," a play—guided solely by fantasy and wit—with artistic form and content and with the reader and the artist himself.

It was the foremost theoretician of German romanticism, Friedrich Schlegel, who applied Fichte's system to aesthetics. He maintained that the continuous yet futile striving for the absolute ideal, which characterizes the subjective self, is also the governing principle of art. In contrast to the culture of Greek and Roman antiquity and its monistic perception of nature and spirit as a unity, Schlegel suggested a "modern" romantic, Neoplatonic philosophy based on Christianity's dualism between nature and spirit, the finite and the infinite. Thus, the purpose of art can no longer be to aim for harmony, objectivity, and perfection, but rather, as expressed by Friedrich Schlegel's brother, August Wilhelm, to reach for the infinite. This striving, which, however, can never reach the perfect state of the absolute ideal, the Schlegel brothers found in the literature of the Middle Ages and the Renaissance, which they both rediscovered after centuries of neglect; August Wilhelm made masterful translations into German of Dante, Calderón, Shakespeare, and Cervantes. The boundaries between dream and reality become blurred; the external world is viewed as a mere allegory of the infinite and divine, which art must attempt to express. In the final analysis, however, such attempts can never fully succeed.

This rejection of any definitive statement and structure explains the predilection of the romantics for the paradoxical and the fragmentary. The short form was much favored by these writers of the so-called Jena Romanticism, or *Universalromantik*: the aphorisms of Fr. Schlegel, the tales by Novalis, and the short stories by Ludwig Tieck. The focus is now on the individual, the artist, and the tradition of the chronologically progressing bildungsroman, as introduced by Goethe's *Wilhelm Meisters Lehrjahre* (1795–96; Wilhelm Meister's Apprenticeship), is rejected in favor of the impressionistic and capricious artist's novel, frequently interspersed with lyrical poetry, as in the works of Novalis, Tieck, and Joseph von Eichendorff. In general, according to Fr. Schlegel's concept of "a progressive universal poetry," the genuine literary work must be free of the rules of genre, mingling and merging prose, poetry, and philosophy as in Novalis's *Hymnen an die Nacht* (1800; Hymns to the Night).

Fichte's and Fr. Schlegel's extreme individualism and subjectivity—previously also present in the writings of the young Goethe, seen, for example, in *Die Leiden des jungen Werthers* (1774; The Sorrows of Young Werther)—were counterbalanced by Johann Gottfried Herder's and Friedrich Wilhelm Schelling's pantheistic theory of the Divine's presence in everything and, in particular, by Schelling's assertion of a now lost unity of nature, history, and religion, a reflection of transcendental harmony, which it is our task to reestablish through art. Thus, it was in accordance with Schelling's philosophy, as well as with the poetics of classicism, that Schiller in a letter to Goethe attacked Fr. Schlegel's unfinished epistolary novel *Lucinde* (1799), a major work in the early stages of romanticism. Against its extreme, almost anarchistic individualism, aestheticism, and unconventional views of sexuality and marriage, Schiller demanded objectivity and moral idealism. And Goethe himself responded by attacking the lack of form and the vapid lack of moral character in contemporary literature in general.

Members of the next generation of German writers also distanced themselves from the early romantics, inasmuch as they rejected their aesthetic and philosophical speculation in favor of belles lettres. Inspired by Herder and his focus on the *Volksgeist*, the collective national spirit, as every nation's creative potential, they developed a strong interest in folk culture and literature (which had been neglected by the preceding Enlightenment). As a result, Jacob and Wilhelm Grimm (1812–14) and Achim von Arnim and Clemens Brentano (1806–8) began to collect folktales and folk songs, respectively, among the peasantry. Brentano, together with Eichendorff, found significant inspiration for his own poetic writings in the plain, unobtrusive, yet intimate and melodious folk song. A strong bond developed between poetry and music, which found its most exquisite expression in the works of Franz Schubert, Robert Schumann, and Hugo Wolf.

Influenced by the political events during the Napoleonic Wars (1796–1815), Napoleon's victory over the Prussian army at Jena in 1806 in particular, and the ensuing demands for unification of the separate German states, these writers of the so-called Heidelberg Romanticism developed a strong conception of historical tradition and a nationalist sense of identity with German history, the Middle Ages being their favorite period. Simultaneously, the earlier pantheistic orientation was replaced by a return to Christian doctrine, exemplified by Fr. Schlegel's conversion to Catholicism in 1808. The same war inspired the corresponding generation of Danish romantic writers in the wake of the country's heroic battle against the English fleet in 1801 and the bombardment of Copenhagen in 1807, which caused a wave of national self-confidence. A school of national romanticism (Oehlenschläger, Ingemann, Grundtvig), with Nordic mythology and history as predominant sources and Walter Scott's historical novels as a frequent artistic model, rapidly replaced the initial, more abstract, and universal romantic outlook, occasionally within the very same authorship.

The reaction in German literature, which denotes a partial return to eighteenth-century classicism centered on Goethe and Schiller, was also strongly reflected in Danish literature after 1800. The early subjective and fragmented German-inspired *Universalromantik* was rather short-lived (Schack von Staffeldt, the young Oehlenschläger) and was replaced even in the first decade by a harmonizing outlook with frequent national orientation, a "poetic" realism, for which some critics have applied the German term *Biedermeier*, connoting the idealizing, often idyllic orientation of these writers (Møller, Heiberg, Hertz). It did not vanish completely, however, but resurfaced both in individual authorships (Ingemann, Hauch) and, during the 1830s and 1840s, as a separate literary development, the so-called *romantisme*, characterized by growing doubts about the spiritual outlook and idealistic philosophy of romanticism. Under the influence of Hoffmann, Heine, Hugo, and Byron, this *romantisme* brought greater psychological complexity and scope to a bourgeois culture and literature marked by a gradually increasing, yet still somewhat idealizing, realism. Whereas for some writers its apparent harmony often covered a hard-won resignation (Winther), for others the contradictions between ideal and reality became irreconcilable (Gyllembourg, Blicher, Bagger, Chievitz). This ethical and religious crisis of the romantic world view could also find expression in the deliberate aestheticization of everyday life, an escape into a worship of beauty (Bødtcher, Aarestrup).

Thus the realistic trend (Goldschmidt, Hostrup, Schack), as it developed during the 1840s and 1850s, decades of significant political and social changes, anticipated—to a much larger degree than is claimed by later critics—the naturalistic rebellion ca. 1870 against political conservatism, metaphysics, idealistic philosophy in general, and the Lutheran state church in particular. Altogether, it is characteristic of the writers of the period 1800–1870 that only with great difficulty can they be classified with regard to specific literary schools. Most of them went through several artistic and ideological stages. Some, like Oehlenschläger and Ingemann, incorporated features from preromanticism into poetic realism and *romantisme*, whereas the greatest prose writer of the period, Blicher, with his existential doubts and pessimistic outlook, even transgressed his own times. Likewise, it is impossible to categorize the three greatest personalities from the mid-nineteenth century: Hans Christian Andersen, Fr. Paludan-Müller, and Søren Kierkegaard. They are all strong-minded individualists who, deeply involved in their own times, call the contemporary Biedermeier culture to account at the same time as they rise above their own times through their universality.

The breakthrough of the romantic movement in England and France was at the same time as in Germany, with Wordsworth's and Coleridge's *Lyrical Ballads* (1798) and Chateaubriand's two lyrical novels *Atala* (1801) and *René* (1802). English and French romanticism was in part based on national antecedents (Blake, Burns, Rousseau). Nevertheless, it was the strong impulses from Germany, disseminated primarily through Madame de Staël's study *De l'Allemagne* (1810; On Germany), which developed romanticism into a powerful, common European movement. It was introduced in Denmark as early as the turn of the nineteenth century (Staffeldt, Oehlenschläger); in Sweden (Atterbom, Tegnér, Geijer) and Norway (Welhaven, Wergeland), ca. 1810 and 1830, respectively; and in the United States, ca. 1820 (Irving, Bryant, Cooper).

UNIVERSAL ROMANTICISM AND PHILOSOPHICAL DUALISM

Denmark's attempt to remain neutral during the Napoleonic Wars by joining an alliance with Russia, Prussia, and Sweden was thwarted in 1801 when England, seeing the strong Danish navy as a threat to her freedom of movement at sea, sent a squadron to Copenhagen to attack the Danish fleet. In spite of strong resistance, Denmark was forced to capitulate. The Dano-English war was resumed in 1807 when British troops surrounded Copenhagen and, after a four-day bombardment, forced the capital to surrender. The entire fleet was carried off, and the defeat was considered the most severe blow Denmark had endured since the Swedish victory a century and a half earlier. The crown prince, later King Frederik VI (1808–39), immediately entered an alliance with France, a decision that turned out to be disastrous. In 1812 Sweden and Russia joined together against Denmark and France and demanded the cession of Norway, a part of the Dano-Norwegian dual monarchy for about four hundred years, to Sweden, which had lost Finland to Russia in 1809. In 1814 Frederik VI signed the Peace of Kiel, whereby Norway was joined to Sweden in a union that lasted until 1905. The tragic outcome of the war was also reflected in a ruinous economic crisis which led to national bankruptcy in 1813. It was followed by general stagnation, which makes the period 1814–30 the poorest in Denmark's modern history.

Altogether 335 Danish merchant ships had been seized during the war, destroying the country's world trade. The simultaneous loss of the Norwegian and English markets, plummeting prices, and the inferior quality of Danish farm products caused an agricultural crisis lasting until 1828. It not only halted the continuation of the reform policy initiated in the late seventeenth century but also exerted a paralyzing effect on industrial output. One reform, however, passed in 1814, made a significant impact on the country's subsequent history. An educational law made schooling mandatory for every child between seven and fourteen years of age, thereby securing the impoverished peasantry the right to basic education. This reform, which also meant a general raising of the quality of education, laid the groundwork for the economic and political struggle of the Danish farmer in the decades to follow, thus preparing for the emergence of democracy in 1849. In contrast, 1814 also saw freedom of the press limited to such an extent that direct censorship was effected. But demands for greater political freedom became louder. In 1819 the writer Blok Tøxen published a letter to the king in which he demanded a free constitution; he was silenced with a royal pension. In 1820 the teacher Jacob J. Dampe likewise advocated the abolition of the absolute monarchy and was sentenced to imprisonment for life.

Copenhagen, the political, financial, and cultural center of Denmark and the home of the country's only university, had in many ways remained a medieval city after 1800, with winding and narrow streets and alleys. Behind its ramparts the one hundred thousand inhabitants (one-ninth of the country's population) were bunched together in a labyrinth of houses, outbuildings, and sheds, and until 1850 every twelfth Copenhagener lived in a basement flat. Sanitation and health standards were horrendous—as late as 1863 more than three thousand head of cattle were still stabled in the city and all sewage ran in open channels through the streets. Poverty was widespread, accompanied by rampant begging, which was punished by imprisonment. Only slowly did the deplorable social conditions—seldom a topic in the literature of the period—improve in the greatly overcrowded city. Not until 1831 did the dwellings reach the number existing before the bombardment in 1807, and not until the 1850s did the city begin to grow outside the ramparts.

The national catastrophes of 1807 and 1813–14 gave rise to patriotism and nostalgia for Denmark's glorious past, a symptom of a general escapism, to which the strict political censorship also contributed. The most significant result was a surge in the arts and sciences, which gave the period its name: the Golden Age. These trends also led to an enthusiastic pan-Scandinavian movement, the so-called Scandinavianism, which grew out of student gatherings in Sweden and Denmark. It manifested itself for the first time in 1829 with the crowning of the poet Adam Oehlenschläger by the Swedish poet Esaias Tegnér in the cathedral of Lund and reached its zenith in the following decades.

In painting, foreign predominance ceased after the establishment of the Royal Academy of Arts in 1754. In 1818 C. W. Eckersberg was appointed professor at the academy, and he exerted a tremendous impact on painters in the decades to come. Eckersberg, like the majority of Danish artists, spent considerable time in Italy, and its colorful nature and folk life became an inexhaustible source for artistic motifs. As in the period's literature, this exotic orientation, whose finest exponent was Constantin Hansen, was counterbalanced by a more local, idyllic school, corresponding to the trend of poetic realism in literature, which found its favorite themes primarily in Copenhagen and North Zealand. Around 1840 a national school in Danish painting was firmly established, focusing on interiors (Wilhelm Bendz), landscapes (J. Th. Lundbye), and portraits (Christen Købke).

While some of the period's leading composers—C. E. F. Weyse, Niels W. Gade, and Peter Heise—often set their texts to music in close cooperation with the romantic poets and thus established a unique Danish romance or lied tradition, Frederik Kuhlau became best known for his music (inspired by old Danish folk tunes) to Heiberg's romantic, national drama *Elverhøi*, which, with its interposed dances became one of the earliest European examples of a gesammtkunstwerk. Gade also created symphonic music of international quality, and his orchestral works were performed under the patronage of Felix Mendelssohn-Bartholdy. Besides opera and song, the ballet blossomed, centered on the dancer and choreographer August Bournonville, whose works reflect demonic *romantisme* (1836; *The Sylph*), romantic exoticism (1842; *Napoli*), and poetic realism (1849; *The Kermis in Bruges*).

While the composers and painters were firmly rooted in the romantic tradition, the period's greatest sculptor, Bertel Thorvaldsen, earned international recognition with his statues in Greco-Roman style. From 1797 to 1838 he had his studio in Rome, where he became an invaluable host and guide for visiting Danish artists and writers. Like his close friend Hans Christian Andersen, he had successfully overcome a proletarian background. In this respect they remain the sole exceptions of the period, but at the same time their careers testify to the possibility that great talents can thrive under an absolute, enlightened monarchy, whose role as a patron of art and literature was only gradually taken over by a bourgeoisie of growing wealth. Neoclassicism was also the guiding style for the architect C. F.

Hansen, who rebuilt the bombarded capital in a monumental classical style.

Within science, parallels can also be found to the developments in literary romanticism. As part of a national revival of interest in prehistory, Christian J. Thomsen, while systematizing archaeological specimens, devised the epoch-making division into Stone, Bronze, and Iron ages. More in line with speculative, universal romanticism is the work of H. C. Ørsted, the brother-in-law of the poet Oehlenschläger. Ørsted's discovery of the principles of electromagnetism in 1820 (in 1824 he also discovered aluminum) gave him a deeper insight into the laws of nature and led him to the idea of nature as a visible expression of God's spirit, as demonstrated by the title of his two-volume collection of philosophical essays, *Aanden i Naturen* (1850; The Spirit in Nature). The pursuit of harmony and unity also characterized the work of the philologist Rasmus Rask. He was the first systematically to describe Old Norse. After travels in Russia, Persia, India, and Ceylon he returned with invaluable manuscripts and was then able to confirm the existence of the Indo-European family of languages. Rask's classification of languages is considered a pioneering work, and he is regarded as one of the founders of the historical school of philology.

Henrich Steffens

It was the scientist and philosopher Henrich Steffens (1773–1845) who introduced the ideas of romanticism to a broader Danish audience. In 1798 Steffens had visited the University of Jena, then the cultural center of Germany, and there attended the lectures by Fichte and Schelling and made friends with the Schlegel brothers, Tieck, and Novalis. Thus Steffens experienced German romanticism in its earliest stage, and his lectures in Copenhagen in 1802 on the romantic philosophy of nature became a true sensation; the first nine were published as *Indledning til philosophiske Forelæsninger* (1803; Introduction to Philosophical Lectures). They recapitulate Schelling's view of the synthesis of nature, art, and history and sharply attack the predominant rationalism, all of which prevented Steffens's appointment to a chair in philosophy in Copenhagen.

In the audience were Oehlenschläger, Grundtvig, and Blicher, all of whom were to become leading writers. In particular, Grundtvig, Steffens's cousin, was deeply inspired by the new conception of history. It was based on Herder's theory of three main phases in mankind's history, reaching from paradisiac innocence over decline because of the Fall of Man to a future glorious Golden Age. Grundtvig shared with Steffens the view that Christ's birth was the decisive dividing line between historical epochs. Whereas the Golden Age, according to Steffens, was heralded by Goethe and German romanticism, however, Grundtvig increasingly associated it with the Coming of the Lord.

In 1804 Steffens returned to Germany, and the rest of his career belongs to German intellectual life. His gradual movement from pantheism toward traditional Christianity, paralleled by Fr. Schlegel's conversion, is documented in his German-language *Novellen* (1837–38; Short Stories, 1–16), actually a series of novels containing passages of brilliantly executed nature descriptions. It is neither as a writer nor as a scientist that Steffens will be remembered, however. His role was that of a cultural and intellectual intermediary, on a par with Ludvig Holberg and Georg Brandes.

Adolph Wilhelm Schack von Staffeldt

It is possible that Adolph Wilhelm Schack von Staffeldt (1769–1826) also attended Steffens's lectures. As early as 1791, however, after having received his military training in Copenhagen, Staffeldt had left for the University of Göttingen, where he spent more than two years familiarizing himself with the works of Herder and Schiller. During a second trip abroad in 1795–1800 to Germany, Italy, and France, Staffeldt was introduced to German romanticism and studied the philosophy of Plato, Kant, and Schelling, which became the foundation for his strongly dualistic poetry.

For posterity it is Oehlenschläger who personifies the breakthrough of Danish romanticism. Indeed, his sensational debut collection, *Digte* (1803; Poems), was the first full-blown manifestation of the new school. Although Staffeldt had published his poems in various journals from as early as 1788, his first and rather uneven collection, *Digte* (Poems), did not appear until 1804 and was generally overlooked and barely understood. Not until the modernism of post–World War II did Staffeldt experience a comeback after having been overshadowed by Oehlenschläger. Staffeldt's poetry—a second collection, *Nye Digte* (New Poems), was published in 1808—is characterized by a Neoplatonic distinction between a material world and an ideal and glorious but past world of the Divine, from which man has fallen. He now lives estranged, in a prison, deprived of that original freedom about which the poet can only reminisce and write. Thus, the poet becomes an intermediary between matter and spirit. But his attempts to reach the ideal, the lost harmony, remain futile, leaving him with premonition and longing, and with an even greater emptiness and pain.

Therefore, Staffeldt's nature poems are permeated not, like Oehlenschläger's, with pantheistic rapture but rather with melancholic contemplation, with weltschmerz. Nature symbolizes the passing of all earthly things, which the poet projects onto his own situation:

Listen to me, fate! Do not let my loss
be little once I vanish.
Let me nourish the leaves on a thousand branches
and yield to an admired spring:
At my feet the wanderer shall then behold
with sorrow the fall of my previous rich life.
        ("I Høsten" [In Autumn], 1804)

From this transitory world Staffeldt turns to the boundless universe, his true realm. As early as in a poem from his stay in Göttingen, "Til den Helliganede" (publ. 1795; To Sanctity Perceived), he lets the macrocosm reflect the microcosm of the poet on a grandiose scale, which was later to be equaled only by Ingemann and Hauch:

The stars cluster themselves around your temple
like a diadem; the ether is your sash.
You twist your arms around all beings like a girdle
O, like a mother's embrace.

The unsurmountable dichotomy between matter and spirit is linked to an erotic longing, which supposedly can bring the individual closer to the Absolute. This longing, which, however, turns out to be futile, finds expression in ecstatic lyrical monologues in Goethean rhymeless poems ("Under Lillas Vinduer" [1804; Under Lilla's Windows]) particularly in the flawless sonnets of the second collection—the first sonnets in Danish literature—addressed to "Lina."

An unsuccessful attempt to appear to be Oehlenschläger's precursor by predating some of his own poems put Staffeldt in a false light among his contemporaries. Furthermore, his early ballads in a preromantic, Gothic style in the tradition of G. A. Bürger, replete with sentimentality and horror effects—a genre also familiar to the young Oehlenschläger and Ingemann—had a negative impact on his posthumous reputation. Nevertheless, the cosmic dimension and abstract speculation of Staffeldt's poetry, its consistent focusing on the vocation of the artist, and, finally, its bold, almost modernist imagery give Staffeldt a unique position in Danish literature which is yet to be fully appreciated. All his life a loner, he left Denmark, embittered, in 1808 and went to Germany. With little success he tried his hand at writing in German and then embarked on a career as a government official. In 1813 he was appointed governor of Gottorp in the duchy of Schleswig.

Adam Oehlenschläger

Well known in Danish literary history is the nightly conversation late in 1802 between Henrich Steffens and Adam Oehlenschläger (1779–1850), after which the latter immediately rewrote an already finished manuscript, *Digte* (1803; Poems), keeping only eight of the original texts; these were narrative ballads in the eighteenth-century Gothic style with only limited artistic value.

Oehlenschläger was born at Frederiksberg Castle near Copenhagen, where his father was organist and later steward. He grasped with amazing intuition and poetic talent the essence of German romanticism, to which he had already been introduced through Steffens's lectures. With A. W. Schlegel's collection *Gedichte* (1800; Poems) as his structural model, Oehlenschläger fully complies with the romantic demand of blending genres. *Digte* is divided into three parts: an epic part, which primarily—often using the medieval ballad as a source—glorifies the ancient Nordic past; a lyrical part, in which Oehlenschläger with sculptural lucidity and melodiousness illustrates the pantheistic concept of nature; and finally, a dramatic part, consisting of "Sanct Hansaften-Spil" (Midsummer Night's Play), the highlight of the volume. It is both a manifesto satirically attacking the previous century's "enlightenment" and a poetic love story glorifying nature, love, and history as one and the same revelation of the divine spirit:

> Bewitching harmony
> in the midnight-dark earth
> blessed empathy!
> Holy poetry
> without words!
> Fusion of grove and lake
> and stars and youth and maiden entwined!
> In deep embrace
> the whole of nature extolls love's name.

Oehlenschläger had learned from Shakespeare's *A Midsummer Night's Dream* to combine low comedy with nature worship. The dialogue is the medieval *knittelvers* whereas the lyrical parts are intricately executed in a variety of meters new to Danish literature.

The attack on petty-bourgeois rationalism, contrasted with a glorified view of poetic intuition and genius, is repeated in the poem "Guldhornene" (The Golden Horns), written in short, irregular stanzas and describing, with historical correctness, the finding and loss of two golden horns from about A.D. 400. They symbolize the union between the golden era of the past ("Ages of gold / flaming forth / light from the north / when heaven was on earth") and the present, and thus they express the romantic longing for historical unity. The same universal spirit also reveals itself in nature, superbly demonstrated in the poem "Natur-Temperamenter" (Nature Temperaments).

In contrast to the earliest dualistic stage of German romanticism, Oehlenschläger's philosophy of nature is basically monistic—that is, the ideal and the real, spirit and nature, constitute a unity, which the poet must perceive and express. Nevertheless, in a substantial number of lesser-known texts, such as "Oldingen ved Werthers Grav" (The Old Man at Werther's Tomb), one encounters characters marked by desperation and spiritual fragmentation, unable to find such harmony. Not always do nature and man merge jubilantly. On the contrary, as in "Den brustne Harpe" (The Broken Harp), chords of isolation and desperation are struck, adding a complexity to *Digte* which among Oehlenschläger's contemporaries can be found only in Staffeldt's oeuvre. Through an overall attempt to bridge any emotional and philosophical conflict and to stress the ethical obligation of the artist, however, in particular through a glorification of Old Norse heroic ideals, *Digte* points ahead. It anticipates both the succeeding, Goethe-influenced bourgeois phase in Oehlenschläger's career and his predilection for national mythology and history, the first manifestations of which can be found in *Poetiske Skrifter* (1805; Poetic Writings, 1–2).

The romantic worship of nature underlies the first volume's two poetry cycles, *Langelands-Reise* (Langeland Journey) and *Jesu Christi gientagne Liv i den aarlige Natur* (The Life of Jesus Christ Symbolized in the Seasons). The first consists of thirty-eight texts describing Oehlenschläger's summer travel throughout southern Denmark. Whereas the outward journey is primarily narrated in hexameters, in which the poet focuses on historical characters and monuments, the scope gradually expands to embrace—in a Schelling-inspired unity—history, nature, and poetry, rendered in a variety of meters, displaying Oehlenschläger's ability to extract from the Danish language a hitherto unseen flexibility and beauty. Nevertheless, the poet has begun to move away from universal romanticism. In the poem "Faareveile Skov" (Faareveile Forest) he glorifies the German rationalist G. E. Lessing, and when in his second cycle he lets the changing seasons illustrate the life and death of Christ, he has clearly abandoned the pantheism of his debut collection. On the contrary, nature merely symbolizes Christ's redemption of humankind, the victory of life and goodness over darkness and death.

The same contrast forms the basis for the works of the second volume, the somber story *Vaulundurs Saga* (The Saga of Vaulundur) and the bright five-act play in blank verse *Aladdin* (Eng. tr. 1857, 1968), whose respective title characters glorify the romantic genius in complete harmony with nature. Whereas the language and characters of *Vaulundurs Saga* are inspired by Old Norse sources, the story's rich use of color symbolism and allegory stems from the German romantic tales, in particular those of Tieck. His fairy-tale play *Kaiser Octavianus* (1804), as well as the collection of oriental stories, *Arabian Nights*, both confronting a petty-bourgeois world with the supernatural, are the main sources of *Aladdin*. In many ways indebted to the Goethean bildungsroman, Oehlenschläger follows the development of a carefree good-for-nothing, "nature's lighthearted son," through experiences of love and hardship on his way to becoming a dynamic representative of goodness. Not until he has reached this stage of perfection does Aladdin deserve his happiness, symbolized in the magic lamp. The ethical element is stressed by the fact that the lamp is pursued recklessly, but in vain, by Aladdin's opponent, "the thinker of the dark," Noureddin, who represents sterile rationalism versus intuition, chaos versus harmony.

In Shakespeare's dramas Oehlenschläger found inspiration for the frequent change between the comic and the tragic as well as the lively, realistically portrayed secondary characters. Shakespeare also influenced his style, especially his forceful and concentrated imagery. But in spite of all models, *Aladdin* stands out—perfectly responding to Fr. Schlegel's concept of *Universalpoesie*—as a unique masterpiece that transgresses all literary conventions with ebullient zest and minute, artistic craftsmanship. The play's superbly executed shifts between fantasy and reality, its penetrating analysis of the tasks of art and the artist himself, and its linguistic innovation make it the major work of universal Danish romanticism, which Oehlenschläger shortly thereafter abandoned.

Nicolai Frederik Severin Grundtvig

Whereas Oehlenschläger became increasingly successful in reconciling Old Norse ethos, romantic nature worship, and undogmatic Christianity, these three spiritual spheres clashed fiercely in the personality of N. F. S. Grundtvig (1783–1872). Not until he experienced a series of severe crises and conversions did he finally arrive at a hard-earned philosophy of life.

Raised in an orthodox, Lutheran parsonage in Udby on Zealand, Grundtvig studied theology and received his bachelor of divinity degree in 1805 but "without spirit and faith." From 1805 to 1808 he was employed as a private tutor at an estate on the island of Langeland. His infatuation with the lady of the estate, as well as intensive readings in works by Oehlenschläger, Schelling, and his cousin Steffens, led to a romantic awakening, evident in the poem "Strandbakken ved Egeløkke" (publ. 1812; The Hill by the Beach at Egeløkke). Here Grundtvig experiences himself as part of the universe or, rather, as someone who is striving to regain the original harmony that, according to Neoplatonic philosophy, through a fall became divided into two opposing forces: base matter and ascending spirit.

Grundtvig sees this split both in his own, present situation and in the historical process. Thus, the fundamental animosity between the gods and giants of Nordic myth is viewed as a symbolic expression of the clash between these two forces. In his article "Om Religion og Liturgi" (1807; On Religion and Liturgy) Christ is portrayed as the reconciler, and in the treatise *Lidet om Sangene i Edda* (1806; A Little about the Songs in the Edda) Grundtvig had merged the poems of the *Elder Edda* into a mythic synthesis. Here Odin, as well as Christ, becomes a manifestation of the same divinity, a view that Grundtvig develops further in his first book, *Nordens Mythologi* (1808; Nordic Mythology), which explains the Twilight of the Gods as caused by moral decay and by deserting "Alfader"—"God the Father." The work was epoch-making in the study of Scandinavian mythology through its attempt at interpreting the Old Norse myths as a symbolic, universal concept of life in the past, present, and future. The decisive step in Grundtvig's development toward an unequivocal Christianity were taken only a few years later, however.

Bernhard Severin Ingemann

Whereas Grundtvig was able to overcome the dualism of this youth (to which he was to return later), a dualistic world view remained the philosophical foundation for both B. S. Ingemann (1789–1862) and Carsten Hauch. Strongly influenced by a Christian upbringing—his father was a Lutheran minister in southern Denmark—Ingemann began in 1806 to study philology and later philosophy at the University of Copenhagen without, however, ever receiving a degree. A generous two-year travel stipend made it possible for him to leave for Italy in 1818, but in the meantime he had already shown an amazing productivity as a poet.

In his debut collection, *Digte* (1811; Poems), which in the years before 1816 was followed by three more volumes, Ingemann settled accounts with the monistic philosophy of Goethe and Schelling. In complete contrast to them, he perceived human existence as a continuous battle between demonic forces and Christianity, Satan and God. On this theme Ingemann based both his epic poem in ottava rima, *De sorte Riddere* (1814; The Black

Knights), and the play *Reinald Underbarnet* (1816; Reinald the Wonder Child). The first work is a rather ponderous allegory, the second a more poetic, indeed fairy-tale-like, profession of Christianity.

The same dualism, but executed less successfully, permeates many of Ingemann's youthful poems, which are influenced by the preromantic Gothic style. Here a preference for the macabre, the instinctive as well as the erotically alluring, type of woman comes to the fore, constituting a predominant thread throughout Ingemann's writings. The battle to liberate oneself from these forces is depicted in the medieval drama *Løveridderen* (1816; The Knight of the Lion), which with its underlying spiritual striving marks a clear repudiation of the German so-called fate drama, as represented by Zacharias Werner's *Der 24. Februar* (1815; The 24th of February) and Franz Grillparzer's *Die Ahnfrau* (1817; The Ancestress). This popular genre strongly influenced several other tragedies by Ingemann, such as *Blanca* (1815), his greatest theatrical success.

Ingemann had concluded *De sorte Riddere* with these lines:

In the distant dark
he sees the star sparkle
hears God in the harmony of the spheres.

Such harmony can be found not in a synthesis of spirit and matter, but in the spiritual world alone. This truly Platonic longing, which makes Ingemann together with Hauch the only successors of Schack Staffeldt in Danish literature, finds expression—sometimes elegiac or overwrought, sometimes sublime—in Ingemann's lyrical poetry, of which parts are included in the verse novella *Varners poetiske Vandringer* (Varner's Poetic Wanderings) in the collection *Procne* (1813). His model is Goethe's epistolary novel *Die Leiden des Jungen Werthers*. A young man leaves insipid civilization and goes out in the countryside, but his idyll is abruptly shattered: "I have seen her, the woman I love, whom I have always loved but not seen before with earthly eyes." She reciprocates his—strictly Platonic—love but falls ill from an infectious disease, and Varner drinks his death from her lips. Whereas Goethe's hero shoots himself, Ingemann lets his couple die, finally to be united in celestial love.

The work is fascinating through its total commitment to spirituality, which occasionally takes it to the brink of abstraction. Not until Ingemann's travel abroad in 1818 can a stronger resonance of the external world be detected. It went hand in hand with the poet's wish for a revival of Denmark's past and made him a leading figure in national romanticism.

Carsten Hauch

External reality, in contrast, had from the outset been present in the works of Johannes Carsten Hauch (1790–1872). He was born in Norway (of Danish parents) and spent his childhood years in close contact with the country's wild nature, which made an indelible impression on him. But like Ingemann, Hauch perceived existence from a dualistic perspective. A fundamental principle in all his writings is the contrast between profound, spiritual values and external, superficial luster. Hauch himself was attracted by both possibilities. In his works as well as in his own life an insistence on responsibility for one's existence here and now predominates. But frequently, in disappointment over what is temporal, an inherent longing for the eternal becomes a strong desire for death.

Hauch's vacillation between reality and the ideal is evident in his first work, with the revealing title *Contrasterne, to dramatiske Digte* (1816; The Contrasts: Two Dramatic Poems). It contains biting satire aimed at exaggerated fantasizing, as Hauch, for instance, perceived it in Ingemann's oeuvre—the first of numerous polemical attacks Hauch later also launched against Baggesen, Heiberg, and Hans Christian Andersen—but to which he knew he himself was also inclined. Thus, the work turns out to be a relentless judgment on himself, expressing a doubt about his own artistic talents. This doubt led to an extended break in Hauch's writing, during which he concentrated on his study of the natural sciences at the University of Copenhagen, which he concluded in 1821 with a doctoral degree in zoology.

During a prolonged illness in Rome in 1825, however, which necessitated the amputation of one foot and brought Hauch close to suicide, he came to a final realization of his vocation as a writer. The first result, written while still in Rome, was the closet drama *Hamadryaden* (1828: The Hamadryad). Inspired by the structure of the folktale, it depicts the battle between good and evil in a pantheistically animated universe. It concludes not only with the hero's victory after having endured several trials, but also—in a secondary plot—in a sharp rejection of irreligious materialism and ethical nihilism. On his return to Denmark in 1827 Hauch was employed as a science teacher at the Sorø Academy, where he became a colleague of Ingemann's. He stayed there until 1846, when he was appointed professor of Scandinavian literature at the University of Kiel, followed in 1851 by an appointment to the chair of aesthetics at the University of Copenhagen.

For several years Hauch was also employed at the Royal Theater as manager and dramatic adviser, and he himself was a highly productive playwright inspired by Greek drama and, in particular, by Shakespeare, whose works taught him the use of contrast in character delineation as well as colorful and forceful imagery in dialogue. Thus, Hauch's tragedies *Bajazet* (1828), *Tiberius* (1828), and *Don Juan* (1829) are all focused on the tragicheroic, psychologically complex personality, as Hauch found it in *Richard III* and *King Lear*.

In the 1840s Hauch returned to the drama, employing motifs from Danish history. However, most of these later plays lack coherence in their character delineation, are without dramatic force, and are burdened by their moralizing. The dialogue is stale, and only in descriptive and lyrical passages is Hauch unreservedly successful. Two exceptions are *Svend Grathe* (1841), which in its discussion of the struggle for power anticipates Henrik Ibsen's *Kongsemnerne* (1863; The Pretenders), and the poetic fairy-tale play with a Norwegian setting, *Søstrene paa Kinnekullen* (1849; The Sisters of Kinnekullen), which analyzes the dangerous power of gold (i.e., materialism) over the human mind.

Hauch reached a larger audience with his novels, which, like his plays, are characterized by a combination of character drawing and an ethical message. Like Ingemann, he was inspired by Walter Scott's historical novels and their cavalier treatment of historical fact. Thus, in Hauch's first novel, *Vilhelm Zabern* (1834), the historical characters and events are, just as in Scott's works, viewed through the eyes of a fictitious person. Local color is totally eclipsed by a series of penetrating character analyses, particularly of the Renaissance king Christian II and his capricious mistress, Dyveke. Her character is further developed in the young woman Veronica in *Guldmageren* (1836; The Goldmaker), whose only goal is to gather riches and live in luxury, a motif similar to that in Hauch's play *Søstrene paa Kinnekullen*. In contrast to the debut novel, however, the characters are presented through their attitude toward one predominant idea: alchemy as a symbol of the romanticists' attempt at transforming nature into poetry. The Jewish title character is guided by an unselfish striving to comprehend the secrets of nature, while others are only seeking gold—once again the contrast between idealism and materialism, on which Hauch also based his contemporary novel about Poland's heroic fight for freedom against Russia in 1830, *En polsk Familie* (1839; A Polish Family). His primary purpose was to write a bildungsroman in the tradition of Goethe, employing its apparently loose structure. Exciting narrative passages alternate with subjective reflections, dramatic dialogues with inserted lyrics inspired by folk songs. *En polsk Familie* exemplifies Hauch's growing skill as a novelist. Whereas *Slottet ved Rhinen* (1845; The Castle on the Rhine) is still burdened by a much too schematic character delineation, among others a malicious Hans Christian Andersen caricature, Hauch's last two novels, *Robert Fulton* (1853; Eng. tr. 1868) and *Charles de la Bussière*

(1860) are written with accomplished artistry and technical skill. In *Robert Fulton* Hauch once again juxtaposes idealism and materialism, and his portrait of the inventor, a genius and an outsider—a typical Hauchian hero who must fight lack of appreciation and exploitation—contains obvious autobiographical traits. In his last novel, at times a veritable thriller, Hauch likewise bases his narrative on an ethical concept. It takes place during the bloody events of the French Revolution, and like the Scarlet Pimpernel, the title hero fights to rescue prisoners from the guillotine and stands out as a Christian humanist fighting against a deceived populace guided by atheist ideology.

The frequently interspersed lyrical poems in Hauch's plays and novels show, however, that his true artistry was to be found in lyrical poetry, which came to full bloom in his later years. In Hauch's three collections, *Lyriske Digte* (1842; Lyrical Poems), *Lyriske Digte og Romancer* (1861; Lyrical Poems and Romances), and *Nye Digtninger* (1869; New Poems), he displays his unique ability continuously to renew his poetic expression. Even though his poetry remained firmly rooted in romantic idealism, the duality of Hauch's philosophical outlook finds an outlet in a desperate sense of weltschmerz. Hauch pays tribute to the period's national romanticism in several epic cycles, inspired by Ingemann's *Holger Danske*, dealing with characters from Danish history. He achieved the superb, however, in some speculative texts that display a deep-rooted melancholy and elevated pathos. For these poems Hauch employed two diametrically opposed metrical forms: the songlike, intimate lied and the free, rhymeless ode modeled on the poetry of Pindar and Goethe. These texts span the passionate love poetry of Hauch's younger years to later expressions of pessimistic resignation. Hauch turns to the universe and cosmic infinity beyond the range of the human spirit in expressing an awareness of humanity's nothingness:

> For us time has hardly begun,
> even though those mayflies of worlds,
> newly hatched,
> flying flakes in the immense space,
> dream about eons and eternities,
> and believe that the end is there,
> even though they have not yet concluded
> one single orbit.
> ("Pleiaderne ved Midnat" [The Pleiades at Midnight])

Here as well as in several other poems Hauch not only points ahead to the formal experimentation of the twentieth century but also becomes the final full manifestation of Danish lyrical romanticism.

The change in Danish literature from universal to national romanticism was due partly to similar developments in Germany, partly to local conditions. It is noteworthy that this change took place in the writings of the *first* generation of romantics.

As early as the eighteenth century Gerstenberg had referred positively to Danish medieval balladry. Generally, during Danish preromanticism a renewed interest in Danish ancient history and Nordic mythology, centered on the medieval chronicler Saxo, had become a major source of poetic inspiration. After 1800 this interest in the early history of Denmark found its first romantic expression in Oehlenschläger's debut collection. In 1812–14 Rahbek copublished a five-volume edition of *Udvalgte Danske Viser fra Middelalderen* (Selection of Danish Ballads from the Middle Ages). These texts, however, were not, as was the case in Germany, directly recorded from oral tradition, but were taken from written sources and were far from philologically correct. They could not, as originally intended, replace Peder Syv's immensely popular ballad collection from 1695, which had been reprinted as late as 1787. It was still this old volume to which the romantic poets turned when they were looking for material. In contrast, the tunes of Rahbek's edition had been collected among the peasantry, a clear indication of the period's newly awakened interest in folklore. This trend culminated in Svend Grundtvig's mammoth project, a twelve-volume edition of *Danmarks gamle Folkeviser* (1853–1976; Denmark's Old Folk Ballads), which because of its methodology became authoritative for all subsequent ballad editions, such as F. J. Child's *The English and Scottish Popular Ballads* (1882–98).

Around 1820 the romantics' keen interest in peasant culture also prompted the poet Christian Winther to collect regional words and idioms; these were included in Christian Molbech's *Dansk Dialect-Lexicon* (1841; Encyclopedia of Danish Dialects). A related project in collecting folklore was undertaken by Just Mathias Thiele, whose four-volume edition of *Danske Folkesagn* (1818–23; Danish Folk Legends), together with L. S. Vedel Simonsen's monographs on Danish nobility, became a main source for many works in nineteenth-century historical fiction.

These folklorist activities demonstrate that an (often orally transmitted) folk literature dating back to the Middle Ages was still very much alive during the early part of the nineteenth century. Winther, who was fascinated by the song traditions of the peasantry, not only submitted a locally recorded medieval ballad to Rahbek, but also found inspiration in one of the most

popular lyrical genres, the broadside ballad. These dramatic and/or sentimental songs were first published in cheap prints in the sixteenth century
and experienced a boom in the decades before and after 1800, when they
were commercially produced and sold for a few cents in the streets and at
country fairs. Together with the so-called chapbooks, primitive prose renditions of well-known topics from world literature such as the stories of Faust,
King Arthur, and Griselda, these broadsides, as well as religious, edifying
treatises, constitute the (often overlooked) chief reading material of the
nineteenth-century non-educated population.

The favorite reading of the bourgeoisie, in contrast, consisted of romanticism's most popular genre, the historical novel. It was introduced by Walter Scott, continued by Ingemann and, after 1850, by Carl Brosbøll and H.
F. Ewald. Among foreign writers during this period, Balzac and Dickens
captivated the Danish reading public, but both were far surpassed in popularity by the somewhat risqué pulp adventure novels by the two French
writers Charles-Paul de Kock and Eugène Sue.

The intensive focus on national history among the Danish romantic poets received a strong impetus from the war against England in 1801–14.
This revival of patriotism coincided with the appearance of Walter Scott's
historical novels. He was the originator of this genre and the most significant foreign model for the Danish writers of national romanticism. Scott's
first historical novel, *Waverley*, was translated in the year of its publication,
1814, and within the next fifteen years more than thirty works were published in Danish. The fascination with Scott's novels, which became best
sellers all over Europe, centered on the one hand on their correctly described and colorful historical milieu, which in Denmark found resonance
in a growing domestic demand during the 1820s for minutely drawn local
and period color, and on the other hand on their dramatic characters and
events, which were fictitious and without historical foundation. Scott's
most talented Danish disciple, Ingemann, looked in vain for an "all-encompassing grand idea" in the works of his model, which he had himself discovered: the revival of ancient Danish values and virtues in order to save his
threatened country. These values Ingemann found expressed in the medieval ballads and in Saxo's chronicle, key sources for him as well as for the
other Danish national romanticists.

Adam Oehlenschläger

It is no coincidence that Hauch, both in his plays and in his poetry, paid tribute to the trend of national romanticism. Oehlenschläger with *Poetiske Skrifter* and Grundtvig with *Nordens Mythologi* were already pointing in this

direction, and even in Ingemann's youthful poetry patriotic chords are touched.

Various texts in *Digte* (1803) and *Vaulundurs Saga* (1805) signify stages in Oehlenschläger's breakthrough as a national romanticist with *Nordiske Digte* (1807; Nordic Poems). With the publication of *Poetiske Skrifter* in 1805 Oehlenschläger was regarded as the leading author in Denmark. He was awarded a royal travel stipend and spent more than four years, from 1805 to 1809, abroad. In Halle he met Henrich Steffens, a professor there since 1804; in Weimar, the much-idolized Goethe; and in Dresden, Ludwig Tieck. He arrived in Paris in the fall of 1806, where he spent more than eighteen months meeting, among others, the Schlegel brothers, and in 1809 he went, via Switzerland, to Rome. Undoubtedly, this long absence from home stimulated Oehlenschläger's feeling for Scandinavian motifs. *Nordiske Digte,* published while Oehlenschläger was still abroad, opens with the epic poem *Thors Reise til Jotunheim* (Thor's Journey to Jotunheim), the account of the thundergod's ignominious adventures and troubles with the giants, which Oehlenschläger found in Snorri Sturluson's *Prose Edda.* In spite of the Germanic meter he chose, Oehlenschläger's great model was Homer, who inspired the Dane to accentuate the "particularly national, the characteristically naive" (preface). Equally characteristic is Oehlenschläger's heroic portrayal of Thor as opposed to the ironic depiction of him in the Old Norse source.

In *Thors Reise* the giants remain only a threat, but in the volume's second work, the tragedy *Baldur hin Gode* (Baldur the Good), Oehlenschläger focuses on the crisis leading to the Twilight of the Gods. This motif he also found in the *Prose Edda,* but influenced by Schiller's fate drama, *Die Braut von Messina* (1803; The Bride of Messina), it is cast as a Greek tragedy with interspersed narrative sections and choir passages of sublime beauty. The same myth had been treated by Johannes Ewald, who described Baldur as a human being who succumbs because of hopeless love. Oehlenschläger, in contrast, calls his work "a philosophical and poetic nature allegory" (preface). It is goodness as a principle that is being defeated by evil, symbolized by the Loki character, whose punishment by the gods in return prepares the ground for their own fall. The final defeat of the pagan North forms the dramatic subject of the volume's third work, the tragedy *Hakon Jarl* (Eng. tr. 1857, 1874, 1905). The blank verse of the dialogue and the mingling of comic and tragic scenes were modeled after Shakespeare. However, Oehlenschläger's decisive source of inspiration was Schiller, whose *Wallenstein* trilogy (1800) also describes the fall of a historical character from power and glory to degradation. In Schiller's *Maria Stuart* (1801), furthermore,

Oehlenschläger found inspiration for the grandiose and decisive confrontation of the two main antagonists of the drama, an encounter that also marks the turning point in the plot. But the defeat of Hakon, representing the Old Norse pagan culture, by Norway's rightful heir to the throne, Olaf, the spokesman of expanding Christianity, is the result not of blind fate but of Hakon's abuse of power. *Hakon Jarl* shows Oehlenschläger at the zenith of his dramatic skill. It is impressive not only for the striking composition but also for the concrete and exhaustive character delineation of Hakon and Olaf, seen against the background of a historical battle between two incompatible spiritual worlds.

Oehlenschläger wrote two more tragedies during his productive years abroad. In Paris he produced *Axel og Valborg* (1810; Eng. tr. *Axel and Valborg,* 1851, 1873, 1874, 1906). The Shakespearean blank verse is combined with the style and form of classical French tragedy: the dramatic unities of time, place, and action are strictly adhered to, and the hero is placed in a conflict between his duty toward his king and passionate love for Valborg; subsequently, he follows the king in a fight in which he is killed. The tragedy successfully balances the sentimental and the heroic and became Oehlenschläger's only drama with repeated stage success. Equally fascinating, but less popular, is the tragedy *Correggio* (1811; Eng. tr. 1846, 1854), composed in Rome originally in German. Clearly, the title character's relationship with the Renaissance master Michelangelo mirrors Oehlenschläger's own attitude toward his admired model Goethe. But the play is, indeed, a more general analysis of the conflict of the artist with a callous environment that does not recognize him until after his death.

After his return to Copenhagen, Oehlenschläger was showered with recognition. In 1809 he was appointed professor of aesthetics at the University of Copenhagen, and throughout his life he received substantial financial support from the government. As Oehlenschläger increasingly became a spokesman for the bourgeois values of the eighteenth century, however, distancing himself from his flamboyant youthful romanticism, his artistic inspiration weakened. His marriage in 1810 and rapid growth of family obligations caused severe financial problems. A decrease in popular appeal was accompanied by steadily growing criticism of his writings, in particular by Baggesen and later by Johan Ludvig Heiberg, which divided the Danish Parnassus into two polemizing camps. But the ensuing hectic productivity—poetry as well as a steady stream of plays, mostly with Nordic motifs—could not conceal a significant artistic decline. The so-called Baggesen Feud began in 1813 and lasted for seven years. If Baggesen in the beginning was objective and somewhat justified in pointing to Oehlenschläger's growing predilection for sentimentality, already noticeable in *Correggio,* he soon lapsed into direct persiflage. His attacks provoked, for instance, Poul M. Møller and Hauch to step forward in defense of Oehlenschläger, while Grundtvig sided with Baggesen. Later Heiberg assumed the role of defender of good taste and elegant form, attacking the numerous epic elements in Oehlenschläger's dramas.

The one masterpiece during this period of uneven productivity is *Helge* (1814), consisting of two cycles of poems—the first in Danish literature—and a one-act tragedy, "Yrsa." Oehlenschläger juxtaposes two brothers: Helge, the viking and warrior, and Hroar, the peace-loving organizer of the Danish nation. Helge sets the plot in motion through murder and rape and thus inflicts tragic guilt on himself. In "Yrsa" he is punished by unknowingly marrying his own daughter, the title figure, and, after the disclosure, by taking his own life. As in *Digte* and *Aladdin*—the highlights, with *Helge,* of Oehlenschläger's lyrical writings—the two cycles display an exceptional command of various metrical forms, mainly Germanic meters, and an impeccable stylistic sense, whereas "Yrsa," in its inexorable pursuit of Helge's tragic destiny, stands out as the most perfect Danish variant of Greek tragedy. Indeed, Oehlenschläger has succeeded in uniting the flamboyant inspiration and sensuousness of his youthful works with the classical demand for moderation and discipline. *Helge* became a source of inspiration both for Esaias Tegnér's *Frithiofs saga,* (1825; Frithiof's Saga), and, to a lesser degree, for J. L. Runeberg's *Kung Fjalar,* (1844; King Fjalar), the two major epic poems in Swedish and Finnish literature, respectively.

Helge and Hroar represent passionate forcefulness and wisdom respectively. To display the union of these two qualities Oehlenschläger added a prose story, *Hroars Saga* (1817; Hroar's Saga), and another epic poem, *Hrolf Krake* (1828). Hrolf is the son of Helge and Yrsa, and not until his death, which means the extinction of the entire family, are Helge's crimes atoned for. Oehlenschläger has thus written a trilogy, undoubtedly inspired by Sophocles' *Oedipus,* which constitutes a harmonized classicist exemplification of Fr. Schlegel's concept of *Universalpoesie,* which incorporates all literary genres.

Whereas the epic cycle *Nordens Guder* (1819; Eng. tr. *The Gods of the North,* 1845) marks a successful return to Oehlenschläger's early mythological writings, his historical dramas from the 1820s and 1830s give evidence of a steadily growing attempt to harmonize the tragic conflict. His works became colored by sentimentality, as criticized by Baggesen. The character delineation is executed without nuances, and the goodness of the title characters, as in *Dronning Margareta* (1834; Queen Margareta) and *Sokrates* (1836), always prevails.

Certainly, Oehlenschläger did not share Hauch's fundamental doubts about the perfection of humankind, nor was he able to match the psychological subtleties of the playwright who completely dominated the stage during these years, Henrik Hertz.

Not until the 1840s did Oehlenschläger regain some of his former popularity. With plays such as *Dina* (1842) and *Kiartan og Gudrun* (1848; Kiartan and Gudrun) he paid tribute to the decade's demand for character development and a more complex psychology. Both dramas were successful on the stage. The first, warmly praised by Heiberg, is a heartfelt defense for the unique individual's rights against a petty-bourgeois environment, and it marks a return to the young Oehlenschläger's advocacy of the artistic genius. The latter, based on the Icelandic *Laxdæla saga,* is permeated with color and compassion, reflecting the aging poet's infatuation with a young woman.

Undoubtedly, Oehlenschläger was at his greatest for only a ten-year period. But although he was often criticized or even ignored in his native country, he was celebrated in Norway and Sweden. Not until his seventieth birthday did Oehlenschläger receive deserved recognition by his own countrymen. After his death he was once again downgraded by critics who took their point of departure in the weakest works of this immensely productive author. Nevertheless, in only a few years he had been able to renew all aspects of Danish belles lettres by intuitively grasping significant concepts of German romanticism and giving this foreign spiritual force a Danish breakthrough. Oehlenschläger had one of the strongest linguistic and stylistic impacts on posterity of all Danish writers, as demonstrated and recognized by the two great innovators of twentieth-century Danish poetry, Johannes V. Jensen and Klaus Rifbjerg.

Bernhard Severin Ingemann

On Ingemann's return from his Italian journey the external world became of significantly greater importance in his writings, as is evident in his collection of descriptive travel poems, *Reiselyren* (1820; The Travel Lyre). At the same time, Grundtvig, who was in the midst of his attempt to revive "the national ethos," in the first part of his translation of Saxo's chronicle urged Ingemann to give poetic life to Denmark's Middle Ages. So when Ingemann in 1822 became lecturer in Danish literature at the Sorø Academy—an idyllic place full of historical monuments—he felt ready to follow Grundtvig's suggestion. His poetic fantasy was then concretized in time and space with a series of historical novels. These became popular reading for the next hundred years and were of particular importance in strengthening the feeling of national identity during the Dano-German war of 1848–50.

Contrary to Walter Scott's novels, which were intended solely for entertainment, Ingemann's novels form a national chronicle with a single didactic purpose, to which, as always in his writings, is added a religious tendency. His program is contained in the introductory epic cycle *Waldemar den Store og hans Mænd* (1824; Valdemar the Great and His Men), in which he states: "What Denmark has once been, it can become once again, / the spirit of our forefathers is still alive." That clearly expresses Ingemann's intent to teach the nation how to relate to the present age by pointing to its past, to the Middle Ages, when Denmark was a great nation because of the union between State and Church rooted in faith in God—the true Golden Age. The dualism of Ingemann's youthful works is present in this concept: the world is seen as a battle between good and evil forces, and frequently the characters of his novels are either stylized heroes or villains. The story starts out in a time of decline and dissolution but is, through battle and heroic deeds, brought to a harmonious conclusion with metaphysical overtones. Ingemann pays attention neither to the correctness of the scenery nor to historical objectivity. His only concern is history's impact on the collective consciousness of the nation or, to be more precise, the process of decline and regeneration of contemporary Denmark after the catastrophes of the Napoleonic Wars.

The first of the novels, *Valdemar Seier* (1826; Eng. tr. *Waldemar, surnamed Seir, or the Victorious,* 1841), opens with a scene permeated with ambience, portraying Saxo—whose chronicle, together with the medieval historical ballads, is Ingemann's main source—working at his desk. Then follows an overview of the entire kingdom of Denmark, and not until one-third of the way into the novel is the title character introduced. Like the heroes in Ingemann's youthful writings, he is a person divided between demonic and ideal forces, which are subsequently projected onto his two queens, the angelic Dagmar and the erotically alluring Berengaria. In the next volumes, *Erik Menveds Barndom* (1828; Eng. tr. *The Childhood of Erik Menved,* 1846) and *Kong Erik og de Fredløse* (1833; Eng. tr. *King Eric and the Outlaws,* 1843), character analysis is eclipsed by a sweeping historical canvas, executed rather splendidly in the tradition of Walter Scott. The first novel deals with a period of decline and disintegration following one of Danish history's most dramatic events, the murder of the title character's father, King Erik Klipping, by rebellious squires. This situation Ingemann traces back to the former King Valdemar, who had neglected his obligations as ruler in favor of the selfish role of warrior and hero. It now becomes the task of King Erik Menved in the novel from 1833 to remedy this situation, a task in which he is not successful. *Prins Otto af Danmark* (1835; Prince Otto of Denmark), Ingemann's last, and largely undervalued, historical novel, also opens at point zero. With intensity and forcefulness the inner dualism of the title character is projected onto the historical events themselves: the hostile German invaders versus the attempts to restore national independence. To further this process, Prince Otto relinquishes his right to the throne and, in Ingemann's interpretation, emerges as a true Christian hero, a martyr. Ingemann has been unjustly criticized for stereotypization of his characters and their speech. First of all, these critics have not taken the overall ideological purpose of these volumes into consideration; second, within this framework Ingemann's attempts at psychological differentiation are remarkable when examined together with the contemporaneous novels of, for instance, Scott and Cooper. Compared with the prose of Hauch and Oehlenschläger, his style is supple and eloquent, a perfect medium for an exciting and entertaining plot.

After concluding his medieval project, Ingemann created a synthesis of its ideas in a cycle of poems called *Holger Danske* (1837; Holger the Dane), the mythical hero from the medieval French *Chanson de Roland,* who was also portrayed in a Danish chapbook published in 1534. This chapbook was still popular in folk tradition and served as Ingemann's source. Holger embodies the Danish national ethos but in a timeless, mythic realm. Like the related hero Viduvelt in *De sorte Riddere,* Holger is a symbol of goodness, faithfulness, and courage. At the same time, he represents a dream about love, which, however, cannot be fulfilled, either in his pagan home or in the service of Charlemagne of France. Holger realizes the futility of his dream in the fifth and last part of the cycle, which Ingemann characteristically entitles "Gjenoplivelsen" (The Resurrection). This realization results not in resignation but in an awareness of the insignificance of this life as opposed to the splendor of eternity. Thus Ingemann in this flawless masterpiece—whose richly varied emotional shifts are masterfully mirrored in the melodious meters—transgressed the boundaries of national romanticism and returned to the metaphysical world of universal romanticism.

This world also forms the underlying basis even when Ingemann takes on a more pragmatic task. In 1822 he had been asked to write seven hymns for the students at Sorø, and then, in 1837, came the high point of Ingemann's hymn writing: the volume *Morgensange for Børn* (Morning Songs for Children) followed by *Syv Aftensange* (1838; Seven Evening Songs). Because of the inherent poetic quality of these texts as well as the appealing tunes by C. E. F. Weyse, they found an enthusiastic audience. With other hymns, such as "Fred hviler over Land og By" (1823; Peace Rests over Country and Town),

"Den store Mester kommer" (1825; The Great Master Comes), and the Christmas hymn "Julen har bragt velsignet Bud" (1842; Christmas Has Brought Blessed Tidings), they are among the treasures of not only the official Danish church hymnal, but of all Danish lyrical poetry. In terms of both meter and phraseology these poems distinguish themselves by their simplicity and naturalness. Rather than being congregational hymns, they make up a strictly personal confessional poetry, based on observations of nature and impressions of everyday situations. We are made familiar with even the smallest detail, but then suddenly Ingemann opens up the cosmic dimensions of universal romanticism:

> In the deeps of celestial streams
> the night now sinks its wing;
> resplendent with stars it gleams,
> and the harps of heaven sing.
> (Tr. Alan Bower)

Not only Holger the Dane, but all of us are merely exiles on earth. Even though God's love is all-encompassing, the Biedermeier idyll is not necessarily permanent:

> Be with us, the day is dying,
> our God and Father of light!
> Be with us when floods of darkness
> break through the gates of night!
> (Tr. S. D. Rodholm)

Ingemann's consistent dualism also manifested itself in his later writings. Again, it is possible to draw a line from his early fascination with Gothic effects to later short stories with self-explanatory titles, such as "Den levende Døde" (The Living Dead) and "Varulven" (The Werewolf) in the collection *Tre Fortællinger* (1835; Three Stories), fantasies, also inspired by E. T. A. Hoffmann's tales of the grotesque, about a world dominated by mysterious, demonic, and macabre events. Gradually, however, and particularly because of the impact of the war of 1848–50, Ingemann's prose moved toward greater realism, depicting contemporary society, a trend culminating in the large-scale novel *Landsbybørnene* (1852; The Village Children). Once again we are confronted with a Holger the Dane figure, but this time the paradise dream is fulfilled in this earthly life. Although Ingemann's ideology is thus a contribution to the realistic taste of the time, he still employs the romantic genre of the artist's novel. With elements from his own life and Hans Christian Andersen's—*Landsbybørnene* is very much related to Andersen's novels

Improvisatoren and *Kun en Spillemand*—Ingemann portrays a great natural talent, the poorhouse boy Anton, and recounts his development into a famous flutist who, on his celebrated tours abroad, does not give in to the temptations of a successful career as a virtuoso but is constantly reminded of the true treasures hidden in the plain but genuine Danish folk songs and ballads and consequently returns home.

Ingemann had no problem identifying himself with Denmark's increasing nationalism. He was also aware of the growing demand for democracy and was able to reconcile this trend with his truly romantic outlook. That is seen in his last novel, whose hero, after all, is a direct descendant of Oehlenschläger's Aladdin. Nevertheless, like Hans Christian Andersen, Ingemann could not reconcile himself with the emerging trend toward atheism and materialism, against which he turned on the philosophical level in the poetic cycle *Ahasverus* (1833), whose title character's homelessness he could identify with, on the satirical level with his dramatic poem *Renegaten* (1830; The Renegade), and finally on the theological level in the poem with the thought-provoking title *Tankebreve fra en Afdød* (1855; Philosophical Letters from a Deceased). This description of his soul's pilgrimage through purgatory toward eternity is a spiritual work that both in its satire and in its metaphysics points forward to Paludan-Müller's epic poem *Adam Homo*. *Tankebreve* is Ingemann's last work of importance, and it forms a remarkable conclusion to one of the most undervalued but nevertheless most fascinating authors in Danish romanticism.

Nicolai Frederik Severin Grundtvig

Grundtvig continued his earlier attempts at reconciling paganism and Christianity, past and present in the dramatic poem *Optrin af Kiempelivets Undergang i Nord* (1809; Scenes from the Decline of Heroism in the North). But a significant shift took place in its continuation, *Optrin af Norners og Asers Kamp* (1811; Scenes from the Battle between the Norns and the Gods), in which he lets the heroes from the *Völsunga saga* be converted to Christianity. Grundtvig's transition from romantic to Christian polemicist was caused by a religious crisis in 1810, when he was asked to serve as a curate for his ailing father. From that point on he abandoned the romantic philosophy of nature and chose Christianity as the constant center of his life.

At the same time, Grundtvig's view of history underwent a change. He still saw its course as an organic coherence but only because of God's intention. In his *Kort Begreb af Verdens Krønike* (1812; Brief Concept of the World's Chronicle), in which he acknowledges his indebtedness to Steffens's concept of history, the incarnation of Christ is seen as the absolute central event in world history, and a nation's future is viewed as totally dependent on its acceptance of the Christian message. Thus, in Grundtvig's rhymed history of Denmark, *Roskilde-Riim* (1814; The Roskilde Rhymes), the country's political periods of glory are seen to run parallel with periods of strong faith. In several inserted romances, such as "Bisp Villum og Kong Svend" (Bishop Villum and King Svend), the king is always depicted as submitting to the representative of the Church. Grundtvig saw himself as the herald of these views, as a prophet, whose task it was to restore Christian values and an alliance between State and Church.

At the same time, he launched the first of several strong attacks on prominent theologians, who in his eyes were attempting to adapt the Bible to a rationalist viewpoint. These attacks caused a scandal. Grundtvig received no incumbency and had to earn his living as a free-lance writer in Copenhagen. His isolation and strong convictions are demonstrated by his medieval mystery play, *Paaske-Lilien* (1816–17; The Easter Lily), written in blank verse. It treats the Resurrection of Christ and various reactions to it: the lily symbolizes not only the Resurrection but also the revival of Christianity in nineteenth-century Denmark and finally Grundtvig's own awakening as a poet and a Christian. During this time he also tried to make his ideas from *Kort Begreb af Verdens Krønike* useful in a practical way. He regarded the years of hardship after the Napoleonic Wars as a trial sent by God and wished to encourage his countrymen by bringing alive Denmark's heritage. The vehicle for these efforts to heighten national consciousness was his journal *Danne-Virke* (1816–19; the title is a place-name, literally "Danes' Bulwark"), containing poems and essays on historical topics, as well as his translations of Snorri Sturluson's *Heimskringla* (1818–22; The Orb of the World) and Saxo's *Gesta Danorum* (1818–22; The Deeds of the Danes), both in a deliberately popular style.

Around 1817 Grundtvig's personal situation greatly improved. He received financial support from the royal court, and so in 1818 he could marry Lise Blicher, the first of his three wives. In 1821 he received a position in southern Zealand and the following year a curacy in Copenhagen. Grundtvig resumed his battle against the rationalist theologians of the state church with increased vigor. Manic-depressive, he was thrown into a spiritual crisis. It led to a discovery of God's "living word," found not in the Bible but in the creed of the primitive Church and to which we are introduced through baptism, handed down in an unbroken chain from Christ himself via the Apostles. This crisis is described in obscure, prophetic visions in the autobiographical poem *Nyaars-Morgen* (1824; New Year's Morning) with symbolic use of Nordic legend and mythology. For some time Grundtvig vacillated between despair and hope, as expressed in the poem "De Levendes Land" (ca. 1824; The Land of the Living), where he uses the meter from Kingo's "Far Verden, far vel." He does not focus on the gulf between heaven and earth, as Kingo did; on the contrary, God's love bridges this gulf, and happiness can be found in this life.

After this "superb discovery" (Grundtvig's terminology)—that it is not the written word in the Bible but the living word given to us through baptism and the Eucharist which confirms and concludes God's covenant with humanity—Grundtvig's subsequent writing follows two paths: one is strictly Christian, expressing itself in the writing of church hymns, and the other takes a popular and pedagogic direction. Grundtvig's hymns, about fourteen hundred in number, half of which are translations and adaptations, were published in *Sang-Værk til den danske Kirke* (1837–81; Collection of Songs for the Danish Church, 1–5), giving him the most prominent position among the other great hymn writers in Danish literature, Kingo, Brorson, and Ingemann. Grundtvig's hymns all have their origin in an existential experience of faith and mission. Unlike the hymns of Kingo and Brorson, they are not based on the concepts of sin and grace, nor do they have moral edification as a goal. And in contrast to those of Ingemann they are clearly intended to strengthen the faith of the *congregation* through Christian fellowship and, through this fellowship, to overcome the fear of death and confirm the hope of resurrection. Grundtvig's first distinctive hymn is the Christmas hymn "Deilig er den Himmel blaa" (1811; Glorious Is the Blue Sky). In this early stage he often used hymns from the Reformation as his source of inspiration. His favorite period, however, was the Middle Ages and its Latin hymns, which inspired him to write "Et Barn er født i Bethlehem" (1820; A Child Was Born in Bethlehem), together with his own "Velkommen igen, Guds Engle smaa" (1825; Welcome Again, God's Little Angels) among the most popular Danish Christmas hymns. The culmination of Grundtvig's hymn writing took place in the 1830s, a decade in which he successfully rewrote some Hebrew, Greek, and Anglo-Saxon religious poems, in which he combines imagery from the Old Testament and descriptions of Danish nature in a unique and convincing manner.

Grundtvig's hymns are forceful and original. They range from the intimate idyll to the prophetic vision. They combine the sublime with everyday situations and are based on a predilection for local color occasionally lapsing into platitude. For church festivals, such as Christmas and especially Pentecost, he wrote a number of splendid hymns, such as the majestic "I al sin Glands nu straaler Solen" (1843; The Sun Now Shines in All Its Splendor). But like Ingemann, he was also able to mirror the infinite in the finite, as in

"Alt hvad som Fuglevinger fik" (1851; All That Which Soars in Upward Flight):

> All that which soars in upward flight,
> and wings its way toward the light
> with notes of joyous singing,
> give praise to God, for good is He
> and by His grace will set that free
> which still to dust is clinging.
>
> My soul, your thought and living word
> are like a young and mighty bird
> with happy songs ascending;
> your breath is always free and strong
> when you express yourself in song
> in praise of God unending.
> (Tr. P. C. Clausen and P. Balslev-Clausen)

Grundtvig's pedagogical thoughts were formulated for the first time in his introduction to the revised edition of *Nordens Mythologi* (1832; Nordic Mythology). This work was occasioned by three trips to England in 1829–31, during which time Grundtvig also laid the foundation for international Beowulf research. In England he received lasting and highly positive impressions of the laissez-faire ideology of liberalism, which, however, was balanced by his fear of a possible dehumanization through industrialization. It was in order to create the condition for a well-balanced and harmonious human development that Grundtvig suggested the establishment of "a school for life," devoid of learning by rote and theoretical knowledge and related to practical life through dialogue between student and teacher. This basic human education may then lead to a realization of Christianity, for, as expressed by Grundtvig, "first a human being, then a Christian."

Built into Grundtvig's program is a democratic revolt against all forms of authoritarianism. The key concept is freedom, and the goal is a common national culture instead of the ruling academic liberalism. Grundtvig expresses these beliefs in various patriotic songs, such as the programmatic "Et jævnt og muntert virksomt Liv paa Jord" (1839; A Plain and Active, Joyful Life on Earth). This song became a favorite in the growing folk high school movement, which in 1844 established its first institution at Rødding—immediately copied in the other Scandinavian countries—based on Grundtvig's views about adult education, which have had a major impact on modern pedagogy. This movement, named "Grundtvigianism," remains a predominant factor in Danish spiritual life because of its optimistic view of life, its concentration on national and historical values, and its rejection of orthodoxy. Thus, both the student rebellion in the 1960s and the fight against Denmark's joining the EEC in the 1970s could cite Grundtvig in support of their cause.

POETIC REALISM; OR, THE BIEDERMEIER IDYLL

Shortly before his death in 1838 Poul Martin Møller wrote a poem entitled "Kunstneren mellem Oprørerne" (The Artist among the Rebels). It constitutes a plaidoyer of the independence of the artist from any political currents of the day and expresses Møller's deep concern with the French July Revolution of 1830 and its possible repercussions in Denmark. At the same time, the poem is a strong defense for an idealistic and harmonious world view that mirrors the domestic political calm and general optimism in the years after the Napoleonic Wars.

Indeed, the July Revolution did shake up political affairs both domestically and externally, and precisely fifty years after the cession of Norway, Denmark suffered a new territorial loss. During the 1830s demands grew louder in the two German-oriented duchies of Schleswig and Holstein, which since the Middle Ages had been in union with Denmark, for a new liberal constitution and unification with the German League, disregarding the fact that the population in northern Schleswig still spoke Danish. The tension increased under King Christian VIII (1839–48). Initially, a group of young Copenhagen middle-class intellectuals, calling themselves the National Liberals, attempted to diffuse the tension by suggesting a closer affiliation between Denmark and only Schleswig, but in the wake of the February Revolution in Paris in 1848 a plan to confirm this affiliation through a new constitution led to open revolt, supported by Prussia. The ensuing war, from 1848 to 1850, which led to Jutland's periodic occupation by German troops, ended initially with a Danish victory. Because of a fatal Danish miscalculation of the political situation, however, fighting was resumed in 1864 against superior Prussian and Austrian forces. Denmark lost both duchies: in all, two-fifths of her territory and one-third of her population of two and a half million.

Domestically, the February Revolution strengthened the liberal opposition, which until 1848 had only slowly gained momentum. The only other political force in Denmark had been the movement of Scandinavianism, which, however, was strictly limited to academic circles. Thus, during a meeting in 1839 Grundtvig had proposed a common Nordic university located in Gothenburg. This plan was never realized, and Scandinavianism on the whole remained an idealistic—sometimes almost hysterical—dream of Nordic unity providing themes for poets but never getting beyond rhetorical inebriation: during a festival at the newly founded Tivoli Gardens in 1845 no fewer than 247 speeches were given on the subject!

Politically, it was a much more significant sign of the new times when C. N. David, publisher of the first oppositional newspaper, *Fædrelandet* (The Fatherland), founded in 1834, was acquitted on a charge of conspiracy; similar democratic voices had been silenced earlier. In 1834 consultative assemblies were set up, primarily representing the wealthy landowners and the bourgeoisie, but with a growing number of farmers demanding the liquidation of the last remnants of their old dependence on landowners. The main object of all the agitation, however, was a free constitution, and a large demonstration outside the Royal Palace on March 21, 1848, persuaded King Frederik VII (1848–63) to appoint a new cabinet of National Liberals. One year later, without any bloodshed, the absolute monarchy was replaced by a democratic constitution.

The political change was accompanied by economic rather than social reforms. Important agricultural measures did increase the social status of the farmer, but the upper middle class still occupied all positions in the state church, the University of Copenhagen, and the administration. Thus, at the election in 1852 the first Copenhagen Socialist candidate received merely 109 votes. Only slowly did the position of women improve, with the introduction of equality in hereditary rights in 1857, the employment of the first female teacher in Copenhagen in 1861, and occasional demands for suffrage. This emancipatory process was furthered by a heated debate in the press and the literature of the day.

The National Liberal party, which dominated Danish politics until 1864, concentrated its reform efforts on modernizing the economic system through abolishing the medieval guild system in 1857 and relinquishing the widespread commercial monopolies, thereby preparing for the industrial revolution of the 1870s. To revitalize commerce, steamship lines and railroads were built to boost the cattle and grain exports to England and shift the trade routes away from Holstein and Hamburg, the dominating trade center of northern Europe.

The defeat of 1864 dealt a final blow to all dreams of political power, and any thought of revenge was put to rest with the German victory over France in 1871. In reaction, all efforts were turned toward the economic reconstruction of the country. This orientation toward concrete, everyday problems had already been anticipated in Danish literature through a general movement away from national and historical romanticism toward a greater focus on period and local color.

This development is noticeable in the shift of scene in Ingemann's novels from the Middle Ages to his own time and in Grundtvig's introduction of the folk high school movement. In fact, this process had been anticipated with Poul Martin Møller's fragmentary novella *En dansk Students Eventyr* (1824; publ. 1843; The Adventures of a Danish Student). Through the author's attack on artificiality, sentimentality, and affectation, portrayed in the character of an eccentric pedant, this work constitutes a general settling of accounts with precisely these elements in the romantic literature of the day. Through its contemporary, realistically depicted everyday scenery and the portrayal of its protagonist, the dynamic and spontaneous student Frits and his pranks in the Zealand countryside, the novella constitutes a perfect paradigm of the school of poetic realism.

According to one of the most prolific representatives of this poetic realism, Henrik Hertz, the task of literature was to render "a clearer but not refined picture" of nature and human existence, to be executed with an elegant taste and a polished sense of form and style. The writer must portray a world that is devoid of extreme viewpoints and that develops according to set rules with due respect to traditional values. There is a predilection for everyday situations, scenes from a secure childhood and idyllic family life, and the characteristic detail. Even with regard to genre the writers favor the small forms: the romance, the singspiel, and the short story. Social problems are ignored or underplayed, political issues rarely dealt with, and even the concept of God becomes idyllized. In general, the writers have no philosophical problems in reconciling the ideal with reality, the supernatural with the worldly. Obviously, such a concerted effort at harmonization could lead to superficiality and simple materialism, which, however, were strictly rejected by the writers of the time and attacked as being inane and Philistine.

Poul Martin Møller
In his poem from 1838, "Kunstneren mellem Oprørerne," in which the revolutionary mob threatens to destroy the works of a sculptor—a portrait combining features from Goethe and Thorvaldsen—Poul Martin Møller (1794–1838) demarcated himself ideologically against any political upheaval in the wake of the July Revolution of 1830. Another poem by Møller, "Glæde over Danmark" (1823; Joy about Denmark), precisely exemplifies the poetics of the time with its patriotic feeling and longing for domestic idyll.

The poem was sent home from the Philippines during a voyage in 1819–21, on which Møller served as a ship's chaplain. After his return he became a teacher of classics in Copenhagen, until in 1826 he received a lectureship in philosophy at the University of Christiania in Norway, and in 1831 he was appointed professor at the University of Copenhagen.

Møller's artistic and philosophical ideals are rooted in Oehlenschläger's and Goethe's idealism, to which must be added a lifelong dedication to classical literature. Møller's own insistence on the uncompromising integrity of the individual led to a psychological preoccupation that turns most of his literary figures into character types. In this way his writings constitute a sharp reaction against the contemporary works of *romantisme* with its strong interest in the split personality and its mood of spleen and irony inspired, in particular, by Byron and Heine.

Møller's psychological orientation made him a brilliant satirist, who eagerly participated in literary feuds; for instance, he vigorously defended Oehlenschläger against Baggesen's attacks. Thus, it is characteristic that although the plot of *En dansk Students Eventyr* is only sketchy and loosely structured, its character delineations are extremely precise with regard to psychological insight. And the various poems, published as *Scener i Rosenborg Have* (1820–21; publ. 1855; Scenes from Rosenborg Garden), consist of psychological snapshots, displaying a strong sense for characteristic detail, executed in a subdued and sometimes humorous tone: an old, impractical pedant (a contrast to Frits of the novella), a beggar, a reconvalescent and his experience of the Danish summer, and the teenaged couple Hans and Trine. The last poem, a dialogue, was performed at the Court Theater in 1826 with a certain Miss Pätges as Trine, on which occasion she was "discovered" by her later husband, the writer and critic J. L. Heiberg.

Møller published very little himself and was notoriously sloppy with his manuscripts. To him, writing was primarily a means of self-realization. Frequently, he limited himself to writing down his observations in concise and pointed aphorisms (1819–36). Most of his early aphorisms are psychological. They analyze and attack affectation as perverting human naturalness. In Møller's later years, in particular after his wife's death in 1834, his focus became increasingly philosophical, showing a shift from a speculative outlook—inspired by the German philosopher Friedrich Hegel—to a firm Christian belief in immortality. This move from abstract philosophical speculation to the existential situation of the individual is demonstrated in Møller's essay *Tanker over Muligheden af Beviser for Menneskets Udødelighed* (1837; Thoughts about the Possibility of Proving Man's Immortality). Through this definitive rejection of Hegel, Møller became an important precursor of his friend and student Søren Kierkegaard and the latter's rebellion against romanticism.

Johan Ludvig Heiberg

The Hegelian philosophy, which Møller so strongly reacted against, initially found a strong advocate in the leading critic of the time, Johan Ludvig Heiberg (1791–1860). He, too, was firmly rooted in romantic idealism and shared Møller's concern for the disintegrating trends of the zeitgeist, but at the same time he was aware of the inherent banality of the Biedermeier culture.

With his wife, Johanne Luise, nee Pätges (1812–90), the leading Danish actress of the nineteenth century, whom he married in 1831, Heiberg dominated the cultural life in Denmark during the 1830s and 1840s. After receiving his doctoral degree in 1817 with a dissertation on the Spanish dramatist Calderón, Heiberg lived in Paris from 1819 to 1822, visiting—and living off—his exiled father, the writer P. A. Heiberg, and seeing for the first time the popular, light comedies by Casimir Delavigne and Eugène Scribe, the so-called vaudevilles. Scribe, in particular, became the all-time favorite playwright of the theater of *romantisme*. His masterly treatment of pointed dialogue and well-tailored intrigue became a model for Scandinavian dramatists up to and including Henrik Ibsen. In 1822–25 Heiberg was a lecturer in Danish language and literature at the University of Kiel, and from 1828 he was employed as a dramatic adviser and translator at the Royal Theater in Copenhagen. After his marriage to Johanne Luise their home became the chief rendezvous for the literary and cultural elite, the closest Danish counterpart to the French salon.

Philosophically, Heiberg was a pure idealist. In 1824 he discovered the theories of the German speculative philosopher Friedrich Hegel, in whose dialectic system everything incompatible becomes reconciled in the absolute spirit, that is, God. Based on Hegel, Heiberg devised a system of literary genres, in which the lyrical is placed on the lowest level, followed by the epic and finally by the dramatic genre. These main genres are then further subdivided, and the vaudeville, which synthesizes poetry and music, becomes the highest form of drama and the model for future Danish comedy. This genre Heiberg analyzed in the treatise *Om Vaudevillen* (1826; About Vaudeville). Here as well as in his *Kjøbenhavns flyvende Post* (1827–28, 1830, 1834–37; The Copenhagen Flying Mail), the most prolific literary journal of the period, Heiberg developed his aesthetic program. He fiercely attacked materialistic trends in contemporary thought. At the same time, he aimed his criticism at all traces of sentimentality, as well as—in the spirit of Baggesen—the tendencies toward the dissolution of formal strictness in early romanticism. Heiberg's favorite target was Oehlenschläger, whom he denied any real dramatic talent. This criticism, expressed in a hitherto unseen elegant prose, was strongly opposed by older writers such as Carsten

Hauch and Christian Winther. In the years 1827–30 it provoked the so-called Three-Year War, which ended with Heiberg's victory.

The highly polemical Heiberg did not participate in the earlier Baggesen Feud. But in 1817 he had launched his first literary attack with his play *Julespøg og Nytaarsløier* (Christmas Fun and New Year's Jesting), a parody of German fate drama in general and Ingemann's Gothic romanticism and sentimentality in particular. Through the work's skillfully executed play with illusion, it stands out as the most convincing Danish example of romantic irony. *Julespøg* clearly displays Heiberg's dramatic skill, and during the following years—under the strong influence of the French vaudeville and the German singspiel, which he had encountered abroad—Heiberg created the Danish vaudeville tradition. The distinctive features of this musical comedy are a light and sprightly intrigue, a simple character delineation, and a fusion of dialogue and music, letting the dramatic climax find its resolution in songs with melodies from well-known operas and operettas or, for instance, by the Swedish rococo poet Carl Michael Bellman and Heiberg himself.

Heiberg's first vaudeville was *Kong Salomon og Jørgen Hattemager* (1825; King Solomon and Jørgen the Hatter). The plot is centered on the mistaken identity of a penniless Jew and his rich namesake, to which is added the obligatory love intrigue. The easygoing tone and superficial character offended several critics. One of them was K. L. Rahbek, a member of the board of directors of the Royal Theater, who regarded the play as inappropriate for the theater. The audience was completely carried away, however, and the play became a box-office hit. During the next ten years Heiberg wrote more vaudevilles, which made him, with Hertz, the leading dramatist of the period. For his future wife he created the leading female part in *Aprilsnarrene* (1826; April Fools), which, employing a somewhat more complex intrigue, mildly satirizes the haphazard nature of the pedagogical methods in schools for girls. *Recensenten og Dyret* (1826; The Critic and the Animal), in contrast, is structured around a rather thin love story, but it contains a fierce attack on dilettantism and snobbery, on that type of critic and journalist who, without the necessary competence, writes only for money. This satirical tendency—and his way of getting back at Rahbek—points ahead to Heiberg's successor in the vaudeville genre, J. C. Hostrup. *Nei* (1836; No) concludes Heiberg's series of vaudevilles. The centrally placed love intrigue is based on different pronunciations of the word "no," an elegant linguistic joke, performed against the background of a dramatic contrast between young lovers and the materialistic bourgeoisie, an obvious attack on the trivialities of the Biedermeier culture.

With great success Heiberg was able to preserve an ingenious balance between romantic fantasy and external reality in a number of large-scale plays. On the occasion of the wedding of the later King Frederik VII in 1828 he wrote the play *Elverhøi* (Elfinhill), with captivating music by Frederik Kuhlau, which is based partly on traditional Scandinavian folk tunes. The complex intrigue, which in a romantic fashion includes folk belief and legend, is solved when the historical figure, King Christian IV, intervenes into this supernatural world and unravels the mystery of a changeling. Heiberg's character delineation is rather sketchy, and the dramatic tension is primarily released through the music. Nevertheless, by involving all three art forms of the Royal Theater—drama, opera, and ballet—Heiberg created an amalgamation, which produces an extraordinary stage effect and has become an overwhelming success as a national festival play, performed more frequently than any other Danish drama.

Contrary to *Elverhøi,* in the fairy-tale play *Alferne* (1835; The Elves), based on a tale by Tieck, the poetic world of the fairies wins over skeptical materialism, poetry over prose. Similarly, the lovers in the play *Syvsoverdag* (1840; Seven Sleepers Day) are removed from petty-bourgeois present time, since it is only in the world of poetry that a recognition of true reality can take place.

In the 1830s this abstract discussion of illusion versus reality, together with a mounting criticism of the middle class to which Heiberg himself belonged, led to a discussion of the question of the identity of the personality itself and its relationship to the finite and the infinite which clearly points beyond Hegel's depersonalized, objective system. Under the influence of the leading theologian (and later bishop) Hans L. Martensen, Heiberg took an increasing interest in Christianity and consequently incorporated Christian ideas in his collection *Nye Digte* (1841; New Poems), his principal work. Its main piece, the satirical comedy *En Sjæl efter Døden* (Eng. tr. *A Soul after Death,* 1991), unmasks the philistinism and insipidities of the time, against which Heiberg calls for an attitude dedicated to ethics and truth. The "soul," a deceased petty bourgeois, can pass neither Saint Peter's entrance examination nor that of Aristophanes at classical Elysium; he feels perfectly at home in Hell, however, where he can continue his fatuous earthly existence. The inoffensive irony of Heiberg's vaudevilles has changed into a strong attack on self-centeredness and mediocrity, which concludes in a demand for an ethically accountable attitude toward life. In that context the play is a major work in the ethical and religious debate of the 1840s and a brilliant counterpart to Paludan-Müller's epic poem *Adam Homo*. The volume's introductory dialogue in verse, *Gudstjeneste* (Divine Service), presents the same message. It centers on a poet who, instead of devoting himself to a pantheistic worship of nature, learns to accept Christianity's teaching of brotherly love. In the romance cycle *De Nygifte* (The Newlywed) Heiberg focuses on this sense of responsibility. A man falls in love with a newly wed young woman and plans to kill her husband. Suddenly he realizes that in a previous life he has committed a similar crime. He changes his mind and thus renounces the woman he loves. This self-reflection through renunciation is discussed on a more abstract level in the final text, *Protestantismen i Naturen* (Protestantism in Nature). Here Heiberg returns to the volume's introductory poem. He rejects nature's divinity and allows the individual personality to realize God through a continuous striving for truth and an act of renunciation of the material world. *Nye Digte* is a profound philosophical work, permeated with a unique spirituality. Apart from the comedy, it is not very accessible, and in spite of its metrical elegance it was neither appreciated nor understood by the author's contemporaries. Consequently, one of Heiberg's last works, the satirical comedy *Nøddeknækkerne* (1845; The Nutcrackers), was aimed at his critics and at the Copenhagen petty-bourgeois audience in general. The attack on the present, however, like the corresponding satirical parts of *En Sjæl efter Døden* written in an Aristophanic tone, is balanced by some lyrical hymns that constitute the zenith of Heiberg's lyrical poetry. Nowhere in his extensive oeuvre is Heiberg's demand for aesthetical and philosophical clarity and balance more convincingly articulated than in this comedy's cosmic visions. With their point of departure in an atmosphere of autumn and death they are directed toward the universe and an eternity in which the poet increasingly—like his contemporary Carsten Hauch—felt at home.

In his later years Heiberg devoted his time to astronomical studies and only occasionally returned to writing. At the same time, he also became increasingly occupied with administrative tasks. In 1828, after the successful performance of *Elverhøi*, he was appointed professor and from 1830 to 1836 taught aesthetics and Danish literature at the Military Academy. The climax of his career as a public servant followed when, in 1849, Heiberg was appointed general manager of the Royal Theater, Denmark's cultural center, where his wife ruled as the sovereign prima donna. After the dictatorial Heiberg retired from this position in 1856, he remained as the theater's dramatic adviser until his death. These later years were marked by conflicts, in particular in his relationship with the acting staff and regarding the choice of repertoire. He patronized the classical but gradually somewhat diluted vaudeville genre, favored Scribe over Shakespeare, tried to keep Hostrup's comedies from the stage, and was generally unsympathetic toward modern drama, rejecting, for instance, the early plays of Bjørnson and Ibsen.

Nevertheless, Heiberg must be recognized as the spiritual leader and the most influential critic of the school of poetic realism and the first significant critic in Denmark who based his aesthetics on firm poetic norms. Although his French-oriented taste for clarity and form was later continued by Georg Brandes, the latter strongly dissociated himself from Heiberg's idealistic and spiritual orientation, with its roots in the philosophy of Hegel, which Heiberg himself had introduced in Denmark.

Henrik Hertz

Among the most frequently performed plays during Heiberg's tenure as manager of the Royal Theater were the vaudevilles of Henrik Hertz (1797[?]–1870). They exemplified Heiberg's own aesthetic ideals, which Hertz, a lifelong friend of the Heibergs, in 1830 had advocated in the collection of *Gjenganger-Breve* (Letters of a Ghost). Actually, these rhymed epistles were written during the Three-Year War as a pamphlet in the controversy between Oehlenschläger and Heiberg; and Hertz, in his insistence on artistic balance between form and content, clearly sides with the latter. With his demand that literature should not imitate nature directly, but give it color by subjecting it to an artistic process, Hertz became a prolific exponent of poetic realism.

Gjenganger-Breve was published pseudonymously, both because it was a strong polemic leveled against the older romantics and because of Hertz's Judaism. To be sure, the Jews in Denmark had become naturalized Danish subjects in 1814, but anti-Semitism was still so prevalent that not only were there violent newspaper controversies (in which, for instance, Bagger and Blicher sided with the Jews) but, in 1819, riots had broken out. Hertz, whose family had distanced itself from Jewish orthodoxy and who himself felt drawn toward Christianity, was baptized in 1832.

His early, somewhat heavy-handed plays—altogether Hertz wrote fifty-four—bear the strong impress of Holberg's comedies, satirically depicting the manners of the Copenhagen bourgeoisie. Hertz's breakthrough came in 1830 with the rhymed, elegantly executed comedy *Amors Geniestreger* (Cupid's Strokes of Genius). It is based on a traditional engagement intrigue, through which the matrimonial plans of a pigheaded father for his daughter are being thwarted. Again, the milieu is that of Copenhagen, as in the great number of facile, somewhat superficial, and increasingly mechanically produced vaudevilles with which Hertz gained his greatest popularity.

Hertz is at his most original in the comedy *Sparekassen* (1836; The Savings Bank), which is still performed, as well as some rhymed plays in a romantic setting. *Sparekassen* builds on the classic motif of the wheel of fortune. Here it is turned by a foster son who, on his unsuspected return from America, lends a hand to his bankrupt family. In spite of the flimsy plot the character delineation is nevertheless remarkably nuanced and thus in complete agreement with the demands of *romantisme* as well as pointing ahead toward the more complex psychology of realist literature. This approach bewildered the audience of the time, and the play initially failed at the Royal Theater.

Complex psychology also characterizes the demonic female protagonist, Ragnhild, in the tragedy *Svend Dyrings Huus* (1837; Svend Dyring's House), a role that, like many others in Hertz's oeuvre, was created specifically for Johanne Luise Heiberg. The inspiration for the medieval setting as well as the meters was the Danish folk ballad. From the ballads he also took the motif of the returning ghost and the use of runes as symbols of erotic power. These features Hertz wove into a dramatic plot about the fight of the proud and ruthless Ragnhild to fulfill her absorbing eroticism. Her attempt does not succeed, however, and her passion becomes destructive and leads to attempted murder and suicide. Ragnhild's attempt at self-knowledge constitutes more than a mere psychological portrayal; it suggests the author's own unsuccessful rebellion against the conventions of contemporary society.

Far more passive is the blind title character, Iolanthe, in the one-act play *Kong Renés Datter* (1845; Eng. tr. *King René's Daughter,* 1845, 1848), set in the Provence of the troubadour era. Here, in diametrical opposition to *Svend Dyrings Huus,* the power of love brings about the fulfillment of Iolanthe's personality, symbolized through the recovery of her sight. *Kong Renés Datter* is a subdued closet play, in which every trace of historical realism, which Hertz in the style of Walter Scott had carefully attempted to carry through in *Svend Dyrings Huus,* has been replaced by a sustained spiritual sublimation and symbolization of external reality, thus making the play a significant forerunner of the symbolic drama of the 1890s, represented, for instance, by Maurice Maeterlinck. As one of the few Danish dramas of the time, it was translated into several languages and performed throughout Europe; it also served as the libretto for Tchaikovsky's opera *Iolanthe.*

A bolder treatment is the reworking of the Ragnhild figure in the title character of the play *Ninon* (1848), the first totally emancipated woman on the Danish stage—intellectual, independent, and, at the same time, totally aware of her erotic attraction. As in the *Oedipus* drama by Sophocles, Hertz lets a young cavalier fall in love with the courtesan Ninon without knowing that she is his mother. His suicide after the revelation of the truth is explained as a nemesis also for Ninon, as she has denied her own maternal calling. Thus Ninon cannot—and is probably not supposed to—liberate herself completely, and Hertz remains within the realm of Biedermeier ideology. This choice is also demonstrated through the genre he has chosen for this tragedy: Scribe's elegant drawingroom play. For once, form and content clash in Hertz's writing.

Likewise, most of Hertz's poetry, primarily collected in *Digte fra forskjellige Perioder* (1851–62; Poems from Different Periods), is rather conventional. Epic poems are predominant along with idyllic genre pieces. Only in a very few strongly personal reflective poems from the 1840s does a tone of desperation break forth in an analysis of the sacrifices that artistic inspiration demands from the poet. These texts share their theme with Hans Christian Andersen's last tale, "Tante Tandpine," but Hertz deliberately avoids the latter's tragic mercilessness. Characteristically, he chooses resignation and a melancholic attitude. An outsider because of his race, Hertz thus opted for safely catering to the taste of his audience, and through this choice he has faded as a literary figure.

ROMANTISME AND THE CRISIS OF THE GOLDEN AGE

Romantisme denotes a departure in the literature of the 1830s and 1840s from the idealistic and spiritual world view of romanticism. This view, when its monistic harmony was questioned, was able to transpose its spirituality into a dualistic but still unquestionably metaphysical realm, as exemplified by Ingemann, Grundtvig, and Hauch.

In a move away from subscribing to the concepts of goodness, truth, and beauty as equally valid manifestations of the Divine, these Platonic concepts were treated either with irony or cautiously questioned. A dualism, restrained by Christian doctrine, was replaced by agonizing disharmony, *Zerrissenheit* (loosely translated as "inner disintegration"). The dark side of existence was emphasized and social issues increasingly came to the fore. Instead of portraying basic psychological types as representatives of certain ideas, Danish writers began to show a predilection for the split, intriguing, even demonic individual character. From a description of local idyll they turned their attention toward foreign, exotic parts of the world, from historical scenery to contemporary times. Literature had to mirror the complexity of life, depict both the grotesque and the sublime.

In England the corresponding poets were represented by Keats, Shelley, and especially Byron. Keats and Shelley entranced particularly because of their uncompromising worship of beauty, but it was Byron who exerted the greatest influence all over Europe, from Leopardi in Italy to Pushkin in

Russia. With Byron a new human type came in vogue: the provocative loner, who in his love for freedom turns against God and society. Frequently, he broods on a secret guilt from the past, suffers from spleen and self-reflection, and treats his fellow beings with cynicism and biting irony.

In French literature Byron had a strong impact on the second generation of romantics and their liberation from the traditional adherence to Crown and Church. In Victor Hugo's poetry collections from the 1820s artistic freedom, with regard to both subject and style, is proclaimed with increasing force. Provocatively, Hugo used contrasting effects, oriental coloring, and exotic words. Similar features are found in Lamartine's descriptions of the Near East as well as Prosper Mérimée's suggestive interiors and exotic novellas from Corsica and Spain, such as *Carmen* (1845).

In German literature the split personality was launched in E. T. A. Hoffmann's *Fantasiestücke in Callot's Manier* (1814–15). With frequent use of the macabre and the supernatural, Hoffmann analyzes the discrepancy between fantasy and reality. A similar perception also characterizes the poetry of Heinrich Heine, finding expression in his unique blend of tender and sublime poetic emotion, biting mockery, and bottomless weltschmerz.

Both Heine and Byron were introduced in Denmark in the 1820s. They replaced Walter Scott as the most popular foreign writers and, for the next decades, became the sovereign models for Danish *romantisme*. Their most talented disciples were Winther, Bødtcher, Aarestrup, the young Andersen, and Paludan-Müller. Heine and Byron inspired not only their poetic style and worship of beauty but also their ennui and skepticism. It was precisely these elements that, in the 1840s, triggered a strong ethical and religious reaction.

Christian Winther

The psychological *Zerrissenheit,* a key feature of *romantisme,* which was only vaguely present in—or rather strongly suppressed by—Hertz became a determining factor in the writings of Christian Winther (1796–1876). It was partly caused by external crises, partly by the tension between the longing for complete freedom and a yielding to societal constraints. This tension occasionally led to a direct disruption of the domestic idyll, leading to a Byronic worship of disharmony and suffering. Not until Winther found his wife-to-be, Julie Werliin, was his agony replaced by serenity and harmony, expressed in tender and intimate love poetry. Emotionally, these years were nevertheless a time of ordeal. In 1836 Winther met Julie, married and the mother of two children, but not until twelve years later, and increasingly a cause célèbre, were they able to marry. The marriage became a happy one but was spent in isolation and on extensive trips abroad; in 1875 Winther, his wife, and his insane stepdaughter moved to Paris, where he died.

Long periods in Winther's life were marked by miserable financial conditions. A degree in divinity in 1824 did not lead to any post, and a succeeding four-year tutorial position resulted only in an unreciprocated infatuation with the student. A considerable inheritance in 1829 gave Winther the opportunity to break away from this relationship. During a two-year stay in Italy, when the poet lived la dolce vita, he had his life's high point of total economic and erotic freedom, which, in a letter to his fellow poet Ludvig Bødtcher from 1831, he nevertheless describes as utterly frightening. And resignation lurked, as voiced with tongue in cheek in the final stanza of Winther's popular romance "Flugten til Amerika" (1835; Eng. tr. *The Flight to America*, 1976), in which the dream of freedom is not realized and the youthful hero "drowns his sorrow and finds his consolation [i.e., raisins] at the bottom of his soup plate."

Winther's early reading was decisive for his later writings. Not only Byron and Heine—whom he translated—but also Walter Scott's historical novels, the German national romantics, and through them German and Danish folk poetry became his sources of inspiration. His debut collection, *Digte* (1828; Poems), was still rooted in poetic realism. The core section, the so-called "Træsnit" (Woodcuts), is inspired by this very folk-song genre. The poems are idyllic pieces, in which Winther focuses on a stylized amorous encounter between a man and a woman in an interior, bucolic, or historic setting. The motif is always that of love's trials. But the volume also contains less naive texts. Thus, in the exquisite love poem "Flyv, Fugl, flyv—" (Fly, Bird, Fly—) a (mostly ignored) dissonance breaks the otherwise amorous atmosphere; the poet's longing and distress can be vented only in "manifold pain." This self-reflection, colored by Heinesque and Byronic irony, becomes the chief ingredient in *Nogle Digte* (1835; Some Poems), a collection that created considerable scandal. The worship of a passionate love affair remains the core experience:

But from our short life
love's existence
has created an ecstatic totality of eternities.

In the same volume, however, this blissful experience can fall prey to the demonic, as shown in the romance cycle "Annette." The somewhat trite love idyll is destroyed when the dark past of the husband is revealed. This past is only vaguely hinted at, however. Indeed, it is the idyll itself that turns destructive. This significant philosophical change from romanticism to *roman-*

tisme is formally reflected in a shift from the traditional *Nibelungen* stanza—introduced by Oehlenschläger and used by Winther in his "Træsnit"—to Byron's ottava rima. And the poem's conclusion stands out starkly, without any note of reconciliation:

> I release the chains of circling embrace,
> and press a burning kiss on your mouth,
> the last one—and this!

In Winther's treatment of historical material a gradual liberation from the traditional, Walter Scott–influenced milieu description becomes noticeable in favor of psychological portrayal and inserted reflective passages. Once again Winther's predilection for erotic and demonic motifs is striking, in particular when he, in the medieval-inspired poem "Vaabendragerens Eed" (The Oath of the Armor Bearer), lets a love relationship conclude in a fatal embrace or, in "Ringens Indskrift" (The Inscription of the Ring), changes a historical anecdote into an artistically detached study of the perverting effects of pent-up feelings.

The focus on the demonic in Danish *romantisme* as well as the writer's deliberate distance to his subject is also exemplified in some of Winther's prose texts, such as *Fire Noveller* (1843; Four Short Stories), with Danish and Italian settings and the theme of happiness disrupted. In "Skriftestolen" (The Confessional) Winther goes so far as to employ thriller effects to tell a story of infidelity. Stylistically more refined and related to Mérimée's sophisticated prose is "En Aftenscene" (An Evening Scene). The episode in which the middle-aged and handicapped suitor catches a glimpse in a mirror of his bride's grimacing mimicking of his limping makes a superbly crafted ironic-tragic climax. These stories, together with the novella *Episode af et Familieliv* (1853; Episode from a Family Life), a profound study of a split personality and moral irresponsibility, constitute a generally overlooked stage in the development of classical Danish prose, anticipating the mastery of J. P. Jacobsen.

With the collection *Digtninger* (1843; Poems) and the epic poem *Hjortens Flugt* (1855; The Flight of the Hart)—characteristically written in the *Nibelungen* stanza—Winther attempts to recreate a Platonic harmony between earthly and divine love. His love relationship with Julie, which was the decisive experience of his life, found its definitive expression in the lyrical cycle "Til Een" (To the One). The first 23 poems were published in the 1843 volume; all 137 were gathered together in the third part of *Samlede Digtninger* (1860; Collected Poems). Without being strictly a chronological diary, "Til Een" traces the development of the poet's love from the initial infatuation and accompanying doubts up to its final realization in a new belief in a totality that encompasses all aspects of sensual and spiritual love. Gone are the doubts, but gone also is the banal idyll. What Winther glorifies in a purified and authentic poetic form—probably the most genuine example of Danish romantic love poetry—is the fervor and integrity of the sentiments of love as they are reflected in the complete union of the hearts of two people:

The hour when my arms closed
around you and my flaming thirst was quenched
only to be strongly inflamed again.
The hour which called our lives to life,
shall become an eternity
and we too shall become eternal through it.

The copestone of Winther's oeuvre was the realization of a plan he had worked on for thirty years, a large-scale epic poem set in the Middle Ages, *Hjortens Flugt*. But the historical color, one major source of which is the medieval ballads, serves only as decor. The language is basically contemporary, and the complex of problems of the whole work is at once autobiographical and timeless. The pinioned Cossack's wild ride, modeled after Byron's romance *Mazeppa* (1818), forms the point of departure for and connecting link with the poem's complex love intrigues. The driving force behind them is the vengeful mistress of King Erik, the Wendish Rhitra, a counterpart to Mérimée's Carmen, while the fickle king himself is an archetypal Don Juan figure. Their love story represents the erotic as an obsession. This demonic element finds its Christian counterpart in the love story of Squire Strange and Ellen. After having pursued Strange in vain, Rhitra maligns him to the king, who has him pinioned onto a hart as a punishment. In the woods he is rescued by the troubadour Folmer, whose Platonic infatuation with the queen is a reflection of the medieval worship of the Virgin Mary. Thus Winther, on a symbolic level, lets poetry—and thereby the artistic vocation per se—appear as the redeemer from demonic forces. To avoid any possible conflict by tying himself up in a love relationship, but also to ensure himself absolute artistic freedom, Folmer (who is partly a self-portrait) seeks solace through a life in nature.

In *Hjortens Flugt,* tremendously popular for generations, Winther's ethical and religious world view finds its most valid expression. But this world view is hard won and under the surface lurk insecurity and fear, with only art itself as a possible point of orientation. Thus this stylistic masterpiece is also significant as a philosophical statement, being a further step in the process of the dissolution of Danish romanticism.

Ludvig Bødtcher

Characteristically, neither an ethical commitment nor expressions of passion can be extracted from the exclusively lyrical production of Ludvig Bødtcher (1793–1874). He lived a quiet bachelor's life in Copenhagen; and a considerable inheritance secured his financial independence and made it possible for him to live in Italy from 1824 to 1835 as a popular member of the Scandinavian colony in Rome. There the sculptor Bertel Thorvaldsen became especially important for the well-crafted and picturesque elements of Bødtcher's poetry.

Bødtcher did not publish any collection until *Digte, ældre og nyere* (1856; Older and Newer Poems), and later volumes contain only additional texts. Reflecting Bødtcher's own course of life, his writings can be divided into an Italian and a Danish part, and the most typical lyrical genres of the period can be found in both groups: romances, epic poems, occasional and commemorative poetry, and, in particular, the genre piece executed either dramatically or as a narrative, employing the structure of the poetic monologue in the tradition of Poul Martin Møller's *Scener i Rosenborg Have*. But it is remarkable that Bødtcher focuses on the aesthetic effect rather than the rendering of reality. That is also the case when he creates his snapshots from Italian nature and folk life, managing to conjure up highly refined rhythmic, colorist, and musical effects—genuine *l'art pour l'art* poetry. It is likewise characteristic that Bødtcher's major central Italian poetry was written *after* his return to Denmark, that is, executed at memory's distance. Thus in "Mødet med Bacchus" (The Encounter with Bacchus) Italian nature receives magnificent treatment, but the experience is immediately aestheticized:

> The golden peak of the mountain
> and the valley with the ruin,
> and the gardens with the vine—
> I closed my eyes
> and sank into my memory
> the entire painting.

Hereafter the genre picture develops into a description of the intoxication as a mythical experience. With self-irony the poet realizes that it is only in the text itself that he can hold onto the experience.

In Bødtcher's poems with a Danish setting the tone becomes less exhilarated and tinged with sadness because of an awareness of his vanished youth. This more personal element appears without aesthetic-ironic distance. Nevertheless in a late philosophical poem such as "Mod Slutningen" (Toward the End)—based on the traditional motif of the Creation as a reflection of the Creator—he focuses not so much on the metaphysical aspect as on the aesthetic experience:

> The earth which you have solaced
> with Shakespeare's golden song,
> where Raphael has painted,
> and Mozart's music resounded.

Emil Aarestrup

Emil Aarestrup (1800–1856) also focuses on the experience of beauty, and in his poetry ethical and religious values are absent to an even larger degree than in Bødtcher's writings. As one of the exceptions among the early nineteenth-century authors, Aarestrup studied not theology but medicine, and he spent his life, after having received his degree in 1827, as a busy country doctor in the provinces. In his limited spare time he wrote his poetry, of which only one volume, *Digte* (1838; Poems), was published during his lifetime.

Aarestrup's writings hardly reflect his bourgeois everyday life. He moves in a prearranged, perhaps almost artificial, and strictly private world of beauty. His poetic technique Aarestrup learned from reading and translating French, German, and English authors (his translations make up an entire volume). Among his favorite poets were Heine, Rückert, Hugo, and Byron, and, in particular, the Irish, Anacreontic poet Thomas Moore, names that show the extent to which Aarestrup was familiar with contemporary European literature. In the works of these poets he found that prosodic mastery that made him one of the most brilliant and elegant versifiers in Danish literature. His formal virtuosity led to experiments with new lyrical forms, such as the Italian improvised stanza in three lines, the ritornelle, which he found in the works of the German romantic Friedrich Rückert and of which he wrote more than 200 altogether. The basic form requires the invocation of a flower, the symbol of a young woman which is incorporated in a more or less overt erotic situation:

> Flower of the sage!
> Even if many call you a prude,
> your little honey hiding-place is known by the bee.

It can otherwise be varied in a more epigrammatic or satirical direction:

> Rosa had nine children, none looking like one another.
> Each child looked exactly like its father,
> but not one looked like her husband.

In his early, traditional poems from ca. 1820 Aarestrup either followed in the traces of the traditional romance, as in "Havfruen" (The Mermaid), influenced by the sensuous approach of the young Oehlenschläger, whose lectures on aesthetics Aarestrup had attended at the University of Copenhagen, or resorted to the preromantic Gothic ballad in the style of Schack Staffeldt or Ingemann, as in "Ridder Bruno" (Sir Bruno). The only remarkable text from this period is "Lucca Signorelli" with its staunch emphasis on the sanctity of art. The succeeding period's orientation toward poetic realism is also reflected in Aarestrup's early poetry, as in "Torsten og Trine" (Torsten and Trine), related to the "Træsnit" of his close friend Christian Winther.

The romance "Tidlig Skilsmisse" (Early Separation) marks a stage of artistic innovation and exemplifies at the same time Aarestrup's second major prosodic model, the plain and melodious four-line stanza of Heine. Purposely the sequence of events is only hinted at; Aarestrup focuses attention rather on the picturesque detail, which he registers with cool objectivity even as he describes the tragic conclusion: "She fainted—fell as if crushed— / you find no marble more beautiful lying in the gravel."

This detached approach, which undoubtedly can be traced back to his medical training, from now on characterizes Aarestrup's erotic poetry, the core of which is a cycle of fifty-one texts, "Erotiske Situationer" (Erotic Situations). These poems are part of a planned episodic novella ending with the death of the beloved. Aarestrup's escort of the sick countess Amalie Raben on a visit to a spa in 1832 has been identified as the inspiration for these texts. Based on this episode Aarestrup has crystallized the central motif and explores it for all its aesthetic possibilities: Eros—interpreted as sexual instinct—as well as death as the prerequisite, climax, and conclusion of this instinct. Aarestrup succeeds in expressing this intertwining of life and death in one single line, one artistic observation, in the otherwise pastoral opening stanza of "En Middag" (A Dinner): "Look, the trout decorates the dish with its last stiff, graceful wriggle." This interrelationship of life and death is treated with more pain in "Angst:"

Hold me tighter,
with your round arms.
Hold tight, while your heart
still has blood and warmth.

Soon, we'll be separated
like the berries on the hedge
soon we have disappeared
like the bubbles in the brook.

Here an existential tone breaks forth, which is both an expression of the costs of Aarestrup's aesthetic world view and the reverse side of his worship of the sexual instinct, the desperate longing for meaning. This longing, however, can only end in emptiness—a duality, which gives his oeuvre a clear tone of modernity and explains its appeal today.

THE BREAKDOWN OF THE BIEDERMEIER CULTURE

P. M. Møller's *En dansk Students Eventyr* serves as a perfect illustration of the transition from romanticism to realism through the stages of poetic realism and *romantisme*. With its contrast between the dynamic student Frits, who throughout the novella grows into a realization of reality, and the indecisive and impractical pedant, it constitutes a decisive attack on the major concepts of Biedermeier: idyllic romanticizing, sentimentality, and escapism. Thus it points beyond the predominant poetic realism of the 1820s and 1830s, to which Møller otherwise belongs, toward the writings of Andersen, Paludan-Müller, and Kierkegaard. In the final account it anticipates the related novel by Hans Egede Schack, *Phantasterne*. Nevertheless, through its idealistic world view as well as its psychology, predominantly based on certain types rather than individuality, the novella remains firmly rooted in romanticism.

As the attempt at harmonization and stylization became increasingly forced, as with Hertz and Winther, if not even outright meaningless, the Biedermeier culture and, as the final step, romantic idealism itself were threatened even further. A defiant attempt in another direction, in a one-sided adherence to the fragmentation and disharmony of *romantisme*, led in the works of Ludvig Bødtcher and Emil Aarestrup to pure aestheticism. As *romantisme* was gradually carried to its final consequence—a process exemplified by Carl Bagger—irony was replaced by skepticism, historical time by present time, the supremacy of Christianity was openly questioned, and social, even political, themes pressed themselves forward, pointing to the realistic and naturalistic literature of the 1870s and 1880s.

Thomasine Gyllembourg

Møller, Heiberg, and, to some degree, Hertz saw their harmonious world view threatened by this development away from romantic idealism. This trend was not only noted but actively, albeit initially hesitantly, advocated by Thomasine Gyllembourg (1773–1856). Her oeuvre of twenty-four short stories was written between 1827 and 1845 under a pseudonym and published by her son, Johan Ludvig Heiberg. Gyllembourg grew up in an academic, upper-class milieu in Copenhagen. When not quite seventeen years old she married her teacher, the author P. A. Heiberg, and thus was introduced to and became the center of a free-spirited, liberal environment. The marriage turned out to be a misalliance, and she took the initiative to divorce her husband. In 1800 he was exiled for political reasons, and the following year Gyllembourg married a Swedish baron (hence her family name) and was forced to renounce the right to bring up the son from her first marriage, with whom she, nevertheless, after her husband's death in 1815, spent the rest of her life.

With Blicher, Gyllembourg introduced the short story to Danish literature. At fifty-four years of age she made her debut with *Familien Polonius* (1827; The Polonius Family), which one year later was succeeded by her most famous work, *En Hverdags-Historie* (An Everyday Story). It tells of the first-person narrator's hasty engagement and of his predicament when he discovers that he really is in love with his fiancée's half-sister, Maja. The plot is complicated further, since Maja is already being courted by two other men. But an apparently insoluble conflict is resolved through resignation, and the idyll thereby restored.

Slægtskab og Djævelskab (1830; Kinship and Devilry) contains a conflict of love, but in this case it is resolved through rebellion against authority. Rosine, a young widow with a little child, protests against her father's plans for a suitable marriage and chooses the man she loves, even though her family turns against her and takes her child away. But whereas Maja in the previous story is just a pawn in the intrigue, Rosine grows out of her passive role as an obedient daughter and becomes aware of her independence as a mother.

The problems of marital relations and sexuality are subsequently analyzed in the story of an upper-class man's seduction of a servant maid, *Drøm og Virkelighed* (1833; Dream and Reality). Here Gyllembourg boldly ventures behind the facade of the period's concept of "ideal love," launching the first piece of social criticism in Danish literature. In *Ægtestand* (1835; Marriage) she recreates the tragedy of her own marriage and thus writes the first work in Danish literature about a woman's conflict between her obligation toward her family and her own sexuality as it unfolds outside marriage. Sophie must choose between her erotic feelings for her lover and the emptiness in her present marriage. Nevertheless, the author does not let her leave her husband. Obviously frightened by the memories of her own scandal, Gyllembourg chooses the status quo—and thus does not transgress poetic realism. Yet she pursues the theme in a secondary plot describing Sophie's friend Karoline and her adultery in pursuit of true happiness. In *To Tidsaldre*

(1845; Two Ages) Gyllembourg takes the final, radical step, inasmuch as the story describes an uncompromising love relationship between a young woman of the Copenhagen bourgeoisie and a representative of the French revolutionary government.

With these stories Gyllembourg anticipated the "problem debate" required by the critic Georg Brandes in the 1870s. And just as in the debate literature of this so-called Modern Breakthrough the message takes priority over artistic articulation. Her major ideological source of inspiration is the prerevolutionary spirit of the late eighteenth century, as represented by Rousseau and his worship of "the natural." Her major literary models are the bourgeois novels of Oliver Goldsmith, Samuel Richardson, and most of all Goethe, in particular his novel *Die Wahlverwandtschaften* (1809; Elected Affinities).

Gyllembourg's stories have their artistic forte in a realistic milieu description, in their scenes of dramatic confrontation, and in the psychological insights they provide into the world of the woman. Their weakness is in their dialogues, which are frequently faltering and somewhat banal. Nevertheless, compared with most early nineteenth-century fiction, her prose constitutes a significant step toward modern, everyday language.

Steen Steensen Blicher

The realistic breakthrough in Danish prose—anticipated by Poul Martin Møller, Christian Winther, and Thomasine Gyllembourg—took place in 1824 with a short story by Steen Steensen Blicher (1782–1848): *Brudstykker af en Landsbydegns Dagbog* (Fragments of the Diary of a Parish Clerk; Eng. tr. *The Journal/Diary of a Parish Clerk,* 1945, 1968, 1991). In spite of his modernism, however, Blicher was probably the writer in nineteenth-century Denmark with the strongest ties to the preceding century. These ties found expression in his interest in topography and the general education of the people (in articles about sheepkeeping and reclamation of moors) and through his progressive involvement in current social and political questions and participation in the pan-Scandinavian movement, interests that at the same time point ahead toward the polemical writers of naturalism.

A degree in divinity in 1809 marked the beginning of a lifelong ministry in Blicher's native Jutland countryside, from 1819 in Torning and from 1825 in Spentrup. With Blicher, a Danish writer emerged for the first time who was anchored neither in the Copenhagen bourgeoisie nor in the milieu of the Zealand parsonages. Blicher introduced Jutland dialect, folk life, and nature into Danish literature. His ministry itself, as well as constant heavy indebtedness and an unhappy marriage, cast a gloom over his life, and as often as possible he escaped on lengthy hunting trips and into heavy drinking.

In addition to the eighteenth-century Enlightenment, the succeeding pre-romanticism left important traces in Blicher's oeuvre, as reflected in the choice of genres in his youthful poetry: the elegy, the occasional poem, and the Gothic ballad. His authorship as such began with a translation of James Macpherson's Ossian poems in 1807–9. Their melancholy nature descriptions and awareness of a past lost forever are frequently present in Blicher's later writings. Later he also translated Alexander Pope and Oliver Goldsmith, whereas German romanticism and its philosophy of nature had no attraction for him. The elegiac tone of the Ossian poems became a significant component in Blicher's own poetry, the culmination of which is the collection *Trækfuglene* (1838; The Birds of Passage). Its underlying mood is struck in the volume's first line: "My hour for leaving draws near apace." The texts constitute a sustained bird allegory that expresses the poet's longing for redemption from his prison, together with a tragic sense of transitoriness—a keynote theme of his entire oeuvre—in both a social and a metaphysical context.

The source of inspiration for Blicher's prose writings is partly his interest in folklore (thus he contributed to Thiele's collection of *Danske Folkesagn*), partly Walter Scott's historical novels, and partly his own desperate financial situation, which made him sign a contract with a provincial publisher to write short contributions for the popular magazine *Læsefrugter* (Miscellany). He began with *Jydske Røverhistorier* (1823; Jutland Robbers' Stories) and *Oldsagn fra Alheden* (1823; Ancient Legends from the Al Moor), in which several of the motifs of his later short stories are suggested. The titles speak their own language: the story and the legend became the basis for Blicher's own realism.

Only a few months later *Læsefrugter* printed Blicher's first totally original prose work, *Brudstykker af en Landsbydegns Dagbog*, a consummate masterpiece. Blicher found the captivating biography of the noblewoman Marie Grubbe (Blicher calls her Sophie), which was later to fascinate both Hans Christian Andersen ("Hønse-Grethes Familie" [The Family of Hen-Grethe]) and J. P. Jacobsen, in some old clerical diaries, which partly explains the eighteenth-century prose style he chose. This historical distance is deliberate, however, and corresponds to a similar distance on the part of the narrator—a fundamental feature of Blicher's work—as the author pretends that the story is made up of diary entries by Morten, the son of a parish clerk. With sophistication, employing a technique that in an astounding way anticipates the linguistic experiments of twentieth-century modernism, Blicher lets this distance mirror Morten's own attitude toward life itself. He is passive, an observer, who himself does not directly experience but is able only to describe the course of events: his service as valet at the manor house, where he falls in love with Sophie; her elopement with the gamekeeper, Jens, after having broken off her engagement to a nobleman of distinction; Morten's military service and captivity; his encounter again with Sophie and Jens as human wreckage; and his final return to his childhood province where, disappointed and resigned, he becomes a parish clerk like his father. Thus, there is no external development in Morten's life, but he has, nevertheless, learned life's bitter lesson: all is transitory and subject to an inexorable destiny. God is distant (although his mercy is invoked in the concluding quotation from the Bible), and the human world is dominated by spite and sexuality. Blicher is a master of psychological realism. His method is one not of laboring analysis but of sudden insights, corresponding to the episodic structure of the diary, into the human psyche, in particular when it is confronted with new, sudden cognitive shifts or catastrophe itself.

The motifs and narrative technique for Blicher's remaining stories are both found implanted in this short text. Documentarism and the diary technique are employed in *Præsten i Vejlbye* (1829; Eng. tr. *The Parson at Vejlbye*, 1945), which is based on a historical occurrence from the sixteenth century involving the clergyman Søren Qvist, who was executed for a murder he did not commit. This part of the story is told by the sentencing judge himself, who is also Qvist's future son-in-law. Just before the execution his diary abruptly ends, and the story's second half is recounted in the words of another clergyman. After a brief introduction it opens as follows: "Lord! How inscrutable are your ways!" The crime has been cleared up, and it comes out that the false accusation was an act of revenge. This exposure brings about the sudden death of the judge, whose marriage with the clergyman's daughter was shattered. Blicher has cleverly used features anticipating the modern detective novel, but only to create a moral tale about the evil of humankind and life's absurdity.

The unmasking of a chaotic reality behind an apparently harmonious surface is also the main motif in *Sildig Opvaagnen* (1828; Eng. tr. *Tardy Awakening*, 1945), located in a contemporary, realistically described city milieu. The narrator, a clergyman, takes it on himself to reveal the truth behind the rumors about the suicide of his friend, a physician. And by using a modern flashback technique, Blicher unfolds a tragic love story between the physician's wife, Elise, and her lover of many years, an officer. The revelation brings about the catastrophe, the deceived husband's suicide, and the clergyman's own strict condemnation. But Blicher himself is undoubtedly fascinated by this attempt at revolting against the ethical norms of the Biedermeier society. It is less a personal revolt, such as undertaken by Gyllembourg and Bagger, than one at a more fundamental level in which he lets a woman (and thus Elise becomes a counterpart to Sophie in *Brudstykker af en Landsbydegns Dagbog*) insist on her own right to love.

The dramatic unmasking, toned down to the motif of the tragic encounter as Blicher had used it in *Brudstykker af en Landsbydegns Dagbog,* becomes the key element in *Hosekræmmeren* (1829; Eng. tr. *The Hosier and his Daughter,* 1945). Like *Præsten i Vejlbye*, this story is told from two different perspectives: that of the narrator, who leads the reader toward the actual plot, thus creating the frame, and who consistently attempts to mediate the conflict, and that of the hosier's wife, who six years later retells the tragic events from the interim period. The love of her daughter, the Ophelia-like Cecil, for the impecunious Esben, witnessed by the narrator at the story's beginning, cannot be realized because of her parents' opposition. While Esben travels abroad to make his fortune, Cecil becomes engaged to a rich farmer's son but goes insane shortly before the wedding. On his return Esben cuts his own throat, and it is Cecil's lament (based on an old folk song): "The greatest sorrow in this world is to be separated from the one you love," which confronts the narrator as he revisits the hosier's home. The theme invites a sentimental treatment, but Blicher is capable of raising the text to a symbolic level. Cecil's father prohibits her marriage because of his love for her. He believes that Esben simply does not have the financial means to support his daughter, and the narrator himself agrees. Cecil's insanity makes the world incomprehensible to her father; he pines away and dies. Only Cecil's mother is left, but like the father, she cannot comprehend the tragic fact that humankind suffers and causes suffering, and the narrator (i.e., Blicher) does not have any explanation at hand.

The relentlessness of existence, coupled with the motif of change, is another of Blicher's major themes. It was introduced in *Brudstykker af en Landsbydegns Dagbog* and is reflected in the very title of *"Ak! hvor forandret"* (1828; Eng. tr. *"Alas, How Changed,"* 1945). The story is narrated by the fictitious Peer the Fiddler, Blicher's alter ego, who appears in some other stories. His function is both to provide the realistic contemporary description and to contrast Blicher's own somber tone with humor and satire. With a friend, a student of divinity, Peer has met the beautiful Maren, with whom he falls in love. He cuts a clumsy figure, however, while the polished student makes a much more favorable impression on the girl. Twenty years later Peer returns to visit the friend of his youth, who is now a minister in a remote province. Peer finds him standing fat and red-faced on a dunghill counting his animals and assumes the man is a tenant farmer. To his great surprise he realizes that it is his friend, married to the very same Maren, with whom he has children, "one for each finger"; she, too, is totally changed. The next day Peer leaves the farm. Even though the mood is somewhat lighter, Blicher's comic approach is unable to cover the tragedy underneath. As the events filter through Peer's mind they turn—and this is the author's artistic coup—into a sort of existential reflection about the impossibility of reaching any insight into God's plan for humanity. This realization forms the basis for Blicher's entire oeuvre and explains its tragic course and profound pessimism.

Around 1840 two unadorned peasant stories show an orientation toward the everyday and popular. Blicher had anticipated this genre with *Røverstuen* (1827; Eng. tr. *The Robber's Den,* 1945), a story of abduction. His attitude toward the plot is somewhat ironical, however, as he scoffs at the romantics' frequent use of this (and other sensational) motifs and at long-winded, descriptive prose in general. In *De tre Helligaftener* (1841; Eng. tr. *Three Holiday Eves,* 1945), whose themes can be traced back to the two collections from 1824, Blicher occasionally resorts to Jutland dialect to amplify his character delineation. The capture by the farmer Sejr of a gang of robbers has been interpreted as a political allegory about dawning democracy's victory over its enemies, but the story is just as much intended as a free and easy account, aimed at a larger local Jutland audience, about the triumph of justice. Blicher takes the final step toward local color with *E Bindstouw* (1842; In the Knitting Room). The frame structure is known from Boccaccio's *Decamerone* (1348–53): some people get together—in this story in order to knit—and as a pastime they tell stories and sing songs in a mixture of comic and tragic texts, all presented in Jutland dialect. Their content gives a cross-section of peasant culture and literature: ballads, jocular stories, and legends. Once again Blicher raises his material above simple entertainment as he brilliantly demonstrates how one text almost demands the next, and a fellowship is born among the people present which corresponds to the democratic dream Sejr embodies in *De tre Helligaftener.*

Nevertheless, many of Blicher's short stories remain on the level of sheer entertainment, no doubt because they were written exclusively to supplement his sparse income. Such is definitely the case with his stories based on foreign material, such as the two long historical works, *Den sachsiske Bondekrig* (1827; The Saxon Peasants' War) and *Telse* (1829), a story from the Ditmarshes. They are both direct imitations of Walter Scott but without his ability to make history come alive.

It is as a local Jutlander and a universal existentialist that Blicher, in only a handful of texts, displays his unrivaled genius. His characters are always portrayed in interaction with—or rather, fighting against—their environment and nature itself. Therefore, it is not only through his analytical exploration of the human mind but also indirectly through precise yet evocative descriptions of interiors or nature that Blicher creates his authentic, intense, and varied gallery of characters. And at the same time, his characters are all symbolic expressions of his pessimism, in which even the feeling of love leads to catastrophe. This obvious antiromantic outlook, combined with a disillusioned skepticism about the possibility of any escape from tragedy, makes Blicher an outsider in the period's literature. One should be most cautious when attempting to find stock ideological messages in his works, a characteristic that points toward the psychological realism of J. P. Jacobsen, Herman Bang, and Henrik Pontoppidan. But in the final analysis Blicher is absolutely timeless and belongs to the great names of short story writers in world literature from Boccaccio to Maupassant.

Carl Bagger

Clear indications of anti-Christian and revolutionary themes are present, by contrast, in the novel of Carl Bagger (1807–46), *Min Broders Levnet* (1835; The Life of My Brother). Born out of wedlock, Bagger grew up with an uncle. A study of law, begun in 1828, was never completed, and Bagger spent the following years as an alcoholic bohemian and writer in Copenhagen, a time reflected in some uneven poems published as *Smaadigte* (1834; Shorter Poems). In 1827 Bagger proposed to Thora Fiedler, the love of his life, but was rejected by her father. A son was born two years later, but not until 1837 could the wedding take place. Only gradually was Bagger able to establish himself for a few years as a journalist and editor in Odense.

Bagger never knew a secure childhood and a stable family life. These were to him a dream, an absent idyll that was alternately glorified and mocked in his writings, revealing an incurable division in his personality. This dream stands in contrast to an almost anarchic worship of provocation, an attempt at liberation from the bourgeoisie, which never accepted Bagger and with which he could never reconcile himself.

This antithesis became the structural basis for Bagger's novel, in which the author has divided himself into two characters, Johannes and Arthur. Johannes, the first-person narrator, a clergyman personifying the upright Biedermeier attitude, tells about the miserable life of his brother, a much more complex character marked by political radicalism, alcoholism, and contact with the outcasts of society—a typical Byron-inspired character. It is Johannes who emerges as the paragon of virtue. Eventually, he becomes the husband of the angelic Mathilde, made pregnant by his faithless brother, while Arthur goes to the dogs and perishes. Only for the sake of his child does Arthur marry Mathilde on his deathbed. Thus the novel ends on an apparently idyllic note, a deliberate effect of scathing irony, which lets the novel's discords remain unresolved. Arthur continues his brooding and self-examination until his death, a scene culminating in a fantasy about an imminent world revolution, which, together with the starkly realistic scenes from Copenhagen slums and nightlife, shocked and repelled contemporary critics. It is quite obvious that Arthur has Bagger's entire sympathy. That becomes even more apparent when he is compared with his strongly caricatured, complacent brother. Johannes, however, is not quite as uncomplicated as he first appears to be. His praise of the idyllic appears almost forced, whereas his invocation of Byron, whom he contrasts to "the miserable Oehlenschläger and the low-flying Neoplatonic Ingemann," seems genuine.

The autobiographical elements are much too unintegrated and the characters too fabricated and unconvincing to make *Min Broders Levnet* a masterpiece. But the novel is of considerable importance in the history of Danish literature. The technique of divided narration was rediscovered later by Holger Drachmann, and both Paludan-Müller and Johannes V. Jensen in their youthful works show Bagger's influence in their description of the seamy side of Copenhagen nightlife. Most significant is the novel's uncompromising rejection of romantic idealism and its description of the Copenhagen underworld, otherwise overlooked by the period's writers. These features, via the writings of Poul Chievitz, point ahead toward the naturalism of the 1880s.

Poul Chievitz

Bagger's immediate successor as a portrayer of life in the big city was Poul Chievitz (1817–54). Like Bagger, he had no higher education and worked as an office clerk. In spite of his involvement with Goldschmidt's journal *Corsaren* (The Corsair), he never became integrated into academic circles, in which he moved only as an observer. Certainly, in his attempts at unveiling the hypocrisy and corruption behind the facade of the Copenhagen bourgeoisie Chievitz emerges as a disciple of Honoré de Balzac. To this literary source of inspiration, however, must be added his strictly personal motives of envy and protest.

A favorite target for Chievitz's satire is the starry-eyed student whose whole life consists of airy and abstract discussions about aesthetic matters. Chievitz firmly rejects any metaphysical structures and points to material conditions as the sole determinant of human interaction in general and the ethics of society and sexual patterns in particular. But Chievitz is more than a champion of sexual liberation. His best-known novel, carrying the programmatic title *Fra Gaden* (1848; From the Street), has a happy ending as bourgeois hypocrisy is being unveiled. In his debut novel, *Saaledes forholder det sig* (1845; This Is How It Is), however, he lets the lover, who has been rejected for financial reasons, draw this dangerous lesson from his defeat: "An unhappy lover can become an excellent revolutionary. If he earlier on had fought as a matter of principle, this principle now receives a strong ally in his hate . . . against the rich and mighty."

Thus, it was not Chievitz's intention to attack the prevalent social ethics from a higher, ideal point of view as Paludan-Müller did in *Adam Homo*. His aim was to protest double standards of morality and the ensuing human tragedies, and he was guided primarily by compassion and solidarity with the victims of this attitude. Chievitz extends a hand to those female writers who in the following decades advocated emancipation. He does not, however, have an eye for the contemporary criticism of the harsh social repercussions of the growing process of industrialization, as found in the works of another contemporary portrayer of big city life, Charles Dickens. Not until Martin Andersen Nexø—with Athalia Schwarz as a link—did the Danish proletariat find a compassionate advocate.

Female Pioneers and the Clara Raphael Controversy

A purely idealistic position is taken by Mathilde Fibiger (1830–72), who with her debut, *Clara Raphael. Tolv Breve* (1850; Clara Raphael: Twelve Letters), initiated Danish women's emancipation. She sent her manuscript to J. L. Heiberg, who wrote a preface and had it published under the pseudonym Clara Raphael. Inspired by P. M. Møller's philosophy of personality, the novel describes a young female teacher's fight to shape a life of independence. This choice leads her to renounce her passion for a baron at the same time as she agrees to become his wife in a Platonic relationship. The novel, especially its overwrought conclusion, provoked a heated debate, and within a few weeks Copenhagen was flooded with articles and pamphlets for and against Clara Raphael's ideas. Mathilde Fibiger herself, strongly supported by Grundtvig, eagerly participated in the debate with a new epistolary novel, *Et Besøg* (1851; A Visit). Here she elaborates her views on the suppression of women, and in the novel *Minona* (1854) she criticizes marriage as an institution, attacking, like Chievitz, the sexual hypocrisy of the time.

Two teachers, Pauline Worm (1825–83) and Athalia Schwartz (1821–71), also participated in the controversy, pointing to an improved education as the first goal of the women's movement. In Worm's novel *De Fornuftige* (1857; The Reasonable Ones) she argues—taking aim at Mathilde Fibiger—for an improvement of woman's material position before an emancipation of the spirit. The novel is written with great passion, but the composition is somewhat chaotic, whereas Schwartz was considerably more successful in realizing her literary ambitions. She was active as a reviewer for Goldschmidt's journal *Nord og Syd*, wrote three dramas that were performed at the Royal Theater, and in the 1860s produced a series of novels, loosely structured and psychologically rather superficial but of interest because they all took up the debate on women's rights. Schwartz focused increasingly on the necessity of providing women with the same possibilities for economic independence as men. In the novels *Stedmoder og Steddatter* (1865; Stepmother and Stepdaughter) and *Enhver sin Mission* (1870; Everybody Has a Mission) she involves the proletariat and focuses on, in addition to women's emancipation, class barriers. These novels anticipate the socialist literature after 1900, even though for Schwartz the solution to sexual and social problems cannot be found in a political revolution but only in self-discipline and reform in the spirit of Christianity.

Frederik Dreier

This spiritual perspective was far distant from yet another participant in the Clara Raphael controversy, Frederik Dreier (1827–53). In a sarcastic pamphlet from 1851 he demanded that before the women's situation could be discussed at all, a new, socialist system had to be brought about, not through revolution but through education. Inspired by the democratic movements leading to the free constitution in 1849, Dreier published two booklets in 1848, *Folkenes Fremtid* (The Future of Peoples) and *Fremtidens Folkeopdragelse* (The Future Education of Peoples). They were aimed against nationalism. They anticipated Darwin's evolutionary theories and, in general, promoted a new educational system stressing social and scientific knowledge. Dreier's principal philosophical work, *Aandetroen og den frie Tænkning* (1852; The Belief in Spirits and Free Thinking), is a polemical pamphlet attacking theology and clericalism as the two conservative factors of power. But it is also a lucid presentation of his consistently atheistic and materialistic world view inspired by the radical thinkers of the time: Max Stirner and his evolutionary socialism, the radical German biblical criticism of D. F. Strauss and Ludwig Feuerbach, and the theories of Friedrich Engels and Karl Marx.

Finally, scattered throughout Dreier's works are radical attacks on philosophical idealism and on the period's romantic literature, in particular poetry, for being imprecise and obscure; Dreier advocates psychological and social narratives. His favorite target was the prose of M. A. Goldschmidt, which Dreier describes as pure rhetoric, and Goldschmidt himself, because of his movement toward conservatism, is denounced as an ignorant political opportunist.

Dreier's castigation of the romantic-idealistic ideology was caustic. His criticism of contemporary literature, however, is valid only when aimed at various secondary, derivative poets, but definitely wrong in the case of Goldschmidt. Other postromantic writers, such as Bergsøe, Hostrup, and Kaalund, were keenly aware of the ongoing social and ideological changes. They all struggled with the dissolution of a previous world view, trying to find footing in a period of transition, and they published works of considerable artistic value. Because of the irregular appearance of Dreier's criticism, it had no immediate impact, but nevertheless in a remarkable way it anticipated the radical and provocative cultural critique of Georg Brandes.

INVOLVEMENT AND TIMELESSNESS:
THREE MID-CENTURY GIANTS

With Dreier, an advocate of women's rights and radical societal changes in general—and with Bagger and Gyllembourg as forerunners—the discussion of religious, sexual, and political issues as demanded by Brandes in 1871 was already in full swing. Thus, Brandes's well-known dictum, "That a literature exists in our time is shown by the fact that it sets up problems for debate," has no validity when applied to Danish literature of the previous decades. Nor was this literature mainly derivative and only dealing with our dreams, as also claimed by Brandes; that is demonstrated by three dominant figures: Hans Christian Andersen, Frederik Paludan-Müller and Søren Kierkegaard. They mark an epoch in Danish intellectual history, standing at the crossroad of the mid-nineteenth century but manifestly pointing toward the future. They are giants because of their innovative thoughts and approaches as well as their passionate or even polemical involvement in the questions of the day. By virtue of their universality, however, they have also raised themselves above their own time.

Hans Christian Andersen
The absolute outsider of the three was Hans Christian Andersen (1805–75), a position explaining the ambition, vanity, and insecurity that accompanied him all his life. In fact, his family background makes him the first Danish writer of proletarian origin. His father was a poor, albeit intellectually gifted, shoemaker in the provincial town of Odense; his mother was practically illiterate and after her husband's death maintained herself as a washer-

woman, spending her last years as an alcoholic in a workhouse. From childhood Andersen was a voracious reader, and when, shortly after his arrival in Copenhagen in 1819, his dreams of becoming an actor at the Royal Theater were shattered, he decided to conquer the stage as a playwright. His first two plays were rejected because they "betrayed such a lack of elementary education." In 1828 Andersen returned to the capital after five years of schooling, funded by a royal grant and helped by various benefactors, one of whom was the influential government official Jonas Collin. Collin became his lifelong paternal friend, and Andersen was more than ever set on a literary career.

Andersen actually never related to Danish poetic realism. On the contrary, from the outset he felt attracted to contemporary European writers such as E. T. A. Hoffmann and Heinrich Heine. And it was precisely Hoffmann's capricious style that he chose for his first major prose work, *Fodreise fra Holmens Canal til Østpynten af Amager i Aarene 1828 og 1829* (1829; A Walking Tour from Holmen's Canal to the Eastern Point of Amager in the Years 1828 and 1829), a loosely structured and witty collection of sketches from Andersen's daily walk across Copenhagen to his tutor. A remarkable number of themes that were later used in his tales and stories can already be found at this early stage of his career. Noteworthy is likewise an unmistakable, almost nihilistic, attack on bourgeois cultural ideals.

Heine was the obvious model for Andersen's youthful poetry. In his first collection, *Digte* (1830; Poems), Andersen ironizes over the romantic genre piece, "There's the setting sun—et cetera!" or he adds a dramatic touch, as in his very first published text, the poem "Det døende Barn" (1828; The Dying Child), a projection of his own loneliness and sufferings. It is characteristic of all these texts that they focus on the poor and those who are overlooked in society. Heine's impact is much more noticeable in the next volume, *Phantasier og Skizzer* (1831; Fantasies and Sketches), both in the nonstrophic attempts at imitating Heine's "Nordseelieder" and in some liedlike love poems, several of which were inspired by his unhappy love for the sister of a fellow student, Riborg Voigt. Set to music by Edvard Grieg, "To brune Øine" (Two Brown Eyes) and "Min Tankes Tanke" (The Thought of My Thought) have gained immortality.

After the breakthrough with his novels and tales Andersen's lyrical production receded into the background and appeared only sporadically in newspapers, plays, and travelogues. It is, however, precisely in the poems from his many travels that Andersen emerges as a bold colorist with a predilection for exotic motifs, making him, more than any other Danish poet, a unique Danish counterpart to the exotic writings of Hugo and Mérimée.

This exoticism also permeates the two plays from 1840. *Mulatten* (The Mulatto) is set on the African island of Martinique. The title character, a social and racial outcast whose love for the white French countess Cecilie is reciprocated, is an obvious self-projection. The play's tight structure, modeled after the works of Scribe, leads with dramatic force to the climax: the final act's slave market at which Cecilie and her rival, Eleonora, fight over the mulatto. Eleonora's sexual obsession makes her the demonic character of the play. A fire ignites in the bold, sensual descriptions of her reckless passion—still only smoldering in Hertz's *Svend Dyrings Huus*—which makes *Mulatten* a revolutionary exception in nineteenth-century Danish drama. It became, particularly because of the slave market scene, a great success, and the always-responsive Andersen immediately attempted to follow it with yet another exotic melodrama, *Maurerpigen* (1840; The Moorish Maid). Heiberg opposed its performance, however, and the resounding failure of the play was partly due to his wife's refusal to perform in the title role, which Andersen had created especially for her after her superb performance as Cecilie in *Mulatten*.

Nevertheless, Andersen continued to write plays during the next ten years and would never admit his failure as a dramatist. By that time, however, he had already established himself as a European celebrity with his novels and tales. It was during his first major journey abroad in 1833–34, particularly his encounter with the glowing colors of Italian nature and its picturesque folk life, that Andersen learned *to see*. Now he could turn his back on his former literary models, and he emerged as a highly sensitive observer with a pointed realistic expression that marks a new departure in Danish literature. It is in his tales and stories especially that Andersen's linguistic innovation manifested itself—in his rejection of literary diction in favor of the spoken language—but it was with his novels that he won his first international laurels.

The immediate impressions from his Italian sojourn, Madame de Staël's technique of combining fiction and travelogue in her novel *Corinne ou l'Italie* (1807), and Walter Scott's detailed milieu descriptions merge in Andersen's debut novel, *Improvisatoren* (1835; Eng. tr. *The Improvisatore*, 1845). It is his own story as it had been and would, he hoped, turn out to be. A poor Roman boy, Antonio, with a gift for poetic improvisation (a talent derogatorily attributed to Andersen by Heiberg), is helped by a distinguished family and succeeds after much adversity, both in his artistic career and in the affairs of love. Andersen, however, was able to reach this harmonious conclusion only by manipulating the novel's plot in order to bring it in agreement with its philosophical idea: to unite the ideal and spiritual with the material and sensual. The novel's colorful snapshots from various Italian tourist attractions made *Improvisatoren* an immediate international success, the audience overlooking Andersen's own occasional sneering at the often too-pastoral atmosphere of such passages. It is characteristic in general of this work, as well as the succeeding novels, that Andersen consistently switches between the milieus of the upper and lower classes, reflecting the hero's own social as well as psychological vacillation between spirit and matter.

Andersen followed up this success with the novels *O. T.* (1836; Eng. tr. 1845) and *Kun en Spillemand* (1837; Eng. tr. *Only a Fiddler,* 1845), both also self-projections but with a Danish setting. In the portrayal of the main character, *Otto Thostrup,* the period's fascination with Byron is evident. Otto is born in *Odense Tugthus* (i.e., jail), where his mother has been imprisoned on false charges, as it turns out much later. The initials *O.T.* have been branded on Otto's shoulder, indicating the social trauma marking him. Finally, and only after numerous mystifications have been cleared up— Andersen's tribute to *romantisme*—Otto is able to free himself from this trauma through a postulated and idyllicized marriage. He does not marry the girl he really feels attracted to, the erotically exciting Sophie, but her sister, the gentle Biedermeier heroine Louise. Compared with *Improvisatoren,* the tone of this novel is much more somber and fateful. With *Kun en Spillemand* Andersen moved close to tragedy. As in his debut novel, Andersen tells the story of a poor but artistically gifted boy, Christian, and his attempt at realizing his dreams of becoming a musician. This time, however, the outcome is negative because of the hero's proletarian origin, his lack of self-confidence, and the unsympathetic environment. Therefore, the talented violinist dies an impoverished village fiddler, a conclusion that strikingly contradicts the optimistic moral of Andersen's autobiographical tale of "Den grimme Ælling"(The Ugly Duckling). Even though Christian has lain in a swan's egg he is not able to rise above the duckyard. The general criticism of *Kun en Spillemand* did not prevent it from becoming Andersen's next best seller. Kierkegaard, however, not without reason, attacked the book as being sentimental, the character for being a sniveler, and the author as lacking a consistent philosophy of life.

Both novels are loosely put together, and in *Kun en Spillemand,* in particular, the narrative falls apart in several places as Andersen changes his focus from Christian to Naomi, the girl Christian pursues in vain and who, in contrast to himself, takes charge of her own destiny and succeeds. Structurally more successful, but less known, is the novel *De to Baronesser* (1848; Eng. tr. *The Two Baronesses,* 1848). Andersen's struggle to assert himself in his relationship with the upper class, which he increasingly associated with, lies behind the idea of this novel: true nobility is not determined socially but depends on the spirit, an idea that is in complete agreement with romantic idealism. In contrast to Christian, the fiddler, the poor crofter's daughter Elisabeth succeeds—through conscious self-education, based on a Christian world view—in raising herself above her childhood milieu and taking her place among the aristocracy as the wife and equal of a baron; thus, the social conflict is dissolved through one's own efforts.

With their mediating conclusions this novel and his next, *At være eller ikke være* (1857; Eng. tr. *To Be, or Not To Be?*, 1857), are much closer to the traditional bildungsroman than Andersen's other novels. The conflict in *At være eller ikke være* between faith and freethinking, between the power of God and the power of man, is embedded in the account of the progress of a young man from atheism to Christianity. His conversion takes place during his participation in the Dano-German war of 1848–50. As a wounded soldier he reaches back to the Lord's Prayer of his childhood in an episode that undoubtedly inspired J. P. Jacobsen to a similar, much better known scene in his novel *Niels Lyhne*. In a broader sense the novel constitutes a strong attack on the emerging materialism of the 1850s, but at the same time it is Andersen's reply to Kierkegaard's attack on *Kun en Spillemand*. With *Lykke-Peer* (1870; Eng. tr. *Lucky Peer*, 1871) Andersen wrote his last novel, in many ways a reversion to his debut novel. Like Antonio, Peer is an Aladdin character, and like Antonio, he represents Andersen's dream about his own career, which by now had been fulfilled. Peer, the son of a poor warehouseman, outdistances Felix, the son of a rich businessman, by becoming a singer and composer, then dying at the climax of his career as he performs the title role in his own opera "Aladdin." In contrast to *Improvisatoren*, Andersen does not allow his hero to savor his success. The experience of happy love is also denied him, and it is with tragic sadness that Andersen, in the final account, lets Peer mirror his own life and actually that of the author himself: true harmony has not been and perhaps never can be established.

The well-known statement that opens Andersen's autobiography, "My life is a beautiful fairy tale, rich and happy," was written in 1855 in idealizing retrospect by a renowned celebrity and is, together with the glorification of his own fate and genius in the tale "Den grimme Ælling" (1844 [translations of Andersen's tales and stories are so numerous that they are not listed]), only partly valid. It should not be overlooked that the magnificent white swan of this tale, after having been ridiculed and persecuted, actually ends up just a domesticated bird taking its food from the hands of children. Here Andersen deals with the relationship with his audience and his social climbing, as he himself ended his career as the favorite author of the upper class. Yet even in this situation Andersen could never forget that he was and would always be an outsider, and in tales such as "Svinedrengen" (1842; The Swineherd), "Nattergalen" (1844; The Nightingale), and "Gartneren og Herskabet" (1872; The Gardener and the Lord and Lady) he aimed his scathing satire at the arrogance and selfishness of the aristocracy and court circles. In addition to being satires, the three tales are also allegories, setting true poetry against rigid academic convention and thus defending Andersen's own writings against his critics. Moreover, exemplifying the intriguing complexity of many of these texts, "Svinedrengen," as well as the less significant but probably most popular of them all, "Den lille Havfrue" (1837; The Little Mermaid), are also comments on the author's own social status. Andersen identifies himself with the swineherd, who is actually a prince in disguise, and the handicapped mermaid. The prince she falls hopelessly in love with and the stupid and arrogant princess in "Svinedrengen," who rejects the beautiful gifts of the prince because they are real, are probably portraits of Andersen's second great but unattainable love, Louise Collin. She was the daughter of his benefactor and in 1833 became engaged to a man of her own social class.

Royalty itself, however, Andersen placed beyond criticism. In spite of his proletarian origin, which he never disguised, he did not become a social writer—like his friend and admirer Charles Dickens, whom he met twice in England, in 1847 and 1857—but attempted to rework his social traumas artistically. Nevertheless, social accusations are hidden everywhere in his oeuvre and occasionally surface, as in the loving portrait of his own mother, given the ironic title, " 'Hun duede ikke—' " (1853; "She Was No Good"), or in his attacks on the ruthless social behavior in contemporary Copenhagen studied through a magnifying glass in the fable "Vanddraaben" (1848; A Drop of Water).

According to Andersen himself, his tales and stories rest on a solid foundation of reality: "Most of what I have written is a reflection of myself. Every character is taken from life." Thus "Grantræet" (1845; The Fir Tree), frequently read as an idyllic Christmas story, is a harsh self-judgment of the ambitious, always discontented artist, afraid of having passed his prime. The fortune-hunting soldier in "Fyrtøiet" (1835; The Tinderbox) and the hypersensitive title character of the one-page masterpiece "Prindsessen paa Ærten" (1835; The Princess on the Pea) are likewise self-portraits, and Andersen's affairs of the heart can also be followed in several tales: the bittersweet "Kjærestefolkene" (1844; The Sweethearts) describes a meeting with Riborg Voigt thirteen years after his unsuccessful courtship. As noted earlier, Louise Collin is likewise portrayed negatively. "Nattergalen," in its contrast of the real and the artificial, is a tribute to his third and greatest love, the Swedish soprano Jenny Lind, whom he met in 1840. She, too, rejected him, and his resignation to bachelorhood is humorously dealt with in the parable "Sommerfuglen" (1861; The Butterfly). Portraits of friends and acquaintances can also be found. The prince in "Klokken" (1845; The Bell), who represents the scientific mode of approaching the Divine, is possibly a portrait of Hans Christian Ørsted, the first to recognize Andersen's genius as a writer of tales. The poor boy, who represents the poetic mode, is another self-portrait.

The tales and stories are more than disguised autobiographies, and more than simple entertainment: "I seize an idea for older people—and tell it to the young ones, while remembering that father and mother are listening and must have something to think about." This statement by Andersen reveals the innermost secret of his tales and stories: their oral quality. When he lets the learned man in "Skyggen" (1847; The Shadow) write about what is true, good, and beautiful, he states not only his own ideal of art but also, in a formula, the values set forth by the romantics of his own time. But the bitter irony of "Skyggen" is that no one pays attention to these values, and people choose instead to follow the title character, the most demonic character of Danish nineteenth-century literature, a being without substance. "Skyggen" is a capital text in the history of Danish thought. Materialism and nihilism are seen as ideologies successfully replacing spirituality, and the Christian God is completely absent. Nothing is left of the romantic belief that the good-hearted person, such as Johannes in "Reisekammeraten" (1835; The Traveling Companion) or Gerda in "Sneedronningen" (1845; The Snow Queen), has nothing to fear from evil: all human efforts are absurd. That is also the main theme of "Historien om en Moder" (1848; The Story of a Mother), a tribute to maternal love but also a demonstration of the mercilessness of life. These texts exemplify how Andersen has replaced the tale with the short story, romanticism with realism, Biedermeier with modernity.

Generally, Andersen's tales and stories are based on a duality between optimism and pessimism, life and death. In opposition to those tales positing a belief in good fortune ("Fyrtøiet," "Reisekammeraten"), in the power of goodness of heart over cold reason ("Sneedronningen"), and in the possibility of human experience of the Divine ("Klokken"), many texts are hopelessly pessimistic about the world in general and strongly skeptical about Andersen's fate and vocation as an artist in particular: "Grantræet," with its conclusion: "It's over! It's all over!"; "Skyggen," in which the learned man ends up being executed; "Den lille Pige med Svovlstikkerne" (1846; The Little Match Girl), an unequivocal and unsentimental condemnation of a callous bourgeoisie; and "Tante Tandpine" (1872; Auntie Toothache), one of Andersen's last tales and through its concluding invocation of death and transitoriness the tragic epilogue to his entire oeuvre.

As a child Andersen had heard retellings of folktales, and he was also familiar with the German literary, romantic tales by Tieck, Hoffmann, and Adelbert von Chamisso as well as the tales collected by the Grimm brothers. These sources are all reflected in the first 4 of the 156 tales and stories written by Andersen, entitled *Eventyr, fortalte for Børn* (1835; Tales, Told for Children). "Fyrtøiet," "Prindsessen paa Ærten," and "Store Claus og Lille Claus" (Big Claus and Little Claus) are all retold folktales. The fourth, and weakest tale, "Den lille Idas Blomster" (Little Ida's Flowers), is Andersen's own invention but dependent on a story by Hoffmann. The discovery of the folktale became a chief element in Andersen's search for artistic independence. Here he found what was lacking in his novels, the short form and the firm structure. Here he found the technique of retelling the same episode three times and using only one main character, while all antagonists of the hero or heroine play subordinate roles.

The first six collections, from 1835 to 1841, were subtitled, "Told for Children," revealing Andersen's ingenious discovery that his tales and stories have to be *told*. He now began to write texts of greater length and of a different, more realistic nature, and the two collections of 1852–53 bear the title *Historier* (Stories). But Andersen did not give up the tale, and his last eleven volumes, from 1858 to 1872, are entitled, *Eventyr og Historier* (Tales and Stories).

What really makes Andersen unique in world literature is not the topics he chose but his inimitable style, his rejection of the conventional literary diction of the romantic era in favor of everyday, colloquial language. His imagination also broke with all literary conventions, animating the inanimate. His acute power of observation endowed the most fantastic beings with realistic traits. Andersen was by no means a romantic dreamer. On the contrary, he welcomed all new events in art and science as long as they did not limit one's spiritual outlook. In the tale of "Den store Søe-Slange" (1872; The Great Sea Serpent) he wrote about the telegraph cable under the Atlantic Ocean, and he even ventured as far as fantasizing, in the science fiction story "Om Aartusinder" (1852; In a Thousand Years' Time), about a group of busy young Americans flying to Europe on the wings of steam with only eight days to spend, a story astoundingly anticipating Jules Verne's 1873 novel *Le Tour du monde en quatre-vingt jours* (Around the World in Eighty Days).

Andersen himself was the greatest traveler of his time, going abroad either to escape criticism at home or to enjoy his international fame. Always on the lookout for poetic motifs, he used material from many of his trips to write travelogues, which stand on their own as accomplished samples of the genre, displaying his brilliant journalistic talent; and they contain episodes and themes that Andersen would draw on for his other works. Even his first journey abroad—to Germany in 1831—resulted in a travel book, *Skyggebilleder af en Reise til Harzen, det sachsiske Schweitz etc. etc.* (1831; Eng. tr. *Rambles in the Romantic Regions of the Hartz Mountains, Saxon Switzerland, Etc.*, 1848). Influenced by Heine's epic *Die Harzreise* (1826; The Harz Journey), its lyrical pictures and fantasies intertwine playfully with impressions of foreign places and countryside as well as new acquaintances. All these impressions culminate in the encounter with the poet Ludwig Tieck in Dresden. In this way the trip, like all the succeeding ones, also became an educational experience, an encounter with romanticism as a literary movement. Likewise Heinesque are the bittersweet sentiments of love. They are overflowing with longing and at the same time shrilly ironic, yet another evidence of Andersen's infatuation with Riborg Voigt, but also an indication of his fascination with the worship of the moods of disharmony present in the emerging *romantisme*. Pointing ahead to the future, Andersen paid tribute to the Greek war of independence in 1821–29 and the Polish rebellion against Russia in 1830–31 and, in a wider perspective, to a new era, in which political freedom, public education, and general enlightenment would rule.

Andersen used a capricious composition for his next travelogues. Of greatest artistic quality is *En Digters Bazar* (1842; Eng. tr. *A Poet's Bazaar*, 1988), the result of Andersen's most extensive journey, to Italy, Greece, and Turkey in 1840–41. It too is sharp and precise in its descriptions of scenery and atmosphere, displaying once again Andersen's talent for catching every detail in all its picturesque qualities and uniqueness. In his capacity as a guide—also characterizing his other travelogues from southern Europe, *I Spanien* (1863; Eng. tr. *In Spain*, 1864; *A Visit to Spain*, 1975) and *Et Besøg i Portugal 1866* (1868; Eng. tr. *A Visit to Portugal 1866*, 1972)—Andersen describes not by reeling off facts but by creating colorful, impressionistic images.

In addition to the fictional works the travelogues are an excellent supplement to Andersen's autobiographies. His first attempt, written in 1832 (publ. 1926), ends with a detailed, psychologically penetrating account of his love for Riborg Voigt; for a German edition of his collected works Andersen wrote another autobiography, published in 1847, which the same year came out in an English version as *The True Story of My Life*. This work was expanded and in 1855 published in Danish as *Mit Livs Eventyr* (The Fairy Tale of My Life). An American edition with additional chapters covering the years up to 1867, when Andersen became an honorary citizen of Odense, was published in New York in 1871 as *The Story of My Life*.

This lifelong autobiographical project, together with his diaries published in ten volumes in 1971–77 (selections in Eng. tr. *The Diaries of Hans Christian Andersen*, 1990), offers fascinating insights into Andersen's psyche. In contrast to the well-balanced, carefully composed autobiographies, the diaries are an inexhaustible collection of raw material, improvisations, moods, and concrete details written in the shorthand style of the moment. Through them we learn of his reading, visits to museums and theaters, and acquaintances with writers and composers, revealing how deeply he was part of the European literary and cultural tradition, indeed the greatest cosmopolitan in Danish literature since Holberg. Nowhere does one come closer to the author than through these entries, in which great and small philosophical speculations and impromptus are experienced and depicted side by side. The diaries shed light on the author's social traumas and document his divided self: his erotic longing and sexual fears, his need for new experiences and his timidity, his optimism and depressions, his hypochondria, vulnerability, and vanity—and most of all his loneliness amid the throng of admirers. Andersen's diaries constitute an exceptionally rich source for the study of European culture and social history throughout half a century. They present one of the strangest and most incongruous artistic portraits in world literature. Here one finds the unique mixture of precision, irony, and naiveté that is so characteristic of Andersen's entire oeuvre and sets him apart from all other writers of his time.

Frederik Paludan-Müller

Even Andersen attempted, in spite of the ideological and social ferment of the time and occasional skepticism in his own world view, to hold on to a concept of external harmony as well as the metaphysics of Christianity as the fundamental determinant of values. Nevertheless, the result of his somewhat dialectic vacillation between contrasting views emerges as a philosophical relativism of a completely modern stamp. In the works of Hostrup the social unrest became increasingly noticeable, Chievitz questioned social morality, Bagger was even less willing to accept the status quo, while writers like Bødtcher and Aarestrup in particular chose art and beauty as values that—at least on the surface—could reconcile humankind with the negative sides of existence.

Against such attempts at reconciliation on one hand and philosophical relativism and ethical nihilism on the other, a sharp criticism and consistent religious commitment emerge with Paludan-Müller and Kierkegaard. During the 1830s Frederik Paludan-Müller (1809–76) was a leading representative of the young, Byron-inspired, and beauty-worshipping generation of writers. As a celebrated poet of the hour, he eagerly participated in Copenhagen social life until receiving his law degree in 1835. With his *Poesier* (1836–38; Poems, 1–2), however, Paludan-Müller's fortunes changed. Besides a Shakespearean comedy, the volumes contain lyrical and epic poems that offer insights into more complex layers of the poet's psyche and—as something new—contain pronounced religious overtones. They were met with surprise and disapproval by the unsympathetic critics. Even more decisive was another event: in 1837 Paludan-Müller was stricken by typhoid fever and nursed back to health by a relative, Charite Borch, whom he married the same year. This marriage, a simultaneous personal crisis caused by his illness, and an innate melancholy resulted in a radical change in Paludan-Müller's philosophy toward an ethical and religious world view. In his writings this change manifested itself in a growing concentration on the themes of renunciation and death.

The first result of Paludan-Müller's infatuation with Byron was the verse epic *Dandserinden* (1833; The Danseuse), written, like several other works from the following years, in the Byronic ottava rima and with remnants from the love story of Don Juan and Haidée in Byron's principal work, *Don Juan* (1819–24). In *Dandserinden* Paludan-Müller depicts the love relationship between the celebrated ballet dancer Dione and the elegant but weak Count Charles, framed by scenes from the fashionable life of Copenhagen high society. Charles deserts Dione when he is persuaded by his mother to marry a woman whose social rank is closer to his. Shortly before his marriage, however, he is killed in a duel, which he fights to defend Dione's honor, and consequently she dies, after going insane. High points of realism are the broadly painted satirical period pictures, but equally significant are the numerous reflective passages or, rather, digressions. Here the author expresses a strong sense of transitoriness, whose dissonant tone is a genuine expression of the *romantisme* movement and of a personal striving for an eternity that is perhaps inaccessible.

This tendency toward philosophical digression—also modeled after Byron—became a permanent feature in the works to follow. The next year Paludan-Müller chose mythological garb for the drama *Amor og Psyche* (1834; Cupid and Psyche), based on a novel of Roman antiquity by Apuleius, *Metamorphoses* (second century). Characters and situations lack the sculptural quality of *Dandserinden*, but both the elegant versification and the basic structure are the same: in three stages Paludan-Müller depicts the brief moment of love's elusiveness, the character's moral failure, and attempted rehabilitation through remorse. A new element is the ethical and religious character of the final stage: it is through endurance and suffering that the true essence of love can be experienced on a spiritual level.

The definitive transition from an aesthetic to an ethical world view took place in the first work Paludan-Müller published after his marriage, another mythological drama, *Venus* (1841). At the same time, this work constitutes a reckoning with the self-centered, demonic, and destructive Byronic hero of the previous decade's *romantisme*. Here Paludan-Müller juxtaposes sensual eroticism with spiritual love. The sexual desire of the hunter Actaeon, a Don Juan character, drives the shepherdess Hermione to suicide. When Actaeon pursues the goddess Diana herself, she transforms him into a stag and he is torn to pieces by his own dogs. Endymion, the bridegroom of Hermione, in contrast, is led to the land of the dead, later to be reunited with his beloved in Elysium. The lament about transitoriness, so pronounced in Paludan-Müller's youthful writing, is here replaced by a forceful condemnation of sensuality and a glorification of asceticism and death.

Whereas *Venus* is a totally abstract drama of ideas, Paludan-Müller in his next work, the dramatic poem *Tithon* (1844), develops individualized characters taken from the legends of Troy. With sublime lyricism he expresses the pain of taking leave of earthly existence and the burden of life's moral obligations, for better or for worse: not only pure materialism but also pure spirituality has its cost.

With reference to his own time Paludan-Müller lets Prince Tithon symbolize romantic poetry and its amoral escapism, and thus the whole work, like *Venus,* can also be read as a significant settlement with the times. In this way it points ahead to Paludan-Müller's definitive work, *Adam Homo* (1842–49; Eng. tr. 1981), which combines the social criticism of *Dandserinden* with a strong demand for ethical responsibility and is given a grand religious dimension. This epic is one of the great masterpieces of Scandinavian literature. Following the tripartite composition of his first two works, Paludan-Müller portrays the life of an average human being (cf. title) from the cradle to the grave and ultimate doom, demonstrating how this opportunist antihero has signed himself away to the present, to pleasure and career, constantly avoiding any ethical commitment.

Like an Aladdin, Adam is born with rich talents, and like a Faust, he finally faces divine judgment for having abused these talents. His childhood in a Jutland parsonage is marked on the one hand by his father's pragmatic attitude and on the other by his pious mother's admonition to live according to the plan of God, an admonition that Adam, on his journey through life, does not follow. He goes to Copenhagen to study theology, but under the influence of a Byronic libertine he is introduced to the pleasures of the capital's social life of easy virtue. In order to be free of his debts Adam becomes a tutor for the flirtatious countess Clara, who only plays with his feelings for her; afterward he finds an outlet for his bitterness by seducing the maid Lotte. In vain he seeks consolation with two prostitutes, in a scene influenced by Bagger's *Min Broders Levnet,* and attempts suicide. After his convalescence Adam meets Alma, a gardener's daughter, and falls in love with her. In a series of sonnets she gives expression to the sentiments of love he has stirred in her. Now Adam develops a new philosophy of life: "He saw that all lay under love's sole mastery."

Finally, he receives his degree, but he is overtaken by his past when he meets Lotte, who is now a prostitute. Nevertheless, as the topic for his first homily Adam chooses the importance of good deeds! Then he learns about his mother's fatal illness, but on his journey home he again sees Clara (now married), is once again attracted by her, and subsequently changes his itinerary. He accompanies Clara back to her castle and exchanges his previous philosophy for an Epicurean view of a life guided by chance occurrence. During an attempt to seduce Clara, Adam is caught by her husband and returns home to his father, now a widower. He abandons his plan to become a clergyman and is supported by his opportunist father, who arranges a marriage with the emancipated baroness Mille after Adam breaks off his engagement with Alma in a letter.

From this point on Paludan-Müller abandons his previous coherent narrative in favor of an episodic composition. Through his marriage Adam has taken a decisive step to further his career, and simultaneously he shifts to an idealistic philosophy. For a time he becomes a philanthropist and establishes a speaker's club with the purpose to promote nothing less than "perfection." But Adam's opening speech is a failure, and thereafter he rejects his former "idealism" in favor of pure opportunism. While Mille commits herself wholeheartedly to the women's movement and her own short story writing, which, because of her bribery of the press, earns her some success, Adam climbs the ladder of society. He is appointed privy councillor, baron, and finally manager of the Royal Theater. In his inaugural speech Adam calls attention to "the ideal" but reduces it to a life on the stage. After a horseback ride he catches a cold and is sent to the hospital, where the doctors succeed in killing him with their ministrations. He recognizes Alma keeping watch by his bed and repents of his betrayal: "Where did the long time go which I had won? / I lived for scarce a minute—it is done!" Shortly thereafter, Alma, who remained faithful to her love for him, dies and leaves behind a collection of lyrical poems and religious reflections. After his death Adam faces judgment, and only Alma's intercessory prayers and love save him from damnation.

Paludan-Müller also passes judgment on his own times. The indirect criticism seen in the account of Adam's external, social success develops—as in Heiberg's *En Sjæl efter Døden*—into a pointed satire on contemporary bourgeois Danish society as an environment of mediocrity, vanity, and corruption. More important are the inserted reflective passages, in which Paludan-Müller develops his philosophy of the personality, thus representing a significant intermediate stage between P. M. Møller and Kierkegaard. In this context his ethical stance takes on a wider perspective as it is turned into an analysis of responsibility versus anarchy in the life of the single human being, a life spent without preparation for its conclusion. *Adam Homo* is above all a grandiose religious didactic epic in which the soul, as in Dante's *La divina commedia* (ca. 1307–20), through purification in Purgatory is led to salvation. But contrary to the related *Faust* drama by Goethe (1808), in which Faust wins salvation through his mere striving, Adam is dependent on grace, won through the love that Alma has never betrayed. Like Beatrice and Gretchen, she represents the ideal woman, the redeeming Eros. Indeed, Alma's poems constitute some of the most exquisite lyrical expressions in world literature of the concept that true happiness can be found only through renunciation.

The three texts in the collection *Tre Digte* (1854; Three Poems) are even stronger expressions of Paludan-Müller's doctrine of self-denial. In *Kalanus* zest for life and asceticism are juxtaposed and represented in the figures of the warrior and conqueror Alexander the Great and the Indian sage Kalanus, respectively. In the final account Kalanus turns out to be the true victor as he seeks his death in flames on the pyre. In *Abels Død* (The Death of Abel), Paludan-Müller's first biblical writing, Paradise is depicted as the realm of true life, whereas death itself, or rather the state of ennui, is directly glorified in *Ahasverus,* which, spurred by the violent cholera epidemic in Copenhagen in 1853, assumes the character of a bitter, almost nihilistic Doomsday vision of a decadent civilization.

Under the influence of the military debacle in 1864, but with the time of the action moved to the war of 1848–50, Paludan-Müller changed signals and wrote a counterpart to *Adam Homo,* the three-volume novel *Ivar Lykkes Historie* (1866–73; The Story of Ivar Lykke), an appeal for national regeneration after the defeat by Germany. Contrary to Adam, Ivar gains inner strength through adversity. His volunteer service during the war rehabilitates him after an unjust discharge from the diplomatic service, and in the final account he wins the hand of his beloved. The novel contains all the necessary ingredients to make it popular: excitement, romantic adventures, and an optimistic line of development in the plot in the tradition of the bildungsroman; Goethe's *Wilhelm Meister* is its unmistakable model. The novel's diffuseness, colorless style, and abstract language have unfortunately consigned it to oblivion.

At the same time, Paludan-Müller, in a number of mythological works, bade farewell to this world. A zest for life is now, in the title character of his last book, *Adonis* (1874), contrasted with renunciation and longing for death, a contrast, in fact, on which his entire oeuvre is based. Adonis has always worshipped both Venus and the goddess of death, Proserpina, but to find peace of mind he finally chooses death, which alone can "bring to an end the conflict of the heart."

It is characteristic that Adonis must make a choice, and this constitutes a crucial concept in Paludan-Müller's philosophy of life. In this respect Paludan-Müller the ethicist holds out his hand to Kierkegaard, who develops this idea further to become the "leap" that must be taken into the religious stage, into salvation. Both men sternly condemn the dilution and vulgarization of the concept of the personality. This they saw as a result both of the aesthetic outlook on life and the abstract Hegelian manipulation of philosophical terms, two phenomena that, in the final account, are rooted in romanticism.

In his youth Paludan-Müller was a celebrated and fashionable writer. Later he avoided all popularity. The contemporary public as well as posterity took revenge by ignoring his message while his critics simultaneously—and justifiably—stressed his mastery of form. *Adam Homo* alone is recognized as a flawless piece of art but can actually be valued and interpreted exhaustively only in context with Paludan-Müller's other and equally significant works.

Søren Kierkegaard

As is the case with Paludan-Müller, the external events in the life of Søren Kierkegaard (1813–55) are few but decisive. The son of a wealthy merchant, he was raised in Copenhagen. His parents' fortune made him financially independent. He never used his degrees to pursue an academic career, although in 1840 he received a degree in divinity and in 1841 a master's degree in philosophy after having studied with P. M. Møller. Three events had a crucial impact on Kierkegaard's life: his engagement to the seventeen-year-old Regine Olsen in 1840, which he regretted two days later, provoking a break by pretending he had deceived her; a confrontation with the writer

M. A. Goldschmidt in 1846; and, finally, his attacks on the official Lutheran state church in 1854.

On the spiritual level Kierkegaard's heritage from his father must also be taken into consideration: a depressive nature and a strict, pietistic Christianity that resulted in crises, the first in 1835, through which Kierkegaard came to understand that "what counts is to find a truth, which is *my* truth." That is the first time Kierkegaard expresses his philosophy of the personality, which he was later to contrast with the abstract and speculative philosophical system of Hegel, in which humankind is only an impersonal pawn in the dialectic development of the human spirit. Shortly after the crisis of 1835 an event took place which Kierkegaard, with the usual technique of dissimulation he used when referring to the most private episodes in his life, labels "the big earthquake." He is probably referring to a shocking insight into the religious world of his father. The result was that Kierkegaard left home, plunging himself into the carousing life of a bohemian. The following year he experienced "an indescribable joy": a reconciliation with his father and a Christian breakthrough.

Shortly beforehand Kierkegaard had made his debut with *Af en endnu Levendes Papirer* (1838; Eng. tr. *Early Polemic Writings: One Still Living,* 1990), a criticism of Andersen's novel *Kun en Spillemand* and its frail title character, against whom he juxtaposes the true genius, who is "a fire, which only the storm can challenge." Kierkegaard saw himself as an exemplification of this definition when, in 1840, he broke off his engagement because of what he, again in enigmatic terms, calls "the thorn in the flesh," which could be an allusion either to his inherited melancholy or to an erotic experience in his youth.

During this period Kierkegaard finished his thesis, *Om Begrebet Ironie med stadigt Hensyn til Socrates* (1841; Eng. tr. *The Concept of Irony with Continual Reference to Socrates,* 1989), a fierce attack on the romantic irony in Fr. Schlegel's novel *Lucinde* (1799) as amoral, negative, and nihilistic. As a contrast Kierkegaard points to Socrates and his "positive" irony, which served to make the opponent insecure at first but only to encourage him to think independently, a method Kierkegaard himself was to employ to force the individual to take a stand and choose a personal attitude toward life.

The tragic events surrounding his unsuccessful engagement as well as a stay in Berlin in 1841–42 were the stimulating forces behind the astonishing productivity that followed, resulting in more than thirty books, thirteen volumes of notes and diaries (Eng. tr. *Journals and Papers,* 1967–78), and numerous newspaper articles in only thirteen years. Under the pseudonym of Victor Eremita (i.e., the one who is victorious in solitude), Kierkegaard first published *Enten-Eller* (1843; Eng. tr. *Either/Or*, 1944). Its first part ostensibly consists of loose scraps of paper on which an anonymous person, *A.*, an aesthete who lives without any sense of obligation and responsibility, has written down in aphoristic form his thoughts about fragmentation and haphazardness as the condition of man, sometimes with a desperate tone: "No one ever comes back from the dead, no one ever enters the world without weeping; no one is asked when he wishes to enter life, no one is asked when he wishes to leave," and sometimes sardonically: "I prefer to talk with children, for it is still possible to hope that they may become rational beings. But those who have already become so—good Lord!"

More sophisticated than the author of these so-called Diapsalmata is the nonreflective character of the seducer, whose life consists of isolated, sensual experiences that end in monotonous repetition. This person's attitude toward the erotic is described through analyses of Mozart's operas, culminating in a brilliant discussion of *Don Giovanni*. The next stage of aestheticism, that of reflective sensuality, is also treated in *A.*'s papers, entitled "Forførerens Dagbog" (The Diary of a Seducer). The highest goal of the seducer, Johannes, is not, as in the case of Don Giovanni, the possession of women, but the strategy leading up to it. Gradually, he lures the young girl Cordelia out of reality and into his erotic fantasies toward the culmination of their relationship, which at the same time is the point of rupture. This novel consists of detached observations of every nuance of Cordelia's emotions, which serve as clues for the seducer's next strategic move. Thus, Johannes is never committed to what he undertakes. He knows of no value system, and in the final account he experiences everything as emptiness and despair. With Paludan-Müller's *Adam Homo,* "Forførerens Dagbog" deals the final, crushing blow to romanticism. In the second major part of the work, however, *B.*, (Judge Wilhelm), presents an alternative. In two extensive letters to his "aesthetic" friend, Wilhelm explains his own ethical philosophy. Through an effort of will the ethicist has moved beyond the stage of aesthetic despair. By choosing obligation and responsibility toward God, his own vocation, and his wife, he has enabled himself to shape his own coherent existence and "realize the universal."

Enten-Eller concludes with an "Ultimatum," a homily in which a third, religious stage is indicated. Together with the aesthetic and ethical stages it is—once more fictionally—analyzed in *Stadier paa Livets Vei* (1845; Eng. tr. *Stages on Life's Way,* 1940), a high point of sophisticated psychology, composition, and style. With Plato's *Symposion* as his model, Kierkegaard, in the section "In vino veritas," starts out by portraying five aesthetes, among them Victor Eremita, and their drinking bout, during which they all present witty but derisive talks about woman in which they see her, and love as well, exclusively from the perspective of pleasure. In an essay that the narrator of "In vino veritas" sneaks from the pocket of Judge Wilhelm, whom he meets the next morning in his garden, love is viewed from an ethical viewpoint. To Wilhelm, woman is not an erotic object but a mother and wife. Nevertheless, he indicates that the ethicist will not necessarily find comfort in his choice but that a third view of life is possible, which is then portrayed in the volume's third part, "'Skyldig?'"—"'Ikke-Skyldig?'" ("Guilty?—Not Guilty?"), with the subtitle "Psychological Experiment." This experiment consists of a love story in the form of a diary, which, like "Forførerens Dagbog," is inspired by Kierkegaard's own life. Because of the male character's melancholy the love relationship cannot be realized. Therefore, "the experimenter" lets him provoke a break so that he can feel guilt and suffering, which constitute the prerequisite for the religious stage. The question of who is guilty is actually not answered but repentance is present, which again is the preliminary condition for the consciousness of sin and thus faith. Thus, the man's misfortune can, on a higher level, turn into his good fortune.

The religious stage had already received in-depth analytical treatment in *Gjentagelsen* (1843; Eng. tr. *Repetition,* 1941). The main character and fictitious author, Constantin, an aesthete, in order to find out if "repetition" is possible at all, goes to Berlin to see if he can repeat his experiences from a previous stay. The experiment fails, and Constantin concludes that no repetition is possible. Into this plot is woven the love story of a young man who is unable to commit himself seriously to his engagement to a young woman. Constantin also conducts an experiment with him, testing him to see if he is able to carry out the "repetition." Constantin instructs the man how to provoke a break with his love—yet another autobiographical reference—in order to relive the engagement and thereby "realize the universal." This ethical repetition also fails, and the young man escapes to Stockholm. In his letters to Constantin he tells about his absorption in the Book of Job, which inspires him to try to regain the girl on a higher level—since repetition is only possible in the realm of the religious. Then he learns that his former fiancée has become engaged to someone else (which in fact had happened to Regine in the summer of 1843). Therefore, he cannot gain her back, but he "wins himself back" in absolute freedom. Like Job, whom the Lord compensated for his repeated sufferings, he "wins his faith."

On the same day that *Gjentagelsen* came out, Kierkegaard also published *Frygt og Bæven* (1843; Eng. tr. *Fear and Trembling,* 1939). The second work analyzes Abraham, "the father of faith," who, by being willing to sacrifice his son Isaac in order to follow God's commandment, overrides all ethical considerations. According to Kierkegaard, Abraham acts correctly by sacrificing everything he possesses, because, by doing so, he wins everything—he wins faith! Thus faith is placed on a higher level than worldly reason and morals. By insisting that "the individual's" absolute duty toward God is more important than the more general ethical demands with regard to your neighbor, Kierkegaard formulates a radical view of the religious, which, in his following works, was to take on the character of the paradoxical. Thus, in *Philosophiske Smuler* (1844; Eng. tr. *Philosophical Fragments,* 1936) he makes a clear distinction between philosophical idealism and Christianity, defining a Christian as a person who, through faith, takes possession of the absolute paradox: that God has become man in Christ, that eternity has entered time in order to grant humankind truth and salvation. This acceptance of the paradox is not connected with reason or limited to history but must take place continually within each single person in total freedom. The prerequisite for faith and salvation is the consciousness of sin, which Kierkegaard analyzes and associates with the concept of original sin in *Begrebet Angest* (1844; Eng. tr. *The Concept of Dread,* 1944). Before the spirit—according to Kierkegaard, the synthesis of body and soul—has become aware of itself, dread breaks forth, which is without an object, as opposed to fear, which is always a fear of something. It is dread that makes us powerless and gives birth to sin. But, as in Paradise, there will come a moment for everyone, when he or she experiences freedom as an ability to choose God. This happens at the same time that we realize ourselves as man or woman. Thus, dread is the first stage on the way that leads to faith. It makes that "leap" possible which leads humankind to the religious, a realm in which the spirit has realized itself.

Philosophiske Smuler was written under the pseudonym with which Kierkegaard associated himself most intimately, Johannes Climacus, and together with its sequel, *Afsluttende uvidenskabelig Efterskrift* (1846; Eng. tr. *Concluding Unscientific Postscript,* 1941), should be counted among Kierkegaard's central works. The *Efterskrift* opens with an attack on all attempts at anchoring Christianity in an impersonalized, speculative system, such as that of Hegel. Simultaneously, Kierkegaard rejects any possible historical proof of the truth of Christianity by invoking the Bible. Thereafter "the individual's" road to Christianity is once again described as predicated on the assimilation of the paradox of faith through a consciousness of sin, which entails a change from objective observation to a subjective and passionate relationship with Christ. Thus, "subjectivity is the truth!"

Efterskrift was intended as Kierkegaard's last work, after which he considered seeking an incumbency in the countryside. But he was now thrown into a fierce literary battle, which only aggravated his thoughts about the martyrdom required to be a true Christian. In 1845 the critic P. L. Møller had ironically and flippantly pointed out the autobiographical elements in the third part of *Stadier*. Kjerkegaard responded indignantly with a violent attack on Møller, concluding by linking him with Goldschmidt's satirical journal *Corsaren* and demanding to be treated by it (i.e., scolded), just as other writers had been. Goldschmidt took Kierkegaard at his word and ridiculed and satirized him. These attacks hurt Kierkegaard deeply and became the cause for his total isolation from the external world, at the same time spurring him to even greater productivity. In *Kjerlighedens Gjerninger* (1847; Eng. tr. *Works of Love,* 1946) he calls attention to the absolute duty toward God, whereas *Sygdommen til Døden* (1849; Eng. tr. *The Sickness unto Death,* 1941) is an analysis of that despair afflicting the human being who attempts to suppress the eternal and of the result of this despair, which is sin. Kierkegaard's views are sharpened even further in *Indøvelse i Christendom* (1850; Eng. tr. *Training in Christianity,* 1941), a work in which he formulates his concept of Christianity as equalling "being simultaneous with Christ," that is, taking on Christ's martyrdom. These two last volumes were published under the pseudonym Anti-Climacus. Whereas Climacus through *Philosophiske Smuler* and *Afsluttende uvidenskabelig Efterskrift* viewed the paradox of faith as the suffering of the mind, Anti-Climacus is already so deeply involved in faith that he realizes the demand for martyrdom.

Kjerlighedens Gjerninger was published under Kierkegaard's own name, and in *Synspunktet for min Forfatter-Virksomhed* (1848; publ. 1859; Eng. tr. *The Point of View for My Work as an Author,* 1939) he makes it clear that his entire oeuvre right from the outset had been religious and that the purpose of all his pseudonymously published works was to educate the reader with regard to Christianity. The development through the aesthetic and ethical stages had never been his own, but a pedagogical preparation for what he truly wanted to demonstrate. *Synspunktet* opens with a fascinating insight into the working methods of a genius, into the process of translating external events into spiritual experiences and even inducing these events in order to experiment with himself.

As early as 1843 Kierkegaard, under his own name, had published a series of sermons, which in 1846 were issued under the title *Atten opbyggelige Taler* (Eng. tr. *Eighteen Edifying Discourses,* 1943–46). Here Kierkegaard employs a direct method of communication, in which he openly expresses his commitment to Christianity. The content is strictly theological and constitutes a crucial component for a complete and correct understanding of Kierkegaard as being neither a psychologist nor a philosopher but a Christian apologist.

Around 1850 Kierkegaard again used the edifying discourse as a vehicle for further developing his ideas on the imitation of Christ. He distanced himself from both the liberal political currents of the day and the nationalistic sentiments rampant during the war of 1848–50, preparing instead for his direct attack on the state church. Kierkegaard was fully aware that he could not live up to the high Christian ideals he had set himself, but neither was this possible for the church, from which he therefore demanded an official admission to that effect. The public was well aware that *Indøvelse i Christendom* had also entailed an attack on the primate of the church, Bishop J. P. Mynster, for his—according to Kierkegaard—merely rhetorical and uncommitted view of Christianity and secular lifestyle. Mynster did not react to this attack, and when he died in 1854 the prominent theologian H. L. Martensen, Mynster's designated successor, gave a eulogy in which he characterized the deceased as "a witness of truth." To Kierkegaard such an epithet was synonymous with being a martyr, and in the same year he published a protest, in which he described Mynster as being "weak, pleasure-loving and great only as a reciter." Protest against this characterization led to a fierce debate in the press followed by ten pamphlets from Kierkegaard's hand entitled *Øieblikket* (1855; The Instant; Eng. tr. *Kierkegaard's Attack upon "Christendom,"* 1944). Here Kierkegaard attacks with scathing satire the entire institution of the state church, its bread-and-butter clergy, and empty ceremonies as simply a great insult to Christianity. It was one of Kierkegaard's principal disappointments that not even *Øieblikket* was able to provoke any reaction from church authorities—to him further evidence of their indifference toward the truth. In a way Kierkegaard was silenced to death. The strain resulting from this controversy took the last strength from him, and before the final installment of *Øieblikket* was published, he died. On his deathbed he refused to receive communion from the hand of a minister of the church, dying with the conviction that his task was completed.

Kierkegaard has had an immeasurable impact on posterity. Ibsen, Strindberg, and Dostoevsky were among the first to be influenced by him; later he had a decisive effect on Franz Kafka, Albert Camus, William Faulkner, John Updike, and Villy Sørensen. Through the philosophers Heidegger and Sartre his *Afsluttende uvidenskabelig Efterskrift,* with its concept of existence as a personal, passionate affair for which humankind alone is responsible, has given impetus to modern existentialism.

In the 1830s the July Revolution in Paris had ignited a political debate in Danish society, which in the following decade came to a climax during the constitutional struggle and national unrest in Schleswig, accompanied by a quixotic and purely academic pan-Scandinavian movement. The victorious war of 1848–50 confirmed national pride and strengthened a romantic longing for new days of glory. The defeat in 1864, in contrast, meant a rude awakening from these dreams to a harsh political and social reality. It was a painful awakening, anticipated in the literature of the previous decades, which was now aggravated and voiced in a fierce philosophical debate about the relationship between idea and reality as it had been foreshadowed by Paludan-Müller and Kierkegaard.

In literature the patriotism and Scandinavianism of the 1840s resulted in a profuse outpouring of ephemeral patriotic poetry and student songs. But as something new this orientation toward a *political* reality was now expressed much more directly through personal involvement by the writers themselves. M. A. Goldschmidt attracted attention as a journal editor initially of a liberal, later of an increasingly conservative, orientation; the most active spokesman of Scandinavianism and a writer of patriotic poetry, student songs, and student skits, Carl Ploug, distinguished himself as an influential and highly polemical journalist and newspaper editor. Hostrup and Schack went a step further and were actively involved in the liberal wing of parliamentary politics.

This orientation toward reality is also reflected in an increasing predilection for the prose genre, as exemplified by writers like Goldschmidt, Bergsøe, and Schack. In contrast, the lyrical poets of the period clearly see themselves as successors of the great poet of Danish romanticism, Adam Oehlenschäger. It would, however, be incorrect to dismiss these poets as derivative writers. Even though their artistic idioms and diction are quite traditional and rooted in the meter and style of romanticism, their poetry distinctly reflects their personal battle between romantic idealism and spirituality and the new era, demanding from them political and social commitment. Most of them, prose writers and lyrical poets alike, have in common a rejection of the predominant doctrines of naturalism and materialism emerging around 1870, and an adherence to a metaphysical world view, most unproblematic in the works of Richardt and Ploug. In the case of Kaalund, Hostrup, and Bergsøe this reaction is an unambiguous expression of a hard-won, existential choice in the spirit of Kierkegaard. Not until Schack was the new era of realism met with resounding affirmation.

Another result of the defeat of 1864, anticipated by Grundtvig's democratic folk high school movement, was a widespread and popular revival, aimed at all strata of society but initially directed toward the rural population. In literature this revival is expressed in the emergence of a so-called schoolteacher's literature, primarily produced by teachers in the countryside, bypassing the academic milieu in Copenhagen. Novels and short stories written by Anton Nielsen (1827–97) and C. A. Thyregod (1822–98) during the 1860s and 1870s seldom rise above the level of pure entertainment. During the next decade, under the influence of the new so-called debate literature, this genre of regional writing, *Heimatdichtung*, became increasingly critical, attacking the exploitation of the crofters and farmhands, climaxing ca. 1900 in the works of Johan Skjoldborg and Jeppe Aakjær and—as the emerging working class was now targeted for artistic treatment—in the socialist writings of Martin Andersen Nexø.

Thus, the years 1850–70 were exciting times with numerous works of superior artistic quality. These years mark a period of transition between conservative idealism and radicalism, in which Danish literature in general had reached an unreserved acceptance of external reality, but when most writers still avoided a direct, ideological involvement in the political questions of the day. This development is best illustrated by comparing Kierkegaard with one of the leading intellectual personalities of the 1860s, M. A. Goldschmidt. In absolute contrast to the secluded and exclusive Kierkegaard—notwithstanding his fierce criticism of the state church—Goldschmidt, during the 1840s, participated actively in the current political debate, attempting to give it a liberal stamp; in his later writings, however, psychological and philosophical questions about the incongruity between the ideal and reality were given chief emphasis. It was this clash that the writers of the Biedermeier era had either ignored or, like Heiberg, attempted to mediate or eliminate by means of a philosophical system, but that from a Christian viewpoint constituted an irrevocable dualism, in which the ideal must be embraced. Paludan-Müller and Kierkegaard had dealt with this question from a strictly ethical and religious point of view. Now it received a much stronger psychological emphasis, and the contrast between the ideal and reality should be seen rather as a contrast between daydreaming and everyday life.

Peder Ludvig Møller and Clemens Petersen

Around 1850 this psychological trend found a talented spokesman in the critic Peder Ludvig Møller (1814–65), whereas the idealistic orientation was brilliantly represented by the other leading critic between Heiberg and

Brandes, Clemens Petersen (1834–1918). Petersen was himself initially a student of J. L. Heiberg but later opposed the strict Heibergian adherence to a perfected artistic form. An outstanding drama critic, writing for twelve years in Ploug's newspaper *Fædrelandet,* he fiercely attacked Hertz's plays for being devoid of ideas. Demanding from a literary work a distinct and well-defined ideology, he championed instead the more realistic Norwegian drama of Bjørnson and Ibsen.

Møller's primary goal was likewise a reckoning with Heiberg's speculative criticism, in which poetry itself was relegated to a secondary position as mere exemplification of abstract theories. Møller demanded a literature that gave imagination and feeling top priority. As examples of writers who comply with this requirement, he pointed to Heine, Hugo, and Byron, and among Danish writers to Oehlenschläger, Andersen, Winther, and Aarestrup.

Instead of fictional characters who were merely representatives of certain ideas, Møller demanded psychological portraits. He fiercely attacked the superficiality of Scribe and pointed, among other playwrights, to the German Friedrich Hebbel but foremost to Blicher, from whom, as a matter of fact, Heiberg had strongly dissociated himself. A selection of Møller's critical studies was published as *Kritiske Skizzer* (1847; Critical Sketches). They are all based on the theory that the literary work should be viewed in relation to society and to its author, and they are inspired by the French critic Sainte-Beuve's psychological and historical method. Thus, Møller must be regarded as a significant forerunner of Georg Brandes, whom he also resembles in his cosmopolitan outlook. Møller, who in 1847 left Denmark—possibly influenced by his confrontation with Kierkegaard—and thereafter lived in Berlin and Paris, was extremely well read in contemporary European literature. In 1838 he called attention to Pushkin and in 1847 to Stendhal, Poe, and Baudelaire.

Meïr Aron Goldschmidt

In addition to his many other activities P. L. Møller also launched Meïr Aron Goldschmidt (1819–87) as a writer, and Goldschmidt's writings were indeed in total agreement with Møller's aesthetics. Møller had also been a secret contributor to Goldschmidt's satirical weekly *Corsaren* (1840–46; The Corsair), largely written by Goldschmidt himself after he had given up his studies of law, begun in 1836. The political orientation of *Corsaren* was liberal and anti-royalist. The absolute monarchy was its favorite target, and conservative authorities of any kind were sharply criticized. At the same time, it promoted freedom of the press, parliamentarism, and universal suffrage. *Corsaren* was taken seriously by the authorities. It was confiscated forty times in all, and in 1843 Goldschmidt himself had to spend time in prison.

After selling his journal Goldschmidt went abroad to Germany, Switzerland, and Italy in 1846–47, primarily to meet with European politicians and collect material for his journalism. On his return he tried in vain to enter politics, and under the influence of the radical changes in Danish society his views turned in a more conservative direction. This orientation is reflected in his new journal *Nord og Syd* (1847–59; North and South), which was totally different from *Corsaren*. Satire was absent, and Goldschmidt focused on informing his readers about foreign events—a result of his many trips abroad—portraying various well-known personalities and presenting political commentaries of a quality hitherto unseen in the Danish press.

Goldschmidt was an industrious writer. Besides editing his journals and writing most of the contents, he published a series of novels and short stories in which a psychological approach, first developed by Blicher, was further refined. His point of departure is childhood and certain intense experiences that later in life take on dominating, almost archetypal or mythic dimensions. Later in Goldschmidt's oeuvre this approach, similar to that of depth psychology, is given increased ethical weight. It is finally formulated in his nemesis theory, according to which a human being in one way or another in this life will atone for the guilt he has incurred by violating the metaphysical order on which life is patterned.

Goldschmidt grew up in a wealthy Jewish business family and soon was in opposition to Danish culture, to which he wanted to belong. But he also opposed orthodox Judaism, with which he broke at the age of thirteen. This conflict is reflected both in the two distinct Danish and Jewish trends in Goldschmidt's writings—his first two books were the novel *En Jøde* (1845; Eng. tr. *A Jew*, 1852, 1990) and the volume *Fortællinger* (1846; Stories)—and in the theme of the tragic outsider, which is treated for the first time in his semiautobiographical debut. In many ways the title character is drawn as a Byronic hero, but the division in him is between Jewish orthodoxy, from which he wants to distance himself, and the Christian-Germanic world, represented by the young Copenhagen girl with whom he falls in love. But he is accepted neither by her nor by society. As an act of vengeance—and here Goldschmidt combines psychological analysis with social criticism—he develops into precisely what is expected from a Jew: a Shylock-like usurer. Influenced by Blicher and probably also Heine, Goldschmidt tried to make his novel "interesting" by including as many details as possible from Jewish milieu and tradition, which indeed contributed to the success of the book.

Fortællinger contains both related Jewish domestic settings and—what is particularly noteworthy—realistic descriptions from the Danish provinces, together with some philosophical stories pointing toward Goldschmidt's later nemesis theory. This theory forms the underlying basis for the six-hundred-page novel *Hjemløs* (1853–57; Eng. tr. *Homeless*, 1861). Contrary to *En Jøde*, the hero in *Hjemløs* has grown up in a Danish milieu and reaches—according to the structure of the bildungsroman (which Goldschmidt deliberately opposes in his first novel)—a state of reconciliation, as mirrored in the novel's subtitles: "At Home," "Homeless," and "Home." Disappointed because the demands he makes on others are not met (demands that he, however, does not make on himself, as he, for instance, does not carry to fruition a love relationship), the disillusioned main character roams about Europe. He finds no peace until, after his return, he accepts his errors and understands that life is made up not of demands but of debts that must be paid.

In 1861 Goldschmidt left Denmark to settle in England, and in 1863 he moved from there to Paris. An encounter with an early love gave him new inspiration that he expressed through a new genre, the legend, generally adding a more mythical, occasionally even legendary, touch to his writings. The first result of Goldschmidt's invigorated productivity was the three-volume *Fortællinger og Skildringer* (1863–65; Stories and Sketches). Here he employs the traditional narrative technique, originating in Boccaccio's *Decamerone* (1348–53), by letting the loosely connected stories be narrated in a circle of friends, a structure that formed the immediate model for Bergsøe's novel *Fra Piazza del Popolo*. The third volume is yet another bildungsroman, *Arvingen* (The Heir), which displays a strong affinity with *Hjemløs*. During their youth the hero and heroine have sinned against love, and thereby squandered it, by not marrying one another. Not until after their respective divorces do they experience a short period of happy love, which she must pay for with her life, while he, the narrator of the novel, must atone for his past by raising her children. As with so many of Goldschmidt's novels, *Arvingen* is also weakened by effects of suspense and too many melodramatic episodes. Nevertheless, the novel ought to be remembered as the first treatment of the problems of divorce in Danish literature.

Still another fictionalization of the nemesis theory followed with Goldschmidt's most successful novel, *Ravnen* (1867; The Raven), which in symbolic form also describes Denmark's recovery after the defeat of 1864, mirrored in the attempt of three brothers to avenge the injustice that has been inflicted on their family. This quest motif is combined with another folklore feature, the belief in the raven as a bird bringing good luck. Hunchbacked like a raven, the Jewish commission agent Simon Levi, the instrument of nemesis, unmasks the swindler who has ruined the family.

The brilliantly drawn Simon Levi appears again in "Maser" (Tithes) in the collection *Smaa Fortællinger* (1868–69; Short Stories), which demonstrates Goldschmidt's artistic maturity in his treatment of the theme of the Jew among Christians: no longer from a somewhat pathetic and sentimental viewpoint but with compassionate humor. The collection also includes the two stories "Bjergtagen" (I–II; Spellbound), which are based on Scandinavian folk legends. This folklorist orientation is carried further in *Kjærlighedshistorier fra mange Lande* (1867; Love Stories from Many Countries), in which legend and nature description are blended into a seamless garment demonstrating love's victory over death.

Taken as a whole, Goldschmidt's writings present a comprehensive picture of Denmark: from Copenhagen, from the countryside, and from the provinces. Jutland, in particular, is of increasing importance. In this respect, as well as in his psychological analyses of the definitive impact of childhood experiences on later life, he anticipates the new era of realism and naturalism. Through his insight into the metaphysical structures that intervene in human life he still remains a romantic. Artistically, this split was immensely fruitful, making his writings the most significant of the 1860s. Goldschmidt's linguistic command is admirable. His diction is precise yet also evocative, and his style lucid yet also suggestive, blending the humorous, sentimental, and exciting into a truly classic form.

Vilhelm Bergsøe

Vilhelm Bergsøe (1835–1911) was Goldschmidt's most talented successor and at the same time the writer who most successfully brought together the various characteristics of the nineteenth-century Danish novel, simultaneously leading the genre to its culmination and writing one of the most popular Danish novels of all times. *Fra Piazza del Popolo* (1867; From Piazza del Popolo) is clearly inspired by Andersen's *Improvisatoren* with its Italian milieu and picturesque scenery, whereas the scenes involving criminals or the poverty-stricken lower classes are possibly modeled after Hugo's *Les misérables* (1862) and Dumas's *Le comte de Monte-Cristo* (1845–46; The Count of Monte Cristo), as well as the popular novels by Eugène Sue. But his main inspiration was Goldschmidt, whose influence spans character delineation, the use of archetypal childhood experiences, plot development, and even the nemesis philosophy.

Fra Piazza del Popolo is a frame story consisting of seven texts told by a group of Danish artists living in Rome, awaiting the release of a young Dane taken prisoner by robbers. While some of the stories are located here, the opening story, "Tordenskyen" (The Thundercloud), which artistically is the most significant, takes as its point of departure the catastrophic cholera epidemic in Copenhagen in 1853. The story, however, switches between the past and the present, with the action moving from one locality to another, and is filled with exciting and mysterious events. Characters from one story resurface in another, and when finally the captured Dane safely returns, the numerous riddles and mystifications of the novel are solved simultaneously.

All incurred guilt is atoned for, according to Bergsøe's—and Goldschmidt's—nemesis theory, and the same philosophical idea determines the outcome of Bergsøe's next novel, *Fra den gamle Fabrik* (1869; From the Old Factory). It is based on the author's childhood memories from Copenhagen, where he grew up, and it contains fascinating insights into the workers' conditions at the time of the emergence of industrialism. Characteristically, Bergsøe does not elaborate on this social aspect but focuses on exquisite psychological details of the child's growing up. Again, Goldschmidt is his model, and the work points clearly toward J. P. Jacobsen's and Herman Bang's subdued psychological studies.

In spite of his own scientific training and penchant for exact observation—Bergsøe was a zoologist—he remained firmly rooted in a romantic world view. Even though several of his characters and episodes are taken from real life, Bergsøe's forte was his ability to evoke compelling mood and atmosphere and release his imaginative powers. Likewise, in his predilection for exotic settings and complicated, adventurous intrigues Bergsøe is a child of romanticism, or rather *romantisme*.

Even though his works do not reach the same linguistic forcefulness and inventiveness as those of his model, Goldschmidt, and his character delineation does not display the same depth and perspective, Bergsøe created works during the 1860s which constitute an overlooked but nevertheless genuine transition to the great prose writers of the next decades.

Carl Ploug, Christian Richardt, and H. V. Kaalund

None of the leading writers of the 1850s and 1860s made use of the lyrical genre, which in previous decades had reached its zenith with Winther and Aarestrup. To Andersen, Paludan-Müller, and Hostrup it remained a secondary genre, and frequently in the form of occasional poetry, patriotic songs, and student songs. It was precisely in these three genres that two of the most important late romantics, Carl Ploug and Christian Richardt, excelled, whereas H. V. Kaalund in his poetry strikes a more introverted and personal note. Of the three, Ploug and Kaalund formed the greatest contrast. Carl Ploug (1813–94) was, after a short period of revolutionary zeal, firmly rooted in a Christian conservative world view, whereas Hans Vilhelm

Kaalund (1818–85) spent most of his life in the pursuit of harmony. Through his work as editor of the National Liberal, initially very progressive, newspaper *Fædrelandet* from 1841–82, as the organizer of the movement of Scandinavianism, and as a spokesman for a Nordic political union, Ploug became one of the most flamboyant personalities over a period of several decades, leaving his stamp on the public debate in increasing opposition to the radical trends of the naturalism of the 1870s.

Ploug's style is highly rhetorical and declamatory, whereas Christian Richardt (1831–92) is a much more supple and melodious versifier in the Heibergian tradition. Indeed, he became one of the Danish poets most frequently set to music and wrote one of the finest opera libretti of all, *Drot og Marsk* (1878; King and Constable; music by Peter Heise). In contrast to Ploug—and Hostrup—he wrote exquisite nature poetry, of which the texts in the collection *Nyere Digte* (1864; Newer Poems) rise far above imitative poetry. Richardt also achieved excellence as an occasional poet, whether his aim was to comfort the nation after the defeat in 1864 or to portray public and private personalities in a series of memorial poems.

While both Ploug and Richardt wholeheartedly identified themselves with the values of romanticism, Kaalund had the greatest difficulty in finding firm footing in the times, and most of his writings are characterized by tragic homelessness. Kaalund began as a student of Oehlenschläger by using Old Norse themes, and of Christian Winther, whose poetic realism is echoed in the exquisite collection of *Fabler for Børn* (1844; Fables for Children)—neither sentimental nor moralizing—with which generations of Danes have grown up.

Kaalund did not find his personal style until the work that led to his breakthrough, the volume *Et Foraar* (1858; A Spring), in which the down-to-earth character of the fables was perfected in a subdued tone. These elements correspond to the topics of the poems, which aim to strike a balance between the author's adherence to political conservatism and his sympathy toward more radical reform movements, and to reconcile spirituality and reality. This attempt is not always successful. In a feud with the naturalist writer Sophus Schandorph in 1878–79, Kaalund clearly professed Christianity and attacked contemporary materialism, demanding from art that it must "raise reality to the same heights as the great eternal values."

Jens Christian Hostrup

Reality as a value and goal in itself manifests itself gradually in the writings of Jens Christian Hostrup (1818–92). With his two musical comedies or vaudevilles, both marked by the struggle between old and new around the breakthrough of Danish democracy, *Gjenboerne* (1844; The Neighbors) and *En Spurv i Tranedands* (1846; A Sparrow among Hawks), which followed some farcical student skits, Hostrup in several ways continued the tradition from Heiberg's and Hertz's comedies, adding, however, an unmistakable democratic touch.

Hostrup received his degree in theology in 1843 and became a minister in 1855, strongly inspired by Grundtvig's ideas. Influenced by his years as a student in Copenhagen, Hostrup based *Gjenboerne* on the clash between academics and the Philistine middle class (against which he aims his satire), between the supernatural and the everyday life in Copenhagen. The student's engagement with the coppersmith's daughter can be interpreted as the fulfillment of the comedy's philosophical objective: "to bind life to the idea," that is, to reconcile realism and idealism. The student's rival, the swaggering Lieutenant von Buddinge, is a descendant of Plautus's Miles Gloriosus, Shakespeare's Falstaff, and Holberg's Jacob von Thyboe. He is drawn with precision and authenticity in dialogue, which also marks the other characters (e.g., Søren Topp, another student, who is a brilliant caricature of Kierkegaard). The original stage version is lost, but it is known to have been crammed with cabaretlike topical references attacking the absolute monarchy in its last stages. But what has preserved the comedy's freshness today is the individualized dialogue, the realistic description of the coppersmith's stolid family, and the catchy tunes, mostly derived from J. L. Heiberg's plays or the Swedish poet Carl Michael Bellman.

En Spurv i Tranedands repeats the theme from *Gjenboerne* but adds a sharper social sting in its revelation of the insipidity and hollowness of the middle class. This characterization is effected by a plain journeyman tailor who, during a period of twenty-four hours, succeeds in deceiving the uncritical public into believing that he possesses rank and riches. In both comedies Hostrup, inspired by Ferdinand Raimund's and Johann Nestroy's popular Viennese fairy-tale plays and farces, employs magic props to start the plot and create dramatic tension. In *Eventyr paa Fodreisen* (1849; Adventures on Foot), the third play by Hostrup which is still in the repertoire, an escaped prisoner has taken over this magic function. In the nuanced portrayal of him as well as in the discussion of society's responsibility Hostrup's ethical commitment and social interest become even more pronounced.

In the succeeding plays this shift from "idea" to "life" emerges in the plot itself. Thus, in the largely overlooked fairy-tale comedy *Mester og Lærling* (1852; Master and Apprentice) a poet is portrayed as a starry-eyed weakling without vigor and vitality, and in the comedy *Æsthetisk Sands* (1849; Aesthetic Sense), as an egoistic, scheming crook. This comedy's fierce attacks on contemporary journalism caused a scandal at its opening night. The primary intention of the play, however, is to depict symbolically the breaking up of the class structure, thereby pointing to Hostrup's late debate drama, *Eva* (1881). This work is strongly supportive of the women's movement and has certain parallels to Ibsen's better-known *Et Dukkehjem* (1879; A Doll's House) in its defense of a mother's voice regarding her children's upbringing.

Thus, Hostrup went through an amazing development from youthful romantic worship of academia to extroverted involvement in contemporary events. This process was, from 1860 onward, accompanied by a great activity as a public speaker and direct political commitment as a candidate for the Liberal party.

Hans Egede Schack

With the only completed novel of Hans Egede Schack (1820–59), *Phantasterne* (1857; The Fantasts), the condemnation of empty aestheticism, initiated with Paludan-Müller's *Adam Homo,* Kierkegaard's *Enten-Eller*, and partly also Goldschmidt's *Hjemløs,* was brought to a conclusion. But in contrast to these works, Schack, instead of posing a superior, spiritual concept as the ideal, demands an acceptance of the reality of everyday life.

This attitude corresponds to Schack's own political activities, which were precisely what made him realize the discrepancy between the clichés of starry-eyed fantasizing and harsh facts, between dream and reality. Thus, he eagerly participated in the movement of Scandinavianism, received a law degree in 1844, volunteered in the Dano-German war of 1848–50, and was elected the same year as the youngest member of the Constituent Parliamentary Assembly. Schack was considered an excellent speaker and an experienced debater with strong democratic views.

Phantasterne was published in the same year as Flaubert's *Madame Bovary*, and like this novel, it deals a crippling blow to the typical romantic fantast. The title characters are three childhood friends, whose development is told by one of them, Conrad, the novel's first-person narrator. He and Christian indulge in daydreaming, first about honor and fame as aristocrats and generals and later, in Conrad's case, about sexual adventures. The third, Thomas, like his biblical namesake, is the skeptic, who does not lose his grip on reality, whereas Christian ends up in a mental hospital, a fate that liberates Conrad from his inclination to daydreaming. Conrad gets his law degree, has a brilliant government career, and marries—in a somewhat labored conclusion—an immigrant Spanish princess. Thus reality, which to Schack is a contemporary, politically liberal reality, has triumphed over a politically effete period and ideological system, the feudal system that the boys had dealt with in their fantasies.

Deliberately, Schack's novel, written in direct opposition to the idealistic bildungsroman, continued the attack on affectation which Poul M. Møller had introduced, and Schack's daydreamers are undoubtedly indebted to the character of the pedant in Møller's novella. The contemporary reaction to *Phantasterne* was indeed strong. Thus Goldschmidt described the novel as "an insult to idealism." Far more positive was a review by Clemens Petersen. He stressed the novel's realistic elements and brilliantly portrayed episodes, but it took several generations fully to appreciate Schack's pungent satire on a wide spectrum of literary and political hollowness. The deliberate rejection of romanticism in *Phantasterne* made it a precursor and model for later works such as Bjørnson's *Arne*, Ibsen's *Peer Gynt*, J. P. Jacobsen's *Niels Lyhne*, and Holger Drachmann's *En Overkomplet*.

After *Phantasterne* Schack began a new novel, *Sandhed med Modification* (publ. 1954; Truth with Modification), which remained a fragment. Its main theme is the hypocrisy of contemporary society. In the tradition of the picaresque novel Schack presents a cross-section of society by letting the young hero set out into the world, where he is confronted by various concretely depicted milieus. By employing a strictly realistic approach, but also by choosing a third-person omniscient narrator, Schack to an even greater extent than in his first novel approaches the trend of realism of the next decades.

Conclusion

The period 1800–1870 obviously cannot be given a label that satisfactorily covers the multitude of literary movements and directions. None of the following terms—romanticism, poetic realism, *romantisme*, or realism—suffices as an all-encompassing designation. These trends, each represented by talented and inspired writers, had much shorter lifespans than often supposed, and in many instances they flourished side by side, sometimes even within one and the same authorship.

This multitude of directions not only precludes set classifications but also contributes to making this period exciting and inexhaustible for future research. The diversity and artistic quality of the six decades provides the guarantee that Danish literature was well prepared to meet the challenge and innovation that came into being with the more ideologically targeted efforts of Georg Brandes. These changes were often anticipated or even present in the previous decades but, because of the inciting and persuasive personality of Brandes, were brought to a definite breakthrough in 1871.

The Modern
Breakthrough

Niels Ingwersen

5

REALISM AND NATURALISM

The term *Modern Breakthrough* has very nearly assumed mythical proportions in Scandinavia. It was coined by Georg Brandes in his *Det moderne
Gjennembruds Mænd* (1883; The Men of the Modern Breakthrough) where
he summarized the triumphant achievements for more than a decade of the
rebellious young generation that he had inspired and that had routed epi-
gonic romanticism.

Most literary historians agree that Brandes was a catalyst for a major aesthetic and cultural reorientation in Scandinavia, but they tend to disagree as
to what extent the subsequent reaction against romanticism was a water-
shed. The rise of realism had been anticipated in various ways; such disparate figures as Blicher, Andersen, Aarestrup, Kierkegaard, and Schack, as
well as the young critic Frederik Dreier, had questioned the romantic vision
and, directly or indirectly, had prodded the reader into seeing the dangers
inherent in romantic ideology. Criticism had been particularly voiced
against that bourgeois form of romantic culture which, rather recently, has
been called Biedermeier, and that criticism was one that Brandes took on
himself vigorously to reiterate and renew. The reorientation of the 1870s
was, thus, prepared.

By 1871, the year of Brandes's first dramatic lecture at the University of
Copenhagen, a new social reality had come into existence. The Industrial
Revolution had reached Denmark in the 1860s—a good deal earlier than in
the other Nordic lands—and was transforming the country. The arrival of a
new technology reshaped the cities: within a few years the old town, with its
medieval layout, was surrounded by a ring of factories and drab, cheaply
built neighborhoods in which the new labor forces lived. The inhabitants of

the swiftly growing cities came from the countryside, whose population was also decimated by the many who chose to emigrate to America. Society was in flux, and to the old patrician families, that era of swift changes seemed chaotic and threatening. With industrialism came banks, trade in stocks and bonds, and that perennial investing and reinvesting of money which signals the change from a feudal to a liberalistic or capitalistic economy. As Hans Christian Andersen had foreseen with some anxiety, the new ruling class had little veneration for the traditions and values of the patricians of the earlier, socially fairly static nineteenth century.

Brandes's major theme in his introductory lecture was the cultural backwardness of Denmark. The country was, asserted Brandes, forty years behind current European thought. To correct that situation Brandes demanded that authors put the problems of importance to contemporary society under debate in their works.

The writings of those young men and women who felt themselves to be bona fide "members" of the Modern Breakthrough show that they sincerely worked to bring about a radical social change. They followed Brandes's call for action by exposing as shams such institutions as the Church and matrimony; they debated the relationship between the sexes; they called for justice for the exploited masses, and so on. Thus, they called for changes that were bound to make the conservative press label them as subversives who threatened the decent, traditional family, the very foundation of law and order in the monarchy of Denmark. Such accusations, of course, only strengthened Brandes's young followers in their purpose and made them feel successful in their attempts to transform society through art.

There can be little doubt that Brandes forged a movement and that he was indisputably considered to be its leader for more than a decade. It is hardly fruitful to debate how original Brandes's ideas were, for those who became his followers felt that they were participating in a march toward truth that would free humankind from the ideological shackles of the past. Young intellectuals from all the Scandinavian countries joined "Brandesianism" in its cultural struggle.

The members of the movement were informed and inspired by European thinkers and authors who had, explicitly or implicitly, redefined human existence in secular terms. Whether or not that transition from philosophical idealism to materialism was intended to shatter romantic ideology, its result was to cause metaphysics—including religion—to be judged as offering outdated and false perceptions of reality. The French philosopher Auguste Comte charted human progress as an advance toward factual ("positive") knowledge of civilization. Such radical German theologians as David

Friedrich Strauss and Ludwig Feuerbach (whose thinking had been debated in Denmark in 1848) reduced Christianity to wishful thinking. Karl Marx (whose influence was quite limited in nineteenth-century Denmark) bluntly made the economy an all-dominating factor in the life of each individual, and he suggested that a struggle against capitalism would not only be inevitable but would bring about the just socialistic state.

A homology between the Modern Breakthrough and the Age of Reason emerges: both ages scorned metaphysics, both saw a moral need to improve society, both questioned authority, and both deemed human beings to be reasonable and capable of taking charge of their destinies. Perhaps that similarity is made most evident in the works of John Stuart Mill, whose utilitarian, ethical ideal is that of a well-regulated state in which the individual is given the highest possible degree of freedom. Mill's most influential work in Scandinavia was *The Subjection of Women* (1869; tr. into Danish by Brandes, 1869), in which Mill claimed that until the female is given the same opportunities as the male, her nature cannot be known.

Brandes encouraged one of his young followers, the author Jens Peter Jacobsen, to translate Charles Darwin, and the ideas of that Englishman were, of course, a shock to the old cultural elite. If the human being was not a divine creation but the product of ages of natural selection, he or she was reduced to a beast; that beast would fight to the death in its struggle to survive, and survivors would be those who were able to subdue the weaker of the species. Darwin's neutral theory was interpreted in a deeply pessimistic way, which overshadowed any possibility of seeing it—in line with the other theories of its day—in an optimistic light that suggested progress toward higher states of civilization. That latter, optimistic reading of Darwin is, of course, also one that can be used to legitimize many of the exploits of capitalism and the specific form of it named imperialism. The old and the new forces interpreted Darwin in two widely different ways.

The fervor and optimism of the early Modern Breakthrough tended to obscure the tension existing between two factions within the body of current European thought, although both were present in the proclamations of the young Brandes. On the one hand, the major concern was the achieving of social reform—the common good—as soon as possible, but on the other, paramount significance lay in ensuring the individual's supreme right to develop freely. These two "demands" are not necessarily incompatible, and were not initially experienced as such, but as political results seemed few and paltry, the interests of the social reformer, who strongly desired a social upheaval, and the wants of the individualist, who primarily demanded to be the master of his or her own fate, were eventually bound to seem at odds.

The writers of the Modern Breakthrough expressed themselves realistically, but some of them were drawn toward naturalism, even if that inclination did not necessarily suggest a naturalistic outlook. As the initial optimism of the movement waned, deterministic naturalism seemed to be a fitting means with which to express the futility of human efforts. If realism-naturalism tended to retain the traditional omniscient narration—even if the all-knowing narrator's authority was diminished—the scenic impressionistic technique, which found excellent proponents in Scandinavia in the 1880s, elegantly played with the illusion that the author had "left" the text in favor of his or her characters' dialogue. From the very beginning of the Breakthrough, lyrical moods, especially when a character dwelt alone in nature, were permitted to temper the work's realism or naturalism. That approach may be seen not only as an echo from the romantic tradition, one that those young rebels knew so well, but also as an influence from the writings of Ivan Turgenev, whose works were closer to the hearts of many Danish writers than were those of the famous French realists or naturalists.

Georg Brandes

The very fact that, as a rule, the name of the critic Georg Brandes (1842–1927) is included among literary artists not only in Danish literary histories but also in most Nordic ones suggests Brandes's stature or the myth of that stature. As mentioned earlier, the swell of modern thoughts and literary forms would have taken place without his presence, but that presence made the swell into a historical happening of years-long duration. Men and women who were affected by the Modern Breakthrough had to choose sides, for or against the "new." Brandes was an inspirer, an irritant, a sensitive judge of art, a rigid arbiter of taste, an idealist, a bully who liked power, and a person whom men and women, both in Scandinavia and beyond, justly disliked or admired. In short, he was—with all the positive and negative connotations that cluster around that term—a cultural forcefield. No other Scandinavian critic has achieved his international reputation.

Brandes's background is that of the cultured, undoctrinaire Jewish intelligentsia; as a young man he wrote perceptively about Danish romantics, was well read in modern French literature, and was influenced by Søren Kierkegaard, as were Ibsen and Strindberg. In 1870, having completed his doctoral dissertation on the French positivistic critic Hippolyte Taine, he toured those countries in Europe whose cultural currents traditionally had formed Scandinavian thinking and art. The effect of that *Bildungs* journey was that Brandes made himself the intellectual chastiser and overseer of his native culture. Through lectures, journalism, and books he bombarded it with criticism and opinions that were intended to cause profound changes in the thinking of those individuals who were willing and capable of waking up. Like the showman he was, Brandes knew the power of the elegantly turned phrase, the stinging remark, the reductive simplification, the condescending generalization, and—not least—the call to arms, that urgent appeal to kindred souls to rally against repression, stupidity, or simply the forces that were against the dream of a free, healthy individual. It can hardly be amazing that the eloquent Brandes became a hero to the impressionable young, who might have felt, even without him, an urge for new visions.

These comments may seem to reduce Brandes to a clever strategist. He was exactly that, but it must be pointed out that his written, jargonless criticism was, and is, immensely readable. Such early articles as the famous "'Det uendeligt Smaa' og 'det uendeligt Store' i Poesien" (1869; The Infinitely Small and the Infinitely Great in Literature) exude sheer enthusiasm, a delight in the subject matter, Shakespeare, and in the critical mission which is highly unusual in criticism. In that instance Brandes's use of Taine's method, superficial as it may be, surpasses in terms of persuasive power those of its originator. Likewise, his later essay on the changing perception of nature in Danish romantic literature—a part of an essay on Christian Winther from *Danske Digtere* (1877; Danish Writers)—shows a masterly ability to offer sweeping bird's-eye views. He may seem to push a certain line of development in nature poetry—from nature being used allegorically to being seen as it is in and of itself—too rigorously. Nevertheless, he creates, in spite of generalizations and omissions, a seductive and valuable example of daring literary history, one not marred by turgid writing or a pedestrian vision. It is quite easy to conjure up a case against Brandes, who manipulated his audience; it is, likewise, easy to remain fascinated by his obvious talents as a critic who enthralled his audience.

His lectures at the University of Copenhagen became the impressive six-volume *Hovedstrømninger i det 19de Aarhundredes Litteratur* (1872–90; Eng. tr. *Main Currents in Nineteenth-Century Literature*, 1903–5). Brandes shows how contrasting currents of revolutionary and reactionary thought dramatically battle throughout the century, and he reiterates that the complacent and provincial Danish culture found itself within the conservative backlash. Influences from Taine's sociological system and Sainte-Beuve's psychological one are felt in Brandes's criticism; not only his tendentiousness but also his keen sense of the individuality of a text set him apart from his critical models and made him transcend their positivism. The very clarity of his language had an impact on many other critics; thus, he was instrumental in changing the critical idiom from the abstract musings of romantic idealists—such as can be found in Clemens Petersen's journalism—to a much more concrete and text-oriented critical practice. Brandes could be an excellent close reader.

When a chair became available at the University of Copenhagen after the death of Carsten Hauch in 1872, it was denied the controversial Brandes, and he spent some years abroad. It may in retrospect seem fortunate that Brandes's roaming mind was not limited to the duties of a university professor but could continue to make all of European literature his object of study. In the new intellectual magazine *Tilskueren* (1884–1939; The Spectator) he reported his impressions of the cultural and literary scene from various European nations.

Brandes's influence grew; he and his supporters found a forum in the new daily *Politiken* (founded 1884; Politics), but after the publication of *Det moderne Gjennembruds Mænd* in 1883, some of his compatriots, such as Holger Drachmann and the Norwegian Bjørnstjerne Bjørnson, parted ways with the literary left. The morality debate that was initiated with Bjørnson's play *En Hanske* (1883; A Gauntlet) tore old alliances apart, and, as was not unusual for Brandes, those who had been friends were from then on considered to be adversaries. It should not be overlooked, however, that new blood was infused into the circle around Brandes, particularly from the neighboring countries. The early works of the young Norwegian Alexander Kielland were a very radical expression of the ideas of the Modern Breakthrough; the naturalist Amalie Skram left Norway to take up what became a permanent residence in Denmark, where she wrote her grim and impressive *Hellemyrsfolket* (1887–98; The People of Hellemyr); and Arne Garborg, likewise a naturalist, explored how a stifling society crippled human beings' potential for happiness. The Swede August Strindberg, like Garborg, sided with Brandes against Bjørnson in the morality debate, as did, if less openly, the Swedish novelist Victoria Benedictsson.

Strife was a way of life for Brandes, and he did not like to see himself upstaged by others. He was prone to lecture newcomers on what was the correct way of writing and, also, to alter his positions. In 1883 he fell into a debate with the rising literary critic Herman Bang. In that scuffle Brandes turned against the naturalistic practice—of Bang and others—as well as against a literature that merely debates social problems, thus distancing himself from his stand in 1871. Brandes's call to order suggests not only his desire to be in command but also the normative restrictiveness of the Modern Breakthrough. Bang was criticized; Benedictsson's works were found to be unsatisfactory; and privately, Brandes disliked several publications (for example, Jacobsen's depiction of a forlorn atheist in *Niels Lyhne*) that he officially praised or had his brother, Edvard, praise. It is thus understandable that some of the younger authors who made their debut in about 1880, such as Henrik Pontoppidan and Bang, as well as even younger literary figures, preferred to keep a certain distance from the powerful and jealous Brandes.

The reorientations in Brandes's views may partly have been caused by personal disappointments, for leaders with visions want results, and those achieved—and they were not few—eventually seemed paltry to Brandes. He was an individualistic idealist who became quite negative in his view of the culture that surrounded him. His changing consciousness may seem to parallel Ibsen's, for in the 1880s Ibsen, the reformist and realist, became gradually the individualist and symbolist, who, therefore, was accused by the critics of the Modern Breakthrough (such as Erik Skram) of turning his back on the right causes. Late in the 1880s Brandes discovered—as had Ibsen, Strindberg, and Pontoppidan—the captivating, poetic voice of the German philosopher Friedrich Nietzsche, and once again Brandes made it his role to signal a change of course in Scandinavian culture.

Brandes was taken with Nietzsche's concept of the great personality as the source of culture, and he introduced the German thinker to the Scandinavians with the article "Aristokratisk Radikalisme" (1889; Aristocratic Radicalism) in *Tilskueren*. The title clearly denotes his wish to remain being seen as a radical, in spite of his loss of belief in the potential of democracy and in the masses. His later career was devoted to studies of great minds—for example, *William Shakespeare* (1895–96; Eng. tr. 1898), *Wolfgang Goethe* (1914–15; Eng. tr. 1936), *François de Voltaire* (1916–17; Eng. tr. 1930), and *Cajus Julius Cæsar* (1918; Eng. tr. 1924)—a turn that had been foreshadowed by his monograph *Søren Kierkegaard* (1877), which was to become quite influential as it was translated into various major languages. That concentration on outstanding personalities did not, however, lock Brandes into a Nietzschean tower of isolation, for he continued to observe and offer his opinions on current events. His adamant neutral stand during World War I and his prophetic criticism of the peace in Versailles made him persona non grata in his beloved France. It suggests Brandes's prominence that even George Clemenceau, the French president, would angrily denounce him with an *Adieu, Brandès!*

Since Brandes was a man of conflicts and of changing convictions, he had as many enemies as admirers. He deserved both. He set an example and demanded that others, in their writings, do likewise. Letters to and from Brandes suggest his power. He could be very constructive, but he silenced some voices and pushed others into modes of writing that may not have suited them. He caused Drachmann and Jacobsen to start their careers as writers; he may have led Bang to switch from his naturalistic exploration of the human mind to his less exploratory impressionism; and he may well have destroyed Benedictsson's career and life. He gave a very positive response to Selma Lagerlöf's *Gösta Berlings saga* (1891; The Saga of Gösta Berling), however, and thereby paved the way for the appreciation of a new talent. In spite of his changes of opinion, his life can be seen as an attempt to realize the dream of a human being to enjoy life in freedom. A sensual desire for a fulfilling existence runs through Brandes's works, early as well as late. For more than thirty years his direct impact on Nordic literature was undeniable. He was a myth in his lifetime, and he remains one.

Jens Peter Jacobsen

Next to Ibsen and Strindberg, Jens Peter Jacobsen (1847–85) is the best-known writer of the Modern Breakthrough outside Scandinavia. The young Rainer Maria Rilke was profoundly influenced by him; and Sigmund Freud, Robert Musil, and Thomas Mann were taken by his novel *Niels Lyhne*. Although many of the erstwhile followers of Brandes have lost their audiences, Jacobsen's works still command critical and popular attention. His major theme—or overriding obsession—of dream versus reality is proffered with so many skillful and heart-wrenching twists, that, in spite of his epochal traits, he transcends his own time.

Jacobsen was born in the provincial town of Thisted. In his youth he wrote poetry of a highly sensual nature—the works of Baudelaire and Poe come readily to mind—but at the University of Copenhagen he was a student of botany and became a close associate of the Brandes brothers. Jacobsen paid his dues to their movement by translating and popularizing Darwin, and in 1872 he published a novella, *Mogens* (Eng. tr. 1921), which has been heralded as the first naturalistic work to appear in Denmark. Mogens, the protagonist, is a young man who, in the famous first scene, is shown to react like the human animal he is by following his instincts rather than social conventions. This young, noble savage loses one love—to death—and after a period of sensual hedonism finds another woman with whom he can combine sexual and spiritual love. Mogens thus overcomes the sexual dualism that had haunted romantic ideology and is able to live happily forever after. In its time *Mogens* may have seemed startlingly new, but in retrospect its naturalism seems superficial, its language quite romantic, and its narrative quite close to that of the romantic bildungsroman or even that of the folktale.

Jacobsen's next major work, the novel *Fru Marie Grubbe* (1876; Eng. tr. *Marie Grubbe*, 1917), may share the optimism he voiced in *Mogens*, for the protagonist is allowed to shape her own destiny, but the author's vision has become more complex and realistic. Superficially, *Fru Marie Grubbe*, which is set in the turbulent 1600s, seems to be a much-needed improvement on the kind of immensely popular historical novel that had flourished in Denmark since the Walter Scott mania of the 1820s. Jacobsen attempted to capture the facts and flavor of the past and added psychological complexity to a genre that had excelled in pageants. Although the title character may seem to resemble Madame Bovary—each is a dreamer whose social status is reduced—Marie Grubbe is rather a contrast to Gustave Flaubert's hapless protagonist. Marie Grubbe, a young woman of noble birth, dreams of a man who can subjugate her, but two marriages (one to the king's bastard son) and one stormy affair are dismal failures; consequently, she takes leave of such men. Her instinctual integrity makes her go against the rules of her rigidly codified society, particularly when, as a middle-aged woman, she elopes with a lowly servant with whom she finds the satisfaction that no one else could offer her.

The ensuing novel, *Niels Lyhne* (1880; Eng. tr. 1919, 1990), is vaguely set in the mid-nineteenth century but fails to capture a sense of the social reality of that era. The novel was intended to be another saga of liberation from the strictures of the past and was to be entitled "An Atheist," but its protagonist, Niels, turned out to be neither liberated nor joyful. On the surface *Niels Lyhne* contains that debate of topical issues which Brandes demanded—such as atheism versus religion, women's emancipation versus marital bondage, and truthful art versus romantic dreaming—but Jacobsen's discussion was inconclusive and thus disappointed the Brandes brothers. The structure of the novel is similar to that of *Mogens* and *Fru Marie Grubbe*, a chronological record of the protagonist's encounters with members of the opposite sex interspersed with only brief summaries of intermediate periods. Niels is attracted to many women, but they eventually reject him; he is rejected even by his wife, who on her deathbed forsakes him for that divinity he had abandoned as a young man. Shortly afterward, when he is about to lose his only child, Niels prays to God, but—as always in Jacobsen's oeuvre—no one answers the prayer, and the child dies. Within a short while Niels himself finds death while doing battle against the German invaders of Denmark in 1864.

In contrast to Mogens and Marie Grubbe, Niels never reaches fulfillment. His fate may reflect the difficulty in becoming a truly modern person by abandoning the values of the past. Niels is and remains an atheist, but he cannot cast off his inclination to dream. Marie Grubbe, too, is a dreamer, but she and Niels use their imaginations in very different ways: Marie unconsciously uses her fantasies to achieve some self-understanding and thus to come to terms with reality, whereas Niels loses himself in vague, quixotic daydreams that distance him from reality. The contrast between Jacobsen's strong, instinctual female of action and his weak, reflective male dreamer suggests artistic impulses derived from Turgenev, but Jacobsen was also analyzing the role that fantasies might play in a human being's—constructive or destructive—striving for self-realization.

The change that took place between Jacobsen's early narratives and *Niels Lyhne* seems rather neatly to reflect the transition from the early optimism of the Modern Breakthrough to a growing doubt as to the movement's effectivity. The young rebels in *Niels Lyhne* become sad and lonely people. Although Niels's melancholy fate can be explained as the result of a flaw in his character, Jacobsen's later works are of undeniably darker hues; harmony is replaced by the somberness of unresolved conflict. That outlook may mirror the personal tragedy of the author, for the last ten years of his life were spent battling tuberculosis. In some works the thought of impending death looms large.

Eros-Thanatos, the proximity of love and death, is another of Jacobsen's major themes, one that dominates many of his short stories and poems. "Fru Fønss" (1882; Mrs. Fønss) can be read as his farewell to life. The story's protagonist, a woman who knows she is dying, is writing her children, who have been appalled at her break with social conventions in order to achieve happiness (once again Jacobsen allows a strong woman to reach fulfillment in life). Mrs. Fønss has no regrets but asks for understanding. Her stoic acceptance of her fate may strike readers as verging on the sentimental, a lurking danger for Jacobsen whenever he allowed himself to judge his fictional characters. No such flaw mars *Pesten i Bergamo* (1882; The Plague in Bergamo), in which Jacobsen coolly and clinically analyzed the intensely dramatic confrontation between a group of debauched hedonists and some religious fanatics, who succeed in casting their antagonists into the damnation of a mental hell. "Pesten i Bergamo" is a masterly study of mass mentality, of mass seduction as well as of lynch psychology, and it suggests that at last Jacobsen might have been viewing Darwin's theories in a nihilistic light: under stress the human becomes an animal; morality is defunct; and the stronger conquers the weaker. Jacobsen's authorial detachment makes it difficult to assess whether the story merely depicts the human animal at its worst or is in itself a warning against those excesses that destroy the humanity of a human being.

Jacobsen explored the innermost realms of the psyche. Initially, it may seem that he restricted himself to the naturalistic formula, which explained the human being as a product of heredity and environment—both Marie

Grubbe and Niels Lyhne are subjects of such an authorial approach—but Jacobsen transcended such simplicity and probed into those recesses of the mind for which Ibsen, Strindberg, Hamsun—and Freud—were to find objective correlatives. That modernity is nowhere more obvious than in Jacobsen's poetry (most of which was written early but, with a few exceptions, not published until after his death by Edvard Brandes in *Digte og Udkast* (1886; Poems and Sketches). Such exquisite texts as the "arabesques" "Arabesk til en Haandtegning af Michel Angelo" (Arabesque on a Sketch by Michelangelo) and "En Arabesk" (An Arabesque) as well as other poems show that Jacobsen's perception of the human being could hardly be captured by the positivistic systems of the Modern Breakthrough. Jacobsen's highly symbolic language, filled with both an intense sensuality and an existential yearning for meaning in life, created a canon for future generations. The young writers of the 1890s took *Niels Lyhne*—the epitome of the dreamer as hero—and the premodernistic poetry of Jacobsen as their models.

Jacobsen continues to puzzle reades and critcs. He seems on the one hand to advocate an integration into society, but on the other to exhibit a deep enthrallment with those aspects of the human psyche which prevent any integration and thwart any easy explanation. That ambivalence may be exactly the quality that keeps modern readers fascinated with his works.

Holger Drachmann

Holger Drachmann (1846–1908) was a prominent public figure during his lifetime; he was feted as Denmark's great lyric poet. As the center of events deemed scandalous by the bourgeoisie, he also embodied the role of the boheme. He was the kind of restless individualist who cannot for long belong to any camp and who, first and foremost, was inspired by his own moods. Drachmann's reputation has faded with the passing of time, but it cannot be denied that he was an impressive lyric talent who gave new cadences to Danish poetry.

If J. P. Jacobsen seemed to herald a sense of a new age and literature with *Mogens,* Drachmann heralded the dawning of a social consciousness with such stirring poems as "Engelske Socialister" (1871; English Socialists) and "King Mob" (1871). Even if such texts in retrospect seem quite romantic, they nevertheless capture the exhilarating feeling of a break with the past. In his early poems, published in *Digte* (1872; Poems), Drachmann, who was inspired by the social turmoil of the Paris Commune in 1871 and by impressions of labor unrest in England, castigates the capitalist system. Then as well as later Drachmann pinned his hopes on the ordinary, healthy people.

Drachmann, both as a man and as a writer, was, however, a person who fluctuated, and like a weather vane, he swung back and forth between radical and conservative positions. In some sense he seemed to flee whatever problems confronted him and tended to find solace, as his lyric poetry demonstrates, in the idyllic, the erotic, or the sentimental. His poetry is often an outpouring of emotion, but such elegiac love poems as "Sakuntala" (1876), in which the mood is brilliantly suggested and supported by the rhythm, show Drachmann's mastery of the genre:

I could not sleep for yearning,
a wind of flowers
awoke my dreams,
pouring warm through my window
in rich Himalayan streams.
I heard the tall palms' music,
and a word
they wept to sing;
I heard it blown on the winds of spring:
Sakuntala, Sakuntala.
(Tr. Robert Silliman Hillyer)

Drachmann's best-known collection of poems, *Sange ved Havet* (1877; Songs by the Sea), suggests why he has been called the poet of the sea, and in both prose and poetry he celebrated the "down-to-the-sea-in-ships" life, but it would be more precise to see Drachmann's use of the sea as symbolic of his ever-changing moods.

Although most of Drachmann's plays and prose now seem rather antiquated, his novel *Forskrevet* (1890; Signed Away), in spite of being overlong and rambling, deserves much more attention than it has received. The novel is given unity by its Faustian quest, and like Strindberg's *Röda rummet* (1879; The Red Room), Arne Garborg's *Trætte Mænd* (1891; Weary Men), and Bang's *Stuk* (1887; Stucco), it captures the atmosphere of the growing, sprawling city. Drachmann's characters are doubters like the protagonist of the Turgenev-inspired *En Overkomplet* (1876; A Supernumerary), and like Jacobsen's Niels Lyhne, they keep searching for that which will allow them peace of mind. In *Forskrevet* the restlessness, the changing moods, and the unending quest for meaning show that Drachmann, a writer who took no final stand, was an astute and sensitive observer of the changing mood of the times. The book, which contains some of the age's most evocative lyric passages, can be read as an introduction to the moods that swept into Scandinavian intellectual life and art in the decade of the 1890s.

Other Men of the Modern Breakthrough

Sophus Schandorph (1836–1901) made his living as a nontenured teacher in Copenhagen and experienced, as documented in his *Et Aar i Embede* (1883; A One-Year Position), how little intellectual freedom was permitted by the ruling cultural elite. He was a steadfast supporter of the ideas of the Modern Breakthrough and a tireless critic of the prevailing double standard. Some of his short stories are a rollicking satire on civil servants, particularly clergy, but his more serious efforts, such as *Uden Midtpunkt* (1878; Without Core)—another novel that emulated Turgenev—failed. The title of the novel, however, suggests one of the age's predicaments: if the belief in a fixed core, the soul, is lost, what then is the human being? That question was brilliantly addressed in the last act of Ibsen's *Peer Gynt* (1867), in which Peer peels an onion as he sheds existentially all the roles he has played in his life, but in Schandorph's works that questioning quality is replaced by quite pedestrian social criticism.

Erik Skram (1847–1923), whose name now mainly survives because he was the second husband of the Norwegian author Amalie Skram, was, like Schandorph, an ardent supporter of the Modern Breakthrough. More so than Brandes's other followers, he took up the leader's message that women should be liberated from the shackles of marriage and be allowed the same sexual freedom as men. His novel *Gertrude Coldbjørnsen* (1879) accentuates, as did Victoria Benedictsson's *Pengar* (1885; Money), that it is a crime against human nature to marry for the sake of security or for upholding the norms of bourgeois society. As a critic in *Tilskueren* he served as a watchdog over the writers whom he considered a part of the movement.

Edvard Brandes (1847–1931), Georg's brother, also served as a doctrinaire critic who kept the troops in line; in addition, he wrote a series of topical plays that carried out, to the letter, his brother's dictum that problems ought to be debated. Those plays, though composed with much less talent, resemble the plays from Ibsen's middle period. It should be recalled, however, that texts that in retrospect seem dusty and lifeless were once the literary journalism of their day and called forth emotion and protest.

Vilhelm Topsøe (1840–81) stands on the edge of the Modern Breakthrough, since his political sympathies were conservative. Nevertheless, as an observer of his day he dealt keenly with its conflicts and, like Jacobsen, knew that dreams must yield to reality. Like Schandorph, he wrote traditional narratives, but in them—as in *Jason med det gyldne Skind* (1875; Jason and the Golden Fleece)—Topsøe dealt with such "modern issues" as adultery. Without being under Brandes's influence (and Brandes never acknowledged Topsøe's contribution to the debate of values) Topsøe's example showed that the time had come for a debate that questioned the values of contemporary culture.

Karl Gjellerup (1857–1919) was initially one of the most fervent admirers of Georg Brandes. His first collection of poetry, *Rødtjørn* (1881; Red Thorn), was a celebration of the radical ideas that would change the world, and his novel *Germanernes Lærling* (1882; The Teutons' Apprentice) contains a sharp attack on Christian theology. Gjellerup, however, like many others, turned against what he saw as the shallowness and materialism of the Breakthrough movement, and he delved, much like the later Ibsen and Strindberg, into exploring the irrational niches of the mind. His novel *Møllen* (1896; The Mill) combines naturalism with symbolism, much in Dostoevsky's manner; besides being a probing study of a passionate man who commits a crime, it is a well-told novel of action and suspense.

In 1917 Gjellerup, who after 1892 lived in Dresden and for years had been the best-known Danish writer in Germany, shared the Nobel Prize in literature with Henrik Pontoppidan; although the latter's reputation has soared in Scandinavia, that of the former has suffered the opposite fate. Gjellerup's declining reputation is explainable in light of his profound concern with philosophical issues, for some of his later novels read more like treatises than like fiction, a tendency that was enhanced by his growing interest in Eastern mysticism.

THE WOMEN OF THE MODERN BREAKTHROUGH

Adele Marie (Adda) Ravnkilde (1862–83) authored three novels, all of which were published, after her suicide, in versions abridged by male editors. Even if her work might have been distorted, those novels show promise, passion, and an astute sense of the problems that the liberated woman must face. *Judith Fürste* (1884)—published with a preface by Georg Brandes—and *En Pyrrhussejr* (A Pyrrhic Victory) suggest that the young author had a sharp eye for the sexual games people play within the bourgeoisie, but in spite, or rather because of, her insights, she shows that a male-dominated culture fosters masochistic inclinations among women.

Astute observations of and sizzling irony against the same provincial bourgeoisie with which Mathilde Fibiger contended during the 1850s permeate Ravnkilde's best work, *Tantaluskvaler* (Tantalus Torments), published in 1884 with her previous novel as *To Fortællinger* (Two Stories). A young female tutor, who dreams of becoming a writer, permits herself to fall in love with a charming, sincere cynic with whom any lasting relationship would be catastrophic. She realizes that this is so, and thus love, possibly doomed already, is sacrificed for the sake of a future artistic career. Both alternatives, mutually exclusive as they appear, are unsatisfactory, and Ravnkilde's protagonist—like those created by Norway's Amalie Skram—seems headed for conflicts that then looked insoluble.

The sense of paralysis that is encountered toward the end of *Tantaluskvaler* seems to point ahead, for the superfluous, self-centered, hedonistic man on whom no lasting hope can rest—a type often found in fiction inspired by Turgenev—foreshadows many male figures of the 1890s. More importantly, the ecstasy that the protagonist experiences as she attempts to record, artistically, her erotic experiences suggests that a passionate devotion to writing could be an avenue for any author's future liberation, one that Adda Ravnkilde sadly did not live to take.

Olivia Levison (1847–94), who came from well-educated Jewish circles, had no formal education, but like many other of the woman writers who quite deliberately joined the Modern Breakthrough, she was culturally well versed. In her short stories, for instance in the collection *Gjæringstid* (1881; Time of Growth), one detects those defense mechanisms that women writers had to invoke to persist: the narrators are male, and their attitude toward the woman whose story is told is ambivalent, thus reflecting the author's own ambivalence toward writing about desires that women themselves may have been unwilling to accept. One such narrator, who witnesses the lust for life in a young woman to whom he is reluctantly drawn, states, "In a woman I expected resignation instead of desperate efforts, and I was astonished to see certain boundaries transgressed."

Levison tends, not atypically, to center on depression, such as in the novel *Konsulinden* (1887; The Councillor's Wife). Her lively narration uses the possibilities opened by the experimental prose of the age for the creation of a dramatic style that could place emphasis on the psychological action of a scene. If Adda Ravnkilde was still expressing herself in a language that seemed (or was edited to be) dated for its time, Levison's clipped prose, especially her dialogue, must have seemed strikingly modern.

Illa Christensen (1851–1922), like Levison, came from well-to-do bourgeois circles. Between 1884 and 1898 she published scores of short stories, four novels, and a few plays, but during the remainder of her life she remained silent as an author, having to care for an ailing mother and falling ill herself. An author like Alexander Kielland might decide, for political or existential reasons, to remain silent, as might, for all practical purposes, such twentieth-century Danes as Jacob Paludan or Tom Kristensen, but their choices were very likely more freely made than Illa Christensen's.

Like Olivia Levison's works, Christensen's writings are topical, for they enter directly into the morality debate of the age by offering the perspective of a daughter caught in the midst of the battle. In her two-volume *Skitser* (1884–86; Sketches) Christensen vacillates among idolization, anger, and desperation as the effects of the deeds of polygamous fathers come home to roost; thus, the ambivalence that could be detected in Levison's works appears also in Christensen's quite tormented depictions of people who lie and suffer. Christensen is, however, a tolerant observer of both sexes, and the pain caused by faithlessness and lies is depicted with a wry irony that may well be a mask. In such a brief but powerful allegory as "Kvinden" (1884; "The Woman") it seems blatantly obvious that the world is not ready to accept or understand that sexuality should be joyfully free. Christensen's work is uneven, for sentimentality sometimes overpowers her delightful irony, but her stylistic vacillation pinpoints, once again, the difficulty of finding the objective correlative that women writers needed.

Erna Juel-Hansen (1845–1922) seemed from her debut to be an author of daring. Her novel *Mellem 12 og 17* (1881; Between Twelve and Seventeen) deals with young girls' puberty. In a short story from *Sex Noveller* (1885; Six Short Stories) Juel-Hansen depicts a young working woman who has gotten pregnant but who manages quite well and even finds a new love in her life.

Most remarkable, however, is the later *Helsen & Co.* (1900; Helsen and Company). Pil Dahlerup has pointed out that although most women authors of the period assume a fairly narrow position as writers, Juel-Hansen embarks on a quite ambitious project in attempting to investigate whether a woman can realize herself—that is, become a whole human being—if given the best possible conditions that bourgeois male society can offer. The protagonist, Terese, whose prior life is depicted in the novel *Terese Kærulf* (1894), wants everything life can and should offer her: work, love, children. Even if she must cede some demands, she is successful and retains the happiness that women authors often feel that society will deny their characters. More than her colleagues, Juel-Hansen seems to take a cautiously optimistic view of women's possibilities of realizing their potential and desires in life.

THE CRISIS OF THE MODERN BREAKTHROUGH

Some of the writers who made their debuts in about 1880 did not share the more or less concealed romantic inclinations of some members of the first generation of the Modern Breakthrough, and in many ways these later writings are more consistently realistic or naturalistic, whether engaged in social criticism or in a quest for truth. Those authors tended to keep some distance from Georg Brandes and might even have been somewhat critical of his ideas.

Henrik Pontoppidan

Henrik Pontoppidan (1857–1943) grew up in the provincial town of Randers, the son of an impoverished minister and one of sixteen children. Later he vigorously rejected his childhood milieu, with its Lutheran Christianity, but he was equally critical of the higher bourgeoisie and was always ready to etch stinging caricatures of any social class with his satiric pen. His humor is reminiscent of Strindberg's and, in its morbidity, is expressive of a similar anger against those whose lives are sheltered in complacency and self-righteousness. Nevertheless, like Schandorph, he "returns" to the provinces—at times he even echoes Blicher's nostalgic descriptions of life there—but as a rule the homecomings result in bitter experiences. The conflict between a life that is free and independent and one that is luringly mundane is a problem that can hardly be resolved satisfactorily. It is embodied in his famous parable "Ørneflugt" (1894; Eagle's Flight): a tamed eagle escapes to the wilderness where by his very nature he belongs, but trapped by a longing for the placid life of the farmyard, he abandons his quest for a free life, only to be shot as a dangerous predator as he approaches the farm. As this sketch suggests, bitter irony and pessimism permeate Pontoppidan's works.

Pontoppidan was a man who made harsh choices. Just before he was to complete his education as an engineering student in Copenhagen in 1879, he dropped out; shortly afterward, he became a teacher at a Grundtvigian folk high school, but that experience soured him on the idea that in the ordinary people lay the wellspring of health. He abandoned his teaching career to pursue the individualistic path of a writer who desired to be the scourge of society. In that desire and in his chosen aloofness he resembles Ibsen more than Strindberg, and like them, he was drawn to Nietzsche's theories. Pontoppidan eventually became Denmark's most devastating and bleakly humorous critic of the spirit of compromise.

Pontoppidan's debut in 1881, *Stækkede Vinger* (1881; Clipped Wings), and his following collections of short stories, some of which depict the rural poverty of hypocritical Denmark with a brutal honesty hitherto unknown, place him firmly within the Modern Breakthrough. Pontoppidan, like Herman Bang, kept his distance from the leader of the movement, and even in his early writings there is plainly a skepticism toward the works of the reformers. His pity and anger—respectively directed toward the meek and downtrodden and against not only their obvious oppressors but also their supposed defenders, the liberals who assume that they are protesting the injustice of the system—suggest simultaneously Pontoppidan's weary and indignant cultural pessimism. At times this attitude veers toward anarchism, such as in the tale "Ilum Galgebakke" (1890; Gallows Hill at Ilum). Many other texts, either short stories or short novels, suggest that those who possess dignity or integrity are fools in a society that is without either of those qualities. The revolutionary in "To Gange mødt" (1886; Twice Met), in his belief that he can change the social order through any means he cares to use, is a fool, like the protagonist in the deeply pessimistic *Isbjørnen* (1887; The Polar Bear). A sweeping condemnation of any attempt to improve the human condition seems to have inspired Pontoppidan to write the nihilistic "En Fiskerede" (1890; A Fisher Nest). The theme of people latching onto illusions that are bound to fail is predominant in Pontoppidan's works.

Just as Ibsen was engaged in exposing sham wherever it could be detected, Pontoppidan emerged as an individualist and a disillusioned idealist whose ultimate concerns could not be contained within the confines of the Modern Breakthrough's reformist goals. Like Bang, Ibsen, and Strindberg, he became a loner who—as Nietzsche would have it—constructively or destructively stands out from, or apart from, the common crowd. That is particularly evident in Pontoppidan's three voluminous major novels, all originally published in installments and later cut down to a more manageable and artistically inferior format. In all three novels although a broad and satirical picture of contemporary Denmark is sketched, the focus is on a protagonist who is a man of extraordinary promise, but whose life becomes a process of disillusionment that leads him to a lonely death.

In *Det forjættede Land* (1891–95; Eng. tr. *The Promised Land*, 1896), a devastating satire of the clergy and the Grundtvigian movement, a young minister seeks the belief that may sustain him in his vocation. That quest, which takes him through various stages, ultimately fails, and he suffers a fatal breakdown.

The hero of the ironically entitled *Lykke-Per* (1898–1904; Lucky Per) is a secular man, but not one who feels at home in a world without spiritual striving. This once-so-promising engineer, a type promoted by modern literature as the hero of the coming century, gives up on many important aspects of life—a budding career, prominence, relationships—and ends up as a lowly civil servant on the austere west coast of Denmark. In that humble role he seems, as his posthumous papers suggest, finally to have found peace of mind. Once again Pontoppidan rails against the hypocrisy of Danish society, and like Schandorph, he is especially sharply critical of the clergy. Nevertheless, this rebellious son of a minister (foreshadowing the later Ingmar

Bergman) could not leave his Christian heritage alone. Some of his most sympathetic figures are those haunted and tragic ministers who possess that purity of heart—to use a phrase of Kierkegaard, a soul kindred to Pontoppidan—that is a curse in a modern materialistic society.

The title of Pontoppidan's third major novel, *De Dødes Rige* (1912–16; The Realm of the Dead), is a devastating reference to the cultural and political life of Denmark. It may be its author's darkest book, for none of the developments of the new century seemed to mollify his doubts about the human race. The characters are mainly fools or scoundrels, and as in the preceding two novels the promise of a sexual relationship that would provide happiness proves to be one more false expectation. As the novel concludes, the misanthropic male protagonist, who is direly ill, refuses to take the drug that might keep him alive. His lover, hearing of his death, rejoices in his having been released from the world and soon joins him in death.

Pontoppidan's major works seem to be more closely related to the mood of the 1890s than to that of the early Modern Breakthrough. Like Ibsen and the Swede Hjalmar Söderberg, he continued to face the social issues of his day, but even though important, they were not at the core of those authors' writing. They created introverted heroes and heroines whose ultimate fate has little to do with the social scene. More than most of the authors of the Breakthrough, Ibsen, Söderberg, and—particularly—Pontoppidan pose the question whether or not the malaise they depict so realistically and astutely is historically determined.

That issue tends to become mute in the case of Pontoppidan's major novels, and in that silence lies his overriding resemblance to the early and late Ibsen. Their protagonists may have left humanity behind in existentially motivated quests for fulfillment in life, and those quests may be deemed by others to be foolhardy or even insane. However, in the characters' departures from life—in their actual deaths or in their Nietzschean rejections of the life and of the common crowd—there is an undeniable aesthetic grandeur or glory that is not nullified by the madness or perversity of the extreme individualist, who meets or seeks the only end that he or she can accept.

Those grand exits grant the Pontoppidan and Ibsen protagonists an aesthetic stature that has nothing to do with the mundane reformist zeal of the Modern Breakthrough. There is much passion in the depictions of doomed idealists, and it is curious that both Pontoppidan and Ibsen, in contrast to Strindberg and Bang, wrote a quite staid and bookish prose that maintained the academic diction of the century; their revolutionary or anarchistic passion was kept under the wraps of the accepted literary language.

Pontoppidan, who in 1917 shared the Nobel Prize in literature with Karl

Gjellerup, wrote some shorter novels and a four-volume memoir (1933–40) which he later, detrimentally, condensed into one volume. The shorter fictions tend to have a sketchy quality that deprives them of the flavor of the three long novels or of the nasty and well-turned sting of the early short stories, but such novellas as *Mimoser* (1886; Eng. tr. *The Apothecary's Daughters,* 1890) and *Den kongelige Gæst* (1908; The Royal Guest) have that unmistakable touch of the ironist, who may hide his compassion behind a mask of misanthropy but does not entertain much hope for the achievement of human happiness. Life becomes art, act becomes gesture.

Herman Bang

Herman Bang (1857–1912) asserted that literature ought not be tendentious; he eventually maintained that instead of expressing opinions, the author should disappear behind the characters and scenes created and thus give a semblance of objectivity. Although Bang was an accomplished naturalist, he has become most famous for his impressionism—his acknowledged model was Jonas Lie—which relies on showing rather than on telling. That scenic or dramatic technique, which suggests Bang's deep infatuation with the theater, gives priority to dialogue and reduces most of the usual descriptive passages to brief statements that often bear a strong resemblance to stage directions—which, of course, although they may seem objective, can be loaded with meaning. If Pontoppidan's narrative can be called epic, Bang's is scenic; the contrast between them corresponds to the one between the Norwegian novelists Alexander Kielland and Jonas Lie. Time-honored narrative tradition, that of the sprawling, nineteenth-century, leisurely-told novel—given form by Walter Scott, Victor Hugo, Gustave Flaubert, and Charles Dickens—is being undermined by a much more nervous, less encompassing, staccato narrative suggesting a less unified vision of life, one reflecting an age of swift and unsuspected change.

In *Det hvide Hus* (1898; The White House) and *Det graa Hus* (1901; The Gray House) Bang recalled his childhood and youth with a somewhat fictional twist. He was the son of a minister on the island of Als who suffered from mental illness and a mother who lost her life to tuberculosis, one of the scourges of the age. Those years, which also figure prominently in the then-notorious novel *Haabløse Slægter* (1880; Generations without Hope), set their mark on Bang and may have reinforced the family belief that the Bangs descended from ancient nobility and were finally succumbing to decadence. Such a myth may seem utterly trivial, but the concept of decline, whether personal or cultural, played a significant role in Bang's works, and it was also in keeping with an age that nourished the naturalistic idea of the decadence of families, regimes, and nations.

That myth may explain to some extent the strong touch of fatalism that can be detected in Bang's works. Fate, whether defined biologically or socially, seemed to be a force whose impact could not be avoided. Bang saw the class from which he came—a gentile, quite patrician, settled group of civil servants of the Crown—lose its prominence to a new rather crass class of what a later age would call capitalist entrepreneurs. That displacement suggests in part why Bang is a persistent recorder of isolation, loss, and alienation, but also why he became a superb observer of the fast life of the new city and of the Danish Gilded Age. In contrast to Pontoppidan, who captures the old ways in the provincial town or at the manor house, Bang records the changing ways of a Denmark in transition and the teeming, restless life of the new cityscape.

Bang tried his luck as an actor, and although he failed, he nevertheless established himself as a consummate performer, for quite often he read his own works aloud to adoring audiences. Thus, from experience he was—like Hans Christian Andersen, another performance author—keenly aware of the effect of word and phrase on the audience. That understanding of the performance aspect of art may partly account for his mastery of a scenic or dramatic technique. During a performance tour through the United States, Bang was found ill on the train from Chicago to California; he died in Ogden, Utah.

The young Bang became a prolific and informed journalist with the conservative Copenhagen press. His cultural specialty was modern French literature, and he upstaged Georg Brandes by advocating Émile Zola's naturalism. Some of Bang's literary articles from that period are gathered in the still highly readable *Realisme og Realister* (1879; Realism and Realists) and *Kritiske Studier* (1880; Critical Studies).

Bang's first significant fiction was the autobiographical novel *Haabløse Slægter,* a fatalistic chronicle of a young man's broken hopes and gradual sinking into a mood of self-destruction. The sensualism of the novel, as well as its relentless naturalistic depiction of human emotion, suffering, and ennui, was deemed scandalous, and Bang had to undergo the humiliation of a court case. Later he was to assume a less deterministic view and to demonstrate the way in which ideologies were shaped by social conditions, not eternal laws, but the pessimism or melancholy of the first novel remained with him throughout his career.

Like some of his fellow writers who found themselves in antagonistic situations, such as Ibsen, Strindberg, and Kielland, Bang traveled a great deal and tried without much luck to have a career outside his native country. On one of his returns to Denmark he published two collections of stories, *Excentriske Noveller* (1885; Eccentric Short Stories) and *Stille Eksistenser* (1886; Quiet Existences), that show him to be a masterly, if tortured, analyst of human sexuality. In the former volume "Franz Pander" is a compassionate but stark study of the reification of a young man who is seduced and destroyed by the glitter of a world of luxury that he never can reach socially. The naturalism of that story is replaced in the following volume, particularly in the short novel *Ved Vejen* (By the Wayside; Eng. tr. *Katinka,* 1990), by an amazingly suggestive impressionism that, seemingly without authorial effort, permits the reader, from a few bits of dialogue or brief "stage directions"— for example, of body language—to glean the personality of the characters and the underlying mood of any scene. *Ved Vejen* engagingly, ironically, and sadly captures the quite trivial life of a rural, provincial community and shows, by focusing on a brief, unconsummated love relationship between two ordinary people, that even if the twain should meet, they will nonetheless never get together. The same point is made in the stylistically equally superb *Tine* (1889; Eng. tr. *Tina,* 1984), which depicts a consummated but doomed love affair during the Dano-Prussian War in 1864. Even if both texts are marred by some sentimentality— Bang managed to incorporate some tear-jerking scenes—they are filled with remarkably perceptive, sharp, and funny details of everyday types and life and remain eminently readable.

In *Ved Vejen* a party at the home of the local minister shows how Bang excelled in impressionism as the voices of numerous guests form a total picture of the event in the reader's mind. The tour de force of Bang's scenic impressionism is his depiction of the retreat of the defeated Danish army in *Tine*: the sound and sight of the tired and wounded men give an unforgettable glimpse of despair, one that ranks with any similar scene in world literature.

Bang's uncanny ability to give an impression of panoramic nature had already been demonstrated in his novel *Stuk* (1887; Stucco). In a sense it is the burgeoning city of Copenhagen that is the protagonist of the novel, for even if the readers are captivated by the plethora of characters, it is the citizenry's collective high hopes for the new financial and artistic projects of the modern city which are at the center of the novel. Not surprisingly, the high dreams (focused on a new theater building) are proven false, for the new age is poisoned by deceit, pretense, and simply greed. *Stuk* may be seen as one of Bang's indictments of rising capitalism—his snapshots of the entrepreneurs are scathing—but at the same time it is obvious that as an author he is always a brilliant journalist ready to capture the mood of any scene and he is infatuated with the teeming throngs and the city lights of what then was the "metropolis."

In those works whose setting is the modern cityscape, Bang introduces the flaneur type, one imported from French, or rather Parisian, literature. The flaneur, a figure later to appear in the works of Hjalmar Söderberg, Peter Nansen, Gustav Esmann, and the Fenno-Swede Runar Schildt, and with a twist, in Hamsun's *Sult* (1890; Hunger), is a man about town who spends his day walking the crowded streets in which he can both hide and be seen. Bang's evocation of such a figure dependent on the daily routine of strolling along the main streets of the city is the most accomplished in Danish literature.

That paradigmatic structure can also be found in Bang's later production, such as the sensual and mannered novels about artists whose excellent public performances form a contrast to their emotional existences. *Mikaël* (1904) and *De uden Fædreland* (1906; Eng. tr. *Denied a Country,* 1927) center on lonely artists who, in spite of the applause they receive, lead marginal lives. In those texts Bang gets as close as he ever allowed himself to discussing the homosexuality that set him apart from the men of the Modern Breakthrough and that posed an existential and aesthetic problem to him throughout his career. Since homosexuality was shunned then as vice and decadence, Bang could only very indirectly address it and was continually struggling to find a language that would address a life lived outside the accepted parameters. His failure to find that objective correlative may limit or mar his works, but what seem to be mannerisms, melodrama, or sentimentality are perhaps cover-ups for desperation and depression. That problem in his art does, however, also imbue it with an unresolved tension that gives it a spellbinding intensity.

Bang focuses rarely on victors, usually on victims. They are often women, like the protagonists of *Ved Vejen* and *Tine,* who both meet with death. Even if that fate is not bestowed on Ida Brandt in *Ludvigsbakke* (1896), the novel once again records the way that the unworthy, the gross, and superficial minds take advantage of those who are sensitive and receptive and thus are bound to be exploited and left in lonely misery.

Other Voices of the 1880s

Peter Nansen (1861–1918) might seem like the very embodiment of the elegant, hedonistic flaneur, even if he in 1896 became a very effective director of the major Gyldendal publishing house, a fact that suggests, together with some of his later writings, that his thumbing his nose at the bourgeoisie might have been something of a pose. In the 1880s he published short stories that tended to record sympathetically the life of the young dandies of ultramodern Copenhagen.

Nansen's forte is definitely the short form, and in the 1890s his brief, stylishly elegant novels, as a rule celebrating the aesthetic pleasures of young individualists of both sexes, attracted attention as being quite frivolous. Although Nansen was not an artistic innovator or a daring political radical, he was, in a sense, one of the most modern authors of his age, for in his narratives he knew how to use the narrow perspectives that were to replace the omniscient narrator: he excelled both in the epistolary and in the presumed diary form. In *Fra Rusaaret* (1892; The Freshman Year), letters between a student who has just entered the University of Copenhagen (then the only university in Denmark) and his traditional, Christian parents delineate how a gap grows, both generational and cultural. Other letters from third parties permit more voices to comment on the private, usually erotic, dilemmas of the protagonists. Nansen's mastery within those limits is proven once again in *Julies Dagbog* (1893; Julie's Diary), in which a young woman, bored with bourgeois confines, thoroughly enjoys an affair with a playboy actor. It was not until *Maria* (1894), translated into nine languages, that Nansen allowed his characters to feel that a permanent relationship might be feasible and satisfying. Nansen was, with Esmann, the sassy dandy of his times. It is worthwhile to juxtapose their works with those of the women of the same period, for they all dealt, more or less intentionally, with the issue at the heart of Brandes's crusade: let us imagine a free individual!

Wilhelm Dinesen (1845–95, aka Boganis) decided to take his own life and thereby made an indelible impression on his daughter, Karen Blixen (Isak Dinesen). Her theme of the male's betrayal of the female has been traced by some critics to that suicide, one that was very likely caused by Wilhelm Dinesen's discovery that, like Ibsen's Osvald in *Gengangere* (1881; Ghosts), he suffered from venereal disease. Dinesen was a good friend of Georg Brandes but hardly a joiner of the Modern Breakthrough. A restless man of action, Dinesen was drawn to wars, and he found it nearly impossible to content himself with an ordinary life. In 1872 he went to the United States (Nebraska and Wisconsin) to settle on the frontier, where he lived close to and felt a kinship with the vanishing Indian. In 1874 he returned to Denmark, married, and served in parliament. Impressions from his roving life appeared in *Jagtbreve* (1889; Eng. tr. *Boganis, Letters from the Hunt*, 1987), in which his subjective, reflective anecdotes and emphasis on moods fit hand in glove with the new prose of the 1890s.

Even if Danish literature does not have an Ibsen or a Strindberg, the stage of Copenhagen during the years of the Modern Breakthrough deserves attention. Not only were Ibsen's and Strindberg's plays performed, thus signaling the advent of a new drama, but plays by less illustrious Danish dramatists were also staged, setting the scene for a battle between the old and the new. Romantic drama could still attract large audiences. In 1873 Ernst von der Recke (1848–1933) had a smashing success with the historical, lyrical drama *Bertran de Born* (1872), and Drachmann's folklore-inspired, taming-of-the-shrew play *Der var engang* (1885; Once Upon a Time) still draws audiences. The representatives of "the new," like Edvard Brandes, were often imitators of Ibsen's problem plays. Among the dramatists who emerged in the 1880s Emma Gad (1852–1921) and Gustav Esmann (1860–1904) have lasted the longest. The latter's frivolous wit is reminiscent of Nansen's prose, and in his "boulevard" comedies, of which the best known is *Den kære Familie* (1892; That Dear Family), he smartly mixes the cynical and the comic.

Although Gad's reputation was not until recently fully restored, her works are more substantial than those of her male colleagues. If her plays seem very tied to their age, so may much of Ibsen's drama. What nevertheless rescues both artists' texts from their time is their quiet but insistent passion, and in Gad's best works the underlying theme is consistently that of survival: how can women manage their lives in sensible and reasonable ways in a world that is hardly inclined to be benevolent toward their dreams and desires?

Gad's dramatic works show that she knew how to fashion a memorably biting piece of dialogue. She seems to bolster herself against disillusionment and pessimism by her sense of humor—her keen eye for comic behavioral patterns—and seems nearly too ready to resolve conflicts, but she gained much attention by contemporary audiences. In the very popular *Et Sølvbryllup* (1890; A Silver Wedding) she is most tolerant of those males who have transgressed Bjørnson's demand for the same moral standard for both sexes. Compromise, as she implies, does not mean approval, however, but should be seen as a means of survival. It became Gad's fate to be remembered not for her humorous and successful dramas, but for an etiquette handbook called *Takt og Tone* (1918; Tact and Manners), which for later generations made her seem a prissy and outdated guardian of stylized behavior. It should be noted, however, that her book was intended to give women self-respect; it advises that rules are not absolute and that risks must therefore be taken.

It is traditional practice in Scandinavian literary history to operate with the last decade of the century as a separate period—the last to be designated rigidly in that manner—and it is telling that the literary historians have had trouble finding the appropriate descriptive or evocative label for the decade.

That problem in designation indicates that unity or common denominators for the literature of the decade are difficult to pinpoint or construct. Europeanists point to the impact of the French symbolist poets (and Edgar Allan Poe) as well as to the drama of the Belgian Maurice Maeterlinck; in other words, to modernist impulses. Moreover, Nietzsche, Dostoevsky, and Tolstoy also appealed to the imaginations of Scandinavian writers. During the fin de siècle, Scandinavia was not merely on the receiving end of Western culture, however, since Ibsen and Strindberg were forming modern Western drama, whether as the realistic-symbolic play of ideas on the part of the former or the realistic-expressionistic play of experience on the part of the latter. It was also during those years that Kierkegaard began to fascinate European thinkers. The works of the late J. P. Jacobsen gained attention in the Western world, his *Niels Lyhne* became a cult novel for young intellectuals who could identify with the protagonist's mental homelessness—as did, eventually, Hamsun's first novels.

As the names mentioned suggest, the vision and mission that the early Modern Breakthrough had promoted, defiantly and somewhat self-righteously, no longer seemed to invest life with a sense of purpose. The achievement of the Modern Breakthrough was not necessarily denigrated, but in about 1890 members of both the older and the emerging generation very consciously sought new departures, calling for new beauty, a transcendence of realism and naturalism, and an emphasis on the individual's uniqueness.

That search was made very evident in some manifestoes, such as Valdemar Vedel's (1865–1942) articles in the short-lived journal *Ny Jord* (1888–89; New Soil), Johannes Jørgensen's articles in his own periodical *Taarnet* (1893–94; The Tower), and in a special way by Brandes's introduction in 1889 to Nietzsche in *Tilskueren*. But as visions of a more colorful and faceted new literature were being conjured up, it soon became evident that their results failed to live up to expectations. A deliverance from the pessimism of the fading Breakthrough did not take place.

If romanticism in its heyday had seemed to offer a metaphysical norm system, the Modern Breakthrough in its eagerness to set the world right had offered different and antimetaphysical values, but they were hardly absolute. As Ibsen's Dr. Stockmann in *En Folkefiende* (1882; An Enemy of the People) asserts, a truth will endure only for a limited span of years. Consequently, the Breakthrough, rather than establishing a new encompassing value system, originated a norm debate that did not result in one norm system's replacing another. Brandes's own disillusioned assessment of his achievement at that stage in his career underscored the intellectual trend of the times, for he recognized that his dream of the free individual had barely been realized during the preceding two decades (a perception that partially explains his turn toward Nietzsche).

It may be that the quick growth of a new social reality caused by the rise of capitalism—made very visible by the changing and expanding cityscape—did not serve the dream of individual freedom well. If capitalism can be said to be individualistic, it was not so in the sense of furthering Brandes's and his followers' ideal of the free human being. In the works of Bang and Pontoppidan a callous, unfeeling world is conjured up; and those images of a world in which the individual seems superfluous also emerge from Amalie Skram's early, brutally graphic short stories, from Hamsun's *Sult* (1890; Hunger), Söderberg's *Martin Bircks ungdom* (1901; Martin Birck's Youth) and *Doktor Glas* (1905), and—for that matter—much later in Runar Schildt's consummate short stories from Helsinki. These texts all suggest that a new, materialistic world is relegating the person of culture, the artist, to the periphery. The artists of romanticism felt that they were the visionaries of their world; the adherents of the Modern Breakthrough recognized their minority status but trusted that the stances they took would have an impact on the future. Now such elevated notions, whether fact or fiction, had faded, leaving the artist in a state of isolation and alienation from the surrounding social world.

One reason for the gradual sinking into a mood of passivity, estrangement, and even mental paralysis may be found in the philosophical foundations of the Modern Breakthrough. The Breakthrough supplied in various ways a new ametaphysical understanding of existence, but even if Mill and Darwin explain much and in specific and scientific detail clarify social life and history, the new explanations have the weakness that, in contrast to romantic metaphysics (or religion), they can offer only partial explanations. No matter how satisfying and stirring those explanations may initially have seemed, their effect was eventually to cause the human being who pondered such matters to feel that there were so many gaps in human knowledge that it was futile to ask questions about a meaningful existence. Although romanticism may have been racked with ambiguities and the young Modern Breakthrough may have been obsessed with analyses of the social world, both imbued life with a sense of purpose. But as the analyses given during the Breakthrough turned into mere observations of life, they began to disappoint, and a sense of futility developed, for the world seemed to be ruled by chance and thus was one over which the lonely human being had little control. That being, whom the Modern Breakthrough had promised would be the master of existence, found himself or herself the impotent onlooker in a life that, at crucial points, was accidental.

If one invokes the Norwegian term for the decade, *neoromanticism*, it should be only to pinpoint that it is the darkest aspects of romanticism that are taken up again. The dualism that reappears in the 1890s is not a shared higher reality to which the mind of the awakened and initiated human being gains glorious access, but rather the private world of the individual's psyche. As J. P. Jacobsen's Poe-influenced poem "En Arabesk" (An Arabesque) had foreshadowed, it was with that journey into the depths of the mind, into niches and corners that hitherto had seemed hidden, that the mind took leave of ordinary, social reality, one deemed flat and unessential. That is not to say that this mental exploration necessarily gave the sense of purpose that the engagement in social issues once had. In fact, the exploration into mental landscapes tended, in many cases, to result in texts that leave the "voice speaking" or the protagonist in a final state of "no return" to a common humanity. A stunning number of antiheroes and antiheroines in the major Scandinavian texts of the decade end or die in deep isolation, in madness, or by their own hands. The 1890s may easily strike one as an epistemological cul-de-sac.

Many authors realized, as their works show, that whatever had earlier granted or given the illusion of meaning had failed, thus leading to the abrupt and brutal demise of all their hopes and aspirations. Apocalyptic images and scenes are thus abundant. Perhaps that vision is summed up most poignantly, as the decade closed, in Johannes V. Jensen's novel *Kongens Fald* (1900–1901; The Fall of the King), with its grotesque vision of the brevity of a human being's life span: human beings live, irrevocably, under the law of the fall and start falling toward their endpoint the moment they are born.

Such nihilism permeated much of the literature of the decade, and some authors tended to sink into passivity or paralysis, whereas others admittedly took delight in delving into that psychic, subjective world. Jensen's gruesome passage referred to above also contains a ghastly beauty, one that other explorers of the mind similarly rendered, through those relative symbols that became a distinguishing feature of the age. Perhaps it is in this particular area that Baudelaire, Poe, and the French symbolists had an impact: they freed the authors from the allegorical symbol of the past and replaced it with the modern, ambiguous, suggestive symbol that reflects not a common cultural frame of reference, but the separate world of an individual. That new relative symbol, the meaning of which must be grasped contextually but is hard to exhaust, flourishes in those Scandinavian texts of the 1890s which may be said to constitute a Modernistic Breakthrough. For some authors, perhaps those for whom art became the only pursuit that would not disappoint, the very experience of charting the "new" created artistic beauty and made art an end in itself.

The accusation of literary decadence can easily be sounded, and some Scandinavian works, including those in the other arts, can be seen as an expression of the decadent imagination. That imagination may seem sickly and reactionary, but it should be kept in mind that such probing may be a quite courageous attempt to gain new ground and deal with hitherto forbidden knowledge.

Of course, many authors took a different path. In some works the intentions of the Modern Breakthrough continued, and poets who found solace or meaning in watching the seasonal cycle of nature gave voice to a pantheism that can hardly be called metaphysical but can prevent the landscape depicted from being merely a reflection of an inner world.

This attempt at charting the 1890s may seem reductive—and peculiar in light of the initial observation that unity is difficult to pin down. Nevertheless, the reader who moves from the Modern Breakthrough to the 1890s is bound to sense a change: analysis becomes observation; plot dwindles in favor of mood; a belief in or desire for norms turns to a bleak acceptance of a void; lyric eloquence returns, but often as an exploration of the separate reality of the mind; and whatever gave or offered guidelines, purpose, or meaning to the human existence is doubted. The cultural heritage was considered utterly suspect.

It may, then, be cautiously maintained that the 1890s represent the beginning of modern Scandinavian literature, in the sense that the decade's modern traits—some of them modernistic—have remained and assume major significance. A part of that modernity, as suggested above, is the questioning of humanistic values or norms, for during the century to come no systems were granted absolute authority by any generation of authors and critics. They became voices reasoning with, and arguing against, one another to the extent that the period concept loses its usefulness. With that background it is thus somewhat ironic that it was during the 1890s that modern Danish literary history was shaped by academicians who firmly believed in a humanistic tradition in which they vested their cultural hopes. Valdemar Vedel's early articles betray his desire to be the Georg Brandes of the dawning decade of the 1890s, but such hopes faded as the literature of the decade failed to live up to his predictions. Vedel, who became professor at the University of Copenhagen in 1918, also served as a perceptive critic for *Tilskueren,* and like the rabidly anti-Brandes critic Harald Nielsen (1879–1957), he was an incisive observer of the age of which he was an integral part.

Vedel has, however, been overshadowed by Vilhelm Andersen (1864–1953), who also served as professor at the University of Copenhagen (1908–30). Andersen authored (with the assistance of Carl S. Petersen in the first volume) a four-volume literary history, *Illustreret dansk Litteraturhistorie* (1929–34; Illustrated Danish Literary History), which for decades became the canon for teachers of Danish literature. It is telling that several shorter literary histories, mainly textbooks for high school use, until the 1970s were condensed versions of Andersen's monumental and nuanced work. Once again historical irony is at play, for at a time when modern and modernistic literature questioned humanistic norms—any absolute value systems—Andersen's literary history advocated, if subtly, an ideal of *Bildung* that left little room for any questioning of it. The impact on academia of Andersen's normative assessment of Danish literature left little space for countermovements; thus, women's literature or working-class texts receive scant attention. That Andersen's vision was challenged by some of his contemporaries did not have for decades much of an impact on the teaching of literature.

Humanism is challenged from within, and even if in its traditional forms it is being shored up by some voices, the lonely, alienated, apocalyptic manifestations of the mood of the 1890s cast a dubious light on the trust in nineteenth-century humanism as a life-sustaining force for future generations. The new century brought social and spiritual changes that to the older generation must have seemed like future shock.

Johannes Jørgensen

Johannes Jørgensen (1866–1956) has assumed a prominent position in Danish literary history because he has been seen as a catalyst for the lyrical renaissance of the 1890s. As the editor of the short-lived but influential periodical *Taarnet* (1893–94; The Tower) he became the central figure in a young generation that was in opposition to the aftermath of the Modern Breakthrough. Some of the articles on symbolism from *Taarnet* are anthologized so frequently that they seem like the signposts of a dawning era. Without denying Jørgensen's impact on his generation, one may view his poetry in retrospect as quite old-fashioned: although he wrote admiringly of the French symbolists, his own poetic practice is quite romantic and hardly innovative. Later in life, in such collections of poetry as *Af det Dybe*

(1920; From the Depths) and *Der er en Brønd, som rinder* (1920; There Is a Flowing Well), he may have been influenced by the simplicity found in Paul Verlaine's poetic language, but the short rhythmic forms that are present in Goethe's striving for eloquence were an inspiration as well.

Jørgensen's early works, such as the poems found in *Bekendelse* (1894; Confession) as well as slim novels such as *Sommer* (1892; Summer), exude a mood of isolation, of premature disillusionment, of a yearning for the lost harmony initially located in childhood, and of a burning sensuality that may abruptly turn into asceticism. That intensity and fluctuation between sensuality and asceticism are reminiscent of the poetry of Schack von Staffeldt and the Swede Stagnelius, who wrote earlier in the century, but Jørgensen's emotional dilemma was eventually resolved by his conversion to Catholicism in 1896, a religious decision foreshadowed by his repeatedly expressed longing for a higher reality. His moods resemble those of his Norwegian contemporary Sigbjørn Obstfelder, but his traditional mode of expression, in poetry or in prose, does not reach the tormented eloquence or the expressionistic discourse of the latter.

Jørgensen's conversion was felt as a betrayal by some of his close friends. Both Viggo Stuckenberg and Sophus Claussen wrote inspired accusations in poetic form against Jørgensen's existential choice. Some of his most gripping poems, however, celebrate his new-found feeling of religious meaning in life and a blissful, nearly jubilant peace of mind.

Eventually, Jørgensen gained an international reputation as a major proponent of Catholicism. His hagiographies, such as *Den hellige Frans af Assisi* (1907; Eng. tr. *Saint Francis of Assisi,* 1912) and *Den hellige Katerina af Siena* (1915; Eng. tr. *Saint Catherine of Siena,* 1938), won wide circulation. His memoirs, *Mit Livs Legende* (1916–28; Eng. tr. *Jørgensen, An Autobiography,* 1928–29), whose title—"The *Legenda* of My Life"—reveals the didactic and confessional purpose of the work, are nevertheless fascinating cultural history. The two first volumes, in particular, offer Jørgensen's slanted but keen observations of a young provincial student's attempts to join, so to speak, the Modern Breakthrough and then gradually to emancipate himself from the movement.

Viggo Stuckenberg

Viggo Stuckenberg (1863–1905) and his wife, Ingeborg (1866–1904), were often hosts for the group of young artists who published in *Taarnet.* Ingeborg Stuckenberg, née Pamperin, has been given an afterlife by her many admirers, who depict her as the muse of their artistic circle but also as one who might well have felt confined in that role. She had artistic ambitions, and she was the occasional coauthor of part of her husband's works, even if credits were denied her on the title page. Eventually, she broke away but soon afterward died by her own hand. A testimony to her fascinating personality is given in Sophus Claussen's mesmerizing poem "Ingeborg Stuckenberg" (1905). If Ingeborg Stuckenberg felt that her life was restricted, her husband, who like Schandorph had to make a living as a schoolteacher, felt the same about his. The home was hospitable, an echo of earlier salons, but daily toil and economic strictures were factors that wore on the marital relationship. That friction is portrayed in all its nuances in the couple's prose and poetry.

Stuckenberg's first works give voice to the opinions of a young radical, but his adherence to the ideals of the Modern Breakthrough seem less than convincing in those early novels. The story *Messias* (1889; Messiah) focuses on a young man who enlists in the radical cause, but whose interests, like those of most authors in the 1890s, lie in personal matters rather than in social ones. In contrast to Jørgensen and others who rejected the social commitment of the Modern Breakthrough, Stuckenberg, like his Swedish colleague Hjalmar Söderberg, remained true to many of the radical ideals of his day.

Nevertheless, the energy in Stuckenberg's quite narrow oeuvre was used on very private matters, and in that lies both its weakness and its strength. It may seem an effort to preserve, in spite of economic, social, and psychological restraints, a sense of self. Stuckenberg was a proud and stoic individualist. A most eloquent expression of that defiant and dignified attitude can be found in his poem "Bekendelse" (1896; Confession), a vehement response to Johannes Jørgensen's conversion to Catholicism, a change of heart totally foreign to Stuckenberg and one that echoes Nietzschean chords.

Stuckenberg's major works analyze in minute detail how and why a marriage works or does not. Such slim texts as *Fagre Ord* (1895; Beautiful Words) and *Valravn* (1896; Wereraven) observe in moody accuracy the nature of love and how it dissolves. If a villain can be found, it is bourgeois society, which prevents freedom within relationships, but in these introverted volumes the major focus is the peculiar, but not always rational, workings of the mind. As is not uncommon among the authors of the 1890s, plot has been reduced to a minimum, so that mood, rendered in a lyrical prose— influenced by J. P. Jacobsen—dominates. There is an emotional, haunting intensity, a sensuality in the text, that has not been properly recognized. That quality is particularly evident in Stuckenberg's poetry, especially when he uses the ballad form, such as in "Tue Bentsøns Viser" (Tue Bentsøn's Ballads) from *Sne* (1901; Snow), which painfully portrays the havoc that sexuality wreaks on the mind.

Somewhat in another vein are *Sol* (1897; Sunshine) and *Asmadæus* (1899), which express a yearning for freedom and a break with bourgeois norms. Those texts can be seen as Stuckenberg's reaction against the claustrophobic atmosphere of his existence, a condition that could not be overcome in life. It is telling that among his collection of parables, called *Vejbred* (1899; The Plantain), he includes "a continuation" of Hans Christian Andersen's "Klods-Hans" (Clod Hans). The hero has become bored with his royal duties and life, plays hookey by going fishing, and meets a teasing, playful young woman from his past, who quite easily lures him into choosing freedom instead of the kingdom. That ardent desire to escape from bourgeois strictures was expressed by many authors of the last decades of the century.

Sophus Claussen

Sophus Claussen (1865–1931) seems refreshingly free and unrestricted in comparison to many of his contemporaries. He possesses a playfulness, a sense of humor, and a keen enjoyment both of the idyllic and of its opposite, giving one the impression that he feels very much at home in this life. His poetry has little in common with Jørgensen's and Obstfelder's pining tones but suggests the same pride in his individuality that can be found in the works of Stuckenberg.

As a young man Claussen worked as a journalist in the Danish provinces, and some early, seemingly loosely composed novels, such as *Unge Bander* (1894; Young Gangs), are erotic, darkly idyllic paeans by a young flaneur who is enjoying his life in spite of its erotic ups and downs. Those works suggest that, although love plays unpredictable and unfair games with the human being, such games ought to be cherished; it was a perception that remained with Claussen as he grew older.

The poems in his first collection, *Naturbørn* (1887; Nature's Children), advocated sexual liberation as the means to a more joyful life, but Claussen joined the *Taarnet* circle and, like Jørgensen, fell under the spell of the French symbolists. In his whimsical travel chronicle, *Antonius i Paris* (1896; Antonius in Paris), he records encounters with Verlaine and Mallarmé, and among Danish lyrical poets of his day, he was undoubtedly the one who best understood the workings and spirit of French aesthetics and practice. More so than his colleagues, he managed to forge a poetic language that did not imitate that of the French authors but came close to their illusive technique.

His second collection, *Pilefløjter* (1899; Willow Pipes), echoed two lyrical ironists whom Claussen admired, Heinrich Heine and Emil Aarestrup, but the voice is very much Claussen's own: although the mood may be somber and the intent serious, a light, even witty touch creates a splendid juxtaposition. Surprising and exquisitely wrought phrases give these texts a playful and lasting innovativeness, and a remarkable ease with metrical form continues to afford the listener pleasure. In the elegant poem "I en Frugthave" (In an Orchard) Claussen infuses an erotic situation with observations of nature on a windy day in a garden:

> Did storm fall on suncalm surface?
> My soul fluttered up like a cloth,
> and a lightning-torn cascade of thunder
> poured rain over green leaves.
> When it grew quiet, you were mine.
>   (Tr. Poul Borum)

As in his early novels the setting is often that of the provinces (the poems selected for this volume span a ten-year period), but the concluding "Røg" (Smoke) records a symbolist's reaction to the bellowing smoke from a locomotive as a train rushes through the landscape. Erotic and philosophical associations and correspondences mix and fuse, but even if the symbolism is quite private and thus not always decipherable, it is a hallmark of Claussen's art that the poem nevertheless intrigues through its strikingly fascinating images and its ability to make visible a very concrete reality.

In *Djævlerier* (1904; Diableries) impressions from his travels in southern Europe function as a background for Claussen's exuberant and devilish commentaries on a life that easily could be made dull but surely can be otherwise if all its possibilities are faced. Claussen knew the lure of hedonism and the moral indefensibility of many of its pleasures; thus, he defiantly delights in the sulphuric smell that accompanies his descent down "the steps into hell" ("Trappen til Helvede") to satisfy his sensual inclinations. Claussen was also a connoisseur of Baudelaire. "Afrodites Dampe" (Aphrodite's Steam) is a poem in praise of passion; although experiences of the body are not depicted, they are suggested or intimated—or replaced by the effect of the experience on the mind—by a cryptic, allusive, symbolic cross-referencing technique that Claussen alone among his contemporaries mastered.

Claussen, for reasons just mentioned, was not a popular poet, but his following collections of poetry, in retrospect, added to his reputation: *Danske Vers* (1912; Danish Verses), *Fabler* (1917; Fables), and *Heroica* (1925) include impressive texts, some very humorous, some chillingly apocalyptic.

Among the latter belongs the late poem "Atomernes Oprør" (1925; The Revolt of the Atoms), in which, apparently inspired by the ominous technical advances demonstrated by World War I, he pleads, "If our star can be saved, please do not cause it harm."

In an entirely different manner an apocalyptic—and cosmic—vision is expressed in the defiantly nihilistic "Imperia" (1912). The poem is a monologue by mother earth; contrary to hallowed tradition, that mother is not a gentle provider but a force inimical to all human aspirations. She feels utter contempt for all human achievements, among them the ridiculous church spires that attempt to reach for a god, and she longs for humankind's violent destruction. The compelling images conjured up to capture that *moment* are, typically, erotic, for earth, who compares herself to ice, eagerly awaits consummation with fire, her lover. The ensuing apocalypse, one that may well suggest a nuclear holocaust to a later audience, seems to be rendered with total detachment from the human predicament, but Claussen, true to his untraditional way of thinking, paints the bang that ends it all—whimpers were not to his liking—as intensely beautiful.

Others confronted with existential chaos had to find some solution to the lack of meaning they saw everywhere, whereas Claussen, although his lack of recognition on the part of an audience annoyed him, patiently found that meaning in beauty and in the act of depicting it. In the poem "Ekbátana" from 1896, an inscrutable text (partly because of the symbolist play with time levels and suggestive correspondences), it is asserted that it hardly matters if life disappoints, for "the word"—poetry—is gained and the writer has "lived one day in Ekbátana." Claussen thus did not join the chorus that begged for meaning.

Such an attitude should not suggest that, as was the case with Jørgensen and Obstfelder, Claussen turned selective as to what the human being should experience. One very early poem, "Buddha" (1888, but published in *Pilefløjter*), foreshadows Claussen's knowledge that life not only may well disappoint direly, but also will surely be worth living. The major part of the text comprises the human lament over a life that has proved to be so disillusioning that Buddha is asked not to let the soul be reincarnated. The list of possibilities that proved to be false is, however, introduced and concluded by identical stanzas, in which Buddha speaks: it may be significant and telling of the limitations of the human mind not only that the divinity takes the human being to Nirvana, but also that the earthly life those disaffected human beings have rejected and are willing to leave behind is rendered as being supremely beautiful.

Claussen is a complex, rewarding, difficult poet whom it is a chore to label (and in that sense he resembles an equally masterly poet from the 1890s, the Swede Gustav Fröding), partly because his poetry, although it surely deals with ideas, is an exploration into experience, real and imagined. What inspired Claussen to disgust might also fascinate and must thus be investigated—with the means of the word. He and Fröding are poets of the highest rank; they belong in the league of Rainer Maria Rilke and William Butler Yeats.

Helge Rode

Helge Rode (1870–1937) is often mentioned as the only genuine mystic of his generation. Others may have longed for visionary insights, but it was the reserved, intellectual Rode who was to write about the moment of revelation. He stood, he proclaims ecstatically in his first collection of poetry, *Hvide Blomster* (1892; White Flowers), "at the brink of the yawning abyss," and that experience endowed him with a firm belief in the human soul. That spiritual awakening eventually made him one of the most ardent opponents of what he deemed to be the materialism of the Modern Breakthrough.

In Rode's early poetry an overpowering intensity and breathlessness express the awe of the mystic when confronted with that which cannot be explained. Rode, whose temperament was hardly that of a William Blake or Stagnelius, did not, however, pursue the path of the visionary who explores the inner crevices of the mind. He established himself as a snappy metropolitan cultural critic, as a playwright (his reputation has now faded), and as a defender of causes threatened by materialism. In his later poetry—one collection is typically called *Ariel* (1914)—he reveals his profound understanding of such minds as those of Obstfelder and Tolstoy, who shared his youthful passion but who chose more dangerous, devastating, or glorious roads. Rode's tributes to them may additionally suggest the reason he seemed preoccupied with death, as revealed in *Den stille Have* (1922; The Quiet Garden).

Ludvig Holstein

Ludvig Holstein (1864–1943) made his debut in 1895 with *Digte* (Poems), but his language is much less allegorical and emotional than that of most of his contemporaries. The pantheism that echoes from the first poems was retained when Holstein resumed publishing after years of silence. In such collections as *Løv* (1915; Foliage) and *Æbletid* (1920; Appletime) Holstein's sheer joy in Danish nature and a sense of its sanctity are combined with a feeling of communion with it. The natural cycle is viewed as a miracle, and such recurrent events as the unfolding of a hyacinth's bud and the splendor of a field of dandelions—pilgrims dressed up to celebrate Pentecost—teach the impatient, reflective human being to accept life and to refrain from asking questions that cannot be answered. In his collection of essays, *Den grønne Mark* (1925; The Green Field), Holstein explains that the person who takes a dubious attitude toward religion must nevertheless admit that miracles, both the mundane and the unique, happen every day in nature.

The longing for pantheistic unification with nature permeates Holstein's poetry. At times his yearning is vague and passive, but the concluding section of *Løv* bears the heading "Paniske Stemninger" (Panic Moods); the ambiguity of that title captures not only the expected yearning for transcendence, but also the passionate desire to cross the border between nature and mind which haunts the pantheist, who cannot be forever content with longing for oneness.

Gustav Wied

Gustav Wied (1858–1914), growing up on the southern island of Lolland, knew the provinces by heart and did not idyllicize them. He had a keen eye for the double standard of the bourgeoisie, and the majority of his works—short stories, novels, and plays—capture with a wicked humor the weaknesses, foibles, and sanctimoniousness of members of good families. Wied spared neither high nor low, even if he did reserve some compassion for those who were made outcasts by not conforming to the accepted codes of behavior. Wied's novels seem to reflect the opinion that all the talk of reform and freedom has had absolutely no effect on Danish society.

As a budding author, Wied had to serve a short jail term on account of his sexual frankness in a short story: he suggested that an elderly female servant was making sexual advances to a young boy. Wied was not, however, a bleeding-heart liberal, and his best-known protagonist, Knagsted, who is featured in the ribald and outrageously funny *Livsens Ondskab* (1899; Life's Malice), the amusing and satiric *Knagsted* (1902), and the savagely bitter *Pastor Sørensen & Co.* (1913; Pastor Sørensen & Company), gleefully announces that his idols are Napoleon and Bismarck. Nevertheless, Knagsted and his creator have a soft spot in their hearts for the misfits who never will be able to achieve the happiness for which they strive. Knagsted's and Wied's contempt for do-gooders, whose efforts are a ridiculous exercise in futility, suggests that Wied's oeuvre has a conservative hue. It would, however, be more precise to see Wied as an idealistic anarchist who easily falls prey to a nihilistic cultural pessimism. The scathing sarcasm of some of his works is reminiscent of the early, bitterly pessimistic stories of Pontoppidan.

Wied's humor became more and more grotesque and desperate as he seemed to try to offend. Such nasty studies of decadence as *Slægten* (1898;

The Clan) and *Fædrene æde Druer* (1908; The Forebears Eat Grapes) manage
to do just that and to suggest that Wied's humor was quite ahead of his
times. He had a compatriot in August Strindberg, whose often-neglected
humor has a similarly bitter sting. Like Strindberg, Wied wrote a series of
plays, labeled "satyr plays," of which *Dansemus* (1905; Dancing Mice)
stands out with its comic force, albeit reflecting the abysmal pessimism of
the author's other prose works. Perhaps both Strindberg's and Wied's galling honesty and wit seem so alive today because the world has become accustomed to the bleak humor of such authors as Samuel Beckett, Edward
Albee, and Lenny Bruce.

Harald Kidde

The major works of Harald Kidde (1878–1918) were published after the
turn of the century, but the mood of most of them relegates their author to
the subjectivity of the 1890s. Kidde depicts nature and advancing industrial
civilization with great precision, but his foremost urge is to capture the inner, mental landscape of his isolated young men. They thirst ravenously for
life, reach out for it, but fail. Their failure is even more striking because they
are supported by strong, joyous women—as in the lyrical *Aage og Else* (1902
–3; Aage and Else)—but in spite of the men's desire for life, their infatuation with death proves to be stronger. As in Obstfelder's prose, sensuality
and asceticism are at loggerheads, but in most cases the outcome seems to be
given, for Kidde's male protagonist chooses death in life, a state of isolation
that will prevent his feverish physical yearnings from ever being fulfilled.

Kidde's attraction to Kierkegaard, which preceded his writing of *Helten*
(1912; The Hero), is highly understandable in light of the conflicts encountered in his early works, and it seems that the philosopher's advocacy of
strict choices that alter life completely is reflected in the novel. Like
Strindberg's novel *I havsbandet* (1890; By the Open Sea), *Helten* takes place
on a lonely island and centers on people from the outside, who never quite
fit in among the islanders. The hero celebrated is one of those weak men, like
Dostoevsky's Prince Myshkin, who humbly accept life's blows. That martyr
figure is surrounded by a surrealistic coterie of restless souls who feel
trapped by the island but who, like Kierkegaard's suffering aesthetes, in reality are prisoners of their private inner hell. Although Clemens Bek, the protagonist, learns to perceive the real and beautiful world around him, the
others become haunting and grotesque embodiments of those characters of
the 1890s who never could break free of the world that their minds created.

With *Jærnet* (1918; The Iron) Kidde started a tetralogy intended to depict
industrialism's effect on culture. Because of the author's premature death,

only the first volume appeared, but its artistic promise was undeniable. Through a small boy's mind, some regional Swedish iron mines and works are conjured up with all the effects that an expressionistic discourse can offer, and they are portrayed with an energy and intensity hitherto unknown in the oeuvre. Simultaneously, the smells, sounds, and sights of an industrial hell that exploits and undermines the health of the human being and the inner, tortured, reflective mind of the boy are captured with spellbinding force. It seems that Kidde once again admits that this world must be observed as it is, but nevertheless, he cannot keep from moving inside the mind of the troubled outsider who longs for, yet cannot be an integral part of, this world. *Helten* and *Jærnet* are peculiar, mannered masterpieces, but so are many of the works of Nathaniel Hawthorne and William Faulkner, both of whom charted the mind that is unable to break away from its own strange paths.

Ernesto Dalgas

Ernesto Dalgas (1871–99) as a very young man experienced the seductive power of Søren Kierkegaard, and the two books Dalgas completed before he took his own life seem to spring from that experience. Like Kierkegaard, he engages his reader in a *Bildungs* process, through which the attitudes that can be shared with others are left behind for totally subjective choices that may have validity only for the singular individual. In *Lidelsens Vej* (1903; The Road of Suffering) the narrator tells of the stages on his life's way, and thus his story embodies not only Kierkegaard's subjectivity, but also the modernism that he foreshadowed, for Dalgas's narrator has tried to find fulfillment through the various attitudes toward life that earlier ages had judged to be creative of meaning in existence. He rejects belief in authority, experiments with hedonism, joins social causes, seeks refuge in love, but realizes that only a solitary life in which he remains truly himself can be called truthful. That rejection of past solutions can be seen as an outgrowth of the human dilemma of the 1890s. In Dalgas the problem is envisioned with uncommon stringency and consistency, but unlike its portrayal in many other narratives of the decade, the dilemma in Dalgas's works is solved—for the narrator.

The same pattern and subjectivity can be found in *Dommedags Bog* (1903; The Book of Judgment), in which Kierkegaard's Johannes de Silentio, the "author" of *Frygt og Bæven*, guides the protagonist through a Dantean tour of Christian worlds which ends in a longing for Nirvana. The rejection of the world of the senses and the apocalyptic fever and visionary power of Dalgas's prose are reminiscent of Kidde, who in his last work, *Jærnet*, reached a similar burning intensity.

Knud Hjortø

Knud Hjortø (1869–1931), whose first collection of sketches, *Syner* (1899; Visions), shows his closeness to the mood of the 1890s, rebelled, like Johannes V. Jensen, against the introversion and cultural fatigue of his age. The title of *Kraft* (1902; Power) suggests its author's intentions, and with the more sophisticated *Folk* (1903; People) Hjortø showed his talent for satire in a manner reminiscent of Wied's portraits of the pettiness of the small provincial town. In the trilogy *Støv og Stjærner* (1904; Dust and Stars), *To Verdener* (1905; Two Worlds), and *Hans Råskov* (1906), Hjortø focuses, however, on the conflict—one never harmoniously resolved—between an inclination toward fantasy and a wholehearted acceptance of the day-to-day world. Hjortø's fine-tuned, reflective language adroitly captures shades of the human mind and takes the reader into the niches that later were dubbed the unconscious; thus, he has earned a well-deserved reputation for his ability to give sophisticated, intricate psychological insights. He particularly attempted to confront and cope with those inner forces that the intellect cannot control. If Hjortø's novels seem to be caught in the webs of the 1890s, his elegantly wrought and wry short stories show a versatile, satirical author. His *Spotske Jomfruer* (1918; Scornful Maidens) pays a witty homage to smart and resourceful women and remains eminently readable.

Jakob Knudsen

Jakob Knudsen (1858–1917), like many Danish authors from the period, grew up in a clerical milieu, of which he became quite critical but never left mentally. Like his father, he taught at a folk high school and became, briefly, an ordained minister. His main criticism of the Christianity of his day was that it denied the human being's sensuality and instincts for the sake of a self-denying spirituality. The characters in his novels are passionate idealists, whose adamant and uncompromising demands on life lead to violent clashes with others and even their own destruction. In the novel *Den gamle Præst* (1899; The Old Minister) a father kills a young man who has tried to violate his daughter and is advised, by a wise, old minister, to take his own life. The minister, who clearly is the author's mouthpiece, firmly believes he is advocating those laws of the Lord that, at critical times, must transcend both secular and clerical authority. The message is that of a relative morality, one that seems to echo, in a distorted sense, Kierkegaard's demands on the individual.

In *Sind* (1903; Temper) one central issue is vigilante justice. The protagonists, in their unshakable righteousness, steer down a path that leads to self-sacrifice and destruction. As in Ibsen and Pontoppidan, but with much less ambiguity, those whom ordinary society has deemed to be fools are heralded as idealists, human beings who insist on preserving their integrity.

Knudsen's vision may seem to be quite conservative, for he is profoundly suspicious of those new ideas that undermine the beliefs and values of the past, an issue confronted in the novel *Fremskridt* (1907; Progress), even if his own insistence on the instinctual and sensual human being appears to echo the ideas of the Modern Breakthrough.

THE EARLY YEARS OF THE NEW CENTURY

In hindsight it makes sense to separate the writings of the 1890s from those of the early twentieth century. Within such prominent oeuvres as Johannes V. Jensen's, Martin Andersen Nexø's, and the Norwegian Knut Hamsun's, there exists a noticeable difference between the youthful works with their distinct Nineties' moods and the later, more extroverted novels. It is, however, hardly possible to find a catchy common denominator that will accurately include the authors of the years leading to and including World War I. As Claudio Guillén has pointed out, Brandes's term *currents* is more apt than the taxonomical *period*, especially at this point, as various classes, with differing backgrounds, found a voice in literature. These classes began to speak as groups, for they were no longer merely represented by one individual who had managed to rise above his or her station. Consequently, literature proffered more incompatible norms and values than ever before.

Of course, many writers still came from the humanistic, intellectual culture that so far had enjoyed a near monopoly on belles lettres, and they continued the psychological exploration of the last two decades of the nineteenth century. Most of them made their debut in the late 1890s and thus are included in the preceding section for practical reasons. An author such as Johannes V. Jensen, who began his career as the epitome of the fin de siècle, eventually vehemently turned against the legacy of the 1890s and embraced a Darwinian view that programmatically allied him with modern technology and with that desire for, and belief in, progress which many of his contemporaries expressed with their political and reformist agenda.

With those authors, such as Johan Skjoldborg and Jeppe Aakjær, the Modern Breakthrough continues. The term *Brandesianism* cannot really be used any longer, however, for even though many socially engaged writers, several of whom had made their debuts in the late 1890s, shared the reformist zeal and indignation of the early Breakthrough, they were not intellectual observers but insiders: they came from families of day laborers or industrial workers. Some of those authors initially paid lip service to the prevailing literary moods of the 1890s but emerged as solid realists who knew that literature ought to promote social justice.

At the time, the working classes had gained a good deal of political power; unions and management had both learned lessons during bitter strikes and lockouts; the conservative ruling elite had been forced to leave the seats of power; and a new moderate government began to enact laws intended to ease the burden of the working classes. The contrast between the bustling industrial cities and the farming culture, still dominated by manor houses and a near-feudal system, was striking, and the conflict between a new technological civilization in flux and an old-fashioned one that resisted change is bound to strike the reader of the works from that time span.

A poignant difference between the Modern Breakthrough and the socially committed authors of the early twentieth century was the new generation's focus on class, rather than on the individual. The realism, or naturalism, of that first twentieth-century generation was, additionally, less doctrinaire than earlier and at that point a natural choice of expression, rather than the embodiment of a literary program. That realism captured, in much more detail than ever before, the farmland, its nature as well as the farmhand's toil, of rural Denmark. The contours of the land and the lives and social conditions of the ordinary men and women who worked it emerge in the works of those authors whom Sven Møller Kristensen has called "the great generation."

If that literature is a protest against existing conditions, so are the works of several women writers, but their battleground remains the home—even if actual or attempted breakaways are recorded. Their works are more individualistic than those of their socially committed male colleagues, but less pessimistic or fatalistic than those of their predecessors. The risk of being ostracized for breaking the rules of the male world remained very real, but the disappointment recorded by those who believed that the Modern Breakthrough would mean a deliverance from bondage seems to have been overcome, and in the works of those female authors strides are taken toward a more individual freedom and a better access to the world outside the home. A promised land—the dream of a more civilized society which permeates many of the works from those years—is by no means reached, but energy, rather than pessimism, underlies the women's writing.

The works of the social critics of the time were often read and discussed at the Grundtvigian folk high schools, which functioned as institutions of "advanced learning" for those young men and women who would never dream of an academic career. From their home regions they had a storehouse of tales, the age-old and ever-current folklore that was a natural and inevitable part of the life of unlettered people or those with limited access to the printed page. Those stories could be splendid entertainment, but they could also voice, often humorously, the anger of the oppressed, and toward the end of the preceding century the folklorist Evald Tang Kristensen (1843–1929) had begun a monumental effort to collect such tales. During a fifty-year effort he succeeded in gathering more than three thousand, a fraction of which was published, partly in the journal *Skattegraveren* (1884–89; The Treasure Hunter) and partly in his anthologies of narrative folklore. Tang Kristensen's endeavor is particularly noteworthy because he respected the voices of his informants and refused to tamper with the stories, since such editorial intrusions would obfuscate the impression of a culture that he intended to present exactly as it was. That respect for the oral text has become a must in modern folklore studies.

At the time, the academician Axel Olrik (1864–1917) was much better known than the humble schoolteacher, Tang Kristensen, for Olrik contributed with imagination to the international knowledge of folklore. He was a prolific writer, and his "Episke Love i Folkedigtningen" (1908; Eng. tr. *The Epic Laws of Folk Narrative*, 1965), published in the journal he founded in 1904, *Danske Studier* (Danish Studies), foreshadowed that structural study of the folktale for which Vladimir Propp gained fame with his *Morphology of the Folktale* (in Russian 1928; Eng. tr. 1958). In their very different ways the two Danes added respectability to a field for which the academic culture had little use. Previously, most folklore, with the exception of the ballad, which dealt with the lives of the aristocracy, had been considered—in a sense like women's literature or that of the working class—to be of inferior quality and generally irrelevant to the person who was seriously engaged in the appreciation of art.

Although folklore as art and as a field of research gained ground, it was simultaneously losing ground because of the advancement of popular modern culture. The exodus of the population from the countryside continued as industry flourished and opened up more jobs. More and more farmhands became a part of "labor" and adjusted to a city culture that craved entertaining reading: a commercial press reached out to the increasingly literate masses and gave them popular novels that idyllicized life at the manor house or on the old family farm; pulp serial minibooks appealed to young readers; newspapers with feuilletons (installment novels of a cliff-hanger cut) and sensational news from all over the world, weekly magazines with photographs from exotic regions of the world and with that new narrative form called the comic strip—all reached the general public. Soon moving pictures, though still silent, and the crackling but not at all silent radio would become a part of life—one that might leave less room for traditional storytelling but could not stop those modern, oral legends that have continued to flourish even after the later advent of television.

During the nineteenth century the distance between highbrow and lowbrow literature, caused by increased literacy and commercialism, had been growing, and thus an abundance of popular publications, which cannot be considered here, filled the windows and shelves of the bookstores. This development may have seemed barbaric to a class that, for generations, had considered itself as having a monopoly on the only, the right culture. That class had been deeply shaken by the Modern Breakthrough and its aftermath, which spelled a rebellion from within by that culture's own sons and daughters. Although the rise of a popular culture could be deemed the blossoming of vulgarity, it can be argued that art nevertheless became liberated from serving a fixed audience, and could diversify and more freely delve into experiments.

The 1890s had been quite conservative in terms of most literary forms, for modernist views were harnessed in time-honored forms, and admittedly, the early years of the new century were not strikingly experimental. Nevertheless, Jensen's poetry, Kidde's last novel, and, of course, the expressionistic, lyrical outburst toward the end of the second decade signal a new freedom for literature, one paralleled in the other arts. As the invention of photography during the nineteenth century left the person behind the camera to produce a true copy of "reality" for the customers, the painters could take leave of that responsibility or chore and permit themselves—as did the impressionists and expressionists—to conjure up more and more daring representations of whatever reality might be.

The beginnings of the twentieth century may not seem all that radical, but its early realism gave minute and quite optimistic insights into ordinary lives, and intermittently, texts suggested a road leading toward modernism. If those authors should be called humanists, their humanism redefined the term for the century.

Johannes V. Jensen

Johannes V. Jensen (1873–1950), the son of a veterinarian, grew up in a windswept rural district, Himmerland, in northern Jutland. His impressions of the people and the landscape of his childhood are powerfully present in several of his works, especially in the three-volume *Himmerlandshistorier* (1898–1910; Stories from Himmerland).

In those stories past ages are invoked, but in several it is apparent that an old-fashioned way of life is giving way to the technology of the young twentieth century. Jensen, however, does not lament that development, which he viewed as both inevitable and necessary. The author, who later became a staunch advocate of Darwinism, was early in his career deeply fascinated with those inhabitants of Himmerland whose destinies took dramatic turns, often in a tragic direction. The outcome of the workings of chance are usually bleak, and at times it seems as if the characters spite themselves by willing their own miserable destiny. In some texts the somber tone is relieved, and some are brief, hilarious comedies that suggest that the practical joke was very much alive among the farmers, day laborers, itinerant workmen, and drifters.

The stories are interwoven, and thus life in Himmerland is mapped out in somewhat the same manner as in William Faulkner's imaginary Yoknapatawpha County, Mississippi. The person who dominates one story will appear as a minor character in another. But the similarity goes deeper than that, for both authors reveal a deep affinity for very diverse characters and capture their lives in a style that is both brusquely realistic and so lyrical and evocative of mood that it transcends realism, just as in modern Latin American fiction. The focus, as in the works of Faulkner or of Gabriel García Márquez, is often trained on a mind unalterably obsessed and thus driven relentlessly and against its better judgment to a bitter destiny.

Jensen went to Copenhagen in 1893 to obtain a medical degree from the nation's only university. To support himself, he wrote some potboilers for newspapers and eventually decided to abandon his studies to embark on a career as a serious writer. Like Martin Andersen Nexø, he wrote novels that placed him in the mainstream of the literature of the 1890s. Human dreams, if not life itself, are seen as futile, and the characters end in despair or madness. The title of the first volume, *Danskere* (1896; Danes), suggests that Jensen sees the inability to live life fully as a national weakness. The second novel, *Einar Elkær* (1898), demonstrates the consequences of unrelenting self-reflection, but both the length of the narrative and its verbal energy imply that Jensen does not share the passivity and fatalism so prominent in the works of Johannes Jørgensen, Sigbjørn Obstfelder, or Hjalmar Söderberg. Even if Jensen's protagonists die pitifully, they have the same paradoxical wish to experience life as do the characters in Strindberg's and Hamsun's works.

The desire to be a part of life, reject introspection, and be a person of action may be seen as a driving force behind Jensen's magnificent, mythical historical novel, *Kongens Fald* (1900–1901; Eng. tr. *The Fall of the King*, 1933, 1992). The king is the historical sixteenth-century Christian II, the ruler of all the Nordic countries during the last days of the Kalmar Union, and the novel depicts his loss of power. More significantly, it juxtaposes the dreamer, Mikkel, and the man of action, Axel, and records how deeply the lives of those two opposites are intertwined. At the level of the text as essay the novel reads as an allegory about a culture that "falls" because the ruler, Christian II, is too reflective to make necessary and timely decisions. An insistent, tightly woven, symbolic structure suggests that the Danish mind has become lost in a metaphysical pondering that leads to historical and personal defeats.

The novel also voices a more drastic, brutal, and ultimately nihilistic view. It seems that no matter what the human being chooses, he or she lives under the law of the fall and will live to see all dreams reduced to ashes. In a brief, grotesque poetic scene Jensen shows how a newborn baby, representing all humanity, swiftly goes through the stages of youth and maturity, to enter, nearly immediately, old age and subsequent death. Perhaps *Kongens Fald* is so striking a work because its consistent and icy nihilism is combined, logically rather than paradoxically, with a profound and sensuous feeling of beauty, of nature, of the human body, of emotion and experience, thus of everything that the human being will soon and, according to the law, inevitably lose. Nihilism is grandly fused with an unabashed sensual aestheticism that celebrates the wonders of the human being's brief life. Although the thought of inevitable mortality may seem to cancel out human aspirations, the person of action, Axel, who has refused to live only in an inner, mental world, is permitted an exit from life that seems to be a triumphant journey toward an ultimate fulfillment of all desire. Eros and Thanatos have rarely been linked in a more accomplished way than in *Kongens Fald*.

Death for the dreamer, who does not see the world, however, can only mean disappointment, and Mikkel's epitaph is that never had the king "seen a person whose features [showed that he] had been more disappointed." *Kongens Fald,* one of the most remarkable novels in Nordic literature, is simultaneously a brusque, if sympathetic, verdict for the dreamer and a paean to an existence that simply is. The novel centers on death, but in its evocative, lyrical celebrations of the natural world that human senses can experience, it subtly admonishes the human being to open up to that land of supreme beauty and utmost happiness—which Axel sees as he lies dying— and which is of this world. *Kongens Fald* may be chillingly nihilistic, but it is not a decadent rejection of the world. In many ways the novel forms a tantalizing transition between the introversion of the 1890s and the open vistas of the twentieth century.

Jensen, however, was set on a very determined path that was meant to deny any association with the attitudes of the 1890s. The newspaper *Social-*

Demokraten (The Social Democrat) sent him to Paris in 1900 to report on the World's Fair. Jensen's articles, published later as *Den gotiske Renaissance* (1901; The Gothic Renaissance), revel in the promise of technology, for it should bring health and wealth to the world. In the same breath Jensen denounced Nietzsche—that hitherto so ubiquitous influence—for failing to grasp the beauty of the world and thus losing out on the only life that the human being has. Facts, objects to be found in this world, even the minutest of them, decreed Jensen, were of much more value than the proudest dreams. He was developing a materialistic outlook that was meant as an antidote, not only to the malaise of the 1890s but also to all that metaphysical dreaming that has plagued Western civilization for millennia and has caused its cultural decadence. It may be that the Modern Breakthrough thereby reasserted itself in its youthful form, for J. P. Jacobsen's protagonist in *Niels Lyhne* demanded that all dreams of going to a higher world beyond ought to be abandoned for the sake of devoting one's energy to living this one and only life. Jensen, however, did not offer any list of reforms to change the social world and create a free human being, but satisfied himself with a no-holds-barred rejection of any kind of metaphysics.

Jensen visited America several times. The Americans' conquest of new land and their will to move westward he saw as a sign of future promise for the human race. Jensen's theories of a decadent Europe and a healthy America may strike the reader as very dubious in retrospect, but his early impressions of America resulted in some sketches, a major poem, and two novels. *Madame D'Ora* (1904) and *Hjulet* (1905; The Wheel) may seem pale in scope and inspiration when compared with *Kongens Fald*, but they offer exciting, if melodramatic, plots and keen observations of turn-of-the-century America; particularly vivid are scenes in the second novel of Chicago deluged by a monumental blizzard. The hero is the New World's man of action, who valiantly combats and defeats the Nietzschean villain.

Jensen staked out his position very clearly in *Digte* (1906; Poems; several of the texts are available in translation). Jensen breaks with the polished form of earlier poetry, in that he resembles Strindberg's quite conscious rebellion against accepted poetic forms in his *Dikter* (1883; Poems). Jensen's texts were not only filled with slang and everyday words, but also scorned conventional meter or rhyme; in addition, they were explosive in mood, angry, frustrated, funny, and infuriating in being both happily self-centered and antireligious. When surface impressions are shed, however, the poems reveal that the poet knows the mood of the 1890s intimately and must fight to defeat it, so that the volume's life-sustaining, robustly healthy, this-worldly message can emerge. The magnificent poem "Paa Memphis Station" (At Memphis Station) captures the development from introverted, suicidal alienation, through a grudging but necessary acceptance of this flawed world, to a pragmatic but enthusiastic realization that Memphis, wherever it is found, is, in its imperfection, the only world we have—to enjoy only briefly:

> *Stay* in Memphis, Tennessee!
> For in one of those poster-howling buildings
> happiness waits for you, happiness,
> if you can only swallow your impatience.
> Here, too, sleeps a shapely young virgin,
> her ear buried in her hair.
> She will come to meet you
> on the street one fine day
> like a wave of fragrance
> with an air as if she knew you.
> (Tr. Alexander Taylor)

The United States also provides the setting for some of the stories in the three-volume *Eksotiske Noveller* (1907–15; Exotic Stories), and it resurfaces as a historical, or rather mythic, entity in the last part of Jensen's six-volume novel *Den lange Rejse* (1908–22; Eng. tr. *The Long Journey,* 1922–24). Most of the "exotic stories," however, are localized in the Far East and are, in their simplistic view of the life of the Europeans among the natives, an example of the strong influence Rudyard Kipling had on Jensen's early writing. In *Den lange Rejse,* in contrast, the dream of America is an integral part of the philosophical subtext. The series, for which Jensen was awarded the Nobel Prize in literature in 1944, is perceived as a history of humankind, based on Charles Darwin's theory of evolution, and thus a scientific counterpart to the biblical Genesis. *Det tabte Land* (1919; The Lost Land) is a Darwinian myth of the transition from animal to human being set in the rain forests of Jensen's native Jutland. In *Bræen* (1908; The Glacier), the first written and most popular of the volumes, the Glacial Age has driven all the people toward the south. Only Dreng stays behind and together with the woman, Moa, founds a new dynasty. In later volumes Jensen demonstrates how the challenge of nature becomes the driving force of progress. A basic trait of the Nordic people, "the Gothic race," is the dream about warmth and sun. This dream, which is Jensen's explanation of religious sentiment, is expressed through a longing for distant places, for "the lost land," paradise. This longing becomes embodied in the structures of the ship and the Gothic cathedral and also manifests itself in the Viking migrations, as well as in the voyage of the Goth Columbus. His attempts at finding legendary lands resulted, however, in the discovery of America, of reality.

The artistic quality of *Den lange Rejse* is uneven and the anthropological theories untenable. Nevertheless, the work must be read and appreciated as a loosely structured, often splendid poetic hymn to humankind, animal, and nature as one close intertwined part of the universe and to compelling longing as a dominant force in the human race. In fact, it should be interpreted as a series of myths, "attempts to focus on the essence of life in a dream," as Jensen himself has tried to define this genre. In *Myter* (1907–44; Myths) he published eleven volumes of such brief sketches, describing animals, nature, and journeys. His point of departure is usually a concrete sense impression from which a spiritual expansion of the perspective takes place founded on Jensen's basic concepts: reality as the source and final goal of all longing ("Fusijama"), balanced by a belief in the cyclic eternity of the revitalizing nature ("Nordisk Foraar" [Nordic Spring]). All of Jensen's myths originate in his belief in the necessity of creating links to the most distant memories from our history in order to enhance a harmonious development ("Darwin og Fuglen" [Darwin and the Bird]).

With the years Jensen's fictional writing decreased. A novel from 1935, *Dr. Renaults Fristelser* (The Temptations of Dr. Renault), is a variation on Goethe's *Faust* (1808) in which Jensen lets the title character—in contrast to Goethe—win over Mephistopheles because he *does* accept the bliss of the moment. Later poetry collections (1917, 1921, 1943, and 1948) are mainly enlarged editions of the debut collection from 1906. They are noteworthy, however, in their gradual shift from the youthful prose poems to alliterating poems in the Old Norse style or traditional verse meters, related to the classic poetry of Adam Oehlenschläger, with whom Jensen felt a strong kinship. Jensen's poetic force did not diminish. His later collections abound with grandiose as well as highly lyrical and intimate glorifications of child, woman, and Danish nature marked by the same mythic quality—the expansion from acute observation to timeless and boundless visions—that characterizes his best works.

Primarily, Jensen turned to the feature article and the essay to popularize the Darwinian view of life. Like *Den lange Rejse*, the content is often based on dubious scientific theories and deductions. Linguistically, Jensen rejected lyrical expressiveness in favor of a matter-of-fact diction. But his stylistic mastery often breaks forth when he opens up vast and haunting perspectives and unsuspected connections.

Jensen was totally without luck within only one genre: his relationship with the theater. Neither his own dramatization of *Madame D'Ora* as *San-*

gerinden (1921; The Singer) nor his fairy-tale play with a Chinese motif, *Darduse* (1937), was successful.

Although insignificant as a playwright and a scientist, Jensen was one of the greatest innovative spirits in Danish cultural life. He was decisive in the turning away from French to Anglo-American culture which was characteristic of the first decades of the twentieth century. His knowledge of American social and political conditions was unique for his time, and he introduced Jack London, Frank Norris, and Ernest Hemingway in Scandinavia. As a lyricist and creator of myths Jensen reached the sublime, in particular when he succeeded in merging these two elements, as in *Kongens Fald, Den lange Rejse, Himmerlandshistorier,* and many of his myths. With *Digte* he laid the foundations of modernism in Danish poetry and generally became one of the greatest influences on Danish literature, on such different writers as Tom Kristensen, Otto Gelsted, Paul la Cour, and Klaus Rifbjerg.

Thøger Larsen
Thøger Larsen (1875–1928) shared his region of origin, northern Jutland, with many of the authors of the time, but even though it is habitual for Scandinavian literary histories to stress the existence of regional literature—as a development that deemphasizes the dominance of the capital—the term is misleading. For only a very few writers is it a major concern to highlight their home regions, and usually the provincial setting is used as a frame of reference for sweeping, if not universal, themes. Larsen's is a case in point: although he stayed in his small hometown all his life and celebrated the nature of that area, his poetry encompasses a cosmic vision. It transcends the local and may have been inspired by the author's profound interest not only in astronomy—those tantalizing other worlds—but also in old pagan beliefs. Once again a brand of pantheism was revived and revised, and Larsen, much more forcefully than Ludvig Holstein, maintains that the continuity of existence can be sensed everywhere in nature. In contrast to Holstein, who gets close to each blade of grass or each flower, Larsen seems to assume a deity's elated, cosmic vantage point and to celebrate the grandeur and beauty of this very real earth; his was a stance that Johannes V. Jensen also assumed in many of his *Myter*.

Like Sophus Claussen, Larsen uses condensed and thus demanding language, and he shares with his older colleagues an exclusive position on the Danish Parnassus: admired but not widely read. Nevertheless, such collections as *Jord* (1904; Earth), *Dagene* (1905; The Days), and *Bakker og Bølger* (1912; Hills and Waves) have won him, like Claussen, a belated reputation as a poet who wrought exquisite verse.

THE RURAL REBELLION
Martin Andersen Nexø

Martin Andersen Nexø (1869–1954) knew the meaning of the word poverty, whether it was to be found in the cavernous modern city or in the countryside, where feudal structures still remained. In his works he recorded how material misery impoverishes the mind and forces people into blind submission and degradation, and how indignation may rise in their hearts and result in militant revolt. He was born into a proletarian family in industrial Copenhagen which relocated to his father's home village of Neksø on Denmark's rocky, easternmost island of Bornholm.

Since Nexø's works are highly autobiographical and since he has written some of the finest memoirs in Scandinavian literature—*Erindringer* (1932–39; Eng. tr. *Reminiscences,* 1946, part of vol. 1, and *Under the Open Sky,* 1938, extracts from vols. 1 and 2)—a remarkable record of his life is retained, a life that by allegorical implication becomes the triumph of the poor, as they struggle to overcome their fatalistic submission to their lot and rise against their oppressors to carve out decent lives for themselves.

After some years spent as a very youthful farmhand, then as an apprentice to a shoemaker, young Nexø discovered the folk high school and spent some terms at the prestigious Askov. His time there enabled him to gain a position as a schoolteacher. A bout with what was diagnosed as tuberculosis sent him to southern Europe, where he not only regained his health but also rediscovered the proletariat. His experience of Spain is recorded in *Soldage* (1903; Eng. tr. *Days in the Sun,* 1929), in which he expresses his belief in and solidarity with the lower classes.

Nexø did not, however, start out as an author in the socialist vein. In his first works he seems, much like Johannes V. Jensen, to be in a kind of literary apprenticeship, for he appears to be set on proving that he can reflect the melancholy mood of the prose narratives of the 1890s. One of his early novels, *Dryss* (1902; Waste), which depicts in textbook fashion the decadent unraveling of a young man, possesses, like Jensen's *Einar Elkær*, a verbal energy that belies the inertia and passivity of the plot.

Of much higher quality—on a par with Jensen's *Himmerlandshistorier*—are Nexø's stories from Bornholm, later gathered with other short fiction in the three-volume *Muldskud* (1900–26; From the Soil). On the surface these tales seem to belong to regional literature, but they are clinically cool, deftly crafted portraits of people whose age-old beliefs and habits form their fates. They lead the lives they want, and no one can force them to change their often self-destructive ways.

Political messages do appear in some of the short stories, and gradually the oeuvre becomes a vehicle for social indignation and protest. That tendentiousness should not, however, be imagined to be detrimental to Nexø's art, for it is the inspiring force in two of his undisputed masterpieces *Pelle Erobreren* (1906–10; Eng. tr. *Pelle the Conqueror,* 1930, parts 1–2 retrans., 1989, 1991) and *Ditte Menneskebarn* (1917–21; Eng. tr. *Ditte: Girl Alive, Daughter of Man, Towards the Stars,* 1931). The message is undeniable; but stark realism, an underlying symbolism, a sense of detail reminiscent of Hans Christian Andersen, and a rollicking sense of humor—all paired with sympathy and compassion for the protagonists—create very vivid narratives.

Pelle Erobreren is a sprawling, epic work filled with a multitude of characters from all walks of life. It takes the reader from farm life on feudal Bornholm, to the island's old-fashioned provincial city, to the slums and factories of Copenhagen, and finally to new industries and neighborhoods created by the cooperative movement as an antidote to capitalism. Pelle, whose father is hired on Bornholm as a day laborer at the decadent Stone Farm, suffers much, but his spirit is never broken, and as the novel takes its protagonist to the modern industrial world in the swarming city, he emerges as a crafty and successful labor organizer and leader. The system he combats strikes back with a vengeance, and on trumped-up charges he spends time in prison. Quieter, humbler, but undaunted—in the novel's fourth, quite utopian volume—he organizes a cooperative venture that bodes well for the future of the working class.

As Pelle conquers the social world for his class, this quite unreflective man begins to understand himself and see his own shortcomings, not least as a husband, and he gains that wisdom a leader must have to ensure the future of his followers. The novel reads as a socialistic bildungsroman, and through the use of that paradigm, which the late nineteenth-century novel dismissed, once again restores, on its own political and social premises, a sense of optimism to Danish prose. The novel's popularity has been immense—in 1989 a film version received the Academy Award as best foreign film—and its rousing action and general readability have made it outlast other tendentious works that once were world-renowned, such as Upton Sinclair's *The Jungle* (1906) and Jack London's *The Iron Heel* (1907).

Ditte Menneskebarn is a much more somber book, for the conquering hero is replaced with the suffering martyr. Ditte's journey takes her in the same direction as Pelle, from the countryside to the big city; and like Pelle, she is supported in her childhood by battered, staunch, and eminently likable figures. Ditte's world seems much more brutal than Pelle's, however, particularly after the dingy slums of the city close in on her. The happy episodes in her life become few as, a victim of the capitalist system, she supports herself and her illegitimate child through sewing. At a very young age, she is worn out by endless work and her boundless compassion for fellow sufferers, which causes her to take on the role of surrogate mother for many others. Ditte acts spontaneously; she is not politically motivated, but the novel is; and as Ditte lies dying, the masses demonstrate angrily in the streets. Their wrath is ignited by the cruel death of Ditte's son, who, when he tried to salvage some coal, was run over by a train—another victim of capitalism.

The passage of time between Nexø's two impressive novels saw not only World War I but also the ensuing political turmoil in western Europe brought on by the revolution in Russia. Politically, Nexø moved steadily to the left and, consequently, revaluated his earlier stances. That process is very obvious in *Morten hin Røde* (1945–57; Morten the Red), which was intended as the third and final part of the trilogy that started with *Pelle*. Morten appears in all three works, first as Pelle's childhood friend and fellow agitator, and then as Ditte's supporter and Pelle's critic, for Morten's former friend has lost his revolutionary zeal. This criticism of Pelle is carried on in *Morten hin Røde,* in which Pelle, in the face of the threat from Nazi Germany, shows himself to be an appeaser and an opportunist. Morten, who like his creator makes a living as a socialist writer, also has grave problems at home, for his marriages seem less than fortunate, until he finally settles down with the rather self-effacing Jeanette.

As a conclusion to the saga of the Danish workers' movement, *Morten hin Røde* is not a success. The qualities of the two former novels are lacking. Both the ebullient fighting spirit and optimism of *Pelle* and the heartfelt compassion and desperation of *Ditte* are gone, and the book reads as a quite personal and cramped effort to register the infighting between the ruling Social Democratic party and the Communists, as well as a dreary account of marriages that have gone awry. Perhaps the main reason for the artistic failure of the book is that the mythical perspective detectable in the two former novels finds no room in *Morten hin Røde*. In *Pelle* one witnesses a march headed for "the promised land," and Pelle knows, as does Nexø, the power of references to the biblical Moses and his people's quest. In *Ditte* the innocently suffering heroine, who is willing to sacrifice all for the sake of others and who thus must sacrifice herself, is, of course, the stuff that has made many hagiographies best sellers throughout the centuries. None of that appeal is to be found in the dry chronicle of Morten and his problems.

In the years between the wars Nexø wrote some poetry, an allegorical play, numerous articles, a travel account of his sojourn in the Soviet Union, and the novel *Midt i en Jærntid* (1929; In an Age of Iron; Eng. tr. *In God's Land*, 1933). The novel attempts, without much success, to capture the effects of the unhealthily wild stock market in Denmark before the financial crash. Of most interest is the probing into the tensions between the sexes, a theme that surfaced early in Nexø's works, was kept somewhat in the background in the major novels, only to reappear painfully in *Morten hin Røde*. It is the unresolved examination of those problems that gives *Midt i en Jærntid* some poignancy.

Nexø's vision became gradually more and more myopic, and his disillusionment with the West grew after World War II. If his later oeuvre is dated, his major works nonetheless retain the freshness and energy—whether caused by optimism or anger—that kept them from sharing a similarly sad fate.

Johan Skjoldborg

Johan Skjoldborg (1861–1936) became the advocate of the cause of the smallholders, a segment of the rural population that was barely organized and, accordingly, remained hard pressed by the land-rich and politically powerful farmers. Skjoldborg's breakthrough happened with *En Stridsmand* (1896; A Fighter), in which he celebrates the tenacious struggle of the smallholder against those above him. An optimistic belief in justice is also reflected in *Kragehuset* (1899; The Crow's Home), in which, as was later the case in Nexø's *Pelle Erobreren*, the hope for a better future is vested in the dawning cooperative movement.

Skjoldborg's realistic prose may seem artless and at times marred by sentimentality, but his straightforward narration, his humor, and his obvious tendentiousness made him popular reading among the students at the rural folk high schools. In some ensuing works, such as *Gyldholm* (1902) and *Per Holt* (1912), he widened his perspective to include life at the manor house. By including more classes, he gave a vivid impression of the rigid class hierarchy on the large estates that then were numerous in the Danish countryside. The social agitation in Skjoldborg's works later became combined with and modified by the author's concern for preserving the spiritual values of those engaged in battle. In *Nye Mænd* (1917; New Men) it seems that a spiritual victory must accompany the political one.

Jeppe Aakjær

Jeppe Aakjær (1866–1930) also became an agitator for the downtrodden rural classes, but his talent was more varied than Skjoldborg's, and his lyric ability, reminiscent of Holger Drachmann's, has especially made him very popular. As a young man he broke away from Christianity, as depicted in the autobiographical work *Bondens Søn* (1899; The Son of the Farmer). He became prominent in the Brandes-inspired radical student organization—he wrote that organization's battle hymn—and even served time. His novel *Vredens Børn* (1904; The Children of Wrath) voices his outrage at the plight of the day laborers and enumerates in stubborn detail the indignities they experienced daily. Those grueling descriptions fired the imagination of his readers and resulted in a stirring public debate that eventually led to significant changes in the lot of hired hands.

The radical author, like the later Martin A. Hansen, was deeply drawn toward the old-fashioned way of life among the rural people. Aakjær moved back to his native northern Jutland, and although he remained a steadfast propagandist for social reforms, the title of his next novel, *Arbejdets Glæde* (1914; Labor's Joy), suggests his love of the daily routine found in the age-old farming culture. Like the later Skjoldborg, he feared the impact of industrialization on rural life, and in some of his short stories he humorously captured, in Jutland dialect, the voices of a fading culture.

His heartfelt feeling for that culture served as an inspiration to his poetry, or rather songs, for inspired by folk ballads, Blicher, Bjørnson, and especially Robert Burns (whom he translated masterfully into the Jutland dialect), Aakjær created some eminently singable poems that evince utter delight in daily life in the countryside and in the nature of northern Jutland. Most famous is the collection *Rugens Sange* (1906; The Songs of the Rye). Some of these texts are tantalizingly sensual, voicing a longing for a lover; in others the angry Aakjær proves that his yearning for the uncomplicated, idyllic life by no means made him forget his social commitment.

Marie Bregendahl

Marie Bregendahl (1867–1940) came from the same region as Aakjær; they married, and for some years she supported the household by running a boardinghouse in Copenhagen. Upon their divorce in 1900, her career as an artist started. One of her late stories, the title story of *Møllen og andre Fortællinger* (1936; The Mill and Other Stories), begins thus: "Fate, that weird, blind God! Where can the region be found that it has not visited? If we could look beyond time, where would we find that spot of earth on which it has not left its traces?" The statement suggests that Skjoldborg, Aakjær, and Nexø found historical, social reasons for the life they depicted and often deplored, whereas Bregendahl focused on a human condition that could not be altered. More so than any of the male authors, she seemed to share the fatalism, a positive as well as a negative force, that permeated the mind of the old rural culture. Such an attitude can be deemed conservative but not reactionary, and it should be kept in mind that Bregendahl's narrative technique was much more modern than that of her, at times, quite pedestrian male colleagues. In her novel *En Dødsnat* (1912; Eng. tr. *A Night of Death,* 1931) the slow and tragic death of a sturdy farm woman is registered through the eyes of her many children. This work may still be a far cry from Faulkner's *As I Lay Dying* (1930), but the changing points of view foreshadow a narrative experimentation to come, one that nineteenth-century writer Steen Steensen Blicher also had foreshadowed with sophistication. This demise of the omniscient author can similarly be found in Bregendahl's major contribution, a series of seven novels with the later, collective title *Sødalsfolkene* (1914–23; The People of Sødal). Here the life of the waning culture and its many destinies, sad as well as joyful, are rendered by various local narrators, so that readers must construct the total picture.

THE NEW FEMALE VOICE

Agnes Henningsen (1868–1962) freed herself from some of the constraints that limited the scope of the women authors of the preceding decade. Her quite outspoken demand for equality between the sexes and a delight in sensuality made her seem frivolous in the eyes of many contemporaries. In her early novel *Strømmen* (1899; The Current) she showed that she was perfectly aware of the dangers that threaten women if they dare to reveal their sensuality in a male world of double standards.

Henningsen's novel *Polens Døtre* (1901; The Daughters of Poland) received much critical attention and acclaim, perhaps because sexuality seemed to be viewed in it as a destructive force that should be harnessed by spirituality. Henningsen seems thus to vacillate, but in *Kærlighedens Aarstider* (1927–30; Love's Season) the conflict posited earlier is, if not overcome, at least handled well by the female protagonist. She breaks out of an unsatisfactory marriage that has reduced her to enacting roles that go against her desires for a fulfilling life. Taking a lover does not lead to fulfillment, however, for being a mistress is another stifling role; thus, Milli Hahn finally establishes herself, to the extent possible for a woman who is an author, with some measure of independence as an artist. She wisely carves a niche for herself, just as Agnes Henningsen did, one that could seem both liberating and confining, but also one she preserved with courage and a zest to persevere.

This zest speaks from nearly every page in Henningsen's marvelous memoirs (1941–55), which recount her early youth as a wealthy farmer's spirited daughter, an exciting marriage that both worked and did not, and her attempts at establishing herself as an author; the memoirs record her success in that endeavor as well as her various, somewhat happy liaisons with several men. The style Henningsen had developed in *Kærlighedens Aarstider*—an impressionistic, seemingly light and chatty, but precise, diction—makes all eight volumes of the memoirs a stunning trip through a life that in spite of setbacks was a triumph, won by a woman who considered herself neither frivolous nor inferior as a writer.

Karin Michaëlis (1872–1950) remained a realist. She made her debut in 1902 with the novel *Barnet* (The Child), in which she focused on the problems of puberty for a young woman. Her most widely known work, *Den farlige Alder* (1910; Eng. tr. *The Dangerous Age*, 1912), which has been translated into several languages, deals with a middle-aged woman who is in the process of obtaining a divorce. She knows that she no longer is considered a sexual object by men, who inevitably seek younger partners. An affair with a younger man does not work out, since he cannot accept their untraditional alliance, but Elsie Lindtner's irony and self-understanding keep the tale from reaching the despair and depression that marked the works of many previous female authors.

Thit Jensen (1876–1957) reached a wide audience not only through her historical novels—a genre that tends to attract a grateful audience—but also through her agitation for a sexual politics of common sense. She was a public figure, often caught in the midst of controversy, who undauntedly pursued causes that would give women more self-determination. Like her brother, Johannes V. Jensen, she wrote about her home region, for example, in *Kongen fra Sande* (1919; The King from Sande), but she remained a realist. In retrospect, it may well be her early novels about contemporary women that will hold modern audiences. In *Gerd* (1918), the most optimistic of those books, as well as in its continuation, *Aphrodite fra Fuur* (1925; Aphrodite from Fuur), it is repeatedly revealed that, even in relationships that seem based on liberal ideas of equality, very destructive conflicts arise and disclose the presence of a double standard. At one point "it dawned on Gerd that the whole misery was caused by her being a woman." That misery, in either the public or the private sphere, Jensen depicted and combated throughout her career. She foreshadowed battles to be fought years later.

Between the World Wars

Sven H. Rossel and Niels Ingwersen

6

DENMARK AND WORLD WAR I

The poet Jeppe Aakjær, in a patriotic song from 1917, hails Denmark: "You tiny country, quietly making yourself comfortable, while the whole world is burning around your cradle." This is an ironical but exactly correct description of Denmark's status during the years 1914–18 after the heads of state in Denmark, Norway, and Sweden made the joint decision to assert the neutrality of all three Scandinavian countries, a final manifestation of the Scandinavianism of the romantic era.

Acceding to German demands, the Danish government at the outbreak of World War I blocked the Danish sea-lanes with mines to prevent the British navy from operating in the Baltic Sea. This step was tolerated by the Allies, and it gave Denmark a unique opportunity to supply both sides with goods, especially food, yielding vast profits for a very few. Agriculture and shipping, in particular, benefited from this position. For some years Denmark became an El Dorado for smart business ventures and stock-market speculation; new wealth was created but could disappear overnight in crashes and bankruptcy. A powerful economic upswing took place in general; wages rose, but prices rose even faster: between 1914 and 1918 the economic index went up from 100 to 182, inflation became rampant, and in the four years of war the shortage of goods, despite stringent rationing, became acute and brought about great social tensions in Denmark and elsewhere.

Denmark could not completely avoid becoming involved in the war, however. As German subjects, thirty thousand young Danes from North Schleswig—since the debacle of 1864 under German rule—were forced to join the German forces; six thousand of them were killed, while many escaped military service by emigrating to the United States. After the German collapse in 1918 the pro-Danish population of North Schleswig demanded reunion with Denmark. A plebiscite resulted in the return of former Danish territory, excluding the major city of Flensburg, in 1920. In South Schleswig thirteen thousand Danes had to remain under German rule and were made to suffer once more under the Nazi regime.

The years 1914–18 were marked by major political and social reforms initiated by the ruling Radical Liberal party with the support of the Social Democrats. A new constitution in 1915 gave women the right to vote and revoked the privileges of the landowning class. Its political power had been dissipated, and the old Right party, so powerful during the last third of the nineteenth century, was superseded in 1915 by the Conservative People's party. Through some far-reaching land reforms, land was procured from the large estates for tens of thousands of agricultural workers. In urban industry the government introduced strict state inspection and regulation of joint stock companies and financial institutions; in 1919 the eight-hour working day was introduced, first in state enterprises and then in private business.

Nevertheless, the feeling of discontent did not fade. Many factories had to close after the war, and unemployment grew rapidly. There were confrontations between workers and the police, stirred by the revolutions in Russia in 1917 and Germany in 1918 and resulting in a wave of demonstrations and strikes. The social unrest culminated in a general strike in 1920, called by the Social Democratic party and accompanied by strong demands for a republic after King Christian X (1912–47) dismissed the Radical Liberal government. The reason behind the king's interference was his dissatisfaction— shared by other influential conservative forces—with the cabinet's unwillingness to disregard the plebiscite in Schleswig and demand further territorial concessions from Germany. The king appointed a new interim government, elections were held, and the Moderate Liberal party formed a new government. This so-called Easter Crisis demonstrated the stability of Danish democracy. Never again has a governing monarch intervened in politics; and the Social Democratic party proved to be nonrevolutionary, which resulted in the founding of a Communist party.

The period 1920–29 was characterized by the same uncertain economic conditions that affected economic affairs in the rest of Europe and the United States. For most of the period Denmark was ruled by Moderate Liberal governments, representing the farmers and advocating economic liberalism. This meant a quick abolition of the wartime restrictions. The previous reform policy continued with regard to general health insurance, unemployment subsidies, and disability insurance. However, Danish industry became seriously affected by dumping from countries with a low currency, and—in part as an aftermath of financial speculation during the war—several major companies failed, together with Denmark's largest bank. When in 1922 the international economic crisis reached Denmark, a major currency crisis (the value of the Danish crown was reduced 50 percent in March 1924) unseated the government. The first Social Democratic government was formed in 1924, with the first woman minister heading the Department of Education.

Apart from the return of North Schleswig two other crucial problems regarding Danish territory were solved. In 1917 the Virgin Islands, a Danish colony for two hundred fifty years, were sold to the United States for $25 million. More problematic was the relationship with Iceland, which had remained with Denmark after the dissolution of the union between Denmark and Norway in 1814. In 1918 the Icelanders, inspired by Woodrow Wilson's fourteen points on national self-determination, demanded independence. As a sovereign state Iceland remained in a union with Denmark until 1944, when it became an independent republic.

The interwar period was marked by an accelerating process of secularization. In Danish spiritual life the decrease in the role of the church had begun with the decline of romanticism in the 1840s. In the following decades the church was targeted for violent criticism by Søren Kierkegaard and attacked frontally by Georg Brandes and the writers of the Modern Breakthrough. The radicalization of intellectual life, accompanied by a growing social awareness in the wake of the process of industrialization, continued after the turn of the century in spite of the literary symbolism of the 1890s, with its clear aesthetic and metaphysical overtones. Nevertheless, Grundtvigianism, including its concept of the folk high school for education of adults, remained strong as a popular movement in the provinces. It, too, was targeted for criticism by the writers of the Modern Breakthrough and, also around 1860, by a fundamentalist movement, the so-called *Indre Mission* (Home Mission). Inspired by Kierkegaard's demand for total personal commitment to Christian faith, the Home Mission remained a strong religious movement in rural areas, particularly in Jutland, throughout the interwar period.

This process of secularization, however, could not be held back, and it was paralleled by increasing emphasis on the natural sciences and technology, also advocated by the Breakthrough movement and hailed by the predominant poet after the turn of the century, Johannes V. Jensen. In 1912 the world's first diesel ship was launched in Copenhagen, and in 1913 the nuclear physicist Niels Bohr published his first epochal theories, which in 1922 won him the Nobel Prize. Other great scientists likewise carried on the tradition of H. C. Ørsted. Around 1900 Valdemar Poulsen made two inventions that formed the basis of modern wireless technique and the tape recorder, and in 1907 he introduced the radiophone. Finally, three Danish scientists—Niels Finsen, August Krogh, and Johannes Fibiger—received Nobel Prizes in medicine in 1903, 1920, and 1927, for treatment of lupus, capillary research, and cancer research, respectively. In 1908 the Copenhagen College of Technology was opened, and in 1928 Denmark's second university was established in Århus.

It was in Copenhagen that provocative cultural changes had taken place in the 1870s and 1880s. And it was also in the capital that two heralds of the twentieth century appeared: the first record player was introduced in 1900, and the first movie theater opened in 1904. And in 1904 the first modern morning tabloid, *Ekstrabladet* (The Supplement), modeled after the American sensational press, was launched. The first shooting of a Danish film took place in 1906 at the studios of the world's oldest film company, Nordisk Film, and the Danish actor Valdemar Psilander achieved universal renown, only to be surpassed in the following decades by the international fame of the film star Asta Nielsen. The tango was introduced in 1913 and discussed in the newspapers as being dangerous for the health of women, and in 1919 the knee-length dress was launched, opposed in the press by twenty-six prominent Copenhagen ladies who claimed it was suited only for prostitutes. Jazz became the predominant fad of the time, and American dance an epidemic. A nouveau riche public demanded lively entertainment. The Roaring Twenties had come to Denmark, and suddenly the entire country was "in the middle of a jazz age"—the title of a book by Knud Sønderby.

CHAOS AND DISILLUSIONMENT

The philosophical outlook of the writers and artists who had their roots in the prewar period and who often were born in the countryside was not deeply affected by their confrontation with the turbulence and materialism and superficiality of the war and postwar era. One exception is Otto Rung (1874–1945), who abandoned his previous fascination with Nietzsche's philosophy of the superman and in his novels *Paradisfuglen* (1919; The Bird of Paradise) and *Da Vandene sank* (1922; When the Water Subsided) depicted—and condemned—with humane compassion and succinct power of observation the criminal exploitation and economic irresponsibility of the period. The most prolific of the symbolist poets of the 1890s could not remain silent either. They chose a more indirect approach by pursuing with determination their artistic ideals in defiance of the trend of the times

(Sophus Claussen, Ludvig Holstein) or by later participating in the philosophical debate of the 1920s (Helge Rode).

Another approach was chosen by the always polemical Johannes Jørgensen, who fiercely attacked Germany, which he otherwise loved so deeply, in two books about devastated Belgium, *Klokke Roland* (1915; The Bell Roland), immediately translated into five languages, and *Flanderns Løve* (1919; The Lion of Flanders). The prose writer Karl Larsen (1860–1931) clearly represented a unique position with his glorification of German militarism. Georg Brandes attacked in a much more balanced fashion both German and French nationalism as well as the horse trading of the Versailles negotiations. This position cost him, however, his long-standing friendship with French intellectuals.

Within the younger generation of writers the protest against the times could take on a clearly anti-American tone. In the works of Jacob Paludan its basis is a conservative-spiritual posture, whereas in the 1930s, for instance in the novels of Hans Scherfig, it becomes a vehicle for socialist propaganda. The horizon is wider in the oeuvre of Otto Gelsted, who in his magazine *Sirius* (1924–25) sarcastically offers a prayer to "the modern mentality," which is in fact a scathing attack on the contemporary, almost postmodernist, eclecticism, superficiality, and lack of commitment. Of the older writers only Johannes V. Jensen, who visited the United States a total of six times, glorifies modern, especially American, technology and big city life, with its traffic, speed, and skyscrapers.

Characteristic of the dominant deprecatory attitude is the fact that when one of the leading Danish architects, P. V. Jensen-Klint, began work in 1921 on a memorial church for the nineteenth-century poet and clergyman N. F. S. Grundtvig, he chose to imitate the style of a medieval Danish village church. Granted, the most prolific and important Danish composer of the twentieth century, Carl Nielsen, departs from romantic tradition in his concertos and symphonies. It is interesting to note, however, that it is primarily with his two hundred fifty songs to texts by Danish poets from around and before 1900 that Nielsen gained widespread popularity and perhaps reached his highest artistic level.

It is natural that numerous writers used the war itself as an artistic motif. Between 1914 and 1917 Jeppe Aakjær wrote several war poems—fiery protests against the horrors of the war—whereas in Pontoppidan's last novel, *Mands Himmerig* (1927; Man's Heaven), the war functions mainly as a corroboration of his own pessimistic outlook as he sets about to analyze the moral and cultural decay of Denmark. In Martin Andersen Nexø's novel *Midt i en Jærntid* (1929; In an Age of Iron) the war serves primarily as the basis for another of Nexø's political attacks on Danish public life in general and the materialistic and corrupt farmers in particular.

It was generally within the younger generation of writers that the war became of existential concern. The prevailing sense of impotence for having to remain outside the theater of war, because of Denmark's neutrality, found a substitute in an intense, often ecstatic glorification of life voiced in poetry bursting with colors and crass effects. This attitude created in Denmark a counterpart to central European expressionism. In opposition to photographic realism, the expressionists asserted the artist's right to depict the objects as *he* saw them. In Denmark this expressionism was permeated by a unique state of tension due to the absence of a direct war experience in the trenches. But the same sense of impotence also created a more openly expressed feeling of meaninglessness, of having lost a chance to face death and thereby experience and test one's identity. Thus the desperation of some writers constitutes a local, Danish counterpart to the international "lost generation," as represented by Ernst Jünger, Erich Maria Remarque, André Malraux, and Ernest Hemingway and corresponding to other Scandinavian representatives such as Halldór Laxness (Iceland), Aksel Sandemose (Norway), and Eyvind Johnson (Sweden). What all these writers could agree on was a realization that the universe inherited from their parents was now shattered.

Three Lyrical Poets
One exception among the lyrical poets of the wartime generation is so notable that he deserves mentioning: Hans Hartvig Seedorff Pedersen (1892–1986). While many of the most significant Danish poets, both in the beginning of the twentieth century and later, have had Johannes V. Jensen's free verse and/or his provocative worship of external reality as their model, Seedorff skillfully pursues a traditionalist technique with regard to form and language. His formal approach is actually rooted in eighteenth-century rococo poetry.

The sense of discord and hopelessness that generally haunted his fellow poets is conspicuous by its absence in Seedorff's wartime collections *Vinløv og Vedbend* (1916; Vine Leaves and Ivy) and *Hyben* (1917; Rose Hips). Their joie de vivre and worship of the carefree life, Venus, and Bacchus enthused a war-weary public. If the popularity of Seedorff's poems can be explained as escapism on the part of their readers, their message was an unambiguous expression of a consistent worship of beauty, exemplifying John Keats's dictum: "Beauty is truth, and truth beauty." In his many later collections Seedorff contrasts this concept of the reality of beauty with the con-

temporary political and social reality, to him a realm of chaos and disharmony, war and demonstrations that he would not accept. This contrast enables him to create a tension that gives his poetry artistic value, especially in
the stirring and disturbing poems about death in the volume *I Dagningen*
(1927; At Dawn). Seedorff's numerous travel poems as well as his sea shan-
ties, whose continuous popularity is due not least to Niels Clemmensen's
catchy tunes, are true romantic expressions of the conquest of a reality not
attainable in present time and space. Not until some political poems during
the German occupation of Denmark in 1940–45 does Seedorff reach the reality that he rejected earlier.

Popularity also surrounded Emil Bønnelycke (1893–1953) after he
made his debut with *Ild og Ungdom* (1917; Fire and Youth), containing the
programmatic lines: "Yes! Life is a party, / and blessed is he who was born
and undeservedly encountered life's miracle." Bønnelycke's rapture for the
world of technology and facts—a continuation of Johannes V. Jensen's
youthful writings but also inspired by Walt Whitman's all-embracing vitalism—reaches its zenith with the important collections from 1918, *Taarer*
(Tears) and *Asfaltens Sange* (The Songs of the Asphalt). What caused a sensation and for some years placed Bønnelycke at the head of literary advance
was his discovery of Copenhagen as a poetic motif, his worship of youth
(learned from Knut Hamsun) and, in particular, his disrespect and his indis-
criminate intoxication with whatever object met his eye: "I love the mast of
a streetcar, an advertising pillar, a cigarette, a match—more than a poem by
Chr. Winther."

Bønnelycke's expressionism, attacking all rationalism and reflection and
advocating intuition and instincts instead, was clearly influenced by modern
pictorial art, and he even contributed several articles to its Danish theoretical mouthpiece, *Klingen* (1917–21; The Blade). Especially clear evidence of
the cubist technique is seen with the novel *Spartanerne* (1919; The Spar-
tans), in which the fundamental idea—the youthful affirmation of life contrasted with the atrocities of war—is examined from three different viewpoints. *Spartanerne* was the first Danish expressionist novel, and its
fluctuating narrative technique and extensive use of lyrical associations were
hailed by the critics. Thereafter, however, public appreciation and to some
degree also the poet's own artistic inspiration diminished.

Bønnelycke's prose works from the 1920s were for the most part failures.
The poetry collections from the same decade, *Gadens Legende* (1920; The
Legend of the Street) and *Hymnerne* (1925; Hymns), openly repeat previous motifs but also reveal that the earlier eulogies to chaos, world revolution, and the streets of Copenhagen had been either an artist's fantasy or a

facade, behind which a troubling religious restlessness was hidden. This restlessness culminated in the novel *Ny Ungdom* (1925; New Youth), Bønnelycke's chief work. Under its violent attacks on wartime materialism and the nouveau riche milieu in Copenhagen it emerges as a deeply committed account of the author's Christian conversion, which, however, was rejected by the public as pure moralizing. Not until the novel *Lokomotivet* (1933; The Locomotive), in which he adhered to the demand for social realism of that decade, did Bønnelycke score another success. In contrast, the poetry volume *Lovsang til Døden* (1939; Hymn to Death), which once again treats his Christian breakthrough, was rejected, and from then on Bønnelycke was ignored in Danish intellectual life: first he had been pampered by the press, then he was silenced to death. Conversions have never been popular in Denmark. Nevertheless, with his friend Tom Kristensen, Bønnelycke was the most prolific lyrical talent of the immediate postwar years. Although he often lacked artistic discipline, he was provocative in his rejection of tradition and rules and refreshing and imbued with a fascination with language that anticipates the linguistic experiments of the 1960s.

Like Bønnelycke, Fredrik Nygaard (1897–1958) displayed hectic productivity in the years around 1920; later he published only with increasing intervals, experimenting with all literary genres. Gradually, he moved into a lyrically oriented journalism of partly topographic nature.

Nygaard is an excellent barometer for the various literary trends of the period under discussion. With carefree youthfulness and virtuosity he improvised on all the various motifs then in vogue: staccato-like, breathless expressionist poems, whose recitations were accompanied by gymnastic shows; ecstatic eulogies to the metropolis and its swirling traffic, executed in prose poems reminiscent of Johannes V. Jensen and Walt Whitman; and jaunty snapshots from theaters, cafés, and dance restaurants rendered in a flippant Copenhagen jargon.

As early as the collection *Opbrud* (1919; Breaking Up), however, a yearning for the peaceful idyll, which Jacob Paludan also sought, becomes noticeable: "Instead of the songs of bicycles and noises from streetcars / a voiceless silence." To this yearning corresponds an emerging wish for a distance in time from the increasingly unacceptable contemporary scene. Nygaard sees his own time as shallow and therefore to be rejected. It must be replaced, in the final analysis, by a romantic concept of a more genuine and truthful reality. Nygaard discovered and described it in a series of travel poems in the volume *Evropaskitser* (1919; Sketches from Europe), rendered in a stunningly executed but seemingly naive and pithy style, snapshots written with the utmost precision:

Green fields.
Yellow flowers.
Blue sky.
Little Luxembourg.

The travel experience as well as the tribute to rural life became recurring motifs in Nygaard's later, voluminous oeuvre, where they are presented in an increasingly accomplished classical form. Nevertheless, the brilliantly written, partly autobiographical novel *Det skæve Foraar* (1925; The Crooked Spring) gives evidence that Nygaard's early fascination with the chaos and upheaval of the war years still had a firm hold on him. With the general strike of 1920 as a backdrop, the novel concludes in a revolutionary vision, not unlike Tom Kristensen's related novel *Livets Arabesk,* in which the working class dethrones the king of Denmark and takes over the means of production. But for Nygaard such a possibility remained a dream, existing as an artistic expression—or artistic expressionism—rather than an existential concern. Thus the work, and in the final account also Nygaard, becomes a striking example of the insecurity, skepticism, and lack of a fixed point of departure which are the main characteristics of the "lost generation."

Tom Kristensen
Unquestionably, the most prominent writer of the wartime generation and, at the same time, its most accomplished writer was Tom Kristensen (1893–1974), who went through a process of development similar to Nygaard's. Kristensen never quite overcame the crisis and the limbo that the war had placed him in, however. The fundamental distrust of his youth toward the traditions handed down manifested itself partly as a deliberate worship of chaos and absurdity, partly as an angst-permeated quest for a firm foundation.

His travel book *En Kavaler i Spanien* (1926; A Cavalier in Spain), with its mix of acute power of observation and lyric sensitivity, a worthy descendant of Hans Christian Andersen's travelogues, contains an exclamation that provides a key to an understanding of Kristensen's predicament: "War! War! The wildest word of my youth! The word which has torn up my mind entirely, because I have never experienced its reality!" This pent-up unrest left its profound mark either in the form of a sense of impotence and resignation or in an overpowering desire for destruction. "The Eternal Restlessness"—the title of one of Kristensen's essay collections from 1958, *Den evige Uro*—accompanies him on his many travels and also in his writings, where it is most compellingly formulated in the novel *Hærværk* and the poetry collection *Mod den yderste Rand.*

After earning a degree in English, Danish, and German from the University of Copenhagen in 1919, Kristensen made his living as a teacher of English, undertook a journey in 1922 to Japan and China, and became a literary critic with the influential Copenhagen newspaper *Politiken* (Politics) from 1924 to 1927 and again from 1931 to 1963. Kristensen's earliest poems, in the volume *Fribytterdrømme* (1920; Freebooter Dreams), are inspired by and constitute a direct and somewhat strained exemplification of Nietzsche's dictum: "One must experience chaos within oneself in order to give birth to a dancing star." Indeed, anarchy and meaninglessness are the main focus of the poet's attention: "Beautiful as a bombed railroad station is / our youth, our force, our wild ideas." Once again the inspiration from Nietzsche is tangible, this time his concept of the "revaluation of all values," in Kristensen's portrayal of the nihilistic freebooter and his attempts to find his identity in a world of constant upheaval. But the effort to restrain the self by means of the creative process proves futile. Kristensen tenaciously seeks to transpose pictorial expressionism into language through startling rhymes, exotic fantasies, and disturbing insights into big city proletarian life—influences from Sophus Claussen and Emil Bønnelycke, respectively—executed with clashing collocations of words. An example is the depiction of "the blossoming scuffle" in the café, where "a green billiard sails between tables and chairs," where a nosebleed is "a poppy that spreads its bloody crown," and a black eye a pansy that unfolds "in colored, flowing rings." This aggressive Dionysian exuberance, yet another Nietzschean trait, leads nowhere in its aesthetic self-sufficiency and is consequently, in the poem "Itokih," enveloped in dadaist onomatopoetic word-paintings:

Now the fleet of the feasts is a fading sight,
tohihah, hiohah, itokih;
but is still as beautiful as a meaningless word
and as clouds and dreams of unknown life,
which I shall never know,
but softly call a-ka
and o-di-mi-venne
and ko-di-fa-na-ka. —

When Kristensen set out on his extensive trip abroad, his motivation was the same unquenchable longing for sensory impressions which drove Johannes V. Jensen, another of Kristensen's major literary models, around the world. In his encounter with the Far East, Kristensen discovered—expressed in the poetry collection *Paafuglefjeren* (1922; The Peacock Feather)—that a different and dangerous realm lurks behind the crude facade of the sensory perceptions, where angst and downfall await him, and that he cannot escape the siren calls of paralyzing reflection, a realization he shared with Jensen. Whereas in *Fribytterdrømme* an embracing meaningless-ness is praised in a carefree manner and conflicts are turned into an ideal, this state of turmoil and absurdity, particularly in the poems about China, is turned into a perilous threat under an apparently quiet surface, waiting to strike. With envy Kristensen finds genuine tranquility in the personality of an old Chinese sage, while he himself, as expressed in the monumental poem "Henrettelsen" (The Execution), remains haunted by an agony and thoughts of death that, on one hand, sharpen the poet's artistic perception and, on the other hand, as the title indicates, destroy him. "But there is a poem which I will never sing," the Chinese sage exclaims in the obscure poem "Li Tai Pe's Død" (The Death of Li Tai Pe), which is a gripping real-ization of the inadequacy of poetry to create meaning and thereby establish human identity.

In Kristensen's prose his novel *Livets Arabesk* (1921; The Arabesque of Life) corresponds to *Fribytterdrømme*. In both works a revolution is carried out, but it takes place only on the aesthetic level. The novel portrays a soci-ety in the process of dissolution. The setting is Copenhagen, but all realistic depiction is absent. On the contrary, rather than a political pamphlet, the novel is a euphoric expressionist fantasy of color and sound. The rebellion is instigated by the working class, which, however, as the action develops, turns out not to be an alternative to the degenerate bourgeoisie, whose cor-ruption it can only imitate. Once again the nihilist message of the freebooter is heard. It is characteristic that the main character, Dr. Baumann, in disgust breaks away from the communism that Kristensen himself at one time felt attracted to, yearning for the tranquility and peace the Chinese sage knew of, and which in the novel gains a religious perspective.

The Chinese poems from 1922 relate to Kristensen's next novel, *En Anden* (1923; Someone Else), in the same way as the two works from 1920 and 1921 correspond to one another. A customs officer living in Shanghai, the novel's major character, Valdemar Rasmussen, analyzes systematically—the detached approach is vastly different from the diffuse linguistic orgy of the first novel—his disturbed youth in a Copenhagen working-class milieu in order to find his identity. The same theme finds a more comprehensive and mature treatment in the culmination of Kristensen's oeuvre, the novel *Hærværk*. Here the despair and chaos is so sustained that no therapy and certainly not the psychoanalytical method, which testifies to Kristensen's temporary fascination with Freud (in-spired by Otto Gelsted's Freud translation from 1920), is adequate. Neither is psychoanalysis especially successful in *En Anden*. Rasmussen attempts to liberate himself from his past by assuming the role of a proletarian expressionistic painter. But this step is contrived, as he, deep down, does not believe in the redeeming power of art, and the attempt at comprehending his perhaps incomprehensible self remains abortive. He returns to Copenhagen, his point of departure and zero point. His wanderings, that is, his quest, which has both a social and—in particular—a psychological and religious dimension, has not helped him to become "someone else."

The identity problem and the religious theme are carried forward in the novel *Hærværk* (1930; Eng. tr. *Havoc,* 1968). Here the inserted poem about the fear of not being able to find oneself, which is "Asiatic in size," calls for a metaphysical solution. By its contemporaries the novel was read as a roman à clef and caused a scandal. Likewise, its major character, the alcoholic literary critic Ole Jastrau has been understood as a portrait of Kristensen himself. Influenced by Nietzsche's concept of "the eternal recurrence," Jastrau and his friend—and in part his alter ego—the poet Steffensen, to a certain degree modeled on the French lyricist Arthur Rimbaud, experience life as a repetition and therefore as meaningless. Neither of them can cope with this realization. It unleashes an angst that they, in vain, try to overcome through systematic self-destruction by means of alcohol. First, Jastrau's marriage falls apart, then he gives up his position at the newspaper. But at the same time, this havoc is carried out in a defiant attempt to reach the core of his personality, his self, and his soul. Jastrau, in his decline, experiences not only joy in his steadily accelerating self-destruction but also a sense of infinity. It is precisely that for which his soul thirsts, but against which the motto of the book warns. Contrary to Paludan's novel *Jørgen Stein*, which also describes such an experience of losing all value norms but whose title character in the final account discovers certain basic values, Jastrau finds that "Jacob's ladder has toppled." But in spite of this nihilistic experience, both Christianity and Platonic philosophy have left their mark on Jastrau as well as on Steffensen. Steffensen, the former communist, finds a foundation and thus an identity in Catholicism, while Jastrau himself, according to how the novel's conclusion is interpreted, realizes a possibility of establishing new values and thereby defining his identity.

Jastrau's obsessive search for truth almost bears the Kierkegaardian stamp of existential quest, a quest he also shares with the characters in James Joyce's *Ulysses* (1922) and Aldous Huxley's *Point Counter Point* (1928). Furthermore, there are formal and stylistic similarities with *Ulysses*. Kristensen masterfully employs the inner monologue, leitmotifs, and repetitions, and he indulges in crass realism. A major motif the two works have in common is the search of the father for his son and vice versa. *Hærværk* is a matchless work in world literature. Its sophisticated, formidably structured, and reasoned composition stands in such a glaring contrast to its inner chaos and desperation that a tremendous tension and ambiguity is created, making *Hærværk* a book that one never puts aside.

It has been maintained that with Jastrau's way out of absurdity the very chaos on which his creativity relied had been overcome and that this should explain Kristensen's silence as a fictional writer in the years to come. The explanation, however, can be found in Kristensen's return in 1931 as a critic to *Politiken*, where he became the principal reviewer of contemporary literature, specializing in Anglo-American and Scandinavian writers, some of his favorites being Kipling, Joyce, and D. H. Lawrence. During the same decade, Kristensen was plunged into an acute ideological crisis that took him from provocative atheism and nihilism in the 1920s, to an approximation of Catholicism and, in the 1930s, to Marxism, and then on to a Christian standpoint based on the theology of Karl Barth and a continuous fascination with the Catholic Church. This attraction is exemplified in another travelogue, from 1951, *Rejse i Italien* (Travel in Italy), which behind its light and entertaining form contains an in-depth discussion of the author's relationship with Catholicism and Greek-Roman art. Kristensen himself maintained that Christian faith is present throughout his oeuvre.

In Kristensen's poetry this religious dimension is anticipated in the reflections in *Paafuglefjeren*, linked to the author's growing doubt about the sole validity of the purely artistic world view. This doubt becomes manifest in the collection *Mirakler* (1922; Miracles). Through an erotic experience with a woman, the poet now tries to find a fixed point in his life. However, his split perception of woman as representing both animalistic, physical sexuality and chaste, spiritual love offers no permanent solution—an experience shared by Valdemar Rasmussen and Ole Jastrau. In the volume *Verdslige Sange* (1927; Secular Songs) this schism, related to Sophus Claussen's view of woman, is analyzed but not until the concluding, crucial poem, "Græs" (Grass), is it vanquished, inasmuch as the life of instinct is replaced by a religious longing:

> Inside the dawning halls of the straws
> there is a voice waking
> calling
> in rising notes: comest thou now,
>
> . . . .
>
> then I shall come, then I'll be small and happy enough.
>
> (Tr. Poul Borum)

In the rather undervalued collection *Mod den yderste Rand* (1936; Toward the Farthest Edge), perhaps the most significant Danish poetry collection of the 1930s, Kristensen subsequently professes Christianity in a series of magnificent death poems. In these texts meaninglessness has been replaced by an affirmation of order, harmony, and self-knowledge. On the social level, homelessness has been replaced by security and assurance, and on the religious level, the fear of an empty universe has yielded to the reinstatement of God.

Kristensen's emotions and thoughts do indeed approach a level of sublime clarification and serenity, but without ever quite reaching it. The freebooter lives on as he looks back on his ventures in the no-man's land of his youth. Nevertheless, Kristensen's break with expressionism, linguistically manifest in *Verdslige Sange,* becomes increasingly tantamount to a stylistic simplification and refinement of form for which Sophus Claussen, once again, served as a model, but with lines reaching back to the classicism of Goethe.

Mod den yderste Rand contains memorial poems often written/drawn directly for next morning's newspaper. In 1940 Kristensen published a collection of these lyrical portraits entitled *Digte i Døgnet* (Poems for All Hours). A characteristic feature of these texts about, for instance, the Arctic explorer Knud Rasmussen or the poet Gustaf Munch-Petersen, who was killed in the Spanish Civil War, is Kristensen's attraction to the man of action—with elements of self-portrait—who, suddenly, is confronted with death. Whereas Kristensen in his poem "Angst" (Fear) in *Hærværk* was desperately forced to exclaim: "I have longed for shipwrecks, for havoc and sudden death," he now approximated the stage of insight of the Chinese sage, while retaining elements of "the eternal restlessness." In his final collection, *Den sidste Lygte* (1954; The Last Lamp), he describes this stage as follows:

> Brutalized, beaten
> I understood too late.
> God wanted me like this;
> but what did he mean?

The concluding question mark is Kristensen's trademark and points to the clash between a chaotic content and a perfected and clarified form, which remains one of the ultimate secrets of his art. It is perhaps, in the final account, only here, in form, that Kristensen was able to discover the structure he was yearning for throughout his life. Like no other Danish writer, but with obvious parallels to the Swedish expressionist Pär Lagerkvist, Kristensen voiced the predicaments and enigma of living in a world of nothingness. A constant quest for meaning, however, made him overcome this absurdity, through an insight that he voiced in a classical form, thus reaching back in literary tradition and uniting past and present in an unceasingly relevant fashion.

THE STRUGGLE FOR AN IDEOLOGY

The ideological chaos of the war and postwar years, hitherto expressed almost exclusively in imaginative writing, culminated around 1925 in fierce public debates. The major battle was waged between a materialistic-biological and a conservative-spiritual outlook, primarily among writers and intellectuals of the older generation.

The slogan "the struggle for an ideology" was used as a book title in 1925, *Kampen for Livsanskuelse*, by the influential critic Henning Kehler (1891–1979). Kehler himself had experienced the breakdown of established values with the outbreak of World War I and analyzed it with brilliance in his semi-fictitious travelogue *Russiske Kroniker* (1920; Articles from Russia). Now, with the symbolist poet Helge Rode, who with his two essay collections *Regenerationen i vort Aandsliv* (1923; The Regeneration of our Spiritual Life) and *Pladsen med de grønne Træer* (1924; The Square with the Green Trees) proved himself a perspicacious polemic writer, Kehler came forth as an advocate of Christian spiritual values against the wartime generation's nihilism and/or political radicalism. Rode, in particular, initiated the criticism of Nietzsche's philosophy of the superman, a criticism that in the 1930s, in the context of emerging totalitarianism, grew stronger among Danish intellectuals. An undogmatic pantheism was being preached by the other two symbolists, Sophus Claussen and Ludvig Holstein, who protested against the contemporary materialistic mentality, a protest shared by the Catholic Johannes Jørgensen. Indirectly, these poets also made their point by publishing some collections around 1920 which are landmarks in twentieth-century Danish lyrical poetry. Tom Kristensen's collection *Verdslige Sange* should also be considered as a contribution to the religious debate.

At the same time, a rationalist—sometimes labeled "scientific" or even "antireligious"—orientation catered to the period's hunger for answers and solutions. Georg Brandes, in four small books from 1925 to 1927, glorified Hellenistic clarity and reason, fiercely attacking the Judeo-Christian tradition. Among the older writers, Johannes V. Jensen also got involved in the debate. After having concluded his novel cycle *Den lange Rejse* in 1922, he began more systematically to focus on his evolutionary, Darwinian theories. With the volume *Evolution og Moral* (1925; Evolution and Ethics) he placed himself heavily on the antimetaphysical side.

Here one could also find two journals: *Sirius* (1924–25), published by Otto Gelsted, and *Kritisk Revy* (1926–28; Critical Revue), published by the architect Poul Henningsen, both advocating a radical and critical approach to aesthetic, social, and political issues. Several articles in *Kritisk Revy* were based on Marxist theory, and indeed, the 1920s saw the introduction on a broader scale into the public debate of not only Karl Marx but also another controversial figure, Sigmund Freud. Freud was then already known in Denmark, but it was Otto Gelsted's translation in 1920 of a selection of his writings, *Det Ubevidste* (The Subconscious), which led to a breakthrough of his psychoanalytical theories. Tom Kristensen found inspiration here; later writers such as Soya and H. C. Branner were decisively influenced by Freud.

Karl Marx had been known in Denmark since the middle of the nineteenth century, but his theories did not have a major political impact until the Russian Revolution in 1917. Shortly after 1900 Martin Andersen Nexø became the first major Scandinavian writer to base his world view on communism. Not until the mid-1920s did communist ideology exert a broader appeal on Danish intellectuals, again with Gelsted as the inspiration, and it became a dominant ideological force in the following decade with writers such as Hans Kirk and Hans Scherfig.

Characteristic of the polarity of the ideological debate of the 1920s are the works of two of the most prominent writers of the younger generation, Otto Gelsted and Jacob Paludan. They share an astute and polemical attitude and venture outside fictional writing to make their viewpoints known. They were succeeded by the somewhat younger Knud Sønderby, who took up a middle position in the interwar period as a balanced, realist prose writer with a skeptical distance to the preceding era.

Otto Gelsted

Like Tom Kristensen, Otto Gelsted (1888–1968) in his youth knew inner chaos and despair. With the writer he admired most, Johannes V. Jensen, he shared an all-encompassing zest for life that instilled in him a strong urge to identify, at all costs, even with such a life of rootlessness and dread. But, a realization that this urge could not be harmonized with the demands Gelsted made on an existence based on responsibility and commitment resulted in a tragic sense of inadequacy, a perception of being a dead man among the living, which several times in his writings was used artistically as a Lazarus motif. In a parallel development, however, the battle against nihilism, anxiety, and darkness turned into a striving toward harmony, which became the mainspring for Gelsted's creativity.

An education at a Copenhagen Jesuit college, from which he graduated in 1907, sharpened Gelsted's critical sense and opened up the philosophy and culture of antiquity to him. Throughout his life Greek clarity remained Gelsted's ideal and source of inspiration (he became a brilliant translator of Homer, Greek drama, and poetry). His most accomplished poems are, indeed, marked by lucidity and balance, but this process of maturation demanded from him a desperate struggle against an innate ecstasy, so much a part of himself, a struggle still predominant in his debut collection, *De evige Ting* (1920; The Eternal Things):

> Let all longings rush toward your heart
> until you are quiet
> like the center of the hurricane.

The split between instinct and rational thought also permeated a series of love poems in the volume *Jomfru Gloriant* (1923; Miss Gloriant), but much more characteristic of this work is Gelsted's sharp criticism aimed at the Zeitgeist. In the poem "Reklameskibet" (The Show Boat), with "clinics for make-up and bureaus for suicide, / which men in despair can consult for a suitable fee," Gelsted, as the first of his generation, reacts against the commercialism, superficiality, and lack of direction of the period, and he concludes his polemical unmasking by blowing up contemporary civilization.

Gelsted's constant striving toward clarity and balance culminates in the volume *Rejsen til Astrid* (1927; The Journey to Astrid). Its exquisite love poems show that the previous dualism has been fully overcome. This hard-won harmony is most convincingly demonstrated in Gelsted's nature poems, not written in the symbolist tradition of the 1890s but rather consisting of a subdued recording of natural phenomena, in particular the changing seasons. Their underlying weakness is a tendency to idealize, which in some texts is successfully counterbalanced by a grandiose cosmic perspective showing a strong influence from another significant Danish nature poet, Thøger Larsen.

Nature poetry increasingly dominates Gelsted's subsequent collections, including his last, from 1961, *Digte fra en solkyst* (Poems from a Sunlit Coast), the title of which exquisitely demonstrates his adherence to the Hellenic ideal of his youth, even though the poet's thoughts increasingly revolve around death, both his own and that of nature. The volume as a whole is yet another manifestation of Gelsted's predilection for formal beauty enveloped in a two- or four-line stanzaic form, as well as a plain metaphoric language reminiscent of the Danish rococo poetry of Brorson and Stub.

Gelsted's desire for clear-cut attitudes and decisions and personal commitment explains not only his viewpoint in "Reklameskibet" but also his future ideological orientation. Against what Gelsted saw as American-inspired commercialism he posits scientific cognition, a demand for synthesis and coherence between and behind the phenomena and for an adherence to critical reason, for which he found decisive inspiration in Kant's philosophy. This rational and critical attitude had already characterized Gelsted's work as an art critic during World War I and, after 1919, as a literary critic for several Copenhagen newspapers. His adherence to this orientation led both in his journal *Sirius* (1924–25) and later during the decade's ideological battle to a rejection of both the religious and the materialistic-biological position. It is also quite thought-provoking that Gelsted now began to voice reservations toward expressionism and cubism in painting, which he had previously advocated in the journal *Klingen*. He also became increasingly critical of the psychoanalytical approach as well as lyrical modernism. With Poul Henningsen, with whom Gelsted collaborated for some years, both as a contributor to Henningsen's journal *Kritisk Revy* and in his musical revues, he emerged as the most prolific exponent of the so-called intellectual radicalism of the interwar period. Gelsted's attempt at combining Kant's epistemology and Karl Marx's materialistic conception of history led him, strongly inspired by a journey to the Soviet Union in 1928, to communism or, with his own words, "revolutionary humanism," and in 1936 he began a collaboration with the communist press which lasted until his death.

Gelsted's political commitment made him one of the Danish writers who most distinctly understood and—already in the volume with the prophetic title *Under Uvejret* (1934; During the Storm)—warned against the impending European fascism. This combative tendency was carried on in Gelsted's poems during the German occupation in World War II and, after he had to leave the country, from his time as a refugee in Sweden. After his return he published the collection *Emigrantdigte* (1945; Emigrant Poems), demonstrating that political poetry never was his true domain. The volume's quality can be found only in texts in which Gelsted's youthful sense of loneliness and homelessness again appears.

Party propaganda is conspicuous by its absence in most—and definitely the best—of Gelsted's poetry. Indeed, in numerous ways he reflects, like many of his colleagues, trends of the times, but he is primarily a philosophical writer.

Jacob Paludan

Whereas both Gelsted and Kristensen were influenced by the crisis of the war and postwar years and responded to it each in his own way, Jacob Paludan (1896–1975) was rather an observer, with such a shy and reserved personality that it took the influence and inspiration of a close friend, the color-ful Erik C. Eberlin, to activate him as a writer. And it is indicative of Paludan that the immediate point of departure for his creativity is a critical and nega-tive yet somehow aloof reaction to contemporary, trendy phenomena. Throughout his life Paludan was an outsider, but Eberlin provided him with material from his own adventurous life which Paludan then shaped ar-tistically.

Paludan met Eberlin in 1914 during his apprenticeship as a pharmacist in Aalborg. In 1918 Paludan received his degree, and in 1920 they both left for the United States. On his own, Paludan went to Ecuador and returned to Denmark after a stay in New York. After 1925 he worked as a literary critic for various newspapers, mostly conservative.

Paludan's stay in America affected his entire conservative and romantic out-look on life and, together with Eberlin's influence, got him started as a writer. He sent his first manuscripts home to his friend, who advised him to overcome his self-centeredness and turn outward toward problems of more general ap-peal. The result was the action-packed emigrant novel *De vestlige Veje* (1922; The Western Roads). On the surface the novel can be read as a satirical, indeed sneering attack on brutality and ugliness as the threatening components of American urban civilization. This attack is launched through the inner mono-logues of a disillusioned emigrant. On a more comprehensive scale, however, the book is a passionate renunciation of the spiritual leveling and superficiality that Paludan saw as a result of the inroads of materialism in postwar Denmark.

As a mirror image, Paludan's continued satire of urban life in the novel *Søgelys* (1923; Searchlight) is set in Copenhagen. The emigrant theme is likewise employed; here Paludan puts his condemnation of this "century of mediocrity" in the mouth of a returning Danish-American war veteran. Pal-udan's pet antipathies are also personified, in the character of the fashion-able but hollow sensational journalist Erup. The harshest—and often unre-strained—attacks are aimed at expressionistic poetry, women's liberation, and the striving for success, all components of what Paludan saw as the "American way of life."

The polemics and the satire result in rather stereotypical protagonists, but the novel nevertheless demonstrates Paludan's increasing skill in charac-ter delineation. In particular, the disillusioned and neurotic emigrant is por-trayed with an understanding and accuracy unique in Paludan's oeuvre, which makes him stand out not only as a romantic and enigmatic Hamsun-like outsider but, indeed, as one of the first Danish representatives of the "lost generation."

In Paludan's next novel, *En Vinter lang* (1924; All Winter Long), the period picture has completely receded in favor of the motif of the outsider, of loneliness and isolation that turn into defiance and frigidity. As in his previous novels the plot remains secondary, and whereas polemic was predominant earlier, now it is the atmosphere, the minute detail, and the nature description—simultaneously in a poetic haze and concretely recorded—that turn the book into a culmination of lyrical expressiveness. In some ways it is related to Herman Bang's tragic, provincial idylls, and like Bang, Paludan also uses indirect psychological analysis, frequently projected onto the reaction of the surroundings, characters, or scenery.

Paludan chooses a similar symbolic approach for his breakthrough novel *Fugle omkring Fyret* (1925; Eng. tr. *Birds around the Light,* 1928), in which, as part of its splendid composition, highly dramatic episodes alternate with poetic and reflective sections. The plot is set in the boom period during World War I. It tells of a monstrous harbor-building project in a small coastal town, the demoralizing effect the construction has on the local population, and finally, the catastrophe when during the inaugural ceremony the ocean rises and takes revenge by crushing the new harbor. This concrete and dramatic juxtaposition of nature and culture—from this point on a main motif in Paludan's oeuvre—serves the symbolic function of illustrating the destructive forces of commercialism, greed, and indeed technological progress. These forces are also reflected in the gallery of characters, who are not, however, as in Paludan's previous books, ruled by irresoluteness and impotence alone. Assertiveness is present in the young woman Bodil, who is inextricably bound to nature. In her, Paludan has created one of his few positive female characters capable of liberating the often reflective and insecure male figures.

Absolute pessimism, in contrast, permeates the novel *Markerne modnes* (1927; The Fields Ripen). For the second time Paludan turns away from the satirical period picture and creates a drama of fate about the victory of superficiality over spiritual values, actually a parable about the battle between goodness and victorious evil. Paludan reverts to the romantic Aladdin myth and turns it around so that the attempt of the poor young man Ivar to realize his musical talent in the final account remains unsuccessful because of too much adversity in his environment, which is devoid of any spiritual values, and a fatal passivity in his character. Ivar reveals his flaws in his relationship with the main female figures of the novel, the idealized Bettina and the emancipated, frigid Ellinor. External success accompanies Ivar's counterpart, the aristocratic poet Ralf, who easily achieves everything Ivar has to fight for. Nevertheless, he also experiences downfall and destruction.

During a five-year pause Paludan worked on the grandiose stock-taking of his times, which also, in its comprehensive scope, transgresses any boundaries of time: the two-volume novel *Jørgen Stein* (1932–33; Eng. tr. 1966). It is structured as a social novel that, with steady acceleration, symbolizes the dissolution of values and attitudes, telling of three generations. The first one, located in the provinces and represented by Jørgen's father, a conservative civil servant, is firmly rooted in the pre–World War I period. His universe collapses with the war, and he himself is financially ruined. His oldest son, the lawyer Otto, belongs to the "lost generation," whose values are destroyed through the war. Initially, he exploits the financial morass as an amoral speculator, but then he falls victim to the materialism and chaos of the wartime era and commits suicide. Jørgen himself represents the third generation, young and disillusioned, taking life's emptiness for granted.

Jørgen Stein is more than a brilliantly drawn period picture. It is also a bildungsroman, but devoid of the optimistic drive that traditionally characterizes this genre. Jørgen is "born under one law, to another bound," as the motto of Aldous Huxley's novel *Point Counter Point* (1928) reads, one of Paludan's most important foreign models. He is weak and passive, emotionally split between the attitudes of all three generations. In Copenhagen, Jørgen first studies philosophy, then art history, then gives up his studies and tries journalism. Neither socially nor in his relationship with women is he able to commit himself. The resulting catastrophe is the suicide of his girlfriend Nanna. Like J. P. Jacobsen's novel *Niels Lyhne, Jørgen Stein* is also a book about death and resignation. In spite of the unconvincing conclusion, which perhaps should be understood ironically—Jørgen chooses marriage with a farmer's daughter and the modest life of a poultry farmer—the work breathes a pessimism that makes it a worthy counterpart to Henrik Pontoppidan's related cycle *De Dødes Rige*. Its underlying theme is the decline and fall of a civilization, the bourgeois Christian culture, and the futile attempt to bring oneself into harmony with a changing world and to accept the frightening relativity of all values. Like Pontoppidan, and before him Paludan-Müller (*Adam Homo*), Paludan deals with the complexity of his work's historical and psychological developments by means of an admirable command of numerous subplots. The narrative technique is much more traditional than in Tom Kristensen's *Hærværk*. Nevertheless, through its relentlessly revealing character delineation, social analyses, and forceful ethical and philosophical statements—Paludan also holds up a moralizing mirror for his countrymen, which might explain the reservation with which his novel was received by contemporary critics—*Jørgen Stein* will stand as a true classic that at the same time is unmistakably modern in its ironic ambiguity and skepticism.

After *Jørgen Stein* Paludan turned to the essay, anticipated indirectly in the numerous commentaries and reflective passages in his fictional writing as well as in a series of sarcastic, gnomic poems and aphorisms in his only poetry collection, *Urolige Sange* (Unquiet Songs), from 1923, and directly in the volume of philosophical reflections *Feodor Jansens Jereminader* (1927; The Jeremiads of Feodor Jansen). Paludan's favorite targets here are once again the "American way of life," feminism, and collectivism, as he attacks contemporary superficiality in particular and moral decline in general. This direction is continued in subsequent collections of aphorisms from 1937, 1943, and 1954. Simultaneously, Paludan worked as a literary critic, guided by detached observation and passionate engagement, a combination also found in his first volume of reflections on nature, *Aaret rundt* (1929; The Year Around) (later collections from 1944 and 1949). Here purely natural phenomena, because of his unique empathy—a talent Paludan shared with his contemporary Knud Sønderby—frequently take on mythic or even mystical perspectives, an orientation that is also documented in Paludan's fascination with metapsychology, which points ahead to the New Age movement.

All of these subjects merge in *Facetter* (1947; Facets) and *Mørkeblaat og sort* (1965; Dark Blue and Black), two volumes that will stand out for posterity as perhaps the best illustrations of the most accomplished in Paludan's work: its thematic span, full-bodied musical style, and subtle interplay of moment and memory. *Mørkeblaat og sort* contains a short story, "Her omkring Hjørnet, her blæser det mindre" (Here around the Corner the Wind Blows Less). It depicts a few days in the life of a scientist, rendered with bubbling humor and grotesque details, but behind the brilliant narrative a billowing and evocative series of mental images emerges, which constitutes the author's own attempt at conjuring up the past. This prose piece demonstrates that Paludan was far from finished as a writer of fiction and perhaps could have achieved the extraordinary if he had overcome his posture as an outsider in favor of an unreserved Tom Kristensen–like self-expression.

The interplay in Paludan's essays between the present and memory takes on an element of personal confession in the analyses of Paludan's own aesthetic experiences in the volumes *Retur til Barndommen* (1951; Back to Childhood) and *Fremad til Nutiden* (1953; Toward the Future), showing the author's compassionate and knowledgeable insights in the world of art and music. Purely autobiographical are the anecdotal memoirs from 1973–76, with which Paludan concludes his oeuvre.

These volumes form a distillation of a lifelong refinement of language, confirming Paludan's extraordinary place in Danish literature as one of its most exquisite stylists. In his best works the bent toward reflection is continuously balanced by irony and skeptical humor. This balance between intellect and feeling mirrors Paludan's own view of life. Until his death he remained a vigilant commentator on contemporary society, but this attitude was always held in check by a passionate love for the arts, tradition, and nature. Here Paludan discovered the harmony and beauty he could not find in his own time.

Knud Sønderby

With Paludan, Knud Sønderby (1909–66) shares a critical distance as well as a—clearly related—mastery of the essay genre. His earlier writing consists of four novels, while later work led to short prose pieces, autobiographical sketches, feature articles, and true essays. Frequently, these were published first in newspapers, of which Sønderby, even before he received his law degree in 1935, was a staff writer.

Sønderby offered a portrayal of the turbulent postwar years, but not until they were at some distance in time. He belonged to a younger generation of writers and never directly felt the desperation of the "lost generation." Therefore, Sønderby's description is executed by a detached but immensely precise photographer or chronicler. Characteristically, it is not the ideological struggle that he depicts in his debut novel *Midt i en Jazztid* (1931; In the Middle of a Jazz Age), but the disillusioned youth of the 1920s, skeptical about grand gestures and banal clichés and therefore throwing themselves into an irresponsible but actually desperate worship of sport feats, movie stars, dance music, and, above all, erotic conquests. The main character, the law student Peter, is analyzed in terms of his relationships with two women from widely different social classes; he feels totally misplaced in both affairs. When he falls out with both of them, however, the reason is less this social aspect than his fear of having to make a binding choice. Thus, Peter is unable to grasp life, and only by means of a series of daydreams can he experience happiness and spontaneity, only then is he able to comprehend his self and his environment as a whole. Thus, Peter's cynicism, and that of the other characters, is partly a pose, and the denial of all ethical norms is only a mask covering a desperate desire to enter into a realistic relationship with life. The dominating milieu of the wealthy and trendy Copenhagen bourgeoisie and the characters' blend of honest self-judgment and pretended indifference are conveyed in a style seemingly naive yet extremely sophisticated and complex. The apparently casual composition, the shifting between sensitive nature sketches, poetic dream sequences, and ironic, ambiguous commentaries, are features that constitute a deliberate and sophisticated reflection of the novel's themes.

The social climate of the 1930s influenced Sønderby's next novel, *To Mennesker mødes* (1932; Two People Meet), about the conflict between young love and different social levels. Sønderby poses the question whether the awareness of belonging to the same generation, apparently so liberated and practical, is strong enough to overcome class barriers and, on the psychological level, loneliness. The author deliberately gives no answer because—and this is his major point—the characters themselves have a confused and fragmented relationship to their own emotional lives. He lets his reader follow the events through the consciousness of several characters, adding only an occasional slight touch of irony. Teeming scenes of metropolitan life, frequently from a bird's-eye perspective, alternate with acutely sensed detail. Each single observation hints at a wide social and psychological prospect. *To Mennesker mødes* has been outshone by *Midt i en Jazztid*, which was adapted for the screen in 1969, but the novel holds its ground as one of the finest love stories in Danish literature.

Sønderby's next novel, *En Kvinde er overflødig* (1936; A Woman Is Superfluous), focuses on the relationship between different generations. Sønderby portrays a mother and widow, Mrs. Tang, the title character, rooted in the bourgeois culture of the previous century, and her tyrannical solicitude for her two grown-up children, an attempt to overcome her realization that she is now superfluous. Her domineering prevents them from developing into independent human beings and ruins her daughter's love relationship. But even as Mrs. Tang does not understand the lives and ideas of her children, she yearns for their love and compassion. They, however, reject her craving for self-sacrifice, which to them appears pompous and conventional, and only through their mother's suicide is the tragic conflict resolved. In spite of the fact that *En Kvinde er overflødig* is Sønderby's most traditional narrative, it is also his finest achievement. Not only is Mrs. Tang his most fascinating piece of character drawing, but the author succeeds in not taking sides with any of his characters, thereby raising his work to a rare level of psychological universality. The children reject their mother, to be sure, but they are at the same time touched by her love; she, in spite of her selfishness, is portrayed as a woman of good intentions.

After three tragic novels Sønderby, with *De kolde Flammer* (1940; The Cold Flames), finally suggests a love relationship that, marked by resignation, nevertheless seems viable. He focuses on a marriage that stands its test when confronted with the magnificent, pristine Greenland nature. The novel opens as an ecstatic Song of Songs, symbolizing the couple's high-strung view of love as a romantic dream. But through encounters with isolation, primitive life, and death this concept matures to a more down-to-earth but sincere affection between two equal people.

The exquisite nature descriptions from Greenland are based on Søn-derby's stay there in 1935, also resulting in the prose sketches *Grønlandsk Sommer* (1941; Greenland Summer), the first of a series of essay collections that were to form the culmination of his later writing. After his return Sønderby dramatized his novel from 1936, performed with great success at the Royal Theater in 1942 (Eng. tr. *A Woman Too Many,* 1955). The conflict of the generations is intensified, while digressions and the narrator's com-ments are omitted. The dialogue is perfected, letting the characters appear with even sharper contours than in the novel. Now Mrs. Tang is freed from any tendency toward whining and self-pity. She appears in all her monu-mental, almost Ibsenesque forcefulness, justifying the symbolic connota-tions of her name (Eng. "pair of tongs"). After writing some one-act plays, Sønderby experienced his second dramatic success with *Kvindernes oprør* (1955; The Rebellion of Women). The plot is based on Aristophanes' com-edy *Lysistrata*, about women who declare a sex strike until such time as their husbands stop their warfare, but Sønderby is actually aiming at the period of the Cold War. In contrast to its much more frivolous model, however, Sønderby lets his work end on a tragic note, inasmuch as the protagonist kills her lover, the prime minister, after he has used and abused her in the play's conflict.

Gradually, the short prose piece—the feature article and the essay—be-came Sønderby's favorite genre. After *Grønlandsk Sommer* he published five volumes of them from 1947 to 1969. They are either semiautobiographical, subdued humoresques, akin to Paludan's essays, or sketches in the tradition of Johannes V. Jensen's myths. Sønderby's expansive outlook on life also recalls Jensen, which with its point of departure in concrete detail, frequently found in nature, transgresses the borders of time and space. Sønderby is a master of memory of great stature, for whom childhood, manhood, and old age con-verge in a realization of the eternal value to be found in the present moment. Thus, reality has received a new dimension—and value—in Sønderby's writ-ings, whose fictional part is otherwise permeated with a mood of pessimism. Indeed, Sønderby is one of the great tragic writers in Scandinavia, a position that has been somewhat overlooked because of the admiration bestowed on his exquisite handling of language, composition, and dialogue.

A LYRICAL MANIFESTATION

Toward the end of the 1920s a wealth of lyrical poets emerged, inspired by the great success of the expressionistic writers around 1920. They did not, like their predecessors, have the war as a common point of reference; it was already at a distance, and the postwar era had established itself as the norm.

These writers employed widely different modes of expression, from the simple and lucid quatrain to surrealist prose poems, and they are, in general, difficult to classify in certain fixed groups or schools. Some experimented with poetry, prose, and drama for a while, like Jens August Schade; some alternated between prose and poetry throughout their careers, like Johannes Wulff; others relinquished poetry by and large in favor of prose, like the Faroese William Heinesen and Nis Petersen; yet others adhered to a purely lyrical mode of expression, like Per Lange, Paul la Cour, and Gustaf Munch-Petersen.

Many of these writers were nothing more than gadflies, elegant but superficial spinners of rhyme and deservedly forgotten today; others for various reasons experienced a brief but intense blooming (Per Lange, Munch-Petersen); and yet others were able to sustain the high quality of their first works until the present time (Schade) or did not write their best until the next decades (la Cour).

If these writers have something in common it is—with Munch-Petersen as a sole exception—a rejection on their part throughout the 1930s of any social concern or political commitment. Likewise, they spurn the expressionists' worship of modern technology as well as the fast, sparkling, superficial aspects of the metropolis. Their poetry frequently revolves instead around the cosmic or irrational, the spiritual or subconscious, or a mystical concept of a communion between humans in their relationship with nature. Sometimes this orientation takes the shape of a D. H. Lawrence–like lust for life, a focus on the instincts similar to (but much less consistent than) the outlook of the contemporaneous group of Swedish authors known as "the primitivists."

Quite characteristic for the outlook of these writers is the title of the Whitmanesque debut collection of Johannes Wulff (1902–80), *Kosmiske Sange* (1928; Cosmic Songs), expressing an optimistic acceptance of life's mystery and at the same time pointing toward infinity:

The riches of our world
only open up their tall gates
for the one, who in gratitude
bows his head
and sprinkles his path
with the wild anemones of feeling.

Jens August Schade

Whereas Wulff's attitude to the world surrounding him remains on the subdued level of the observer, a state of ecstasy characterizes the period's most colorful and artistic temperament, Jens August Schade (1903–78). Schade grew up in a provincial, middle-class milieu in Jutland, which he rebelled against throughout his life. Following his matriculation in 1921 he studied economics for one year at the University of Copenhagen. Thereafter he lived a bohemian life in the capital's Latin Quarter, often without a roof over his head.

His career—or lack thereof—Schade describes in the epic poem *Sjov i Danmark* (1928; Fun in Denmark [Sjov is also the name of the hero]), a hilarious satire on the bourgeois society of the interwar period but also an attack on any revolutionary political movement. Schade builds up an eroticized universe inspired by D. H. Lawrence's sexual vitalism, which acknowledges no conflicts, in accordance with Taoist philosophy, letting life unfold in an ecstasy that creates cosmic coherence. In this universe all rational, human dimensions are abolished with regard to time and space. Eros inactivates all traditional measures of value.

This unique philosophy is already developed in Schade's debut poems, *den levende violin* (1926; the living violin). In a colloquial, deliberately naive style, mainly unrhymed prose poetry, Schade conveys his subjective experience of the cosmic coherence in nature and the universe, made possible through the expansive miracle of love:

> Of gold and fire is the feast of my thought —
> why then is fear in your heart?
> behind your breasts flowers are growing
> you smell of apples and eternity.
> (Tr. Poul Borum)

Schade's eroticism receives its most succinct expression in *Hjerte-Bogen* (1930; The Heart Book). Here he emerges as a modern mystic who experiences one vision after another of earthly as well as celestial love in a universe devoid of the Fall of Man. In later collections, such as *Kællingedigte* (1944; Hag Poems), however, a predilection for vulgarity overshadows the previous poetic flight and linguistic imagination.

Schade's fiction has unique lyrical qualities but lacks coherent narrative structure, which results in a series of sketchy, almost fairy tale–like texts. Typical titles, such as *Den himmelske Elskov paa Jorden* (1931; Heavenly Love on Earth), indicate the thematic scope. Schade's major prose work is *Mennesker mødes og sød Musik opstaar i Hjertet* (1944; People Meet, and Sweet

Music Fills the Heart), which brought him a charge of writing pornography. Once again time and space are suspended in dreamlike, erotic fantasies. The characters are transformed or doubled as an effect of the activation of their subconscious minds.

This Freudian impact is also present in Schade's experimental dramas of only minor artistic value. It is as a lyrical poet that Schade was prolific, and his poetic powers did not diminish with the years. From his debut to his last collection, *Overjordisk* (1973; Supernatural), he proved himself, with Munch-Petersen, the most significant Danish representative of surrealism. But in contrast to its French counterpart—and Munch-Petersen—Schade's brand of surrealism is devoid of any social or political reference. It contains, however, clear religious connotations. The uniqueness of Schade—his continuous rejection of any public party political stand (later shared by the *Heretica* poets of the 1940s) and his panerotic, indeed romantic attitude—is furthermore shown by the fact that he has had no direct successor in Danish literature; only Jørgen Nash and, to some degree, Jørgen Sonne have been influenced by his erotic world view.

Per Lange

The absolute contrast to Schade is Per Lange (1901–91). Whereas Schade subscribes to an all-encompassing, almost pantheistic harmony and his poetry is open and easily accessible, Lange is an exclusive classicist and adheres to a non-Christian philosophical dualism, the result of which is tragic disharmony.

Lange has issued only three volumes of poetry, distinguished by formal beauty and musicality of language, their titles indicating the major themes of his writings; *Kaos og Stjærnen* (1926; Chaos and the Star), *Forvandlinger* (1929; Metamorphoses), and *Orfeus* (1932; Orpheus). With Otto Gelsted he shares a restless, inquiring mind, which he attempts to conquer through an orientation toward the Greek ideal of clarity and order.

After a pause of more than twenty years Lange continued his authorship with a series of essay collections, likewise permeated with classical spirit, that often have as their point of departure current sentimental and superficial phenomena. These are discussed with subdued yet cutting irony, but subsequently Lange focuses on eternal questions about God, death, and art. His texts are formed after Michel de Montaigne's essays and La Rochefoucauld's maxims, and with Sønderby, Lange must be considered the renewer of the essay genre in Danish literature.

Continuously, Lange yearns to transform chaos into Apollonian beauty—obviously, the title of the debut refers to Nietzsche's thought that only a personal experience of chaos can lead to sublime creativity—but the process is ultimately forced through in vain, and the result is thus disillusion. The duality between life and art cannot be overcome, and the underlying mood of pessimism in Lange's oeuvre originates in a sort of renunciation of the life forces that humankind reaches out for but can grasp only through their reflection in art. A recurring motif is the lonesome wanderer, the outsider, who has perceived the splendor of the world but ensconces himself in his reticence, finding consolation in the notion that everything is just a dream. The infinite beguiles, but it, too, can be explored only through art and cannot be directly conquered in a universe in which God has hidden his face. Thus, when Lange in his poetry seeks to overcome chaos to attain a state of harmony, this attempt is accompanied by a tragic awareness—identical to the Orphean division between life and art—that this goal cannot be reached.

Whereas for Gelsted reason is the sustaining force, behind the classic and perfected form of Lange's poetry a Dionysian unrest is always present, adding a strong tension from the inside, as it were. If Gelsted was able to find consolation and healing in nature and Schade to incorporate and thereby neutralize it in his own cosmos, with Lange nature remains an alien and disquieting force, actually a metaphor for insecurity and loneliness. This view makes it possible to define him as a modernist and a sophisticated one to boot, as he attempts to express his despair in a tight form of beauty in order to accentuate his existential predicament.

Paul la Cour
While Lange, at least on the surface, personifies the detached and ironic observer, whose themes have not changed since his debut, Paul la Cour (1902–56) was a many-faceted writer (and a prolific art critic and translator from French literature) who constantly developed thematically and stylistically. His most significant collections were not issued until after World War II.

La Cour's early, immature poetry, published during a prolonged stay in France in 1923–30, when he made a living by doing odd jobs (decorations for the film maker Carl Th. Dreyer, for instance), echoes Danish symbolism of the 1890s but is dominated by purely pictorial, occasionally *l'art pour l'art* motifs. Back in Denmark, la Cour's poetry was colored by the reexperience of the Danish countryside in poems that in their preciseness are indebted to Johannes V. Jensen and in their merging of nature and Eros to the symbolist poet Ludvig Holstein. Increasingly, new themes are incorporated, such as the poet's longing for his lost childhood, when life was experienced spontaneously and as a totality. Partly to blame for this loss of harmony was World

War I, against which is set the plot of the semiautobiographical novel *Kramer bryder op* (1935; Kramer's Departure). It is a psychological study about how compassion and solidarity can be changed into hatred and aggression, attitudes that la Cour finds expressed with increasing force in the zeitgeist of the 1930s. At the same time, his own poetry turns toward political reality, posing questions about the role of an active humanism. In la Cour's two main collections from the 1930s, *Dette er vort Liv* (1936; This Is Our Life) and *Alt kræver jeg* (1938; I Demand All), he articulates a strong sense of guilt toward the coming generations, a feeling of responsibility for the wars, the previous one and the one to come. With World War II la Cour's poetry develops into a merciless judgment of himself for not having warned strongly enough against and actively fought back brutality and evil. There is a tragic awareness that people can no longer control the world surrounding them.

Levende Vande (1946; Living Waters) is one of the few poetry collections that immediately after the war gave an artistically valid reflection of the exhilarated mood of the liberation after the German occupation of Denmark in 1940–45. At the same time, its texts constitute an orientation away from the ethical questions of the interwar period and toward speculation about aesthetic experimentation, the function of literature in the cognitive process, and the impeding effects of reflection in conveying the intention and message of the poet and the poem. In 1948 la Cour published his poetic manifesto, *Fragmenter af en Dagbog* (Fragments of a Diary), which exerted a tremendous impact on the new poetry of the 1940s. In a series of aphorisms he attacks the bare life of reflection and intellect: "To be a poet does not mean making poems, but creating a new way of living." People have become estranged from one another, and materialism has shattered the vision of the irrational and divine. The "new way of living" is found in an existential feeling of responsibility and in a struggle to overcome the postwar crisis caused by the breakdown of ethical and spiritual norms. La Cour urges his fellow humans to seeks the simple, creative forces at the root of existence, to unite the rational and irrational, which is the task of all art, best executed by means of the concise poetic image. This new harmony permeates both the poems from 1946 and la Cour's last collection, *Mellem Bark og Ved* (1950; Between Bark and Wood):

O you who bind the living and the dead
to this great strange game
your will be done.
Let the air heal its path behind me,

but before I fall let me sing,
let me once in eternal song
be faithful: close to your lives
live bound one last time. Wholly free . . .
                    (Tr. Poul Borum)

La Cour is more than perhaps the most important and indispensable link between Danish prewar literature and the later poetic modernism. The shadows of the Cold War, which could lead him to a state of desperation and renunciation, also brought about an orientation toward the culture of Greek antiquity. Continuously looking for new avenues and sources to enhance the quality and possibilities of life, also constantly changing himself and demanding the same of his fellow beings, la Cour holds a prominent position as the prototype of a humanist, continuously searching and fighting, in a battle against coldness, artificiality, and fossilization.

Gustaf Munch-Petersen

The number of lyrical poets did not increase significantly during the 1930s, a decade dominated by drama and prose. The most fascinating of the young poets who made their debut in this decade is Gustaf Munch-Petersen (1912 −38); he was so much ahead of his time, however, that he was not accepted until the modernists of the 1940s recognized him. In the writings of Munch-Petersen, la Cour's brand of humanism received a more active form. The demand of André Breton, the chief ideologist of French surrealism, to change poetry and dream into reality became a major source of inspiration:

Powers, I beg you in my pain,
grant me a light for my activities,
let me not die useless.

This demand as well as a strong personal yearning for a direct immersion in reality led Munch-Petersen, who had broken off his study of philosophy and psychology at the University of Copenhagen, to Greenland in 1932. Thereafter he vagabonded throughout Europe; in 1937 he joined the International Brigade in the Spanish Civil War and was killed in action.

Munch-Petersen's debut collection, *det nøgne menneske* (1932; naked man), describes his own attempt at breaking up and transformation, at liberating himself from the bourgeois and conventional norms in which he had been brought up in Copenhagen academic circles. In the two next collections the poet focuses on individual rebirth, frequently depicted through the metaphor of a closed egg that bursts. This effort at liberation develops into a more universal attempt to establish first a new, collective human consciousness and then a new society ruled by freedom and brotherhood. In *det underste land* (1933; the land below) Munch-Petersen abandoned external and recognizable reality in favor of the subconscious, the realm to which the positive forces of humanity have hitherto been repressed, the dream to which freedom and goodness have been exiled. In hymnlike visions the process of liberation and the possibilities of transformation are now depicted:

You should go to the land below—!
o you should see the people of the land below,
where the blood runs freely among them all—
men—
women—
children—.

In the experimental collection, which inspired the Danish avant-garde of the 1960s, *mod jerusalem* (1934; toward jerusalem), Freud's theories and D. H. Lawrence served as models for a growing advocacy for the release of the instincts and a general primitivist concept of life as the optimal unfolding of these instincts through a spontaneous invocation—an evocative quality, which also distinguishes Munch-Petersen as a painter. Not until this revolution of the consciousness has been accomplished—and here Munch-Petersen unmistakably adheres to the theories of surrealism—does the political revolution become possible, that is, the rebellion of the oppressed proletariat.

In posthumously published poems written in Swedish and English in 1934–35 Munch-Petersen continuously revolves around the possibilities of the free scope of the self. In the likewise posthumously published *19 Digte* (19 Poems) from 1937, however, a political orientation in a Marxist direction can be noticed, a growing impatience to act concretely. The previous typographical experiments are abandoned, and the poems are firmly rooted in a physical and recognizable world, which is recorded precisely and graphically through concentrated sense perceptions. Artistically, the volume displays the earliest impact of Ezra Pound's imagist technique. The texts appear on the page as concise, rectangular squares, condensed wholes of material and form, of controlled energy:

The sun's spear, slanted at dusk
swings and stabs the sea,
the skin of glass swells and trembles
and is flattened out.
(Tr. Alan Bower)

Munch-Petersen's poetry was rejected as being madness by his contemporary critics, and his books did not sell. Not until his collected works were published in 1959 was he fully recognized as the precursor of Danish lyrical modernism. Apart from French surrealism and Freud's psychoanalysis, Munch-Petersen was influenced by and felt akin to the Fenno-Swedish modernists Edith Södergran and Elmer Diktonius, with whom he shared his free verse, an ecstatic and prophetic tone, and metaphorical forcefulness and complexity. These were the elements that attracted the next generation of Danish poets, who, however (with a few exceptions, such as Erik Knudsen), did not adopt Munch-Petersen's determination to see poetry in a concrete social and ideological context.

FROM PSYCHOLOGICAL DRAMA TO POLITICAL MANIFESTATION

Since the mid-nineteenth century Danish drama had been waning. Particularly during the periods of realism and naturalism it was conspicuous by its absence compared with the thriving theater in the other Scandinavian countries. Neither during World War I nor in the following years did Danish drama experience a heyday. The major commercial theaters performed a traditional, naturalistic repertoire adhering to the realistic style of acting of the nineteenth century. The only two significant playwrights, Sven Clausen and Svend Borberg, both rooted in the war years, were (contrary to their fellow poets, Bønnelycke, Nygaard, and Kristensen) largely ignored.

Among the younger, contemporary playwrights the Icelander Guðmundur Kamban (1888–1945) enjoyed huge popularity with his well-crafted domestic plays, focusing on ethical and marital problems but lacking Ibsen's genius at character delineation or Strindberg's passion. The general public hungered for light entertainment, however, and found it in the works of writers of slick plays, in light-hearted comedies, in lavish shows and operettas.

Some small experimental theaters tried to introduce expressionistic avant-garde pieces and foreign plays of social engagement, for instance by Bertold Brecht and Nordahl Grieg. One stage in particular, Arbejdernes Teater, a cooperative amateur theater organized by the labor movement and headed by Bertel Budtz-Müller (1890–1946), became the driving force behind the performance of contemporary Danish drama. Budtz-Müller's own plays, mirroring German expressionism through their worship of the vital forces of the instincts and their attack on tradition and authority, but also advocating pacifism and a dream of universal solidarity, had no impact on

Danish drama. But the theater he managed was of decisive importance for the artistic development of Sven Clausen, as four of his plays were staged here. Clausen did not have his breakthrough until 1948, however, when the Royal Theater in Copenhagen performed his historical drama *Paladsrevolution*, written as early as 1923.

Svend Borberg and Sven Clausen

The rebirth of original Danish drama was heralded by Svend Borberg (1888–1947) with his 1919 article "Skuespillets Forfald" (The Decline of Drama). In it he attacks the dominant psychological realism and seeks a modern theater marked by "a world in ruins, of enormous insecurity, wild instincts, fog and doubt"—in a formula describing the situation of the "lost generation." Instead, Borberg demands a mixture of ecstasy, imagination, violent action, historical topics, and a symbolic approach. This program, in an astounding fashion, was realized by Kaj Munk and Kjeld Abell, whereas Borberg's own plays anticipated Soya's oeuvre.

In 1920 Borberg made his contribution to this new drama with *Ingen* (Nobody). World War I serves as a frame, and the motif is that of the Greek Amphitryon myth. A soldier thought dead returns unrecognized from the war to find his wife in love with another man resembling the soldier's former self. He is haunted by the piercing question of whether or not human character is anything but an illusion, an accumulation of impressions, or a mere manifestation of the opinion of others about oneself. In his attempt to analyze his situation as well as his divided self in order to find a human identity behind the facade, the soldier discovers only a void, a "nobody." Borberg dramaturgically anticipates the Italian playwright Luigi Pirandello as he violates all rules of the theater. His play is not divided into acts and contains no psychologically credible characters; scenes of violence and murder alternate with poetic passages; and the coherence between the cinematically changing episodes is established only by means of leitmotifs. With sophisticated skill Borberg employs all conceivable stage effects, creating with a blend of reflective and spontaneous elements a unique masterpiece in the history of Danish drama and beyond doubt its finest work of expressionism.

Psychological, or rather psychoanalytical, analysis—indeed, Borberg was the first to discuss Freud in Danish in his philosophical treatise *Krig og Køn* (1918; War and Gender)—also forms the basis for his two following plays. In *Cirkus Juris* (1935; The Juridical Circus) Borberg questions the possibility of juridical justice and of making moral judgments per se. In *Synder og Helgen* (1939; Sinner and Saint) he juxtaposes Don Juan and Don Quixote, two fantasts who are chasing an impossible dream, in a discussion of whether life must be viewed as a dream or if it is possible to make one's ideals come true. The ironic point in the play lies in the fact that the girl who has disappointed Don Juan is the same who in Don Quixote's imagination becomes the ideal of a woman. Whereas the drama from 1935 is sophisticatedly abstract and speculative, appealing directly to the intellect, the second work is a grandiose tragedy of occasionally extraordinary poetic power and beauty. Because of his sympathies for National Socialism during World War II, Borberg, one of the few twentieth-century Danish playwrights of international stature, is still persona non grata in Danish cultural life.

The human psyche is also the focus of Sven Clausen (1893–1961), who after a career in a credit association in 1950 became a respected professor of law at the University of Copenhagen. Clausen did not experience significant success on the Danish stage in spite of a dazzling mastery of acute and witty dialogue and a transparently devised composition. Perhaps in Clausen's case the lack of appeal was primarily due to the analytical and stringent rationalism underlying his plays, together with a relentless satire that does not recoil from any taboo.

Favorite targets for Clausen's satire are abuse of power and envy among employees, both in the private sector and in public life. These attitudes form the background for the bitter tragedy about contemporary alienating and inhuman society, *Bureauslaven* (1922; The Office Hack), in which a cowed clerk—the prototype of the perpetually bullied individual—lets himself be tyrannized by his superiors and finally commits suicide. Similar themes characterize the historical play *Paladsrevolution* (1923; Palace Revolution). Here the upright and rational human being, embodied by the German eighteenth-century statesman and reformer Struensee, falls victim to the lust for power, egoism, and stupidity of the courtiers at the royal palace in Copenhagen. In spite of the ambience—the splendid setting, the colors, the passions, the absorbing intrigues, making *Paladsrevolution* technically one of the most brilliant plays in Danish drama—it is the pessimistic nihilism that leaves the greatest impression on the audience. The only way out of the folly and evil of this world is found by the king, the historical Christian VII, who escapes into insanity.

Clausen as the strict satirist is again apparent in *Vore egne Mandariner* (1920; Our Own Mandarins), which attacks bureaucracy and patronage, and in *Kulturaben* (1927; The Cultural Monkey), depicting opportunism in public Danish cultural life. Formal experimentation marks *Nævningen* (1929; The Juryman). By using allegorical figures the play is enacted in the mind of a juror in a murder case and thus has a motif in common with both Borberg's *Cirkus Juris* and Soya's *Hvem er jeg?* The sophisticated dramatic technique and symbolic weight estranged the audience, and after the 1930s Clausen devoted himself to his juridical writings and an attempt at establishing a common Nordic language as a counterweight to the increasing influx of foreign, especially German, loanwords.

Carl Erik Soya

The attack on the traditional naturalistic theater, initiated in the 1920s, was brought to victory in the following decade by three playwrights, whose finest plays—and this was also something new—became media events and hits with the theatergoers. Carl Erik Soya, Kjeld Abell, and Kaj Munk chose totally opposite directions, each representing different ideologies: skepticism, humanism, and Christianity, respectively. While Munk learned from Ibsen, Oehlenschläger, and Shakespeare, and Abell from contemporary German expressionism, Soya was influenced by the turn-of-the-century Danish satirist Gustav Wied, with whom he shared a deeply pessimistic view of life. But whereas Soya and Abell portrayed the ordinary person, Munk's favorite characters were grand, willful personalities. As the political situation in Europe became increasingly tense, all three turned their attention to contemporary problems, rallying in a defense of human freedom against oppression.

The first play by the journalist Carl Erik Soya (1896–1983), *Parasitterne* (1929; The Parasites), was closest to the naturalistic tradition. Although early, the play is typical of Soya's dramaturgy: skillfully structured, candid, and shunning no effect of gore and violence. *Parasitterne* is a macabre and stinging satire about human meanness set in a petty-bourgeois milieu. Soya is a pronounced moralist who wants to change the establishment. It became his destiny in Danish belles lettres never to be taken quite seriously, but to be regarded rather as a cantankerous writer, speculating in sensation and scandal.

Soya was immensely productive, branching out into poetry, essay, novel, and short story, but the quality of his work is quite uneven. He did not experience his actual breakthrough until the 1940s with a dramatic tetralogy and the semiautobiographical novel *Min Farmors Hus* (1943; Eng. tr. *Grandmother's House,* 1966). In a middle-class Victorian setting in Copenhagen, Soya lets a five-year-old child interpret an adult world with the author's characteristic keen eye for human foibles, discovering malice and devilry lurking everywhere behind the childhood idyll. The satirical line continues with the comedies *Umbabumba* (1935), a Brecht-like revue set in an African country, which deals with the impotence of democracy and seizure of power by the Nazis (the play was banned by the Danish government), and *Chas*

(1938), which pokes fun at the mania for sports and journalists' exploitation of the idealized athlete.

During the 1930s Soya found inspiration in psychoanalysis and began to experiment with theatrical effects, in which he was influenced by Pirandello and Abell. Thus he approaches the aspect of Danish drama which in the previous decade was represented by Svend Borberg and Sven Clausen: a projection of humanity's inner, often subconscious moral dilemma onto the stage. *Hvem er jeg?* (1932; Who Am I?) is a comedy in fourteen scenes which enjoyed a major European success. Its object is to analyze the struggle between instinct and ethics, vice and virtue in the subconscious of a young man divided between two women. The Devil offers to get rid of one of them, and the Virgin Mary, Don Juan, and Bluebeard, among others, participate in a discussion pro and con.

In the less successful *Lord Nelson lægger Figenbladet* (1934; Lord Nelson Takes Off His Fig Leaf), a definite Freudian experiment, a kind of grotesque puppet show about human inhibitions, Soya lets a series of historical celebrities such as Cleopatra, Nietzsche, and Lenin play. As in Borberg's *Ingen,* war and heroism are interpreted as projections of suppressed sexual instincts. In *Don Juan som Ægtemand* (1932; Don Juan as a Husband), like the nineteenth-century writer M. A. Goldschmidt, Soya experiments with the nemesis motif, with ethical retribution in yet another discussion of the complex of problems predominant in his oeuvre about life's regularity or fortuitousness, justice or injustice, reflecting the duality of his own nature: the moralist versus the nihilist.

This complex of problems underlies Soya's main dramatic work, a tetralogy entitled *Brudstykker af et Mønster* (1940; Bits of a Pattern), *To Traade* (1943; Eng. tr. *Two Threads,* 1955), *30 Aars Henstand* (1944; 30 Years' Deferral), and the final farcical piece *Frit Valg* (1948; Free Choice). These plays are held together by an attempt to find a pattern in the apparent lack of meaning and cause in a series of accidental events behind which looms an inexplicable nemesis that seems to avenge all guilt on earth. The tetralogy, characterized by a skillful composition, a terse and idiomatic dialogue, and scenes highly effective on the stage, constitutes a dialectic structure that, considered from the standpoint of irony, tragedy, and melodrama, seeks to illuminate a series of intricate philosophical questions rather than provide convincing solutions.

World War II and the German occupation is directly treated in the prose allegory *En Gæst* (1941; A Visitor), about a Danish family visited by an earwig, representing the occupational forces, which grows to a threatening size before it is killed. In the play *Efter* (1947; After) Soya takes a strong stand against traitors, especially those opportunists who profited from the war and after 1945 began glorifying the Resistance. Finally, *Løve med korset* (1950; The Lion Wears a Corset) deals with the causes of war from the perspectives of a romanticist, a psychologist, and a materialist in a series of episodes from ancient Greece to the office of a director of a contemporary arms factory. Here Soya employs striking theatrical effects such as a stereopticon and cinematic pictures to facilitate the usual dialectic approach to find answers.

In contrast, in his last major plays, *Vraggods* (1965; Wreckage) and *Brevet* (1966; The Letter), written for television, depression and the disillusionment of old age reign supreme. Soya the skeptic, who in his constant search for answers revealed himself after all as a true humanist, has now become nothing but a bitter moralist, feeling his isolation as a martyrdom. Posterity, however, will certainly place Soya among those writers who are constantly probing to find answers to the never-ending philosophical and ethical problems of humankind. Soya made use of a genre whose technique and essence he knew and explored with expertise, achieving sometimes the excessively complex, sometimes the perfect.

Kjeld Abell

In comparison with Soya, Kjeld Abell (1901–61) is an exclusive, immensely critical writer who nevertheless published plays that were less labored and more accessible. Because of their poetic atmosphere and boundless imagination as well as their quick-witted dialogue, they readily appealed to theatergoers and achieved immediate success. Abell received a degree in political science from the University of Copenhagen in 1927 but decided against a civil-service career. The same year, he traveled to Paris and London to study modern theater and acquired a thorough knowledge of contemporary playwrights, such as Jean Giraudoux and Bertold Brecht, and renowned directors, such as Max Reinhardt. During this time he supported himself as a supernumerary, scene painter, and costume designer. In 1930 Abell returned to Copenhagen and joined the Royal Theater as a stage designer; from 1941 to 1949 he was director of the famous Tivoli Gardens.

The sensational success of his first play, *Melodien der blev væk* (1935; Eng. tr. *The Melody That Got Lost,* 1939), was probably due to the application of the genre of the revue comedy (with roots in the singspiel of the 1830s) to a serious social topic. From the outset *Melodien* was planned as a ballet, and it also contains some cinematic features. With this work Abell got to the heart of the social problems of the 1930s. The twenty-one sketchy episodes, interspersed with songs, are only loosely connected by a scant plot. Abell introduces the white-collar proletarian, the clerk and slave of routine, Larsen—a relative of Hans Fallada's well-known protagonist in the novel *Kleiner Mann—was nun?* (1932; Little Man, What Now?). The same question— "What now?"—Abell asks about the little man caught in an environment permeated with prejudice and social imbalance, which prevent him from grasping life at its fullest, finding the melody. The play concludes on a note of hope and a new start, however. After all, Larsen's wife happens to find "the melody" first with a child, then among the working class.

Abell's next play, the comedy *Eva aftjener sin Barnepligt* (1936; Eve Does Her Duty as a Child), is based on similar Marxist sympathies. It carries further the attack on what the author sees as outdated and inhibiting routine, satirizing the bourgeois ways of child rearing. As in *Melodien* the atmosphere is light, but a more serious tone is also heard, pointing to Abell's next and most significant work, the symbolic drama *Anna Sophie Hedvig* (1939; Eng. tr. 1944), in which Abell warns against the threat from Nazi Germany, growing because of the passivity of the bourgeoisie. The title character is a timid provincial schoolteacher who musters the courage and strength to kill a tyrannical and much-feared principal who is about to destroy her happy little world. In the conclusion political reality and its symbol are merged in a scene of transfiguration. Anna Sophie joins a freedom fighter from the Spanish Civil War about to be executed. Her story is related by using a complex cinematic flashback technique and only gradually, as in a detective novel, is her murder revealed, preceded by a discussion in a Copenhagen upper-class family about the ethical implications of killing.

During the German occupation Abell wrote two plays, *Judith* (1940) and *Dronningen gaar igen* (1943; publ. 1955; Eng. tr. *The Queen on Tour,* 1955), both of which urge resistance in an indirect manner. In January 1944 Abell stopped the performance at the Royal Theater to announce the execution of Kaj Munk and immediately had to go underground. *Silkeborg* (1946) became a tribute to the Resistance but, at the same time, the most stinging denunciation of the general attitude of appeasement and collaboration with the enemy during the war.

Dage paa en Sky (1947; Days on a Cloud) takes place in the mind of a pilot during the seconds in which he falls to the ground, intending to commit suicide. He embodies the humanist disappointed with the Cold War ideological development after World War II but nevertheless seems to refuse to accept any responsibility. Abell once again makes an appeal to direct action in order to maintain human freedom. The pilot is not killed, because in the clouds he is talked into returning alive to the earth by the goddesses of Greek mythology.

The major problem discussed in Abell's postwar plays is the danger of the intellectual's isolation from a general fellowship with all of humankind; the predominant conflict is that between the death wish and the will to live. In *Den blaa Pekingeser* (1954; The Blue Pekingese) this isolation leads to suicide. Like *Dage paa en Sky, Den blaa Pekingeser* is a dreamplay, brilliantly exploiting all the technical means of the stage. Time and space are dissolved, and in a visionary fashion memory and imagination are woven together into a consummate masterpiece.

The redeeming force of love, which in *Den blå Pekingeser* is juxtaposed to destruction, becomes the all-encompassing focal point in Abell's penultimate play, *Kameliadamen* (1959; The Lady of the Camellias), inspired by— yet totally different from—Alexandre Dumas's sentimental novel. In addition, the work once again settles accounts with the passivity of postwar humanism, which is also an integral part of the author's own personal dilemma, as well as an appeal to overcome man-made regulations and systems that inhibit freedom, openness, and life's dynamic forces. The same topic is treated in Abell's last drama, *Skriget* (1961; The Cry), which moves on three levels: in a world of birds, in a contemporary human world, and in an Old Testament setting centered on the story of Jephta's daughter.

To Abell, writing was a political tool. Nevertheless, he succeeded in avoiding dogmatic preaching, the pitfall of all political art, and he was therefore often reproached because his plays ended ambiguously. But behind his playful and capricious imagination and witticisms, sometimes touching on artificiality, as well as his remarkable juggling of stage techniques, one always finds a serious insistence on freedom and the individual's development toward greater dignity and responsibility. Until his death Abell continued his theatrical experiments with the form and expression of the dramatic genre—he also wrote revues, filmscripts, and ballets—and with regard to the technical development of Danish drama, he must be acknowledged as the major innovator of the twentieth century.

Kaj Munk

In the dramatic writing of Kaj Munk (1898–1944) innovation is found more in content than in form, in which he did not show much theoretical interest. Munk went his own way in the literature of his time, not representing any trend or school, not having any direct Danish predecessor or successor. Nevertheless, he was a child of his time, of its unrest and doubt. Feverishly productive, he wrote close to sixty plays as well as numerous essays and sermons.

The pietistic atmosphere of his home left a strong mark on Munk and influenced his decision to study theology at the University of Copenhagen, where he received his degree in divinity and was ordained in 1924. He became a minister in the poor parish of Vedersø in West Jutland, remaining there until his arrest and execution by the Nazis. Because of his contempt of the enfeebled democracies as well as political chaos after World War I, and guided by his admiration for the ruthless but also self-sacrificing man of action and power, he was initially receptive to the totalitarian ideologies of the 1930s. Although he maintained his hero worship, before the war Munk revised his views of Mussolini and Hitler. He became the spiritual leader of the Danish Resistance movement, and he ended his life as a martyr, clearly a destiny he consciously sought for himself. But Munk was primarily a Christian, an idealistic writer, and it is the Christian faith that gives his writings their most profound perspective. It was from this perspective that Munk viewed humanity as engulfed in a tragedy determined by a perpetual battle for power among human beings themselves and between God and man, the spiritual and material, good and evil.

The first of Munk's dramas to be staged was the powerful historical play *En Idealist* (1928; An Idealist; Eng. tr. *Herod the King*, 1953). It was a colossal fiasco, partly because of mistakes in its production, partly because the grand pathos of the play was so far from the expectations of the audience. Episodically, Munk depicts a man of power, related to the Nietzschean superman, who without any scruples becomes a criminal in order to fulfill one single idea: the obtaining of absolute power. To achieve this goal, he sacrifices his happiness, his beloved wife, so that his love for her will not distract him from his political endeavors. Herod is not successful in fully exterminating the goodness in his own heart, however. Therefore, in the gripping concluding scene the dying king must, at the height of his triumph, submit to the look of purity of a young woman and her son—Mary and the Christ Child. In the final account Herod is defeated by God.

Munk's analysis of the heroic character is continued in *I Brændingen* (1929; In the Breakers). The drama's passionate and bellicose protagonist, also an "idealist" (modeled after the radical critic Georg Brandes), faces nothing but defeat: the suicide of his favorite son and another son's conversion to Christianity, which the father has fought his entire life. The tragedy only causes him to rise to the occasion, however, adding even greater stature to his personality.

In *Sejren* (1936; The Victory), based on material from Italy's war against Ethiopia in 1936, a purely political aspect is added to Munk's hero worship. The protagonist is a Mussolini-like ruler who is described with critical admiration, but Munk in the final analysis renounces the pure lust for power, pointing to the individual's need for God's mercy. Munk's concept of the hero changed during these years. He passed from the worship of power to pure humanism, from Herod to Professor Mensch, in *Han sidder ved Smeltediglen* (1938; Eng. tr. *He Sits at the Melting Pot,* 1953), the first in a series of plays in which Munk discusses the matter of vocation. Criticizing the persecution of Jews in Nazi Germany, Munk lets the scientist Mensch discover that Jesus was a Jew, which brings him into conflict with the government. Granted, Mensch destroys his proof, but he marries his Jewish secretary, not just out of protest but as a realization of God's love. Chosen by God, a fragile human being gains the strength to assert himself against the powerful of this world.

Similarly, in the historical play *Niels Ebbesen* (1942; Eng. tr. 1944), written to stir his fellow Danes into action against the occupying German forces, the somewhat indecisive title character represents humanism in its protest against tyranny. And in the curtain raiser *Før Cannae* (1943; Eng. tr. *Before Cannae,* 1953) Munk lets the Roman commander Fabius (i.e., Churchill) be his mouthpiece in an unequivocal renunciation of power and authority, personified in the Carthaginian general Hannibal, a boasting Hitler figure.

Three years after the fiasco of *En Idealist* Munk won a decisive victory with *Cant* (1931; Eng. tr. 1953), a historical play about King Henry VIII and the hypocritical, theological, and political dodges he uses to reach his erotic goals. *Cant* is the most cheerful of Munk's plays, with colorful and lively scenes modeled after Shakespeare. Nevertheless, it is a penetrating analysis of a human character who seeks to bestow on his selfish actions a noble, ethical justification, but thereby only deceives himself and others.

If the greed for power and the craving for love are the two forces balancing each other in *Cant,* Munk in two other plays focuses exclusively on the commandment of love seen in the light of faith. *Kærlighed* (1926; Love) portrays an ambitious young man who, without faith and only for pecuniary reasons, accepts an incumbency in a distant West Jutland parish. An insidious disease shatters him physically, but the faith of his parishioners and a reciprocated love for the married daughter of a farmer give him the strength to carry on his work. Because of this relationship, however, the external framework of his life crumbles: the congregation turns its back on him, the ecclesiastical authorities intervene, and his disease worsens; but throughout the catastrophe the feeling of love remains the absolute source of strength right to his deathbed. The last encounter between the two lovers is portrayed with a purity and tenderness which make it one of the most gripping love scenes in Danish literature and raise the pastor to a heroic level, if not in faith then in love—for Munk, actually two manifestations of the same love of a gracious and thus victorious God.

The pure gift of grace becomes the center of Munk's attention in his modern miracle play, likewise in a West Jutland setting, *Ordet* (1932; Eng. tr. *The Word,* 1953; filmed by Carl Th. Dreyer, 1955), Munk's greatest stage success. Its first acts are almost comic in their description of the disagreements between two different religious orientations—the more extroverted and superficial Grundtvigianism and the stern fundamentalist members of the Home Mission movement—which also lead to social and family conflicts. Unexpectedly, a young woman, Inger, dies in childbirth, and then Munk exposes various attitudes toward death, ranging from the physician's materialism to the orthodox Christian hope of reunion in the beyond. Only the mentally ill son on the farm, Johannes, once a student of theology, dares to ask the decisive question of whether death is a beginning or an end, thereby raising the problem of the play: Is it possible for God to give human beings such a strong faith that they can bring the dead back to life? In contrast to Bjørnstjerne Bjørnson's related but rationalistic play *Over Ævne, Første Stykke* (1883; Beyond Our Power I), Munk's answer is affirmative. In the final, overpowering scene, Johannes, who identifies himself with Christ, surrounded by believers and nonbelievers, resurrects Inger through his own boundless faith, and once again God has won a victory over humanity but through a human being.

In scenes such as the conclusion of *Ordet* Munk demonstrates the powerful dramatic tension he is able to create. Whether it is the confrontation between God and individual or the conflict between humans with their passions and attitudes, he is able to keep the undivided attention of his audience, aided by an unerring instinct for building up excitement and concentrated atmosphere, occasionally by using somewhat vulgar shock effects.

His breakthrough with *Cant* opened the theater to Munk, and during the 1930s he was performed as no other Danish author had been before. Between 1932 and 1940 one Munk play per evening, on the average, was performed on a Scandinavian stage. To his contemporaries, Kaj Munk was both a celebrated and a controversial figure. His stage success, strong personal charisma, and national martyrdom formed the background for what amounted to cult worship of him well into the years after World War II. Since then the evaluation of the quality of Munk's oeuvre has become more critical, occasionally downright condescending, because of his sketchy psychological character drawing and provocative Christian message. But Munk was a dramatist who always sought out the dialectic tension between ideas in order to challenge his public. This goal enabled him to create works for the stage which undoubtedly have secured him a position as the most significant twentieth-century Danish playwright.

It has become truistic to label historical periods, especially recent ones, eras of crisis and to state, dramatically, that all values were questioned and turned topsy-turvy. Even if there can be little doubt that the generations in focus experienced a mental upheaval and eloquently depicted its consequences, this type of periodization, which for more than a hundred years has led to the registration of crisis after crisis, tends to trivialize literary or intellectual history. If the literary historian states that the works of a certain era express a sense of deep cultural disillusionment, the reader may sigh and wonder what else is new.

Of course, intellectual malaise could be found in the 1930s, but harsh economic realities resulted in a drastically new epochal awareness and assertion of values. The medium chosen for that awareness was, as a rule, narrative prose, especially that of the realistic or naturalistic novel. The writers of the decade may not have expected the world to change soon, but the ideal of social justice—one combined with a hope for psychologically freer human beings—is overtly or covertly expressed in many of their works. Perhaps they were so strongly expressed because the conflicts of a turbulent world ominously seemed to endanger any hopes of justice or freedom. Their prophetic sense of danger was tragically proved right when World War II broke out and soon after arrived at Scandinavia's doorstep.

Consequently, it makes sense when the Danish critic Peter P. Rohde maintains that the period under consideration started on November 29, 1929, with the notoriously famous crash on Wall Street, for him the greatest of all economic crises and ended with World War II and the German invasion of Denmark on April 9, 1940.

Even if one takes exception to Rohde's view of the depression as the greatest of all economic crises, the generation that was exposed to the effects of it would very likely agree, for the crash was felt in the minutest details of everyday life. The rate of unemployment was not quite as high in Scandinavia as in America, but the feeling that it was hard to manage the next day economically permeated Scandinavian society. There may not be a Scandinavian counterpart to John Steinbeck's depression epic, *The Grapes of Wrath* (1939), even though some of the so-called proletarian Swedish authors come close, but such Danes as Hans Kirk, Harald Herdal, and Mogens Klitgaard, although they were temperaments apart, register how difficult it was for the ordinary wage earner to make ends meet.

If such hardships tended to make bread-and-butter issues overshadow those of the mind, that mind had nevertheless to make ideological choices.

Developments outside Scandinavia urged people to take a stand politically, one that often was meant to improve their daily lot by removing its economic frustrations. To put it simply, Scandinavians who were not satisfied with the traditional political systems of their native nations looked south, east, or west, respectively, to Hitler's Nazi Germany and Mussolini's Fascist Italy, to Stalin's Communist Soviet Union, or—it should be kept in mind— to Franklin D. Roosevelt's democratic New Deal America.

The first two of these remedies not only promised, in different ways, to hold the depression at bay but also rhetorically enticed the people to take a shortcut to better, if not glorious, days. Kaj Munk's admiration for the strong leader and the existence of conservative youth organizations that were imitative of the Nazis, suggest that Hitler's example had made a strong impression. Few Danish authors joined the National Socialist movement, but some were drawn to the Communist example set by the Soviet Union. Harald Herdal and Hans Kirk, like the increasingly radical Martin Andersen Nexø, saw salvation in Lenin's and Stalin's drastic restructuring of society. But both camps received severe shocks and became disillusioned: Munk realized how the Jewish people were treated in Nazi Germany, and some of the Communist sympathizers were rudely awakened by Stalin's Moscow trials (1936–38), whereas others continued to toe the party line.

The authors of the 1930s were different from the experimental daredevils of the 1920s: they were often earnest moralists; they were mostly solid realists; and they were anti-intellectuals, in the sense that they grasped—to refer to T. S. Eliot—the hollowness of those who played the role of intellectual guardians. The angry authors of the 1930s, whether optimists or pessimists, had a keen eye for double standards, and even if that decade was not one that particularly forcefully promoted equality between the sexes, it seems quite clear that, by some male authors, such as Jørgen Nielsen and Mogens Klitgaard, women were praised for their integrity without being put on that infamous pedestal.

Maybe that bit of common sense was owing to the fact that some of the best of the young authors of the 1930s concentrated on life among the rural population, a feature that should not, however, lead to a facile categorization of them as regional writers. In that everyday world of constantly necessary toil both sexes worked together strenuously; thus, equality, to the extent that ideological censors, wittingly or unwittingly, permitted, could emerge. But as several texts show, the semiofficial censors, whether representative of pietistic forms of Christianity or bourgeois moralism, were hard at work to promulgate the woman's subservience.

Even though such authors as Herdal, Erling Kristensen, Kirk, Jørgen

Nielsen, and Knuth Becker are quite unrelentingly critical of the repressive forces in their milieus, they nevertheless and ironically may now be read as unwilling—maybe unwitting—literary preservationists of a way of life that was waning. The hard work in the fields, the claustrophobic life in the provincial towns, and Copenhagen with its unemployed or underemployed masses are described in eloquent detail, thus reflecting a way of life that was eventually to fade in favor of a consumer society.

The concern of the authors of the 1930s with everyday life, with the ordinary person rather than with the outstanding one, made well-tried narrative paradigms seem outdated; thus, the hero-oriented novel, especially the elitist bildungsroman or its likewise individualistically envisioned, negative mirror image, gave way to the collective novel. The social class in a milieu or the milieu itself replaced the protagonist(s); that form could result in a strictly realistic novel (e.g., Kirk or Herdal) or in a patchwork scenario (Klitgaard or Jens Gielstrup), receiving inspiration from John Dos Passos's kaleidoscopic tour de force.

Of course, not all writers became erstwhile realists or collectivists—Karen Blixen became famous, after all, in the 1930s—but Denmark took hardly any part in the primitivist movement that made inroads into Sweden, and even if Freud had significant impact on some authors, Danish writers did not take as strongly to him as was the case in Norway. Some authors nonetheless admitted, if not in manifestoes, that toil with the soil and the dull pain of making a few cents more as a working person were not sufficient subject matter for art. Inspired by the workings of the mind, especially that shadowy realm of the unconscious, a few women made remarkable modernist forays, and some ironic, satiric, or melancholy minds—male and female—gave the psychological narrative new impetus.

As one works one's way into the 1930s, one finds that the homogeneity of the period slowly becomes, as might be expected, an image rather than reality, but an image that clings quite stubbornly to the era. That image of stolid and solid realism and moralism has not served the period well, for not only has its homogeneity been overstressed, but it has also found reluctant readers.

If the period seems too glumly serious, it should be recalled that the theater revue—that humorous, often satirical mixture of skits, monologues, and songs—remained prominent, and the radio carried those disrespectful sketches and catchy songs to people all over the nation, for in spite of the economic misery, the radio was being purchased. On that radio the person isolated far from any cultural centers could listen to the top twenty songs of the day, as well as radio plays (some of which were written by top-notch authors), and cultural, ideological debates—and, of course, endless entertainment. The distance between capital and farmland, as well as provincial town, was being decreased.

To grasp not only the impact of the media of the day but also its role as an antidote to the seriousness of the times, one must remember that in the 1930s the "talkies" were introduced and became the dominant entertainment of the day. Movies were prominent before, but not until they "spoke" did they assume their momentous power over the minds of their audience. Like much of American literature that appealed then, Hollywood movies were immensely popular. If Hemingway, Steinbeck, and Dos Passos were influential, so were Frank Capra and Ernst Lubitsch, and as the decade wore on, a lighter touch became discernible—the leeway to address or ignore problems and to do so with a sense of humor—and that ability graces in very different ways such Danish authors as Klitgaard and Hans Scherfig. In the works of the gifted and prematurely deceased Jens Gielstrup, who owes nearly too much to Hemingway and the hard-boiled American school, a sense of a darker convergence of novel and movie suggests itself, not least in those lyrical, moody scenes in which the characters are seen pathetically roughed up by fate—the *film noir* effect.

On the lighter side, perhaps, the spirited heroines of American movies, from Mae West to Carol Lombard and Jean Arthur, also helped give the plucky, commonsensical Scandinavian antiheroine—experienced sexually, but not considered a fallen woman—more of a chance in contemporary fiction. She holds her own in a male world.

Poul Henningsen

A glimpse of the decade's complex mixture of the serious and the comic, of the heavy and the light, may best be given by cutting to Poul Henningsen (1894–1967). His satirical or bittersweet songs, composed to be performed in revues, paved the way for an oral diction that effortlessly and elegantly used the slang and jargon of the street. A collection of his poems appeared in 1951, *Springende vers* (Leaping Verse). Without being modernistic, he reflected the rebellious modern spirit of the day, and like Johannes V. Jensen before him, he made a case for casting off the needless cultural baggage of the past: outdated habits, opinions, tastes. In many ways Henningsen, who was educated as an architect and professed to the ideas of functionalism in art and life, restated the Modern Breakthrough's ideals with the slangy, democratic language of the 1920s; labeled cultural radicalism (*kulturradikalisme*), they have remained an influential factor in Danish intellectual life. Henningsen started out in the short-lived but influential magazine *Kri-*

tisk Revy (1926–28; Critical Revue) and soon became a prominent cultural critic who set out to expose snobbishness, prejudices, the galling desire "to fit in," and all that stood in the way of the human being's sense of freedom and joy. He was an unpretentious moralist with humanist inclinations, and his dictum, "We believe in art with human content, art for the sake of society," sums up the outlook of many of the politically radical artists and critics of the 1930s. A teasing, sharp debater, he was often embroiled in controversies, and like the "Mot Dag" group in Norway, he detected early ominous signs in nazism and fascism. His pamphlet *Hvad med Kulturen?* (1933; What about Culture?) is as sharp a warning as the works of the Norwegian writers Sigurd Hoel and Arnuld Øverland.

If the literature of the 1930s is often considered to be socially committed, serious, and bleak, it should be recalled that there is another side to it, one that Poul Henningsen represents well. The humanistic battle for freedom, be it social or psychological, which so many of the authors of the 1930s were engaged in was fought with talent, anger, and humor in many of the radical magazines of the decade.

Such voices were stilled when Danish reality suddenly changed on April 9, 1940. Those that spoke up after a period of silence were much more serious, much "heavier," and the "lightness" that was also to be found in the 1930s—in some of the fiction, in revues, in movie comedies, in Abell's experimental plays, and in spirited cultural debates—did not return.

CRITICAL REALISM

Hans Kirk

Hans Kirk (1898–1962) writes compellingly about his childhood in the collection of sketches/memoirs entitled *Skyggespil* (1953; Shadowplay), a book that rivals Nexø's memoirs. With warmth Kirk tells about his father's pietistic family and his mother's wealthier and more secular kin. Kirk's own home was atheistic, and his father, an esteemed country physician with a strong sense of social responsibility, objected in particular to the injustice of the class hierarchy. The son followed in his father's footsteps.

Kirk received a law degree in 1922 but soon turned to journalism and, as a cultural critic of Marxist leanings, became a frequent contributor to radical magazines. Like Johannes V. Jensen, for his bread and butter he started publishing short stories in popular magazines. Some of those texts reveal a robust sense of humor. With *Fiskerne* (1928; The Fishermen) came his breakthrough. In this collective account of a group of deeply religious fishermen and their families who move from a coast battered by the North Sea to a more hospitable fjord, Kirk used his familiarity with his childhood milieus. The stern Christians do very well, for they have the conviction that their uncompromising belief is right and are strengthened by a deep-seated solidarity within their group. As the novel unfolds in mosaic form—brief glimpses from individual lives—two developments are charted: the material success of the newcomers and their spiritual victory over the habitual but weak Christianity of the original residents of the parish. Kirk cleverly draws out the reader's sympathy for the steadfast fishermen's families, but behind the well-told, seemingly quite unbiased account of the strong conflicts they find themselves in, one detects the Marxist and also a familiarity with Freud's theories. The newcomers have considerable strength through their belief that all is the will of the divine being—nothing that occurs is accidental—and thus all misfortune is explained. It becomes obvious to the reader, however, since Kirk stacks his narrative cards very cunningly, that the pietists are beset by a conflict between religion and sexuality, not only one that they are incapable of solving, but also one that causes tragedies and deaths that were totally unwarranted. Earthy comic episodes are used to allow the reader relief, whereas the characters are steeped in the turmoil of the moment. Gently, Kirk implies, as the narrative draws to a close, that some of the offspring of the pietists will become less inhibited and intolerant than their parents, and the book concludes by suggesting an optimistic belief in future developments.

If *Fiskerne* had not been such a striking book, perhaps the best collective novel in Danish literature, the following works in the same vein, technically and ideologically, might have assumed a higher profile in literary history. In *Daglejerne* (1936; Day Laborers) and *De ny Tider* (1939; New Times) Kirk depicts the effects of industrialization on a rural region as the building of a concrete factory changes the smallholders into industrial laborers. They experience the effects of capitalism, form a union, engage in strikes, and endure unemployment. Kirk portrays characters as vividly as ever and shows, once again, his sensitivity toward people who would never embrace or understand his Marxist convictions. Both books are marked by the sure storytelling instinct that Kirk displayed in *Fiskerne,* but the deep-seated tension of that novel is lacking, and thus they seem less compelling than his debut work.

During the 1930s Kirk continued to consolidate his position as one of the most outspoken journalists on the left. Like Nexø, he defended the Moscow trials, and again like Nexø, he was arrested in 1941, when Hitler invaded the Soviet Union. Although interned, the irrepressible Kirk continued to protest in writing against the illegal actions of the occupiers, and later he managed to escape.

Kirk's postwar works—for example, *Vredens Søn* (1950; The Son of Wrath), which makes the story of Christ and Judas a parallel to the days after World War II—have often been accused of substituting tendentiousness for artistic quality. Kirk would hardly disagree but certainly not renege, for like many other members of the resistance against the Nazis, he felt disillusioned by the aftermath of the occupation. Both *Vredens Søn* and *Slaven* (1948; The Slave), a fascinating mixture of action novel and essay disguised as a historical narrative, may well be read as the works of a disappointed but not embittered humanist who continued his efforts to steer his audience toward a saner and sounder society.

Knuth Becker

Knuth Becker (1891–1974) is first and foremost known for his momentous and impressive cycle of novels—consisting of eight volumes—about the young Kai Gøtsche, a likable misfit whose hunger for life not only leads him into endless difficulties with the repressive world that surrounds him, but also gives him the ability to endure and continue his quest for a fulfilling life. In the two first and best entries in the series, *Det daglige Brød* (1934; The Daily Bread) and the two-volume *Verden venter* (1934; The World Waits), Becker delves into the ways in which the milieu shapes the mind and behavior of a child, a topic that gained prominence in the 1930s, perhaps partly owing to a growing knowledge of psychoanalytical theory and, consequently, a greater understanding of the significance of the formative years. In depth, Becker's charting of Kai's early years does not measure up to Sigurd Hoel's *Veien til verdens ende* (1933; The Road to the End of the World) or to a similar portrayal by the Swedish proletarian author Ivar Lo-Johansson in *Godnatt, jord* (1933; Goodnight, Earth), but Becker's realistic depiction of life in a small provincial town and of an institution for boys is vivid and filled with minutely delineated minor characters. Kai emerges as a victim who knows, defiantly, that he is one. He is a boy of action, of playfulness, one easily led astray by his instinct for fun and troublemaking, and he readily takes refuge in lies and fantasies, which become an escape valve and may foreshadow Kai's eventual debut as a lyric poet in the last volume, *Marianne* (1956).

Even though Becker shows a great deal of understanding for such repressive figures as Kai's father and mother—they, too, have been victimized—his world is nevertheless quite black and white. The schoolteachers, the pietists, the merchants, and others who want control over their fellow beings may have decent traits, but they create a world that threatens to crush the playful human, *homo ludens*. That such forces do not always succeed testifies to Becker's essential optimism; in the first volume that optimism is touchingly embodied in Kai's aging, compassionate grandmother, who, in spite of being ill, fights against Kai's being sent away to a boys' home, and in Sine, the sensual, commonsensical maid who emerges as a healthy antidote to the home, in which everyone, as the voice of the town expresses it, "is screwed up."

The hope that a wayward world can be put straight is reflected in Becker's poetry. His anger against exploiters and hypocrites had already surfaced in his debut, *Digte* (1916; Poems), and in the three volumes of *Silhouetter* (1921, 1923, and 1928; Silhouettes) he focuses on ordinary workers and with humorous generosity suggests their basic humanity.

Harald Herdal

Harald Herdal (1900–1978) also started his career as a lyric poet, and some of his short-lined texts, a form he excelled in, are highly personal love poems that give no hint of his strong moral indignation. The collection *nøgne digte* (1933; naked poems), however, voices the proletarian's solidarity with the underclass of his time and is a cry for political action. Like Nexø, Herdal never had much belief in any party ever so slightly to the right of the Communists, and some of his works are imbued with the hope of waking the slumbering workers to take charge of their own destiny. In several of his works, maybe most impressively in *Man skal jo leve* (1934; Live One Must), he depicts through a collective narrative the sordid and dull lives of the inhabitants of a slum dwelling in Copenhagen; they tend to sleepwalk through their lives, they feel little fellowship with others, but their cheap tricks and schemes may be seen as survival mechanisms against a numbing poverty. Nevertheless, this work and Herdal's many autobiographical or semiautobiographical writings seem quite bleak in outlook and have made him somewhat suspect in the eyes of Marxist critics. The strength of his works, even if they lack Nexø's or Becker's vivid characterization, is their authentic portrayal of the milieus of the downtrodden.

Erling Kristensen

Erling Kristensen (1893–1961) was, like Becker, brought up in the rural poverty of northern Jutland, and he, too, had to take a risk in becoming an artist—the mechanic dared to publish a novel in 1927, *Støtten* (The Pillar), a study of a shady opportunist. That novel was the beginning of an uneasy career, for even if the angry Kristensen was exceedingly critical of romanticized rural life, a yen for the simple country life occasionally surfaces, such as in the early part of *Stodderkongen* (1929; The Pauper King), which eventually demonstrates, however, that solidarity is a sham. That outcome may partly be caused by Kristensen's lack of hope in political engagement and in his nearly obsessive fascination with egoists who have no redeeming features, misfits who with their perverse inclinations and ambitions poison the lives of others. The collective novel *Drejers Hotel* (1934) and the sternly moralistic *Ler* (1930; Clay) both embody a drive to show the worst aspects of human behavior and to do so to the point that realism is undermined by allegory or caricature, as Drejer's Hotel becomes a metaphor for bourgeois losers. The protagonist of *Ler* has been called a Peer Gynt figure by the critic Hans Brix, but the trouble with Kristensen's fantasts is that they do not possess the charm with which Henrik Ibsen endowed his dreamer but only a viciousness and ridiculous lack of perception. Kristensen's preoccupation with such types lends stature to his claustrophobic, but uncompromising works that gloomily look into sleazy, petty minds. Some late narratives, not least the short stories in *Den sidste færge* (1954; The Last Ferry), show the same fascinations, but these leaner, less obsessive stories have an appeal reminiscent of Johannes V. Jensen's and Nexø's dark tales from their home regions.

PSYCHOLOGICAL REALISM

Jørgen Nielsen

Jørgen Nielsen (1902–45) was rooted in the remnants of the old peasant culture of the Jutland heath, which was probably the area least affected by modern technology. The age-old fatalism and pietism of those farmers, who manage a living but without gaining any economic or social advantage, come to life in Nielsen's simultaneously compassionate and critical depictions of members of that particular class. That dual quality suggests that Nielsen had left his roots behind, and tragically, the distance he thereby created to his source of inspiration became both an artistic and an existential barrier: his fiction suffers from an authorial removal from its characters; and in his life as an author he suffered from a sense of homelessness among the intelligentsia, to which his inclination for reflection rather than analysis had drawn him.

Nielsen is a considerable talent. His first short stories are linguistically indebted to Johannes V. Jensen's *Himmerlandshistorier,* but in terms of attitude—or of understanding of the temperament of the rural proletariat—they have more in common with Nexø's early short stories. They are terse and/or humorous statements about the mindset of people formed and limited by their milieu. These are people who have absolutely no use for the morality or opinions of others. Later collections of stories, such as *Figurer i et Landskab* (1944; Figures in a Landscape), solidify Nielsen's reputation as a raconteur who knows that there are quick short-cuts between comedy and tragedy. For the sake of truth—and Nielsen is painstakingly and painfully searching for truth—both poles must be presented.

Nielsen's novels are often explorations into the lives of those who realize, without surprise or outcry, that they must resign themselves to less than satisfying fates. In several of his novels his protagonists are women, such as in *Offerbaal* (1929; Sacrifical Fire), *De Hovmodige* (1930; The Proud), *En Kvinde ved Baalet* (1933; A Woman by the Bonfire), and *En Gaard midt i Verden* (1936; A Farm in the Midst of the World). In some of these novels the road toward resignation may seem easier going than in others, but the borderline between victory or defeat is blurred. Such ambiguities are barely experienced by the protagonists, but they haunt Nielsen and have a profound effect on his technique: he probes his characters' states of mind with rigor, compassion, and insight, but in the final analysis he can merely record their paths through life, not steer them or offer solutions to their claustrophobic destinies. Nielsen's approach to the characters in his novels is as far from the spontaneous as can be, for the omniscient narrator has a disturbing inclination to intervene—often to ask questions that he cannot answer—and thus readers are prevented from experiencing Nielsen's characters from within.

Nielsen's books have, nevertheless, a restless, very nearly obsessive quality that takes them from the realm of social realism (although Nielsen records the daily, endless toil in detail) to the tormented world of the mind of a man who had left his origin and could not find a home in the once-tantalizing world of the intelligentsia. It is understandable that Nielsen's junior, Martin A. Hansen, understood him well, for he, too, found himself between two such worlds, and in the works of both authors the protagonists are consistently people who are caught in that limbo. As realistic novels about the drudgery of life in the countryside between the world wars, Nielsen's novels may not warrant much attention, but if his own agonized quest for a place to breathe freely, where the demons of his origins could not reach him with their crippling pietism and fatalism, is sensed as the primary underlying errand of these books, they acquire a desperate and tragic urgency as the oeuvre darkened.

The critical realists of the 1930s were all to some degree psychological analysts, but Nielsen's example suggests that probing into a mind could become the major project of the oeuvre. That was true of some authors whose background was bourgeois and who felt more at home with the educated world, but who in some ways shared the fatalism that burdened Nielsen's figures. Those authors have less concern, however, for the social dimension that grants authenticity even to the works of the lesser of the social realists.

Aase Hansen

Aase Hansen (1893–1981) wrote about women who found themselves simultaneously liberated and trapped. Her protagonists are well educated and aware of the issues but feel that knowledge rarely leads to a fulfilling life or a heightened insight as to how such a life might come about. Hansen records that dilemma, but her oeuvre does not suggest solutions to it. The dilemma surfaced in the accomplished *Ebba Berings Studentertid* (1929; Ebba Bering's Student Days), in which one character, a young woman, sharply derides an emphasis on theory, which leads only to frustration for the so-called liberated woman, for she loses contact with the sensuality of life—a theme also found in the writings of Jacob Paludan. Hansen registers that frustration in exquisite detail and leaves the reader with the sad feeling that her characters, in spite of their obvious intelligence and sensitivity, accept the male view that the intellectual woman loses her femininity.

The same themes reappear in many of Hansen's ensuing novels, and although *En kvinde kommer hjem* (1937; A Woman Returns Home) has been heralded as a renewal, the attempts at achieving some integration into life remain dubious. In this novel the academic narrator has returned to her home and her religious mother, a woman with entirely different values from her "modern" daughter. The problematic role of the new women of the age is reflected in several fates, as it is in *Drømmen om i Gaar* (1939; The Dream of Yesterday); in this novel the attempt to reach beyond that frustration and sense of entrapment voiced in *Ebba Berings Studentertid* also fails, and what awaits ahead seems to be resignation mixed with an attraction to death. Like Jørgen Nielsen, Hansen registers and reflects, but the analyses implicit in the oeuvre were rarely completed, and it may be that her life's center, like that of the very different Karen Blixen, became the very act of writing. In that transference from life to paper the person who felt homeless could build an edifice.

Aage Dons

Aage Dons (1903–) shares the psychological approach and, like H. C. Branner, focuses on emotional lives that were thwarted in childhood. The analysis of the past of his protagonists is often given in a narrative close to that of a mystery, a choice of form that may reflect a growing reliance on Freud's theories. Dons's characters tend to be talented and doomed misfits who are very aware of their situation, and the final impression left by several of his works is that of a fatalism that cannot be overcome. Dons's first novel, *Koncerten* (1935; The Concert), contained that mood, but it was *Soldaterbrønden* (1936; The Soldier's Well) that revealed his talent for depicting the fate of the outsider who refuses to be part of a trivial life: a woman, whose life has turned empty, commits a crime of passion but lives to feel regret and desperation. That sense of past guilt tends to torment Dons's protagonists and may become their undoing or exile them from ordinary life. Dons sends his martyred protagonists out into a world of psychological and actual exile by locating the plot in exotic settings—for example, Tangiers, in the suspenseful *Haand i Haand med en Fremmed* (1968; Holding Hands with a Stranger)—and may at times remind readers of Paul Bowles.

Dons is a skillful writer who sometimes seems so smooth that he appears superficial. That judgment is, however, unfair, for the artfully constructed surface, glittering with impressionistic dialogue and clever plot twists, masks a searching mind that, like Aase Hansen's, does not seem to arrive at a destination. Maybe if Dons had allowed that surface to crack, to show what it concealed, his oeuvre would have achieved more.

THE INCLINATION TOWARD FANTASY

For some authors the realism of the decade may have felt like a tether, but it should be kept in mind that even during the 1920s literary experimentation, with some notable exceptions, had mainly been confined to poetry. That experimentation was continued by some poets in the next decade and, less obviously, by some writers of prose. Although no major break with past tradition was articulated, the highly conscious anachronism and distancing irony of Nis Petersen's novel *Sandalmagernes Gade* undermined the authority of realistic narration. Similarly, Karen Blixen's reliance on mythic patterns and Gothic elements questioned the belief in a reality that can be adequately rendered by realistic practice. Petersen, Blixen, and the women modernists had little in common, but they were all inclined and inspired to transcend realistic aesthetics, and it is noteworthy, in retrospect, to recall that Petersen and Blixen both immediately achieved success away from Denmark.

Nis Petersen

Nis Petersen (1897–1943), whose attempts to fit into the bourgeois world did not work, made a name for himself outside of Scandinavia with the panoramic, digressively composed historical novel *Sandalmagernes Gade* (1931; Eng. tr. *The Street of the Sandalmakers,* 1933). The location is ancient Rome during the time of Marcus Aurelius, an age of political and spiritual flux. A parallel to the Western postwar cultural climate is made quite obvious through references to modern phenomena such as weaponry or the media of the twentieth century. The novel is humorous, whimsical, cynical, subjective, and ultimately sad, as the humanist's hopes for the future seem foolish. Petersen's second novel, dealing with the Irish civil war of 1922, *Spildt Mælk* (1934; Eng. tr. *Spilt Milk*, 1935), is generally considered inferior to *Sandalmagernes Gade,* but its nihilism is tempered by Petersen's compassion for the innocent victims in a world that is decidedly not fair.

It was Petersen's lyrical production, however, that made him such a popular writer, even among many who normally would not deign to read poetry. His appeal was similar to that of Robert Service or Rudyard Kipling. He shares with Service not only pathos but also sentimentality, and unfortunately some of Petersen's poems, such as the famous "Brændende Europa" (Europe Aflame) from the collection *En Drift Vers* (1933; A Drove of Verse), tend not to wear well, for they ring hollowly as oratory. The inspiration from Kipling is obvious in some of Petersen's "ballads," but Tom Kristensen, who translated the Englishman with amazing flair, had a better ear for Kipling's subtleties and nuances. Petersen's first collection of poetry from 1922, the ebulliently youthful *For Tromme og Kastagnet* (For Drum and Castanet), was not published until 1951, and his official debut as a poet was made with *Nattens Pibere* (1926; Eng. tr. *Whistlers in the Night,* 1983). With that collection, as well as the following three, Petersen took his place as one of those crisis-ridden loners who saw apocalyptic signs in the times but could not feel at home with any outlook. In humor, in lovingly idyllic scenes, and in the celebration of the heroic deed—often by unassuming figures—Petersen found respite from the anguish that seemed to haunt him until his early death. There seems to be something incomplete about the oeuvre, for playacting—assuming and posing in roles—tends to replace the existential engagement that some early texts richly promised.

Beginning Modernism
The desperation that can be felt in some of Petersen's best texts also burns in the poetry of the three most prominent women lyricists of the decade. It may be facile to lump them together, but the parallel that exists with the situation of the 1880s and 1890s is so striking that one must take note of it. Adda Ravnkilde's, Victoria Benedictsson's, and Amalie Skram's desperate texts testified to unresolved dilemmas, and the writings of Hulda Lütken, Bodil Bech, and Tove Meyer suggest that the male voices of the age were not able to render women's experiences. Thus, these poets ventured out on a

modernistic path, the former two partly guided by the example of the Fenno-Swedish poet Edith Södergran.

Hulda Lütken (1896–1946) was influenced by both surrealism and expressionism, and her poems can be seen as an exploration into the unconscious. Her passionate, tangled, complex poems tend to veer toward an ecstatic, if tragic, experience of Eros-Thanatos, as, for example, in the collection *Elskovs Rose* (1934; Love's Rose). That living within of a private world was shattered by the outbreak of the war, which in *Skærsilden* (1945; Purgatory) made her see inner destructive forces as the cause of the global catastrophe. After her debut as a poet in 1927 she also wrote several novels; the most daring, if least accessible, is *Mennesket paa Lerfødder* (1943; On Feet of Clay), a highly personal, relentless analysis of a person split between various impulses—the spiritual being is lost in the gaudy material world—which concludes in a visionary, Christian scene of crucifixion. It seems that the homeless, desperate, and anguished soul must strive for a sense of ending to give its existence a semblance of purpose.

The early poetry of Bodil Bech (1889–1942) is often compared to that of Schade, for erotic themes, sensual longing, and humor prevail, as in her first collection *Vi, der ejer Natten* (1934; We Who Own the Night). Impressions received from Edith Södergran, however, gave Bech's later poetry a metaphoric richness and a metaphysical coloring that are very distant from the early sensuousness, but the ecstasy remains. The image from Södergran of the bride who awaits her liberator takes on Christian hues of longing for the heavenly groom. The exploration of the unconscious, as in *Ud af Himmelporte* (1941; Out from Heavenly Portals), once again had to find objective correlatives in the myths of salvation.

Tove Meyer (1913–72) showed from the very beginning, in *Guds Palet* (1935; God's Palette), a metaphysical inclination and gave voice to the soul whose longing cannot be satisfied. Like Lütken, she focuses on the dark side of the mind. But even if her diagnosis does not lead to the same passionate diction as in Lütken and Bech, Meyer's later works make it clear that life's many tensions are not resolved.

These three women writers, together with Gustaf Munch-Petersen, indicate the future artistic paths to be taken, and the women's choice of form—breaking with the norm—suggests strongly that the literary conventions of the male establishment were insufficient for the depiction of their experience of life and their vision of what life should be.

Karen Blixen

Karen Blixen, née Dinesen (1885–1962; pseudonym Isak Dinesen), published her earliest literary efforts in Danish periodicals under the name "Osceola." The choice of an Indian pseudonym was, in part, homage to her father, Wilhelm Dinesen (1845–1895), who had published under the Indian name Boganis. However, the adoption of literary masks also came to play an important role in her later writing. The Gothic delight in the supernatural, insanity, and the dangerous powers of nature is evident in both "Eneboerne" (1907; The Hermits) and "Pløjeren" (1907; The Ploughman), where the young Blixen had not yet found her tone of tempering irony. In "Eneboerne" a neglected young wife living with her intellectual husband on a desert island finds companionship with the ghosts on the island and is inexorably drawn toward death to the accompaniment of a violently raging storm. In "Pløjeren" an innocent young woman is able to lift the curse from a mysterious man she meets at night by the gallows. More playful and less melodramatic than these other early tales is "Familien de Cats" (1909; The de Cats Family), written more in the style of the mature Blixen with its ironic treatment of bourgeois manners. It is the fate of the de Cats family that every generation produces a black sheep, who gathers within himself all the family's vices, so that the other members of the generation may live piously and prosperously. When one black sheep decides to reform, he sends the family into a crisis, which is resolved by paying him to continue his dissolute ways.

Sandhedens Hævn (1926; Eng. tr. *The Revenge of Truth,* 1971) is a "marionette comedy" with elements from the commedia dell'arte tradition. The play is peppered with anachronisms, and the unruly characters sometimes stop to criticize how their roles have been written. The theme of the marionette as an entity whose actions are in the hands of a higher power is a central feature of Blixen's later writing. God is both puppetmaster and author, and human beings are his marionettes and characters in his tales, who enact their roles either competently or clumsily. Fiction becomes a metaphor for life; life is a grand artistic creation.

Blixen is one of those rare figures in world literature who are able to write masterfully in a language not their native tongue. After the failure of her coffee farm in Kenya, where she had lived for eighteen years, Blixen made her world literary debut in English with *Seven Gothic Tales* (1934). The Danish version—translation is hardly the appropriate term—*Syv fantastiske Fortællinger,* appeared a year later in 1935. Against the gray background of world economic depression Blixen produced an exotic collection of tales combining settings and moods from the English Gothic, the narrative irony of Søren Kierkegaard, and the German romantics, as well as the inventiveness of *The Arabian Nights'* Scheherezade. Blixen's tales explore the vicissitudes of an aesthetic, aristocratic approach to existence, as well as the quirks of fate generated in a world designed by an artistic deity who loves a good joke. The name Isak in Blixen's pseudonym means, after all, "laughter."

In "Syndfloden over Norderney" (The Deluge at Norderney) the heroic Cardinal Hamilcar von Sehested, the slightly mad Malin Nat-og-Dag, the melancholy Jonathan Mærsk, and the silent Calypso are perched in the loft of a barn that threatens to collapse into the rising waters of a great flood. Like the noble narrators of Boccaccio's *Decamerone* (1348–53) and Scheherezade herself, the inmates of the loft tell tales as a source of diversion and a means of warding off impending death. The end of a narration brings closure and death; therefore, one must keep the tales flowing. These odd individuals tell stories about themselves which function as tools for answering the question, Who are you? In the end, the cardinal reveals himself to be an actor, Kasparsen, who has murdered the real cardinal in order to adopt, literally, his life's ultimate role. Kasparsen has played his role so well that he accepts death to remain true to his character. Truth is secondary to style and fidelity to the ideas of the divine author of existence.

The theme of the existential masquerade is pursued even further in "Drømmerne" (The Dreamers), where it becomes a means of dealing with crisis. In a complicated narrative of tales within tales the destiny of Pellegrina Leoni unfolds. When the life of Pellegrina, a famous opera singer, is laid waste by the loss of her voice in a fire, she vows never to invest as much passion in a single existence again. She assumes various identities until her new role loses her interest or discovery threatens. The dreamer of the title is an individual who allows himself or herself to be swept along in life by the Imagination of the Universe, that is to say, Blixen's artistic deity. "Dreaming is the well-mannered people's way of committing suicide," since one has ceased insisting on one's own identity and one's personal demands on life. The dreamer possesses an ironic distance to his or her own actions and fate, since both are dictated by the dream itself.

Out of Africa (1937; *Den aftikanske Farm*, 1937) is a stylized account of Blixen's life on her coffee farm in Kenya from 1914 to 1932 which opens with a note of loss: "I had a farm in Africa, at the foot of the Ngong Hills." The novel describes a gradual fall from paradise. The narrator observes that whenever necessity enters into a dream, it becomes a nightmare. Necessity is introduced into the paradise of the farm by a shooting accident, the repercussions of which Blixen is unable to deal with by herself. From this point on, conditions on the farm deteriorate until Blixen is forced to leave for economic reasons.

The fall from paradise constitutes the narrative thread that holds the work together; however, the weight of the novel lies in Blixen's lyrical and affectionate descriptions of Africa and the people she knew there. The narrator crafts a mosaic of the denizens of the country: the natives, the immigrants, and the animals. Blixen marvels at the culinary genius of the peculiar little Kamante, the dignity of Farah, the majesty of the Masai, and the feminine mystique of the Somali women. In recent years, however, her work has been criticized for its romanticization of colonial Africa.

Art is a metaphor in Blixen's tales. After the loss of her farm in Kenya, Blixen set about transforming her life into a work of art. She loved to claim that she was a witch who had sold her soul to the devil for the ability to spin life into tales or that she was three thousand years old and had dined with Socrates. Blixen's exotic biography has proved to be of compelling interest. The immensely popular film about her life from 1985, which took its title from her book *Out of Africa*, was based less on this work than on the myth of Blixen, which she herself helped to foster. As further fuel for the burning interest in Blixen's life, a collection of her letters from Africa was published in 1978 (Eng. tr. *Letters from Africa: 1914–31*, 1981). In the tale "Det andet Møde" (Second Meeting) from *Efterladte Fortællinger* (1975; Eng. tr. *Carnival: Entertainments and Posthumous Tales*, 1977) a man tells Lord Byron that in a hundred years his works will scarcely be read, but his biography will be reproduced in new editions every year. Blixen may well prove to be kin to Byron in this respect.

SATIRICAL REALISM

Mogens Klitgaard

Mogens Klitgaard (1906–45) was an autodidact who as a hobo saw a good deal of Europe and whose account of the life of the drifter applauds young people who break out of the bourgeois harness. His main focus is that of life in the city, a life that he records with his generation's sense of its drabness for the victims of the depression era. To a much higher degree than most of his compatriots Klitgaard retains his fascination with the passing seasons—the flowering bushes of May and the ripe apples of August, as well as the way in which light is reflected on human faces on a main thoroughfare in Copenhagen in late April. Such evocative passages of sharp, minute, yet lyrical observation and sheer delight in the world can rarely be found with the same playful intensity in the work of his contemporaries.

Klitgaard made his debut with a surehanded depiction of a sadly typical fate during the 1930s. *Der sidder en Mand i en Sporvogn* (1937; A Man Sitting in a Streetcar) refers to a sadsack former store owner. The economic decline has forced him to become a collector of debts, a poorly paid, depressing job that leads to minor, secret debauchery and thus to debts and to manic attempts, bitterly funny and pitiful, to cover those debts by accruing new and more taxing ones. The protagonist sinks slowly and surely socially and economically, and he knows it quite well, even in his euphoric moments. Although Klitgaard does not take the reader as close to his major characters as did some of his contemporaries, his gallery of losers or semilosers often seems more poignantly etched. The artistic means to create distance and proximity are used very effectively.

There is in Klitgaard much sympathy for the man without much format, the bit player on life's stage, one who would never dream of occupying center stage, but such a person does not have much chance of living a fulfilling life. The economically dire times were partly to be blamed for that failure, but Klitgaard insists—so often that the insistence seems vehement—that bourgeois upbringing stifles the human being's sense of self-worth and ability to be daring, and thus such a person becomes an evasive, petty self-deceiver who quite regularly has to admit that he is exactly that. Those qualities or lack of them in the protagonist in *Der sidder en Mand i en Sporvogn* imbues that sorrowful character with a quiet pathos.

The narrator-protagonist of *Gud mildner Luften for de klippede Faar* (1938; God Tempers the Wind for the Shorn Lamb), supposedly a quite autobiographical novel, admits readily that he is a shifty, manipulative failure as he tells of his past life, and just as readily, he blames his strict bourgeois home not only for his less than admirable character traits, but also for his failure as a rebel. He has become a drifter, a liar, a beggar, a smuggler, and whatever else has seemed convenient, to be able to lead a life in freedom, which, ideally, has meant lying in a field and looking at the fleeting clouds. This ideal that sloughs off any demands or duties—as well as other human beings—is, as he experiences again and again, impossible to realize, for his upbringing forces him to take on work, to be enterprising, and eventually to rebel against the bourgeois norm and throw whatever he has gained overboard. The narrator admits very honestly that he is a failure, but he has absolutely no intention of regretting the path he took or of mending his ways, for his life, even if at a dead end, is to be preferred to petty-bourgeois ways. As a rebellion, if it can be called that, the narrator's stance is completely individualistic. The novel in its casualness may seem slight, but it is not, and it would be difficult to pinpoint a more competent and seemingly effortless narration elsewhere within the 1930s.

As war loomed threateningly and then became a reality, some authors, including Klitgaard, turned to the historical novel, which was a handy instrument for commenting on current times in the guise of portraying the past. Neither *De røde Fjer* (1940; The Red Feathers) nor *Ballade paa Nytorv* (1940; Trouble at Newmarket) may have the philosophical weight of Martin A. Hansen's historical novels from the 1940s, but they share a spicy wit and delve with verve into the Danish past. In *De røde Fjer* a meek tutor, who has been cowed by his upbringing, finally learns to stand up for his beliefs; thus, the novel could be read as a call for resistance against the powers of occupation. *Ballade paa Nytorv* is an erotic comedy—with some skewed similarity to Jørgen-Frantz Jacobsen's novel from the Faroe Islands, *Barbara*—that records mischievously how the lusty and promiscuous wife of the warden of the Copenhagen jail brings about the ruin of a righteous minister.

Some of Danish literature's major works have been commissioned by the Danish State Radio, such as Martin A. Hansen's *Løgneren* and Klitgaard's *Elly Petersen* (1941). The latter tells a story that could barely be more typical of its times: a young girl from the country comes to the big city, where she becomes a maid in various homes. Elly goes through some very credible experiences and crises, but when she leaves Copenhagen, she is wiser but not disillusioned. It seems that Klitgaard's perspective was widening as he no longer obsessively focused on failures.

Klitgaard tended to mix close portraiture with sweeping, authoritative views offered by the omniscient author, but in the last, very accomplished, work that he completed, *Den guddommelige Hverdag* (1942; The Divine Everyday), he changed and used a narrative technique resembling that of the modernist John Dos Passos, one previously used by Jens Gielstrup. The book seems to consist of unrelated sketches or short stories without closure, tied together by actual quotations from newspapers of the time. Those "clippings" relate, in the factual manner of the press, the horrors of the day—grand or seemingly trivial—the effects of war, or the plight of working women. Gradually, the seemingly unrelated texts of the book merge and, both artlessly and artfully, form a narrative approaching that of a novel without ever offering full information or the endings that readers of the genre expected. The answer to the question, What happened next? must be furnished by each reader. Whether or how the sensual Agnete will manage the abortion that is imminent, or whether Jørgensen, a shopkeeper being put out of business by a conglomerate, will succeed in rallying his former customers—both remain to be seen. Klitgaard's last book is a well-executed experiment in form: it records the ordinary lives and tragedies of people who merely wish to experience their share of life in a decent manner and whose unstated desire to do so is thwarted. These mosaic or patchwork pieces, in their tantalizing suggestiveness, startlingly remind readers of Peter Seeberg's precise short prose pieces. They refuse to pinpoint the blame for misery in simplistic ways.

Klitgaard is a rare writer; he tends to be applauded and yet neglected. Maybe that is because he does not fit nicely into critical categories. In that, of course, lies much of his appeal.

Leck Fischer

Leck Fischer (1904–56), who made his debut as a poet and who wrote some well-tailored realistic plays, is deservedly best-known as a novelist. Like Klitgaard, he focuses on the economic crisis's victimization of the common people, but his touch is heavier. Like Branner's later *Legetøj*, the collective novel *Kontormennesker* (1933; Office People) depicts the poisonous atmosphere of the hierarchical miniuniverse of the white-collar section of an industrial firm. In *Det maa gerne blive Mandag* (1934; Let Monday Come) the cruel effects of unemployment on a working-class family are shown vividly, but the novel ends on a hopeful note. Fischer also tried his hand at the historical novel, leading up to contemporary times and dealing with crucial moments in Danish history from 1899 to the German occupation; the concluding volume was entitled *Dette latterlige land* (1950; This Ridiculous Country). That grand plan, comparable to Becker's series on Kai Gøtsche, lacks the immediacy and social engagement of the early novels.

Hans Scherfig

Hans Scherfig (1905–79), through his irrefutable satiric talent, has reached many readers with his merciless reports on the bourgeoisie. He came from such circles himself but broke away to pursue an artistic career, and he eventually shared Otto Gelsted's and Hans Kirk's political convictions.

Scherfig writes a bit drily—he comments with intentional pedantry from his omniscient, quite snide vantage point—on the folly of his society and his characters. He knows exactly what ails them, and that knowledge, without much change, inspired Scherfig throughout his career. But his sarcasm and heavy irony often seem to be accompanied by a Swiftian and, to cut to the future, Hellerian (Joseph Heller of *Catch-22*, [1961]) glee in his observations of ghoulish and stupid human behavior. Scherfig and Kirk may have shared the same political outlook, but their temperaments are far apart.

Scherfig's narratives are indebted to popular literature, especially to the detective novel; more often than not a crime is committed, and the plot is the unraveling of it. No dapper detective is present, however, and when the criminal is revealed, if that occurs, there is no grand hope offered for a better future. In fact, the solution hardly matters, for what is of consequence are the steps taken by the author toward the solution. In them the less-than-discreet moral flaws of the bourgeoisie stand exposed as the real criminals.

Scherfig's debut, *Den døde Mand* (1937; The Dead Man), had already staked out that path.

Most prominent among Scherfig's novels are *Den forsvundne Fuldmægtig* (1938; Eng. tr. *The Missing Bureaucrat*, 1989) and *Det forsømte Foraar* (1940; Eng. tr. *Stolen Spring*, 1986). The former depicts a conscientious, pedantic civil servant's attempt to escape to a free life—away from office and wife— by pretending to have committed suicide. He is so set in his ways, however, that his newly gained freedom is in vain (a theme that Klitgaard would have recognized), and he returns to society. By pretending to have murdered the man who really committed suicide (and with whom he switched roles), he manages to escape completely from freedom and ends up enjoying the neat routines of prison. Jonathan Swift and the elderly Mark Twain would have approved of that bleakly humorous ending.

Det forsømte Foraar captures beautifully and utterly convincingly the feelings of all students who have felt that life passed them by as they were cramming for a subject in which they had no interest and which seemed to have no relevance to their future lives. Some potentially gifted high-school boys are squeezed through the Danish educational system—one that N. F. S. Grundtvig's liberal spirit has scarcely seemed to affect—and gradually lose their spontaneity, integrity, and curiosity. They end up as sad mirror images of the generations before them that went through the same saddening and maddening process. They become, sneers Scherfig, like their sadistic and warped teachers. In the following novels Scherfig kept some of the vivid characters from those two books around and managed, in some cases, to show how the mind, thwarted by a ghastly educational system, reflecting a sick and exploitative society, could easily accept nazism and fascism. In such works as *Idealister* (1945; Eng. tr. *The Idealists*, 1949, 1991), *Skorpionen* (1953; The Scorpion), and *Frydenholm* (1962) Scherfig unleashes his anger at and contempt of the corruption and callousness of the Danish legal system, during and after the German occupation. *Frydenholm*, a stinging roman à clef, is an indictment of official Denmark during the occupation as Scherfig relentlessly depicts the many ways in which various Danish institutions collaborated with the Nazis.

Scherfig was an angry rationalist with a scathing wit, one that was meant to hurt and did so. The problem with his works is that unlike Gustav Wied's—which they resemble—they seem cold, in the sense that the sympathetic characters are in a distinct minority and that all his characters are highly stylized and lacking in nuances. Scherfig may well be wishing and striving for a fair world, one freed of bourgeois shackles, but it is difficult to overlook the misanthropic tone in his admirable satires. That judgment should be tempered by the knowledge that writing was only one of Scherfig's careers and that his humor may have seemed much warmer and more fabulatory in his paintings. It may be telling of Scherfig's intentions that he drew and retold Holberg's satirical science-fiction novel *Niels Klims Reise Under Jorden* as a comic strip in the Danish communist newspaper *Land og Folk* (Country and People). Holberg could also seem misanthropic, but as was the case with the social critic Scherfig, his exposure of fools and folly was meant to bring his readers to their senses.

BEYOND THE SOCIAL PERSPECTIVE

Two writers whose stature was not to be recognized until the years of the occupation made them find new themes and ways of expressing their experiences were H. C. Branner and Martin A. Hansen. Both started out as social realists. In the works of both, as well as in those of Jens Gielstrup, an underlying theme of the need for a more fulfilling existence can be detected—as it can in the poetry of Tove Meyer and Bodil Bech—a need that could not be eased substantially by social or political engagement or a psychological probing into the mind.

That yearning for transcendence of the social perspective of the age was addressed by Vilhelm Grønbech (1873–1948), professor of history of religion at the University of Copenhagen. In *Kampen om Mennesket* (1930; The Struggle for the Human Being) he stressed the possibility that human spiritual needs could become creative impulses; they should exist not in individualistic isolation, but communally. In his voluminous oeuvre Grønbech emerges as a sweeping critic of Western culture for both its inwardness and its materialism, and he calls for new sustaining myths that will give humanity a sense of communal values. In that sense he resembles the poet and clergyman N. F. S. Grundtvig, whom he admired, and (as Martin A. Hansen has asserted) Søren Kierkegaard, whom he disliked for his excessive individualism. Moreover (as P. M. Mitchell has pointed out), Grønbech could recognize the strength of Marx's call for solidarity. Grønbech is an inspiring writer. He had more than a touch of a poet, and if he never constructed a philosophical system, he brilliantly summed up the past in grand syntheses that seemed to promise a wholeness missing in the sober 1930s. Thus, that fighting humanist caught the imagination of several of the young writers who no longer could compose in the ways of the 1930s, notably Martin A. Hansen and the poets who gathered around the journal *Heretica* in the late 1940s.

Hans Christian Branner

The origin of H. C. Branner (1903–66) in academia is reflected in an oeuvre that is intellectual, skeptical, and deeply involved with the humanist cause. He wrote some short stories and radio plays in the early 1930s, but he did not attract attention until he published the collective novel *Legetøj* (1936; Toys), which renders the hierarchical daily life in a small toy factory, a life that turns distinctly unpleasant as a new manager comes into power and sets colleague against colleague. That destruction of well-being and solidarity can easily be seen, allegorically, as a parallel to developments in Nazi Germany: the new management wants conformity and no criticism.

If *Legetøj* seems very tied to the age, it should nevertheless be given credit for inaugurating its author's painstaking search for the psychological causes of his characters' deep-seated problems. The Norwegian Sigurd Hoel and the Dane Branner shared some territory in that area, for both were staunch humanists who early on saw the Nazi menace and who fought it, but who also grasped the fact that the mean spirit of fascism or nazism was a general mindset that might thrive well in the Nordic countries. Both authors—and that comparison can be extended to another Norwegian, Johan Borgen, as well—were, however, mainly intent on exploring the whys and hows of the psyche of the person attracted to the totalitarian temptation.

A more pronounced psychological interest surfaced in Branner's next novel, *Barnet leger ved Stranden* (1937; The Child Is Playing by the Beach), in which a first-person narrator relates his miserable childhood, his failed marriage, and his child's death, all caused by his own shortcomings as a parent. The narrator seems self-destructive, but the existentialist sense of responsibility that tends to dominate Branner's fictional universe does not permit self-destruction, and in this modern type of the bildungsroman, new hope is gained at the close of the text.

The same hope is voiced toward the conclusion of *Drømmen om en Kvinde* (1941; The Dream of a Woman). Five minds reveal, through inner monologues, their fears as they are engaged in or observe a game of bridge. Their attitudes, quite clearly discernible, once again suggest Branner's allegorical bent. Nevertheless, the novel, with its stream-of-consciousness passages, plotlessness, and Freudian imagery, shows that Branner widened his perspective from his early works and, as the title suggests, tended to idealize woman as the savior of the male.

If Branner's early novels seem to fade, his short stories do not. Such collections as *Om lidt er vi borte* (1939; Soon We Are Gone) and *To Minutters Stilhed* (1944; Eng. tr. *Two Minutes of Silence,* 1966, which includes translations from other collections) in particular are striking in their sensitive portraits of children's tangled inner lives, which mature people often fail to grasp or consider. Branner tends to focus on that hidden territory of the mind, on those wounds and angers that may thwart the human being later in life. Even if Branner suggests rather than analyzes, some of these stories seem like a call for an undogmatic, commonsensical Freudian to intervene, but in others Branner's customary seriousness is abandoned for a nostalgic and humorous approach. Branner is here, as well as in his postwar works, the existential humanist who admonishes the human being to live up to his or her responsibility, but who at the same time sheds doubt on humanism's ability to make life more purposeful.

Martin A. Hansen

Martin A. Hansen (1909–1955), a son of smallholders, grew up in an old-fashioned, rural setting on Zealand that remained, the rest of his life, a yard-stick: the ethos of that rural culture, one that Hansen felt was lacking in modern civilization, became the underlying inspiration in his oeuvre. Hansen, like Branner, may be called a humanist, in the sense that in an age tending to doubt and degrade values, he, too, maintained that the human being must retain an attitude of responsibility for neighbor as well as for nation. Hansen's Kierkegaardian Christianity and inherited nationalism endowed him with a heavy existential burden. It was a burden that he never managed to cast off or lessen, although the wry humor in some of his earlier works suggests some kinship with Cervantes and folklore.

Hansen's two first novels, *Nu opgiver han* (1935; Now He Gives Up) and *Kolonien* (1937; The Colony), are an attempt to realize a Marxist quest: to create a collective farming venture. The characters aim for a new world, re-structured and just; they fail, but that decline, recorded in the second volume, indicts not the cause but rather the people, who were not sufficiently prepared to carry out the Marxist promise. That is, at least, how one of Hansen's sages, Jacob, judges the failure of the "colony." Hansen did not experiment any further with the Marxist solution, and in the postwar era he emerged as one of the great Christian humanists of Danish literature.

Jens Gielstrup

Jens Gielstrup (1917–43) lived to complete two novels only; the warnings of war that echo in his narratives came to fruition, and Gielstrup, who had enlisted in the British air force, was killed in action. His startlingly promising debut, *Kys til højre og venstre* (1939; Kisses to Right and Left) belongs in the tradition of Knud Sønderby's works, which center on the erotic and existential problems of the young. The dreary side streets and the economic misery are there but are nearly reduced to background for the erotic adventures and misadventures of young people, the best of whom are engaged in a semiconscious search for meaning, thus foreshadowing the intensity and desperation in Morten Nielsen's poetry. The book is written in an effective, peculiar mix of the sensitive and the hard-boiled style and is thus somewhat reminiscent of Sigurd Hoel's early novels and F. Scott Fitzgerald's stylish sadness. Much as in Klitgaard's works, many fates are intertwined, and each chapter is tied together by vignettes of other fates made bitter by the inevitable force of sexuality. The undeniable influence of Hemingway is felt even more strongly in *Det gode Hjerte* (1939; The Good Heart), which in a low-key manner reports on the effects on some young people of the outbreak of the war.

Tove Ditlevsen

Tove Ditlevsen (1917–76) knew from her youthful years in a gloomy part of Copenhagen how discouraging and somber life could be in the working class, and she repeatedly returned to that milieu to render the loneliness and disappointment of the child. For her the written and published word became a ticket away from that misery, to what eventually was to become other forms of it. Like many other young women of that generation, she published her first poems in the magazine *Vild Hvede* (Wild Wheat), but her actual debut occurred with *Pigesind* (1939; A Girl's Mind), which earned her a wide audience, one that she seemed to retain even though her works turned much darker. Her poetry is straightforward, traditional, stanzaic, and rhymed, but it does not take the reader into fictional worlds of modernistic complexity or ambiguity, as did the works of the women poets of the 1930s.

Even in Ditlevsen's first collections of poetry a melancholy sense of loss dominates, one that is never quite overcome, for the voice speaking seems fearfully estranged, and that estrangement is most frequently experienced in what should be love but becomes loss. The variety of moods clustered about that experience was captured in detail. In a sense her poetry and young Jens Gielstrup's detailed charting of the pain of sexuality can be recorded as two voices on the brink of World War II which expressed for both sexes the torments caused by the erotic.

Both Gielstrup and Ditlevsen poignantly captured the somber Copenhagen of the age, but the reader cannot help feeling that matters of the mind have gained a higher priority than they did earlier in the decade and thus that these authors foreshadowed the introversion that was to come. The 1930s were receding into memory and, because of the turbulent history of the 1940s, were quickly becoming a distant age.

Danish Literature, 1940–1990

Poul Houe

7

THE 1940S: WAR AND POSTWAR—
LATE SYMBOLISM AND EXISTENTIALIST HUMANISM

In the spring of 1940 the European political storm arrived in Denmark. It had been brewing throughout the 1930s and broke internationally with the declaration of World War II in September 1939. On April 9, 1940, German troops transgressed the Danish borders and occupied the country until the end of the war in Europe in May 1945.

The first years of German occupation were relatively normal and peaceful, considering the circumstances; but during the later years, in particular after the pursuit of Danish Jews, the resignation of the Danish government in 1943, and the spontaneous general strike in 1944, both national resistance and the German policy of retribution were dramatically intensified. Although earlier anti-German sentiments in defiance or escapism could be worked off in furtive entertainment, or undisguised zoot suits, jazz bands, and ballrooms, conditions eventually deteriorated to the extent that many writers and cultural personalities were forced to go underground. And from having accommodated German censorship—or practiced preventive self-censorship—increasing numbers of journalists and authors were published anonymously or illegally.

A case in point is the so-called occupation literature, which was directly in the service of the Resistance and originally a resourceful gift of tongues. The clandestine anthology *Der brænder en Ild* (1944; A Fire Is Burning) became a landmark for spiritual resistance: a whole array of Danish authors spoke their minds under its cover, whether in the form of ephemeral propa-

---

Secondary sources cited in this chapter are listed in "References" at the end of the chapter.

ganda or of less perishable poetry. Contributors included distinguished writers of drama and prose such as Kjeld Abell, H. C. Branner, and Martin A. Hansen, and some younger lyrical poets such as Tove Ditlevsen, Halfdan Rasmussen, Poul Sørensen, Piet Hein, Ole Sarvig, and Morten Nielsen. Most of the poets already shared in the community spirit that characterized so many literary circles and periodicals during the occupation, and most of them continued their literary activities on an individual basis after the liberation.

One exception is Morten Nielsen (1922–44), who stood his ground as a poet but fell victim to an accidental shot. His life and work are inextricably associated with the Resistance, and the only volume of poetry that time permitted him to publish is entitled *Krigere uden Vaaben* (1943; Warriors without Weapons). It shows in flashes how the young man's intense desire for life is inseparable from his disillusioned and defenseless awareness of death. Similar experiences are recorded in works by other writers who died young, as shown in the novel *Syv Aar for Lea* (1944; Seven Years for Lea) by Sonja Hauberg (1918–47) and in the posthumous letters of the freedom fighter Kim Malthe-Bruun (1923–45).

With complete disregard of danger the poet and clergyman Kaj Munk spoke out against the Germans until they executed him in 1944. In a variety of historical novels by Martin A. Hansen and others the ordeals of the occupation are suggested in representative parallels to previous instances of foreign rule. Under the sarcastic title *En Gæst* (1941; A Visitor) the playwright Soya penned a different kind of allegorical narrative on the basis of anti-German sentiments, and even late symbolistic lyrical poetry made for ill-concealed innuendos concerning the evil and frozen climate of the war. Ole Sarvig's "Drømmekerne" (Seed of Dreams) from the collection *Grønne Digte* (1943; Green Poems) reads:

Light seed
in your cloak of chaffs

Saint *Georg*
in your armor,

resounding hard
full of frost
was your helmet
and your coat,

then came summer
with its green tree!

The poem clearly incorporates the gruesome wartime conditions in an atmosphere of utmost benignity with its faith in growth, redemption, and liberation. This symbolic course of events marks several wartime works by Danish authors, even those by the humanistic realists of the 1930s. Martin A. Hansen deals a blow to modern evil in *Jonatans Rejse* (Jonatan's Journey)from 1941, and H. C. Branner confronts the universal theme of life versus death in his novel from the same year, *Drømmen om en Kvinde* (The Dream of a Woman). Under the impression of war and brutality these writers turned their rational humanism in the direction of an irrational existentialism.

Like many others, they had already experienced a shift of their priorities by the end of the 1930s. A predominant interest in the everyday problems of the lower middle class had gradually yielded to more abstract, universal concerns, and with the intrusion of wartime reality this displacement of intellectual accent came to tangible fruition. Notwithstanding a certain realistic continuity across the 1940s, the typical innovation of the period was focused on a spiritual crisis spanning the depths of human commonality and fellowship to the heights of metaphysics. Writers in the vanguard attempted to reconcile the inevitable physical and mental confinements of the war with renewed expansions of their cultural horizon. The French writers Jean-Paul Sartre and Albert Camus became the portal figures as Danish authors looked beyond the war into the postwar community of European culture.

German capitulation meant that the war was over. But only in a narrow sense, and not in literature. Instead of a new age, the remainder of the 1940s became a postwar period. Not until the end of the decade did the shadows of the war years disappear as rationing and other restrictions were lifted. In matters of law the judicial purge of occupation authorities and their Danish collaborators presented another lingering affair. By contrast there was a rapid dissolution of the national government; hardly was the common enemy defeated and the ecstasy of liberation over and done with before the petty party strifes of the 1930s reentered political life, somewhat intensified by growing East-West tensions on the international scene. In cultural terms the impression of a shady judicial process paralleled a sense of defaulting self-examination. The postliberation hangovers caused many intellectuals to lose their illusions about a new and better society.

When the consciousness of war almost inevitably became part of the postwar scenario, the principal reason was not that the war remained a compelling issue per se, as was the case in Hans Scherfig's polyphonic showdown with the inhuman bourgeois society in *Frydenholm*, his semidocumentary novel from 1962; rather, the reason was a combination of the actual aftermath of the war and a postwar climate that both allowed for and called for a painstaking digestion of war problematics. This atmosphere is evident in H. C. Branner's short story "Angst" (1947; Anguish), in which the trauma of war surrounds a new brand of humanism in its infancy, and in the anthology of poetry and prose with subjects from the war, *I Ti-Året efter* (1955; The Following Decade).

The immediate reason for the framework of this process to be labeled humanistic is the conspicuous absence of religious, fascist, communist, or any other fundamentalistic line of interpretation. Such postures may have been competing, but they were not competitive on the ideological stage of the 1940s. Some marginal adversity or antihumanism is discernible in certain areas of mass culture, as in Sven Hazel (1917–) and Morten Korch (1876–1954). However, the unconditional worship of authority that unfolds in Hazel's widely read and translated books about his experiences as a volunteer soldier on the German front in Russia belongs primarily to the 1950s and onward. And concerning Morten Korch, it is true that his countless popular novels and plays provide the foremost satisfaction of mass cultural demands and petty-bourgeois inclinations in the 1940s. Nevertheless, his surface romantic settings and peasants in nature portrayed with a slight religious touch merely give a patina to a trivial display of idyllic stereotypes; it is no surprise that as soon as a new generation of younger city dwellers had replaced the intended older, rural audiences, the books in question were readily available for profitable modernization for the film screen.

Only in postwar mass culture was there noticeable dissent from humanistic standards, and few of these exceptions to the rule were taken seriously in critical discourse at the time. By the same token, in the area of high literature humanism was the foundation of both critical debate and artistic performance. The fact that humanism incorporates serious misgivings and conflicts that to some extent dispute its very validity only underscores its overall bearing on the postwar period of literary history.

Kjeld Abell

Marked scruples already haunted the leading playwright of the period, Kjeld Abell (1901–61), whose prewar play *Anna Sophie Hedvig* (1939; Eng. tr. 1944) in its female protagonist personifies a "fighting humanism" in the progressive and antifascist spirit of the 1930s. When in 1946 Abell published his play *Silkeborg*, written underground during the last part of the war, this humanism has become problematic insofar as the prospect of a future without a common enemy tended to dissolve the combative spirit that formed humanism's backbone and the identity of its proponents. While the struggle against the external enemy (the Germans) and the internal conventions (in family life) appears quite straightforward in political and human terms, the future objectives in both respects seem far more intricate.

As proletarian preparedness gives way to the returning bourgeois society, the fighting humanism turns into a major problem. In Abell's next play, the drama of ideas *Dage paa en Sky* (1947; Days on a Cloud), the concrete struggle for liberation has been replaced by an abstract invocation of the idea of liberty. In the existentialistic manner of Sartre and the Norwegian writer Nordahl Grieg the author endeavors to combine his actual critique of humanism with the anticapitalism of his early years, while in the meantime seeking to avoid Marxist unambiguousness. The slightly hazardous formal inventions that distinguish the scenography of his play are precariously indicative of disorders in contemporary reality. The dramatic situation in which the individual is supposed to face his choices on a symbolic cloud between heaven and earth inadvertently testifies to a political situation mired in obscure choices.

A major objective in Abell's art is the bourgeois repugnance to acknowledge the indelicate means that respectable ends sometimes entail. A case in point is *Den blå Pekingeser* (1954; The Blue Pekingese), in which the bourgeois world is directly compared with antiquity's kingdom of the dead. In a formal sense the play is perhaps even bolder than its predecessor, and yet the author now succeeds in articulating bourgeois claustrophobia and desire for death as a reality that only the utmost zest for life—in fantasy or telepathy—can surmount. And fortunately, the outcome is not unequivocal. Humaneness must transgress the boundaries of the bourgeoisie in order not to perish; however, the transgression is an allegorical maneuver on a suspended level of consciousness, and it points to a concept of humanism that is much more spacious than Abell's private political philosophy and left-wing ideas of action.

Until the end of the 1950s, when inspiration from abroad finally catapulted Danish theater out of its postwar isolation, Kjeld Abell was the preeminent innovator of modern Danish drama. Major performances of foreign drama on Danish stages after the war—notably by Tennessee Williams, Sartre, and Jean Anouilh—had little impact on the domestic production of dramatic texts. Nevertheless, this production included counterparts to Abell's humanistic drama of ideas authored by H. C. Branner.

Hans Christian Branner
It was Danish radio that challenged Hans Christian Branner (1903–66) to become a playwright, and it was his work for radio that prepared this medium for its important role as an independent forum for Danish drama.

Branner's almost visual radio drama has an impact on his experimental narratives from this period but, interestingly enough, not on his works for the regular stage. As a traditional playwright he is quite—traditional: in form he is a student of Henrik Ibsen, in substance he is an advocate of humanistic faith in life and a sense of responsibility. In *Søskende* (1952; Siblings; Eng. tr. *The Judge,* 1955) there is ostensible strength behind the family revolt against the petrified father figure and superego, but it is undermined by the unmistakable weakness of the family members' faith and their gifts for self-determination in the future. These problems concerning humanism are the very themes in *Thermopylæ* (1958; Eng. tr. 1973) and later the television drama *Matador* (1965; Monopoly); in both plays the notion of humanism is ingrained in blind idealists who self-righteously desert the very same people and family members they allegedly wish—and claim—to serve.

Since promulgation of humanism posits an integral part of its problem, it is particularly problematic that Branner in these dramatic works refrains from transcending the world of promulgation and its naturalistic-symbolic language. The ideology of humanism is an impasse that Branner cannot escape without the guidance of prose experimentation. His novels, *Rytteren* (1949; Eng. tr. *The Riding Master,* 1951) and *Ingen kender Natten* (1955; Eng. tr. *No Man Knows the Night,* 1958), represent the first steps in that direction; the last and decisive steps are taken in a series of short stories written between the end of the war and the end of his own life.

In *Rytteren* the basic humanistic attitude rests on both Christian and psychoanalytical imagery. Like other trend-setting artists from the postwar period, Branner is skeptical toward ideologies and political matters and more inclined to consider human nature as the stage for the battle between good and evil. His utopia is a moral conception embracing goodness alongside an idea of freedom and an unconfessional philosophy of charity with Christ as its paragon of virtue. Ultimately, his vision is a mixture of Western individualism and Eastern community spirit on the basis of which political life in both East and West can be rejected.

The novel's religious-humanistic protagonist is the physician Clemens Weber. His personal religious development in Branner's view encapsulates the entire development of Western culture from Christianity to a form of humanism that will gradually incorporate cardinal Christian values. Clemens Weber's name discreetly suggests that this weaver of God's mercy and people's lives is a clown; and his feeling of inadequacy (as a doctor) does, in fact, stem from his divine ambitions (as a humanist). Moreover, his conspicuous lack of sensuality is related to this spiritual surplus. Clemens is all too human. His excessive weight conforms with his superego.

His girlfriend, Susanne, is his psychological opposite. She is a barren woman who lacks maternal feelings, and her bond to the id is a trauma that needs to be resolved with the assistance of the superego if she is to develop a personal identity (with a certain emphasis on the superego). The principal object of Susanne's (and others') subconscious desires is Hubert, the riding master; in Branner's psychological universe Hubert is destined to relate to his horse the same way the other characters relate to their subconscious.

Hubert is more—or less—than a symbol of desire for sexual freedom in other people, however; he further represents their emotions in a regressive, distorted form. Like Nietzsche's Man-God, he is from before the Fall, a demonic phase in Susanne's life that she must live through before she is ready to accept salvation from Clemens, the man of conscience. Her cure prescribes that she learn to take responsibility for Hubert's death; only thus may she rid herself of libidinous bonds and prove herself open to Clemens's Christian humanism and its notions of guilt, atonement, and responsibility for others. Hubert is the necessary evil, the devilry every true humanist must vanquish and exorcise. Consequently, Susanne's attempted suicide represents a way to salvation analogous with Christ's way to the Crucifixion.

Susanne and Clemens then meet like subconscious and superconscious in a total but frail formation of ego. Psychoanalytical determinism and Christian transcendentalism merge into an immanent existentialistic humanism. But the road to fully realized human nature has its pitfalls. It is not a matter of controversy that the author is intent on providing room for libido within his humanism, nor can it be disputed that his novel fails its objectives in that respect. In *Daguerreotypier* (1951; Eng. tr. *Daguerreotypes and Other Essays*, 1979) Karen Blixen noted maliciously that Susanne's encounter with Clemens's superego was at the expense of the lower part of her body, and obviously the Hubert myth disintegrates concurrently with an affirmation of Clemens's idealistic view of man: in the image of an abandoned child of man left behind in place of the myth. Decomposing one myth adds to the composition of another.

Humanism in *Rytteren* does not dissolve into art, but the evil of life dissolves into humanism in accordance with psychoanalytical formula. The same applies to evil as an external reality. Both nazism to the right (in the guise of Herman) and parlor communism to the left (in the shape of Michala) undergo individualization. The forces of action that stem from fear are unveiled and supplanted by a sense of change originating from love. Goodness and democracy prevail as a so-called third point of view, as they did for the bourgeoisie after World War II. Branner has unmasked the mental basis for nazism, which he felt had remained unchallenged before its violent takeover in the 1930s, and with his solution to this urgent problem his novel attained the status of a principal contribution to Danish cultural life in the postwar years. Even Karen Blixen in her sharp criticism of *Rytteren* admitted that "in a hundred years a weighty judgment may be passed on the intellectual life of our time in Denmark: 'It was in *The Riding Master* that this generation found release for its essential being'" (Dinesen 158).

Nevertheless, its position was never undisputed. Blixen's critique deals especially with the fact that the novel's pronounced concern with human conscience is a puritan affront to erotic fulfillment; and even though the curtailment is undertaken by a clown—seemingly at authorial distance—the reality of the matter still speaks of refined intellectual rape and manipulative humaneness on Branner's part. The purported Christian dualism is without alternatives, and the transformation of eroticism into Christian psychoanalysis further foregrounds psychoanalytical assumption of political power, within the auspices of the third point of view. An undialectical humanism of this nature is defenseless against interests and sentiments discordant with humaneness.

Ingen kender Natten shares *Rytteren*'s moral and existential problematics, and the way the later work's principal theme bifurcates into patterns of Christian and psychoanalytical allusions is also reminiscent of the precursor. Yet the artistic arrangement of the thematic agenda is more comprehensive in several respects. The actual plot is anchored in the war and the Resistance, but the novel is no less devoted to postwar conditions. Its pivotal point is the involvement of the intellectuals, and its location is the intersection between wartime demands for responsibility and cold war prerequisites of fear and anxiety.

While the soundboard of the novel is unadorned, like the frame of a void, the resounding effect of the characters' inner monologues and streams of consciousness is exuberant, unschematic, and symbolic. Thomas is the intellectual centerpiece of *Ingen kender Natten,* brought up on cynicism and well on his way to drowning in alcohol and social indifference when one evening his shady father-in-law collapses in his arms. The man is named Gabriel—a Christian name like the other characters'—and he has tried to play the whole gamut of ideological cards of his time to his own advantage, but to no avail. He is also, however, a messenger in the more surprising sense that he elicits feelings of tenderness in his son-in-law. When Thomas later falls in love with Martha Maria Magdalena, he is able to share these emotional qualities with her—the woman as protector, mother, and lover. Reborn as a human being by this exchange, he is finally prepared for a responsible and meaningful encounter with death side by side with the freedom fighter Simon.

This symbolic and sacrificial death presents a beautiful but also tragic end to the problems of reality and the substance of conflicts in *Ingen kender Natten*. It has to do with an escalating crisis in Branner's entire work. In short, the empirical psychology of the author's insight is exposed to severe philosophical and ideological pressures. On the surface his artistic productivity remains intact, thanks to stylistic and aesthetic agility, but fundamentally the artistic procedures inadvertently mark a departure from the production line of longer narratives and an approach to the artistic autonomy of shorter narrative forms. Branner's short stories after the volume *Vandring langs floden* (1956; Walking by the River) betray a growing undercurrent of modern mythical experiences. Insofar as texture is concerned, these texts are markedly open to wide European horizons, but thematically they shut themselves up and almost situate their visions of human destiny in modernistic or script-thematic self-sufficiency.

In H. C. Branner's last works humanism tends to coagulate into false idealism. But characteristic of the author's attempt to relieve or isolate humanity from its deplorable circumstances is that the attempt stultifies itself. His glib philosophical speech subsides into desperate art or provokes an aesthetic idiosyncrasy. Humanism as a philosophical construct has proven impossible. Truth is ambiguous, and humanism is altogether part of the ambiguity.

Martin A. Hansen

The crisis of humanism is both an important bridge and a divider between Branner and Martin A. Hansen (1909–55). It may with some justice be said, as one critic, Frederik Nielsen, has done, that they are the "two most skilled writers of prose" in the postwar period and that "together they conquer the world for culture. In a way they have written to each other in each their 'dialect'" (p. 40). At least the beautiful idealism of humankind's prospective community spirit is a dilemma they share: without engagement, ideals turn sour; with engagement, they become tainted by reality.

Both in Branner's *Rytteren* and in Hansen's contemporary novel *Løgneren* (1950; Eng. tr. *The Liar,* 1954) the human appears as a paradox linked biologically to an amoral nature, yet separated from nature by a knowledge of good and bad which is alien to nature. And both Hansen's "Eneren og Massen" (The Individual and the Mass) and Branner's "Humanismens Krise" (The Crisis of Humanism), published together in 1950, advocate faith in man in the most elaborate, semireligious terms. Hansen's salvation is tantamount to the salvation of humankind, and the rhetoric proclaims that a human being dies of his victories but is victorious when defeated. Marxism, Darwinism, and other ideologies are subject to suspicion while the authors share in the conviction that they themselves are above ideological constraints. This very self-deception has proven to be the ultimate foundation for the crisis of humanism.

Hansen had devoted his collective novels in the 1930s to the external struggle for societal changes. Under the impression of World War II he enters human psychology in order to expound the internal strife between good and evil. As opposed to the menacing defeatism and futile controversy about guilt and punishment in the early novels, his later works promote a responsible existentialism on Christian grounds. Eventually, his development meets with the spirit of self-sacrifice known from the Resistance, and in the final analysis this connection induces an important transformation from the sphere of absurdity to the purified forces of life.

In the course of the 1940s the meaninglessness of war offsets the postwar exuberance of meaning in Hansen's prose, and the concept of neighbor supersedes the representative of social class in his conception of humans. An old culture has waned, but in the light of this modern insight it becomes important to defend human beings against the inhuman rationalism of modernity. Divine simplicity is destined to substitute for reflected wisdom. The artistic task thus implies a moral obligation to bring about religious humanization of life. But the actual piece of art often declines to accommodate this message. In accordance with its own form of spirit or lawfulness, the poetic inspiration frequently incited Hansen to depart from his alleged intentions. Only later did he learn to shelter his indigenous sense of responsibility from artistic surprises; his method was to keep the creative process out of reach of his daring fiction.

The literary achievements of Martin A. Hansen—and the entire decade—range from the burlesque novel *Jonatans Rejse* (1941; Jonatan's Journey) to the radio novel *Løgneren*. Both were inspired by nineteenth-century writer Steen Steensen Blicher but were conceived in the context of World War II. The former, influenced also by Herman Melville's *Moby Dick* (1851), is involved directly and outwardly in the belligerent clash between good and evil. The latter, told in the manner of André Gide's novels *Les Nourritures terrestres* (1897; The Fruits of the Earth) and *Les Faux-monnayeurs* (1926; The Counterfeiters) and published as the last of Hansen's major works of fiction, is by far more inward and complicated, as could be expected in the meditative aftermath of a period of war. The comparison shows how the crisis of humanism spills over into an aggravated artistic crisis.

The title character in *Jonatans Rejse* is the blacksmith of the old fable who has bottled the devil and qualified himself to conquer the world. But contrary to the narrative's modern hero, with the folktale name Askelad, both the smith and the king to whom he offers his diabolical powers are responsible and considerate characters. Both represent the uncorrupted old ways, and both are portrayed in contradistinction to Askelad, who has the future ahead of him because he has no history, and to the irresponsible intellectuals who are unable to agree on the nature of evil but are perfectly able to let evil loose in the course of their quarrels.

Throughout his life Hansen's ideas of tradition were in favor of the old culture of peasantry and Christianity but did not dispute the demise of this culture. His sympathy for traditionalists like the regional writer Thorkild Gravlund (1879–1939) was never unconditional. While they faced backward, Hansen saw tradition as a promise for the future, and although the basic values in *Jonatans Rejse* are outdated and modernity comes out of its struggle victorious, the novel is not nostalgic. The old authorities face up to the evil spirit with staying power, and they are representatives of both an old conception of the law and a modern democratic humanism. Evil is not what hurts; evil is when political ideologies and utopias renounce the existence of hurt in life. Shut up in a bottle, evil represents a vile temptation to anyone scheming with humanity as a means, not as an end. Conversely, "in the confluence of Christianity and humanism Martin A. Hansen finds the answer to the modern, rootless, superintellectual and merciless world in which war and misery originate" (Møller 129).

Was an active and responsible humanism on undogmatic, evangelical grounds sufficient to fend off the intrusions of an atrocious war? Yes and no. During the spontaneous general strike in July 1944 the common urbanites revolted against the Germans as the villagers had done in Hansen's fiction. But this source of encouragement met with an onerous inability after the war to scrutinize the level of responsibility on which a series of drastic emergency measures were exercised during the war. Hansen's share in the responsibility for liquidating wartime informers contributed significantly to a lasting crisis in his later life and art. But before this crisis joins with his growing misgivings as to the appropriateness of art as a means of cognition, he issues another novel on the war, his masterpiece *Lykkelige Kristoffer* (1945; Eng. tr. *Lucky Kristoffer*, 1974), completed just before the time of liberation.

Situated between the times of war and postwar, the book is a centerpiece of Hansen's writings in the 1940s. Its explicit narrator, a clerk named Martin, is an anticipation of the narrator in *Løgneren*, though less outspoken than the latter in part because of *Lykkelige Kristoffer*'s historical disguise. It stands to reason that the outcome of the war accounts for the aesthetics and wording of the novel, as intimated by an old huckster's rendering of

Kristoffer's life while the city around him is being leveled. Incidentally, the last three chapters of the book came about during the popular uprising in 1944, at the same time as Hansen's vindication of the liquidation of informers appeared in the anthology *Der brænder en Ild*.

Lykkelige Kristoffer's indirect picture of its period of publication implicitly refers to these epoch-making events as the backdrop for paramount existential ambiguities that were not subjected to public debate until the end of the decade. The novel's medieval Nordic ambiance on the level of plot could not infinitely conceal the topicality of its atmosphere and problematics. Hansen himself calls attention to the anxiety of the period demonstrated by the title of Branner's contemporaneous short story *Angst* (also published in *Der brænder en Ild*), but further artistic parallels come to light in Swedish literature, for example in Sivar Arnér's *Knekt och klerk* (1945; Knight and Clerk) with its comparable intercourse between modern existentialism and medieval fiction and motif. A brief short story entitled "Offer" (Sacrifice), which was left over from Hansen's novel and included in his collection *Agerhønen* (1947; The Partridge), accentuates the thematic scope. Its title refers to two orphans that some plague-stricken peasants bury alive. Their act of sacrifice is both godless and meaningless, but it leads to a faith in resurrection that is beyond comprehension and to a sense of responsibility that is indistinguishable from a true will to sacrifice oneself.

The richness of *Lykkelige Kristoffer* is due to its poetic and narrative complexity and to the depth of its outlook. Its images of world and humanity emerge on several levels because of the same artistic capacity that was later a burden to the author. A case in point is the way its rich instrumentation—embracing medieval faith in God alongside modern problems of existence—stands out in characters typifying bodily and spiritual energies within the universal drama of life. It is of particular interest to observe how Hansen wedges the theme of responsibility between the sexes and how women and female infidelity play the decisive roles in this context. Hansen's novels have been accused of an arid fear of sexuality and of old Lutheran prudery in delineating women characters, and rightly so insofar as even Kristoffer's luck depends on an ability to outdo demonic female nature with a pure and innocent calling in the service of death. All the same, the effacement of responsibility blamed on the women is part and parcel of the total image of Man. Good and bad are united in a higher pact according to which the triumph of evil inevitably vouches for the existence of good. Kristoffer dies—a lucky death.

Clearly, the complexity of the novel crosses the boundaries of naturalism. The principal short story, "Midsommerfesten" (The Midsummer Festival), from *Tornebusken* (1946; The Thornbush) submits an explicit antinatural-ism and an extensive experimentation with the narrative form. The author and his female reader are both part of the fiction, together, next to, and in conjunction with the apparent characters of the story; the point of the entire arrangement is to occasion the involvement of these "outsiders" in the internal debate of moral issues. The result is both ambiguous and strained. To be sure, the human dimensions stretch well beyond the concepts of inheritance and environment but also into the seductive realm of eroticism. Art in itself is a form of seduction delivering from crippling moralization but also leading into patterns of immoral sensations. The decay of culture and the disintegration of personality meet with a purifying pang somewhat akin to sado-masochism and not very redeeming. Hansen submits his characters to passions that are bound for reduction to maternity and charity. The affectionate Alma is a descendant of her namesake in Paludan-Müller's nineteenth-century epic poem *Adam Homo*, a savior worthy of an evil adversary. But her male counterpart is not evil, merely a divided mind more in need of love as healing than salvation.

Both in his collections of short stories from the mid-1940s and his cultural critiques in the periodical *Heretica* later in the decade Hansen takes the field—in the manner of Vilhelm Grønbech—against the naturalistic depictions of humanity. Nature is immoral throughout, and if the natural human surrenders his sense of justice, he will succumb to the violence of reason. Individualism, loneliness, and agony, along with proportionate sentiments of bitterness and egotism, make up the offspring of this demon to which the humanistic response is responsibility, self-criticism, and belief in the resurrection with a view to a sense of societal community. It is the problems of existentialism that concern the poet and thinker Hansen, and it is characteristic of him to interpret the myth of resurrection in existential terms and to relate it to the demonic so as to demonstrate its victory over death. In essence we are facing the "will to goodness" that prevails in the philosophy of Søren Kierkegaard. But within this frame of reference Hansen has taken on the business of the poet and clergyman N. F. S. Grundtvig, *his* allegiance to the earth and *his* allocation of traditional meaning to life at present. He believes in resurrection as a relief not from the chaos of death but from the fear of death's very reality.

The entire formation of such issues is convened in *Løgneren*, from original sin and the reality of evil to a sense of guilt and a consciousness of sin. Also present are forms of anxiety and a common spirit of reconciliation. The novel's simulated diary account of a lonely parish clerk on an island—placed between more or less common islanders, but particularly between two women, a former student and a married woman—is worded with astonishing narrative distance and subtle artistic intensity. Its terse style has led to comparisons with the sagas and the Old Testament; its declared listener Nathanael is reminiscent of a similar figure in Gide's *Les Nourritures terrestres*; and its protagonist Johannes has both Blicher's Morten in *Brudstykker af en Landsbydegns Dagbog* and Harald Kidde's Clemens in *Helten* among his literary ancestors. Its reactionary scent of lavender, as one critic called it, abounds in allusions to both Danish and foreign works of literature. The novel is one of the most widely read and discussed in Danish letters, and the vast patterns of literary associations underneath its alluring simplicity offer a suspensive synthesis of images from Hansen's entire oeuvre. Ambiguousness is omnipresent in the book, and critics have disagreed accordingly, about both its meaning and its value.

Some have seen—or heard—*Løgneren* as the ideal novel for broadcasting, while others have deplored its obligations to the radio; critics have praised its form of diary and dialogue as earnest dialectics, or they have found its style labored and stale. Its entire mode of expression may seem both pathetic and sentimental but not necessarily without artistic justification. On balance it comprises attitudes that are typical of the postwar period; at least the fact remains that it has stood its ground remarkably well, especially if compared to a kindred text like Branner's *Rytteren*. Yet to expound its pervasive ambiguousness is a different matter and calls for considerable caution. One of the most balanced verdicts from the time *Løgneren* was published reads that it is the fate of the humanist that has befallen its narrator and that he finally takes responsibility for his destiny. But this is a typical, average reflection, and more recent critics have not found it difficult to disintegrate its message. In its form the novel is smooth and classical, breathing the air of Danish national lyricism from Blicher's *Trækfuglene* onward. But in substance it is exclusive and desperate, torn between a great desire for life and petty opportunities to live it, a matter of deforming modernism conforming to classicism.

Divided against itself, this attitude is rooted in the narrative situation inasmuch as a shortage of good qualities in the narrator corresponds with a surplus in his declared listener. The deceitful Johannes Vig (*svig* = deceit) addresses the guileless figure Nathanael, but all that he tells him happened a long time ago and has already passed away. The rest is a shadow of life. The ideologies, at least those of the fortune hunters, are tottering to their fall while the old ways come true anew as gateways to personal wholeness. This insight is precariously dualistic, though. On the level of both symbols and psychology—personified in the snipe and the girl Annemari, respectively—

the consciousness of the narrator is haunted by the unclean spirit of the Gospel. Halfhearted and self-deceiving, he is not without aesthetic capacity but quite at a loss as to ethical competence. Although tempered with some self-irony, the narrator maintains an illusion of his own innocence to protect himself against subconscious feelings of guilt. Typical of his decade, he is under the law of perdition and even deprived of the hope of mercy. With his brand of Cain he insists on writing a story without having it on his mind.

Once again the scenario indicates Kierkegaard's influence on Hansen's horizon. The narrator's guilt, or lost opportunities with respect to the women in his life, is demonic in nature; Johannes is the victim of an infinite fear of goodness until in the course of his aesthetic frustrations he begins to see a method in his madness. His self-comprehension recedes but instills a pattern of awareness that eventually breaks the spell of repetition and the power of the evil spirit. Subconscious seductions and other pitfalls thus prepare him—and us—for a growing insight into the conditions of truth as the book approaches its conclusion. By the end of the book this development has unfolded an all-embracing aptitude for human love and a pact with the entire sphere of the actions, the island of Sandø. Not salvation but experiences of life eventually permit the narrator to transcend his selfishness. And *this* echoes, once again, the antimodernistic sense of roots in Grundtvig.

But the question remains: How durable is this purge of or exemption from Kierkegaard's demon and obsession with nature, this emergence of a common horizon of humaneness—artistically speaking? Is the narrator's original proclivity for enjoying the pleasures of giving himself at no cost an effect of the work of art itself, and does lying unfold in a way that is drawing toward its self-revelation? Or is, by contrast, the liar's original fear of human contact a simple fabrication designed to attract dramatic notice of better morals and conduct? Are the art and narrative of the novel, in other words, indicative of a devotional book, or do they qualify it to face its reader with the real untruth and not simply the unreal truth? If so, finally, is the reader likely to see through its tricks? The choice seems one between plague and cholera or between preaching and seduction. Hansen tried to escape the dilemma between its horns by replacing lies, no matter what their origins, with solid knowledge in which the common people could have faith.

Hence his departure from art in *Orm og Tyr* (1952; Serpent and Bull) is a continuation of his experimental endeavors in "Midsommerfesten." Modernistic elements of danger seem to form part of the author's awareness of tradition. The ostensible purpose of the book is to demonstrate how the new Christianity originates not merely from Hebrew but from Nordic tradition, a rural tradition devoted less to sin and atonement than to Grundtvig's sense of life, death, and resurrection, a tradition that is faithful to the earth. The latter is of particular interest if compared to the object lessons of Hansen's fictive works in which agony and deprivation are the principal sources of purification.

Hansen may have escaped this conflict, but not without a price. His later book is a pseudoscientific substitute for good fiction and shows how the author is bound to tradition more than he realizes. Although an admirer of Johannes V. Jensen, Hansen has none of the winds and fresh air of the works of the Jutland poet. It is no matter for surprise that Knud Leif Thomsen in his film version of *Løgneren* (1970) easily managed to reduce the sexuality of the novel to the level of a pornographic magazine, albeit with Christianity as part of the reactionary design. Throughout the 1960s and 1970s Hansen's rustic style and vital liars were met with general fatigue in his audience—to which must be added that this period saw a specific and political distaste for his pent-up glorification of the gospel of suffering and the allegedly inevitable misery in society. By the end of the 1980s, however, around Hansen's eightieth birthday, political frontiers seem to have mellowed and religious experiences resurfaced in public debate, along with a rising interest in the narrative as a genre. This set of circumstances accounts for a renewed preoccupation with Hansen's concept of culture, his profound sense of the dark sides of life, and his courage not to grace them with refreshing and fashionable expressions. For all the onslaughts on the notion of "personality," his has proven resistant to most critical angles of incidence.

Personality, according to Hansen, is threatened mainly by ideologies, in particular if the ideologists consider the necessity of history to be on their side, as both Marxists and materialists do. Writers such as Hans Kirk and Hans Scherfig did not share in this view, nor did the young Hansen himself. But although he was to revise his writing after 1940, his Marxist colleagues continued their postwar production in the same ideological vein as before. Thus *Vredens Søn* by Kirk is the typical counterpart to Hansen's *Løgneren*. Whereas the ideology critique of the latter is religious-existential and rather limited in its optimism, the former displays a sociohistorical and quite optimistic concern, with contemporary matters in religious guise. Nonetheless, both authors are critical of culture and trustful of human nature. Progress in human affairs presupposes either introverted heart searchings or extroverted social protestations, and the two procedures are concomitant throughout the postwar period of fiction and cultural debate, as illustrated by the periodicals *Heretica* and *Dialog,* respectively.

Willy-August Linnemann

One writer at the center of this period and spanning its many diversities is Willy-August Linnemann (1914–). His image of Denmark combines existential introspection with social criticism and Christian trust. Born and raised in South Schleswig and later the European immigrant incarnate, Linnemann in his essays, stories, and novels even geographically testifies to the significance of boundaries and to the potential for expansion of the images they define. Typical in this respect are his essays entitled *Sønderjyllands fremtid* (1972; The Future of North Schleswig), in which he inquires specifically into cultural boundaries and their values. For him it is the borderline regions of Europe that are truly conducive to future societal developments, and the various national borders are justified mainly as means to safeguard the integrity of national characteristics, without which cultural communication across the borders is destined to fail. Linnemann's first two novels, from 1939 and 1945, circumscribe both the Danish-German border and the time frame of the German occupation in such a way that intrinsic limits for human development at the time are called into question.

In *Natten før Freden* (1945; The Night before the Peace) the very title centers the tension between war and postwar times within this context. The novel is about the Danish Resistance during the Nazi occupation, but it is dedicated to the memory of the rank and file of young freedom fighters who were killed in the course of its action. With death being its most decisive sign of life, the book's humanistic epic is generally dualistic. When the protagonist offers an explanation of his view of love to one of his girlfriends, he sounds like an impossible cross between a cultural radical of the 1930s and an existentialistic humanist of the 1940s, firmly convinced that within the otherwise elusive moment of togetherness, intimate devotion merges into a larger spirit of community. The expression of one's own humaneness forms the lifeline to major forces of both unification and liberation of the nation. The confrontation between this young freedom fighter and his Nazi adversary elicits yet another attitudinal dichotomy in the novel. The Nazi character is possessed by ideological megalomania, but before he bowls himself over, and deservedly so, the author avails his acerbic skills to launch a critical attack on the freedom fighter's altogether Danish vagueness, naiveté, and fellowship-meeting rhetoric. The point is to demonstrate that the freedom fighter's weakness is his strength. His anachronism and idealistic mysticism may be dubious strongholds, but with all his qualms and doubts he literally crosses the border to die for what he believes in. At the end the novel demonstratively testifies to the value of a combative humanism, full of resolve, yet almost devoid of the kind of resolve that we term *resolution*.

During his later years of self-imposed exile and loneliness, wander years and apprentice years at a safe distance from the Danish Parnassus, Linnemann matured to the point where his attempts at artistic synthesis came to fruition within a genre of his own that he properly called *Europafortællinger* (1958–66; European Stories). A group of people in a Flensburg shelter during the war kill the time in the manner of Boccaccio's *Decamerone* (1348–53) by telling each other stories. The situation exposes their secrets, and with the shelter as microcosm of the larger bewildered world outside, the tales manifest the attitude that under the influence of a menacing destiny, conflicts of life crumble into a melting pot of community spirit. As in Martin A. Hansen's case Linnemann's narrative undermines its own naturalistic surface level to touch on hidden sources where liberation from the blind forces of nature originates and where humanity becomes part of the inexplicable paradox of eternity. Moreover, as cycles of tales or collections of short stories, these books open upward and outwardly, not to linear progression, but to spacious expansion. In essence, human beings transcend matter. Only spirit and divinity are beyond doubt and cannot be done without. The vanity of reason in all its nihilistic and aesthetic disguises is like the emperor's new clothes. Faith in humanity should connect with belief in God. In Kierkegaard's words, spirit, not soul, is the noble sign of the European, and by the same token his and her tie to pessimism.

With this idea in mind Linnemann, in a final seven-volume series of major novels about the Sunesen-Schleswiger family (1968–74), returns to his native Schleswig. His artistic transgressions of boundaries now meet with dual fulfillment. He affronts the outer limits for human self-realization imposed by the modern industrial society but also the inner limits preventing humans from consummating this process; by disbanding these boundaries Linnemann reinforces his humanistic visions.

Karen Blixen

Just as World War II occasioned a change in the writings of H. C. Branner and Martin A. Hansen, the literary production of Karen Blixen (1885–1962; pseudonym Isak Dinesen) also lends itself to a prewar and a postwar phase. Her two principal works from the 1930s reflect the reciprocal action between European and African myth and reality and between male and female imagery. These aesthetic-moral works of fiction are patterned on autobiographical adaptations of myths of creation. After the outbreak of the war Blixen issued, aside from a belated epilogue to *Den afrikanske Farm* (1937; Eng. tr. *Out of Africa*, 1937), three collections of tales and a pseudonymous novel in which the artistic process of creation is at center stage, in a suspenseful relation to the implied notion of humaneness. While her prose writings—in that they comprise extensive elaborations on European humanism and cultural interpretations—are somewhat compatible to Linnemann's, they are markedly different from Branner's and Hansen's, the leading authors of the period.

Branner's stand-in salvation of man in distress is the target of Blixen's criticism concerning *Rytteren,* and Hansen's ethical orientation is no less at odds with the brilliant aesthetic response to the human condition in her works of fiction. Yet her aesthetics is not dispassionate, her humanism not passive. The pseudonymous novel *Gengældelsens Veje* (1944; Eng. tr. *The Angelic Avengers,* 1946) seems an allegorical sneer at the vileness of war. But not only does its evangelical message of love amount to an evil being exorcised by good, this version of active humanism is further substantiated by aesthetic means akin to those of Kierkegaard. While goodness and love come true through self-realization, artistic boldness is called for lest self-realizations remain out of reach. Consequently, what separates Blixen from Branner and Hansen in terms of aesthetics and morality is her lack of compromise, her celebration of the Fall, and her daring artistic combinations or, simply put, the audacity of her sense of humanism.

Unlike Hansen and the other members of the *Heretica* circle who were seeking an untraditional combination of Christian existentialism and democratic revisionism as the remedy for human agony, Blixen did not view the throes of life as an absolute evil; she rather perceived such conditions as inextricably related to the strength of whatever values humans felt compelled to suffer for. Her all but classical emancipation from the effeminate scruples of contemporary humanism marks the difference between the human and unheroic narrative and the divine and heroic tale. The latter seems adverse to modernism since it does not indulge in art as a problem in itself, as Martin A. Hansen had encountered with despair, but rather explores its representative potentials. Representation of African nature entered the framework of western European civilization in Blixen's works from the 1930s, and it later stood behind her religious ideas, for example, that the Christian conception of charity in "En Herregaardshistorie" ("A Country Tale") from *Sidste Fortællinger* (1957; Eng. tr. *Last Tales,* 1957) did not disintegrate into "Christian existentialism and democratic revisionism." Blixen's images of life rest on a "Philosophy of Nemesis" according to which objective lawfulness may turn into subjective freedom.

Although Blixen's point of departure is quite different from modernism and from writers who, like Branner, Hansen, and members of the *Heretica* milieu, were struck by modernistic scruples, she is nonetheless heading for modernistic postures. In her later works this cultivation of aestheticism reached such a point that it created its own objections and eventually must rectify itself. Her depictions of human features may thus seem inhuman, but thanks to their self-contradictions, they come across as human after all. Blixen considered art to be a security against moralism, whereas her contemporaries used it to further moral views. From her perspective they spoke with two tongues, while her own ambiguous efforts to undermine moralization were unequivocal. Rather than positing a contradiction in terms, this confrontation between modernism and humanism is quite typical of the epoch.

The question remains when Blixen's original notion of life as a piece of art gives way to a contradiction between life and art and to a conception of art as manipulation rather than comprehension, as in the later Henrik Ibsen. At least in the famous tale "Sorg-Agre" ("Sorrow Acre") from *Vinter-Eventyr* (1942; Eng. tr. *Winter's Tales,* 1942) it is still a fact that modern humanism is led into a larger artistic model of the human condition. The young Adam returns from the modern world of enlightenment to the feudal world of his family only to experience a mixture of uplifting and alarming sentiments as he watches the old mother of a young suspect commit her suicidal act of sacrifice on behalf of her son and in grim connivance with the feudal lord, Adam's uncle. Torn between the humanistic commandments of his heart and an inclination to subject himself to the calling of his feudal family, Adam finally realizes that only within the larger context does individual passion become meaningful, and only in the light of the individual sacrifice does the superior law become humane. Both self-realization and higher obligations are prefigured in the immediate stylistic figuration of the tale, and eventually they protrude as the total exposition of its patterns. This all happens when the old woman's vicarious act of sacrifice occasions the norm and is the point of departure for the self-realization of young Adam.

In the long story "Ib og Adelaide" ("Copenhagen Season"), from *Sidste Fortællinger*, the title characters are typically Blixenian children of men with divine dispositions who become themselves as humans only when they begin to realize how the divine and aesthetic frames around their lives are devoid of meaning. The framework is merely to posit a demand for existential surrender and an obligation to invest one's life in the human tragedy, although this tragedy presupposes and is part of the divine comedy. The overall humanism in a story like this is a sign deprived of its social and metaphysical references. On the level of plot and characters this humanism unfolds as a matter of tension between the two protagonists. Ib is a humanist in touch with two equally important things. He acknowledges and accepts that Adelaide is intent on transgressing her own nature as well as any given natural human boundaries. But while he observes this buoyancy toward civilization and self-importance in her, his own submergence into nature and sub-consciousness indicates what he has forsaken by submitting himself to her transgressions. No way of life obtains access to his personality without entailing notions of life foregone. Ib is familiar with the existential power of abandoned forms of life.

An analogous familiarity with new forms of life is conspicuous by its absence in Adelaide's mind; she is precariously further behind her age than Ib is ahead of his. Adelaide early knows a lot but is late to learn of life, in fact so late that her early knowledge is indistinguishable from wisdom after the event. Hence the two youngsters come to share what in Blixen is both the destiny and dignity of nobility, the ability to convert historical defeat into existential grandeur, impersonal necessity into personal virtue. But this compatibility is first arrived at in the cemetery. The idea of how to gain one's life does not come true until it is lost; tragedy is self-affirming before it is life-affirming. While still full of life Ib and Adelaide were basically out of step with each other and would meet only in passing.

The last story, "Ringen" ("The Ring"), in Blixen's last collection of stories, *Skæbne-Anekdoter* (1958; Eng. tr. *Anecdotes of Destiny,* 1958), rekindles the idea that losing the foundation of life is a prerequisite for human maturation. The protagonist, Lise, is a newlywed immersed in marital bliss and an alarming illusion of harmony between herself and her surroundings. Yet like a big Red Riding Hood, she is led out of her chronic innocence into a seductive setting of nature; and miles from anywhere her bourgeois and comforting pact of marriage gives way within a minute to a pact outside of law and order. Her stroll into the woods and her abrupt encounter with a lawless thief and murderer turns into an experience beyond all limits and all imagination. Not in the sense that she gets eaten, as in Charles Perrault's tale, or saved at the last minute, as in the Grimm brothers' version, but in the sense that she is left with an incredible insight into the gulf between life as she knows it all too well and life as the unknown, of which she has a foggy notion, at best.

This is not a classical position to find oneself in, but rather an uncomfortably humanistic one; in fact, only modernists may be wrecked on such rocks. In Danish literature Blixen was long the strange bird on the rock, but as times caught up with the range and depth of her radiating power, she gained international acclaim and eventually some recognition in Denmark as well. In the 1950s her national fame had reached the point where she occasionally attracted clandestine satires and caricatures, but in the 1980s it was the screen versions of *Out of Africa* (1985) and *Babette's Feast* (1986)—based on the story *Babettes Gæstebud* (1950) and winner in 1988 of the Academy Award for best foreign film—that somewhat paradoxically solidified her position both abroad and at home.

The Heretica *Circle*

While humanism in these important war and postwar authors remains characterized by an ambiguous awareness of problems rather than an unambiguous philosophy of life, most of the attitudes and tendencies of the period meet and collide decisively by the end of the 1940s in and around *Heretica* (1948–53) and in the conspicuously absent dialogue between this journal and its antagonistic counterpart *Dialog* (1950–61; Dialogue). But the interrelationship between the two periodicals does not simply mark the culmination of the war and postwar years with Denmark's joining of NATO in 1949; its aftermath can be traced far into the 1950s.

Ideologically, it is the awkward juxtaposition of class cooperation on the domestic political scene and lack of cooperation on the international scene of cold war affairs which accounts for many intellectuals' distaste for ideology as a concept. Both Christian and Marxist standpoints generally meet with reservations in most artists, and even middle-ground positions of a humanistic nature tend to be undermined by skepticism. A principal volume on cultural politics, *Mennesket i Centrum* (1953; Man at the Center), in which, for example, the leading Social Democrat politician Julius Bomholt advocates an "active humanism," is indicative of how cautiously proponents of more radical ideological stances had to promote them in the postwar years; it also illustrates how even limited steps in that direction rested with practical politicians, at least until the end of the 1950s. As late as 1960 Bjørn Poulsen, formerly an editor of *Heretica,* issued a book entitled *Ideernes krise i åndsliv og politik* (The Crisis of Ideas in Intellectual Life and Politics), which was largely a reflection of his cultural pessimism in ten-year-old articles.

More abstract discussions of humanistic ideas are prevalent, however, and while poetic discourse is for the most part more concrete, its ties to the debates are nonetheless noticeable. The interdependence between the genres clearly comes across in *Heretica*'s antinaturalistic, if not altogether anti-ideological, crusade and in several attempts to formulate poetic alternatives to ideological intrusions (even from humanism). Martin A. Hansen's essay "Konvention og Formånd" (Convention and Spirit of Form) from 1948 was merely an attempt to depict the innermost character of the new poetic art; a more comprehensive effort appeared with the publication of Paul la Cour's *Fragmenter af en Dagbog* (1948; Fragments of a Diary) in *Heretica*.

Though Hansen and la Cour were seemingly at the same game of art in-terpretation, la Cour's particular approach to the secrets of his craft made Hansen uneasy and basically inclined to view his colleague's pathetic-vision-ary and philosophizing tract as a lovely collection of poetry. The scenario shows how artistic reflections and creative elements merge in the surround-ings of *Heretica*; a solemn and cryptic commitment on poetry's behalf was the trademark of its contributors, with regard to both their theories and practice. Powerful forces of creation are at stake here, but considering how exposed they are to ideological and naturalistic infringement, they must be approached with caution. The open expectation, the advent position, is a typical response to the mystery of poetry, and also typical is the use of the word *holdning* ("attitude"), as opposed to more ideological terms such as *anskuelse* ("views") and *livssyn* ("outlook"). In continuation of the tradition of romanticism, authors approach the boundaries of reality by means of a discourse charged with symbols and imagery; they wish to prevent the pe-culiar nature of their poetry and visions from being affronted by naturalis-tic-ideological pawing and intellectual constrictions.

Recapturing the whole reality is the objective. Authors set out to include in their discourse spiritual forces that would otherwise disappear in repres-sion and merely appear in demonic forms. And their advent sensibilities en-tail evangelical, transcendental, and spiritual conceptions of what it means to be human. Most of *Heretica*'s anti-ideological lyrical poetry flows into this framework of humanistic-religious complexity, notably assuming its global dimensions in the works of la Cour and no less conspicuously the anti-Hellenistic influence of Vilhelm Grønbech. And again, it was a long time before the political radicals in the counterpart splinter journal *Dialog* could get a word in edgewise.

Art, and not society, is the framework for the individual in her quest for self-comprehension, and the abstruseness of art, as circumscribed by la Cour, and by Bjørn Poulsen in his essay "Elfenbenstårnet" (The Ivory Tower) from 1949, is quite indispensable as a safeguard against rational in-trusions on this process of cognition. Branner's humanism and Martin A. Hansen's faith in personality both owe a debt to this concept of art. When, for example, personality is the ultimate goal in Hansen, the individual char-acter attains its objective only by living through an artistic cognition that goes beyond personality. Romanticism's creed in life's wholeness has moved through symbolism's longing for wholeness into modernism's scru-pulous gift of tongues and despaired proclamation of wholeness in the light or shadow of wartime experiences.

From an international point of view the Danish *Heretica* positions are perhaps not particularly advanced. Many ideas were foreign loans, from Sartre to Franz Kafka and T. S. Eliot, and even at close quarters, in contemporary Sweden, artists had arrived at attitudes and formal experiments that preceded the developments in Denmark by a decade. All the same, the generation of poets that centered on *Heretica* has demonstrated considerable artistic quality and variation.

Thorkild Bjørnvig

The fact that Thorkild Bjørnvig's (1918–) perception of reality is different from la Cour's relates to diverging conceptions of art and implies different views of humanity as well. La Cour considers poetry to be free and independent of perceived reality and merely bound to the artist's "I." Bjørnvig, by contrast, considers art the incarnation of perceived reality, something outside the artist himself. The title of a large collection of his essays is *Virkeligheden er til* (1973; Reality Exists), and it stipulates that reality is what the poet must relate to and articulate in his writing. If la Cour purports directly to investigate the world of human interrelationships, Bjørnvig's aim is to explore a world outside of humans that humans nonetheless have in common. First and foremost, this is a world of nature, but second, it is religion, which also contains otherness we cannot do without and should not try to subdue. Ultimately, though, it is cosmos and death that enrich our lives by challenging us with fertile otherness. Bjørnvig's humanism is threatened by the crisis of self-doubling, but a possible resolution awaits it in terms of reconciliation with the world outside the human sphere of power.

Before this redeeming artistic insight in the human conditions outside the exclusive domain of humaneness, art and reality appear bitterly opposed to each other. As early as in *Stjærnen bag Gavlen* (1947; The Star behind the Gable), Bjørnvig's first work of poetry, his poems secrete a series of cosmic images of their ego's original life. As the star behind the gable offers a synthesis of these fragmented life experiences, however, it also implies segregation of human consciousness from its previous contact with the circumstances of life. The lyrical ego's initial loss of wholeness has been compensated for, though merely in the form of autonomous art.

Begyndelsen (The Beginning) is the name of Bjørnvig's collection of essays from 1960, but the point of departure and growth referred to in its title is one that allows for repetition of life without intellectual or ideological restrictions and one that Bjørnvig refuses to commit to an encapsulated existence within the incorporeal autonomy of modernism. The perfectly exclusive poem is a rather questionable expression of his lucid state of mind, and in his next collection, *Anubis* (1955), the title poem refers to the Egyptian god of death, who embodies this narrow and suppressed world of thoughts, this dehumanization of the memory of cosmos and of life as it was at the beginning. When, however, Anubis's jackal head suddenly reveals a face, its divided poetic observer experiences a healing, and all that was confined to his mind disperses organically throughout his entire person.

Bjørnvig knows of other images of this condition of wholeness and equilibrium. One, exposed in the essay *Kentauren* (1983; The Centaur), is the centaur with an animal body of sensations and a brain of thoughts; another, and more exemplary, is the ellipse with the poet at one of its centers and nature at the other, together stipulating where the inspiration of the beginning attains its power and form. But whatever the model, modernism is being ransacked. Bjørnvig's work (in dissertations and translations) on the German poet Rainer Maria Rilke's incorporeal verse has negatively challenged him to reach for a cosmic concretion of his own, and of equal importance is his preoccupation with Martin A. Hansen's works of fiction, culminating with his doctoral thesis, *Kains Alter* (1964; The Altar of Cain), in which he observes how nature under control in *Løgneren* becomes nature under human care in *Orm og Tyr*.

Bjørnvig's new concept of nature settles in the poems of *Figur og Ild* (1959; Figure and Fire). His language purports no longer to structure a pervasive sense of nothingness but to shape a fullness experienced in nature. Poetry has become the medium for cosmic radiation and has anticipated the essayistic verdict that reality exists, not as a void for art to replace, but as a presence for it to mediate. Significant in this context is Bjørnvig's rejection of the purely aesthetic fascination he had encountered in Gottfried Benn, and his alternative reference to the seer and moralist Charles Baudelaire.

Yet to realize his childhood inspirations Bjørnvig remains tied to art and nature as his sources of inspiration. How he extricates himself from these ties and enables himself also to view the cultural and historical dimensions of life as emancipating is the central theme in a central collection of poems, *Ravnen* (1968), named after Edgar Allan Poe's "The Raven." Although the volume's breathtaking lyrical instrumentation is based on a personal and biographical history of development, its Faustian dimensions of language and insight preclude easy accessibility. After having tried in vain—in *Vibrationer* (1966; Vibrations)—to break away from his almost classical poetic form and style, Bjørnvig in *Ravnen* succeeds in distancing himself from his earlier mode of writing while still preserving a firm and orderly poetic structure. The poems at hand constitute a twelve-part suite, each consisting of four-lined and rhymed *knittelvers*. With their powerfully coherent vision unfolding like a history of heart searchings, they depict a journey of the soul from the nightmare of disruption to a stage of reconciliation with body and cosmos. They are not about art, but about morality, guilt, and conscience. In answering the major question pertaining to the identity crisis of youth— Who am I?—they submit to a new life in reality and love. The raven, like the star behind the gable a cosmic image resurrected from the ashes of earlier life, compounds the symbolic elements of this work of poetry and earlier works of the author as well into a lasting sign of integrity and wholeness in the universe.

Ravnen is charged with countless references to European mythology, gnostic speculation, and older and younger works of fiction from Goethe to Poe, not to mention suggestions of works by Grundtvig and Rilke, the Swedish and Danish poets Ekelöf and Rifbjerg, respectively, and others. Further charged, by way of association, with an abundance of loosely connected meanings, the entire work appears almost impenetrable to many of its critics and readers. Superficially read, it readily confirms the impression of Bjørnvig as an Alexandrian poet, a preacher full of pathos and Olympic humor, if humorous at all. His language is studded with scientific and historical allusions, yet it is remarkably compact. There is an unmistakable air about it, but then again its train of thought is quite majestic. The same can be said of Bjørnvig's own edition of selected poems (1970) in which his materials readily conform to section headings on the grand themes of Childhood, Nature, Love, Titanic Theme, The City, The Ecstasy, Death, and Cosmos. *Ravnen*'s heroic diction of destiny is seldom void or trumped up, and it must be reckoned as epoch making in modern Danish literature in general and in Bjørnvig's poetic oeuvre in particular.

First, here is a poet whose somewhat outmoded insistence on the virtue of communicating reality reverses the propositions of young linguistic contemporaries who claim that only examples of language make up reality. Second, in acknowledging reality per se, *Ravnen* prepares for an opening of his entire authorship toward environmental concerns as seen in the subsequent collections of poems written under the influence of an imminent global catastrophe. Their expressions of care for nature are not unknown in his earlier works, but the solicitous attitude has expanded from formerly individual domains to the purview of humanity as a whole. At the same time, they strive to sustain their descriptions of nature with concrete historical evidence; the impact is intended to be of current interest while still of lasting importance. Several poems appeared initially in the daily press, but even they were usually up to the artistic mark, thanks to a rare mixture of matter-of-fact information, memorable poetic imagery, and well-retained indignation and compassion. These qualities were inherently scattered in Bjørnvig's more monumental works of lyrical poetry but are now released from his personal and visionary recesses to the benefit of public debates over the environment.

His poems from 1970–75 were called *Delfinen* (1975; The Dolphin); they were followed by *Abeguden* (1981; The Monkey God) and *Epimeteus* (1990). But Bjørnvig also participated in the environmental debates with collections of essays, such as *Også for naturens skyld* (1978; Also for the Sake of Nature) and *Barnet og dyret i industrisamfundet* (1979; Children and Animals in the Industrial Society). The former includes an essay called "Hvalerne har sange og naturen har rettigheder" (Whales Have Songs and Nature Has Rights) in which the author launches the concept of "ecological socialism," that is, the idea that not only does nature have a functional value, but it has a value of its own, and if it is deprived by humans of that essential value, humans have thereby deprived themselves of the foundation of their existence. To be oneself in Bjørnvig's world of ideas still means to be identified with something beyond oneself, only now the implications of the attitude are clearly political.

Bjørnvig's ecological socialism met with both approval and disapproval. Among his critics were regular socialists who accused him of letting the threat of the environment place everyone in the same boat at the expense of a necessary class struggle. Others charged that his principal defense of the use of violence against destroyers of the environment was a symptom of a dangerously naive extremism. Nevertheless, Bjørnvig remains a writer who may seem exclusive and serious about himself at a distance but in reality is prepared to take anything but himself more seriously than most other writers have dared.

A collection of poems called *Morgenmørke* (1977; Morning Darkness) is written in the same key as the environmental poems; based on personal divorce experiences, it is, of course, more introverted, but nature and cosmos still make up the frame and perspective. Not surprisingly, though, Bjørnvig's preferred outlets in recent years have been reminiscences and memoirs. After all, his personal myth in *Ravnen* was conceived as a sequence or transposition of memories, and even his general experience with memory is one of access to the present, a mental repository of immense importance to an individual whose purpose in life is bigger than himself and whose microcosmos reaches out for cosmos. Memory expands the topical perspectives; the inner universe endows the experience of the universe as a whole with profound significance.

Bjørnvig's first volume of memoirs was *Pagten* (1974; Eng. tr. *The Pact*, 1983), about his friendship with Karen Blixen. Despite the tragic end to their relationship and its modest importance to his artistic development, he found in her inconveniently "unchronological" way of being an inducement to look for greater perspectives, for higher and more rigorous measures for human existence than he knew from his own humanitarian experience. In his more recent volumes of memoirs, published since 1983 and spanning his life from birth to the present, the expanded perspectives are, needless to say, of a more composite nature, more deeply torn and more profoundly reconciled within the larger context. The title and cover of *Solens have og skolegården* (1983; The Garden of the Sun and the Schoolyard), dealing with his earliest years and the first to be published, provide the illustration. The garden of the sun is the idyllic childhood and green beginning; the schoolyard is the gray substitute for true continuation. These are starkly dissociated worlds until the adult recollection with its claim to continuity reunites them. Connections allow life to proceed, whereas divisions eventually regress to traumas. Thorkild Bjørnvig was one of *Heretica*'s first editors and has since proven to be one of the unavoidable poets of his times.

Ole Wivel

After Bjørnvig (and Bjørn Poulsen) edited volumes 1 and 2 of *Heretica*, the editorial responsibilities (for volumes 3 and 4) were transferred to Ole Wivel (1921–) (and Martin A. Hansen). Both the connections and the discords are remarkable. Like Bjørnvig, Wivel authored a monumental work on Hansen (in two volumes, 1967 and 1969), but unlike his predecessor's controversial and audacious "explication de texte," Wivel's study is a classical biography suited to deemphasize Bjørnvig's tenets concerning the frustrating impact of Christianity on Hansen's production; Wivel argues instead that Hansen's crisis of conscience was triggered by the liquidation of wartime informers. And while Bjørnvig in his book on Karen Blixen from 1974 presented a friendship brought to an early close, Wivel fifteen years later issues what he calls her "unfinished self-revolt": *Karen Blixen: Et uafsluttet selvopgør* (1987; Eng. tr. *Karen Blixen*, 1990). There remains, within the same horizon of interests, a noticeable difference between Bjørnvig's all-absorbing engagement and Wivel's cooler overview, between the exhausted drama and the unceasing efforts to arrive at critical harmony.

The similarities speak to the power of gravity within the *Heretica* circle, its role as a gathering point, whereas the dissimilarities indicate the degree of variation and potential for development within the milieu—even before it broke up or became outdated. In further reference to Bjørnvig, it should be recalled that his prophetic and visionary abilities prepared him for an ecological socialism without reducing his gifts for seeing the past in dense and profuse memories. Wivel, too, departs from *Heretica*'s chalked circle and sets out for wider social and political commitments; but his course is determined by given liberal and socialist alternatives, and his three volumes of memoirs harbor more elucidating breadths of view and less original and penetrating insights than one is likely to find in Bjørnvig. Wivel writes deftly, often beautifully, but reading him is rarely a harrowing experience.

That has to do in part with his exceptional talent for combining private and public service. Not only was he the editor of *Heretica*, he was also its publisher, and soon he became the general manager of Gyldendal, Denmark's leading publishing house, not to mention his many other cultural assignments. The title of his memoirs, *Tranedans* (1975), literally means "crane's dance," but in Danish the word usually appears in a phrase with a sparrow as the dancer, a sparrow among hawks. In a different manner of speaking the author sees himself at the big and lively switchboard of communication; intellectually, he is the "intersecting point between lines leading away into extreme opposition." These are informative images. They immediately show Wivel's readiness to mediate between circumstances before they arrive at consequences from which he would have to recoil. They also show that although the point of mediation may be fixed, this individualist is not prepared to leave it resting assured in self-sufficiency. In his last volume, *Kontrapunkt* (1989; Counterpoint), he speaks of reaching "the discords of my own times and my own mind and [making] them coalesce, if not into a fugue, at least into a counterpoint."

That is the core of Wivel's humanism, especially if one adds that a discussant must answer for his precious words and readily put his body and money where his mouth is, as Wivel does himself when he describes his path in "Fra elfenbenstårnet til barrikaderne" (From the Ivory Tower to the Barricades), an essay in *Poesi og protest* (1971; Poetry and Protest). It is no mere coincidence that the riddle of the human face is what Wivel most keenly seeks to resolve in his memoirs. It expresses humane uniqueness in its full, centripetal complexity, and it affords sustenance to the resistance against inhuman demands. Thus, when Wivel later searches for the identity of his entire country, in a collection of poems entitled *Danmark ligger her endnu* (1979; Denmark Still Lies Here), his procedure typically results in what his subtitle labels a series of "Postcards and Portraits." It is the strength and weakness of these classical-modern works of writing, including the first volume of memoirs, *Romance for valdhorn* (1972; Romance for French Horn), that their harmonies come forward with almost complete naturalness and yet a slightly melancholy tone of loss and distance.

This tone is part of the *Heretica* period's signature as it can be heard in *I*

Fiskens Tegn (1948; In the Sign of the Fish) and *Jævndøgnselegier* (1949; Equinoctial Elegies), Wivel's first, small collections of poems; and it is the intensification of the same tone, for instance in *Gravskrifter* (1970; Epigraphs) and its Vietnam poems, that signals his departure, or attempt to depart, from his comfortable bourgeois milieu and aesthetic-existentialist turn of mind. A station on the way, at the crossroads of his development, is *Templet for Kybele* (1961; The Temple for Cybele). Along with the other collections of poems it shows how Wivel overcame the crisis of the 1940s and resisted the temptation to survive the ideological terror of the cold war years from within a state of inner emigration. The experiences of Vietnam and of the exploitation of the third world eventually supersede the psychological aftermath of World War II.

During his formative years as a poet Wivel envisioned both a way of escaping from the wasteland and a savior who would outlaw the conceited mercenary souls from the realm of humankind. What he expected was for humanity to receive the brand of Cain before humankind would receive the verdict that life must be continued. In a quiet and earnest manner we are told that life is impossible but still worthy of fearless pursuit. There is no understanding of life, merely an effort to accept its course as a stone must do when hit by the cold gravity of cosmos. It is like falling into a well and not grasping what has happened until a moment before the fall is over. The poet's attempt at comprehending the world hinges on self-comprehension.

Wivel maintains, in *Gravskrifter*, after less and less metaphysical beating about the bush, the idea of an "always vainly requested identity." But despite an increasingly striking confrontation between the falsehood of inhuman oppressors and their victims' helpless bid for truth, the author persists in refusing to place his writing in the danger zone. No matter how honest his intentions or how eloquent his pronouncements, when Wivel takes sides, his bent for personal quest and self-perception is all but concealed by a calm stylistic surface. His many smaller portraits are elements of a major self-portrait. The advantage here is that the portrayal is never completed; the disadvantage is that its various parts only vaguely appear to be fragments. Perhaps this intricacy is intimated by Wivel himself as he makes the ensuing assessment of his experiences with the Danish Resistance during the war. In *Poesi og protest* he writes, "Everything changed. The problems of responsibility, choice, and action disrupted my bourgeois ideas and estranged me from the way of life I was brought up with. I was bound to engage in ceaseless self-criticism and to question my entire upbringing and state of mind."

Departing from familiar circumstances rather than accommodating the unknown is the trademark of this poet. His artistic and social adaptability notwithstanding, he remains in a certain state of suspension. A case in point is his Nordic sense of justice and balance between concerns for the individual and concerns for society. Both he and Martin A. Hansen were proponents of this idea, and yet it was held in low esteem within contemporary bourgeois and liberal circles. No matter how deliberately and radically Wivel distanced himself from the influence of these circles, the ideal harmony was irretrievably lost. He was probably even looked on as somewhat of a traitor by those whose treason he himself had felt. But that, too, forms part of his insight. In a way even his frustrations seem placated and reconciled, although the question remains whether this makes him a radically established author or a modestly established radical.

Frank Jæger

The last two volumes of *Heretica*, 5 and 6 (1952–53), were edited by two younger and less established authors with less radical ideas. The academic critic Tage Skou-Hansen would not become a published writer of fiction for another five years, and although Frank Jæger (1926–77) had already demonstrated his talents in both artistic prose and lyrical poetry, he was not a radical in any traditional sense of the word. Nor was he a traditionalist but, as perhaps he would call himself, a reactionary (with reference to his rejections of technology, summer tourism, and other forms of modernity). In the context of *Heretica* he is best described as the jester at the solemn court. It is no accident that one of his works of fiction, *Alvilda. Sengelæsning for unge og gamle* (1969; Alvilda: Bedtime Reading for the Young and the Old), includes a priceless satire on la Cour and his *Fragmenter*.

The complexity of Jæger's artistic expressions goes even further. A subtle blend of zestful mirth and moribund brooding is discernible in his early collections of poems, where refreshing and purified poetic sensations occasionally collide with signs of doubt and spleen. In his last collection, *Idylia* (1967), this balance of attitudes is upset by examples of increasingly problematic poetry of ideas and decreasingly articulate poetry of emotions. The green and innocent side of Jæger's personality, as expressed in his collections *Dydige Digte* (1948; Virtuous Poems) and *Morgenens Trompet* (1949; Morning's Trumpet), dates back to the eighteenth-century arias by Ambrosius Stub; the sensuous side, to Sophus Claussen; but the intervening period of bourgeois romanticism provides the sounding board for his entire production. At his best he intermingles with effortless ease these assets with his personal characteristics and exceptional sense of rhythm, sonority, and semantics. But whenever his aesthetic performance is upset by a sense-jarring emptiness, his romantic tonality is a double strain; the public image of his romantic drapery is at the same time that of a carefree bohemian goliard and a demonic artist disguised in virtue.

It is typical of Jæger to have written his memoirs at the age of twenty-seven and to have given them a fictive and pseudobiographical form. A classical piece in *Den unge Jægers Lidelser* (1953; The Sorrows of Young Jæger [Hunter]) seemingly contributes to the popular image of the poet's personality, but read more carefully it rather rectifies the myth. "Djævelens Instrument" (The Devil's Instrument) is about a young man who is head over heels in love but understandably perplexed at realizing that the woman he was supposedly embracing in the darkness was in fact his double bass, the instrument that set his mind in erotic movement. He had intended to park it in a hallway but wound up confusing it with the actual female object of his affections. This is suffering and coyness at once, Werther's pain in Jæger's heart. And it is self-revelation with self-irony, harmonic and demonic forces in devilish intercourse.

A special cadence and unpretentiousness, a bellicose and yet jaunty zest for life are Jæger's distinctions within his generation. Most members of the *Heretica* circle wrote autumn poems, and so did Jæger; but unlike his contemporaries, he also crafted some winter poems purporting to cool off a vigorous sensuality. For the majority of young poets in the 1940s the mythical heretic stylites and ascetic spirits were light-years away from the world of everyday B-movies and bashful dancing ordeals at the local hotel. Jæger (incidentally, a jazz and dance musician himself) was refreshingly devoid of mythical pomp, although in other respects he was a child of his age. His lyrical qualities were actually broadcasted—in several radio plays—and even his works of prose often testify to how he demythologized the heavier late symbolism of the 1940s.

The odd or crazy characters in the seven stories of *Provinser* (1972; Provinces) share their defiance and uncouthness with the narrator of Jæger's travel books. The poet hated travel and therefore was unusually aware of its conditions. When a physical trip was thwarted, an inward journey would take off in its stead and lead toward the exposure of characteristic traits of the author's artistic physiognomy. In *Naive Rejser* (1968; Naive Journeys) the title thus refers to a mental process by which the traveler is moved toward a durable basis for his existence at the same time as he experiences an external world of ubiquitous homelessness. The core of personality was a concept so important to Jæger as to occasion his readiness to sustain it by defying any material obstacle on his way. His other collections of essays also cater to this dichotomy. The fact that one is called *Velkommen Vinter* (1958; Welcome Winter) and another *Drømmen om en Sommerdag* (1965; Dream of a Summer

Day) merely puts the general pattern into a contrapuntal perspective.

By eventually leaving the big city for the quiet countryside, Jæger both escaped and embraced his alienation. It was not a simple place to live, but a good place to write, and his books of prose, if viewed in chronological order, unveil the underlying contradiction. The first small volumes, the novel *Iners* (1950) and the stories in *Hverdagshistorier* (1951; Everyday Stories), are dangerously playful romantic epics and folktales. Later the author ventures into more realistic genres, for example, a sort of biography of Joan of Arc, *Jomfruen fra Orleans* (1955; The Maid of Orleans) and a collection of short stories, *Kapellanen og andre Fortællinger* (1957; The Chaplain and Other Stories); but not until *Danskere* (1966; Danes) and *Døden i Skoven* (1970; Death in the Forest) does he accomplish an up-to-date and timely composite form, a spacious realism with room for fantastic elements, satirical pungency, and gentle humor. Here the opposites of his complex personality combine with reasonably effortless ease and without betraying their innermost disharmonic nature. A certain resemblance to Peter Seeberg's and Gynther Hansen's provincial stories comes to mind.

The conflict between intimate and alien is essential to Jæger's production. Its tension is between sensations and matters that cannot, or can no longer, be perceived. The development of his writings in prose thus corresponds with the course of his lyrical production, in which the most daring display of transgression and depersonalization is to be found in *Tyren* (1953; Taurus), *Havkarlens Sange* (1956; Songs of the Merman), and *Cinna* (1959). Eroticism is the central force of tension, both the core of human personality and its point of decay, inasmuch as it saturates, overwhelms, and depletes the senses. It equates the ambiguousness by which Jæger in his so-called Sidenius poems (named after the hero of Pontoppidan's novel *Lykke-Per*) disputes the Lucky Per side of life with profound spleen. And yet the ambivalence fails to blast the idyll. It affects it piecemeal but not in full measure. As a whole the idyllic remains a distant figment of the *Heretica* imagination, like the vital death of a good poet.

Leif E. Christensen

A kinsman and contemporary of Jæger's romantic prose idylls—and of Blixen's aristocratic conception of art—was Leif E. Christensen (1924–), who made his debut with short stories in *Heretica* and in a collection called *Tyven i Tjørnsted* (1951; The Thief in Tjørnsted). But here the play with myth and pastiche is free of risk rather than free. A thoroughly reflected novel of war, *Træslottet* (1964; The Wooden Castle), comes closer to contemporary reality and to the technical innovations of the French *nouveau ro-*

man, and in *Kvinden fra Østen* (1967; The Woman from the East) the author further supplies his notions of humanity and art with various oriental contrasts. And yet, as Blixen noted, the existentialistic dialogue of his narrative compositions remains largely within the *Heretica* world of imagination.

The problem is evident in *Esben Grønnetræs puslespil* (1959; Esben Grønnetræ's Jigsaw Puzzle), a collection of short stories in which the title story is about a family's obsession with jigsaw puzzles. Generation after generation do the puzzle, and though repeatedly unsuccessful, they all find the process meaningful. In fact, the most remarkable thing about the method in their madness is its ties to their past. In another story, about a shipboard fire in supposedly safe harbor, the narrator is almost killed. On his way through the emergency exit he is reminded so vividly about an interior from his childhood that he almost fails to get ashore alive. As the past in these instances is a fettering trauma, the present in other stories can be incredibly elusive and mean at the same time. Whether real or imagined, the reign of evil makes life a strain—at least in Christensen's rendition.

Ole Sarvig

None of the many poets rallying round *Heretica*, without belonging to its inner circles, was as unusual and gifted as Ole Sarvig (1921–81). To many readers he is the most modernistic poet of his age. Contrary to Jæger, who astonished Bjørnvig by declining to write about childhood and yet was so perceptive in his writing about it, and who astonished everybody by declining to travel and yet was such an astute writer on travel motifs, Sarvig is every—modernistic—inch a poet of both beginnings and travel.

When Sarvig says in *Igår—om lidt* (1976; Yesterday—In a Little While) that in "the beginning were the places, because there is nothing but the places—and we who live there create and dream in the language of the places," he is not professing regional poetry (although he respects it). Sarvig traveled through and lived in Europe, particularly Spain, over extended periods of time, and his writings bear witness to that effect and to the more general effect that places are his points of passage. He resists the temptation to dwell on certain places, because most places are unreal, empty shells; left behind by life, they become subject to even the poet's abandonment in his continued quest for places at which provisional life may still take place and encounters with other people may still afford some meaning.

Nevertheless, redemption from a meaningless reality is possible but in a spirit of metaphysics or, in Sarvig's case, within a personal conception of Christianity, remote from church, cult, and other human remains devoid of meaning. Sarvig's prospects of redemption lie outside the realm of human personality; his place is the place of modernism and as far away from political ideologies as any metaphysics of the 1940s could be. In temporal terms he calls his evangelical place a time for second thoughts, a time and space between the world of ruins that we all inhabit and the hope for a new beginning or a point of consciousness which Sarvig, nonetheless, cherishes and seeks to fulfill. He states that one "must incessantly depart or take leave of one place after the other. As time went on I came to experience this movement as a journey, an obligatory journey, an ethical necessity for my mind," adding, however, that "there is an end to the journey: the encounter with Man, with the Son, eventually with the Son of Man" (Borum 38).

As a poet Sarvig patrols the borders of history and consciousness; his artistic search for a new lease on life comes about on the brink of disaster and disappointment. In the spirit of the age this new faith in life arises in a predestined encounter between "I" and "You." One's innermost self comes into being outside oneself as one's consciousness partakes in a larger sense of spirit. As a stranger among strangers the individual seeks nearness and naturalness. Art is understanding one's self by way of understanding humanity. Roughly speaking, this process originates in the 1940s as a cycle of lyrical poems in five parts, and it continues with five novels written from the mid-1950s onward. As for the elaborate works of art philosophy and cultural criticism that accompany these works of poetry and fiction, the author himself calls them footnotes to the primary texts (and to their implicit message that humans are seeds that have landed on an alien planet); perhaps one could also talk of prosaic reflections. In any event, the spread of eschatology and images of growth over such a wide variety of genres testifies to Sarvig's comprehensive approach to the media as well as to the surrounding world; after all, his different genres share both properties and potentials for interaction. Not only poems by Sarvig, but novels as well, appear in cycles, often centered on the same places and the same motifs of travel. Their images, too, are interrelated (as emphasized in Sarvig's essayistic interpretations) and dedicated to possible encounters and interplays. And the imagery comprises three dimensions: a sight (of visible reality), an in-sight (in the immediately invisible), and an out-sight (in terms of a philosophy of life and art).

Within the poem cycle, *Grønne Digte* (1943; Green Poems) articulates creation and innocence; *Mangfoldighed* (1945; Multitude), growth and variety; *Jeghuset* (1944; The House of Self), the ego-identification; and *Legende* (1946; Legend), a dream of life coming full circle, anticipating the real redemption in *Menneske* (1948; Man), a book about the "I" meeting with "You," or the ego identification fulfilled as self-realization. A pattern of harmony between the individual and his world clearly disintegrates to the point where only the lyrical ego is able to restitute the lost totality in a new whole-ness, a new poetical language of images. This drive toward the image is ulti-mately aimed at the human subconscious, where love can thrive and the in-dividual again can meet her fellow human being, relieved from the crisis of individuality and intellect.

"The Late Day," as this cycle of poems has been named (selections pub-lished in 1962 as *Den sene Dag*), is meant not to escape the absurd but to penetrate its countless potentials. In its final poems Sarvig attempts to take the process even further, beyond the lyrical monologues of his autonomous creation. His solution, however, consists of dramatic and symbolic forms merely suited to bestow reflective language on his pictoral images. His de-parture from lyrical poetry becomes inevitable as his coherent but dramatic tour de force through the crisis of Western civilization approaches its provi-sional ethical solution. And it becomes even more dramatic as the ensuing series of novels seems to reverse the poetic process. The ultimate result is a universe of interchangeable forces and forms in which everything and noth-ing has happened. Notably, the alienation of the cities and the confiden-tiality associated with nature have been separated only to prove inseparable.

The range of this world of imagination emerges quite clearly from a sur-vey of Sarvig's genre models. Besides revising and restructuring his lyrical masterpiece so as to enrich its intertextuality, Sarvig has engaged himself in exciting mixtures of genres. His anachronistic philosophy of life notwith-standing, he is one of Denmark's most time-perceptive writers, somewhat an evangelical interpreter of modern signs. His first novels, *Stenrosen* (1955; The Rose of Stone), *De Sovende* (1958; Sleepers), and *Havet under mit Vin-due* (1960; The Sea below My Window), are daring adaptations of the de-tective genre, written abroad before this popular genre attained critical ac-claim in Denmark and held up as mirrors to Sarvig's existentialistic contemporaries and their concerns. But far from resolving the enigmatic problems of human identity that are on the author's mind, these novels make it perfectly clear that the causes of such problems lie outside the pur-view of the sleeping narrative characters referred to in the title from 1958. Hence the detective genre is a vehicle for Sarvig's quest for reality.

This quest continues in *Limbo* (1963), written for broadcast on radio and considerably more experimental in both lyrical and visual terms than the earlier novels. It is told, and was read, by a female voice and unfurls the en-counter between a male who displays power and desire for conquest and a female enacting the role of savior and redeemer. As elsewhere in Sarvig's work the depiction of gender roles and political orientation is not of this world. But if the oppression of women is viewed as a reflection of the incapacity of men, and if women as a whole are seen as mirrors of the novel's entire understanding of human life, it becomes clear that even works of prose by this author are essentially propelled by autonomous forces away from the reclusive nature of lyrical poetry. While Sarvig's poetic form of consciousness largely deprives the individual of escape routes to social interaction, his works of prose, despite their autonomous fabric, afford an outlet for mental round trips to other forms of consciousness.

This artistic autonomy—even inspired by graphic works of art—can lead a narrative into the very focus of political events, as is evident in the long short story *Jantzens sommer* (1974; Jantzen's Summer); but the example merely shows how artistic energy is inextricably related to the process of factual recollection. Even Sarvig's most disrespectful work, the burlesque novel *Glem ikke* (1972; Do Not Forget), posits the question of memory and its bearing on the notion of identity, and leaves it suspended in midair after a frivolous display of mirth and satire. An expatriate Dane has come home with a lack of memory and sense of identity. But will his contact with the past provide replacement for his loss or has the riddle of his life already been reduced to an abstract geometrical formula?

In *Limbo* the very title suggests a Dantean pilgrimage through the mist of memory toward a frontier where man and woman can meet and share in a spirit of transmutation. By comparison, *Glem ikke* is a teasing provincial odyssey in which people eventually gather around the small-town fleshpots. The two novels relate to each other—with Dante's *Divina commedia* (ca. 1307–20) as their symmetry plane—as a proper mirror to a magic mirror of the poet's visions. Woman seeks man, man seeks woman, and the problem of identity is their shared property.

In a series of later works Sarvig extended his experiments with genres to include collaboration with other artists; his natural environment initially comprised pictorial artists of his own age, especially members of the famous *Cobra* group. Both his view of himself as a visual person and his empathy with the unconventional ways of artistic life can be traced to his works of fiction, whether in their illustrations or in their pictorial discourse, and to his figurative language and style in general. A striking example of media expansion and media cooperation is *I Lampen. en skærmnovelle* (1974; In the Lamp: A Screen Story), written in and around a lighthouse and intended for performance on television. Earlier in plays for both radio and regular stage Sarvig made the audiovisual dimensions of language his experimental basis, and after enactment of *I Lampen* failed to materialize, two photographers joined forces with the poet in the lighthouse to use its nightly flare and dramatic contrasts as a way to highlight the conditions of human encounters. As shown in the black and white etchings by Palle Nielsen illustrating some of Sarvig's other texts, the locations for such encounters are places of abandonment and conquest, of harsh and challenging nakedness.

Sarvig's last novel, *De rejsende* (1978; The Travelers), has a Danish-American protagonist whose name, Dan T., once again is reminiscent of Dante's work. The novel also features a modern Beatrice, but as seen previously, Sarvig's travels go against the current, away from modern Hell. The homeless traveler rushes along in the poet's film, passing through a senseless space of decaying ideologies, truncated images, and sharply isolated phenomena. Only obscurely worded internal connections come to his mind. Yet drifting toward the depth and limits of this universe, his quest for spatial and transcendent insight is unmistakable. The traveler is in a thousand fathoms of water, but so are the other failures in life, and hope is all they have in common. The strength of this modernistic novel is its allegiance to the incomprehensible, its relentless quest for a meaningful sense of community in the midst of meaninglessness. And the author's ability to see through the eyes that he craves to meet, to see Denmark from the outside, makes this allegiance a matter of confidence in the unknown. Perhaps even confidence in the apparently known. The aim of the journey is the journey itself.

An attainable goal beyond that—perhaps closer to his inverted heavens—eluded Sarvig; *De rejsende* became his last novel. Under the weight of personal grief and sorrow—a year before he took his own life—he resumed, instead, his earlier writing of modern hymns, that is, religious and traditional poetry in the present age with its animosity toward religion and tradition. *Salmer og begyndelser til 1980'erne* (1981; Hymns and Beginnings to the 1980s) is a recondite work in which the author is respectful of tradition while critical of its limitations and decrepitude. Its attitudinal compromise is angular and objectionable, and its lyrical voice repeatedly transgresses the very boundaries and connections by which the author establishes his meaning. He is intent on imparting a total view of a world that is devoid of totality and visible only in fragments.

A number of Sarvig's collections of essays bear titles that corroborate this sense of crisis, of being out of place, at a time of change: *Krisens billedbog* (1950; Picture Book of the Crisis), *Midtvejs i det 20. århundrede* (1950; Halfway through the Twentieth Century), and *Stedet som ikke er* (1966; The Nonexistent Place). But in images, in particular *Evangeliets billeder belyst af denne tid* (1953; Images of the Gospel Illuminated by This Time), and in *Glimt* (1956; Glimpses), these crisis symptoms are counterbalanced by glimpses of reflection, insight, and creation that passeth all skeptical (and bogus) wisdom. Both the visual and musical powers of Sarvig's production are inextricably related to this spiritual and sensual synthesis based on pervasive dissolution and alienation. It stands to reason that many of Sarvig's texts have been set to music (by Per Nørgaard) and that Sarvig himself set works by the great transitional, synthesizing poet Shakespeare to verbal music in the Danish language.

From Heretica *to* Vindrosen

Heretica was essential to Danish letters in the postwar years both in the sense that it captured the spirit of promising writers and in the sense that its influence extended beyond its actual years of publication. Not only did it assemble the vanguard achievements of the 1940s under one umbrella, but reverberations from its discussions and polemics could be felt far into the 1950s. Although the front lines of the cold war eventually became markedly obvious, the immediate postwar bent toward inner emigration and stylistic obscurity did not vanish overnight. Resistance to ideology remained intact despite insurmountable international front lines, and moreover, the domestic development toward a social-liberal welfare state was both alarmingly materialistic and ideologically confusing. The situation was altogether untenable and, at the same time, destitute of alternatives.

It is typical that *Heretica* poets such as Paul la Cour and Erik Knudsen escaped the magic circle around 1950, but it is also typical that their Marxist opposition remained without consequences for more than a decade. The rationalistic-humanistic journal *Dialog*, with its attempts throughout the 1950s to continue the ideological culture struggle of the 1930s, never managed to compare favorably with the anti-ideological humanism of *Heretica*; and its intended dialogue with *Heretica* barely came into play. Not until the 1960s, when both periodicals had ceased publication, did certain people from the two camps engage in less artificial encounters than those afforded by the adverse editorial guidelines of the magazines. In 1954 Wivel Publishers merged with a reorganized Gyldendal Publishing House headed by Ole Wivel and his associates, and hence the heresy of *Heretica* was even technically forced to give way to more objective commitments. Its replacement bore the broader name *Vindrosen* (1954–74; Compass Card) and was edited from the outset by representatives of both its predecessors. Even so, its influence remained ephemeral until the late 1950s, when a new generation of authors began to relinquish the confines of the cold war mentality and to launch instead an increased concern with third world countries, a radical and timely critique of the welfare state ideology, and an effort to demythologize the *Heretica* version of modernism.

This revolt, though both political and artistic in nature, was not entirely at odds with humanistic positions; despite some ideological dislocations, humanism appears to remain a constituent part of most constellations of intellectual life in Denmark. As a matter of conjecture, its dogged perseverance may be seen as an offspring of longstanding efforts to consolidate democratic-humanitarian center ideals, most recently within the framework of the welfare state. As a matter of fact, reality expanded as Denmark entered the 1960s (cf. the anthology *Virkeligheden som voksede. Litterær kulturdebat i tresserne* [1970; The Reality That Expanded: Literary Culture Debates in the 1960s]). The growth began as early as the 1950s, but the growing pains could not be felt on a larger scale until around 1960.

For one thing, the combined impact of American mass culture and domestic welfare developments after World War II significantly undercut the high literary tone and profundity of the *Heretica* period; one sign of this change is the gradual takeover of market shares by imported fiction in Danish translation at the expense of poetry and fiction written in Danish. In the 1940s it was still possible to reconcile influences of translated fiction with contemporary idioms in the recipient culture; cases in point are writers of Danish fiction with American leanings such as Finn Gerdes (1914–) or Jens Gielstrup. From the 1950s and onward the traditional language of form is no longer on a par with these conditions.

Consequently, some Danish authors who reached their years of discretion in the vicinity or shadow of *Heretica* succeeded in maturing to independence in the course of the 1950s, while for the most part their artistic breakthroughs were long in coming. For practical reasons they will be discussed alongside the 1960 generation of younger modernists. Others did make their debuts or gain recognition in the 1950s without altering their course significantly at a later point; they will be discussed beforehand. Finally, it deserves mention that despite the alleged pervasiveness of *Heretica*'s spirit throughout the postwar years, this spirit was not universal. Traditional writers of different orientations asserted themselves continuously, some of them with quite noticeable artistic achievements despite their limitations.

Traditional Writers of the 1940s
Ove Abildgaard (1916–90) is a lyrical poet who was somewhat in touch with *Heretica* and whose limited production is also marked by *Heretica* themes. Since his convincing breakthrough with a collection of poems called *Uglegylp* (1946; Pellet), his calm perceptions and reflections have yielded the spirit and mentality of the 1940s in concentrated lyrical forms. But underneath his rhymed stanzas on nature, woman, and soul, a social outlook and an awareness of tradition merge with his omnipresent humor

and make for a traditionalism that has a character of its own and is worth preserving.

Other lyrical poets who give traditional voice to the spirit of the 1940s are Grethe Risbjerg Thomsen (1925–), Birthe Arnbak (1923–), and Lise Sørensen (1926–). Sørensen, however, was forceful enough to keep up with the times and contribute decisively to the gender-political debates of the 1960s with, for example, the essays in *Digternes damer* (1964; The Poets' Ladies). Traditional more in the sense that they add to the conquests of writers in the 1930s are such incompatible characters as Hilmar Wulff (1908 –85) and Jørgen Nash (1920–). Wulff writes a sociocritical, sociological prose in the manner of Hans Kirk, though with a touch of petty-bourgeois nostalgia and sentimentality. Nash, a brother in flesh and spirit of the noted *Cobra* painter Asger Jorn, is the author of both prose and verse in the surrealistic and vitalistic style of the 1930s; his program includes pictorial art as well as political anarchism, as shown in titles such as *Atom-elegien* (1946; The Atom Elegy) and *Galgenfuglen* (1949; The Gallows Bird). Eventually, Nash's crossings of boundaries took him into a variety of artistic happenings and, more permanently, across the Øresund to Sweden; he is an alien residing in the vicinity of home.

Among the traditionalists of this generation three in particular have become both beloved by the people and respected by the critics. Their no-nonsense attitudes to life and ways of expressing themselves are sometimes so direct that they come across in nonsense forms. Piet Hein (1905–) is an idealistic commercial artist and jack-of-all-trades, a humanistic designer and nuclear physicist whose hundreds of charming aphoristic and philosophical poems, *Gruk* (1940–63; Eng. tr. *Grooks*, 6 vols., 1966–78), have been translated into English by himself. The poems are on the same wavelength as the 1940s but have nonetheless captured the attention of the world. Hein's humor and lenient irony appear to move freely and harmoniously on the face of all sorts of ideological waters, as suggested by the title of his debut book in 1941, *Vers i Verdensrummet* (Verse in the Universe).

At that time he was the lover of Tove Ditlevsen (1917–76), whose husband, Viggo F. Møller, was the editor of *Vild Hvede* (1930–51; Wild Wheat), a magazine around which the young poets of this generation were first to rally. Triangle dramas of this nature haunt Tove Ditlevsen's poems and rather confessional prose, but her daring innocence and unobtrusive honesty usually guard against sensationalism and pathetic sentimentality. Her last volume of memoirs is called *Gift* (1971), a typical title that has the double meaning of "poison" (drugs) and "married." Her many depictions of marriage and childhood—in poems, short stories, novels, and autobiographies—center on feelings of susceptibility and vulnerability.

Ditlevsen grew up in a poor, working-class district in Copenhagen and never left her background behind. A recent popular movie about her life has appropriately been named after her second novel, *Barndommens Gade* (1943; The Street of Childhood), which was preceded by *Man gjorde et Barn Fortræd* (1941; A Child Was Hurt). The fear of being different is a basic motif, and changes over time only in the sense that it matures. A case in point is the excoriated self-analysis in the novel of marriage and crisis *Ansigterne* (1968; Eng. tr. *The Faces,* 1991). Its conflict matter is firmly fixed, even from a formal point of view, and it offers no redemption in terms of a modernistic breakthrough. Rather, in Ditlevsen's claustrophobic experience of life there is traditional evidence of harshly modern conditions. Her world is one in which people use and abuse one another, but more out of necessity than out of choice, more as victims than as executioners. They burn their candles at both ends, but the author is fully aware of the great existential expense, and until the candles burn out—as it happened when Ditlevsen took her own life—they keep the sparks of life painfully alive.

Halfdan Rasmussen (1915–), a contemporary of Ditlevsen, shared her social background and point of departure, but his experiences of poverty and war made him more pugnacious; during the German occupation his poetic struggle against social injustice naturally extended into a struggle against political and military dehumanization. It is typical that his first collection of poems was called *Soldat eller Menneske* (1941; Soldier or Human) and that he was the most widely published underground lyric poet in Denmark during the war. His conscientious feeling for humankind's struggle for life was later transformed into a feeling for life itself in the shadow of the atomic bomb. Life proves fragile and constantly overshadowed by fear and doubt and death, but its fragility only makes it more deeply appreciated, as suggested by his collection *På Knæ for Livet* (1948; Kneeling Down before Life).

Rasmussen advocates an intimate contact with the basics of life and shuns philosophical abstractions. Exploring tradition is his gateway to new circumstances and his way of being in touch with new generations. His many children's books and nursery rhymes may well be read as a continuation of his more serious and less durable works for adults. And his books and poems about Greece, Greenland, and Vietnam may be viewed as extensions of his (ab)original social and political involvement. He is a studious and concerned traveler whose horizon has become worldwide without moving its center from the back streets of Copenhagen. Readers of all ages love

Rasmussen for his naivistic charm, and he is respected by many for his genuine expressions of human and social commitment.

Concern about society's destitute outcasts also distinguishes some minor prose writers of the 1940s and 1950s. The plight of children and young adults, and of the Greenlanders, is the trademark of Jacob Bech Nygaard (1911–88); the problematic status of many women in society, of Eva Hemmer Hansen (1913–83); racism and discrimination, of the Jewish author Pinches Welner (1897–1965); and the unfair treatment of the physically handicapped, of the older and blind Karl Bjarnhof (1898–1980). These writers side with the victims of "development" according to an established humanistic notion of commitment. In yet another vein of the socialist-realist collective novel of the 1930s Ditte Cederstrand (1915–84), whose memoirs portray the years of World War II in Germany, authored a series of novels from the 1950s and onward. Unlike her contemporaries, she devotes her narrative to a class analysis of oppression, but her comprehension of class distinctions is utterly fragmented, and her writing inadvertently shows how it is possible to overstep the boundaries of one's class and yet succumb to its influence.

Regardless of their different political orientations, these writers all use traditional, established modes of writing to give voice to the weak in society. That said, we can turn now to writers who gain their independence in the wake of the *Heretica* years and have closer connection with their own times than with the war and postwar atmosphere of the 1940s. We can call them authors of the 1950s, even though they are both facing backward and pointing forward; most of them are prose writers in their own right with an ability to renew themselves, but they are not metaphysicians, as were their famous precursors, nor are they neorealists, political documentarists, or modernists, as were their colleagues in the 1960s.

THE 1950S: YEARS OF MATERIAL, SOCIAL, AND CULTURAL TRANSITION

Hans Lyngby Jepsen

The large body of work of Hans Lyngby Jepsen (1920–) is well suited to illustrate the new epoch. It is almost entirely prose, and its distance to the mentality of *Heretica* has been measured retrospectively by the author himself in his postscript to the second edition of *Håbet* (1976): "As to the domestic (duck)pond, the piety and the ivory tower self-sufficiency of the *Heretica* years were still hanging as mist in the naked trees." To be sure, Lyngby

Jepsen's own career began in 1945, but the short stories in his first book, *Kvindesind* (Woman's Mind), as well as the ensuing novel *Stenen i Strømmen* (1948; The Stone in the Stream) are indebted rather to older artistic forms, such as the realism of the 1930s and the Jacob Paludan–type novels of development, transposed to the times of the German occupation. More directly typical of its own time is the novel *Rød Jord* (1949; Red Earth). It, too, describes the occupation—and the feelings of despair and disaster that so frequently occur in Lyngby Jepsen's universe—but its release of emotions is unusually explosive, and it is quite extroverted, and modern as well, in its narrative form.

It is clear that Lyngby Jepsen's work does not lend itself readily to a formula description. It takes off immediately in different directions, and even when reminiscent of established patterns of writing, it tends to mark a path for itself without giving rise to substantial innovations. For instance, the author had his breakthrough with *Håbet* (1953; The Hope), a collection of short stories in which one text, with the characteristic title "Savn" (Want), is about an alcohol-addicted woman's grinding consciousness and desperate clinging to times past her recall. The story blends the inner monologue and dialogue techniques of modernism with a traditional portrait of psychological-realistic proportions. That texts of this nature pertain to the concept of hope derives from the protagonist's perception of reality as well as from the ironic attitude to this perception implied by the narrator. Moreover, the hope brings to mind a famous novel of revolution with the same title, André Malraux's *L'Espoir* (1937). Lyngby Jepsen intended to elicit its political associations at least to suggest a way out of his own despair. Leftovers from the original manuscript of *Håbet* are included as short stories in the collection *I kærlighed* (1959; In Love).

Though not acknowledged by many of his contemporaries, the political background for these texts was the author's experiences of the cold war, especially as it affected the United States; by his own account even the novel *Vintervej* (1955; Winter Road) and the short stories in *I solnedgangen* (1960; In the Sunset) were products of the icy atmosphere. The former is merely a futile attempt to surmount the despair of the times, whereas the latter at least submits an irrational optimism as a faint possibility. Even in the light of humor, though, these were cold times, and "the cold would sneak into the language," as Lyngby Jepsen wrote (in the second edition of *Håbet*) of his work from these years.

By the end of the 1950s Lyngby Jepsen's writing seemed to take on larger formats and to center on more popular forms of realism, perhaps a sign that despair is on the decline after all. *Paradishuset* (1963; The House of Paradise), *Træerne* (1965; The Trees), and *Jorden* (1966; The Earth) are a trilogy of novels later followed by serene volumes of memoirs in which the author deploys a realism of milieu that also marks *Din omgang* (1972; Your Round), a novel of moral critique on the subject of artists in Copenhagen. Add to this list some semidocumentary historical novels, travel descriptions of Eastern Europe, monographs on Social Democratic leaders, and books of general debate, and a connection emerges to the overall politicization of Danish intellectual life which commenced in the 1960s and continued throughout the 1970s. Bear in mind, though, that the author, now a Sicilian resident with a pronounced European perspective on the domestic scene, displayed political inclinations from the very outset of his career. Besides, just as his realism was aimed at illustration rather than illusion, his political criticism was harsher than was customary in the 1950s and yet less one-eyed than what became the fashion of the political left in the 1960s and 1970s. Lyngby Jepsen is an author of the 1950s going forward, a rather central figure of transition.

Erik Aalbæk Jensen

Erik Aalbæk Jensen (1923–) was initially closer to *Heretica* than was Lyngby Jepsen, and yet his work eventually better realized the attitudes and modes of expression in the 1960s. Despite its considerable artistic scope, Aalbæk Jensen's originality is genuine. He combines, from his debut in *Heretica* and his earliest novels, an existentialism colored by Christian views with a scale of realistic distinctions rooted in the realism of the 1930s, if not downright in the tradition of Henrik Pontoppidan. None of these prosaic impulses was held in high regard in the postwar years, but even so, in the author's series of three remarkable novels from the 1960s and the 1970s, the artistic connection with the past offsets a body of modern regional works of fiction. Its broadly composed realism is not unlike Lyngby Jepsen's in his trilogy of novels, which was not in fashion either when it first appeared.

In this sense Aalbæk Jensen in his own sober and reliable way forestalled the conceptual extension of reality introduced in the 1960s, if only for nostalgic and political reasons at that point. Modern development's very disregard of certain areas, groups of people, and attitudes to life constitute the subjects of his depictions and of his sympathetic, yet unsentimental, literary records. While his personal points of departure often conform with his subjects, his points of arrival are usually more advanced. The humanistic ambition to capture, with moral insight and suggested critical distance, what is alien and different is the pulse of Aalbæk Jensen's writing. His first novel was called *Dommen* (1949; The Judgment) and deals, as its title signals, with guilt and punishment in the spirit of its times (as applied to a sex crime). In *Dæmningen* (1952; The Dam) the period's cultural pessimism and hostility toward ideology attain historical legitimacy—at least in disguise. On the level of fiction the novel critically reveals how Danish capitalism after the national disaster of 1864 attempts to reclaim internally what was lost externally. But just as in the ensuing novels its underlying experience derives from the German occupation during the war. Aalbæk Jensen wrote two other novels in the 1950s, *Gertrud* (1956), in which the questions of guilt and responsibility do not convincingly conform with the realistic plot, and *I heltespor* (1960; In the Steps of Heroes), in which the author merrily succeeds in demythologizing the Resistance.

The best ingredients of these early works blend together in the sterling composition of Aalbæk Jensen's major breakthrough novel, *Perleporten* (1964; The Pearly Gate), and its two sequels. The title refers to the threshold between the sacred, who live in faith, and the heathen, who live in the world, both within the location of the author's childhood in northern Jutland. The world, allegedly, is "all the others," and it is the feat of the author to have passed the threshold of this ostensibly narrow understanding of life and to have demonstrated that despite its limitations it does provide space for true humaneness and strength. Conversely, it is within the bigger world, as it were, that confusion and decay prevail and that people on social borders tend to succumb to the Nazis' truly inhuman substitute for religion.

Many literary traditions—from nineteenth-century so-called schoolteacher's literature to regional writings at the turn of the century and on to twentieth-century collective novels by Hans Kirk—form the backbone of this novel's motley and complex images of life. Amalgamating these traditions in his own rendition, Aalbæk Jensen further derives from their intersection a variety of individual and social psychologies, and his delivery of tradition is generally fraught with an awareness verging on criticism. The milieu of this narrative has absorbed considerable authorial sympathy for the past, yet the author had little compassion for the cultural narrow-mindedness that in the decade to follow would make its publication painfully topical. *Perleporten* was to reach unusual numbers of readers and enthusiastic critics.

The second and third volumes of the trilogy appeared in reverse order. In *Kridtstregen* (1976; The Chalk Line) the two young Nazi protagonists from *Perleporten* enter the Danish Legion on the German eastern front, and we learn of the individual and social mechanisms that take them that far, across the chalk line and back again with their tails between their legs after the defeat of the Germans by the Red Army. The time of the plot is World War II, but the time of the novel is the political 1970s, as seen in the final update of the author's—and the *Heretica* years'—discussion of guilt and responsibility; just as in *Perleporten* the portrayal of the past in *Kridtstregen* has proved to be of current interest in today's Denmark.

The last volume of the trilogy, *Sagen* (1971; The Case), deals with Denmark in the 1960s, where the misery of war clearly has been superseded by the crisis of the welfare state. With his minute history of consciousness Aalbæk Jensen has unmasked the conditions of public irresponsibility and the general deprivation of personal control over one's destiny which in recent years have inflicted new social frustrations and elements of crisis on democracy. Even the techniques of his discourse are quite up-to-date; in the semidocumentary form of *Kridtstregen*, for example, there are traces not only of Scherfig's semidocumentary *Frydenholm*, but of authentic sources of military history, as was customary in the report and documentary genres of the political 1970s. Furthermore, in this novel the boundaries of the Danish province and what remains of its lifestyles and conditions are being fairly and squarely transcended by an author who had become conversant with local circumstances through his ministration, a literary conquest that was in keeping with the broadening appreciation of culture in the 1960s and 1970s. Aalbæk Jensen's last achievement is typically a monumental book about life on the Danish islands, based on personal inspection and written sources. Man may well be an island, but an island consists of men—men and women—and Denmark consists of many islands.

Tage Skou-Hansen

It was early prophesied of Aalbæk Jensen that if Martin A. Hansen's mantle of literary leadership would fall on anybody, it would most likely be on him, and his principal trilogy has indeed been proclaimed a masterpiece of postwar Danish literature. Meanwhile, another Jutland writer of prose, Tage Skou-Hansen (1925–), reckons Martin A. Hansen as an obvious predecessor, and *his* sequel of novels, about Holger Mikkelsen, has also gained recognition as a postwar magnum opus of Denmark. In addition to these points of resemblance the two authors share a background in the *Heretica* circle—Skou-Hansen even as a member of the journal's last editorial staff—and throughout the 1960s, and on the basis of war and postwar experiences, they both proved capable of bringing their writing abreast of modern times. Open to new attitudes, they readily included new angles of incidence and new modes of writing in their broadly defined projects of realism. A subtle combination of empathy and critical reservation with regard to milieu and characters is their shared distinction.

In addition to these similarities there is also a series of differences. Aalbæk

Jensen's artistic power appears to sustain rather than remove an outmoded attitude of style; whereas in Skou-Hansen's case the writing is less coherent, but all the more susceptible to radical contemporary developments. They are both writing in continuation of the Pontoppidan tradition in Danish letters, especially as it appears in the rendition of the 1930s, but unlike Aalbæk Jensen, Skou-Hansen was early seriously interested in newer English-language literature, film, and other genres of contemporary mass culture. It seems that while Aalbæk Jensen's strength is sociological and ingrained in the depiction of milieu, the focus of Skou-Hansen is political and mostly on the description of characters. The view of humanity is central to both, but in Skou-Hansen's work politics of all items hold the quintessential view of human nature; it posits a provisional balance between introvert moral obligations and extrovert obligations to take on reality.

Skou-Hansen's first publication was an article in *Heretica* 1950 called "Forsvar for prosaen" (In Defense of Prose), and from the outset the defense was a matter of rising above the self-absorbing "Heretic" meditation and of supplying instead an epic overview and a placement of the human in a wider context. This might be interpreted as a sign of widespread lyrical claustrophobia within the *Heretica* circle, but it is rather a testimony to the opposite effect that, after all, the milieu encompassed a variety of mentalities. At least Skou-Hansen did not consider its discrepancies to be irreconcilable, and his prose perspective was thus far not engendered by social or political reflections. What it implies, though, is an outspoken interest in reality, and the belief that reality, including nature, always exists outside the reality and the people found in art. Art does not exist in its own right, and only in the form of prose does it really pertain to the real world. Skou-Hansen considers this connection a somewhat symbolic realism.

This approach mainly consists in transforming poetical metaphysics into ethical matters with a personal touch and is evident in Skou-Hansen's first novel, *De nøgne træer* (1957; The Naked Trees). A student, Holger Mikkelsen, enters a resistance group led by Christian, whose passionate wife, Gerda, eventually has an affair with Holger. After an act of sabotage in which Christian is wounded, Gerda returns to her husband. This is a wordy and sometimes stale account of love and war in which a budding "Heretic" poet is among the victims and in which the title signifies how the promises of spring eventually collapse into the resignation of fall. In the perspective of war, love is what initiates human being's mission and renunciation; the experience of deeper commitments than the pleasures of the moment offsets the humanistic creed of this book. In his second novel, *Dagstjernen* (1962; The Morning Star), Skou-Hansen follows directly in Martin A. Hansen's footsteps. The subject matter is the same liquidation of informers that marred his predecessor and also poses a problem of responsibility. Without resolving the problem, his novel intimates that responsibility can be shouldered and that shirking it definitely presents a weightier problem. At least the book liberated its author temporarily from the imposition of wartime motifs—and from the structural confinements of the first-person narrative.

After dealing with a typical history of marriage in the novel *På den anden side* (1965; On the Other Side) Skou-Hansen seriously and with artistic ramifications cuts a larger slice of contemporary reality in *Hjemkomst* (1969; Homecoming). He had recently traveled to India on behalf of Danish State Radio, and the outcome of this trip was significantly to alter the course of his development. His novel portrays a Danish peace corps worker's homecoming. As this individual experiences his native country for the first time in a critical and political perspective, the ethical dimension in Skou-Hansen's work finds its truly political superstructure. What appears from the overall construction is a notion of the wealth-without-welfare society of the middle class—scanned by a fashionable ideology critique and revealed in a five-dimensional narrative that is probably indebted to yet another fad of the 1960s, the concept of "attitudinal relativism," a notion of concurrent and equally valid mental postures.

The artistic and human process of maturation in *Hjemkomst* becomes the vehicle for Skou-Hansen's next two novels as they set out to update the young protagonist Holger Mikkelsen and his surroundings. It first happens in *Tredje halvleg* (1971; Third Half), where sport is at the center of Mikkelsen's reminiscences. He is now a middle-aged attorney, and his memories are colored by the youthful slang of the novel's title, which refers to the obligatory round of beer and chat—at the expense of the home side—that follows a soccer game. In *Medløberen* (1973; The Follower) the sport of soccer is the principal issue, partly because of the author's comprehensive knowledge of the subject, partly because he views the game as a core example of reality when it hits the spectator with all its concrete and sensuous weight. Underneath the level of plot, however, it is the thematics of *De nøgne træer* that has been brought up-to-date in the shape of eroticism wrestling with politics.

What this author is intent on charting is conflict-ridden bourgeois consciousness in its making, and it is a special sign of his ideology critique that it does not prevent him from sympathizing with the issues he takes to task. Orthodox Marxists have found this varied ambivalence typical of a bourgeois humanist, while other left-wing writers have praised Skou-Hansen for his dualistic disposition. What happens in the course of his sequel of novels is that Mikkelsen moves in with the left-wing daughter of his late senior partner in the law firm, and he gradually sees himself able to accommodate her attitudes as an (un)pleasant contrast to his own bourgeois upbringing. In Skou-Hansen's principal work, *Den hårde frugt* (1977; The Hard Fruit), Mikkelsen slides even further away from his past, toward something resembling a signal for departure. His marriage with the former student rebel was merely a station on the road to radical liberation; the marriage dissolves, and in *Over stregen* (1980; Over the Line) Mikkelsen teams up with Eva, a daughter of his early love, Gerda, who has turned terrorist and now depends on his professional and existential defense abilities.

A dramatic reflection of a shift of mentality in Danish society and culture between the battle for freedom in the 1940s and the hope for equality in the 1970s is suspended in this series of novels. The gradual emergence of an anti-authoritarian way of life slowly enlists a bourgeois-liberal in its field of force while vaguely suggesting a promise of human and political understanding across generational and cultural boundaries. The slightly antiquated ambiguousness of the protagonist serves both as a drag on his involvement and as a susceptibility to its potentials, a fragile bridge across the years. As for the artistic value of these novels, a similar ambiguity in the predisposition of the author himself is quite decisive. Skou-Hansen is both thorough and handy as a craftsman of novels but is probably most convincing where his indelible subjectivism upsets meticulous documentary arrangement, an effect of disruption, incidentally, that he greatly appreciates in the works of P. O. Enquist, the Swedish master of sport documentaries. In his most recent series of novels Skou-Hansen examines how the 1980s in particular appear in the mirror of World War II and the Danish Resistance.

Poul Ørum

Another prose writer who has realistic roots in the provincial environment of Jutland and who is both progressive and preoccupied by the moral problematics of the postwar period is Poul Ørum (1919–). But compared with the works of Skou-Hansen, his production is more versatile and his semimodernistic experiments more pronounced. He constantly calls attention to the autonomous, self-producing character of his books and to their genesis as self-effacing splittings of the deep structure of the authorial personality. Intrigued by a life-enhancing uncertainty, Ørum clearly writes in the manner of Kierkegaard and existential psychology. He does so, like Sarvig, by using the detective novel as one of his artistic tools, although the solution is relegated to secondary importance or simply given in advance. His point is to show precisely how technical insight does not disentangle the irrational knots of guilt and destiny underlying a criminal intrigue. In fact, the detective usually arrives at his solution to the external problem only by identifying himself with the criminal as a person. After all, it could be himself, and perhaps it is. It is this interplay between internal and external circumstances, at the point where the detective starts spying on himself, that is most exciting in Ørum's work.

In early novels such as *Ulveleg* (1954; Wolf's Play), *Sidste flugt* (1955; Last Flight), and *Slet dine spor* (1956; Remove Your Traces), and in later ones such as *Ukendt offer* (1967; Unknown Victim), *Spionen ud af den blå luft* (1968; Spy Out of a Clear Sky), and *Hjemkomst til drab* (1970; Return to Murder), the very titles betoken criminal acts with moral undertones. Other titles, such as *Den stjålne ild* (1971; Stolen Fire), *Syndebuk* (1972; Eng. tr. *Scapegoat*, 1975), *Kun sandheden* (1974; Eng. tr. *Nothing but the Truth*, 1976), and *De uforsonlige* (1975; The Implacable), unequivocally stress moral problematics. Finally, psychological ambiguousness comes to the fore in *Et andet ansigt* (1970; Another Face) and, less conspicuously, in *Nattens gæster* (1969; Guests by Night), a book about the "I" behind the "I," the motif of the double or "she-shadow."

These different thematic and formal components are lucidly collected under one hat in the novel *Hanegal* (1965; Cock Crow). Its narrator is a crime reporter, as Ørum himself had been earlier, but rather than solving the crime from the outside, he is inclined to draw himself into the plot as guilty. His proclivity is well articulated insofar as a stream of consciousness technique prevails on the narrative to the same extent that the narrator's subconscious prevails on his acts and actions. The connections between his inner and outer worlds are dubious, if not directly distorted. The man is cooped up in himself—and cut off from others by suspicion—to the extent that only his delusions seem alive. Whereas a less dauntless narrative technique would likely have left the false impression of a possible survey of the personal circumstances and traumas involved in his rendition, it is Ørum's project to leave the potential resolution of conflicts with the protagonist himself. Dare he take the plunge and embrace himself in the upheaval of his destiny? The answer blows in the wind, yet it reveals a writer in the process of transferring the metaphysics of souls associated with the 1940s into something reminiscent of the confrontational techniques of the 1960s.

Thorkild Hansen

Few writers of Danish prose with a background in the postwar period sneered at his colleagues so often as Thorkild Hansen (1927–89), a prose writer in his own right who criticizes his peers' depictions of the Danish Resistance for being erotic-existential rather than matter-of-fact-realistic. On the face of it, his books appear to foreshadow the breakthrough of documentarism in Danish literature, while in fact they, more than any other body of fiction, adhere to existentialism drawn to its extreme; they share the inspiration from André Malraux with Lyngby Jepsen. This tension and ostensible contradiction are what make their discourse both intriguing and controversial.

What is remarkable here is not that the voice of individualism comes across in spite of a documentary form; that scenario also applies to authors like Aalbæk Jensen and Skou-Hansen, who use it for the purpose of extending their delineation of characters to include a societal perspective, and it further applies to the political awareness of documentarists of the 1970s, who want to strike a blow for the concept of class struggle. These authors are all intent on using documentarism to facilitate overstepping the boundaries of individualism. Hansen, by contrast, deploys his documentarism to show that the boundaries in question are impassable. His travel books—with himself or historical characters in the role of the traveler—make the point especially clear. Fraught with documentary ballast, they demonstrate repeatedly how the avowed intentions of traveling spirits come to naught while this very defeat permits the enquiring individuals to find rehabilitation in themselves.

A case in point is the historical-documentary novel *Det lykkelige Arabien* (1962; Eng. tr. *Arabia Felix,* 1964). It is about a Danish eighteenth-century expedition to Arabia, whose members include a variety of honor- and fortune-hunters, all of whom are disappointed and killed, and a lonely seeker after truth, the young German Carsten Niebuhr, who survives disaster and experiences a purification. In earlier books on Danish writer Jacob Paludan (1947) and on literary variations on Shakespeare's "To Be or Not To Be" (1953), Hansen ushered in his idea that strong individuals in defeat outrank weak soldiers of fortune, and in his later work this priority setting is radically elaborated.

His second novel, *Jens Munk* (1965; abridged Eng. tr. *North West to Hudson Bay,* 1970), is in the same genre as *Det lykkelige Arabien* and has as its title character an even more marginal individual than Carsten Niebuhr. Munk is sent out to find the Northwest Passage, but rather than reaching his destination he is on the high road to ruin. Seek and ye shall not find. The book testifies to Hansen's sympathy for Nietzsche's *amor fati* and Camus's Sisyphus; life is absurd and history devoid of values, and the human's rebellion must lead to an acceptance of the absurd and to gestures in which this acceptance finds its expression. That, on the other hand, endows history with an existential meaning; an abundance of connections between the naked life and other modes of existence dislodge the muddled waters of comfort and of life as a kind of tourism. And already close to the bottom the hero has full freedom and a perfect view of whatever rubbish of history that the surface community merely wants to disown. It is the useless and discredited existence on the fringes of society that constitutes true humaneness and affords the individual an opportunity to reconcile herself with her destiny and experience her death as meaningful.

Technically speaking, the book about Jens Munk conveys this insight by means of a double stop. On the one hand we find an apparently authentic character dealing with reality, and on the other hand a chronicler who is for the most part a loyal mouthpiece of the documentary author: a seeker after truth in sources and facts but whose authority the author occasionally calls in question. The arrangement benefits the moral complexity of the book. The author can use the chronicler's eloquence to instill in the reader's mind his fundamental philosophy of life. And when that manipulation has served its purpose, he can question the chronicler's perspective and sense of reality and eventually confess to his merely fictitious approach. Such concern about truth and self-revelation will in no way disrupt the effect of his philosophical maneuvers; in fact, it is likely to add the impression of a ubiquitous documentary validity to this effect.

In the English and American editions the role of the chronicler has been reduced to a minimum and the author's final dissociation from his performance totally eliminated. The narrator's precarious position between fiction and reality has become a very simple position in travelogues called *North West to Hudson Bay* (Eng.) and *The Way to Hudson Bay* (Am.). Unlike this trivialization, and the deconstruction of moral ambiguity it entails, Thorkild Hansen himself clearly moved in the direction of a mine field of moral issues, especially in his monumental work *Processen mod Hamsun* (1978; The Trial of Hamsun).

The title refers to the judicial purge, after the occupation of Norway, of the country's world-famous author, who stood accused of collaboration with the Nazis. If Knut Hamsun and his activities had already been the subject of mixed feelings in Norway, Hansen's book about his trial almost made the controversy explode. As in *Jens Munk,* Hansen has provided partly a representation of factual evidence, partly a literary interpretation extracting existentialism, mythology, and analogies from reality. Together these elements lead to the well-known conclusion that the only real thing is agony, oblivion, and death. The style of the book fortifies Hamsun's case, and the fortification reflects the strength of Hansen's case and the kind of case study he cultivates. In defending Hamsun the man, Hansen alludes to the grandeur of Hamsun the artist. Artistic capacity serves as an excuse for human incapacity in that it reveals an ambivalent and less reprehensible mind than narrow-minded moralists can conceive and appreciate. As the artistic genius becomes a tragic human being, aesthetics becomes a convenient transformation of unpleasantly straightforward moral problems into ambiguous moral problems easily adjustable to more pleasant frames of moral interpretation. The question of moral indifference at stake here could be just a matter of amorality but is rather a matter of immorality, because in the last resort it makes it better to be a good fascist than a bad stylist.

Processen mod Hamsun reveals the roots of moral ambiguity in Hansen's entire authorship. In defending Hamsun, Hansen for the most part lays claim to the man's absolute greatness in moments of failure; however, when occasionally his thesis collides with the facts, he fails to resist the temptation to find excuses for his protagonist. Hamsun has to be priceless at any price. Another self-contradiction stems from the fact that the humaneness of an attitude cannot be derived from an artistic performance exempted from human responsibility in the first place. In fact, if artistic freedom, as seems to be the case in Hansen, automatically means freedom from responsibility, this freedom is of no use in a serious consideration of morality. And finally, it seems quite self-contradictory to exempt a genius from the verdict of the public by writing an enormous and enormously entertaining apology for that genius that is tailor-made for public attention.

Why has Thorkild Hansen made an artistic principle out of Hamsun's human lack of principle? The answer is intimated in a diarylike self-documentary about the years 1943–47 called *De søde piger* (1974; The Sweet Girls). The bittersweet innocence of its title suggests the personal background for Hansen's brand of existentialism—sweetness of impotence, chronic innocence, blessings of nuisance. While others had their fingers interlaced with the Gestapo's thumbscrews, this young lad and his friends had theirs interlaced with sweet girls' fingers.

In between Munk and Hamsun, Hansen published *his* suite of novels: a large historical-documentary trilogy on the Danish slave trade. In *Slavernes kyst* (1967; The Slave Coast) we learn of the capture of the slaves in Africa; in *Slavernes skibe* (1968; The Slave Ships), of their transportation to the Danish West Indies on slave ships; and in *Slavernes øer* (1970; The Slave Islands), of conditions in their new "homeland," from where gold and raw sugar eventually was shipped to Denmark. This is documentary fiction that circumscribes its subject, and its point remains to demonstrate what actually takes place underneath the surface of official history. Relying on the objectivity of his style, as it were, Hansen sets out to reveal how objectivity in reality—behind the most beautiful slogans to the opposite effect—serves to systematize both evil and inhumanity; it has also been the case in Denmark.

Hansen is one of Denmark's most widely traveled men of letters, and alongside his works of fiction he issued some travel books and diaries; they amplify and clarify themes in his other publications but really deviate from the course of those works. Several of them keep close to the novels on Arabia and the Northwest Passage, whereas others are works in their own right. A composite volume, *Rejsedagbøger* (Travel Diaries), including three previously published separate volumes, was published in 1969, and in 1982 there followed another composite volume, *Kurs mod solnedgangen* (Destined for the Sunset). The title piece, which concludes the book, has as its motto a stanza by Hansen's older colleague Johannes V. Jensen, which says that young men go east, but old men go west, into the sunset.

Concretely, the essay is a matter-of-fact report from the author's tenure as educational officer on the training ship *Denmark*, but it also presents an existential exposition in the spirit of *Jens Munk*. A mythical leitmotif or figure is the biblical Jonah, a man who prefers to turn his back on the world but never gets permission, neither from the whale nor from the Lord. In terms of realism, Hansen makes it clear that conditions on board for the young naval cadets are more stupidly authoritarian and less human than our dreams of training ships allow us to imagine. Meanwhile, Jonah, who is half a jinx, half a banshee, mysteriously changes identity on the level of myth before he finally settles in the shape of a ficticious friend of the narrator. At this point he is definitely on the downhill slide, but he accepts his destiny with humor and with his head erect. While the world is heading for the dawn of moralism and politics, he is heading for the sunset, at his own risk. Disillusioned on the verge of cynicism, or simply human to the bitter end, he is without extenuating circumstances.

Elsa Gress

Traveling was perhaps even more a way of life for Elsa Gress (1919–88) than it was for Thorkild Hansen. She is the intellectual, artistic vagabond incarnate. The first volume of her memoirs—the principal genre within her large and motley oeuvre—is characteristically named *Mine mange hjem* (1965; My Many Homes) and devoted to a childhood constantly destined for departures and a way of life devoid of roots. Although it was for better more often than for worse, death was indeed among the frequent guests in her life, and the thin-skinned and nervous lifestyle further induced an almost insatiable desire for recognition. In the ensuing volumes, from *Fuglefri og fremmed* (1971; Fancy Free and Foreign) to *Compania* (1976), Gress depicts a development from the loosely knit fabric of her homes to her own complete independence on the highways of Europe and America, where the community spirit of her homes as a child is eventually restored on its own adult and loose foundation: the Gress family's international art milieu and creative "Decenter" (cf. *decentral*, *decent*, and *dissent*).

In order not to leave the reader with the impression of a successful educational development with a traditional harmonious ending, it deserves mention that this history is written with both an outspoken female consciousness and an unmistakable ability to take destiny in one's own hand. Gress's view of women as actively challenging their circumstances was markedly introduced as a philosophy of androgynous life in *Det uopdagede køn* (1964; The Undiscovered Sex), an original contrast to Simone de Beauvoir's *Le deuxième sexe* (1949; The Second Sex). Zest for life was the source of Gress's always restless and indomitable urge for action. It impels her best works of art, and it overflows her less accomplished pieces, in which one must include her dramas. As the centerpiece of her decenter, she naturally took a fancy to the dramatic form of art, but it was a love that most critics, to her great displeasure, found unrequited or one-sided.

The core of Gress's artistic activity is humanistic in the original sense of human-oriented. She says of her memoirs that man and message are central and constant categories and that she does not care much for academic disputes over genres and forms. Yet even assuming the importance of the message from a creative individual to a receptive fellow being, humanism can mean different things. Karen Blixen, though, is viewed as a true humanist, as opposed to the miserable and tormented H. C. Branner, and this appraisal is somewhat indicative of Gress's norm. On another occasion she counts herself among the anti-humanistic humanists (in a collection of essays called *Fanden til forskel* [1978; The Hell of a Lot of Difference]) so as to liberate her humanism from the ideology of humanism, be it political or religious. Basically, it is the ideals of eighteenth-century Enlightenment, mediated by the critics Georg Brandes and Poul Henningsen, that she espouses, but as mentioned before, espouses with a zest for life that tends to overflow the factual boundaries of humanism; Gress was first and foremost a personality.

Elsa Gress was one of many young people who after World War II was dreaming of a more spacious and creative way of life than the restrictive years of German occupation had allowed for and than she had personally encountered on her early journeys through fascist Europe. Instead of dreams coming true came the narrow-mindedness of the cold war, which she encountered in McCarthy's United States and was directly affected by to the extent that years later she would make her Danish "Decenter" a sanctuary for "the other U.S.A." Meanwhile, the home front was dominated by the introverted metaphysics of *Heretica*, converting icy politics into gilt-edged security. Gress's disappointed lust for life turned into a defiantly polemical and aristocratic lust for art. Initially an antiauthoritarian and demythologizing cultural radical, she ended up outbidding her own functionalistic conception of art by worshipping artistic geniuses in exile from abroad, such as the American Tom O'Horgan, or others in inner exile from the Lilliput state itself, such as Karen Blixen and the film director Carl Th. Dreyer. This cult took place under quite different circumstances—in novels, essays, opera, television plays, and so on—and ultimately it induced the author to throw herself into the art of martyrdom and self-staging with an energy that was deserving of a better cause.

Few deny that Elsa Gress was a zealous discussant, articulate but abrasive. But aside from that, her authorial personality will continue to attract attention. Her books contain cheap polemics and a peculiar sense of proportion but also a colorful sense of life and a great quickness at repartee; she is at once impressively experienced and unpretentiously well read (especially in modern American literature, but generally in subjects from the Stone Age to the camp of the 1960s). Jumping at fixed points in human life, this rootless humanist gets disappointed and lashes out or gets enthused and hangs on. What else can a modern artist do? Commonplace talk about the function of art is easily frustrated by art's real lack of function; hence her tendency is to fall back on the very myths that this function was meant to outdo. Gress's dilemma would recur time and again after the breakthrough of modernism, and interestingly enough, she would frequently take pleasure in aiming a blow at what she saw as the superficiality and solemnity of the modernist movement. Even its demythologizing efforts became a myth; even its critique of institutions an institution. Perhaps, after all, the more sedate and pensive 1950s were to be preferred. Sometimes eager to carry the matter of humanism to an implacable conclusion, Gress at other times makes it placate confrontations around her. Her view of women is a dialectical view of humans, clarifying the issue in some people's opinion, obscuring it in others'. Again the heritage of Blixen is perceptible, although the sovereign passion of the baroness is discharged as impulsive independence in Gress.

Hans Mølbjerg and Finn Søeborg

Finally, a brief mention of two authors who, each in his way, round off and supplement the picture of Danish creative writing in the 1950s. One is Hans Mølbjerg (1915–), whose first books give impressions of rustic life; critics have regarded the novel *Gården* (1949; The Farm), which is both critical and emphatic in its treatment of the subject, as the young generation's most important work of prose. The author, who is also a teacher, has since been writing lyrical poetry of his own and analyzing poems of others, Danish as well as foreign. His approach is deliberately aesthetic but also indebted to the history of thought. It is somehow reminiscent of the *Heretica* circle but at the same time knowingly and responsibly informed by more recent artistic trends. Not a modernist himself, Mølbjerg has, unlike Gress, made respectable efforts to be on speaking terms with modernism. His weak point is not that he is short of humor, but that sometimes his humor is insufficient to make his personal commitments digestible to a third party.

Finn Søeborg (1916–) has a different problem with humor; somewhat unfairly, he has been dismissed by the critics as merely a humorist. He *is* a humorist, but not in the superficial sense of the myth about him. Ever since his writing took off in the wake of Evelyn Waugh—his debut was in 1950—his humor has been mingled with tragedy. The result is a special brand of melancholy; it influenced other works throughout the 1950s and 1960s, including several noteworthy pieces of fiction, from Leif Panduro's first novel to typical characters in Benny Andersen's verse and prose.

In the fictive world of Søeborg two tracks intersect. One is social-realistic and has its point of departure in the 1930s; it is marked by sympathy for the little person, the eccentric or the apparent maniac, and it castigates the unfortunate inclination of the middle class to step on little people in an effort to reach up to the big people. The other track is humanistic in the general sense that it bestows an unreserved sympathy on all the small people in an unsympathetic world. Søeborg's style may not be particularly subtle or poignant, yet he succeeds in depicting, for instance, a lonely woman's candlelight dinner for two with her plastic dildo without making it a caricature or an overly sentimental piece. The popularity of this cocktail of ingredients in Denmark—across generational borders—is evident from the fact that sales of Søeborg's books have surpassed one million copies. That readers abroad concur in the appreciation of this underestimated writer follows from the fact his books have appeared in more than ten languages other than Danish, including English.

THE 1960S: MODERNISM AND NEW REALISM

Modernism

The 1970 anthology *Virkeligheden som voksede* (The Reality that Expanded) was about the cultural debates in the 1960s; but even the new poetry and fiction that came to fruition around 1960 inevitably reflected the expanding reality. Coincident with the surge of new realism, however, there was a tendency in modernistic art to shut itself up in autonomous forms. Compared to the cosmic and metaphysical perspectives envisioned by the *Heretica* generation, this tendency seems to mark an artistic curtailment. Both the new realism and modernism, and their mutual interaction, presumably unfolded in connection with social and political developments at the time. While negotiating a different time-spirit in a different manner (compared to previous decades), the advanced positions of modernism in the early 1960s were nonetheless part of the legacy of the 1950s and the postwar years. This applies to the extent that the overall picture came to include a continued rebellion against tradition alongside an ongoing expansion of the image of reality and of the artistic specialization required for the expression of that image.

The so-called crisis of humanism appeared to be constantly changing, culminating in a variety of antihumanistic attitudes and art forms in the late 1960s. With a view to the death of humanism found in the works of Grønbech in the 1930s, and the severe disease of humanism depicted in the fiction of Branner in the 1940s, the most remarkable thing about it was still the endurance of the patient and the recurrent resurrection of the deceased. One almost gets the impression that even criticizing humanism became an act of humanism (or of antihumanism, as Elsa Gress said). Seen in retrospect, the 1960s featured an abstract humanism not unlike its postwar forerunner, although an important displacement of accents has happened in the meantime.

All things considered, distinctive changes occurred in Danish literature in the late 1950s, and around 1960 we find a confluence or comprehensive manifestation of individual efforts. One of the earliest harbingers of the new climate is Villy Sørensen's collection, *Sære historier*, from 1953. Save for certain similarities with the *Heretica* style, these "strange stories" seemed so peculiar that Ole Wivel, who was the publisher of the prestigious journal, declined to put out Sørensen's first book (a decision he later admitted to regretting); it deserves mention that Wivel in general was known to be open-minded and that departures from the sphere of *Heretica* were not new to him (Erik Knudsen's "defection" to the political left is only one example). On the prose front Sørensen's stories were followed by Peter Seeberg's (from 1956 and 1957) and later by Leif Panduro's and Klaus Rifbjerg's first and neonaturalistic novels (from 1958). This was a choir of voices different from those people were accustomed to hear.

Lyrical poetry was undergoing radical changes, too, as shown by Rifbjerg's fresh and youthful debut in 1956 and by the fact that poets such as Per Højholt and Ivan Malinowski, who first appeared on the periphery of *Heretica*, gained full artistic independence or recognition around 1960. Perhaps, though, the most disrespectful and boisterous departures from the spirit of the 1950s were launched in drama, where little of original importance had seen the light since the 1940s. Ironic and satirical revues by Panduro, Rifbjerg, and Jesper Jensen (1931–) marked a considerable hiatus between this and the preceding generation; the solemnity of *Heretica* was no longer respected as sacred. At the same time, it is characteristic that almost all works of drama in the 1960s were offshoots of major authors' productions of prose and verse. The only exceptions to this rule that are of some importance are *Teenagerlove* (1962) by Ernst Bruun Olsen (1923–) and a few plays by Leif Petersen (1934–).

Just as *Heretica* was the trend-setting journal in the late 1940s, *Vindrosen*, edited by Rifbjerg and Villy Sørensen from 1959 to 1963, profiled the generation ten years later. Its first editors were Peter P. Rohde (1902–78) and Tage Skou-Hansen, but they were basically solicited by the publisher as a compromise team and were somewhat caught between periods. One of the few memorable contributions to the journal during this transitional phase was Ivan Malinowski's essay "The Empty Pedestals" (1958), which later became the title essay of the author's collection *De tomme sokler* (1963). The essay conforms easily with the attitude of the new *Vindrosen*, and if positioned next to the program of the first editorial team, it signals a remarkable distance between the cultural positions of "now" and "then."

The editorial program of Rohde and Skou-Hansen was clearly a compromise between the cultural left and the people from *Heretica* (represented by the two editors, respectively). It talked of humanism in the active and combative sense of the term that cultural radicals relish, but it also paid lip service to the tone of *Heretica* by mentioning personal responsibility and the unknown objectives of the struggle ahead. Malinowski, by contrast, was uncompromising. He deliberately wrote off his first collections of poems from the 1940s because of their universally human dispositions, and as a matter of course he set out to debunk the easy and lofty humanistic promulgation of the Dignity of Man and the Veneration for Life, an artistic challenge to these general concepts that proved irresistible and brought them down to earth.

That was precisely their destination under the auspices of Rifbjerg's and Sørensen's *Vindrosen*; and how they got there has to do with the image of reality as being curtailed and expanded at the same time. The author was expected at once to restrict his relations to metaphysics and to open his analysis of reality. Artistic modernism went along with cultural radicalism. Since the initial departure from *Heretica*'s circle, the latter position has been associated with the journal *Dialog*. But with the incorporation of neoradical forces in *Vindrosen*, *Dialog* was to some extent rendered superfluous and consequently ceased publication in the middle of Rifbjerg's and Sørensen's tenure as editors of its competitor.

One of *Dialog*'s last editorials, "Humanismen i vor tid" (1960; Humanism in Our Times), shows the same difficulty in formulating a coherent conception of humanism which earlier troubled the authors of *Vindrosen*'s program article. But while the editorial also demonstrates that the problem of humanism remains essential no matter how you look at it, it goes beyond the program's language of compromise by formulating a more clarified conception of the interrelationship between the opposites involved. It typically arrives at this resolution by leaning closely to Villy Sørensen's "Neither-Nor" philosophy; in fact, it was his astute approach to welfare-state problematics that pulled the problems of humanism out of the backwater, at least temporarily.

In the early 1960s reality literally grew in the sense that the welfare state and society made their breakthrough in grand style. Good times lay ahead, unemployment disappeared, and the increase of prosperity became tangible. The political parties could no longer go to the polls on the cry of crises; rather, they followed inflation and promised to make good times even better. Even art and literature came to benefit from the economic prosperity in terms of direct state support, and the educational system saw an equally dramatic expansion. Meanwhile, it became clear what was wealth in the Danish class society and what was not; it was not necessarily tantamount to everybody's welfare.

Villy Sørensen is to be credited for having upheld the dual view of the new societal circumstances that they should not be met with anxiety but neither should the material profit they bring be allowed to trigger complete satisfaction: we should recognize that certain societal forces go beyond human reach but not let this recognition truncate human values. Similarly, science should be considered a good thing but also a thing that sometimes invites positivistic simplification. In this spirit the editorial in *Dialog* is inclined to say both yes and no to the welfare state, to appreciate its merits and yet warn against its perils. The same spirit came to bear on *Vindrosen* and the new radicalism.

On the international political scene the cold war was still a fact, but whether because of habituation, more thick-skinnedness, or increased resistance occasioned by social improvements of everyday existence, the atmosphere seemed less paralyzing than in the past. With the writing on the wall of imminent nuclear danger, especially after the Cuban missile crisis in 1962, the first popular marches against nuclear weapons, led by authors Carl Scharnberg (1930–), Halfdan Rasmussen, and Erik Knudsen, were right around the corner. They marked the beginning of the 1960s' and 1970s' many extraparliamentary manifestations, the most vociferous of which were the protests against the World Bank and the Vietnam War (1958–73). Also spilling into the public sphere of the 1970s were the striking events of youth and student revolts and the active feminist movement. The welfare state had offered such a heightened level of expectation and greater sense of freedom that eventually people turned these gains against the state itself. The political orientation of the new radicals intensified into Marxism, and within contemporary art and cultural debates a combination of increased artistic consequence and increased prospects of expression accompanied the expanded image of reality.

The decade began almost according to program with the revues by Panduro, Rifbjerg, and Jesper Jensen assaulting the debasement of intellectual standards by popular art forms. Although launched in the name of democracy, this criticism seemed rather highbrow; critics spoke in the abstract over people's heads and elicited a taste of populist objections that later became politically significant. Another effect of this critical enterprise appeared at the end of the decade as various forms of popular art got house manners: pop art, neoromanticism, and so on. Allegedly, the proponents of this development were very respectful of their popular base, but in reality it seems that their main incentives lay in the potentials for artistic expression, for example, in the supple application of clichés.

The breakthrough of neorealism in the mid-1960s rested on the appearance of a new middle class, and this slice of the population was the subject matter as well as the audience. The documentary forms of writing, which extend into the 1970s, had different popular objectives, usually political as well. Documentary reports and other seemingly nonfictional products were interventions in the class struggle (inspired, for example, by the Swedish writer Sara Lidman's reporting from wildcat strikes in the state-owned Swedish mines). While bourgeois state institutions and literary forms pretended to serve the public weal, Marxist ideology critique showed that only the ruling class and its interests were well served.

The Marxists' own one-sidedness was presented as a virtue; that they openly sided with the proletariat in its struggle against the hegemony was supposed to separate them favorably from bourgeois thinking. In fact, since their one-sided aim was to abolish *all* social classes, it was not even one-sided! This conclusion proved to be merely a new illusion, though. With all their criticism of the bourgeois society the Marxists themselves were quite firmly rooted in certain segments of the dominating middle class, and their ideas of class struggle appeared precariously abstract in the context of contemporary Danish reality. That did not prevent some artists and other cultural personalities from lashing back at what they saw as Marxist obtrusiveness. More typical for the cultural scene, though, was a patchwork of mostly left-wing attitudes that put the formations of the middle class under constant scrutiny.

These intricate but not illogical alliances were most noticeable in the area of lyrical poetry. The new poetry around 1960 seemed quite unconventional; at least it did away with the artistic circumspection about which Torben Brostrøm, the foremost modernistic critic, used the term "the immoderate Danish moderation" (in the first issue of the new *Vindrosen*). The new generation of poets made radical attempts to distance itself from both the metaphysics of *Heretica* and the expectations of the bourgeoisie; the abstract lyrical "I" was stood in the corner, and the world of body language was put in its place. The new tide was often referred to as "poetry of confrontation" (after a 1960 collection of poems by Rifbjerg).

Art purified language at the expense of attrition, convention, and illusion. The procedure was to discharge artistic references from cosmic as well as recognizable circumstances, which means that symbols and metaphors no longer signified coherence and cohesion and that literary work became increasingly self-sustaining and self-preoccupied. Apparently, it was a most unpopular inclination, but according to the new "language poets" (around 1965), it was rather a question of completing what the poets around 1960 unsuccessfully set out to do in response to the poetics of *Heretica*: demythologizing the conception of art. By treating poems as texts, examples of language, linguistic games, worlds, or prospects, rather than as pretentious forms of attitudes and cognition, writers removed a barrier between themselves and their readers. Ideally speaking, the sophisticated artist became a sober language worker, while in reality poetry got disconnected from everyday expressions and referential forms to the extent that any claim to popularity had to yield the right-of-way to specialized "linguistics" for the initiated.

Without attempting to distinguish here between the intentions behind new simplicity and so-called concrete and systemic poetry, exploring, respectively, poetry's material and structural basis, or between concomitant journals such as *ta'* (1967–68; take) and *Mak* (1969–70; Odds and Ends), we should note that all of these forms of language poetry have been labeled the third phase of modernism. The *Heretica* group marked the end of the tradition of late symbolism and the beginning of Danish modernism and its departure from metaphysics; the generation around 1960, which finally left "immoderate moderation" behind, marked the second phase of this development (about one generation later than modernism had its formidable breakthrough in Swedish and Fenno-Swedish lyrical poetry). In the third phase Danish poets concluded a rebellion against vertical and humanistic ideas of the subject that were still intact in Rifbjerg and his generation. The result was a displacement of the anthropocentric model of the world, and familiar forms of subject and identity went down under a new horizon of attitudinal relativism, role games, and fields of possibility (as it happened in

Swedish "language poetry" about ten years earlier). The world is not a given thing; it is in consequence of—and limited by—language.

Looking back on the genius for crisis and tragic abstractions that is so characteristic of the early modernists, a younger poet, Vagn Lundbye, inspired by the French philosopher Michel Foucault and various other structuralists, disowns lamentations over this meaningless world. He proclaims instead that humaneness has always been conspicuous by its absence under circumstances of this nature and that only faith in communication and language is human-making. This is not to say that rigorous models of language and accelerating political demands were in simple concord in the late 1960s. When Hans-Jørgen Nielsen, the author and instigator of "attitudinal relativism," also became a Marxist, he began to use a sort of bookkeeping by double entry to make the most of his talents. While his lyrical examples defined their own relativistic boundaries, his political essays expressed themselves within less flexible boundaries defined in advance by the materialist analyses of classes.

In sum, the legacy of the 1960s includes an opening of literature's field of possibilities and a complex network of literary manifestations. The decade left the impression of boundaries being overstepped, not least the boundaries between literature and criticism. In the long run that transgression may well overshadow more spectacular political events of the times; literature no longer stands out from other types of letters insofar as critical or pedagogical mediation goes. A case in point is the appearance in 1967 of the journal *Kritik* (Critique); it came out with the express purpose of combining literature, research, and teaching. Also, the instruction of Danish in the schools was required to integrate poetry and fiction in the framework of a so-called expanded conception of texts.

Viewing its characteristics through social codes, critics of this scenario have seen it as "soci(et)alization" of literature; some have emphasized what they call "deaestheticizing" consequences of the process, which continued into the 1970s within material and functional types of literature such as blue-collar literature, women's literature, confessional literature, and artless, unrhythmical so-called broken prose. Much of the increased political awareness, however, was in continuation of the highly specialized language poetry of the mid-1960s. More important than these labels is the fact that the various currents appeared in a universe marked by an explosion of the media as well as of reality. Relatively speaking, the role of literature since the early 1960s was probably on the decline, whereas visual media were making headway.

Finally, the significance of the political radicalism of the period lies in its desperate attempt to acknowledge and at the same time oppose this irresistible move toward intellectual technocracy. The radicals wished to safeguard those opportunities of life and growth of society that in the eyes of many artists were incompatible with the process of modernization. First, there was the demand that the welfare state commit itself to cultural politics; second, there were the Marxist analyses of the class society behind the facade of wealth and welfare. In the course of the 1970s the fruits of this criticism fell to the ground as windfalls. Both the weakness and the strength of social capitalism frequently defied the interpretational models of the left. Meanwhile, more perceptive forms of literature met with little defiance of that nature.

Klaus Rifbjerg
No one embraces so many new artistic opportunities and approaches, so many genres and forms of expression as Klaus Rifbjerg (1931–). His literary production, intellectual appetite, and public influence have been provocative and legendary, and they extend far into the next decades, when he becomes a literary institution of his own, for example, as honorary professor and leading publisher. He has authored around one hundred books: novels, collections of short stories, collections of poetry, and travel books, as well as films, revues, feature articles, literary criticism, and dramas for the stage, radio, and television. In quantitative terms his major works are his novels; in qualitative terms, his collections of lyrical poetry. He has himself defined his artistic role as opposed to the *Heretica* spirit, which he found self-complacent and humorless; in fact, his many journalistic and artistic activities result from a practical sense of reality unknown to *Heretica*. Even in defiance of given genres, he has frequently explored potentials that his predecessors would shun, as illustrated by *Rifbjergs lytterroman* (1972; Rifbjerg's Listener Novel), created as an experiment in collaboration with his radio listeners and initially aired on Denmark's State Radio. Even thematically, in his attitudes and artistic forms, he is an agile poet of his times. Actually, there are critics who repeatedly rebuke him for blowing about on every fashionable breeze and for belching forth publications in all possible and impossible directions. As a criticism of the uneven quality of his work, the point is well taken. But his mode of production is inextricably related to his temperament and fluency; Rifbjerg is a writer, it seems, of whom one must take all or nothing.

Moreover, his writing is at its best when it takes off from personal experiences, especially from experiences of puberty; his resources in this area clearly outweigh his ability to fabulate. He has often described his individual novels as chapters in a giant developmental novel; in other words, as a kind of literary memoir, in which the same elements of experience appear in new constellations and interpretations under the impression of the author's situation at this or that particular writing. The novel *Tak for turen* (1975; Thanks for the Trip), for example, is about a school trip that took place at the same time as the fictive period of time dealt with in the author's first novel, *Den kroniske uskyld* (1958; The Chronic Innocence). The theme of loss of innocence in this novel resurfaces much later in the bleak science fiction frame of *De hellige aber* (1981; Eng. tr. *Witness to the Future*, 1987). What these examples show is how new artistic angles of incidence can invigorate old areas of matter and conflict.

These memorial thematics make Rifbjerg a poet of his times in more than a topical sense of the phrase. At the core of his writing is a momentary experience of eternity, a mixture of boundless sensuous fulfillment and a lurking sorrow over its coming to a close. In its sexual form the experience threads the short stories in *Og andre historier* (1964; And Other Stories). It is the awareness of death that warrants the eternal perspective, the emptiness that stakes out the terms of fulfillment. And it is Rifbjerg's forte that he is able to elicit this dialectical pattern from his memory and to take his momentary experience of life beyond the commonplace. To invoke and avert the menace of oblivion is undoubtedly a major source of his need to produce; moreover, it is a matter of moral concern insofar as the entire occurrence of values is provoked by an experience of nothingness. The concrete experience of immediacy becomes a maximal experience of clashing with reality or of *Konfrontation* (1960; Confrontation), as Rifbjerg named one of his lyrical masterpieces (incidentally including several travel poems from the United States). A catchword for the Rifbjerg generation, "confrontation" is at odds with the notion of life's being in vain, and suggests that the very formulation of a personal image of life is the real alternative to this outcome.

In his own words Rifbjerg's experience of moments of eternity is "almost hysterically existential," but in this intensity also lies a defense against the tendency of the "I" to pacify the artistic impulse. The usual mask in life is to make a proper face. As a convenient act of escapism, it merely prevents the individual from being positively overwhelmed by otherness or from "developing," as the title of a play, *Udviklinger* (1965), reads. As a prototype of the process of development Rifbjerg often resorts to motifs of travel and journey, insofar as both the inner and outer planes of his books are concerned. But whatever the artistic level in question, we are talking about travel as either a panoramic accomplishment of a process (rather than as a matter of means to an end) or a movement toward a new perspective on the point of departure.

Most of the ingredients of this notion of art and life are already present in *Den kroniske uskyld*. The book is a Danish neoclassic, translated into several languages (not including English, though). As reflected in the novel *Leif den lykkelige jun.* (1971; Leif the Happy Jr.), Rifbjerg spent a year as a student at Princeton University (1950–51), and he has clearly testified to his preoccupation with modern American literature ever since. It is not inconceivable that the resemblance of *Den kroniske uskyld* to J. D. Salinger's *Catcher in the Rye* (1951) may have prevented an English edition. Its very title posits innocence as an uncorrupted openness as well as an indissoluble trauma. The former is a sign of maturity, although few adults can boast it. The latter is a stigma of immaturity, which few adolescents can outgrow. The novel's narrator and protagonist is a high school student by the name of Janus; the double entendre of his name and the book's title signify perfectly both the youngster's contempt for his parent generation's loss of innocence and his own inability to secure it. If we consider it further, it is the eternal moment that stands out as the twofold unattainable experience in this novel, rather than the innocence, which merely represents a possible compensation for this ideal. But only in memory can innocence become a substantive replacement. A comprehensive experience of the moment, in which the "I" can feel itself undivided, requires the kind of unconsciousness or immersion in the past that only mythology provides. Janus idealizes his classmate Tore and *his* relation to their common girlfriend Helle, but underneath the ideal lurks the duality between a dream of pure and heterosexual love and the perception of truly destructive ties to latent homosexuality. Eventually, the regression to the past brings to heel an ideal that in its utmost realization would become inhuman. After the intervention of her demonic mother, Helle commits suicide, and Tore ends up in a mental institution where Janus visits him and says goodbye to him with the words "See you." This sounds quite encouraging, both in that Tore is likely to get out and in that Janus, despite his many weaknesses, has pulled through what Tore had not. Furthermore, the author has repeatedly said that he finds it difficult to conclude a book on an entirely pessimistic note; after all, he wants to go on writing. But whether his promising words go beyond yet another chapter of his great developmental novel is an open question.

Before his first novel Rifbjerg had his debut as a poet with *Under vejr med mig selv* (1956; Getting Wind of Myself), in which he literally gives poetic birth to himself. His self-understanding or self-confession is biological and bright, lively and sensual, narcissistic and cool, and, last but not least, humorous. It is chronic innocence at its best. Although obviously different in many respects, Rifbjerg's poems and novels seem to share from the very inception of his career an attitude of style that could be called "realism with style." It means that his works are indeed based on concrete and personal experiences, of which the core or some characteristic detail must be minutely recorded and identifiable to others; but once this element has been restored to life, it is the author's flair for stylizing the experience that endows it with the flight and weight of expression, with both suppleness and explosive force. That certain works eventually attain a total effect of realism, whereas others turn modernistic to an extent that almost defies intellectual transliteration, may be merely a sign of different inducements at the various points of writing and of Rifbjerg's versatile talent for preserving his initial impulses. His style ranges from technical objectivity to ready religious wit, but the decisive common denominators underneath the diverse appearances of his works make it understandable that, rather than invite his readers to an exhaustive analytical exercise, he prefers to have them keeping time with his verbal and mental rhythm.

In the large poem *Camouflage* (1961) there is an attempt, as in the early novel and collection of poems, to get underneath the mask, down to the prepersonal foundation of personal identity. Whereas *Under vejr* moved the conception forward, *Camouflage* takes it in the opposite direction, and the kind of camouflage that is being unmasked here is a disguise of profound significance. Consequently, as a matter of linguistic form this book has become a demanding search for subconscious and ambiguous mental landscapes, full of images of taboo and guilt but also of points of growth. The sources of sexual angst and fertile zest for life lie side by side in the poem's mightily shattered language, and without arriving at any complete understanding of their mutual positions, the reader can follow the author's description of the double functions of his camouflage. This disguise is both an impediment to openness and a means of self-protection, and if it is removed, it only reappears as a new disguise with the same characteristics. Screening and expounding this fundamental dualism, Rifbjerg is constantly induced to go beyond its confines and yet compelled to recede. Small wonder that he felt attracted to Johannes V. Jensen's combination of sensual vigor and puritan shyness.

Seemingly in contrast to the extremely modernistic *Camouflage* is the minimalistic-realistic novel *Arkivet* (1967; The Archives), in which hardly a word is beyond the reader's recognition. Nevertheless, it is still the formation of style that distinguishes the text. Composed of endlessly varying reiterations, the book gives minute testimony to the fear of change that prevailed over even social relations in the 1950s. It is an archival period of waiting and dragging on that *Arkivet* calls to mind, and it envelops the same kind of angst that conditioned ominous chronic innocence and that later possesses the opera-loving math professor in *Operaelskeren* (1966; The Opera Lover); the only difference is that in *Arkivet* the angst is relieved from the viselike grip of mythology.

Still, mythology remains an important factor in Rifbjerg's work. One collection of poems is directly entitled *Mytologi* (1970), and in novels such as *Operaelskeren* and *R.R.* (1972) the basic mythic structure is inspired directly by such classic characters as Don Juan and Faust. In other works mythology is the code word for Rifbjerg's dual relations with Denmark and the Danes. In *Marts 1970* (1970; March 1970) he delivers an invented and satirical version of the youth rebellion, interwoven with a fantastic love story between Sweden's prime minister and the Queen of Denmark and with the plight of a haplessly utopian Danish Joe Average, who plays the role of the ardent supporter for the two notables. The book is a sneer at some of the artistic fads of the period, but as an antikey novel (with the names of known people unconcealed) it is especially an attempt on the author's part to do away with the freewheeling utopianism of many intellectuals and instead to embrace common man and woman. This ambition is unabated in *Lena Jørgensen, Klintevej 4, 2650 Hvidovre* (1971), in which Rifbjerg's artistic alter ego Kjeld Deeners's and the cab driver's wife, Lena (living at the inconspicuous address of the novel's title), converge to an intellectual fellowship that both of them fancy but only Deeners's fiction can afford them. It is not enough to know that reality exists; they need to remember and insist on its existence to make it serve as the foundation of their lives.

Taking Rifbjerg's prose realism in the direction of the neorealism of the 1960s and making his lyrical poetry—from *Amagerdigte* (1965; Amager Poems) about the island of his childhood to the shots of everyday life in *Scener fra det daglige liv* (1973; Scenes from Daily Life)—virtually filmlike in character, the aforementioned theme basically constitutes the boundaries of modernism. What looks like realism is a plain discourse that has been confronted with emptiness and become fully enriched by the confrontation. In the novel *Brevet til Gerda* (1972; The Letter to Gerda) the relation between the hairdresser of the title and her itinerant spouse is determined by his (in)ability to formulate himself across the distance to her. But when his letter to her finally arrives, its message is one of suicide. Preceding the anticlimax he has mythologized her outrageously and thereby made this personal contribution to the overall mythology of Denmark, for which the entire narrative is responsible and to which the uncommonly common Gerda is devoted as a guardian angel.

As seen in this book, many of Rifbjerg's portraits of women show worship of angels on the one hand, dislike of feminists on the other. The author explains this slanting of the issue as a result of his overprotected upbringing in surroundings dominated by women. All the same, he is quite right in pointing to a development of his views that culminates in novels such as *Anna(jeg)Anna* (1969; Eng. tr. *Anna(I)Anna,* 1982) and *Vejen ad hvilken* (1975; The Road along Which). In the former the title character travels toward a qualified understanding of her own life; and although the female protagonist of the latter, as spelled out in its title, goes toward a more hopeless openness of mind, the narrative is legitimately covered by a self-ironical motto to the effect that when men write about women, it is like hearing the blind discussing colors. Just for once the author has transcended his male chauvinistic view of women and eliminated the need for it to be guarded by false modesty.

When utopia is cultivated and reality disguised, as in *Brevet til Gerda,* it remains an act of defiance against emptiness. Danish reality is full of stifling contractions, and nothing short of the myth of the blonde Danish virgin can keep the King of Terrors away. The dialectics recur, as a mixture of solidarity and distance, in the poems of *Fædrelandssange* (1967; Patriotic Songs), in which all of Denmark is like a dog that is averse to getting out of its kennel. Not until all symbolic and traditional patriotic images have slipped off and the dog has been enticed to come out of its hole, does a plausible image of Denmark come across. The image of Denmark in this poetry is stripped of official myth.

There are other stifling contractions in the picture of the period and its media against which Rifbjerg has felt called on to react. He has exposed the aggressive man hunting and cynicism of the tabloids to public contempt in a so-called pamphlet novel, *Du skal ikke være ked af det, Amalia* (1974; Do Not Feel Sorry, Amalia). A different newspaper milieu is subjected to more harmless satire in *Spinatfuglene* (1973; The Spinach Birds), and when navel-gazing confessional literature came in fashion, Rifbjerg retorted with a tricky novel called *Dobbeltgænger* (1978; The Double), in which the author—with seemingly unfeigned sincerity—confides that he is not at all the person he has been taken for. But what gives this novel artistic preference over the others is that its unmasking of the indecent exposures in some confessional writing does not prevent it from standing its own ground and liberating itself from its narrow point of departure. It is an energetic but also serious book that shows that Rifbjerg's indomitable will to challenge the restricting whims of fashion is a will that hits both ways. For who, after all, is more fashionable than Rifbjerg himself? His critical impetus is most interesting when it boomerangs.

There is in this author an introverted attraction to self-comprehension that, combined with a considerable resistance to meaninglessness, is typical of modernism of the 1960s at the same time as it is reminiscent of earlier Danish writings on identity. And then there is an exceedingly realistic and extroverted interest in current affairs, in the reality and people of the times, in species and subspecies. But the two tendencies are not disconnected. In consequence of earlier generations' humanism they intersect in major subject matters and patterns of life such as sexuality, family, and similar developmental categories, and the attitudinal approach to these matters is a radical humanism that remains in touch with cultural conceptions of the 1930s. Everything changes, but in defiance of the void that development leaves behind, art is still a powerful voice and an advocate of memory. Disillusioned and aware of its crisis, it nonetheless speaks with an optimism as ultimate and lasting as the authorship itself and makes its case for persevering on the rock in the ocean. Is the artist the fool of the system, according to Rifbjerg? Perhaps, but if the fool can fill the instant between past and future, and fill it with an instance of eternity, no one can complain about his role. Rifbjerg may write the myth of the artist with lowercase letters, but the Role of the artist he capitalizes.

Leif Panduro

Leif Panduro (1923–77) was eight years older than Rifbjerg, who looked up to him just as Janus (in *Den kroniske uskyld*) with jealous admiration looked up to Tore as the incarnation of true, mature innocence. But other than that, in the eyes of the public, these two enfants terribles were so much alike that they were often referred to as the Katzenjammer kids in Danish cultural journalism. Also, they had their literary breakthrough about the same time. Panduro's first novel was composed as a collection of satirical short stories about provincial life, and its title, *Av, min guldtand* (1957; Ouch, My Gold Tooth), recalls directly that the roguish and observant author was originally a dentist by profession. But his real breakthrough and departure from the prevailing mode of writing at the time came with *Rend mig i traditionerne* (Eng. tr. *Kick Me in the Traditions*, 1961) in 1958, the same year that saw the appearance of *Den kroniske uskyld*. Rifbjerg later told how embarrassed he felt when he realized that someone else had undertaken something that was as novel as what he had cooking. But he has also described with loyalty and precision in what way their works were similar: "The struggle against the world of masks and what later Panduro labeled 'the stone faces,' were things we had in common, along with the use of jargon, overtly spoken language, and, most importantly, *the theme of innocence*, viewed as a phenomenon with both positive and negative connotations" (Hammerich, ed., 56).

They were also partners in dissociating themselves from the previous period. Both Rifbjerg and Ole Wivel relate what Panduro said about Wivel and his generation of poets: "Yes, it is possible that you are wiser than us, but I'll be damned if the talent is not on our side" (Hammerich, ed., 66). By that he meant, as did Rifbjerg, that the young generation was ready with drums beating and flags flying to enter modern life, unlike the "Heretics," who were more inclined to shirk modernity. Panduro and Rifbjerg were united in provocative and productive activities in a variety of media and genres, sometimes in direct collaboration, for example, on revues and speaking engagements. To emphasize these similarities is to point to the importance of close personal relations and to the existence of a distinct generational profile in Danish literature by the end of the 1950s; it is not to underestimate individual artistic contribution to the common stamp of the times.

Panduro's individuality contributed a rare combination of a spontaneous and inquiring spirit on the one hand and the resigned maturity of previous knowledge on the other. It is probably true that he kept his vital senses alert right until his premature death, but also that he gradually became more disillusioned. The balance of his mental state was always precarious, but its anxiety and vulnerability became more pronounced in the course of time. A certain unrest is always present behind the bourgeois facade in Panduro's universe, but by the end of his life he witnessed a regular eruption of militant political commotion wherever he looked; in the meantime his personal outlook had become more centripetal and socially concerned. The disintegration of the bourgeois world in Panduro's work is unrelenting. Although both the causes and the consequences are political, he does not allow them to politicize his fiction or engage it in misplaced didactics; rather, his battleground remains psychological. This humanistic location was considered a sign of artistic strength by writers of his own generation, such as Villy Sørensen and Rifbjerg, but a sign of ideological limitation by younger and more Marxist-leaning writers and critics, such as Hans-Jørgen Nielsen.

Panduro's perspective *is* humanistic, in the optimistic sense of the 1930s, but also in the sense that external progress without dissolution of internal repressions is deemed impossible. Humanism is a matter not of suppressing the political, but of furnishing an unbiased display of its connections to people's state of mind. That was manifested also in Panduro's disrespectful treatment of the Resistance. He had just made it to the movement before the war was over and managed to get shot the day after the liberation—by accident! The heroic existentialist Thorkild Hansen made connections between this episode and Panduro's death thirty-two years later, but for Panduro himself it afforded grounds for antiheroic attitudes and relinquishment of myths. His basic motivation, however, was that even though the war had been won, peace was still at large. The victory was external, not internal.

When Panduro opts for exploring conflicts between people rather than between classes, and yet places his thematics within the bourgeois class, his purpose is probably to show that human problems resist the benefits of social progress. The welfare society leads to emptiness, not fulfillment, and the higher one's position on the social ladder, the more empty one must feel at being powerless. Panduro approached these conditions in the early 1960s, when times were good and the cold war less pressing; needless to say, during these years literary works with problems as an agenda were predestined to unpopularity. By the end of the 1960s the good times seemed to have reached their limit, if not their end; then the artist attracted an audience, either because his demonstration of the absurdity in life and humanity had finally struck a chord or because the general public found consolation in the fact that pain and misery in his work, for the most part, were earmarked for the privileged. People's angst for the unknown, the revolt, or just change had at least become palpable.

The individual feels that his surroundings are mad and that he—it is usually a man—will grow mad if he adapts, which he often does, or become fearful and amenable to the point of absurdity. And even if he gets off his docility, he is likely to encounter the craze within himself. The bourgeois and the anarchist suffer from the same alienation, and neither in repression nor in liberation is there comfort, or normality, to be found. As an outward manifestation of this inner fragmentation the male (and female) protagonist is usually accompanied by an undesirable youngster who engages the attention of the lead character in the most obtrusive way. The neurotic and rebellious youngster and the psychotic bourgeois are interdependent humans rather than human alternatives. Normality, then, is perceived as fragmentation itself, an imperceptible guilt feeling, an undefinable angst. These are the basic conditions that appear with different accentuation in various parts of Panduro's work. In the short stories, his earliest work, which he continued up to the mid-1960s (a selection of which, *Den bedste af alle verdener* [The Best of All Worlds], was published in 1974), absurdism is most conspicuous, ranging from ironical forms of fairy tales to rattling forms of monologues. In the novels, which he produced to the end of his career but mostly in the 1960s, a subjective realism is noticeable throughout. Finally, in the dramas for television, which dominated his production in the 1970s and became his most significant innovation, he writes his most objective and realistic discourse.

When the world is confused and unpredictable, a young person easily loses track of his identity and innocence. That happens in the early novels, notably in *De uanstændige* (1960; The Indecent Ones). In later novels the harm is done and the middle-aged protagonists *have* lost track of themselves in alien social circumstances, as clearly indicated by such titles as *Fejltagelsen* (1964; The Error) and *Den gale mand* (1965; The Crazy Man). In the first novel of this group, *Fern fra Danmark* (1963; Fern from Denmark), the identity problem has its background in the author's own depressing experience of being a displaced person; in order for him to feel truly homeless, he paradoxically had to feel at home somewhere, and once that feeling was at home, the story—or the total experience—was at an end! In *Daniels anden verden* (1970; The Other World of Daniel) the *whole* thing means nothing; the character in the title is frightened by everything diverging from norm and order. Hence he of course attracts what he fears the most. Even farther removed from total perspective, in the literal sense of the word, is the protagonist of *Vinduerne* (1971; The Windows). He is a middle-aged, unwed high school teacher who spends his lonely days looking at life through the hole of his telescope, a domesticated window peeper following events at a dubiously safe and (dis)respectful distance.

A relatively harmless version of the theme of displacement unfolds in *Vejen til Jylland* (1966; The Way to Jutland), about an old Danish-American and his encounter with the old country; the projections of Panduro's image of America on the background of Jutland make for a prank. Quite hapless, in contrast, are the interrelationships in *Amatørerne* (1972; The Amateurs), whose protagonists are middle-aged editions of the two youngsters, Thomas and Topsy, from *De uanstændige*. In his big box of a villa Thomas keeps track of his life in solitude by fastening on petty and easy-to-grasp details. But neither his adolescent son, the young rebel David, nor the indecently lovely Topsy, with whom Thomas—better late than never—has plunged into life, fits into this world of tiny gadgets. Each in his or her own way pushes Thomas out of his isolation, after which he dies. Topsy's husband arranges for an accident that puts a stop to the "old youngsters'" belated attempt at liberation. In *Den ubetænksomme elsker* (1973; The Thoughtless Lover) Sanna, the secondary character escorting the protagonist, is mad, but as her name suggests in Danish (*sandhed*, "truth"), for good and true reasons. And there are further indications that the protagonist takes on responsibility for her insanity. In Panduro's last novel, *Høfeber*

(1975; Hay Fever), such a solution is out of the question, however. The nearest the author comes to resolving his books' dilemmas is when, in keeping with the antipsychiatry of Ronald Laing, he opens up the prospects of greater existential and human diversity, and of critical and social awareness, within his own psychoanalysis.

Panduro's radio plays deal with the same problems and problematics as his novels, but in his many television plays—twelve between 1963 and 1977 —the medium is the message to a larger extent, for instance in the sense that the realism of the screen takes over the symbolism of the narratives. Perhaps the author's unusual ability to accommodate the new media sometimes had consequences that were not to his artistic advantage. But he had half of Denmark's television eyes starting out of their heads, especially when his crime serials were on the program. A list of his many successes would deepen the impression of his field of activities considerably (though not of his field of thematics); and besides, it would highlight how his writings on the unpopular themes of disruption and disintegration, both the epic and dramatic versions, from the late 1960s and onward proved capable of merging into one body of visual and popular fiction. It often happened in the form of humor. It seems that Panduro's humor, while subjected to the same incurable split of mind that marks his characters, contributes both healing and wholeness to his portrayal of characters. *Et godt liv* (1971; A Good Life) was one of his most beloved television plays, about a middle-aged, middle-class man who is finally ready to begin a new life when he learns that his heart is no good. A good life is what he will not get. And yet, once he realizes that, the life he still has becomes a good deal better.

Villy Sørensen

The most earnest endeavor within the generation of the writers of the 1960s to tackle the concept of cultural cleavage and to penetrate the entire theme of innocence, the whole conflict "between childishness and stagnation," belongs to the author and philosopher Villy Sørensen (1929–). His narrative was an entirely novel absurdistic or fantastic art form, preceding, for instance, Samuel Beckett; and its presumably decisive influence on other writers such as Panduro is only one of many pieces of evidence that Sørensen was the most astute and awesome cultural personality in Denmark in the heyday of modernism.

Although Sørensen, with his debut *Sære historier* (1953; Eng. tr. *Tiger in the Kitchen and Other Strange Stories*, 1957), was at another game than the *Heretica* writers, his point of departure was closer to this group than was most of his generation. With the latter he shares the sense of humor that it "is an attitude that is necessary to keep the fragments together" (Clausen 25) but his humor is of a special nature, influenced by Kierkegaard. And because Sørensen is so philosophically inclined, there is, after all, a conspicuous train of ideas connecting him to the gravity of *Heretica*.

When Bjørn Poulsen, in his book *Ideernes krise i åndsliv og politik* from 1960, recapitulated the anti-ideological program of *Heretica* by speaking against a variety of current intellectual and rational repressions of ideas and symbols, Sørensen, as mentioned earlier, responded with an article in one of the last issues of *Dialog* which later came to serve as the concluding piece in his collection of essays, *Hverken-Eller* (1961; Neither-Nor). The gist of his answer was to point to the tradition of old cultural radicalism (as opposed to Poulsen's criticism of rational humanism) while proposing an extension of the concept of tradition from its unequivocal left-wing form in the 1930s to a more complex and ideology-transcending design in the future. All in all, the two debaters concur in critiquing ideology, but while Poulsen speaks of the crisis of culture and against democracy, Sørensen sees in art and literature a solution to the cultural crisis on the basis of democracy.

The cultural criticism fueled by *Heretica* around 1950 was being consummated in Sørensen's humanism a decade later. In his art and criticism throughout the 1950s, he reformulates his intellectual background to the point where it becomes a modernistic and neoradical basis of interpretation and an intellectual platform for the new generation of writers. With his critical concept of neither-nor, which also encompasses a both-and, he writes himself into the 1930s' and 1940s' tradition of a so-called third standpoint, a point of mediation between cultural and ideological opposites.

The single individual of the day is split from the innocence of childhood just as European man as a single type of mankind since the Renaissance has been split from the totality of the feudal world. To return to a time before this fall, Sørensen resorts to myth as he alludes to primordial conditions preceding the beginning of time, experience, and history. His restoration of unity and totality takes place in art and literature and links the individual not to the sphere of politics, but to universal and general matters. The existential course of *Heretica* has set off an artistic practice by means of which he transforms politics into psychology and psychology into interpretation, not action. While drilling into the problems of fragmentation, his stories provide ample insights but few resolutions.

Disillusioned silence had descended on the intellectuals that were caught between the front lines of the cold war in the 1950s. At the beginning of the next decade, as the either-or simplifications of the world picture start losing authority and the Danish welfare state proves to be consolidated, Sørensen's work brings their voices back. Being itself a modernistic interlude, *Heretica*'s metaphysical version of the third standpoint finally comes across with new, political accentuation. Its novel tone may sound slightly different from that of *Dialog*, yet the notions of humanism both in the journal and in Sørensen's work have class cooperation as their prerequisite and consideration of the public weal as their incentive. Concurrent with the depoliticization of communist and anticommunist front lines, a critical and radical politicization befalls the third standpoint's notion of human personality.

These parameters stay intact until the late 1960s, that is, throughout the welfare period between the international "stabilization" of the cold war and the reemergence of class struggle on the domestic scene. As the period comes to a close, Marxism imposes itself as a new either-or form of intellectual exposition. But after that flood has receded, too, Sørensen's third standpoint recurs, now clarified by historical experience and updated in the format of a major work, *Seneca: Humanisten ved Neros hof* (1976; Eng. tr. *Seneca*, 1984), and a programmatic text named *Oprør fra midten* (1978; Eng. tr. *Revolt from the Center*, 1981); the latter is against thinking in terms of special interests and for a humane society of equilibrium, although the implementation of this society seems to assume or anticipate the framework of a corporative state.

From having originally interpreted his age by interpreting himself, Sørensen advances his myth-thinking toward utopian thinking and achieves, as his total effect, a humanism that emanates from the order of nature, which is prior to the disorder of society. His humanism further suggests that humans can overcome the splits in themselves and live with the splits in society, given the fact that societal norms no longer define the value of a human being. Whereas *Heretica* rejected civilization because it had ostracized the human, Sørensen affords it a critical reception because his understanding of nature allows him to view it as a challenge he can accept. However, the split constitutes no longer an insurmountable existential crisis, but rather a step on Sørensen's way to realizing the third standpoint or the political utopia of a society of equilibrium, based on natural and ecological principles. Sørensen has been labeled "the humanist between Kierkegaard and Marx," and at least his third standpoint can be explained in this context. In his reading the two philosophers both start with the individual: Kierkegaard from the individual's internal problems, Marx from the individual's problems with society. Subordinating the two precursors to his own thinking, Sørensen manages to include them in the same formula. As for Marx, the formula prescribes that more credence be given to his juvenilia (of which Sørensen in 1962 issued the first selection in Danish) and that the concept of human alienation be detached from the theory of class conflicts; in this way societal problems turn into (social) traumas. And as for Kierkegaard, whose *Begrebet Angest* (The Concept of Dread) Sørensen introduced in 1960, it is the other way around; one's freedom from alienation is the condition in which one's lack of freedom is seen as self-inflicted. Indeed, the concept of alienation in Marx and the concept of sin in Kierkegaard could be seen as two sides of the same concept in Sørensen. And freedom is not so much a matter of community spirit as it is a matter of personal insight and fulfillment.

In characterizing Sørensen as the poet of the welfare society, we should keep in mind that he is also the critic of this society: the two roles are interconnected, as are all of his artistic and philosophical endeavors. But the interconnections are constantly subject to change. In his works from the 1950s human disintegration is rooted in time, and the author's interpretation of the historical causes is psychological, not political, although the social awareness in *Ufarlige historier* (1955; Eng. tr. *Harmless Tales,* 1991) and the essays in *Digtere og Dæmoner* (1959; Poets and Demons) are greater than in his first stories from 1953. In the 1960s the disintegration of personality is seen within a historical context of considerable political complexity and discrepancy. But since the discussion of political problems does not lead to political resolutions, this additional perspective only frustrates the work of the interpreter. Modernistic insights in psychological and societal conflicts are typically inclusive and self-intensifying, and a movement in the direction of neoradical politics remains a mere possibility. Until this possibility materializes, Sørensen's discourse remains a matter of fiction—accompanied by critical-philosophical expoundings.

The latter form part of the essays in *Hverken-Eller,* whereas the fictive texts are located in *Formynderfortællinger* (1964; Eng. tr. *Tutelary Tales,* 1988), of which Sørensen has admitted that it took him by surprise to find their innermost logic in compliance with the actual social circumstances at the time they were written. Sørensen is not a writer who hitches his art to the carriage of politics; in a late postscript (1976) to his first book he underscores that "the literature that is best suited to inform about economical conditions is not poetry but social reportage." In the 1970s, when Sørensen escapes the sterility of left-right political confrontations by formulating his utopian revolt from the center, his works of fiction give way to philosophical products, including, for example, *Uden mål—og med. Moralske tanker* (1973; Without Goals—and with: Moral Thoughts).

As reflected in this development of his production, the author's defense of the welfare society is based on his confidence in this society's ability to secure the social functions of its members. But even energy disengaged from social problems does not necessarily benefit more basic existential problems; it may as well be invested in the repression of these problems. That was the view in the early 1960s of such phenomena as pop, mass culture, and the guardian society. The masses were considered the totality of single individuals who were not, but still had the opportunity to become, themselves. And the task for the artist, now that the external problems were solved, became to transfer the kulturkampf, or the peace dividend from former social struggles, to the internal human realm. The artist and the politician ought to be in the same boat and aim at the same public sphere—above special interests and private sentiments and devoted to emancipation and general concerns.

As a philosophical reaction to the conflict between art and its audience, Sørensen converted C. G. Jung's metaphysical language of symbols into a more secular conception of art, one in which the internal and the external, psyche and history, were supposed to be analogous entities. And as a political reaction, in compliance with his own thoughts on morality from 1973, he confronted the conventional thinking about special interests with the argument that since nature is the same to everybody, everybody must have the same interests and, hence, be interested in seeing the institutions of society rest on general principles. The treatise in which these ideas were definitively formulated was *Oprør fra midten,* which was later to be supplemented by *Røret om oprøret* (1982; The Controversy around the Revolt). The tenets were coauthored by Sørensen and proved to be of general interest indeed: they were read by many but had little impact on concrete reality—the humane society of equilibrium remains a utopia.

Sørensen's stories caused considerable consternation at their first appearance. An immediate concern was the story "Kun en drengestreg" (Only Child's Play) from his first collection, because of its matter-of-fact description of the attempt by two little boys to use a fretsaw to remove the leg of a third little boy to stop the spread of an infection. Besides that, it took readers a good deal of time to get accustomed to Sørensen's "fantastic" stories. And when finally some familiarity seemed established for his readers, the tutelary tales arrived as a surprise, in spite of the important keys to Sørensen's world of ideas which had been revealed in his essays in the meantime. At this writing, when his self-interpretations have been widely supplemented by works of other scholars and critics, a coherent understanding of his entire production should be well within our reach.

The first key is to be found in his elected affinities among European poets and philosophers. His large book *Kafkas digtning* (Kafka's Fiction) was published in 1968, his biographies *Friedrich Nietzsche* and *Schopenhauer* in 1963 and 1969, respectively, and treatments of Kierkegaard and Hans Christian Andersen, Thomas Mann and Herman Broch, among others, appeared in *Digtere og Dæmoner*. His probing into the philosopher Martin Heidegger also deserves mention. In terms of philosophy and ideas, these individuals have all had an impact on Sørensen's approach to division and unity in psyche and society, but even in stylistic terms, several of these writers have served Sørensen as useful points of departure or measures of his scruples. While, for example, the experience of division and collapse, in cultural history as well as individual psychology, is articulated most clearly in Thomas Mann and his epic version of the Fall of Man in *Doktor Faustus* (1947), it is in Herman Broch, the poet of repetition, that reconciliation between modern conditions and this lost harmony is the key motif.

With history as its starting point Sørensen's writing is charged with an existential interpretation of history as discontinuity. At the same time, his works are intent not on refurbishing past totalities, but rather, and this applies to the tutelary tales in particular, on maintaining the conditions of discontinuity so as to fend off false resolutions. The separation between past and present was brought about by the Fall, but reunifying the past with its present subject—be it individual or historical—is a matter of interpretation. When Sørensen refers to poets and demons, the latter are his signs of disjunction, the demoniacal feeling versus the demoniacal intellect, and the former are the authorities who can interpret, or reunite, the emotional and intellectual fragments in a historical context without concealing that this context has no reality.

The story "Tigrene" (The Tigers) from *Sære historier* is a recreation of the Faust myth, and like Mann's novel *Doktor Faustus,* it illustrates how the demons, in the shape of ravenous tigers, have been turned loose in modern society. Also, it is obvious that the dangerous tigers symbolize repressions, and when the Faust character of the story, Fif, sets out to contain the demons, his efforts are doomed to fail because his overdeveloped intellect—in the guise of tigers—is itself part of the problem that haunts his existence. Contrary to the character in Mann's book, though, this Faust at least realizes that to resolve repressions is not to dissolve or release them, but merely to interpret their meanings.

When art can put the problem of reality on the right track without resolving it, the reason is simply that it relates to reality by embodying it without depicting it. When the problem is intellectualism in particular, Sørensen brings his reader within its range by playing tricks on the intellectual discourse. Filled with irony and puns, his stories keep the reader in ambiguous uncertainty while putting him with certainty on the scent of the conflicts he has earlier repressed. Underneath linguistic logic an abyss of irrational potentials opens up in the very moment that language contradicts itself and its images familiarize the alien and alienate familiarities. Sørensen calls this "reflection on language an unhappy love affair with innocence" (Clausen 23). This unrequited love often shows up in his stories in the shape of double characters or twins, for example, in the allegedly harmless story "Duo" (from *Ufarlige historier*), which in reality is a perilous story about truth and how a conference on truth "succeeds" in taking its ambiguity apart and separating the inseparable parts. The portrayal of this surgical incision, however, by which dualism truncates reality, is done with such painful insight and compassion for the double truth that it fully vindicates its undivided veracity, and the concept of love as wholeness, too. Commenting on another harmless story, "Fjenden" (The Enemy), Sørensen himself said in a newspaper article that "it is an internal deficiency that provokes an external enemy. Love is ambiguous in the same sense: it is both what you escape from and what you long for. You love your enemy and cannot at all be without him—because you are in a conflict with yourself. This love of the enemy—and hostility to him—is what the story is about, both on its psychological and social level; and, needless to say, it is impossible to keep these levels artificially apart" (*Aarhus Stiftstidende*, June 21, 1968).

When an artistic interpretation that deals with the schism between emotions and intellect is itself situated at the center of this conflict, it is important that it includes a warning against its own authority as a guide to the truth, that is, against its own romantic superiority. Such a warning is given in *Formynderfortællinger* as the tales encircle the tutelary as an individual who acts with the best intentions on another person's behalf and thus deprives the person in question of her freedom. As his artistic means Sørensen here more often than earlier avails himself of literary prototypes, for the most part old legends or biblical stories, to make his entire (re)creation depart directly from the notion of authority.

Even Hans Christian Andersen can be rubbed the wrong way, as seen in the first story, "En glashistorie" (A Glass Story). Whereas in Andersen's "Sneedronningen" (The Snow Queen) God and a loving human being together save a lost intellect, the reverse takes place in Sørensen's text as it demonstrates how a human being and intellect gets lost on its own. First, the division of the human as *Mellem fortid og fremtid* (1969; Between Past and Future) comes to mind in the form of a myth and in the healing form of the author's interpretation. Second, this personal realization of social traumas enables private conflicts to appear in a rather general form. Third, lending its name to the title of the essays in *Den gyldne middelvej* (1979; The Golden Mean), the same process of realization eventually becomes instrumental for the revolt from the center. Altogether, Sørensen combines the mythical fixed points of the past, and of primordial nature, with their future equivalents in the utopian society of human equilibrium. In his most recent collection of philosophical essays, *Demokratiet og kunsten* (1988; Democracy and Art), he has characterized this democratic state of affairs as a framework for the physical and spiritual exercise of human faculties—at a safe distance from both capitalism and socialism.

But along with this promotion of his interpretations Sørensen has recently reestablished their personal, if not private, foundation, initially in individual essays and later in the poems and sketches of *Vejrdage* (1980; Weather Days), an entire book accounting for the personal expenses incurred by his movement through the process of symbolic writing. After all, the only way for the author to follow the path of artistic salvation away from the confines of privacy was to leave privacy behind. In a diary from the *Heretica* period called *Tilløb: 1949–53* (1988; Attempts) it is possible for the reader to get closer and deeper into the kind of schism in the author's intellectual and emotional life on which his work is based. Reading this material confirms Sørensen's spiritual affinity to the *Heretica* circle and tones down accordingly his connection with the cultural radicals. The reading also suggests that the philosopher precedes the poet in this case. Conceptualizing and generalizing profoundly personal conflicts—the agony of love, for instance—have always come before artistic attempts at resolving the matter. Control prevails over movement in Sørensen's work, like a bridge over an abyss of despair.

Besides the works pointing forward and backward, respectively, Sørensen has written some upward and outward reaching texts, adding further dimensions to his humanistic outlook. In recent years he has retold Nordic, Oriental, and Greek mythology to establish as a fact that the myths about gods are in reality images of humanity. Thus, his *Ragnarok* (1982) has appropriately been translated into *The Downfall of the Gods* (1989), and in *Apollons oprør: De udødeliges historie* (1989; The Rebellion of Apollo: The Story of the Immortals) he speaks of the Greek gods as follows: "They were different—at a certain point—from mortals in that they were immortal, not in that they were divine. They did not so much become prototypes of the mortals as they became immortal images of their human(e)ness."

As a matter of partial resemblance, another prose writer by the name of Sørensen, Preben Major (1937–), deserves brief mention. He shares Villy Sørensen's philosophical inclinations and was under his influence when his first book came out in 1965; in recent years, however, Major Sørensen's freewheeling imagination has taken a more metaphysical course, for example, in the novels *Af en ærkeengels erindringer* (1976; Of an Archangel's Memories) and *Søvnen og skyggen* (1987; The Sleep and the Shadow).

Peter Seeberg

Admitting to his own disposition for fantasy and imagination, not for sensation and realism, Villy Sørensen once said in an interview, "I really *don't* know how to describe." If there is anything his contemporary Peter Seeberg (1925–) can do, it is describe, visualize concrete surroundings in time and space, nail the precise detail. And yet even his narratives are fantastic. His intellectual physiognomy is probably more poetic and less philosophical than that of Sørensen—for instance, he has written no philosophical essays—but the more important difference is between their artistic and philosophical foundations.

Unlike Sørensen, who saw culture and humanity divided from an original context, that is to say, a particular problem of reality, Seeberg presupposes that reality as such is the problem, and a general one at that. And whereas Sørensen started out realizing how the fragmented individual was related to the initial conception of unity, and ended up envisaging the universal and central position of humaneness in the future, it is Seeberg's basic assumption that individuals are and will remain secondary characters separated from existence as such; there is no universal resolution to their plight, only a religious atonement. This is an *amor fati* attitude to the world that comes close to the attitude in works by Seeberg's colleague Thorkild Hansen, with whom Seeberg arranged the commemorative expedition to Jens Munk's winter harbor in Canada in 1964.

No wonder that Seeberg's first book was named *Bipersonerne* (1956; Secondary Characters). It is based on personal experiences from a labor camp in Berlin at the end of World War II and is about a group of youngsters from different countries assigned to second the shooting of a Hawaiian film in German operetta style. The purpose of inciting an audience that has virtually seen its country lose the war is unreal, to say the least, and for someone in the camp who has literally hunted up the action in order to experience reality bodily, the result inevitably falls short of expectations. Still, it is not sheer madness that shines from the pages of this book, but everyday, gray meaninglessness and fortuitousness. Its realism is indisputably sober, and yet it is fantastic in the penetrating sense that it not only concerns this randomly composed group on its trivial pursuit in the midst of war, but delineates the situation of every human being in every kind of life. That the characters of the novel are secondary means that they are all equally insignificant and that their attitudes are all equally valid or invalid. Only one of them, a certain Balt, is able to take the triviality of things at face value and then endow it with meaning instead of inquiring after a meaning in vain. To this man, reality is not absurd but merely a fact.

What little recognizable milieu realism was discernible in Seeberg's debut was effectively excluded from his second novel, *Fugls føde* (1957; Eng. tr. *The Impostor,* 1990). Its setting can be anywhere on the outskirts of a typical city with housing developments, construction sites, and so on. In a trivial house in this faceless cityscape sits a burnt-out writer—his name, Tom, means empty—who tries to write something real to the order of a so-called friend for ten thousand Danish crowns. It turns out neither more nor less real than the writer's immediate and quite unpredictable moods. Unable to use his words to disentangle himself from his problems with reality, he is deprived of the only possible solution, namely, to accept that reality is no more problematic than people make it. While reality has called on other modernists for poetry and interpretation, it calls on Seeberg for action. The problem is not that reality is not readily available, but that it is not readily real. And the solution to that problem is simply to take the plunge into reality—at one's own risk. Tom is unable to do it, but Seeberg himself has done it with emphasis (and with the philosopher Ludwig Wittgenstein as spiritual backing), as, for example, a practical museum director in Viborg since 1960 and head of the Danish Writer's Union from 1981 to 1984.

Several characters in his collection of short stories *Eftersøgningen* (1962; The Search) tend to follow suit. In "Hjulet" (The Wheel) the man with the Beckettian name of Djap obtains relief from the loss of his wife by playing around with a wheel that friends have given him. Then one day, many years later, a three-wheeled car comes by, and Djap sees the prospects of drawing his wheeling happiness to a meaningful conclusion; by giving his old toy to the driver, he naturally expects it finally to serve a practical purpose. In that respect he is disappointed, however, and is mildly rapped over his knuckles by the narrative. The man in the car is grateful for the present but still prefers his three-wheeled transportation. Good for Djap; his earliest passion was chess, and precisely this logical game made his feelings subside until his wife was dead and it was too late to express them. The story is not intent on reprieving this rational mistake by letting Djap fall victim to its last temptation. Quite similar to this text is "Patienten" (The Patient), which is about a man whom transplantations have changed completely, including his head. Deprived of this last fixed point of identity in his life, he naturally feels driven into despair. Although there is seemingly no way back to his old identity, he is indeed presented with it by his wife as she insists with tears in her voice that "it is you. It is you." And he repeats, "Then let it be me," as if it were a definition. Perhaps it is; at least he must repeat it every day. All the same, a frail identity is better than no identity at all.

The important thing in these stories is not what reality is; the riddles of existence are usually insoluble. What is important is to invest oneself under the given circumstances, no matter how dubious they may seem. That makes reality real. Or as the title story, "Eftersøgningen," shows: it is not what you search for that makes your search meaningful, but the fact that you do search. With an emphasis like this, these short prose fictions are considerably less hopeless than the novels that preceded them, and their more distinct orientation toward communication and action, not to mention situation and delineation, has since become increasingly pronounced in Seeberg's works, as has a more empathetic humor.

In his next book, the novel *Hyrder* (1970; Shepherds), it is still the interaction with other people that liberates an individual from his truncated and blunt existence; we are each others' shepherds and sheep. But in this book the interplay comes about in religious and mysterious ways as the novel makes a high virtue of the low necessity of isolation. Like Panduro, Seeberg would earlier make his amateurs of life fling themselves into life, a maneuver that often went wrong. Now he instead introduces metaphysical values and incentives to stay alive for. Marxist critics have repeatedly accused Seeberg of reconciling himself with reality, but never have they felt the thorn in their flesh as such a nuisance as in the cases of *Hyrder* and *Ferai* (1970), a play for the experimental Odin Theater in which the playwright allows all reason to be absorbed in religious mysticism.

That his critics were prematurely writing off his development as somehow stuck in false consciousness is suggested by three of Seeberg's more recent books: *Dinosaurusens sene eftermiddag* (1974; The Late Afternoon of the Dinosaur), *Argumenter for benådning* (1976; Arguments for Mercy), and *Om fjorten dage* (1981; In Two Weeks). They repossess the same pattern of ideas and the same basic attitude to life distinguishing Seeberg's first books: that the world is everything and nothing until you passionately plunge into it and take possession of it. But at the same time, the new books include some hitherto unknown textual types and genres, and display a variety of discourses in which the semantic accents have been transmuted to underscore lopsidedness, oppression, defenselessness, and commonly neglected ordinary matters. Sides and ways of life that get either stifled by norms and regulations or looked down on by decent people are at center stage. The death of the last dinosaur in the first book is a monumental example of such an anachronism, rendered superfluous by development but still worthy of an argument for mercy.

The formulation is an adaptation of the second book's title, *Argumenter for benådning*, which is otherwise coined to signify a murderer who incidentally was the best bass singer in the choir. Hence the arguments for his reprieve: music comes before murder. Maybe not, if one goes by the book, but reality has different concepts of truth. Even the last of these three books is devoted to matters that are at odds with developments or have been bypassed by them. People and things that modernity does not have time for are quietly and anonymously ready for someone like Seeberg, who has an ear for other voices than the authorities'. While the protagonists skim life on the surface, he once again gives voice to the secondary characters and their life on the bottom and in the shadow, the remarkable life of the unremarkable. On his own terms and with his own understated Jutland humor Seeberg has been quite instrumental in opening the public sphere to subcultural forms of life. Provincial literature like his made headway into the literary institution of the 1970s.

The three books at hand are related in a formal sense, too. They are all tripartite compositions and contain within their framework a spread of genres that entails other important points of resemblance. In a fourth volume, *Ved havet* (1978; By the Sea), the subject is a normal summer Sunday at the beach. But even though the many incidental glimpses of life come across as a minimalistic mosaic reminiscent of some of the previously mentioned texts, the flashes are so brief, on the one hand, and the total ocean fiction so overriding, on the other, that a larger epic span was to be expected. The point is the opposite, though: that its span and suspension are unusually usual, and perhaps decidedly unexciting from the reader's point of view. But along with the other extensions of Peter Seeberg's books from the 1960s, *Ved havet* makes it abundantly clear that modernism could conquer reality or develop the ability to do so, and in doing so it becomes a realism with high overtones and deep undertones.

Sven Holm

Among the younger prose modernists who made their debut after 1960, Sven Holm (1940–) is probably the one most strongly influenced by Villy Sørensen's understanding of European identity crisis and conflict thematics. It shows in the stories of his first book, *Den store fjende* (1961; The Great Enemy); the title story, which is in modernistic opposition to the realism of Steen Steensen Blicher, refers to a cleavage of mind that is magnified and aggravated by belligerent operations in the outside world. The next collection by Holm, *Nedstyrtningen* (1963; The Fall), is a mature extension of his debut and of both Danish classical realism and French prose modernism.

The novel *Termush—Atlanterhavskysten* (1967; Eng. tr. *Termush,* 1969) is yet another first-person narrative in which external threats excacerbate internal conflicts. Like some of Holm's prose books, it is only about one hundred pages long, and the taut format has to do with its concentration on the mythical and mystical core of its conflict matter. The external danger is the atomic war, against which a group of well-to-do people have insured themselves in time by making reservations at Hotel Termush, a veritable radiation shelter on the Atlantic Coast (with associations to both thermo-[nuclear] and mush[room cloud]). Pressed by a threatened and threatening local population, the hotel guests must consent to leave the premises and sail to their uncertain fate on the ocean. The narrator is a skeptical and self-critical humanist, yet he hesitates on the brink of a precipice to acknowledge the limitations of his humanism. In a later postscript to his book (1976) the author confesses that his narrator's confusion of insight and paralysis face to face with a collective crisis is his personal dilemma as a humanistic writer.

Deft variation in and concentration on myth distinguish most of Holm's prose. In *Min elskede—en skabelonroman* (1968; My Beloved: A Template Novel) the mixture is accomplished through brief colloquial chapters on the theme of Copenhagen, Holm's hometown. The style is chatty and satirical, elegant and fun, and the compositional connection a grotesque intrigue and caricature of the agent novel. But the essence and leitmotif is depersonalization. This effect remains after the many typical images of big city situations have faded. Holm's characters are modernistic figures or itinerant principles, more evident as models than as self-evident humans. Their bearing is one of restricted and melancholic humanism, of myth rather than life. In *Syv passioner* (1971; Seven Passions), too, both people and the world hang by a thread between order and chaos, and yet in this critical interspace an encounter takes place between the psychological and the political. The book's seven passions are pieces of prose convening to encircle symbolically this uncertain position with all its good or bad qualities. It is a place where life and myth perhaps can meet.

In the novels *Det private liv* (1974; Private Life) and *Langt borte taler byen med min stemme* (1976; Far Away the City Speaks with My Voice) the split and composite locations of myth are the nuclear family and the city of Copenhagen, respectively. In the former novel, as later in the sarcastic *Ægteskabsleg* (1977; Marriage Game), family and private lives are the victims of disintegration, while the text itself and its women seem able to make up for the ineptitudes of male culture. In the 1976 novel disintegration has invaded the very role of the author. The voice of the city is actually that of the author, who must listen to the outside to hear himself speak. The images of big city isolation and depersonalization laid out in the abstract by *Min elskede* have now become family matters and authorial concerns. And abstract cultural imperialism is in evidence throughout, from *Hans Egede* (1979), Sven Holm's play about the first recorded Dane on a mission to Greenland in the early eighteenth century, to *Koster det sol?* (1981; Does It Cost Sun?), about Danes on the Spanish Sun Coast much later.

Ulla Ryum

The special field of interest of Ulla Ryum (1937–) is a borderland. People in her books long incessantly for love and interdependence, but they are lonely and isolated, stretched between emptiness and fulfillment, night and day, in a world where everything is relative, if not directly false. Like Sven Holm, Ryum resorts to myth and (re)production of myth to find a fixed and gathering point in this confused and unpredictable concourse of subsidiary characters. Her first novel, *Spejl* (1962; Mirror), is a modernistic self-reflection on different planes. Its two parts mirror each other, and in the prose of the first part the characters are in the so-called mirror room of reality; it is not until they enter the reading drama of the second part, where they appear in a dream play outside time and place, that they can see themselves as they really are. In *Natsangersken* (1963; The Night Singer) it is a seedy female artist who experiences the isolation and thirst for love in her frail body; the novel formally wraps itself around this ill-fated individual by delivering a double montage of her hardships and declarations of love. A third novel, *Latterfuglen* (1965; The Laughing Jackass), recreates the Orpheus myth and presents the reader with a moralistic criticism of the betrayal of love.

As bold experiments with the human image, Ryum's first books are tainted with technical peculiarities and considerable sloppiness. In her fourth novel, *Jakelnatten* (1967; Punch and Judy Night), she definitely has the knack of it; still, critics have complained that the hermetically closed form remains unmotivated. Why even attempt to conceal the truth when you don't believe it exists or is accessible in the first place? Whatever her reasons, the fact is that Ryum this time retells the Odysseus myth in the manner of James Joyce's stream of consciousness, and then it is probably up to the reader to decide if the result is of current interest. At least the novel's title, with its reference to the marionette tradition, leaves several possible readings open.

With the exception of the recent novel *Jeg er den I tror* (1986; I Am Who You Think I Am), Ryum's production since the 1960s has been concentrated on short stories and dramas; triggered by the youth revolt and the Vietnam demonstrations, she became intimately involved with left-wing politics, and by her own account, her first child further reduced her time-consuming novel production. Some of her short stories have found their final expression in dramatic form, where once again the myth of love and its conditions, demands, and potentials are her preferred subjects. Just as in her other writing she has moved toward political discourse, and her principal dramatic work is a five-part cycle about the victims of war in our civilization, written throughout the 1970s and breaking the ground for the 1986 novel; the cycle's final piece, a radio drama called *Og fuglene synger igen* (1980), appeared in English as *And the Birds Are Singing Again* (1989). Precisely this persistent concentration on the theme of love takes her plays from the last two decades beyond the borders of her initial artistic field. One of these plays, an intimate scene, and still not even published as of 1991, is directly named *En kærlighedshistorie* (1981; A Love Story).

Svend Åge Madsen

In a critique of the early prose of Svend Åge Madsen (1939–) it has been suggested that for this author successfully to continue his efforts to objectivize the field of privacy, he would have to claim new land in the surroundings and the milieu of his characters, perhaps in some dramatic form. Viewing the older Madsen's production in retrospect confirms that his land reclamation has led to favorable results, even in his prose. His talent for using linguistic and narrative games to transcend the human subject has been concentrated increasingly on disclosing both psychological and social conflicts; a direct political involvement gradually becomes discernible. But the decisive politicization is essentially implied in the way he opens up linguistic structures and debunks the authorial role. Madsen, who studied mathematics at the University of Århus, is a systemic writer, and unusually humoristic and exuberant at that.

In the system lies a risk of specialization and constriction; in the humor, a potential for emancipation and engagement. And both are connected to the conception of the human in systemic poetry. In Madsen's view the question of identity is not the traditional "Who am I?" but "What I can do?" Instead of one given identity, the individual is confronted with several potential roles of which she can choose the one she sees fits in a given situation, at a given time and place. The same scenario applies to the writer, who can meet his artistic needs at a certain juncture by choosing between different genres and modes of expression, and it applies to the reader, whose needs are met correspondingly as she is afforded an array of linguistic alternatives on which she can test her prospective intellectual and emotional functions. To writers of an earlier date, who think of literature as a trustworthy caretaker of the depths of the soul, this may seem an unacceptable reduction. If, however, the human's identity is no longer believed to be an established fact, it must be to everyone's advantage and relief to entertain and appraise an experimental display of human roles. Madsen's strategy may sound like a frontal attack on humanism, but actually its justification is to liberate both human and poet from the straitjacket of identity and to make both responsible for the consequences of choice—and narrative.

This author does not express knowledge in his books; he looks for it. In his first novel, *Besøget* (1963; The Visit), akin to works of both Villy Sørensen and Seeberg, the basic situation is the one in which the novel is written; that is what the text elaborates and plays on. The "I" visits with a family, but is he intruding on them or are they intruding on him? Is his identity threatened by the surroundings or is it precisely when the boundaries between the "I" and the others disappear that the individual begins to partake in his world? Madsen calls his next novel, *Lystbilleder* (1964; Pictures of Lust), an "*uroman*"—a nonnovel (or a disturbed novel?)—to indicate that a normal relation between the "I" and its surroundings has been replaced by a description of the surroundings in which the "I" is only indirectly present as an abstract gathering point. Like *Besøget*, the *uroman* has three narrative tracks, and they coalesce at the quasi-personal gathering point and assume a kind of subject-object character. But is the character an intermediary of communication or rather its victim? The question remains unanswered.

While these books drive a normal situation to extremes, the short stories in *Otte gange orphan* (1965; Eight Times Orphan) are mentally ill extremes viewed from a normal perspective. The language of the title is schizophrenic, but the first-person narratives in the book normalize its disorders to an extent that appears more disturbing than the disorders themselves. Boredom becomes exciting, as so often happens in Madsen's books. The cassette novel *Tilføjelser* (1967; Additions) consists of five independent booklets in different colors. The order in which they should be read is not given in advance but must be decided entirely by the reader on the basis of his momentary needs. His decisive share in the responsibility for the ultimate reading experience becomes a moment of excitement in itself, completely emancipated from the kind of tragedy that is incident to, say, Beckett's modernism.

This devotion to the world of abstractions and linguistic games forms the basis of *Liget og lysten* (1968; The Corpse and the Desire), in which a new lust game, or comedy, is so disengaged from all previous reality that the traditional omniscient narrator can return and make his own terms—mind you, for the convenience of his readers. The author's authority is particularly called on when games and coincidences need to be systematized; after these measures the book ends up, anyway, resembling reality and *its* many moments of uncertainty. Crime novel, pornographic novel, science-fiction novel, and romance novel—they all emerge again as intermediate links in this sovereign construction of potent and impotent relations. Conventions and alienations are deliberately exploited to an extent that mocks at any illusion of human faces behind the masks; in return, the prospects of the mask game itself exult over a world that claims to be but no longer *is*. The artistic procedure reverberates in later titles such as *Maskeballet* (1970; The Masked Ball) and *Sæt verden er til* (1971), the latter title meaning either "Assume That the World Exists" or "What if the World Exists!"

If the world's existence is questionable, one way or the other, it is only natural that the author demonstrates how questionable it is. It happens in his play on the genre of crime fiction in *Tredje gang så ta'r vi ham* (1969; We'll Get Him the Third Time), where on close examination the seemingly coherent detective story dissolves into sheer ambiguities. By turning even motifs from other works, such as Kafka's *Das Schloss* (1926; The Castle), upside down, Madsen's novel shows how our dearest pictures of reality, rightly considered, are linguistic constructions of a different breed. In *Dage med Diam eller Livet om natten* (1972; Days with Diam or Life by Night) the individual's lack of history is once again what breaks the ground for life's innumerable role potentials. Throughout the book the narrative comments on itself, and the many narrative tracks reflect the span between the day and the night of the title. This reflection, in turn, mirrors the challenge of an impossible dualism, to which the author has responded by constructing a bigger world than the one that exists under dualistic restrictions.

Madsen's largest book so far, *Tugt og utugt i mellemtiden* (1976; Decency and Indecency in the Meanwhile), draws his systemic discourse to its conclusion as it applies to history, the present times, and the social settings. His abstractions no longer lead away from human conditions; in fact, they point to these conditions' most central and incompatible points of conflict. It is a world that Madsen has invented, but his inventiveness covers and at the same time eclipses most people's imagination. Such is the case in most of his books, from whodunits like *Hadets bånd* (1978; The Bonds of Hatred) to later historical plays about royalty (1986). Increasingly polyphonic, their echo-space constructions of reality entail ever more reality: more concretion and more readers.

With Rifbjerg as the all-embracing exception, the aforementioned modernists have first and foremost, though not exclusively, been writers of prose. Some have written drama, but with Panduro as the possible exception, their plays have been by-products of their talents. Svend Åge Madsen goes beyond the artistic limits of the modernism of the 1960s, and so do Cecil Bødker and Dorrit Willumsen, although in a less radical sense. Both of them write lyrical poetry as well as prose, but their modernism remains essentially prosaic.

Cecil Bødker and Dorrit Willumsen

Cecil Bødker (1927–) had published three collections of poems in the 1950s before her breakthrough as a prose writer with the short-story collection *Øjet* (1961; The Eye). Her poems span the nearness of nature to the remoteness of myth, especially in *Anadyomene* (1959), but sometimes they are weakened by obviousness and long-winded monotony. Bødker's short stories are better focused and more concentrated; many are centered on the unacknowledged or repressed side of human nature and show how it breaks apart when confronted with nature outside of humanity. Most of the stories let off their steam without pedagogical meddling by the author, and this modernistic practice applies to their depiction of environment, too. There is little local color in Bødker's fiction; the world in her prose is without a center and somehow without life and communication. Perhaps her occasional desire to overinterpret her experiences has to do with the degree to which they appear inexplicable.

One of the harshest stories in *Øjet* is "Vædderen" (The Ram). This stubborn animal with its latent force of nature also shows up in the title of Bødker's latest collection of poems, *I vædderens tegn* (1968; Under the Sign of the Ram), and once again the signifier points to the unrealized nature of the human (incidentally [?], Bødker was born under the zodiacal sign of the ram). The bulk of the author's more recent writing consists of children's books, about half of her entire production. Her recent works for adults include two plays, two narrative cycles, and in the 1980s two novels about women's liberation, *Evas ekko* (1980; The Echo of Eve) and *Tænk på Jolande* (1981; Remember Jolande). Finally, two narratives put the character of Jesus in the light of modernity: *Drengen* (1983; The Boy) and *Manden* (1984; The Man), creating altogether new angles on humanity.

An artistic travel book based on a three-month stay in an Ethiopian village, where Bødker adopted two children, finally unleashes a pressing urge in her earlier works to transgress cultural boundaries. *Salthandlerskens hus* (1972; The House of the Salt Dealer Woman) is, for the most part, a first-person narrative in second-person form. It is an inner monologue, as it were, deployed as a means of overcoming distances and applying to readers or a way of subjecting cultural boundaries to artistic scrutiny. Its clash between the Danish and African worlds results in a mixture of cultural chasm and cultural communication. It can be fatal, as it is for the woman in the title, or it can be enriching, as for the time being it is for the author. Her experiences combine an act of writing with an act of social and ethical dimensions, and her journey can continue even after it has literally ended with her and her new children's departure from Ethiopia. As for its final result, the verdict is still out. But people have reached each other far way from home; in fact, it was first at a distance that closeness occurred.

Dorrit Willumsen (1940–) made her debut in 1965, at a time when young writers were on the move toward systemic poetry, neorealism, or other manifestations of relativism. Willumsen, however, is firmly rooted in the world of imagination and artistic practice associated with the modernist movement of the early 1960s; her particular departure from this foundation consists of depictions of depersonalization and alienation of women in a male- and consumer-oriented society. Her subject matter perhaps puts her readers in mind of Ulla Ryum, but her style and conception do not. In the title story of her first collection, *Knagen* (1965; The Hook), the female part of the couple it describes is only once depicted as something reminiscent of a human being, in the next to the last line, which says that "her shoulders slipped out of their hooked position." Even this description leaves her quite objectified, mentioned only indirectly by a part of her body, which has been relieved as a rare exception from its strenuous physical position. Already in the next, and last, line about the next day, "it" (the female part) reappears totally reduced to the same kind of insectlike entity "it" has been from the very beginning of "its" existence in man's world.

This modernistic representation of an alienated woman is given extensive orchestration in *En værtindes smil* (1974; The Smile of a Hostess), which is in two parts, each consisting of several short texts. The first and longer part is called "En sluttet kreds" (A Closed Circle), which refers both to the circle of texts and to the characters' circle of acquaintances. In both senses of the word the circle is constituted by a permanent gallery of persons, and it is definitely a closed circle. But by addressing this closed world from different angles and changing perspectives, the book's versatile composition underscores precisely how boundless its alienation and modern everyday milieu are. In its second part the alienation is inserted in an utterly sterile vision of the future. The stifled tears and superimposed smile of the hostess now being their connecting emblem, its chapters still overlap. Both the woman's age and sexual appearance undergo drastic changes, which are nonetheless alarmingly futile. Normality, in endlessly repeated variations, flattens all differences and potential shock effects, and psychological deficits are immediately and mechanically compensated for by means of chocolates and novelty toys. The only reason for optimism purveyed in the entire book is a possible, belated contact between the members of its alienated cast. Their world is really void, though not blissfully void, of everything but things, and the empty and loveless life here stretches into later titles such as *Modellen Coppelia* (1973; The Model Coppelia), *Manden som påskud* (1980; The Man as Pretext), and *Programmeret til kærlighed* (1981; Programmed for Love). But in the large novel *Marie* (1983; Eng. tr. 1986), about Madame Tussaud, Willumsen convincingly makes the case that love can be more than mutual stunting of the sexes and that art can reach beyond the absurdity in reality.

Jørgen Gustava Brandt

Returning to the starting point of predominantly lyrical modernists of this generation, one realizes that—just as in the area of prose—some writers from *Heretica*'s circles became modernistic pioneers around 1960. Why they arrived at artistic prominence so late was either because their writing remained under *Heretica*'s sign for years or because their early originality remained unnoticed. It seems fair to say that the earliest and most visible departure from the artistic climate of the 1940s occurred in prose (the most widely read genre), whereas the most daring and confident departure was seen in poetry.

One spokesman of this appraisal is Jørgen Gustava Brandt (1929–), and his own development is, indeed, in agreement with its characterization. In his collection of essays, *Udflugter* (1961; Excursions), the departure from the past is evident in two seminal pieces. "Den geniale monotoni" (The Monotony of Genius) makes its pledge to Bjørnvig's and Sarvig's invocation of art as a subtle and exclusively separate world, whereas "Kunst og virkelighed" (Art and Reality) professes a creed in exchanges between artistic autonomy and ever-present reality. To the extent artistic autonomy remains intact, it is in the form of clear-cut, but provisional, consciousness. If the artist withdraws from the real world, it is merely for the purpose of confronting its reality with extra alertness. It is not to take refuge in a higher world of imagination, but to be able to risk his life head first and eyes open without a dulling, worldly safety net.

In Brandt's poetic practice this development between late symbolism and modernistic confrontation takes place between his debut in *Korn i Pelegs Mark* (1949; Grain on Peleg's Field) and *Fragment af imorgen* (1960; Fragment of Tomorrow). In *Dragespor* (1957; Dragon's Tracks) the self-reflecting attitude is still predominant. The dragon's tracks lead up to, say, Panduro's saurian days, as the title reads of his novel *Øgledage* (1961), and they mark whatever obstinate reality the artist is inclined to expel from his artistic world. But his awareness of the conflict at least prepares for the breakthrough of his confrontational energies, and in *Janushoved* (1962; Head of Janus) he has adapted them for his poetic practice, in the midst of everyday life; the face of Janus points both backward and forward. The fettering past has not yet been unfettered, but knowing that gives strength to an open encounter with the present. An overview of this early poetic history is surveyed in Brandt's *Digte i Udvalg 1949–62* (1963; Selected Poems).

The outcome of his development so far is an unpredictable and painful insight that cannot be compromised or reconciled with his initial aesthetic cohesion. In *Etablissement* (1965; Establishment) this aesthetics collapses, and his syntax and metaphors disintegrate. Quite a few of his later works, for example, *Ateliers* (1967), continue to advance the duality between outward consciousness of everyday life and almost sacral artistic authority. Brandt is a quick-change artist and a man of versatility, an undaunted experimenter with an interest in bold identifications and mixtures of style. His Janus head continues to behold opposite directions, but more and more lines of communication occur between his observations. Angels of Easter and devils of tomorrow, Byzantine ornamentations and Danish trivialities collide or commingle at a rapid pace in longer or shorter poems by this poet.

Taken together, his artistic expressions speak of the fullness of time, *Tidens fylde*, as he has named a selection of his poetry from 1979. It means they are the right poems at the right time and that they articulate the fullness of time to boot. This provisional balance between his authorial personality and his times has distinguished Brandt's writing since the 1960s and has more recently influenced titles such as *Ophold* (1977; Stay), which, after all, means a temporary stay. And the unconfessional religiosity of time's fullness found its fullest expression when in 1987 the author collaborated with the composer Ole Schmidt on a book of hymns called *Giv dagen dit lys* (Give the Day Your Light). On the whole, it is Brandt's conviction that if poetry has difficulties communicating, the blame is not in a specialized text, but in a specialized reader; in fact, the general qualities and fullness of the former are the ultimate challenge to the constraints of the latter. Consistent with this perception, Brandt has unswervingly refused to render artistic services to political and propagandistic ends, as so many writers of the 1970s decided to do.

The lyrical trilogy *Mit hjerte i København* (1975; My Heart in Copenhagen), *Jatháram* (1976), and *Regnansigt* (1976; Rain Face) pivots on the center of Brandt's Copenhagen, but in such a way as to give the author's personal experiences a fullness of tone and rhythm far beyond the routines of contemporary social analyses. An article by the poet in the newspaper *Information* (Sept. 6–7, 1975) concludes that "art is rebellion. Art is closeness. And in closeness there is always parting." Like an erotic tension, provisional fullness is the trademark of Brandt's best books, especially his best poems, and their fullness is more than sufficient to prevent them from being merely self-sufficient.

Erik Knudsen

The years of *Heretica* formed the lyrical background for Erik Knudsen (1922–), too, but more so because of the postwar traumas than because of the aesthetic and religious ideas of the time. Notwithstanding his continued and avowed interest in existential questions, Knudsen's poems were addressed not to the hidden God of Ole Wivel's poems, but to an unknown God, as in the title *Til en ukendt Gud* (1947). His poems signal a discharge of, rather than a quest for, religion, and shortly after their publication the author openly left *Heretica* in favor of directly political activities. Not surprisingly, a review of his total production demonstrates a preponderance of lyrical poetry throughout the 1950s, while his later years have seen a shift of genres toward various brands of critical debate and satirical drama. As for his plays, Erik Knudsen ranges from historical to topical settings and from quick-witted revue comedies such as *Frihed—det bedste guld* (1961; Freedom—the Best Gold) to critical pieces about the Social Democratic party.

By no means is that to say that Knudsen has put his art in cold storage or trampled it under political foot. In fact, he has respected both politics and art by keeping them clearly separated in a mutual relation of tension. This approach is in keeping with a dualism that runs through everything he has written and done and that appears, in his own words, both "fruitful and accursed." In essence, it stands out in the very title of the collection of poems named *Blomsten og sværdet* (1949; The Flower and the Sword), which must be called one of the earliest harbingers of modernism in Danish lyrical poetry. The flower is a reference to past and idyllic times; the sword, to the harsh realities of the day; finally, the conjunction between them marks the position of the poet within this conflict. He is loosely and provisionally suspended between opposites, which he does not attempt to escape, but does not pretend to enjoy either. From reality he learns that idealism is false; from idealism, that reality is not much better. Disillusioned satire and valiant defiance become the conjunctional or central conditions.

It is possible to ring the changes over this basic theme, as Knudsen has skillfully done. Poems about nature occasionally make it sound as if this is a place that permits the subject to forget himself for the world and the world for himself. Dualism is a happy separation of the concepts. But the goal is restitution. Things come apart only to induce the world to change and the subject to fight for himself. In the words of the satirical and harsher poems, he is fighting for a position at the focus of events, and *Brændpunkt* (Burning Point) was the telling title of these poems from 1953. Not until capitalism is ablaze does the flame of freedom flare up. Knudsen generally views life as hopeless and purified of wishful thinking, but he keeps his spirits up anyway. He quotes Camus and Sartre, saying, "We shall not allow ourselves to be stopped. Pride is a will to live that outsmarts despair."

From the 1960s until today Knudsen has applied his dualism to both political propaganda and nihilistic satire, as, for instance, in the collections *Journal* (1963), *Forsøg på at gå* (1978; Attempts to Walk), and *Ord fra Humlebæk* (1986; Words from Humlebæk). What consolidates his role as a leading lyrical modernist at the same time is that his fearless message rarely drowns his linguistic boldness. Save for the value of his current agitation, his language comes across at its best as it transcends the limits of its intended purpose. Its formulations are vehicles for what is known, but they often arrive at unknown places. Knudsen's forte is his surprising demolition of societal superstructures; it supersedes by far his weakness for basic edification. His talent for keeping matters separate and for letting contrasts cut the loose connections is an artistic feat insofar as it raises the standard of revolt without losing the earth connection.

Ivan Malinowski

Ivan Malinowski (1926–89) is a great modernistic and political poet whose ideas have considerable resemblance to Erik Knudsen's. He later erased his first two collections of poems, from the 1940s, from his records, perhaps because they were artistically immature, or because they were products of the *Heretica* spirit, or both. Notwithstanding their clear disposition to modernism, Malinowski postponed his official debut to 1954, when he issued a collection of short stories named *Vejen* (The Road). It is, indeed, a black and nihilistic book in the most exacting manner of modernism. Yet it was not until 1958 that Malinowski's development took its decisive direction and marked a turning point in Danish literature. In his essay "De tomme sokler" (The Empty Pedestals) he codified nihilism as an alternative to well-meaning postwar humanism, and the well-seasoned poems in the thin collection *Galgenfrist* (1958; Short Respite) became a major lyrical work and breakthrough within the modernism of the 1960s.

Both in Erik Knudsen and in Malinowski, nihilism results from disappointed idealism, and both authors have written poems that bisect romantic unity in the vein of Schack von Staffeldt. Malinowski's most graphic and uncompromising poem of disruption and discord is literally called "Disjecta membra" and stands as an introduction to *Galgenfrist*, whereas another central text of the book, "Myggesang" (Mosquito Song), confirms that the only true feeling of wholeness under the sun is provisional. The text hovers as a structure between dream and consciousness and between life and death; its point of rest is the quivering moment of tension in which the opposites meet— the short respite. Charged with significant dialectics, even this is a point reminiscent of Knudsen. The frame around it is more universal in Malinowski's case, however. His dialectic is no less political or conscious, but the underlying ideas are more deeply rooted in existentialism and ontology.

Between his poems in the 1940s and the later *Galgenfrist* Malinowski went round by way of the Swedish poets of the 1940s for artistic inspiration (he later settled in Sweden and translated his Swedish sources of inspiration—Erik Lindegren, Karl Vennberg, and others—into Danish). The kind of value-nihilistic purification of poetic language that he advocates in *De tomme sokler* (1963; The Empty Pedestals) and later practices in subsequent collections of poems is much indebted to Swedish intellectual life and, for that matter, to international modernism as well (introduced in his important anthology *Glemmebogen* [1962; Book of Oblivion]). His own concentrated poems make their first appearance in *Poetomatic* (1965); their poetic precision mechanics manifests itself in ultrabrief and haikulike verse, though not in political neutrality. On the contrary, both purification and concentration afford an irresistible effectiveness to attitudes otherwise tainted with clichés and sentimentality. The eternal perspective of the haiku, for example, is seen to evoke a massive political threat, not a poetic redemption.

In the meantime, the poet's message oscillated between artistic mediation and directness, between the modernistic catalog poetics of *Romerske bassiner* (Roman Basins) and the political discourse of *Åbne digte* (Open Poems), both from 1963. Their dual commitments have been compacted into one in *Leve som var der en fremtid og et håb* (1968; Living as if There Were a Future and a Hope). The title alone makes it clear that there isn't, but that life must go on all the same, as Erik Knudsen would say, too. The book does not take refuge in art as a haven for survival, however, nor does it accuse art of attempts to escape from reality. Instead, the author devotes himself to art and language—from excerpts of his own poems to samples of current concrete poetry—as formulated attitudes to reality, and moreover, not simple-minded attitudes that might find other forms of expression. The poems in question are often political, but rarely party political, unambiguous, or facile.

But how does one intervene in political reality with such intricate weaponry? In a collection of poems entitled *Kritik af tavsheden* (selected Eng. tr. *Critique of Silence,* 1977), issued on May Day 1974, the author tries to take his contradictions beyond the confines of political apathy and paralysis and subject them instead to political criticism. The question is whether or not he succeeds, and if he does, whether or not he jeopardizes his artistic capital by investing it in anticapitalistic emergency poetry or by using his language as a hatstand on which to hang his propaganda. The answer is yes and no. There are still poems in the style of *Poetomatic* which, in a single flash of lightning, can elucidate some shady political connection; but then there are other poems that reduce the reader's experience by keeping themselves predictably close to reality rather than viewing it independently. *Kritik af tavsheden* was followed by *Vinterens hjerte* (1980; The Heart of Winter) and *Hvad nu* (1983; Now What).

It is Malinowski's problem, as it was Erik Knudsen's, how to inject political vigor into art without ejecting its artistic capacity; how to experience life in a thin-skinned manner and yet be able to hit back with a thick-skinned fist; and how to witness impotence without allowing the potent testimony itself to claim our attention. Our language posits the boundaries of our world, as Ludwig Wittgenstein said, but can the language of poetry transcend these boundaries, and if so, will it merely posit its own? Malinowski has no resolution, but he insists on addressing the dilemma. Being the fool of capital, the artist is qualified to receive its reward for his criticism, but at the same time justified in trying to cut his master's throat at the first opportunity. Judging from later publications of poems in beautiful books of calligraphy, such as *Fuga* (1985; Eng. tr. *Fugue,* 1986) with its illustrations by Dea Trier Mørch, we find that Malinowski has nonetheless maintained the artistic quality and sense of unity that distinguish his central lyrics as the basis for rebellion against forces threatening to disintegrate and obliterate all distinctions.

Jørgen Sonne

In his first collection of poems, *Korte digte* (1950; Short Poems), Jørgen Sonne (1925–), as in the ensuing books, *Delfiner i skoven* (1951; Dolphins in the Forest) and *I en levende tid* (1952; In a Living Time), straddles the transition between the themes of the 1940s and the artistic forms of later modernism. The last two titles point to Sonne's unconventional conception of nature and his pronounced and vital sense of time, but his early faith in love and growth is soon overshadowed by the poems of crisis in *Italiensk suite* (1954; Italian Suite) and *Midtvejs* (1960; Midway). Sonne writes with erotic pleasure about the sea, and it is this eroticism, among other things, that comes through in his later texts. His best nature poems encompass eros and death united in tension, and they offset an unendurable agony that endures nonetheless.

Sonne is an erudite and widely traveled poet. He has skillfully translated and learned from classics—from John Donne to Ezra Pound—and taken artistic impressions from the remotest corners of the world. In various symbolic lights, travel is the most frequent motif in Sonne's oeuvre. It is the poet's hypersensitive and intense imagination that encircles this motif, a nervous mobility combined with an extraordinary linguistic ingenuity and sense of precision. Qualities such as these do not make a poet easy to read; but Sonne's artistic audacity is not baseless, and eventually the astute and durable insights of his best poems are destined to settle in the reader's mind.

From his early collections of poetry and throughout *Rejsekoncert* (1972; Travel Concert) European destinations define his framework; but in the novel *Blå turist* (1971; Blue Tourist) and the poems in *Thai-noter* (1974; Thai Notes) Sonne's linguistic originality summons remoter lands. The strange words and sentence constructions in these poems once again testify to the author's ability to profit from jumping out of his skin into a meeting with otherness, a maneuver, incidentally, on which he has reflected in the essays called *Horisonter* (1973; Horizons). The experience is akin to Erik Knudsen's dualism, but Sonne somehow ventures farther out—and farther into the process of self-realization. He said in an interview that "transgressing boundaries is the only cliché about modernism that I concur in."

The questing attitude does not only extend into time and space and into the nooks and corners of the soul, however. In the important poem "Foldemændene" (The Folding Men) from *Krese* (1963; Circles) the artistic probing gets underneath the "I" feeling, and as a result its privacy is fruitfully objectivized. Sonne's consciousness is dualistic, but in his major works he transcends the dual parameters. His aptitude for poetic associations allows for more prolific and more compounded combinations of more dissociated circumstances than any late symbolist could conceivably assemble under his umbrella. Sonne's strictly artistic attitude gives rise to a world that exists on its own and yet is not an escapist aberration from reality, but merely a reflection of reality from surprising angles.

In a collection of idylls called *Huset* (1976; The House) the author has rooted his vision in a concrete locality, and in *Eroterne* (1977; The Cupids), where the rooting is erotic, he has demonstrated how intensely and unceasingly he can move around his point of departure, and how dynamic and comprehensive a picture of the world this movement brings to his mind. In a recent book of poetry entitled *Nul* (1987; Zero) he has finally in manifold ways made clear how emptiness and fullness, starting point and end point, chaos and cosmos form part of each other. Sonne can both unfold and infold, and still avoid becoming a folding man.

Uffe Harder and Poul Borum

Uffe Harder (1930–) is slightly younger than Sonne and had only a single book behind him when the 1960s began. In academic background, reading, and travel experiences the two poets are akin, save for the fact that Harder has put his extroversion to use for extensive introductions of Latin American and southern European poetry and fiction. In the latter domain he has worked and translated with his Sardinian-born wife, the author Maria Giacobbe (1928–), who has used her own bicultural horizon of experiences for the artistic and pedagogical purpose of communicating culture in both directions.

Harder's artistic position is stated clearly in his third collection of poems, *Positioner* (1964; Positions). It is typical that it opens with a suite of travel poems—in this case from Greece—and that its conclusion is the title poem, preceded by the poem "Begynde i midten" (Beginning in the Middle). Harder himself has indicated, and others have agreed (with certain reservations), that modernistic rhetoric supplies the link of the opening parts of the book to its middle and its end. Its basic scenario, on which the author has commented as well, shows emptiness calling on fullness and silence challenging the word. This is modernism by the book, but how do words in practice add meaning to void? From where do the poems speak and in which direction? That is where the author is making little headway, but relying all the more on a variety of surrealistic inroads and sorties, or whims propped up as rhetorical clarity, to purvey his orientation. "Begynde i midten" thus offers an invitation to be seen as a clever encirclement of existential problematics. Several linguistic variations on the basic conditions of existence eventually stabilize a subtle balance between life and death. Death (and emptiness) must be acknowledged, but for life's sake sent into oblivion right away. Living *with* death as a fact of life, not *against* death in a state of fear, becomes both the beginning and the end of existence. The position in the middle is, then, the position of the poet as he realizes his existence.

"Beginning at the beginning / beginning to understand," says Poul Borum (1934–) in the poem "Min verden" (My World) from his collection

Sang (1967; Song). It suggests a more forward and optimistic outlook than that of Harder, and there are other titles in Borum's large production of lyrical poetry that point in the same direction, from his debut, *Livslinier* (1962; Life Lines), via *Mod* (1965; Courage) and *Dagslys* (1966; Daylight), to *I live* (1972; Alive) and *Sang til dagens glæde* (1974; Song to the Joy of the Day). But the suggested joie de vivre is neither naive nor one-dimensional. In the last collection, for example, the final poem is about borders being effaced and organic and inorganic matters melting together; and in the collection *Kendsgerninger* (1968; Facts) one poem says "be able to date / one's first death." In the little book *Alting* (1987; Everything) the author translates his awareness of death into confirmation of life, but the turning point is clearly his personal exposure. Although stupendous confrontations with things are rare, Borum's basic position is quite modernistic; his dualistic ideas of life and death are beginnings rather than ends, but he, too, wants to develop "the absence of the world in the presence of language" (*Havfruens ansigt* [1978; The Mermaid's Face]).

That Borum's attitude of style seems moderately confrontational is probably due to his linguistic orientation. He is a well-read and influential critic and cultural personality, and his many publications and special interests include rock music, American literature, and international modernism. He has also written a (very personal) "short critical survey" of Danish literature (1979). His own brand of modernism in the 1960s is essentially determined by attitudes to the world, incorporated in language. But he is well acquainted with the so-called language poetry of the later 1960s, which turned attitudes *in* language into attitudes *to* language and then back to the world. *Kendsgerninger* is perhaps not written in this spirit, but its poems are experiments in the same direction. Their subtleties sometimes border on studied elegance, which now and then endows them with an evasive and cunning earnestness. At best Borum's naivism is so learned that it seems all but imperceptible, or merely perceptible as vision and tone.

Benny Andersen

The trademark of Benny Andersen (1929–) is versatility and humor, but the complete picture of his work is more detailed. It is true that he has tackled the most varied genres and media throughout his artistic career—eventually even a novel called *På broen* (1981; On the Bridge)—and his audiences for his children's works and ballads are very large. But lyrical poetry and to some extent short stories have remained his principal area of creation since he made his debut with the poems in *Den musikalske ål* (1960; The Musical Eel). As his starting switch, he has referred to, besides personal circumstances, favorable growing conditions around the Danish Parnassus and productive influences from Fenno-Swedish and Swedish poetry and balladry. And as for his humor, he has called himself "a pessimist, who survives thanks to his high spirits." Others have more directly called him an optimistic pessimist, which he finds very much to the point. "Light and darkness in my poems go together and condition each other," he says (*Aarhus Stiftstidende*, June 3, 1973), and adds on another occasion, "I am a citizen in the land of smiles, and that is not funny at all" (*Berlingske Tidende*, Nov. 5, 1989). Just as with other authors of modernistic disposition in the 1960s, there is another side to Andersen's humor, and it is one of deep anxiety and uncertainty.

Andersen is remarkable for the way he concretizes abstract concepts and depersonalizes human traits. His technique and diction create distance, and the alienation brings the prevailing misery into reality at the same time as it animates the hackneyed sides of life. He shares the general modernistic perception of the world as a void, but his displacement strategy fills the gap with both life and disorder without dispensing of it. He is primarily a small-scale operator. His heroes are not glorious, but little, disheveled people like you and me, and their linguistic universe abounds in the commonplace and trivial, which he takes at face value with jaunty innocence. His many puns and plays on words should not be confused, however, with the concrete and systemic poetry of the late 1960s. While open to these new linguistic tactics, Andersen in his own practice uses them moderately. They presuppose that poetic texts define their own artistic rules, whereas the usage in his poems is guided by psychological and existential correlates and by an attitude to the world.

This is to say that the pessimism in his texts is a challenge to the world, not simply to other textual elements. And a cure, whether social or political, is not on Andersen's menu. Resignation, occasionally with a touch of bitterness, instead appears as the permanent reverse of his humor. The world is simply not together, and the only bridges over its chasms are humorous observations and unpredictable experiences of nature. And how long do they last? The poet's expressions of these abysmal circumstances will likely last a good deal longer. His ability to understate desperation and to portray everyday silent madness as a simple matter of course is triumphant in various degrees in such collections of poetry as *Kamera med køkkenadgang* (1962; Camera with Kitchen Privileges), *Den indre bowlerhat* (1964; The Inner Bowler Hat), *Portrætgalleri* (1966; Portrait Gallery), and *Personlige papirer* (1974; Personal Papers). There is a method in their images of madness, and the author's ability to decoy the reader into a mine field of depressed emotions is indebted to his unpretentious solidarity with the plight of both his characters and his audience. His collections are well composed.

In his short stories, also well constructed, the themes fall in line with those of his poetic works. "Lagkage" (Layer Cake) from *Puderne* (1965; Eng. tr. *The Pillows*, 1983) is about a deplorable woman whose husband—emaciated from nausea—eventually leaves her because she cannot resist the temptation to force-feed him with her layer cakes and cream puffs. Only this power over her sole dependent prevents her empty life from falling to the ground. Andersen's empathy with life's anonymous victims is devoid of sentimentality, and if there is some nostalgia in his most popular work, *Svantes viser* (1972; Svante's Songs), it is of the slightly ironical and bittersweet kind. The songs of the book—Andersen is an accomplished pianist and composer—are connected by prose in the style of everyday absurdity, and singer Poul Dissing's squeaky voice has done its best to add to the popularity of Andersen's inscription of the little man's struggle for life in the tradition of Nordic songs and ballads.

Jess Ørnsbo

In terms of appearance there are light-years between Benny Andersen's low-keyed humor and the shameless iconoclasm in the works of the slavophile poet Jess Ørnsbo (1932–). But the distance is only apparent. Andersen's pessimism is, indeed, no joke, and at the bottom of Ørnsbo's raging anarchy some fairly romantic tones can sometimes be heard. But where the rule of the land is tidiness, Ørnsbo incontestably and infallibly finds rottenness. His modernism is relentlessly defiant of all living death, whether within bourgeois institutions and social protocols or within the prudery and taboo areas of conventional Christianity, and he expresses his slashing criticism in both pungent newspaper polemics and far-reaching lyrical poems. He prefers to articulate his idiosyncrasies in images of so-called distasteful bodily functions and lower-ranking animal life; once he called the poet an open knife for the reader to step on, and that is indeed how it feels to go through his work.

Not surprisingly, discord in this body of work is both method and result; the author splits cadaverous harmonies to their roots in order to show that they are worm-eaten covers of incurable conflicts. His usage is antithetical on all levels, but unique both in the sense that his gall rises from uprightness and in the sense that his ferocity is capable of unleashing unheard-of beauty. A major piece of his poetic breakthrough, *Myter* (1964; Myths), is "Sæbesalme" (Soap Hymn), about the concentration camp prisoner's road to lampshades and soap bars, a modern myth of resurrection compared with the image of a cast-off Christ. This is confrontation without mercy, and merciless if not downright martial confrontations speak out from such titles as *Digte uden arbejde* (1977; Poems Out of Work) and *Mobiliseringer—lige og ulige digte* (1978; Mobilizations: Even and Uneven Poems), and from the subtitle "24 desperationer" (24 Desperations) of a collection called *Kongen er mulat men hans søn er neger* (1971; The King Is a Mulatto but His Son Is a Negro). Both romanticism and realism get impaled in a surrealistic collection named *Hjertets søle* (1984; The Slush of the Heart).

In his only novel, *Dullerdage* (1976; Duller Days), Ørnsbo describes with brutal precision the alliance between human infantilism and over-developed technology. A primitive and monstrous mentality of violence penetrates the entire text and its images, and yet its baroque situations and expressions are drenched in sarcastic humor and poetic beauty, somewhat like the setting in Alfred Jarry's drama *Ubu roi* (1897; King Ubu). This immaculate alloy of extreme opposites is also the objective of Ørnsbo's many plays, although they have met with a mixed reception. They may still be transcendent, but of no avail, since their sarcasm often transpires into monotony, as in *Livet i Danmark* (1981; Life in Denmark), and their milling nihilism often turns self-sufficient, as in the play *Majonæse* (1988; Mayonnaise). In Ørnsbo's work it is possible for the reader to enjoy an acid bath, but if he is almost drowned in the tub and all his flesh is eaten off his bones, he is unlikely to be concerned with the action for very long.

Per Højholt

One of modernism's older poets and one of its younger both distinguished themselves within their generation by anticipating a new poetic practice in close connection with the third generation of modernism, the so-called systemic and concrete poetry. Outstanding artists in their own right, they advanced the development of Danish modernism in the 1960s to a climax, at which point they then staked out certain trends for the 1970s.

Per Højholt (1928–) made his debut as early as 1949 with *Hesten og solen* (The Horse and the Sun), influenced by the aesthetics of *Heretica* but still a rather bold and profane erotic book of poetry. At intervals of seven years he published *Skrift på vind og vand* (1956; Writing in Wind and Water) and *Poetens hoved* (1963; The Poet's Head), and the year after that *Provinser. Digte og fotografier* (1964; Provinces: Poems and Photographs). It is very slim and yet its ten short poems and eleven pictures give ample verbal and visual evidence of Højholt's basic approach to language and reality. The poem "Indskrift" (Inscription), for example, transforms the experience of an evening to linguistic form, literally to the form of a cube inasmuch as the text shows graphical resemblance with a square and constantly points out how its language annuls reality. More and more words referring to reality literally lose their meaning, either by having their shapes and forms truncated or by the poem's making it expressly clear that items referenced within its framework no longer *are*, but merely are *said to be*. Reality, as it were, recedes to the same extent that awareness of language proceeds: literally, in a manner of speaking! The actual experience of the evening becomes nothing, and the poem about it, everything. While the dream in Malinowski's "Myggesang" became insight as the description of its character progressed, the evening in "Indskrift" becomes language or inscription from the moment the poem "takes form."

Most of Højholt's poems are about themselves and only indirectly about human existence. The philosophy behind this practice has been expounded by Højholt himself in two essays: *Cézannes metode* (1967; Cézanne's Method) and *Intethedens grimasser* (1972; The Grimaces of Nothingness). Both volumes discuss modernism as its tradition unfolds from Stéphane Mallarmé to *Heretica*, if not all the way to, for instance, Rifbjerg. Højholt says it is accursed to represent transcendental reality as more and more of a demon or thingification. God has died, true enough, and transcendence has become empty, but the void left still testifies to the loss of value; metaphysics, then, has not died, but has been turned upside down, and the scattered cosmos has been reinstated in artistic form. Højholt, with Cézanne at his hand, objects to this kind of artistic imagination and manipulation. The impulse of reality in an artist's work must be handled on strictly linguistic grounds and not for the purpose of miming or in other ways tampering with reality, but for the purpose of realizing the autonomous existence of language. The poem is, then, destined not to fall back on the world, but to manifest a world of its own within its limits. Whereas la Cour was intent on going behind the poem in quest of the poetic in reality or to become one with the intrinsic silence of things, Højholt is prepared to give silence form by taking it out of the world as language.

Turbo (1968), published between the two essays, displays a poetic "praxis" in agreement with Højholt's essayistic poetics. The text is full of concrete and systemic particulars, and surrealism, dadaism, and other gadgets from modernism's collection of curios abound as well. The entire text is a form of prose-lyrical, self-conscious so-called metapoetry moving, as the title says, onto the pages at full blast. It is manifested presence, here and now, and detached as fully as possible from the perspectives and referential functions of outside reality. And its liberated existence is supplied as a model or an example on which the reader can test his own existence. Everything has been done to let go the moorings of the text to norms and concepts of everyday life; emptiness under these textual circumstances has become a field of possibilities.

This practice means freedom from nihilism. The reader is not supposed to get results from the text; it is writing in wind and water, and only in flashes does it show what is possible. Showing it, however, without the stifling reservations of reality, renders it possible for the reader by textual means to transcend her own *being* and to begin to *become*. It is like a *Show*, as Højholt labeled his poems from 1966, and as he made it graphically clear in his media-minded book of collage, *Volumen* (1974; Volume). In *Intethedens grimasser*, too, he lets the title bear witness to the show as an empty and absurd communication of substance; language, though, makes the emptiness substantial. But unlike the substance of reality, the substance of the poem does not impede the reader's self-expression; texts are binding only as potentials. A madly funny systemic novel from 1969, *6512*, illustrates perfectly well how the reader is invited by the text to use her own potentials for imagination. The world of the book is still within the wide and white framework of attitudinal relativism, an empty, trivial, and meaningless world that is, all the same, tempting for the reader to explore and shape.

Højholt is a poet who makes major vaults; in a series of small, numbered collections of poems with the common title *Praksis* (1977–89; Praxis) he basically takes a piece of reality into language to demonstrate that in this way the piece disappears—in reality—or enters the indefinite. But the more the poet approaches silence, the more intensely his texts communicate. Occasionally, they come close to social compassion or the life of an everyday individual, as in another, and more popular, series of books (and records) of poetry: *Gittes monologer* (1981–83; Gitte's Monologues). But *Praksis* can also mean to approximate silence—in the briefest possible textual forms—to the extent that the very incision between emptiness and existence, reality and language becomes the only real thing. "Only with my back to the world can I play its games as games into the world! / If I turn around I see the world with goose-eyes," he says in *Praksis, 2* (1978). But that he is consciously self-conscious only follows from the fact that "with goose-eyes" in Danish means "with quotation marks," not simply looking through the eyes of a slow-witted bird.

Inger Christensen

Inger Christensen (1935–) made her debut much later than Højholt, in 1962, with a collection of poems called *Lys* (Light), and her artistic victory came quickly with the systemic poetry in *Det* (1969; It). As suggested by the titles of both her debut poems and the next collection, *Græs* (1963; Grass), the author's attentive and sympathetic insight combines with notions of creation and growth. It is remarkable, though, that in the central lyrics of the two books a further connection is established to both everyday trivia and cosmic space. There is an ever-present tension between simple and unsophisticated sensations and utterly distant inklings in these volumes, and their occasional monotony conceals an intriguing musical variation.

In her two experimental novels, *Evighedsmaskinen* (1964; Perpetuum Mobile) and *Azorno* (1967), the author uses her stylistic suppleness both as a means to target the interplay between narrative and narrated and as a way to blur the distinction between the two. In the creative process one character is defined vis-à-vis another, and their worlds coalesce or intersect. In the meantime the artistic awareness of this occurrence increases and attains a form of lyrical prose that is tailor-made for merging the pettiness of normal life with the overviews and insights inherent in resurrection and salvation mythology. Politics and eroticism whirl around in torrents of sensations and clash with streams of consciousness and childhood memories and dreams, all signs of aging and decay. Meanwhile, a symphony of narrative voices collaborating with somnambulistic cunning succeeds in shaping the many courses of events and the many fragments of life into a framework of resolution, a philosophical pattern of realization. Together the pseudosystematic composition of the eternity machine and the artful filing system within *Azorno*'s narrative introduce the same display of social and existential metamorphoses that Christensen was to complete in *Det*.

When this book of poetry became all but popular literature, the reason was probably the author's ability to make its systemic poetry produce meaning. Its systems liberate, rather than restrain and inhibit, the immanent life of language, and they enhance its potentials for development. This is creation for no apparently mystical reason, but that does not mean it is pure mechanics. Christensen knows how to program her language machine with intuitive presentiments of the outcome. She runs through it a semantic repertory with far-reaching implications and sees to it that the system with its unerring certainty brings to light a world of deceptive uncertainty. The volume can be read as one long poem, but also as a collection of poems within a pattern of cognition. Its centerpiece is the Western myth of creation, and logos, preceded by prologos and succeeded by epilogos; the centerpiece in itself is systematically divided into components that are textually interrelated along the lines of pre-positions in modern linguistic theory. If the input into the process consists of the eternal existential questions, the output is the modern, relativistic view of the world. In her long, illustrated art story *Det malede værelse* (1976, The Painted Room) Christensen invites the reader to compare this insight with the tenets of Karen Blixen's stories. Although the lawfulness of the latter is based on *amor fati* rather than systems, it seems both stricter and more straightforward than the rule of law in the modern text. The dialectics between the creator and the created is complicated in today's ungodly art.

This complexity has been demonstrated more recently in Christensen's suite of poems *Brev i april* (1979; Letter in April) and in her collection *Alfabet* (1981; Alphabet), where words, like surviving animals, march on board Noah's ark of poems. They are granted admission in alphabetical order, up to *N*, and their value for preservation is viewed on the background of the author's impassive registrations of external threats to the various species. Big words are spoken: the words of basic existence that we cannot do without, and the cerebral words of myth that we are not permitted to do without. The conflict between art's power to preserve what in reality its lack of power compels it to let go never escapes Christensen's attention.

In a play from 1972, *Intriganterne* (The Schemers), she creates, with yet another allusion to Blixen, an absurdly distorted world in which all identity and all common sense are tottering to their fall. The ironic point, though, is that death under these circumstances becomes a release from the everyday backwater. The intrigue, like the mask, invites us to a life richer than an honest face, and art leads toward, not away from, reality. Artistic dreams are the cure against daydreaming as a consolation for those who might fear that systemic poetry is in want of a creed.

Two Poets of Concretism
Højholt and Christensen account for the principal works of late modernistic "language poetry" in Denmark. But the last years of the 1960s saw other examples of concretism, systemic poetry, and new simplicity. Concretism, with several precedents in both Sweden and Germany, was preceded in Denmark by, for example, Palle Jessen (1920–62). Its most ardent spokesman, both in theory and practice, was the linguist Vagn Steen (1928–), who has made considerable effort, as a critic, teacher, and cultural politican, to animate self-creativity in the material of words. Titles such as *Riv selv* (1965; Tear Off Yourself) and *Skriv selv* (1965; Write Yourself) were direct invitations to the reader to do the author's work, a democratic appeal that was not always received in the spirit it was put forward. At exhibitions Steen would hang his poems like pictures for the visitor to look at, and in *Et godt bogøje/A Hole Book* (1969) he literally makes the reader of the book see right through it to people on the other side. The mythology of reading has been perforated, and so has the myth of both the poem and the poet, for example, in

Digte? (1964; Poems?), *Jeg er ingen/digtsamling/af Vagn Steen* (1967; I Am No/Collection of Poems/By Vagn Steen), and *Digte uden samling* (1976; Poems without Collection [or: Poems That Are Not Together]). Language is like clay that everybody can knead, and while the procedure in its simplified form can lead to much formless chat and amateurism, the sheer awareness of the verbal material in Steen's teaching is both catchy and instructive. Moreover, in his own practice it has served as a stimulating point of departure for quite different artistic ventures into such genres as historical-topographical-documentary novels about his personal cultural background. These "dig where you stand" books are nonetheless marked by linguistic finesse and authenticity.

Concrete poetry verging on systemic poetry with a touch of new simplicity can be found in the works of Charlotte Strandgaard (1943–). Her first collections are typically called *Katalog* (1965; Catalog), *Afstande* (1966; Distances), and *Uafgjort* (1967; Unsettled); the titles point to her formal registrations, her distant and impersonal perceptions of the world, and the manner in which the artistic message became increasingly subordinated to the medium as a message in itself (these were the years of Marshall McLuhan's triumphal progress). Abiding to the grammar book's definition of a pronoun as an empty frame, Strandgaard deliberately cultivates the third-person pronoun; and her lyrical ascertainments do indeed fall in place as unprioritized entities within a universe devoid of values. At the same time shunning the use of metaphors, she relishes in automated syntax, leaving the overall impression of a horizontal and undifferentiated world. This pervasive sense of indifference is reinforced by such a title as *Indimellem holder de af hinanden* (1969; They Love Each Other at Times); one realizes that Strandgaard's unpolemic but persistent pronouncements are lending credibility not to the openness of democracy but to its decline and despair. Her documentary books from the 1960s about society's losers are in the same vein, whereas most of her works from the 1970s and 1980s are political in a more feminist sense.

Three Systemic Poets

Kristen Bjørnkjær (1943–) is systemic and neosimple in his own naivistic manner. He is understated somewhat like Benny Andersen, but his world is a seemingly flat, pop-art place, filled with clichés and comic-strip heroes and villains, until at closer inspection its simple puns and small displacements of accents reveal their deeper perspectives. An important book is *Min landbrugsleksikalske barndom* (1969; My Agrilexical Childhood), in which childhood memories are imparted in alphabetical order just as in an old specialized dictionary, with quaint pictures and illustrations inserted. At first it seems ingenuous, then extremely crafty, and finally some of the ingenuity returns. It looks simple but is all tongue in cheek. And where is the tongue? Bjørnkjær has written about revolution in Peking in another book, *Aramis i Peking* (1971; Aramis in Peking), and in a third, the novel *En vild tid* (1985; A Crazy Time), about café life in Copenhagen. The intangible doubleness of matter-of-factness and jest, of empathy and irony, knows of few cultural or geographical boundaries. Political commissars cannot feel comfortable about this poet, but neither can the apolitical highbrow intellectuals. And for the poet himself there is little comfort in being classified at all, artistically or politically. Our world is cruel and complex, but Bjørnkjær prefers to meet it with open arms, as he has done, for instance, in his collection of poems, *Kærestesorg* (1976; Unhappy Love), which occasioned both muted shock effects and solid feedback.

Two poets of this generation have made headway into the international scene in other art forms. Already a painter of note, Per Kirkeby (1938–) is as a poet more of a phenomenon, incredibly productive, traveled, and complex. His texts are original and eclectic, collages of words and pictures, poetry and prose, romanticism and systematism, aesthetics and philosophy. He audaciously blends systemic mechanics and romantic myth, and his controversial mind takes pompous symbols down and endows clichés with pomp and color. Spleen and zest convene in his work.

Jørgen Leth (1937–) is a noted director of both short and feature films and a poet in his own right, too. His poems first appeared in the 1960s and were pale reflections of works by those of Rifbjerg's generation. But in 1967, two years after the publication of Rifbjerg's *Amagerdigte*, Leth issued a collection called *Sportsdigte* (Sports Poems), which was quite original and heralded both what was to become the author's special field of interest—sports—and a new sensibility akin to the trends in concrete poetry and pop art. The setting is once again a world that is empty and can be manipulated, and with the techniques of systemic poetry, Leth avails the short moment of his text to elicit a cognitive structure from its empty recourse and uniform field of potentials. His cultivating of artificiality transpires through a poem like "Jeg bevæger min hånd og min fod" (I Move My Hand and My Foot) in the collection *Lykken i ingenmandsland* (1967; Happiness in No-Man's-Land). Its affinity to attitudinal relativism is quite unmistakable, and the ensuing *Glatte hårdtpumpede puder* (1969; Smooth Hard Inflated Pillows), with its slick blue cover and golden letters, adds an excessive surface aesthetics. In *Hvordan de ser ud* (1987; How They Look) and in other books the author continues to deconstruct conventional relations of language and reality and inflate instead normal meaningless language with the airy meanings of linguistic aesthetics. His cinematographic view of language is given special treatment in *Filmmaskinen. Udvalgte historier om film, 1965–78* (1979; The Film Machine: Selected Stories about Films).

Hans-Jørgen Nielsen

In the same way that Vagn Steen was the concrete poet incarnate, the critic Steffen Hejlskov Larsen was the most outspoken proponent of *Systemdigtningen: Modernismens 3. fase* (Systemic Poetry: The Third Phase of Modernism), as he called his critical survey from 1971, and the go-between was Hans-Jørgen Nielsen (1941–91). He was coeditor, with Vagn Steen, of the concretist journal *Digte for en daler* (Poems for a Quarter) and (with Erik Thygesen) of *ta'* (1967–68; take), an organ of both concrete and systemic poetry. He also was the editor of *Exempler* (1968; Examples), an anthology of poems, or "examples," as it were, by writers of his own generation. Using another demythologized term for fiction and poetry at the time, *texter* (texts) is the title of an anthology edited by Vagn Lundbye in 1969, which includes texts of Nielsen and others; its introduction discusses the underlying attitudinal relativism, which term, incidentally, was coined by Nielsen to signify a new, open, horizontal image of the world. It is a world in which values—just as in the haiku poems introduced by Nielsen in 1963—are without preconceived order of precedence and in which their alleged crisis is a contradiction in terms. This entire world is flooded by an omnipresent and neutral electronic culture, unobstructed by traditional cultural boundaries. During the next couple of decades Nielsen partook in most literary innovations—artistic, critical, and political. He is impossible to overlook.

Besides according most of modernism's third phase to artistic forms and aesthetic and theoretical formulas, Nielsen transgresses the boundaries of the 1960s with zealous and spectacular participation in left-wing politics. The new sensibility and various strategies of language poetry expressed a sense of general exodus from bourgeois confinements and a desire to explore potential freedoms and alternatives within the special world of language. But starting with the youth rebellion and continuing into the next decade, a conflict evolved between the utopias nurtured by language and a more impervious social reality. Obviously, confrontation of this nature required both political analysis and societal involvement, and Nielsen was the first to accept the conditions at hand. At the same time, he sought to preserve whatever sensibility and creativity he had inherited from the more exclusive activities of modernism in the 1960s. It became a difficult task to reconcile the incompatible roles, and even though organic unity was not exactly the catchword for the high priest of attitudinal relativism, there were some limits as to how interchangeable roles could be.

Examples of Nielsen's own language poetry abound in his first books, *at det at* (1965; that it that), *konstateringer* (1966; statements), and *output* (1967). This is concrete poetry (by German standards!) and systemic structuralism (by French?) with a vengeance, and yet it occasionally puts out attitudinal potentials beyond the purview of language. It seems that, after all, the linguistic happenstances have been cleverly calculated and put at the reader's disposal. As the author puts it himself, his experiments in language are "in the last resort also an experimental view of reality in a given historical situation" (Schnack 125).

In a collection of essays called *"Nielsen" og den hvide verden* (1968; "Nielsen" and the White World) the author cited in the title explains the philosophy behind this poetry. As merely one of many potential roles the authorial identity obviously must be taken with the reservations of quotation marks. This is a nonperspective world where all colors have merged into one great whiteness and where sociality in a neutral sense has replaced existential individualism. A short biographical novel, *diletariatets proktatur* (1969; the proletatorship of the dictariat), shows how the author envisions the alliance between his linguistic experiments and raw reality. By "systematizing" the unruly youth rebellion, he has accomplished a brazen challenge to a political "system" intent on stifling the rebellion. *"Den mand der kalder sig Alvard"* (1970; "The Man Who Calls Himself Alvard") is called a "piece of fiction," not a novel, and its systemic composition spirals this fragmentation into vertiginous height, not to mention into an empty gesture. The book gives ample evidence of a vociferous genre, but also of one that breathes with difficulty.

As many airy left-wing strategies and analyses were crashing in the late 1970s, Nielsen, too, came back to earth, falling on his feet, though. His regular novel *Fodboldenglen* (1979; The Soccer Angel) is at once self-critical and critical of the perpetual, yet so narrow-minded, politicization of the recent decade. There is much chastising going on between the analyses in this book, but at least the one comforting fact is that the book was written. As suggested by the title of his collection of essays from 1968–80, *Billeder fra en verden i bevægelse* (1980; Pictures of a World in Motion), Nielsen's mobility is unimpaired; in fact, it has finally brought him beyond the linguistic equilibrium of both poetry and politics and in touch with more irremovable forms of reality. His congenital talent for intolerance has struck a well-directed blow at his personal limitations, and his no less congenial suppleness has made him recognize the opportunities he has forfeited. By relating his political experiences to his hero's loss of identity, Nielsen comes out of his long period in the theoretical wilderness safe and sound.

The New Realism

Modernism with its linguistic peculiarities was the breeding ground for new (critical) alternatives to the bourgeois way of life in the 1960s. Conversely, it is in contemporary neorealism and its deliberate omission of peculiar forms that we find most (critical) empathy with the bourgeois way of life. That is not to say that neorealists are necessarily more bourgeois than modernists, but rather that they unveil the frailties of bourgeois life indirectly, with an eye to its discrete charm, whereas modernists with no charm in mind do not mince words in their treatment of this world, but bleed it white, directly, bluntly. The neorealist attitude and practice—of which the critic Hans Hertel has been the foremost spokesman—is in continuation of the epic tradition of Herman Bang; its goals are perfect illusion and immediate recognition, and its means the transparent and art-less forms of language. Both goals and means, however, are updated sociologically so as to represent urbanites of the middle and upper middle classes in the modern welfare society. As stylistic idiom, neorealism is sympathetic in its subject matter, but often at a critical, skeptical, or ironical distance. Its pseudo-objective discourse is stylized in a general direction. The bourgeois world is both defended and attacked with its own form of consciousness as weapon.

Christian Kampmann

Christian Kampmann (1939–87) gave his books titles that are precise indications of their author's objectives and attitude. His first book was a collection of short stories, *Blandt venner* (1962; Among Friends), as was his second, *Ly* (1965; Shelter). Both have a ring of good, (petty)-bourgeois security, and yet there is a disquieting undertone of hype in the words. At closer scrutiny individual texts elaborate the point. One of the stories in *Ly* with the direct title of "Fravær" (Absence) tells about the frightening emptiness between spouses; he tries to quietly walk away from the void, whereas she takes a more dramatic refuge in painting. But the escapism and the expressionism are merely opposite reflections of mutual victimization. Everything but a feeling of presence is present in this little bourgeois world. Even as they respond to their common plight, the two are hopelessly alone.

Kampmann's next books were novels, but their characters' strained security complex, sometimes expressed at the expense of others' security, is undiminished. At stake is the most incurable Danish social disease, *hyggen,* a special form of coziness, and the price paid for it. The title *Sammen* (1967;

Together) has its own touch of forced community spirit, and in *Nærved og næsten* (1969; Near and Nearly) things sound almost as perfect as, say, almost pregnant sounds pregnant. In Kampmann's next collection of short stories, *"Vi elsker mere"* (1970; "We Love More"), the optimistic words in the title are in quotation marks. The title story reveals that the emphatic expression is the motto of a weekly magazine's Letters to the Editor page about cohabitation problems. The editors, with the fictitious names Pia and Poul, are real enough, but their own image of ideal cohabitants is a best-selling make-believe. The straw that breaks their real relation—and her life at that—is added when she takes the motto seriously and goes out on her own really to "love more." In "Tvivl" (Doubt), another story of marriage, the wife of nineteen years of marriage suddenly has no doubts that her husband "was the person in the whole world she knew the least. Then she realized that what she felt was rather a consequence of their many years together so close to one another. All that time and closeness had made it impossible to take in his whole person. That is the way it will always be with the man in one's life." Bourgeois life, whether lower or upper middle class, is an empty space with the apparent distinction of no space at all.

In *Nok til hele ugen* (1971; Enough for the Whole Week) Kampmann's impressive awareness of the genre of documentary fiction is put to use to depict the marital crisis of an older female reader of weekly magazines. He focuses on the conspicuous absence of particular characteristics in this "normal" individual, and forwards the case in a pedantic and impartial headline style by use of compositional means inspired by game theory. The alleged intention is "to create communication with the reader in order to entertain so as to hereby stimulate an attitude to the above-mentioned reality." It reminds one of the logic of systemic poetry as Kampmann's narrative begins with a sketch of a dark background and then goes on to sketch a light one, then another dark one, and at the end a more realistic one. But clearly, since the outcome has already been decided, little tension is coupled with the reader's choice among these options. What is exciting, though, is to observe the contrast between the experimental narrative and its completely unimaginative protagonist. The petty bourgeois claims to live her "festive" life—in the middle of the void. This is the schism of the book and perhaps of the life of its reader.

The masterpiece of Kampmann—and of all neorealism—deals with the upper half of the bourgeoisie. It consists of four novels about the Gregersen family and is like a modern version of Thomas Mann's *Buddenbrooks* (1901), a contemporary narrative on bourgeois Denmark, 1954–74. It is about love and money in a well-to-do suburban milieu, but also about everyday life and social conditions, ideological knots and political crises in the rest of the country. Kampmann himself compared the series with American musicals or Hollywood comedies and emphasized the vaudeville style of their seriousness. Precisely the right style can demonstrate how the base of the bourgeoisie caves in while its facade still appears intact or only slightly cracked. The development of the four sequels is marked by their titles. *Visse hensyn* (1973; Certain Considerations) intimates problems, but merely intimates; in the 1950s the key word for crisis management within the family circle was "discretion." In *Faste forhold* (1974; Firm Relationships) and *Rene linjer* (1975; Clean Lines) we have left the suggestive mode behind us and entered the boom of the 1960s. The cover flies off the intimate sphere, although firm relationships, in private life or elsewhere, do not seem to be a lasting answer to the new daylight; some cleaner lines are the most one can hope for. In *Andre måder* (1975; Other Ways) the downhill ride of the 1970s has commenced. With optimism, regret, or simply sobriety the reader can entertain the dissolution of old mores and the sketchy appearance of other ways of life.

The latter is the subject of Kampmann's final achievement as a neorealistic writer, an autobiographical novel in three serials (1977–80) about his personal journey through the bourgeois world of imagination. They show him gradually disengaging himself from the conformity of his surroundings while correspondingly confessing to a "new" bisexual identity of his own. The books have been read as important contributions to the expansion of the cultural public sphere that occurred with the advancement of confessional works of literature in the late 1970s. Kampmann was murdered by a friend in 1987.

Anders Bodelsen
Anders Bodelsen (1937–) made his debut with a rather muzzy student novel in the late 1950s. He later said that he found the decade gray and uninspiring and that he made a long detour round *Heretica* and what it stood for; what he was attracted to instead was the culture of the 1930s, jazz, Poul Henningsen's lamps, and Knud Sønderby, not to mention the English novelists of the 1950s and their angry young men. Also, he had witnessed how Rifbjerg's poems of confrontation, and the 1960s in general, were bright spots among all the dullness and modesty. That perhaps explains why his second short-story collection, *Rama Sama* (1967), turned out more energetic and precise than his first book. One of its most frightening texts depicts a frustrated bourgeois's destructive reaction when "The TV Shimmers" (as the story "Fjernsynet flimrer" translates). Bodelsen's basic out-

look is the same as modernism, but his language and conception of life accord with neorealism. Like Kampmann, he is preoccupied with the welfare
society's middle class and its average individuals. Uninterested in the outsider but all the more intrigued by the common person, he is an acute but
loyal and sympathetic portrayer of the bourgeoisie, and when he throws
stones, it is from his own glass house. To meet his objectives, he writes increasingly in the thriller genre. As a movie buff he is enthused and knowledgeable about Alfred Hitchcock, and it shows in his books. Their ideal of
cool passion is otherwise inspired by Vladimir Nabokov.

Bodelsen's first hits with his audience, even internationally, were two
novels, *Tænk på et tal* (Eng. tr. *Think of a Number,* 1969; *A Silent Partner,*
1978) and *Hændeligt uheld* (Eng. tr. *One Down,* 1970; *Hit and Run Run
Run,* 1970), both written in 1968 (and later adapted for the screen). They
are realistic, not in the documentary sense of the word, but in terms of verisimilitude, as convincing depictions of the possible. "What next if . . . ?" is
the author's question as he lets the unknown into the everyday life of a normal person. In the former novel a person like you or me accidentally becomes a bank robber; in the latter, and under comparable circumstances, a
hit-and-run driver. And just as in classical novels of the same mold, suspense
builds up as one little step inevitably leads to the next, until the protagonist
has become a criminal all the way to his fingertips. It was never the decent
man's intention to go that far, but once sidetracked, he is less concerned
about doing away with a fellow man than about being caught himself. That
is one moral point. The other is that readers instinctively feel sympathy with
the unfortunate perpetrators and perhaps discover a similar inclination to
save their own skins at any price.

The prime movers of the action, then, are psychological; but the psychology is convincing only because it is matched by precise descriptions of milieu and environment. And included here are the general movers and
shakers of bourgeois society: greed for money and the need for safety. The
advantage of the thriller genre is that it combines the two, but its disadvantage is that it limits analysis of the combination. To accomplish its thrilling
effects, it is prevented from disclosing much of the information needed to
understand the characters' innermost motivations. The basic conflict in
Bodelsen's books about the bourgeois world, however, is the one between
law and order (*Lov og orden* [Law and Order] is the title of a volume of short
stories from 1973) on one side and madness or chaos on the other. His
heroes are unlucky, to put it mildly, but they are decent people; by contrast,
their evil spirits are the scum of the earth, or termites undermining these pillars of society.

On the basis of this taxonomy Bodelsen drills into the psychology of anxiety and hidden frustrations and the sociology of welfare Denmark's middle class. *De gode tider* (1977; The Good Times) was his (first) counterpart to Kampmann's Gregersen series, and while avoiding explicit analyses, it, too, ventures a style with both surface impressions and deep dimensions. The crime motif shows up again in the title *Bevisets stilling* (1973; Eng. tr. *Consider the Verdict,* 1976), a novel in which the author has shifted his focus to a hapless member of the lower middle class who is in trouble because the zealous judicial system is reluctant to admit to a miscarriage of justice. In *Alt hvad du ønsker dig* (1974; All That You Desire) the title essentially alludes to money, and in *Pengene og livet* (1976; Your Money and Your Life), to blackmail as well. Finally, in *Frysepunktet* (1969; Eng. tr. *Freezing Point,* 1971; *Freezing Down,* 1971) and *Straus* (1971; Eng. tr. 1974) Bodelsen applies his insights in the bourgeois world to the wide perspectives of the science-fiction genre and to the narrow perspective of a personal grudge.

More on target are the short stories in *Hjælp* (1971; Help). Their common motif is angst applying to high and low alike. A story with this title is about an individual's ups and downs as well as about individuals who are socially upstairs and downstairs. Bourgeois safety and familiarity are fine bubbles that can burst when one expects it the least. But what is worse: fearing the enigma or fear itself? Or fearing to let go of this very fear? The title of the book echoes the dilemma. It can be a cry for help, but it can also be the help that finally arrives. Art can register the angst as a destructive incapacity, but it can also face what its fictive characters tend to deny.

Henrik Stangerup

Henrik Stangerup (1937–) is an out-and-out neorealist. That is to say, he passionately professes neorealism as an art form, but his own application of this form has been considerably more subjective and polemic than Kampmann's and Bodelsen's. Stangerup is both an insider and an outsider in this group and is proportionately intriguing as a borderline case. Like Bodelsen, he is a cultural journalist and has in no uncertain terms argued for literature to be an extroverted activity, concerned with reality. Interestingly, though, in his polemics he contrasts neorealism with an allegedly metaphysical and soul-searching tradition that he finds pervasive in Danish letters from Branner and Martin A. Hansen to Rifbjerg, while in his other writings he practices his own introspection and subjectivism to perfection. Even though the apparent paradox has proven less inexplicable than it sounds at first, the author's idiosyncrasies and narcissism clearly do not pave the way for his connection to neorealism, or for his disconnection to modernism, for that matter.

Stangerup's authorship dates back to the end of the 1950s when he basically wrote short prose like his hybrid of short-story fiction and reporting "faction" in *Veritabel pariser* (1966; Veritable Parisian). But his breakthrough was the novel *Slangen i brystet* (1969; The Snake in the Breast), which has a Parisian setting as well and which launches the conflict matters and personality problems that were to become so ingrained in most of Stangerup's later work. Here is the guilt problem, based on self-contempt but blown out of individual proportion to serve as a national characteristic called The Danish Disease. And here is the media man's special exposure to this guilt complex and its consequences.

In *Løgn over løgn* (1971; Lie upon Lie) the author has dug into the question of why Danes feel so perpetually ashamed and guilty over their very existence. The complex is said to be rooted in their thousand-year history as a pietistic farming country and to have saturated their epic tradition. The latter allegation, at least, is corroborated by the novel at hand, and in a double sense at that. One of its vital liars is a fictive middle-aged film director, and the other is a discernible side of the author himself. The semidocumentary form enables one of these media imperialists to serve as the pacemaker for the other and to outdo the other's lies with better ones. But apart from that, the form permits the narrator to transfer his guilt complex to the very art of writing. "Who gives me the right to invent a person and then pretend that he is real and to blame for the fact that he approaches the abyss and, hence, the end? What kind of surroundings do I take for granted when I describe them realistically? What kind of imaginary production circumstances am I putting myself into?"

Those are the questions, and that is how Stangerup, in contributing to the endless succession of Hamlet-sick Danish men, rather than evolving from his guilt feeling, involves himself further in its quagmire. But in doing so he is calculating and conscious of his medium; even while getting the worst of his guilt feeling he has a good time revealing how. Perhaps, then, the only thing that can be trusted in *Løgn over løgn* is this: regardless of how dastardly the impact of its guilt complex, without it the author would be mute.

Stangerup's next novel is called *Manden der ville være skyldig* (1973; Eng. tr. *The Man Who Wanted To Be Guilty*, 1982), and it is about someone who is not allowed to be guilty because the zealous tutelaries of the social state deprive the individual of responsibility for his own life. Confronted with this guardianship, he suddenly experiences guilt as something positive. The author's troubles with finding an excuse for his umbilical studies have reached a point where suddenly the risk of losing sight of his navel becomes a compelling reason for preserving it as a focal point. The psychological mechanisms—both individual and social—behind this dilemma have been explored at (too) great length in the novel *Fjenden i forkøbet* (1978; Anticipating the Enemy), which has the subtitle "En roman om angst og skyld og sjælens misère" (A Novel about Fear and Guilt and the Misery of the Soul). It is at once an apologia for the author's late father, a self-analysis of his own wrecked marriage, and a gaudy image of the fiasco of his lifetime— film shooting in Brazil. But documentation and autobiography are mythologized; instead of getting to the bottom of the fear and guilt and misery of the soul, the book projects the authorial problems into the wider collective screen. The creator of the man who wanted to be guilty—at any price—is amazingly apt at shifting his own guilt onto circumstances.

The limitation of Stangerup's realism is that it does not open up prospects of insight in his sense of martyrdom, but rather encloses it. The essayistic and polemic versions of his intellectual claustrophobia are especially cases in point, as shown by such sensitive titles as *Kunsten at være ulykkelig* (1974; The Art of Being Unhappy), *Retten til ikke at høre til* (1979; The Right To Not Belong), and *Fangelejrens frie halvdel* (1980; The Free Half of the Prison Camp). Like Elsa Gress, Stangerup is always inclined to nurse a grievance. The strength of his art comes across when it unmasks the notion of the good bourgeois world as exceptional people's hinterland. His books about the victims of this illusion are among his best. The novels *Vejen til Lagoa Santa* (1981; Eng. tr. *The Road to Lagoa Santa*, 1984) and *Det er svært at dø i Dieppe* (1985; Eng. tr. *The Seducer: It Is Hard To Die in Dieppe*, 1990) are both documented, widely translated, and reputed portraits of nineteenth-century extraordinary Danes, the scientist P. W. Lund and the critic P. L. Møller, respectively, who felt compelled to find themselves in a world entirely different from Denmark.

Bent William Rasmussen
The main characters of Bent William Rasmussen (1924–) rarely travel beyond Danish borders or become mythical. They are more typical than Stangerup's Danes, which is not to say, though, that Rasmussen's image of Denmark is more inspiring. Their bourgeois dream of order and propriety is best suited for the past, or the future in the cemetery, and only on rare occasions of intimate contact and love do they encounter the present as a refuge of quiet and comfort. For the most part they are on the run or chasing a possibility of continuity in their lives. Their sense of details is typically a sense of order that dissolves all order into scattered impressions and experiences. They look for surfaces of contact but are lucky if they find a single point.

Sensitive in style and narrative technique, Rasmussen has characterized this world since his debut in 1963. In *Til venstre for Virum* (1970; Left of Virum) the typical middle-class Dane is on a citizen's course among like-minded citizens, but he is not the same person when he returns home. Whether he is truly different and more himself is an open question, though. In *Uge 38* (1985; Week 38) he *is* different, and himself, when the book ends. But his transgression of previous boundaries is not much of an achievement since it came about as he joined his family's tradition of treason; he simply became himself by entering a context of disruption. Only an act of paralysis—suicide—is left, and then a picture of bourgeois Denmark in which love belongs to the past, death to the future, and a man who wanted to be guilty is the only one present. Judging from the author's most recent novel, *En dag i Amerika* (1986; A Day in America), this character is still standing. Or is it just the novel about him that does?

Outsiders

Like all classifications, this outline of Danish literature in the 1960s has several limitations. It attempts to define various principal trends, but needless to say, in many ways they are inseparable. Neorealistic features can be traced in Rifbjerg and Panduro, while traces of concrete poetry show up in Benny Andersen, Gustava Brandt, and Harder; and these are merely some obvious cross-references. In addition, some authors are difficult to group, some of them significant. The reasons may vary; in fact, they are often individual. A few examples illustrate the point and do some justice to authors outside the categories.

Ole Henrik Laub (1937–) has, since his debut with the short stories in *Et sværd dyppet i honning* (1967; A Sword Dipped in Honey), been on a cruise across boundaries of style and genre. His stories, for example, range from neorealism via tales and fables to fantasy proper, but his novelistic realism holds odd ingredients, too. Angelo Hjort (1924–) has been published since the 1950s, but his principal work is a series of novels from the late 1970s about the German occupation. Before this series he wrote a novel about Copenhagen named *Skråt op* (1976), a double entendre including the disrespectful meaning "up yours." After the novels of the 1970s he wrote a collection of poems called *Firben og grønne høns* (1980; Lizards and Green Chickens). Hjort is an inveterate Copenhagener, and yet the last poem in this collection, a travel poem about Italy, gives the best impression of his standpoint between illusions and realities. Its unassuming humanism consists of knowing how little one knows and then in loving that little even more dearly. A man with as many years and genres behind him and as committed to a philosophy of life like this is obviously hard to classify.

Also difficult to capture in a few lines is Palle Fischer (1928–84). He is akin to several modern humorists—Panduro and Benny Andersen, for example—but though a pessimist at bottom, he is more unruly and less disciplined, and occasionally completely self-ironical. He has published a handful of novels since the early 1960s. Henning Ipsen (1930–84) is a prose writer and translator whom other historians of literature have called difficult to classify, which is true. But his large and solid production over a generation qualifies him to be mentioned. Anna Ladegaard (1913–) was fifty-three years old when she published her first novel in 1966. Since then she has written more than a dozen. She is difficult to place because she has never had an eye on literary fashion trends but has always written her own kind of action stories about love and death. In a formal sense she is not exciting, and her presentation is often grossly idealized. But feminist critics have read her as a gender-specific writer, and her many German-Jewish novel settings make her equally readable from a cross-cultural standpoint.

Poul Vad

Educated as an art historian and the author of significant works about modern Danish artists, Poul Vad (1927–) is a fiction writer of considerable caliber as well. He made his literary debut with an essay in *Heretica* in 1953, which criticized airy metaphysics, and with the poems in *Den fremmede dag* (1956; The Strange Day) in the same year as Rifbjerg's debut in verse and Seeberg's in prose. As a lyrical poet Vad is more realistic than the authors in *Heretica* but less experimental than his modernistic peers. The alienation intimated in the title of his book recalls the 1940s, but at the same time, its big city images are perceived from the outside and without the underlying empathy with strangeness that distinguished the poets of the 1940s. The rest of Vad's work is in prose and no less difficult to classify.

His first three novels are *De nøjsomme* (1960; Modest People), *Taber og vinder* (1967; Loser and Winner), and *Dagen før livet begynder* (1970; The Day Before Life Begins). An expectant attitude is still noticeable, but it is not the *Heretica* hope for a definitive breakthrough, merely a waiting for *something* to happen. The plots are set in the quiet and eventless 1950s, which were also the backdrop of Seeberg's debut and later the setting of Rifbjerg's *Arkivet*. Thus, it is lack of action that marks the books at hand, along with an understated—and in itself pointless—way of depicting what does not happen. The poet and critic Poul Borum claims that Vad appropriates his book covers to signal a development within the texts from the gray everyday portrait in *De nøjsomme* via the black-and-white *écriture à la nou-*

veau roman in *Taber og vinder* to the blue-green stream of consciousness in *Dagen før livet begynder*.

In any case, it is only behind the deep blue cover of the novel *Rubruk* (1972) that Vad, escaping his muted and compromising style, begins to meet his *readers'* expectations. Akin to contemporary documentary works in both Sweden and Denmark, the book was based on a publicized travelogue by a Dutch medieval monk. But its documentarism is devoid of political ambitions and quite imaginative in the way it shifts attention from journey as an end to journey as a means (to self-comprehension). One is reminded of the Swedish writer P. O. Sundman's neohumanistic search for man's "hard-to-get-at fellow being": identity is unlikely to be found in a given, hidden context, in what is actually found; rather, it lies in the will to search. Vad's major achievement is quite a colossal novel called *Kattens anatomi* (1978; The Anatomy of the Cat). Its fantastic and fantastically complicated narrative of the course of events cannot be accounted for within a brief exposition, but it does, indeed, venture another fruitless search for the truth. There are no answers, neither in this world nor in the next, neither in realism nor in grotesques. But the effort of searching for answers is its own reward. The entire book can be read as evidence that life is richer than the prophets proclaim and most literature can imagine, but first of all, it must be read. Works of literature with such comprehensive and undecided concerns easily escape the attention of most readers.

Albert Dam

In 1980 Poul Vad was the coeditor of a book about Albert Dam (1880–1971) and his literary work, *Den lodrette bestáen,* the title meaning both vertical existence and endurance. Dam's oeuvre dates back to the turn of the century but culminates with a close formation of publications in the 1960s, when the times finally caught up with his peculiar and self-taught narration. It was initially *Vindrosen*, in the early 1960s, and later the organs of the systemic poets that rehabilitated Dam's name after years of oversight and thus contributed to his late-coming reputation as one of Denmark's major writers of the twentieth century.

In some respects Dam went his own way the same way as Karen Blixen, who found *her* late response in the *Heretica* circle. In neither case did the recognition obtained from younger colleagues imply complete acceptance of the older writers' ideas. But both Dam and Blixen are writers of myth who have confronted modern depictions of humanity with a daring stringency that no honest modernist can disregard. In the case of Poul Vad, for example, both his relativistic search and scrupulous description of the process of the search are closely related to Dam's artistic method in his largest novel, *Mod det ukendte mål* (Toward the Unknown Goal). Published in 1986 as part of the growing interest in Dam after waiting for half a century, the novel illustrates how difficult it is to situate Dam in literary history. Its central chronological position is between the early twin novels *Mellem de to Søer* (1906; Between the Two Lakes) and *I den firlængede gård* (In the Four-Winged Farm; written 1906–13, but not published until 1988) on the one hand and old-age "pictorials" like *Menneskelinien* (1965; The Line of Man) and *Menneskekår* (1967; The Conditions of Man) on the other. Far from upsetting the concepts in the titles of these frame works, three or four of Dam's novels dispersed over the intervening years tend to elaborate the entitled concepts. Clearly, he himself felt most comfortably and productively at home in the 1960s, and his surroundings confirmed him in this opinion. It is, therefore, appropriate to let his final breakthrough be the conclusion of this section.

While in Dam's very first novel the irresistible powers of a man's instinct make him slit the throat of a sensuous woman so he can live a decent life with a motherly woman privy to his designs, the novel's sequel confronts this bloody dualism with the author's mental framework and cultural point of departure, the four-winged home of his childhood. The result is altogether tragic, but the double consciousness that it sets free gradually assumes the form of a dialectic process. While in the course of this process the human's untiring craving for something beyond his existence repeatedly falls short of success, this very defeat becomes his inducement to continue his indefatigable defiance of the life he knows. Traveling through life on the bumpy roads of destructive self-indulgence and constructive dissatisfaction is the individual's reality. Meanwhile, his spirit and imagination spiral above and beyond the earthly conditions without ever leaving them completely behind. In Dam's style, process and dialectic train of thought appear as verbal oddities, elements of separate languages from Danish dialect to Latin, and a querying syntax in affirmative disguise. It is a style that stutters and groans in its own irresistible rhythm, lumpy and tortured, but energetic and relentless as well. Mired in impossible conditions, Dam reaches out for unconditional possibilities—a reality that we shall never procure in this world, but that the deficiencies of this world compel us to search for so long as we desire to endure as humans.

When Dam later refers to the line and conditions of man, he merely stretches his imagination to include the present moment with both its eternal perspectives and its remotely distant prerequisites. Searching for the unknown goal, in past and future, his works maintain a purpose that never becomes clear, a transcendent notion of humanity that is always at the human's own risk, and an activeness that in spite of despair knows no limits, not even the limits of illusion. Our only strength and safety is to be helplessly in the power of contradictions. This is Dam's awareness of "the deep crisis and inner divisions of the Western European," as Poul Vad has labeled it in *Den lodrette bestäen* and as Dam has interpreted it in *Vesteuropæers Bekendelser* (1963; Western European Confessions).

That existence, both the individual's and humankind's, is split to the ground is a fact that should not be assuaged. Compared to the modernist conception of empty transcendence, it is, moreover, a fact that does not imply any tragic decline of values. Dam's disharmonic universe does not contain lamentable matters; its boundless abyss of debacles and prospects goes to the bottom of every concrete individual and her life, and its dialectics are reality here and now. In its most palpable form and with its most far-reaching consequences this dualism comes across in a famous Renaissance picture called "Alrune" (The Mandrake), from Dam's breakthrough book *Syv skilderier* (1962; Seven Pictures). Compared to the bourgeois world, the world in Dam's work is unknown and ultimately unknowable; hence it never leaves the individual in the lurch of satisfaction. Perhaps this disillusioned zest for life and this harsh abundance of potentials were the refreshments that modernists in the late 1960s found most attractive in Dam. At any rate, he adheres to human complexity as an implacable design against the simplified models of life on the market. His line of humanity is the broken lifeline of modern humanism brought back to date and up-to-date.

THE 1970S: POLITICIZATION AND SOCIAL EXPERIMENTATION

In literary history there is not the same discernible dividing line between the 1960s and the 1970s that there happens to be between the 1950s and the 1960s, and again later between the 1970s and the 1980s. Whereas both of these lines are marked by an entire phalanx of young authors typical of their generation, a similar generational uniformity is conspicuous by its absence around 1970. Demarcation by the late 1960s is largely a reflection of the overall politicization of intellectual and societal life in the wake of youth and student rebellions, and a variety of extraparliamentary forms and grass-roots movements continued to serve—far into the 1970s—as bases of recourse for many writers and cultural personalities; these were the arenas that took up most of many people's energy.

At the time of the events, consensus undoubtedly was that the main political trend in the 1970s was left-wing and militant. But for one thing, a right-wing populism already had made inroads in parliament in the early 1970s and with no fewer repercussions than its left-wing counterpart. And besides, the turns to the left that did occur did not occur in unison. In simple terms, while everyone on the left was in favor of deposing capital, there was a major disagreement between those who wanted fantasy empowered in its stead and those who planned for the working class to seize power. The two objectives proved hard to reconcile, and many left-wing formations broke apart because of infighting between the lax children of flower power and the rigid proponents of Leninism; eventually, neither group came into power.

The total picture, then, shows a society being increasingly politicized and polarized but not making much political headway in the long run; the optimistic 1960s turned pessimistic quite early in the 1970s. It is instructive at this point to listen to Viggo Kampmann, who had been minister of the treasury in the 1950s and in his capacity as prime minister in the early 1960s contributed to getting the new decade out of the 1950s' mire of stagnation and unemployment; in addition, he was the foremost advocate and he bravely suited the action to the word of government support for the unpopular modernistic art and literature. On New Year's Day 1970 he said: "I believe that the youth rebellion in 1968–69 was merely an overture here and there in the world. In the 1970s the symphony of destiny will set in full slide" (*Berlingske Tidende*, Jan. 1, 1970).

All the same, both political and cultural spheres expanded and became more complex, and many new forms of organization and expression were collective, not only as a matter of appearance but in terms of ideological position. It is remarkable, for example, to watch the free flight of imagination on the cultural level coincide with the rigorous "capital logic" and social criticism on the level of political economy. The entire scope reflects that the crisis of society is the crisis of a welfare society. Economic progress during the 1960s had at the same time fulfilled the boldest promises and raised the popular level of expectation to euphoria. Yet it soon became clear that the welfare society was more a society of wealth than a society of welfare; everybody got a slice of the cake, but the relative social inequalities remained unchanged on the higher level of affluence.

Criticism of societal deficits, then, originated from experiences of surplus. In the meantime the most articulate youngsters and intellectuals arrived at schools and universities from hitherto unfairly treated, petty-bourgeois backgrounds. The criticism leveled at the bourgeois state institutions was all but destined to become intransigent. Conversely, when the rise in welfare procurements began to level off and the high level of expectations that had nurtured revolutionary optimism and critical energy faded correspondingly, critics began to realize that the alleged crisis was perception more than reality. The deflated rates of increase notwithstanding, welfare developments continued throughout the 1970s, and despite all the slogans calling for class struggle, most people continued to become somewhat better off.

This progress had a high price, however, which many people felt embittered their joy. While the majority's standard of living continued to improve, a considerable minority was reduced to continuous unemployment. Another minority was still part of the rat race but tended to drop out easily. And last but not least, to sustain families' and society's progress, women entered the work force in large numbers. Still, with all these accommodations, the national debt continued to increase in a vicious spiral, and a tendency to sidetrack the notions of solidarity and social utopia and to compete instead for the best conceivable niche in the marketplace became perceptible in the late 1970s.

Before that happened, though, the public arena of the 1970s displayed a motley patchwork of politicized culture. Some of its patterns were quite clear. Led by the Red Stocking movement, the entire Danish women's movement got into motion, and a rich cultural and literary sphere with connections to the movement itself and to new centers of feminist studies in the universities began to mushroom. Female consciousness in particular was central to discussions of sex and gender roles, of women's groups and island camps, of ecological matters, and so on, more or less in association with the general politicization of society. Many held that women's liberation was meaningful only within a larger left-wing political strategy; they proclaimed that without class struggle, there is no women's struggle. At the same time, the women's struggle was commonly seen as a necessity for the class struggle to escape fossilization and the charge of oppressing women in the same way as capitalism and patriarchy had done.

Some women's literature was written *by* women *about* women *for* women; with such exclusive parameters the authors prioritized the values of function and consumption in a given social situation over broader and deeper aesthetic appeals. A case in point is confessional writing—in either prose or versed prose—in which formerly repressed and privatized female experiences were brought to public attention with the intent to demonstrate just how difficult it can be to be who you are. Publications of this nature were buttressed by the predilection of the 1970s for documentary discourse. Documentary forms had been used to various degrees by authors in the 1950s and later (not to mention earlier), but in the 1970s they were used with the particular purpose of publicizing previously marginalized or disenfranchised social groups. In doing so the authors contributed analytical evidence to the political struggle for societal changes. Reports on women's lives in homes, in factories, and in politics were merely excerpts from the gamut of documentary opportunities, but they exemplified how gender-specific suppression could be entered into larger social contexts and how the ensuing experience of reality as a whole was entitled to public appearance outside the framework of the bourgeois public sphere.

An entire formation of working-class literature, written *by* workers *about* workers and sometimes *for* workers, appeared under these conditions, and in a broader geographical—and social—context so did a body of provincial literature serving primarily to document suppressed, overlooked, or directly moribund forms of life outside the urban centers. As mentioned earlier, such incompatible older writers as Seeberg and Bjørnkjær had been at it again and foreshadowed the trend; but as a regional political movement, provincial literature did not gain momentum until the 1970s, when its social psychology reechoed the same frustrations that rural constituencies then mandated in parliament. Finally, ecology and environment as movements attracted their own form of consciousness and public opinions in the 1970s. Bjørnvig has been mentioned as an early pioneer, but in the 1970s a whole ecological movement began riding the crest of a wave. Some writers even went beneath and beyond familiar ecological concerns to evoke the myth and existence of primitive peoples and cultures.

That they were not reformatory but committed to critical or imaginative alternatives to the existing (dis)order formed part of the untraditional or extraparliamentary character of the various movements. Several were engaged in revolutionary and social experiments, and the very concept of alternative society was frequently used, for example, in deference to communes and more or less permanent camps and folk high schools outside the established society, notably the Christiania colony in Copenhagen. A flowery patchwork of new experimental, communal, group, courtyard, and children's theaters originated from this social fabric. Not only were they formally detached from the bourgeois world of theater, but some of them, like the Christiania-based Solvognen (chariot of the sun, or sun disc with horse), caused great direct disorder in decent bourgeois minds when, disguised as Santas, the group entered a Copenhagen department store to distribute Christmas presents free of charge. On another occasion—during the war in Vietnam—they challenged the traditional Danish-American festivities on July 4. As part of such activities new forms of popular music were performed, which became a revolutionary force in the 1960s, diversified into a variety of beat, rock, and punk styles in the 1970s. They, too, were "social recitals" outside the confines of bourgeois or middle-class taste.

Open political commitments were the order of the day in the early 1970s; in substance they were anti-imperialist, mostly condemning the Americans in Vietnam, occasionally the European Economic Community (EEC), which Denmark joined in 1972. Some writers of the decade had closer attachments to more local and less profiled circumstances, and a few seemed almost exclusively artistic in their practice. Nevertheless, their bases of writing were usually political extensions, if not remote controls, of intellectual positions in the 1960s. The distance factor pertained, in particular, to the so-called scripture thematic poets, who placed their societal revolt in completely textual terms or in what they conceived as the guerrilla warfare of scripture against the terror of language. On the journal front, left-wing dispositions came to the fore with new editors of *Vindrosen* and with a new publication called *Hug* (1974–; Slash, or Beating); formerly formalistic, the journal *Poetik* (1967–76; Poetics) made a significant change of its name to *Kultur og klasse* (1977–; Culture and Class), and with no less pertinent changes of its subtitle (from "Journal for Existentialistic Debate" and "Journal for Phenomenological Debate" to "Journal for Literature and Semiotics" and "Journal for Text Theory"), the existentialistic mouthpiece *Exil* (1965–76; Exile) gradually became an organ for new semiotics and scripture orientation. By the end of the 1970s the journal *Chancen* (1979–80; Chance) had bobbed up as a sign of more pluralistic—happenstance—times. The political trenches became less appealing.

A closer inspection of this front of journals shows quite precisely the ideological transformation that came to pass in the course of the decade. On the book front the ideology ranges from, say, Thorkild Hansen's Hamsun hagiography on the right to ideology critique on the left. In the journals, however, the ideological signals were more up-to-date, and once again they pointed to humanism as the compass; by the end of the decade Villy Sørensen's variant of bourgeois humanism, the third standpoint between Kierkegaard and Marx, had captured the attention of most intellectuals and many others. His and his associates' revolt from the center was not an exercise in class struggle or in rejecting the welfare society and state; it was an effort to further social and human equality on the (revised) premises of this society and state. Political consciousness in the 1970s was heightened on political and ideological wings, to the left and to the right, but it was adapted to a balanced revision of insights and experiences from the 1960s. A revolt in Denmark had to be a revolt from the center, and at best, it delivered a constructive crisis awareness, while at worst, it became a debate about revolting.

What caused women's literature to balance between extreme simplicity and complex aesthetic achievements was, among other things, a fertile historical and critical hinterland for the practical feminist movements. One of the pioneering critics and scholars was Pil Dahlerup, with studies of sex and gender roles in literature and later with a seminal work about previously neglected women writers of the Modern Breakthrough. She and colleagues such as Jette Lundbo Levy, Toni Liversage, Anne Birgitte Richard, and Susanne Fabricius, just to mention a few, exercised an extensive critical activity in the newspaper *Information*.

A case in point is Lundbo Levy's elaborate review of Maria Marcus's *Den frygtelige sandhed* (1974; Eng. tr. *A Taste for Pain,* 1981). The book was controversial because of its author's personal confession to masochist inclinations and because of the extra painful fact that this taste for pain so clearly was at odds with her feminist advocacy of women's independence of men. Lundbo Levy, in her review, added to the complexity of the book by acknowledging and penetrating its problematics rather than trying to rule out its disturbing message as gender-politically inappropriate. Celebrating the centennial of the most famous woman writer, Karen Blixen/Isak Dinesen, the book *Out of Denmark: Danish Women Writers Today* (1985) was an attempt to make selected representatives of this literature, who transgress cultural boundaries, cross the Danish frontier as well.

Kirsten Thorup

The utmost complexity is to be found in the work of Kirsten Thorup (1942–). On a superficial viewing it seems to be in the late 1960s mode of language poetry and attitudinal relativism with texts that are seemingly superficial and trivial themselves, dangerously beautiful, unreal, and impersonal. But Thorup knows what she is doing. *Indeni-Udenfor* (1967; Inside-Outside) is her first collection of poems, and whether its title is meant as a juxtaposition or a confrontation, it clearly enunciates a dual world. Underneath the textual surface is an almost schizophrenic inner world, and a world of social disenfranchisement to boot. In *Love from Trieste* (1969; Eng. tr. 1980) and *Idag er det Daisy* (1971; Today It Is Daisy) the impression of surface, aesthetic monotony and depersonalization prevails (at least on critics with personal stock in language poetry), but in the novel *Baby* (1973; Eng. tr. 1980) it becomes clear that the reductive and seemingly dispassionate style is a vehicle for conditions of existential loss and alienation. The impeccable surface is like the silence before a storm of emotions, a vulnerable, provisional safety measure before an eruption of inner and social life.

That is what happens in two novels from the 1970s, *Lille Jonna* (1977;

Little Jonna) and *Den lange sommer* (1979; The Long Summer). Realistic novels about an adolescent girl's development from the age of ten to twenty-two and about her childhood on the social outskirts of Denmark in the 1950s and 1960s, these are typical documents of the 1970s: concrete, historical, and engaged. But Thorup's development is not toward simplification; in her two large and powerful masterpieces from the 1980s she brings her realistic outreach to bear on her earlier modernistic explorations of the human psyche and existence. *Himmel og helvede* (1982; Heaven and Hell) updates the realistic novels and parts of their settings to the world of the 1960s, and at the same time, it reevaluates the relationship between the individual and the world. Depicting a fascinating, alien world of meaningless beauty, Thorup's first two books reflect the spirit of their times and take it to task. Turning a fictitious world into obvious fiction, they mark the boundary of reality and prepare for the liberation of an individual inclined to succumb to the world as it was. In the novels written in the 1970s this individual develops further, and in *Himmel og helvede*, as Inger Christensen has noted, its development finds artistic room for its inner life; no longer alienated by the surrounding world, it takes the world on itself and makes its own authority—a defiant claim to life despite inevitable death—replace the false and so-called real authorities of traditional economics and politics.

In *Den yderste grænse* (1987; The Outer Limit) Thorup takes her project from the utopian late 1960s of *Himmel og helvede* to the period of disappointment and disillusionment ten to fifteen years later. But reaching the outer limits does not limit her insistence on behalf of love and life against stagnation and despair. Without compromising her insight into the human conditions of discord and unreality she mightily allows herself to venture into wholeness and reality. As Inger Christensen has also said, in awarding Thorup a literary prize, she makes her characters mature to the point where they no longer can forget they must die; and at that point she makes them live as if they were immortals. This way Thorup transgresses the boundaries between the 1960s and the 1970s and between the 1970s and the 1980s. She also transgresses the boundaries of women's literature, to which her central works in many ways have affinity. She is a bridge over generations, sexes, and social realities, an overwhelming author.

Inge Eriksen and Suzanne Brøgger

Inge Eriksen (1935–) has been much more closely associated with left-wing feminist movements than Kirsten Thorup, and her first and most important novel to date, *Victoria og verdensrevolutionen* (1976; Victoria and World Revolution), is actually her own revolutionary experiences in Copenhagen in the 1970s projected onto the colorful scene of a revolutionary country in Latin America in the 1950s and 1960s. Nevertheless, Eriksen, like Thorup, is essentially intent on authorizing the inner self of her protagonist and other characters as the beautiful movers and shakers of the world. Her novel is a hymn to life, and its colorful patchwork of beautiful people and good deeds interweaves some victorious individuals. It has been criticized for its bountiful trivia, idealizations of characters, soap-opera self-confidence, and what have you, but Eriksen has responded that true revolution unites people in action across conventional boundaries, whether defined by bourgeois capitalists or regimented feminists. Her images of human love do not have Thorup's critical deep dimension, but somehow her optimism compensates for existential shortcomings. With all its own stereotypes, this socialist entertainment novel defies stereotyping from both right and left. Typical and yet atypical, it functions well in its own right and its own way.

For Suzanne Brøgger (1944–) the prime target is the bourgeois family and the cancerous culture that it epitomizes, not the mere oppression of women or the struggle against it in women's groups. Like Sven Holm in his family novels, Brøgger lashes out at modern private lives as a kind of business secrecy that no longer serves its purpose in a society of normal wage earners. Part of this privacy is monogamous love, which is too specialized and exclusive and perfectly suited to prevent love from elsewhere to enrich our lives (particularly the lives of children). These are the principal themes in Brøgger's first book, *Fri os fra kærligheden* (1973; Eng. tr. *Deliver Us from Love*, 1976), which articulates its experimental philosophy of life in a "mixture of genres." In her later work she has written predominantly in the first-person mode in an effort to reach the collective subconscious while remaining herself; but many readers have read her against the grain and confuse the authorial "I" with the private person behind it.

A different confusion characterizes the dialogue between Brøgger and her feminist critics. She has accused them of revolting against male society on that society's terms, and they have replied, in turn, that she is the victim of bourgeois individualism and male fixations. The controversy appears similar to the one between Inge Eriksen and the feminists, that is, between an author who goes her own complicated and sometimes irregular way and an academic enterprise that knows the law. *Kærlighedens veje og vildveje* (1975; The Ways and Wrong Ways of Love) and *Brøg* (1980; Brew) are titles that in themselves defy superior knowledge of the right economy, political strategy, and psychological or moral principles. *Brøg* alludes directly to witchcraft as a law-defiant way of going about love in Western culture, and in *Crème Fraîche* (1978; Sour Cream) Brøgger delights in a story about a Chinese potter who threw himself into the flames so as to provide his glaze with the right amount of oxygen. Brøgger has eloquently started many brush fires in Danish public debates and has readily thrown herself into the flames. Yet she only contributed the moral obligation to break an outworn camel's back.

Other Women Writers

Two writers whose works Inge Eriksen defended against Pil Dahlerup's allegedly doctrinaire criticism are Jytte Borberg (1917–) and Jette Drewsen (1943–). There is not only a considerable age difference between the two, but also a very different outlook. Borberg made her debut in the 1960s with a collection of short stories, *Vindebroen* (1968; The Drawbridge), followed by a novel, *Nældefeber* (Nettle Rash) in 1970, both of which submit that modern existence is a general experience of isolation and coincidence; her stylistic capacity ranges from realism to fantasy, and occasionally she cross-breeds the two. Drewsen made her debut in the 1970s with *Hvad tænkte egentlig Arendse?* (1972; What Did Arendse Actually Think of?) and has been from the beginning a writer of women's literature; throughout her career she has created female protagonists, usually a single mother with children, and her style is mostly realistic and direct.

These differences notwithstanding, Borberg and Drewsen got caught in the same critical cross-fire for good reason. In the 1970s Borberg, too, became an author of women's books, and Drewsen's compositions and social scenarios became increasingly complex. For different reasons the two authors approach the feminine world with a view to its open-ended ambiguity that is not necessarily in tune with gender-political strategies at the time of writing. *Rapport fra havbunden* (1978; Reporting from the Sea Bottom) is Borberg's variation of the famous medieval ballad about Agnete and the Merman, but the adventurous and fantastic human imagination is confronted with rigid social barriers and wrongdoings and makes the future course of Agnete's life an open question. In Drewsen's *Tid og sted* (1978; Time and Place) the single protagonist and single-level plot have been four-doubled, and a series of family histories unfolds its own open-ended and relief-giving course of events. Both Borberg and Drewsen accord their individual characters a social or collective space in which individuality can be either lost or fulfilled.

Marianne Larsen (1951–) believes that because of their special gender roles and family experiences women write in a different manner than men. Her first books call to mind the first of Kirsten Thorup's works in the sense that they, too, are abstract and almost unreal on the surface but political in their deep dimension. But while Thorup was inclined toward the attitudinal relativism of the 1960s, the younger Larsen's formal affinities are versed prose and scripture-thematic poetry; likewise, her sociopolitical allegiance is, indeed, to the underdog, but her adversary is chiefly the entire society of commercial exploitation. Poetry and prose are intermingled in her books, and her formal originality, and its connection with her political tenets, is part of her protest against the classical, orderly world. Her collection *Billed-tekster* (1974; Pictorial Texts) has the subtitle "Un-Calligraphy," and the idea behind the deliberate disorder is to combine prosaic political analysis with sensitive reflections of human loneliness. Larsen wants to liberate the abandoned individual, but concurrently she must redefine the societal frames in order to give her liberation an outlet. Increasingly concrete, her texts, like Thorup's, incorporate her abstractions and leave the reader with an unobtrusive, surreal combination of political criticism and political uto-pianism.

Vita Andersen (1944–) is the epitome of a versifying prose writer. She has confessed to a deep fear of writing real verse, and the simplicity that re-sults from just chopping off the lines before the margin has not been unre-warding. Vast numbers of readers have bought her books and presumably recognized themselves in the insecurities, the urge to eat for comfort, and other modern addictions that fill the pages of her first book, *Tryg-hedsnarkomaner* (1977; Security Junkies), published while the insidious welfare crisis was beginning to strike inward. The harshness of emotional life under competitive, desocializing conditions also comes across in titles such as *Hold kæft og vær smuk* (1978; Shut Up and Be Beautiful) and *Hva' for en hånd vil du ha'* (1987; Which Hand Do You Want), a collection of short stories and a novel, respectively. Andersen writes about people, not just women, but as victims her women characters are more exposed. Their feel-ing of thingification reminds the reader of Dorrit Willumsen, but in place of Willumsen's subtleness and suppleness, Andersen simply leaves the impres-sion that she herself is one of "them"—and that the reader is another.

Discomfort in the work of Vibeke Grønfeldt (1948–) is caused by human closeness rather than distance and isolation, and in a trilogy of novels from the late 1970s she shows her characters escaping from this claustrophobia into a language that is both dense and opaque and free of stressful normality, whether in vocabulary, syntax, or associations. Only verbally can recurrent desire for love come to fruition. The situation in the books of Dea Trier Mørch (1941–) is completely different. She has long been a good, solid Danish communist with boundless faith in the (working) people, and her graphics and writings beam simplicity and celebrate with no misgivings the collective virtues of the commoners; *Vinterbørn* (1976; Eng. tr. *Winter's Child*, 1986), about mothers-to-be in a prenatal hospital ward, became an immediate success. Compared to this display of convincing sister-solidarity, *Kastaniealleen* (1978; The Chestnut Lane) is an anticlimax, though. Mørch's positivism in these childhood recollections is too idyllic and nostalgic to make any petty-bourgeois daydreamer uncomfortable. A worshiper of life, this writer sometimes seems to forget what her political vision imparts: there is no sunshine without shadows, and no life without struggle.

Otherwise, the very productive genre of women's literature in the 1970s and after range from the brilliant novel *Guldkuglen* (1985; The Gold Ball) of Hanne Marie Svendsen (1933–) to the predictable products of Herdis Møllehave (1936–). The majority of titles, though, are functional and useful statements about their chosen social background, rather than aesthetically, intellectually, and emotionally ground-breaking texts in a larger cultural sense. Examples are *Vent til du hører mig le* (1983; Wait till You Hear Me Laugh) by Bente Clod (1946–) and *Søstrene* (1979; The Sisters) by Ulla Dahlerup (1942–). Both are historical retrospectives; but whatever their insights, understanding the past as it shaped a certain group of women serves the explicit purpose of giving the same group, or its equivalent in real life, an incentive to move on in a feminist direction. Clod looks back on three generations of women to reinforce an alternative society for the latest generation. Dahlerup looks back only to 1970, when an early feminist base group took off; reconstructing what followed regroups this group's identity.

More interesting than these prototypes are texts such as the novel *Konen og æggene* (1973; The Woman and the Eggs) by Grete Stenbæk Jensen (1925–) and novels by Ragnhild Agger (1918–), for example, *Pladser* (1973, meaning both "Places" and "Jobs"). Both are written by women about women, but they are not exclusively for women. Their subject is not an urban middle-class inner circle, but lower middle-class women's working lives and conditions, often in rural or provincial areas. Situated between women's literature, working-class literature, and provincial literature, these fictive reportings endow the public experience with a multitude of disenfranchised experiences. Alluding to a satirical poem by Hans Christian Andersen, Jensen's title refers to a middle-aged woman working at an egg-packing station, and the question it raises is, "Why are the eggs treated so much better than the people who pack them?" (Hans Hertel; in *Information*, May 14, 1973). In Agger's book about a maid in the 1930s there is more mobility, both geographically and mentally, but the plight of her character (herself in disguise) is no less painful. Caught between her dreams of books, film, and music, and the erotic and social oppression in her real life, she eventually becomes realistic to the extent that she at least knows when she daydreams! But she remains between a rock and a hard place; to be accepted on her own terms seems impossible, and to be accepted on the terms of the men around and above her is an uphill battle. How can she strike the balance while preserving her self-respect? Like Maja Ekelöf's Swedish cleaning woman, she is hungry for knowledge and freedom because she is so deprived. Rather than ending on a positive note, the novel makes this condition an irrevocable fact; its altogether pale and nonatmospheric discourse becomes the tone of a nonnegotiable determinism. The protagonist can move and go and do, but her plight is inescapable. And she accepts it.

Blue-Collar Literature

In working-class literature this individualistic acceptance of fate is not uncommon. A woman in a menial position in the 1930s highlights a troublesome conflict between ideology and reality in much more recent work-place settings as well. To this day the ideal of solidarity and organization has not eliminated the vestiges of bourgeois mentality. In fact, the soaring exploration of working-class literature in the 1970s may well be a political attempt to solidify the cultural identity of this class at a time when its socialist integrity looks rather dismal. At least, this was the suspicion arrived at by certain established writers, some of whom had themselves endeavored to turn their bourgeois language into proletarian discourse. After having given up on that project in his book *Festen er forbi* (1974; The Party Is Over), Lars Bonnevie (1941–) thus sarcastically writes of working-class literature that "this trend in the intellectual life of the 1970s had the particular purpose of giving the [left-wing] academics *first-class information* from the blue-collar reservation" (*Politiken*, Aug. 14, 1983). Be that as it may, the many anthologies and other publications of working-class literature may not have offset a stronger socialistic platform—and class members for the most part ignored its existence—but the effort in itself and its mixed results speak quite eloquently of the ideological dilemmas of the decade.

Ulrik Gräs (1940–) illustrates this point with books in which workers, mired in generational conflicts, are themselves conflict-ridden characters in terms of both class and gender identity. One collection of short stories is called *Historiens Gang* (1980; The Course of History), and in the novel *Her og altid* (1987; Here and Always) Gräs portrays the bourgeoisization and historical defeat of the working class. In the first and prime novel of Per Larsen (1937), *Krapyl* (1977; Rabble), a thorough and genuine insight into current blue-collar consciousness and life experiences is forwarded in a manner of modernist complexity, against the background of a keen awareness of neglected historical roots.

Complex in a different sense is the debut novel of Bent Vinn Nielsen (1951–), *Arbejdssky* (1978; Work-Shy), in that it juxtaposes the passive narrative of its lead character and the active reflections of its author. In the autobiographical books of John Nehm (1934–) the first-person narrator is painfully trapped between his own individuality and his oppressing social circumstances. In a sense his personal makeup is frail and constricted, but in dealing with these deficiencies and writing them out in fictive forms, he counters the impossible social odds with partial success. *En gren af nerver* (1977; A Branch of Nerves) is clearly about a mental breakdown, but it is also about a branch of nerves with an offshoot of green leaves. Its somewhat disjointed double entendre suggests that Nehm has not fully accomplished repossession of his personality in artistic form, but that his writing at least leaves him with some hope and sense of direction.

Provincial Literature

Provincial literature, too, addresses popular culture severed from its roots and subjected to oppression. At its best it laments the fact without sentimentality and constructively looks for alternatives that are compatible with downtrodden tradition. Unlike several minor writers, whose ineptitude in transgressing the provincial borders is a provincialism in itself, Gynther Hansen (1930–) is a true border(line) case. He quotes William Faulkner in saying that "he will depict the universal reflected in the local," and adds, "That is what I want to do, too" (*Dansk Udsyn* 65[1985], 45). Hansen was born of German minority parents in southern Denmark (North Schleswig), where he stayed in order to convert his semi-German ancestry into full-scale Danishness. In his writing he only slowly captured the Danish tongue. His first book, in standard Danish, took him a long time to write, and it literally left him all but speechless. By his own account it was not until his second volume, eleven years later, that he found a voice of his own, the southern Jutland regional variant of Danish. Transgressing this linguistic boundary at the same time was a matter of crossing the line between written and spoken language and, hence, the need to use dialogues or monologues as spoken by common people in the countryside: *Stemmer fra provinsen* (1976; Voices from the Province) and subsequently *Jeg. Jeg. Mig. Mit* (1978; I, I, Me, Mine), four monologues or four variations on stifled and stifling individualism. Hansen later deepens and widens these eruptions of words into autobiographical expressions of European traumas, in *Hitler, min far og mig*

(1988; Hitler, My Father, and Me), for example. His province, then, is not the place where people have their roots, but the place where they have lost them, and his humanism is modernistic insofar as it turns the decline of the native soil into the rise of a restless and ambiguous consciousness.

A special Danish province exists in the neighborhoods within Copenhagen's city limits. Peter Poulsen (1940–) has captured the spirit and atmosphere of the working-class quarters in Vesterbro in a series of down-to-earth books of verse and prose in oral vernacular. And Lean Nielsen (1935–) has in even less roundabout ways expressed his strong emotions in poems and novels, epics and memoirs, and genre mixtures such as *ballader om vold og ømhed* (1976; ballads on violence and tenderness). Nielsen has been hurt, and it sometimes hurts the reader to learn about it; his lyrical narratives are not documentarism but they document real life—a worker's life at that—and sometimes make it memorable. The province of Steen Kaalø (1945–) in the capital is the inner city, where his first poems were sold from an artist's pram in the streets of Copenhagen in the early 1970s. His simplicity is not pronounced; in fact, he likes to give his imagination free rein both within and across the genres, including modern hymns; his province is alive. To modify what a critic has said of the difference that still exists between urban and rural culture, Kaalø's outspoken experiments highlight the otherness of rural provinciality and its understatements and dislike of conflicts.

Scripture Thematic Literature

Not to belabor the point, there are provincial differences even among the most scripture-oriented writers in the 1970s. Approaching the world through an explicit struggle with language, these poets do not immediately reveal any dialects; nonetheless, the sociopolitical implications inherent in their writings are marked by their respective theoretical environments. Some of them associate with Denmark's second largest city Århus, notably the critic Niels Egebak, and the semiotic milieu around the journal *Exil*. Others are centered in Copenhagen. What they have in common is a high degree of sophistication and inaccessibility; throughout the 1970s the bulk of their works appeared in underground format or was issued by special avant-garde publishers. Only slowly have a few of them made inroads in the larger public sphere, and then usually by way of more appealing writing styles.

In itself quite a hermetic text, the book *Skriften, spejlet og hammeren. En kritisk analyse af en række nyere eksperimentelle danske forfatterskaber* (1972; Scripture, Mirror, and Hammer: A Critical Analysis of a Number of Newer

Experimental Danish Authorships), by Hugo Hørlych Karlsen (1948–), gives a general sense of the artistic enterprise in this group of writers. The centerpiece of his title, the mirror, reproduces the existing world. Hence the mirror must be crushed or divided in two separate parts: the real praxis or the hammer in the hand, and the formal praxis or the scripture in operation. In its dialectical interplay these two functions will replace "the metaphysical mirror of language and its prerequisites in the existing society." To illustrate the point, Karlsen's title reads as a mirror image on the shiny, silver cover of his book; his material praxis is visible. Neither the critique of ideology nor the critique of myths will suffice to ensure a new revolutionary praxis. Praxis depends on scripture, and before language becomes action-oriented, no real action, as it were, is going to make any difference.

Leif Hjernøe (1938–) made a confident debut with a thin novel called *En tid lang* (1968; For a While), the first volume of a trilogy ending with *Fra tid til anden* (1971; From Time to Time). Like several of his contemporaries, Hjernøe gets his critical impetus from Michel Butor and other French *nouveau roman* authors. Many have time as their main concern, and as suggested by Hjernøe's titles, time is not purposeful, goal-oriented, action-minded; it is slack, casual, protracted. Gradually deprived of its objects, its chronology, and its occurrence outside of language, it becomes omnipresent and evasive—at the same time. Since text production is their principal theme, these texts arrive at meaning by decomposing meaning as it was, and as it were; in doing so they inform a consciousness of the real world, which is the only thing they believe in. The illusion of textual representation of reality, which informs traditional novels, has given way to an awareness of that illusion in Hjernøe's antinovels. The last novel of his trilogy has three so-called tracks; in another, *Romanen om Vitus Bering* (1972; The Novel about Vitus Bering), we find five tracks and an exceedingly elaborate exhibition of time. A series of more recent novels, notably *Hverdag* (1976; Everyday), has labored to wear down the conventional images of life even further; the benefits from this process are still to be found in the ability to convert the deficit of realistic illusion into a surplus of dis-illusioned consciousness.

Jens Smærup Sørensen (1946–) is one of the quintessential authors of the 1970s. He made his debut in 1971 with a book of poetry, *Udvikling til fremtiden* (Development into the Future), in which the confrontational poetic style of the early 1960s was put into the systemic mode of the later 1960s. And his most recent book, *Katastrofe* (1989; Catastrophe), is a showdown with the generation of the 1970s, his own contemporaries. Not surprisingly, it confronts their past idealism and community spirit with their current sentiments of egotism and material obsession; but more interestingly, it shows how their turnabout is ingrained in words and language postures. Smærup Sørensen is a prime example of the Århus brand of scripture poetry; provincial roots and Niels Egebak's semiotic guidance are typical of his publications. His second book, and first novel, *At ende som eneboer* (1972; Ending Up as a Hermit), unfolds a conflict in a character who collapses in reality but takes refuge in myth; somehow the person's writing unites these conflicting processes. A comprehensive and complex collection of epic and lyrical texts, the ensuing *Gøremål* (1973; Doings) is still fettered in its own scripture. By contrast, Smærup Sørensen's breakthrough, the elaborate novel *Byggeri* (1975; Building), is a mixture of science fiction and realism, critical of a violent society but somewhat optimistic on behalf of its victims. Even more realistic is *13 stykker af en drøm* (1976; 13 Pieces of a Dream), yet more hopeless at that.

Skoven nu (1978; The Forest Now) is his first complete description of the entire country, which is in crisis and on the downhill side, but not yet corrupted by future "opportunities." In *Mit danske kød* (1981; My Danish Flesh) the narrative point of view is after the Big Bang, although confusing memories from life in old Denmark continue to intrude. The text digests our culture and defecates the result. Only in this process do we live, and only the discourse brings the process to bear on our body of language and culture. It is called *Det menneskelige princip* (1985; The Human Principle) in one of Smærup Sørensen's latest pieces of writing.

The death of civilization is the recurring theme in the many publications of Henning Mortensen (1939–). Mortensen was the publisher of numerous underground works of the 1970s, and his anarchistic mediating takes place in his own texts as well. They have been called psychophysical, anarchosurreal, or examples of synaesthetia, meaning they short-circuit or commingle both genres and aesthetic impulses. Mortensen is an energetic, playful desperado rushing through the artistic time machine. His fast consumption of systemic, scriptural, and political procedures occasionally leaves the reader with a feeling of indigestion or of being part of a circus performance; Mortensen, incidentally, has humor. And apparently, the most striking problem—how to align artistic means with critical, let alone realistic, ends—is felt no less by the author himself. He repeatedly writes that he no longer will write about writing. And so be it.

The production of Peter Laugesen (1942–) is extensive, too, and for many years was essentially an underground activity (on Mortensen's duplicator). The continuous flow of texts is hard to subdivide into separate entities; and insofar as titles are concerned, they are situated in the same universe as Mortensen's. *Anarkotika* (1975) is a synthesis of anarchy and narcotics, and *Kakatonien* (1970) is a phase of schizophrenia. "Composed" of an abundance of linguistic debris, the latter impossible collection of poems and notes nonetheless reveals a desperate and moving love story. Laugesen revolts with frenzy against the straitjacket of modern society, and his fervent attacks on its norms and normality are aimed at liberating life from claustrophobia. Political anarchism and psychological insanity are complementary tools to be used in the service of love and freedom. Laugesen wants to reach the point where language becomes impossible because reality is impossible. His experiments are attempts to spot the psychopathic potentials of language wherein scripture can unfold, hence his repeated references to mental dissolution and breakdown. More consistently than most of his colleagues he implements this constructive demolition with disciplined bulldog tenacity. In one of his books, called *72 håndskrevne sider* (1970; 72 Handwritten Pages), material awareness is under the microscope; in an inserted letter to one particular reader, the "printer," the writer divides his development into ballpoint periods and fountain-pen periods. The writing is not calligraphic, corrections and deletions are not omitted, and the pages are unnumbered; in fact, the cover informs us that the author has forgotten their order of appearance (and would have distorted it if he had not). Once you look at the longhand, an extra disturbing dimension is added. The writing of one page either reads HA HA HA, or it pictures a series of crosses in a cemetery. Should we laugh or die? Laugesen's answer is a title such as *Hamr & Hak* (1977; Hammer & Hack). An unending revolution in language and text is all that preserves life and death.

Among Mortensen's and Laugesen's selected affinities were the Swede Lars Norén and Jack Kerouac, respectively. The idea to institute a sociopsychological rebellion in language, rather than take issue with the normal humanistic subject, was not of Danish origin. In the case of Dan Turèll (1946–) the foremost inspiration is American, as he has testified in *Amerikanske ansigter. Udvalgte artikler fra 70'erne* (1979; American Faces: Selected Articles from the 70s). A conglomerate of American popular culture, books and films, media and music, says the author, has "given me more, in terms of consciousness, conceptions" than good and respectable Danish traditions.

Turèll's production must have reached one hundred titles at this writing, and like Mortensen's and Laugesen's, it is largely one gigantic, ever-flowing text. The title of a book from 1972 illustrates the point: *Sidste forestilling bevidstløse trancebilleder af eksploderende spejltrics igennem flyvende tidsmaskine af smeltende elektriske glasfotos* (Last Performance Unconscious Trance Images of Exploding Mirror Tricks Through Flying Time Machine of Melting Electric Glass Photos). The book itself consists of more than four hundred pages of text masses in various IBM printout fonts, each reflecting a program or a synthetic vernacular. Knocking off its verses or rattling off its speeches, the book characterizes itself (via the author) as an act of revolution: "It is your madness I knock off and rattle off." The alienating language is exposed to its own obsessively beautiful self-destruction, and even the splintering of the mirror, suggested by critic Hørlych Karlsen, has reached the title; for the pillars of society this is the end, while for the children of flower power it is an unintermittent hallucination, the intoxicating downfall of language and capitalist gods.

There is another Turèll, though. A man that everybody knows because he has punk hair and black nails and a weekly column of chat in a leading paper and has written a series of suspense-filled thrillers and a no-nonsense, down-to-earth bestseller of childhood memoirs, and, and . . . As suggested by a critic, Turèll has long ago become a literary cliché. One could also say that despite the outrageous transgressions of national and cultural boundaries, this wild beast has become a very domesticated animal. Turèll would probably say that revolution begins and ends in a text. He appears to be proven absolutely right.

The popularity of Michael Buchwald (1943–) is less conspicuous; in fact, he has no public image whatsoever. He is one of the scripture-thematic poets with models in French philosophy and critique, and his rather small production has not given up on the textual revolution, which more or less follows the trend of his generation. His first book, *Afsøgningsmønster* (1970; Pattern of Reconnaissance), is a reflection on the youth rebellion; his second, *Genudsendelse af en båndlagt snak* (1972; Rebroadcasting a Taped Chat), discusses the necessity of a permanent social rebellion; and in *Blokland* (1975; Block Land) he embarks on myth and reality, fiction and faction, to describe an area of concrete suburban slum in which rebellion is obviously called for but remains unexpressed. Just as *Genudsendelse* resembles Smærup Sørensen's *At ende som eneboer*, *Blokland* is quite like Smærup Sørensen's *Byggeri*. Both of Buchwald's novels seem to depict reality, and both insist that it only looks that way and that the difference—the awareness of the illusion—literally makes all the difference. Approaching the revolution engrosses the text.

In the case of Klaus Høeck (1938–) the marked difference between the illusion of art and the illusion-breaking awareness of art is extreme. Høeck is a revolutionary romantic who puts his sonnets into a computer program that allows the discarded elements to replace the orderly parts in the final scheme. The effect brings about a disturbing awareness of romantic form at the expense of the innocuous form itself. Høeck's inspirations range from William Blake to beat, with Heinrich Heine's *Deutschland. Ein Winter-märchen* (1844; Germany: A Winter's Tale) at the center. Høeck is a traveler himself (*Rejse I–V* [1971–73; Journey]), and his lower-class Copenhagen neighborhood forms the background of revolutionary encounters, in spirit, with terrorist Ulrike Meinhof and PLO leader Yassir Arafat, but essentially with himself. The journey into romantic identification returns the traveler to his naked self. As a trip—an ego trip—it was all right, but at the end of the line there were only lost illusions. Draining the cup of romanticism to the dregs is merely to entertain a lesson about reality.

As a vignette to this list of language-philosophical poets, brief mention should be given to two remarkable outsiders, Svend Johansen (1922–) and Per Aage Brandt (1944–). They represent not two provinces within the scripture-oriented landscape, but two extremely international—French—orientations in both poetry and humanistic scholarship. Johansen is an acclaimed specialist on symbolism and structuralism and made his poetic debut at the age of fifty-five. Brandt is a profuse writer, as both a semiotic scholar and lyrical poet. He has been accused of being too scientific as a poet and too poetic as a scientist, but maybe the jury is still out. So far, Johansen and Brandt, in their own ways, appear to represent an unparalleled combination of exclusiveness and inclusiveness.

Myth and Mythology in Literature

Alongside documentary fiction and various forms of language and scripture poetry the 1970s witnessed a remarkable surge of literature inspired by mythology or committed to the criticism of myths. Several writers of this category were originally in the language and scripture circles, but as their priorities shifted to mythological writing, this artistic trend eventually—by the end of the decade—took priority over documentary forms.

Mythology was already a factor in the late 1960s. Roland Barthes's famous book *Mythologies* (1957) appeared in Danish translation in 1969, and a Danish book by Poul E. Andersen, *Det myteløse menneske* (1969; Man without Myth) gave additional impetus to discussions of the issue. Danish mythological poetry and fiction was published by poets like Rifbjerg and Leth at the same time, and an entire collection of myths and stories by Per Kirkeby, *Jüngling auf der Wanderschaft* (The Wanderings of a Young Man), appeared in 1970. Mythology in beat music was analyzed by Peer E. Sørensen, and in popular weekly magazines and books for children and young adults by other scholars at Århus and Copenhagen universities.

The interest in myths and mythologies in the 1970s springs from the general critique of late capitalism and emerging technocracy, and it points in two directions. First, the bourgeois individual is supposedly a person without myth and without irrational or transcendent inclinations. This individual has no desire to go behind or beyond the actual world or in other ways partake in mythical revolts. On the contrary, he aims at human rationality, economical growth, and technical perfection, and discussions are only about the appropriate means to this end. Outside the purview of rationality, bourgeois language is stereotypical, dominated by clichés, and devoid of emotional nuances.

Occasionally, however, the absence of myth does engender a sense of void in the individual. And with true myth out of the question, the imposition of false ideological myths typically fills this void. But the false myth, although quite similar to its real counterpart, has no functional value. It meets a need but offers only mystification to the needy. Instead of giving meaning to actions it simply leads to irrationalism. A period of this nature is "late mythical" in the sense that only remnants of original myths are available. But met with critical awareness and skepticism, the late mythical period also affords opportunities, both to reassemble a genuine language of metaphorical and pictorial depth and to counter falsifications of older myths. Modern writers of myth do not reach for artistic illusion; on the contrary, it is by pointing to illusive representations of the world that they indirectly point to the world itself. They write with a view to political and cultural restoration in a period of decline of the public sphere.

The first novels of Vagn Lundbye (1933–) appeared in the late 1960s and were all exclusive narrative experiments à la Alain Robbe-Grillet. One is mostly about the uneventful life of a cow and simply called *Roman* (1968; Novel), but they all subordinate apparent concerns with sex and death to questions of point of view and other technical matters. Then, in 1969, Lundbye wrote *Nico*, which was the first opening of his work to myth, in this case the Andy Warhol singer who was herself a myth of beat culture. Lundbye in his use of eclecticism and pastiche both celebrates his subject and makes the reader aware of its nature. Its title, a loan from Leonard Cohen, *Smukke tabere* (1970; Beautiful Losers), is devoted to the mythology of the young political left and to hippie mentality and nature romanticism, but the narrative experiments get stuck in tradition. At this point, however, Lundbye begins to relax his experiments and to talk, for example, about experiences "before language." He clearly moves out of linguistic circles and approaches an entire realm of myth, as his next titles indicate. *Her ligger min yuccafrugt* (Here Is My Yucca Fruit) is from 1972, *Den indianske tanke* (The Indian Thought) from 1974, and *Et indianersamfund i USA* (An Indian Society in USA) from 1976. Along with Indian cultures and myths, Lundbye develops an interest in a variety of mythical alternatives—domestic or foreign—to the existing societal order, and the perspective is generally ecological; in books from the 1980s he speaks up on behalf of both Alaskan whales, *Fra verdens begyndelse* (1982; From the Beginning of the World) and the Arctic peoples, *Mytologisk rejse i et grønlandsk landskab* (1985; Mythological Journey in a Greenlandic Landscape).

Lundbye's most important works, though, are three novels about the myth and mysticism of a Danish island: *Tilbage til Anholt* (1978; Back to Anholt), *Hvalfisken* (1980; The Whale Fish), and *Den store by* (1982; The Big City). This is domestic and cosmic, mythology and ecology, narrative experiment and new realism in one alternative structure. Although both romantic and didactic in its advocacy of back-to-nature ideals, Lundbye's mythological critique of civilization is more than tradition revisited. At least his democratic ideas are not unlike those of Villy Sørensen, Thorkild Bjørnvig, and the members of an organization called The New Society.

The younger Ib Michael (1943–) has a sphere of interest quite similar to Lundbye's. After short flirtations with flower-power mythology in his first book, he, too, turned his interest to the American Indians. The country he chooses is Mexico, and *Mayalandet* (1973; The Land of the Mayas) and *Rejsen tilbage* (1977; The Journey Back) are dramatic and most readable travel books about his personal experiences. They are myth and reality completely interwoven and original critiques of Western civilization to boot. By contrast, the discourse of *Rejsen til det grønne firben* (1980; Journey to the Green Lizard) is a semidocumentary. But the mythology is right around the corner in his next book. Like Lundbye, Michael takes an interest in Arctic people, and his Nordic version of his American documentary is no less mythological than the composition by Hans Christian Andersen on which it is molded: *Snedronningen* (1981; The Snow Queen). Michael's hit with both readers and critics is a mythical tale as well. In *Kilroy Kilroy* (1989) he enunciates an American popular myth to demonstrate how the American go-getter mentality defies the constraints of identity. Myth is an exploration of larger patterns of life than rationalism and naturalism can deal with. To do justice to coincidence and adventure, a comprehensive and synthetic poetic language is necessary. Myth cannot be understood, but it cannot be done without.

Lundbye's *Smukke Tabere* from 1970 is supposedly about guerrilla war but in reality is about love and the youth culture at the time. The constellation of war and beauty is about the same in a book by Rolf Gjedsted (1947–) from 1970 called *Krigen er smuk* (The War Is Beautiful) (cf. also the title of his first book, *Englefronten* [1969; The Angel Front]). Psychedelic flower power spiced with French poet Arthur Rimbaud (and Charles Baudelaire) is Gjedsted's special recipe—even the cover of *Krigen er smuk* is a colorful piece of romantic war trivia—and he follows it throughout the 1970s; incidentally, he was one of the founders of *Superlove* magazine. Gjedsted's many genres include novels, poems, and diary novels, and their mythical and metaphysical trips in time and in space are not hampered by realistic boundaries.

Gjedsted's predilection for angels was shared by the older writer Preben Major Sørensen, but Knud Holten (1945–) ventures also into myth and metaphysics on angels' wings, for example, in *Englen med det langsomme smil* (1975; The Angel with the Slow Smile). Unlike Lundbye and Michael, Holten travels almost exclusively in the vertical dimension. As a poet with such vivid imagination, he has become a noted author of children's books.

But travels do not require defiance of gravity to transcend the limits of either experience or imagination. Proof of that is available in the works of Jørn Riel (1939–), who has explored the world for almost forty years and written popular, humorous, and weighty books about it. His principal works are series of narratives, or tales, about the Eskimos of America and Greenland. Unlike Lundbye, he does not use the term *mythological* about his journeys through Greenland, but that is, nevertheless, what they are. Summing up his *Skrøner fra et rejseliv* (1989; Cock-and-Bull Stories from Traveling), he says that through his traveling, he has constantly "been on the border of dream and reality," and about the cock-and-bull story he adds that it is "precisely truth that could be lie, or is it the lie that could be truth? Nobody knows for certain. Least of all I." This comment defines the modern myth.

Finally, three writers of the 1970s are difficult to group with others, either because they are outside group formations entirely or because they encompass several groups at once. Their range, quality, and impact make them quite universal, each in his own way. In simple terms, Henrik Bjelke, who writes both prose and lyrical poetry, is universal within the framework of European modernism. Henrik Nordbrandt, who writes lyrical poetry from a self-chosen Mediterranean exile, is universal and Danish (in this order) in the sense that he unfolds his modernistic language in central lyrical poems of emptiness. And Ebbe Kløvedal Reich, who mostly writes prose, is universally Danish in the sense that he explores Danish history and destiny in contradistinction to European and international history and politics.

Henrik Bjelke

The modernistic ambitions of Henrik Bjelke (1937–) are obvious already in his first books, and his artistic frenzy does not fall short of his level of ambition. These books are merely preludes to his breakthrough with *Saturn* (1974), however. Without much plot of significance, this colossal novel is an exercise in modernistic styles, sensations, reflections, and thematizations which is unparalleled in Danish literature and has counterparts only in the major works of European and American letters: Lautréamont, Whitman, Joyce, Eliot, Nabokov, and many others. The novel's subject is the European wasteland and its cultural malaise, its boundless echoes in the human psyche and in the constellations of cosmos. An experimental tour de force the novel turns the complexity of the world into a problem of the integrity and identity of the character who writes the world. And that is no simple matter. In his first collection of poems, *Arcana* (1978), Bjelke's elaborations on styles and genres reflect the same schizophrenic condition of Western culture, but at least here the title suggests a secret solution that might remedy Europe's disastrous one-sidedness, a point of balance in the midst of chaos. Judging from Bjelke's last novel, *Togplan for Otto* (1990; Train Schedule for Otto), and his own comments about it, the formal artistic resolutions in dealing with this disabling culture remain intact. Bjelke's language is not running amok, although its relevance to the subject matter lies more in its rhythm and tone than in its mere signification.

Henrik Nordbrandt

Discussing the poems of Henrik Nordbrandt (1945–) entitled *Syvsoverne* (1969; The Sluggards), the critic Steffen Hejlskov Larsen asserts that Nordbrandt is a systemic or "example" poet like Jørgen Leth and Hans-Jørgen Nielsen (Larsen, 106–8), and in a composite work about Nordbrandt the same critic carefully examines Nordbrandt's Danishness as if it were an issue worthy of special attention (Holk, ed., 23–34). There is some merit in Larsen's observations, but they must nonetheless be validated. It is true that alienation and emptiness are everywhere in Nordbrandt's poetry, not in its references or allusions to reality, but in its language and linguistic self-awareness. But this truth has to do with a dialogue between identification and alienation that Nordbrandt for years has experienced firsthand as a voluntary expatriate from Denmark living in Greece and Turkey. A book containing his impressions from the two countries is called *Breve fra en ottoman* (1978; Letters from an Ottoman). Alluding both to a Turk and a couch, the title of these letters to Denmark establishes Turkey as the poet's elected identity and his state of mind as that of a relaxed and contemplative dweller in his chair at the time of writing; on closer inspection the book makes clear that its title represents the link and equilibrium between Turkey and Greece, the author's other elected home. His otherness is harmonious, and his traveling persona an extension of his psyche. At the same time, one text reveals that he is simply a second in an Oedipus drama that is a matter of life and death. The freedom of his role is inseparable from the coercion of his role.

This duality of Nordbrandt's otherness is what sets the stage for his dialogue between identification and alienation; it gives it an unmistakable pulse, and yet is the kind of chilling creativity that comes from unsentimental melancholy. Denmark, then, is the ever-present absence in Nordbrandt's poetic workshop. Whereas Bjelke revisits European culture as it pivots on chaos, Nordbrandt walks the tightrope between Danish and European and European and Oriental; one thing in his universe elicits another only to register its beautiful disappearance, and vice versa. In one of the four-line poems in *Håndens skælven i november* (1986; My Hand Trembling in November) the author says,

> My words are accidental. Not symbols
> Yet I sometimes recognize something
> as contours of a fish drawn on the ground
> in a Roman camp, in Brittany.

Only words, yes. Yet neither symbols nor examples, but precisely identification and alienation, or captured absence. This experience is both visual and musical in Nordbrandt's poems, and their rare centrality becomes more indisputable with every book he publishes.

Ebbe Kløvedal Reich

Ebbe Kløvedal Reich (1940–) was everywhere in the 1970s: at demonstrations, on editorial boards, in socialist communes, and so on. His physical presence was an integral part of many grass-roots movements and anti-American, anti-EEC, and antiauthoritarian platforms. He is a remarkable link between the youth and student rebellion on the one hand and many popular and extraparliamentary activities on the other. And his writings are intertwined with these physical circumstances, both in terms of their origins and in terms of their ideas and formulations and the tone they set. His so-called popular book about N. F. S. Grundtvig's life and times, *Frederik* (1972), is typical. It is an extremely intelligent, bizarre, and loving text, composed of free imagination and numerous historical sources, mixing biographical anecdote with current political polemics. Grundtvig's periods of insanity, by normal standards, are his healthy periods of cultural and political defiance, according to Reich, and they set the norms for the 1972 national battle against the EEC, the modern Roman Empire. Overall it is a matter of destiny, and the superstructure in *Frederik* is astrological (with graphological subterrain). Topsy-turvy throughout, its peculiar language is its prime mover: a new academic-popular style, a fluent, unpretentious tongue-in-cheek mode of telling with slightly archaic connotations. Although the spirit of the people was not aroused by the spirit of the book— Denmark did enter the EEC in 1972—Reich's view of both history and democracy is very Danish and has influenced many bourgeois Danes.

Reich's oeuvre also includes an early book of poetry, journalistic books on China and Vietnam, historical interpretations of revolutionary characters in domestic and international history, and a variety of topical articles and essays on cultural and political issues. But the bulk of his work is on Danish history—and mythology. The latter, which was part of *Frederik*, is the principal subject of a slim book about another popular Danish hero, *Holger Danske* (1970; Holger the Dane), and it is inseparable from the (hi)story telling in all of Reich's voluminous historical works. Essentially, these narratives are based on a unique interpretation of Isaac Newton. In *Rejsen til Messias. Tre bøger fra enevældens tid* (1974; The Journey to Messiah: Three Books from the Times of Absolutism) Reich manages to deprive historical discourse of any systematics and to accord it individual virtues instead. In practice his texts unfold like Jørn Riel's cock-and-bull stories with an emphasis on veracity, not verisimilitude (by which Reich became disappointed when he studied history at the university). In *Fæ og frænde* (1977; Cattle and Kinsman), a complicated narrative and travelogue from Roman times, he boldly, if not recklessly, suggests that historical truth is accessible only behind several walls of historical appearances and certainties. Only by transgressing these walls does one arrive at "dreams and truths and lies and desires and black stains of angst." As the historian *and* storyteller moves backward in time, through layers of sources and evidence and toward the beginning of national culture and history, he moves underneath the very concept of history toward a total human experience, and his "I" becomes gradually part of the people's collective past and original identity. Telling the people their history, then, is becoming part of that history and that people.

With this mythology as his tool, Reich succeeded in speaking for the political (and not very popular) left of the 1970s while furnishing the people at large with a plausible image of themselves. He became the eye of the storm or the genial democratic mediator in a culture priding itself on diversity. Reich went beyond the divisions in national culture, not by evading them but by taking them to extremes with generosity and faith in an underlying unity. In this way he became rather paradoxical: a revolutionary guarding the past, and a grass-roots person finding his roots in the highest spheres. His writings reveal the dichotomies of the 1970s, in particular the efforts to arrive at the future by rewriting the past. Reich, with all his metaphysics and popular deeds, is not a humanist, but his collective subjectivity and his way of interrelating opposites without moderating them have strong humanistic prerequisites.

THE 1980S: POSTMODERNISM—AND SO WHAT?

It goes without saying that the literary innovations of the 1980s cannot be characterized historically at this writing. Faced with either turning out shy generalizations or hazardous individual portraits, one is tempted, though, to extend some historical lines of development into the 1980s and then support the result with selected examples.

The specter of humanism continued to haunt Danish letters. Cases in point are some critical interpretations of the past. Culminating with the bicentennial of his birth, N. F. S. Grundtvig had long been a rallying point for modern critics concerned with Danish national and popular identity, whether in Poul Borum's modernistic, Ebbe Reich's astrological, or Ejvind Larsen's Marxist way of interpreting it. In some instances humanism was the decisive demarcation line between interpretations. For example, the high school teacher Poul Engberg found Grundtvig devoid of humanism inasmuch as he subordinates his human inclinations to his relation to God. Contrary to this view, the university teacher Flemming Lundgreen-Nielsen argued that future Grundtvig scholarship must focus on Grundtvig the humanist; after all, Grundtvig did say, human first, Christian second. Finally, the famed cleric Johannes Møllehave, in *Hvad er et menneske?* (1984; What Is a Human Being?), preached that Christianity and humanism are concomitants: "Man is a divine experiment of dust and spirit."

In more topical and international debates disagreement pivoted on humanistic concepts. When the theologian Søren Krarup in his book *Det moderne sammenbrud* (1984; The Modern Breakdown) determined the conditions necessary for the Gulag to occur, he found them inherent in godless humanism, while in the meantime another conservative cultural critic, Per Stig Møller, in his book *På sporet af det forsvundne menneske* (1976; Tracing Man Lost), found the very same misery occasioned by unrestricted antihumanism. The confusion seemed total and conceptual but was rather a trait of reality, whereas humanism was essentially visited as one possible fixed point in the midst of the blur, although it was by no means above it.

What humanism—present or notably absent—seemed to offer was unity in this plurality. In the 1970s Villy Sørensen assembled his artistic insights around a program of action that outlined a natural balancing act between elements of discord in human life and society. In the 1980s this social humanism was challenged by postmodern poetry and thinking, which basically rejected the notion that a fragmented existence allows for any balance that has not already been subsumed by long-since-discredited metaphysics. Instead, postmodernists made a virtue out of the necessity of discord, played with it, sneered at it, exploited it to their own ends, in short, relinquished the idea of any stability underneath the fluctuations of appearances. Hans-Jørgen Nielsen's attitudinal relativism was a prelude to this form of cognition, whose practitioners in the 1980s, such as Søren Ulrik Thomsen, claimed that any notion of humanity is a menace to transient life here and now, a metaphysical reduction.

Once again, however, humanism proved disinclined to attend its own funeral. It is suggestive, for example, that the critic Johan Fjord Jensen, whose critical work on Villy Sørensen's humanism and third standpoint appeared in the early 1980s, issued a book called *Det tredje: den postmoderne udfordring* (1987; The Third: The Postmodern Challenge) in the late 1980s in which he argued that the discrepancy between instrumental reason and aestheticized humanism which marked intellectual life for two hundred years had reached a turning point where postmodernism stood out as the primary symptom. Rather than have us clinging to previous philosophies of growth, which caused the discrepancy to occur in the first place, Fjord Jensen proposed that we recognize the limits we have reached and that we aim at a future existence based on a critical equilibrium. He called it *dialectical humanism* and credited it with continued allegiance to instrumental and material reason but also with a fixed position—or fixed place of absence—outside and independent of this reason. Ultimately, the place is nature as it extends beyond the order of both culture and transcendent reason and thus supplies the framework for any sensible critique of reason.

Much innovative writing in the 1980s occupied the space between the postmodern challenge and this reply to the challenge. And writing in the sense not only of cognition and result, but of medium and public discourse as well. A book debating the matter of reading has the telling title *Bogens fremtid er ikke hvad den har været* (1988; The Future of the Book Is Not What It Was), and although its statistics and other information may be debatable, it obviously shows that the art of reading is dramatically influenced by the same conditions that the authors interpret. An important outline by the editor Hans Hertel is subtitled "From the Philosophy of Growth in the 1960s to the Limits of Growth in the 1980s," and its main observation, as previously noted by Fjord Jensen, is clearly the appearance of "a saturation point: a limit of growth. From the early 1980s studies showed stagnation and later decline in the literary activity of the adult population—and a marked decline in book reading and book buying among young people."

Conducive to writing and thematized within it, the postmodern conditions of the 1980s also applied to books and reading per se. Sharper competition from electronic and visual media, new educational patterns and consumer habits, and less lenient forms of mediation and cultural policies—in other words, an entirely different sociology of literature—surrounded the literary work of the 1980s. New prospects and media may have profited from the society of recreation, but new challenges in terms of "time-efficient" reading habits had come along. It was conceivable that both the novel and the book itself would succumb, together with the implicit notion of individual development to which both the genre and the medium tended until the advent of the challenge of postmodernism. But it was also conceivable that both the book and its content would set the stage for a dialectical and humanistic reaction to this challenge. On the one hand, more literature was published than ever before; on the other hand, literature's monopoly in the public sphere of arts was a thing of the past.

What was truly new was not that certain forms of literature, but the entire cultural transmission of letters, was under scrutiny. While critics earlier took exception to the immodest modesty of Danish literature, the new challenge to its institutional framework was so serious that sheer protestation no longer sufficed to remedy the situation. Humanism, as it runs through Danish letters, represents both the pervasive modesty and a supple aptitude for responding to new circumstances. The duality may not be a national characteristic, but it does distinguish the bulk of modern Nordic literature. Some marked tendencies and bodies of writing within Danish literature in the 1980s are outlined here against this background.

Simply put, whereas the 1970s were dominated by prose or versed prose or open, functional poetry, most of these genres ran to seed in the 1980s. Prose in this decade generally was secondary to lyrical poetry, which marked a generational breakthrough not unlike that of the 1960s. In extension of earlier statements on the ascendancy of the media in the 1980s, also in terms of their impact on literature, it deserves mention that the crisis of prose, and of the novel in particular, expressed itself in a torrent of texts by media workers about media workers, journalists, and so on. Problem awareness turned entertainment was the typical scenario in these slick products by Johannes and Herdis Møllehave, Lise Nørgaard, Poul Henrik Trampe, Jørgen Thorgaard, and others. Loss of meaning in the world of media became a media event to the second power, and the modes of the 1970s lost momentum in the 1980s. More qualified transformations of previous idioms occur in the field of women's writing. Kirsten Thorup, for one, went beyond the political and social realistic maxims of the 1970s in her later works, and Mette Winge went all the way back to eighteenth-century Charlotte Dorothea Biehl for inspiration. New and prolific writers of prose were few, however, and Jørgen Chr. Hansen, Klaus Lynggaard, and Jens Christian Grøndahl are probably three of the best.

Jørgen Chr. Hansen (1956–89) published his major work, a trilogy of novels about children and their world, in the early 1980s, and later he wrote novels and cycles of short stories in which motifs and conflicts in the trilogy were gradually subjected to adult conditions. He has been called the romantic of modernism, and his short stories illustrate quite well how the socio-historical climate turned harsh and disillusioned in the 1980s. Klaus Lynggaard (1956–), too, thematizes these epoch-making circumstances or "paradigm" changes. He is essentially a lyric poet and made his debut as such in 1981; but his principal work is a large—and lyrical—double novel about typical youngsters of the 1970s, the two sweethearts Martin and Victoria. Lynggaard places himself between hippies and punks, a kind of flip-out artist or observant intermediary, and his literary baggage contains Rimbaud as well as Knut Hamsun and Bob Dylan. He is a romantic only in the sense postmodern youth culture conceives this tradition, but his portrait of people who were young in the 1970s is certainly indifferent to that decade's own ideology critique and structuralist fashions. Lynggaard's characters are alive and defy compartmentalization, and his art transcends the scheme of things in both misanthropy and antihumanistic theory. Jens Christian Grøndahl (1959–) completes this trip out of square social identification and into the so-called inner landscapes of the body. Already highly regarded, his major work is called *Rejsens bevægelser* (1988; Movements of the Journey), and its actual train trip does not merely translate into meetings with a new corporeal identity. Embarking on the noble tradition of Danish travel fiction, Grøndahl expands the symbolic notion of a personal journey through life into an abstract, experimental journey through time and space and several linguistic identities. His style is inspired by the French *nouveau roman*.

Most impressive, though, is a book of prose published in 1985 by an older writer, Peer Hultberg (1935–), called *Requiem*. In the 1960s Hultberg wrote two difficult experimental novels that few understood, and hence the author withdrew to an academic career abroad. His late comeback and breakthrough in 1985 consists of 537 musical and prose lyrical monologues in which the cultural atmosphere of the 1980s—its seemingly personal anonymities and unstructured complexity—is given its richest mouthpiece. This is postmodernity captured and mediated by an empathetic outsider, an older contemporary, and a traveler in emptiness and discord who has profound understanding of wholeness and connectedness. Combining transgression of given boundaries with its own lines of demarcation, *Requiem* offers a Janus profile of the decade.

In facing the past the profile reveals a contrast to the 1980s, but it is too early to say how significant it is. Perhaps the apparent confrontations were simply noisy transgressions of boundaries. What did cease to prevail in public attention in the 1980s was the 1970s' torrent of confessional writing and socialist agitation. Also the neorealist tradition in prose and television drama à la Panduro seemed unable to rejuvenate in the 1980s. Writers of the student-revolt generation licked their wounds, and so did the front-line soldiers from the heyday of the men's and women's movements. Sometimes the result was paradoxical in that the older generation that pledged to make politics at the expense of art became more artistically inclined, whereas younger authors with aesthetic concerns made their art emit political sparks. In general, the world had decayed like an old tooth, and alternatives were needed to fill the void. Historical fictions were one alternative; science fictions, as in a recent trilogy by Inge Eriksen, another; but more fillings were done with experiments in language, as in, for example, Jørgen Chr. Hansen's images of the unspoilt world of the child surrounded by dilapidated adultness.

The most interesting fillings, though, were furnished by the many lyrical talents of the decade. And their substance was usually the language of the body and sensuality or expressions of similar concrete sensations. The seven-volume poetic cycle of more than thirteen hundred pages by Bo Green Jensens (1955–) called *Rosens veje* (The Roads of the Rose) is a manifest and very wordy example of the kind of fullness that the emptiness of the 1970s elicited in the young generation; the 1984 volume is, in fact, named *Undergangstestamentet* (Testament of Destruction). Interspersing neoromantic syntheses in postmodern decenters is not a simple task, though. A major note apparatus and a rather stilted authorial role seem to be the price for having, in Johannes V. Jensen's words, "the stillness spreading rings."

In the works and life of Michael Strunge (1958–86) the battle against emptiness ends in suicide; first the author literally decided to close his books, then he closed his life. Another clash between fullness and void occurs in the writing of Pia Tafdrup (1952–), for example, in a title such as *Intetfang* (1982; Nothing-ference), whereas in the texts of Thomas Boberg (1960–) the world in itself is a minor problem, even though it is in crisis, without a center, and evasive and distant. The main thing is that it exists and that the "I" transcends itself and its own limitations in an effort to incorporate it in artistic expressions—on art's terms, but not for art's sake. What-ever living in this world is—and the author harbors few illusions in that re-spect—it is a task that can be dealt with. *Ud af mit liv* (1985; Out of My Life) is the telling title of one of Boberg's worldly collections of poems, and in *Hvæsende på mit øjekast* (1984; Wheezing On My Glance) he shows his re-lentless and merciless sensibility in dealing with this confusing impulse of reality.

Because of his essay *Mit lys brænder: omrids af en ny poetik* (1985; My Can-dle Burns: An Outline of a New Poetics), Søren Ulrik Thomsen (1956–) has gained recognition as the theoretical or programmatic spokesman of this generation. Despite the sketchy genre term he uses for this text, Thomsen, who is a lucid poet in his own right, has been perceived as a norm for the 1980s. It should be emphasized, though, as Boberg has done, that the com-mon denominators for the poets of the 1980s have been extremely exagge-rated and are essentially media ploys. Especially by the mid-1980s, individ-ual differences had become obvious. Niels Frank (1963–), for example, is a much-acclaimed opposite of, say, Green Jensen, in terms of how he articu-lates his lyrical voice and authorial identity. As often was the case in this pe-riod, abstraction is the basis, frequently emanating into fascinating and complicated images of life. A special case in point is Juliane Preisler (1959–), in both her poems and her novels. Construction and language acts, along with the abstraction, are propellants in her works; the "I" unfurls in predomi-nantly narcissistic and alienating ways, whereas the interplay between char-acters' inner void and linguistic props results in sublime reading experi-ences. One of her novels is *I en anden* (1986; In Another), and its very title indicates the formless mode of sliding beyond the limits of individual per-sonality which clearly signifies the artistic outlook from attitudinal relativ-ism and throughout postmodernism and deconstruction.

A majority of the poets of the 1980s are included in Pia Tafdrup's genera-tional anthology *Transformationer: poesi 1980–85* (1985; Transformations: Poetry 1980–85). One of the earliest "transformers" was F. P. Jac (1955–); one of the latest, Camilla Christensen (1957–); and in between the two are the aforementioned names and another handful who have also proven artis-tically durable. Suffice it here to conclude this outline of transformational trends and individual milestones with a tentative peek beyond the 1980s. In fact, Camilla Christensen has since the end of the decade reviewed the next generation of postmodern lyrics. In Carsten René Nielsen's *Postkort fra månens bagside* (1990; Postcard from the Back of the Moon) Christensen de-tects the entire postmodern gamut: the recycling of historical set-pieces, the vagabondish trespassing on established hierarchies, and the unpretentious *look* at the world—all diluted to immediacy and entertainment, to superficial mirror effects. It almost seems as if postmodernism is being caught in its own net of games and plays, to the extent that even slightly older post-modernists feel turned off. Has the game begun to approach the endgame, or the limit where some dialectical humanism may be in the position to respond to the postmodern challenge?

An answer in the affirmative is suggested by the young Jens-Martin Eriksen (1955–), whose remarkable novel trilogy from the late 1980s carries the same tune to the point that the author has felt the need to distance himself from his allegedly old-fashioned role as a human storyteller. The question is particularly relevant, though, in light of the fact that Denmark's most popular writer by the end of the 1980s was Martha Christensen (1926–), a sixty-four-year-old working woman whose twelve novels passed relatively unnoticed until the late 1970s, but whose breakthrough with *Dansen med Regitze* (1987; Dancing with Regitze) put her name on everybody's lips (and brought an Academy Award nomination for the screen version of her book). Why is an easily read social realist with roots in the Herman Bang tradition and with a message centered on petty-bourgeois humaneness the big success in a period mired in high technology and postmodernity? Is it simply proof of the fact that any time is far behind its vanguard and that older and younger authors are always contemporaries? Or is it, rather, testimony to this particular period's interplay between incompatible artistic forms, and its disregard of historical and formal dividers, in other words, to postmodern eclecticism in a nutshell? If so, perhaps the lesson to be learned is how decentered postmodernity may evolve into its own opposite: an artistic concern with all the major issues of today—from women's liberation to family harmony—that are threatened by depersonalization or effacement tomorrow. Perhaps that is the dialectic and humanistic response—in practice—to the vagueness and elusiveness of our time. And a response the majority of readers dare consider a fixed point.

REFERENCES

Borum, Poul. *Samtale med Ole Sarvig*. Copenhagen: Gyldendal, 1960.
Clausen, Claus. *Digtere i forhør 1966. Samtaler med tolv danske forfattere*. Copenhagen: Gyldendal, 1966.
Dinesen, Isak [Karen Blixen]. *Daguerreotypes and Other Essays*. London: Heinemann, 1979.
Hammerich, Paul, ed. *Panduros verden*. Copenhagen: Forum, 1977.

Holk, Iben, ed. *Ø. En bog om Henrik Nordbrandt*. Odense: Odense Universitetsforlag, 1989.

Larsen, Steffen Hejlskov. *Systemdigtningen*. Copenhagen: Munksgaard, 1971.

Møller, Per Stig. *Nat uden daggry*. Copenhagen: Gyldendal, 1985.

Nielsen, Frederik. *Fra Martin A. Hansens værksted*. 2d ed. Copenhagen: Gyldendal, 1971.

Schnack, Asger. *Portræt. 40 danske digtere efter 1968*. Copenhagen: Gyldendal, 1981.

Faroese Literature

W. Glyn Jones

8

THE PRELITERARY PERIOD: 800–1850 (by Patricia L. Conroy)

The Faroes, a small group of eighteen islands located roughly two hundred miles northwest of the Shetlands, were first settled sometime during the eighth century by Celts who established at least one village in the northern islands. By the early ninth century, however, the Celtic settlement had been overwhelmed by a new wave of Viking immigrants from Norway, who clustered their homes at sea level around natural harbors or on clifftops above rocky landing places. The cool and windy weather of the islands did not favor diversified agriculture, and the Viking settlers became first and foremost sheep farmers, supplementing their living by fishing, fowling, and whaling. They were from the very beginning heavily dependent on imports of Norwegian timber, grain, and metal wares, for which they chiefly traded woolens.

Initially independent, with their political center located at Tórshavn, the Faroese were soon absorbed into the Norwegian empire. Thanks to an evolving Norwegian royal policy of Christianization and unification, the islanders found themselves subsumed under both the Norwegian bishop and the Norwegian Crown when they accepted Christianity through the agency of King Olav Tryggvason in A.D. 1000. They also lost control of their export trade to Norwegian merchants because they lacked their own timber for the building and maintenance of a fleet. The union with Norway lasted until the late fourteenth century, when Norway and its tributaries became part of a far-flung Danish empire. Trade and the Faroese church continued to be administered from Bergen until ca. 1620, however, when control was shifted to Copenhagen. Although essentially Norwegian, as time went on Faroese language and culture came increasingly under Danish influence: the official language of the church was Danish and virtually all communication with the outside world was via Copenhagen.

Apart from two short runic inscriptions from the twelfth and thirteenth centuries, *Seyðabrævið* (1298; The Sheep Letter, [a Faroese appendix to a medieval Norwegian code of law]), and several diplomas from the fifteenth century, there were no extant documents in Faroese until Jens Christian Svabo (1746–1824) assembled from oral tradition his two manuscripts of Faroese ballads—a smaller collection of three ballads from ca. 1773 and a larger one (52 ballads) from 1781–82—inventing his own orthography in order to do so.

Ballads probably first reached the Faroes from western Norway as early as the fourteenth century. Like the Norwegian heroic ballad, Faroese heroic ballads, at the core of Faroese tradition, are long narrative songs about the victory of heroes against overwhelmingly powerful, often supernatural adversaries. Characters and plots alike are highly conventional—a young hero journeys to a foreign land to seek a suitable wife, a country to rule, or wrongs to set aright—and are realized to a high degree by means of commonplace stanzas. Composed in quatrains with a four-line refrain, Faroese heroic ballads can consist of as many as four hundred stanzas and be subdivided into a maximum of nine *tættir* (subballads).

In the Faroe Islands the performance of ballads as dance songs has persisted to the present day. Until the first decades of the twentieth century the high points of social life in many villages were weekly dances, commonly held on Sunday evenings from Christmas until Lent, as well as the dance fests held in celebration of holy days, weddings, and whale hunts. In performing the ballad dance villagers form a chain or ring as one or two of them, usually men, take the lead in treading the simple steps of the dance and chanting the opening stanzas of the ballad. Other dancers often join in the stanzas familiar to them and then lustily take over the chanting of the refrain, while the leaders rest their voices.

In the nineteenth century it was chiefly outside interest in Faroese ballads that inspired islanders to record and collect their oral literature of ballads, legends, and folktales. While studying algae in the Faroes during the summer of 1817, Danish naturalist Hans Christian Lyngbye recorded a few fragmentary ballad texts, which he showed on his return to Copenhagen to the antiquarian scholar P. E. Müller, who recognized in piecemeal form a version of the Germanic legend of Sigurd the Dragon Slayer. Müller wrote immediately to two churchmen in the Faroes to procure additional texts of "Sjúrðar kvæði" (The Ballad of Sigurd). Johan Henrik Schrøter (1771–1851) of Suðuroy, also known for his Faroese translations of the Book of Matthew

(1823) and the medieval Icelandic *Færeyinga saga* (1832; Saga of the Faroe Islanders), was able to oblige Müller, enabling Lyngbye to publish his find in *Færøiske Qvæder om Sigurd Fofnersbane og hans Æt* (1822; Faroese Ballads about Sigurd Fofner's Bane and His Kin). The pastor of Sandoy delegated Müller's assignment to one of his parishioners, Johannes Clemensen (1794–1869), who provided a collection of eighteen ballads in 1819 and then continued to collect on his own behalf, producing a fair copy of a collection of 93 ballads, "Sandoyarbók" (Sand Isle Book), in 1831.

In the 1840s two Faroese students at the University of Copenhagen began to take an interest in collecting ballads. Napoleon Nolsøe (1809–77), a medical student, began his three-volume collection by copying ballads from Svabo's manuscript in the Royal Library; he later expanded this work by copying ballads from the collections of other Faroese ballad enthusiasts, such as Johannes Clemensen and Hanus Hanusson (1794–1854) of Fugloy.

The second Faroese student, Venceslaus Ulricus Hammershaimb (1819–1909), was encouraged by the Danish folklorist Svend Grundtvig to take up the project of a national ballad collection incorporating all existing manuscript collections and modeled on Grundtvig's edition of Danish ballads, *Danmarks gamle Folkeviser* (Denmark's Ancient Folk Songs). While visiting the Faroes in 1847–48 Hammershaimb began his own collection of ballads, publishing "Olufas Kvad" (The Ballad of Óluva) in the Danish periodical *Antiquarisk Tidsskrift* (Antiquarian Journal) in 1848, followed by a small sampling of ballads, "Færøske Kvæder med Oversættelse" (Faroese Ballads with Translation), in 1849. In 1851 his edition of "Sjúrðar kvæði" appeared in the first volume of *Færöiske Kvæder*, followed in 1855 by a second volume containing a thematically varied anthology of ballads. In 1871 he turned over his collection of ballads to Grundtvig, who with the aid of Jørgen Bloch completed a fair copy, *Føroya kvæði [Faroese Ballads]: Corpus Carminum Færoensium*, in fifteen volumes (1876). After Grundtvig's death Bloch turned out a sixteenth volume (1889) and two supplements (1896 and 1905) containing additional texts collected in the 1880s by the Faroese philologist Jakob Jakobsen. The compendium, edited by Christian Matras and Napoleon Djurhuus, was published in six volumes (1941–72).

Grundtvig and Bloch's *Corpus Carminum Færoensium* (abbr. CCF) contains a total of 236 ballad types, all of which were composed before 1850. CCF numbers 1–105 are heroic ballads, but their ordering is somewhat arbitrary. CCF 1–13 are the ballads published by Hammershaimb in the first volume of *Færöiske Kvæder*, selected by him as the most important ones dealing with the hero Sigurd the Dragon Slayer. Best known of these is "Sjúrðar kvæði" (CCF 1) in three *tættir*: (1) "Regin Smiður" (Regin the Smith), about the death of Sjúrður's father Sigmundur, Sjúrður's youth and acquisition from Regin of the sword Gram, his vengeance on his father's slayers, and his killing of a dragon to win a treasure; (2) "Brynhildar táttur" (The Ballad of Brynhild), about how Sjúrður wins Brynhild but, because of a magic potion, forgets her and marries Guðrún and how Brynhild takes revenge by inciting her husband Gunnar and his brother Høgni (both Guðrún's brothers) to kill Sjúrður; (3) "Høgna táttur" (The Ballad of Høgni), about Guðrún's marriage to Artala, her successful plan to kill her brothers, and the vengeance of Høgni's son on her and Artala. All three *tættir* probably had their immediate sources in Norwegian ballads reflecting a combination of Scandinavian and northern German reflexes of this Germanic legend.

CCF 14–32 are the ballads published by Hammershaimb in the second volume of *Færöiske Kvæder* (1855); they tell an assortment of stories about heroes and events also known from the medieval Icelandic legendary sagas, family sagas, and sagas of the Norwegian kings. As suggested by a legend from Sandoy about an Icelandic manuscript rescued by villagers from a foundering ship, the Faroese ballads with close parallels in Icelandic sagas may well have originally been composed from literary sources. This is true, for example, of "Kjartans tættir" (The Ballads about Kjartan, CCF 23), which follows the events of the central part of *Laxdæla saga* very closely, and of "Gunnars kvæði" (The Ballad about Gunnar, CCF 21), which retells the story of Gunnar's last stand in *Njáls saga*.

The remaining heroic ballads in *Corpus Carminum Færoensium* (CCF 32–105) are arranged alphabetically by title. While many of these may well be of medieval provenance, others show signs of having been composed during the late eighteenth and early nineteenth centuries. "Hildardalsstrið" (The Battle of Hildardal, CCF 91), for example, was probably composed ca. 1820 on Sandoy. In general, the relatively few heroic ballads composed in couplet stanzas also seem to be of late origin, reflecting the impact on Faroese tradition of the couplet ballads in Anders Sørensen Vedel's and Peder Syv's editions of Danish ballads, which were performed widely in the Faroes.

CCF 106–113 are ballads about the heroes of legends and romances originating south of Scandinavia. Most important of these is "Karlamagnusar kvæði" (CCF 106), a cycle of ballads about Charlemagne and his champions, with Roland foremost. Most of the ballads in this cyle reflect features of both the Old Norse *Karlamagnús saga* (ca. 1250; The Saga of Charlemagne) and the Danish *Karl Magnus' Krønike* (ca. 1480; The Chronicle of Charlemagne). Of special interest are "Koralds kvæði" (The Ballad of Korald, CCF 111) and "Bevusar tættir" (The Songs of Bevus, CCF 112), both of which reveal in their high incidence of alliteration and unballadlike rhyme schemes that they originally were Icelandic *rímur*.

CCF 114–178 are for the most part ballads of mixed thematic content which have been translated and adapted from printed Danish ballads known to Faroese tradition. CCF 179–236 are a mixed group of ballads considered to be of relatively recent composition. A few of them are not ballads at all but have nonetheless been performed in the ballad dance; one such example is "Ljómurnar" (Rays of Light, CCF 220), a religious poem composed by the last Catholic bishop of Iceland. Some of them are ballads from more recent times. In the early nineteenth century, for example, Jens Christian Djurhuus (1773–1853) composed from literary sources several ballads on historical themes, the best known of which is "Ólavur Trygvason" (CCF 215). The bulk of this mixed group, however, consists of satirical ballads (also called *tættir*), lampooning the foibles of various residents of the Faroes. In "Ániasar táttur" (The Ballad about Ánias, CCF 192), one of the oldest extant satirical ballads, a villager from Suðuroy blows himself up by drying some wet gunpowder over a fire. The satirical ballad continued to be a productive genre, and nineteenth-century poets such as Poul Nolsøe (1766–1808) and Jens Christian Djurhuus directed their satire against Danish rule in "Fugla kvæði" (The Ballad about Birds, CCF 190) and "Páll i Leivík" (Páll in Leivík, CCF 203). More recently, Tróndur Olsen (1875–1958) and Tummas Napoleon Djurhuus (1928–71) published collections of satirical ballads, which also emphasized political themes.

MODERN FAROESE LITERATURE: THE BEGINNINGS

Despite the legacy of medieval ballads, constituting one of the greatest treasures of Faroese culture, literature in its modern sense did not emerge in the Faroes until the latter half of the nineteenth century. The Kalmar Union of the Scandinavian countries (1397–1523) brought the Faroe Islands under Danish rule, and for many years they were a closed country subject to a royal trade monopoly. The difficulty of access, due partly to Danish policy and partly to the remoteness of the islands, meant that they failed to keep up with general cultural developments in Europe, and when the monopoly was abolished in 1856 the Faroe Islands were still virtually a medieval society with oral literature as the only indigenous tradition. Danish was the language of religion, education, and administration, while Faroese itself occupied a position of inferiority from which it did not completely escape until the twentieth century. Until the end of the monopoly the Faroese economy had been based almost exclusively on agriculture, but the emphasis began to shift to fishing, which, again by the mid-twentieth century, became the main source of income for the islands. The ending of the monopoly had a further radical effect in that it enabled a sense of national identity to develop, closely linked to efforts to establish Faroese as the official national language. World War II, during which the islands were occupied by British troops, allowed these nationalist feelings to gain momentum, and the Faroe Islands came to enjoy an increasing degree of local self-government until 1953, when they were granted their present status of a self-governing region of the Kingdom of Denmark, with their own national flag.

Until 1846 there had been no established Faroese orthography. Jens Christian Svabo (1746–1824) and later Johan Henrik Schrøter (1771–1851) had attempted an orthography based on phonetical principles, but thanks to regional variations in pronunciation, the experiment failed. In 1846, however, V. U. Hammershaimb (1819–1909) produced three Faroese folktales written in a new orthography based on philological principles. They appeared in the Danish *Annaler for nordisk Oldkyndighed* (Annals of Nordic Antiquity) under the title of "Færøske Folkesagn med tilføjede Bemærkninger om den færøske Udtale" (Faroese Folktales with Added Comments on Faroese Pronunciation). Hammershaimb's orthography bore in certain respects little relationship to pronunciation, but it could equally well be used by any of the existing dialect forms and thus quickly became a vehicle for written communication. He modified his system in the 1850s, and the results largely represent the system still in use.

Orthography was not the only obstacle to a literature in the vernacular. Danish was firmly established as the language of culture, administration, and church life in the Faroe Islands, and the Faroese language was in the eyes of many little more than a local dialect doomed to extinction. Thanks to the efforts over many years of Faroese patriots, this situation gradually changed. Nevertheless, Faroese completely replaced Danish in schools only in 1938, in church in 1939, and in the courts in 1944. Today it is the national language, used in all fields, and Danish is now a foreign language, though the first one to be learned. One consequence of the once-dominant position of Danish is the emergence of some literature written in Danish but essentially Faroese in character. The novelists William Heinesen and Jørgen-Frantz Jacobsen are the main exponents of this usage, but they are not alone, and both Guðrið Helmsdal Nielsen and Regin Dahl have written poetry in both languages.

Meanwhile, Hammershaimb's significance for Faroese letters went far beyond his orthography, and he played an important part in the cultural developments that came in the wake of its establishment. The time of his efforts coincided with the nineteenth-century interest in the culture of former ages and with an emerging international awareness of the Faroe Islands, and Hammershaimb set about collecting and publishing traditional oral literature, some of which he also translated into Danish. In 1848 he published "Olufas Kvad" (The Ballad of Óluva) in *Antiquarisk Tidsskrift*, followed in 1849 by "Færøske Kvæder med Oversættelse" (Faroese Ballads in Translation by V. U. Hammershaimb). Then came a series of fairy tales and legends, proverbs and children's games. In 1851 Hammershaimb's edition of the greatest of the Faroese ballads, "Sjúrðar kvæði" (The Ballad of Sigurd), was published, followed in 1855 by yet another collection of ballads. In 1854 Hammershaimb had also been responsible for the first Faroese grammar.

After spending some years as pastor and then dean in the Faroes, Hammershaimb settled in 1878 in Denmark, there continuing his studies and the publication of Faroese literature. It is from this period that his principal work stems: the *Færøsk Anthologi* (Faroese Anthology), published between 1886 and 1891. It is a much fuller anthology and account of Faroese literature, containing further ballads, folktales, and proverbs as well as descriptions of Faroese life written by Hammershaimb himself.

By this time a more modern kind of literature was beginning to emerge, centered on a group of Faroese students living in Copenhagen. Though much smaller, this group can loosely be compared with the so-called Norske Selskab (Norwegian Society) of a century earlier, a gathering of culturally and nationally aware students with a gift for writing. Their work consisted largely of drinking songs and poems in praise of their native land and is more akin to the Danish poetry of the late eighteenth and early nineteenth centuries than to that being written in Danish by their contemporaries.

Most important among these writers was Fríðrikur Petersen (1853–1917). Born in Saltnes, where Hammershaimb was pastor from 1862, he was the son of the local teacher. He went to high school in Iceland and studied theology in Copenhagen. In 1880 he returned to the Faroe Islands, finally becoming the Faroese primate. His original inspiration to write patriotic poetry seems to have come from his stay in Iceland, where he was present at the festivities to celebrate the thousandth anniversary of the founding of Iceland, with their attendant patriotic overtones.

Petersen's production was not large and stemmed mainly from his time in Copenhagen. Nevertheless, among this poems are several that have become some of the most widely loved patriotic poems in Faroese. His work is unpretentious and of uneven quality, but at its best it is musical and shows a deep love of his native land. There is little precise or detailed description, but rather a generalized reflection of an archetypal landscape:

Faroe, my mother, fair art thou indeed
When dressed in winter's garb.
Splendid, Mother, art thou indeed
In linen of shining white.
Then the starry hosts are resplendent in the heavens
The Northern Lights dance round the mountain tops.

For all their modesty, however, Petersen's stand as the first "modern" poems in Faroese to project a sense of the Faroese landscape and occasionally Faroese history in a way designed to promote a sense of national pride. The significance of the Faroese language for this upsurge of national feeling—a feature of much Faroese writing even to this day—is reflected in two poems from the late 1870s, "Hvat kann røra hjartastreingir" (What Can Touch the Heartstrings) and "O, móðurmál, stort var títt fall" (O, Native Tongue, Great Was Thy Fall).

A sense of nationalism, in particular linked to a fervent wish to save the Faroese language, lay behind the activities of many of Petersen's younger contemporaries. Though Faroese poetry had so far been the product of a group of students centered in Copenhagen, the desire to defend and further Faroese culture began to spread to the islands themselves. A group of nine signatories called a meeting for December 26, 1888, inviting the participation of anyone concerned with "defending the language and customs of the Faroe Islands." The immediate result was the founding of the Føringafelag, the Faroese Association, aimed at promoting that cause, especially through the introduction of Faroese as the language of education and religion. The second achievement was the launching in 1890 of *Føringatíðindi* (Faroese News), the first periodical publication ever written in Faroese. In the twelve years of its existence it came at first monthly and subsequently biweekly. Its aim was to awaken the national awareness of its readers and to combat the widespread influence of Danish language and culture in the Faroe Islands. Nevertheless, like many a Faroese nationalist since, it declared itself not to be anti-Danish.

One of the signatories of the manifesto and the first editor of *Føringatíðindi* was Rasmus Christoffer Effersøe (1857–1916). Born in Trangisvág on Suðuroy, Effersøe went to school in Tórshavn and later studied agriculture in Denmark and Scotland. He settled in the Faroes in 1884 and worked in various capacities to improve Faroese agriculture. From 1886 to 1889, and in 1902, he was editor of the Danish-language newspaper *Dimmalætting* (Dawn). With the establishment of the Faroese Association and *Føringatíðindi* he threw himself wholeheartedly into the work of the new movement.

Not only did he write many of the articles in the journal as well as doing the practical work of editing, but he was also a prolific poet and dramatist and a keen and efficient translator.

Effersøe's early poetry, much of it written in Copenhagen, is light and optimistic, often aphoristic, more intimate in its imagery than that of Fríðrikur Petersen, but no less patriotic. He writes in praise of his native land, remembers it, longs for it in poems such as "Heimið" (Home), "Kvæði til Føroyar" (Song to the Faroes), and "Vesturætt" (West Wind).

The later poems are different in character, more solemn, more somber in mood, and although the patriotic tone is still present, there are echoes, too, of differences of opinion that had emerged in the Faroese Association, whose members were now clearly divided into radicals and moderates. The moderate Effersøe was unhappy with this dissension, especially the different stances adopted by himself and the other dominant figure, Jóannes Patursson.

Effersøe's most lasting contribution to Faroese letters is his poetry, but he was also important for his work for the theater in Tórshavn. Plays had been performed there throughout the century, but they had been in Danish. Effersøe, together with other, minor, writers of his day set about establishing a dramatic repertoire in Faroese. He translated Holberg's *Kilde-Reysen* (1725; Journey to the Spring) and Hostrup's *En Nat mellem Fjeldene* (1852; Night in the Mountains) from Danish and added to them with original works: *Gunnar Havreki* (1889), *Magnus* (1892), and *Best man vera sum er* (1895; Things Are Best As They Are). All the original plays are on Faroese subjects of a more or less historical nature, while maintaining the tradition of the Danish *singspiel*. They lack tension and tautness, and apart from historical interest their main contribution is their songs.

One of the other original signatories to the 1888 manifesto, and with whom Effersøe's relations subsequently became strained, was Jóannes Patursson (1866–1946). The two men had entirely different natures; while Effersøe was gentle and restrained, Patursson was fiery and impatient in the nationalist cause. Born in Kirkjubøur, he went to school in Tórshavn. Then, instead of taking the customary practical training in Copenhagen, he went in 1882 to the agricultural college in Stend in Norway, where he was fired by the ideas of Norwegian nationalists. On returning home he took up the nationalist cause in the Faroe Islands, signed the 1888 manifesto, and became a leading figure in the Faroese Association. He soon felt the association to be too moderate, however, and resigned from it, turning to politics instead.

The difference between Effersøe's and Patursson's work is clear from the start. Instead of Effersøe's gentle songs in praise of the Faroe Islands and the

Faroese language, Patursson wrote energetic poems calling for action. "Nú er tann stundin komin til handa" (Now the Hour Has Come), the poem he wrote on the occasion of the 1888 meeting, struck the tone of his writings as a whole and has since become identified with the Faroese language movement. As a poem it leaves much to be desired, and aesthetic niceties are put aside in favor of the message to be conveyed; however, the very strength of feeling behind it sometimes raises the agitation to lyrical heights. The time has come, the poet says, to take up arms in the cause of this language, which is now filled with foreign words.

Poems like this inevitably led to controversy with more conservative-minded Faroese, and Patursson's work is often polemical in nature, revealing the Faroese propensity for lampooning one's adversaries. His poetry can at times produce effective metaphors and linguistic expressions, but it is of more importance for its agitation than its aesthetic qualities. Nevertheless, not everything Patursson wrote is of this kind: there are gentler expressions of his love for his native country, often written while he was abroad, and tender poems of a more personal nature.

In spite of their qualities and their importance for Faroese culture, all the writers so far considered have been minor in an international context. It was not until the appearance of Jens Hendrik Oliver (Janus) Djurhuus (1881–1948) that the Faroes saw their first poet of international format. His gifts were appreciated even while he was at school in Tórshavn, where he was introduced to Latin and Greek. His teacher left to take up a post on the Danish island of Bornholm and took Djurhuus with him. Djurhuus then proceeded to the University of Copenhagen, finally deciding to read law. He worked as a lawyer in both Denmark and the Faroe Islands until 1928, when he was accused of dishonest practices. He was barred from further legal work and even spent a short time in prison, after which he settled in Denmark. In 1938 he was again given permission to practice and returned to Tórshavn, where he spent the rest of his life.

At the age of twenty Djurhuus published his first poem, "Gandakvæði" (Sorcerer's Song), in the newspaper *Tingakrossur* (Assembly Cross). With its intense use of alliteration and its irregular, short-lined stanzas it was immediately reminiscent of Eddic poetry, while with its references both to Old Norse mythology and the gray area between Faroese history and Faroese legend it established the continuity of Faroese culture with the ancient civilization of the North. The sense of rhythm, the resounding language, and the skill with which it was fashioned into poetry betokened a writer of a new kind. If it can be said that his predecessors had written in the style of minor national romantics, it is equally true that the sounds of the great Scandinavian romantics are echoed in Djurhuus's own work. It is impossible not to see the parallel between the publication of his first poem and the appearance of the Danish poet Oehlenschläger's "Guldhornene" (The Golden Horns) in 1803. Djurhuus is otherwise the poet of the sea, of battle, of life in its ecstasy as well as its sorrow, and in this he can fairly be compared with a Danish neoromantic such as Holger Drachmann.

Djurhuus's national feelings were akin to those of his predecesors, as is indicated not least in his poem to Jóannes Patursson, "Til Jóannes Bónda í Kirkjubø" (To Jóannes, the Yeoman of Kirkjubøur), or in his three-verse poem on the language, "Málið" (Our Language), but his aesthetic sensitivity was of a different order. Other writers had urged the defense of the Faroese language, but Djurhuus actually demonstrated its capabilities. There is in his mode of expression a new dynamism and musicality, combined with a linguistic inventiveness that raises his work far above anything written by his older contemporaries.

Much of his poetry is rhetorical in nature, and the unusual preponderance of alliteration inspired by Norse tradition can lead to a certain heaviness. By no means all his poems, however, are of this kind. His "Kvæði til Apollon" (Song to Apollo), which makes free use of Greek mythology, is written in well-turned hexameters, while in "Atlantis," likewise in classical verse form, he combines Greek and Nordic mythology in a vision of the Faroes as the lost Atlantis.

Janus Djurhuus also wrote poems of a deeply personal nature, such as the melancholy love poem "Til K." (To K.) or the allegorical "I Búri" (Caged), in which sympathy for the caged bird clearly echoes the poet's own feelings during his time in prison. In "Ver sterk mín sál" (Be Strong, My Soul) he expresses his own deepest feelings in a hymnlike poem reminiscent of the seventeenth-century Danish hymn writer Thomas Kingo, whose profoundly felt and grandiose hymns had a formative influence on both Faroese religious life and, in the twentieth century, Faroese poetry. In 1914 the Faroese Students' Association in Denmark published a selection of Djurhuus's poetry under the title of *Yrkingar* (Poems). Thus Djurhuus became the first Faroese poet ever to have his work published in book form.

A complete contrast to Janus Djurhuus was his brother, Hans Andrias Djurhuus (1883–1951). Born in Tórshavn, Hans Andrias went to sea at the age of fifteen but gave up the venture two years later. He went first to the folk high school, which has been a source of much inspiration for Faroese letters, and then to the teacher-training college in Tórshavn, subsequently entering a career as a teacher. His literary tastes were soon clear: the Danish romantics on the one hand and the great Russian novelists and contemporary Danish and Norwegian dramatists and novelists on the other. He was not, however, in his major work to follow in the footsteps of the realists.

Instead of Janus Djurhuus's rhetoric and the somber thoughts it often contained, Hans Andrias's work reflects an optimistic view of life, often expressed with disarming simplicity. As a consequence of this approach and of the immediacy of his work—which encompassed poetry, short stories, and drama as well as hymns—he has become one of the most beloved of Faroese writers. His training as a teacher, his natural understanding of children, and an innate ability to write poetry led to a collection of poems and songs written expressly for children, often portraying Faroese characters past and present in a language easily assimilated by the young.

Djurhuus published his first poem in 1901, but it was not until 1914 that he began to publish his most representative work. *Barnarímur* (1915; Poems for Children), intended for use in school, and other children's poems were collected in *Søgumál* (Issues) from 1922. From an early age Djurhuus tried his hand at dramas; by 1908 he had produced *Marita*, based on a Faroese ballad. Other plays, such as *Annika* (1917) and *Traðarbøndur* (1933; Smallholders), also derived their contents from Faroese legend and myth. Legend was likewise to form the inspiration for his novel *Beinta* (1927), whose theme is the same as in the better-known *Barbara* by Jørgen-Frantz Jacobsen (1939). *Beinta* was intended for the adult reader, as was a short story such as "Duruta" (1922), but even here Djurhuus strayed in the direction of the fairy tale. His reputation, not unnaturally, rests principally on his writings for children, on the collection of fairy tales to which he gave the Hans Christian Andersen–like title *Smásøgur og ævintýr* (1924; Stories and Fairy Tales), and on his poetry.

Hans Andrias Djurhuus's production spanned many years, and he was the first Faroese to establish himself as a writer of prose as well as of poetry. His novels were not the first to be written in Faroese, however. That honor went to Regin í Líð's *Bábelstornið* (1909; The Tower of Babel). The author was the folk high school teacher Rasmus Rasmussen (1871–1962), writing pseudonymously. In view of the fact that there was no novel tradition in the Faroe Islands, and that would-be writers there were cut off from the mainstream of Scandinavian literature, this is a remarkably successful novel. To some extent its purpose is national and didactic, seeking to define the differences between Faroese and Danish and to awaken the Faroese to the need to move with the times. There are clear political overtones, not least through the presence as a minor character of the Faroese reformer Niels Winther (1822–98), but these perspectives are encompassed within a family saga centered on a feud stretching from ca. 1840 to ca. 1900. When the son of one family refuses to marry the daughter of the other, he breaks with tradition, and the woman he has refused vows vengeance. And despite later intermarriage, she attains her goal. The interplay of family feud and sociopolitical development is an interesting one, clearly an offshoot of the major Scandinavian naturalist novels from the turn of the century, partly because of its insistence on the Darwinian theme of inherited characteristics.

Regin í Líð's *Glámlýsi* (1912; Dazzling Light) was the first collection of Faroese short stories to appear in book form, similar in import to his novel but without its inner strength. Líð also wrote a play, *Høvdingar hittast* (1928; Meeting of Chieftains), based on the legend of Sigmundur and Tróndur, as well as a volume of memoirs, *Sær er siður á landi* (1949; Each Country Has Its Customs). None, however, has enjoyed the status of his sole novel.

The Djurhuus brothers were not, of course, the only writers of their generation, though they were undoubtedly the most important. Of their contemporaries, two stand out: Hans Marius Ejdesgaard and Rikard Long. They did not write much, but both have maintained their positions, and in particular Rikard Long had, in his capacity as publisher and literary critic, great influence on the course taken by Faroese literature.

Hans Marius Ejdesgaard (1887–1966) was born in the village of Oyndarfjørður, the son of a teacher. His life, like that of many of his contemporaries, was uneventful. He attended school in Tórshavn, spent two years at the folk high school, and qualified as a teacher. During his career he began writing, and he published for the first time in the periodical *Varðin* (The Cairn) in 1924. He regularly used *Varðin* as his medium, and with the exception of the somewhat static play *Ein myrking* (1937; An Eclipse), it was not until he had retired that he began to publish in book form. His novel *Hitt ævinliga gonguverkið* (The Perpetuum Mobile) appeared in 1952, twenty years after the first extract had been published in *Varðin*; it was followed by *Lívsins rættur* (1953; Life's Dues) and his most important volume of short stories, *Ein stjørna er tendrað* (1962; A Star Is Lit).

The novel *Hitt ævinliga gonguverkið* is the most substantial of Ejdesgaard's prose works, a somber story of a descent into madness, with the implied message that one cannot recompense for past crimes. The central figure is Birgir á Hamri, whose mother was once wronged by Elspa. In an attempt to put things right Elspa takes Birgir into her home with the intention of ensuring his marriage to her daughter Katrin. Birgir, however, is obsessed with the idea of perpetual motion, and Katrin's attempts to combat his incipient madness come to nothing. It is not inconceivable that the element of family guilt in this novel owes something to Regin í Líð's *Bábelstor-*

nið, but there the similarity stops. Stylistically, Ejdesgaard's novel has considerable qualities, and it has been praised as an accurate portrayal of the Faroese way of life of his time, though structurally it suffers from the fact that it appeared in parts over several years, resulting in a desultory, episodic quality that its style fails to overcome.

Rikard Long (1889–1977) was born in Tórshavn of a Faroese father and Danish mother. After his schooling in Tórshavn he went to Denmark, starting but never completing a university study. In 1914 he returned to the Faroe Islands to work as a teacher, entering politics later in life. Long's importance to literature is twofold. First, there was his original poetry, a contrast to the romantic, highly patriotic poetry in vogue at the turn of the century. Certainly, he was fond of painting the Faroese landscape, with its light, its color, and its vistas, but he did so in a more subdued manner, far more in keeping with the approach to landscape poetry current in mainland Scandinavia in his day.

Second with the exception of Janus Djurhuus, Long was without doubt the most intellectually gifted of the writers of his time, and this quality he put not only into his own poetry, but also into his activities as editor of *Varðin* from 1921 to 1931 and 1935 to 1965. He wrote trenchant yet positive criticisms of Faroese literature and contributed long articles on contemporary foreign literature, which in themselves added impetus to Faroese writing. He thus had an important formative role in the path taken by Faroese literature as it sought to move in the direction taken by literature abroad.

FAROESE LITERATURE COMES OF AGE

It was a slightly younger generation of writers that was to bring Faroese letters to the level of contemporary literature in Scandinavia. Within a space of some two and a half years at the beginning of the present century five men were born who together were to have a profound effect on the future of Faroese letters. Two of them, William Heinesen and Jørgen-Frantz Jacobsen, wrote in Danish. The other three, Christian Matras, Heðin Brú, and Martin Joensen, became pioneers, Christian Matras in his poetry, the other two in their prose works.

Cultural and social conditions in the Faroes were not such as to lead to the establishment of a "school," and indeed, the five men show very different characteristics. Jacobsen was a historian and journalist, and his work bears clear traces of this background; Heinesen was a man of vivid inspiration whose works are an idiosyncratic mixture of poetry, realism, and fantasy; Heðin Brú was a great stylist, a devoted portrayer of village life, the man generally acknowledged to have turned the Faroese language into a medium for literary prose; while Martin Joensen, whose work has some affinity with that of Brú, was a rather less conscious stylist but a more deliberate psychologist. Christian Matras, the only one of the five to write poetry using Faroese as his medium, is in a category of his own.

Christian Matras

Christian Matras (1900–1988) was born and spent his early childhood in the most northerly village in the Faroes, Viðareiði, on the island of Viðoy. The impressions he there derived of the majestic scenery, the variations between idyllic calm and tempestuous storm, the swirling mists around almost perpendicular mountains, the utter darkness at night and the loneliness of the outlying village marked him for life and put their stamp on his poetry.

At the age of twelve Matras went to school in Tórshavn, where he met William Heinesen; in 1917 he moved to Denmark to attend boarding school and subsequently the University of Copenhagen. By 1936 he was appointed lecturer in Faroese, and in 1952 he became the first man ever to hold the position of professor of Faroese. In 1965 he returned to Tórshavn to head the Department of Faroese Language in the newly formed Faroese Academy.

Matras was a philologist, responsible for much basic research in the Faroese language past and present. He published a pioneering work on place-names in the northern Faroe Islands and was responsible for the publication of Svabo's collection of Faroese ballads (1939) and the monumental *Føroya kvæði: Corpus Carminum Færoensium* (1944–72). With M. A. Jacobsen he compiled a Faroese-Danish dictionary, and as early as 1935 he published a short history of Faroese literature.

Matras's first published volume of poems was *Grátt, kátt og hátt* (1926; Gray, Playful, and Solemn), in which many of his major themes appear, though not yet in full flower. For a poet who later talks of simplicity of language as his goal, these works have a long way to go, and the symbolism and language of some of them can be complex. Nevertheless, in "Hitt blinda liðið" (The Company of the Blind) the allegorical nature of the blind, who walk along without knowing where they are going but experience momentary glimpses of understanding, is clear and effective. This motif of the brief glimpse of inspiration or insight is characteristic of much of Matras's work and appears in many of his poems.

In this theme, as in his general approach to poetry, Matras was related to the Norwegian poet Olav Aukrust, whose work he read while studying in Oslo. Aukrust seeks to capture poetically the spiritual essence of Norwegian village life; with his own insight into village life in the Faroes and his feeling for the natural scenery and the hidden forces of the elements, Matras set about a similar task in relation to the Faroe Islands—though without the religious perspectives of Aukrust. Matras is also associated with Robert Burns, much of whose work he translated into Faroese. Particularly in his middle period he can, in seemingly simple poems reflecting the village, express himself in a way—and indeed, a verse form—not far removed from Burns, perhaps reflecting his search for pregnant simplicity.

In *Heimur og heima* (1933; The World and Home) a historicocultural perspective emerges directly. In "Neytakonur" (Milk Women) the group of women returning in single file from the pastures where they have been milking the cows assumes an almost ritual significance for those who have known the historical pattern of life in the Faroes. And the constant refrain tells, significantly, that the baby meanwhile lies sleeping at home, combining the motif of the child with the refrain technique of the medieval ballad:

Milk women come now south to the bourns,
goose-file they come, like hill marker-cairns
that started to walk when light left the heaths.
Gates open for them and wide village paths.
Home lies the little one and sleeps.
        (Tr. George Johnston)

At times Matras achieves an epic grandeur in poems that not only present but interpret nature, poems such as "Úr upprúnaheimi" (From the World of Origin) or "Á hellu eg stóð" (On the Firm Rock I Stood), but in his late years he moved into a new simplicity, experimenting with radical forms of free, pregnant verse. Many of the poems in *Úr sjón og úr minni* (1980; Seen and Remembered), to which he gave the modest subtitle of "Verses," show a clear affinity with the Japanese haiku. The shortest of them consists of a mere five words and is a brief glimpse of the scene after a fowler has fallen to his death over a cliff, leaving his fowler's net lying behind on the ground. It is a poem with an implicit image of a very Faroese activity; the catastrophe reflects the nearness of death that is also a feature of Faroese life and consciousness; and the fact that the net is left behind on the ground points to cultural continuity, for someone else will pick it up and continue the work. To these elements can be added the directional hints in the poem, also reminiscent of the haiku.

Over the sixty years during which he wrote, Matras progressed from ornateness and complex vision to a simplicity of language and vision unique in Faroese poetry. In so doing, and in his many translations of foreign poets from Thomas Kingo to G. K. Chesterton, from Edgar Lee Masters to the ancient Egyptian emperor Akhnaton, from Sappho to modern Polish and Romanian writers, he helped fashion the language of modern Faroese poetry.

Heðin Brú

The part played by Heðin Brú (Hans Jacob Jacobsen) (1901–87) in molding Faroese literary prose was similar to Matras's. Brú was born in gentler natural surroundings than Matras, in Skálavík on the island of Sandoy. He spent a period in the folk high school before studying agriculture in Copenhagen, returning to the Faroe Islands as an agricultural consultant. In 1930, only three years after Hans Andrias Djurhuus had published his novel *Beinta*, Brú published *Lognbrá* (Mirage), the first part of a two-volume novel, to be followed in 1935 by the second volume, *Fastatøkur* (Firm Grip). Through these works we follow the life of the sensitive Høgni from childhood to manhood. As a child he is misunderstood by his family; he reacts against home life and goes to sea on a fishing smack. In the background is his romantic love for a fair-haired girl, whom he finally marries on his return to take over the family farm. The dreamer of the first volume has become the realist of the second.

The novel is a curious mixture of romanticism and realism. It is realistic insofar as it is an accurate portrayal of life in the Faroe Islands in the first half of the twentieth century and also in the hint of family disagreements arising from the social changes to which the Faroes were subjected. Yet there is a romantic element about the aspirations of the young Høgni, in particular his falling in love at the age of five with the fair-haired Gunnvá, whom he then recognizes when he meets her years later and whom he finally marries. Perhaps this romantic element can best be reconciled with the realism of the novel if it is seen in a symbolic light, representing Høgni's ideals and aspirations, which he finally achieves. It thus harmonizes with other symbols: the distant mountain Vestfelli on the island of Oyggja Stóra or the waterfall to which Høgni repairs when despondent.

In 1936 Brú began publishing parts of a new novel, which he completed in 1940. *Feðgar á ferð* (Eng. tr. *The Old Man and His Sons*, 1970) is generally considered his masterpiece. Shorter than the earlier novel and without its romantic element (though not without certain symbolic traits), it is concerned with the generation gap emerging in the Faroe Islands with the transition from the old survival economy to the modern money economy. The older generation prefers to exist on what it owns and can achieve, while younger people finance their aspirations by borrowing. Brú writes of the resulting problems with sympathy and understanding as well as a good deal of humor.

Brú's later novels were less successful as works of art. The roman à clef *Leikum fagurt* (1963; Fair Play) has some successful satirical qualities and is deeply concerned with social and political changes in the Faroes earlier in the century, while *Men lívið lær* (1970; But Life Smiles) is a historical novel set in the early nineteenth century and clearly inspired by that century's more romantic novels, despite its undoubtedly genuine individual pictures of Faroese life. Little better is the romanticized and unhistorical *Tað stóra takið* (1972; The Great Undertaking), which is concerned with the twentieth-century transition from a farming to a fishing society.

It is in the short story that Heðin Brú excels. Some, like "Einbýli" (1936; Eng. tr. "Lice," 1972), are related to *Feðgar á ferð* in their portrayal of a vanished and anything-but-romantic society (this humorous story is concerned with an old man who is deloused by his new and modern daughter-in-law and consequently dies of boredom); others are tender presentations of characters whom Brú has met in years gone by or fond sketches of Faroese nature. There are portrayals of village society, too, in which an underlying brutality sometimes disturbs the idyll in stories such as "Krákudóttir" (Crow's Daughter) or "Búravnurin" (The Caged Raven)—both from the collection *Búravnurin* (1971)—which verge on the demonic. The same qualities, including the humor, are also in Brú's memoirs, *Endurminningar* (1980; Memoirs).

Martin Joensen
Martin Joensen (1902–66) also sought to portray Faroese society in the first half of the twentieth century. Like Brú, Joensen did so to a large extent through a two-part novel, *Fiskimenn* (1946; Fishermen) and *Tað lýsir á landið* (1952; The Land Grows Bright), and in a series of short stories published in four volumes (two posthumously) between 1949 and 1977.

Born in Sandvík, Joensen went to sea at the age of seventeen, returning four years later to study at the folk high school and then at the teacher-training college. He taught in various villages until ill health forced his retirement. Like Heðin Brú and Regin í Líð before him, Joensen was fascinated by the major realist novelists, and he names Dostoevsky as one who exerted a decisive influence on him. Like Brú, he traces the change from an agrarian society to a fishing community, and from the efforts of the individual to the employment of those individuals by a wealthier—and more ruthless—shipowner, reflecting the emergence of the capitalist system in a community that had hitherto been organized along individual and even medieval lines. In the second of the two novels the indecisive Símun (not entirely unlike Brú's Høgni) moves firmly into the center of the action, and we follow him through the stresses and doubts that he experiences on various levels. A love theme is intertwined with a presentation of the sectarian problem, which is never far below the surface in Faroese literature (though scarcely touched on by Brú), and it is also linked to the question of trade union organization in an unsophisticated society. Perhaps it is in the portrayal of Símun's divided nature that the Dostoevskian influence is to be found, transplanted to the gentler, simpler society of the Faroe Islands in the first half of the twentieth century. The romantic element noted in Brú's work is absent here, and the portrayal of conditions on board the fishing vessel is more detailed. Chance plays an important part in the novel, an element best explained through the fatalism that is clearly discernible, in both religious and profane guise.

As a writer of short stories Joensen lacks the poetry of Brú but is more socially aware. Whereas Brú in *Feðgar á ferð* can throw a partly humorous light on the social tensions creeping into the Faroe Islands, Joensen, who shows a more obvious, but not obtrusive, political bias, paints them in darker tones. A story such as "Húsvillur" (Homeless) is an unrelieved portrayal of a young husband and wife forced out of their home because they are unable to pay their way. A story such as "Gamli maðurin og varðin" (The Old Man and the Cairn) shows a profound insight into the mentality of the isolated communities of the Faroes in former times. An old man sets out to walk across the mountains to his home village but is overtaken by a blizzard and has to spend his time taking the marker cairn to pieces and building it up again in order to keep warm. Here Joensen shows the same awareness as both Brú and Matras of the significance of the unknown men of the past who built the cairns to mark the paths and whose anonymous efforts helped fashion the land.

There is an occasional glimpse of humor in Joensen's work, for instance in "Heimadoktorin" (The Home Doctor), but it is more subdued than is the case with Brú. Nor is there the same demonic element. Joensen does manage to combine a certain grim humor with a study of obsession in "Tanntongin" (The Dental Pliers), however, while "Maðurin ombord" (The Man Aboard) is an ambiguous study of a seamen's superstition.

William Heinesen

Both humor and an awareness of demonic forces are present in the work of the Danish-writing William Heinesen (1900–1991) and they are successfully blended with an element almost entirely lacking in his two contemporaries: satire. Heinesen was born in Tórshavn and as a teenager moved to Denmark, where he was trained in the school of commerce with a view to joining his father's business on returning home. Instead, he turned his mind to philosophy and writing and journalism, and he eventually became the first Faroese to live entirely by his own artistic efforts, not only as a writer but also as a painter.

Heinesen's first novels, *Blæsende Gry* (1934; Windswept Dawn) and *Noatun* (1938; Eng. tr. *Niels Peter*, 1939), were akin to the Danish collective novel, broad portrayals of Faroese village society during the period of change. *Blæsende Gry* is concerned not only with changing patterns of commercial and social life, but also with the advent of the sectarian movement, which has played a major part in Faroese society in the twentieth century. *Noatun* is centered on the implications of the new land laws introduced in the islands in the 1930s, allowing the previously landless village dwellers to buy land in outlying areas and settle there. *Blæsende Gry* is shapeless but dynamic, full of memorable events and characters, some of them larger than life. *Noatun* is written in a much more sober style, clearly influenced by the Dane Hans Kirk's novel *Fiskerne* (1928; The Fishermen), but nevertheless showing traces of the fantasy that is part and parcel of almost everything Heinesen has written. After the publication of *Noatun* there was a gap of eleven years before the appearance of the next two novels, *Den sorte Gryde* (1949; Eng. tr., *The Black Cauldron*, 1992) and *De fortabte Spillemænd* (1950; Eng. tr. *The Lost Musicians*, 1972). Both show affinities with the collective novel in that it is the group, of one kind of another, that is at the center, but whereas the collective novel by tradition is sober and factual, Heinesen has here moved in a totally different direction.

Den sorte Gryde is set during World War II, when British troops occupied the Faroe Islands and Faroese fishermen were risking their lives and making huge fortunes (for their employers rather than themselves, according to Heinesen) by sailing fish to British ports. It is a novel that shows the hypocrisy of the employers, especially one Opperman. Opperman gradually emerges as a symbol of death, finally seducing Liva, the symbol of life, whose relationship with the sectarian leader Simon the Baker has been fraught with erotic overtones. She ends her days in the mental hospital that Opperman has built in memory of his wife.

Through a taut and quick-moving novel Heinesen not only presents a picture of wartime life in the Faroe Islands, but with his newfound skill at grotesque caricature he introduces a completely new dimension into Faroese literature. That dimension is further extended in *De fortabte Spillemænd*, with its plot centered on the struggle to achieve total abstinence on the islands. (Historically, that occurred in 1907.) Heinesen's abstinence movement, which he mischievously names after a Faroese brewery, does finally triumph, bringing about the death or downfall of the group of musicians who represent the unspoiled forces of life. *De fortabte Spillemænd* is a tragic novel that nevertheless ends on a note of optimism, when the child musician Orfeus leaves to take up a musical training in Copenhagen.

Of particular interest is Heinesen's free fantasy on a historical theme. The novel is set at the time of the abstinence struggle, and some of the characters are recognizable, not least the musicians themselves. Yet the various historical strands are woven together to produce a pattern that is not representative of the actual historical events. Such cavalier treatment of history was to be repeated in the historical novel *Det gode Håb* (1964; Fair Hope).

Heinesen's next novel, *Moder Syvstjerne* (1952; Eng. tr. *The Kingdom of the Earth*, 1973), contains some of the same characters, including the sectarian leader Ankersen. It is not, however, properly speaking a sequel, but is concerned with the girl Antonia and her illegitimate child, Jacob. There is little action; Antonia dies, and Jacob is brought up by the strict sectarian Trine, who feels responsible for Antonia's "fall." The attack on narrow-minded sectarianism is secondary to Heinesen's dithyrambic praise to Antonia as the archetypal woman. The work has much more the character of a hymn to womanhood, woman as the bearer of life, than of a novel properly speaking.

There was again a long gap, during which Heinesen wrote short stories and poems, but in 1964 he published his longest novel, *Det gode Håb*. It is based on the story of the Danish pastor Lucas Debes, who lived and worked in the Faroe Islands in the seventeenth century, and is written in the form of a series of letters. The principal character, here called Peder Børresen instead of the historical Lucas Debes, finds himself battling with the authorities and gradually comes to be seen as the leader of the opposition, until finally the regime falls in a minirevolution. The novel can be seen as an allegory of the defeat of a dictatorial regime by a popular uprising, and it is probable that this is how it should be read. The confrontation between life and death motifs, which had been a feature of earlier books, is also present, while the criticism of sectarianism is given a new guise in the portrait of early and fictitious sectarian movements. The state church, which never wins favor in Heinesen's eyes, is sharply attacked for its sycophancy.

Heinesen's novels were interspersed with several volumes of short stories with qualities similar to those of the novels. They are set in a fictitious Tórshavn and often, through characters reminiscent of Heinesen himself as a child, reflect the social changes, social exploitation, sectarian activities, and eccentric characters he experienced in his own childhood. At the same time, the confrontation between life and death motifs is raised to mythical levels; Heinesen was earlier influenced by the Danish poet and novelist Johannes V. Jensen, and stories such as "Det vingede mørke" (Winged Darkness) and "Historien om digteren Lin Pe og hans tamme trane" (The Story of the Poet Lin Pe and His Tame Crane) from *Det fortryllede lys* (1957; The Enchanted Light) reflect something of Jensen's penchant for the concentrated, pregnant prose form to which he gave the name of myths. This same tendency toward myth and abstraction, first found in its unambiguous form in *Moder Syvstjerne*, is likewise of central importance in the later *Tårnet ved Verdens Ende* (1976; Eng. tr. *The Tower at the Edge of the World*, 1981), *Her skal danses* (1980; Here We Must Dance), and *Laterna Magica* (1985, Eng. tr. 1987). Although the first and the last of these works are superficially given the aspect of novels, they are at times more akin to interlinked short stories, but they show Heinesen at his most inventive and, in the case of the title story of *Her skal danses*, his most Faroese. With its study of the Faroese mentality, its reflection of ancient Faroese customs and of the cultic, ritual significance of the Faroese chain dance, this piece stands as one of the most intensely Faroese stories ever produced.

There is as much variety in Heinesen's poetry as in his prose. His first volume, the introspective *Arktiske Elegier* (1921; Arctic Elegies), is in the tradition of Danish neoromantic or symbolist poetry from the turn of the century. *Højbjergning ved Havet* (1924; Harvest by the Sea) shows an approach to a philosophy based on the idea of rebirth and the continuing cycle of life, an idea permeating much of Heinesen's later poetry. Because of the death of his brother, Heine, in 1927, the next two volumes, *Sange mod Vaardybet* (1927; Songs in Spring Depths) and *Stjernerne vaagner* (1930; The Stars Awaken), show a return to introspection, often with religious overtones. *Den dunkle Sol* (1936; The Dark Sun) sees a transformation. Here, partly at the urging of the Dane Otto Gelsted, Heinesen uses poetry for a social or political purpose, reflecting the oppression and fear felt at the emergence of nazism. He continues in this vein, blending political and social satire with a devoted portrayal of his native islands and also reflecting his awareness of the life-death confrontation and of the vastness of the cosmos. There is humor in some of the poems, but it is used in the service of satire. In 1972 a volume entitled *Panorama med Regnbue* (Panorama with Rainbow) appeared, combining the satire of the middle period with a series of dignified retrospective reflections and a philosophical evaluation of life and the aging poet's position in it:

Slowly darkens
March evening's frost-clear sky.
Sun has gone down.
Stars light up behind the black fells.
Low in the east over the horizon
can be felt the new moon's airy
spiderweb-fine sickle.

All the roads and paths that I have gone!
Now there is only one left,
the last wild path
over the dusking sea and into the dark.
That shall I walk with thanks in my heart.

That shall I walk
and think with tenderness of you
who are yet young on the earth—
you who have the sunset
and your longing and ache.
You who have evening star and your hope.
You who have new moon and your love.

                    (Tr. George Johnston)

Jørgen-Frantz Jacobsen

Jørgen-Frantz Jacobsen (1900–1938), a distant relative of Heinesen, was also born in Tórshavn, where he went to school. In 1916 he went to boarding school in Denmark and subsequently studied history and French at the University of Copenhagen. He turned to journalism, writing for a time in the newspaper *Politiken* (Politics). At an early age he was found to be suffering from tuberculosis, and the rest of his life constituted a long and losing battle against the disease.

Jacobsen's production was small, consisting of a study of the relationship between Denmark and the Faroe Islands entitled *Danmark og Færøerne* (1927; Denmark and the Faroes), a topographical-cultural study of the Faroe Islands called *Færøerne. Natur og Folk* (1936; The Faroes: Nature and People), and the novel *Barbara* (1939; Eng. tr. *Barbara*, 1939), which lay almost complete on his death and was prepared for publication by William Heinesen and Christian Matras. In 1943 Matras published a selection of Jacobsen's best newspaper articles under the title of *Nordiske Kroniker* (1943; Nordic Articles), and in 1958 Heinesen published a selection, with commentary, of Jacobsen's letters under the title of *Det dyrebare liv* (Precious

Life). Virtually all Jacobsen's work was written with a view to making the Faroe Islands known and understood in Denmark; while that is clearly the intention with his first book and his essays, it is also implicit in the novel, though in no way can *Barbara* be called a didactic work.

It is *Barbara* on which Jacobsen's international reputation is now founded. Published in 1939, it quickly became a best-seller in Denmark and has remained so ever since. It is based on the Faroese legend of Beinta and Peder Arrheboe, which tells of the evil Beinta, who was thrice married to Danish pastors and thrice responsible for their deaths. Jørgen-Frantz Jacobsen transforms the story of the evil woman into that of an enchanting but totally amoral counterpart, Barbara, whose marriage to Pastor Poul is at the center of the action. Pastor Poul arrives in the Faroe Islands from Copenhagen, believing that he is thereby turning his back on the world. Instead, he finds Barbara, who comes to represent this world as opposed to the other-worldliness on which he is supposed to be basing his life. It is the work of a historian, an accurate account of life in the Faroe Islands at the end of the eighteenth century; it is a fascinating study of a woman who loves Poul but has to follow her bent when others appear on the scene; but it is above all a poetic presentation of the dichotomy between the love of this world and the renunciation of it, a hymn to life by a writer who is about to leave it.

Jacobsen's letters in *Det dyrebare liv* are similarly an homage to life, and they act almost as a commentary on the novel. They show Jacobsen's almost ecstatic enjoyment of life, whether in the south of France, in Denmark, or in the sanatorium where he uncomplainingly underwent much suffering. Strictly speaking, the book is a collection of letters, but by his selection and his sensitive comments Heinesen turned it into a moving human portrait, a work of literature ranking alongside the best in Denmark from the middle of the present century.

Other Writers

Although these five writers—Christian Matras, Heðin Brú, Martin Joensen, William Heinesen, and Jørgen-Frantz Jacobsen—tower above their contemporaries, they were by no means alone. Chief among the second rank of writers born at the turn of the century is the enfant terrible of Faroese poetry, Poul F. Joensen (1898–1970). Born in the southern village of Sumba on the island of Suðuroy, Joensen went to sea at the age of fourteen but returned to study at the teacher-training college in Tórshavn. His career as a teacher was short, and by 1927 he was living as a smallholder, which he continued to do until his death.

His first published volume of poems came out in 1924 under the title of

Gaman og Álvara (Fun and Seriousness). It was followed by *Millum heims og heljar* (1942; Between Earth and Hell), *Lívsins kvæði* (1955; Song of Life), and *Ramar risti hann rúnirnar* (1967; Strong Runes He Carved). There are three strands to Joensen's poetry. First, well versed in classical mythology and ancient history, he was, like Janus Djurhuus, able to fuse his knowledge of the distant past with his pictures of the Faroe Islands. One one occasion he sees swirling mists approaching at breakneck speed and compares them with the hordes of Genghis Khan. Second, there was the tender poetry inspired by Robert Burns and Heinrich Heine, poets for whom he had great affection:

> Do you remember, dear, that summer eve
> When I awoke your slumbering womanhood—
> High 'tween fell and sunset's splendor
> Lay the land of Faroe—sacred memory.
>
> When the blushing sun departed,
> The all-knowing moon smiled on us,
> And the stars twinkled merry and gentle
> As we sank into heavenly joy.

Third, Joensen was also inspired by other aspects of Burns and Heine. One suspects the inspiration of Burns's "Tam O'Shanter" behind "Jarðarferðin" (The Funeral), a balladlike poem depicting a grotesque funeral in which the bearers drink schnapps to help them on their way, arriving drunk at the cemetery, where they perform a wild, intoxicated dance. Likewise, Heine's irony is seen behind many of Joensen's brief and sometimes wounding poems. He has been called the first social critic in Faroese, but that is only partly true. He is no social critic in any organized sense but attacks vehemently any sign of hypocrisy or corruption, whether in the official church, the sectarian movement, politicians of local or international varieties, or well-known figures in the Faroe Islands. No one, from Winston Churchill to a local politician, was safe from his biting satire.

Hans Dalsgaard (1899–1970), like many other Faroese writers, went to sea as a boy, but he returned in 1919 to spend a period in the Faroese folk high school. He later returned to his native Skálavík, where he worked in various capacities. He was the Faroese representative in Iceland during World War II. He did not have the same flow of language as Poul F. Joensen, but he wrote a small number of carefully chiseled poems whose principal inspiration was the poetry of Janus Djurhuus but which also show the influence of Icelandic poetry. His first publication was in *Varðin* in 1923, and he continued to publish in this way until in 1966 he collected his poems and published them in book form as *Av mannagøtum* (Off the Beaten Track). As the title of this slender volume (consisting of fourteen original poems and sixteen translations) suggests, Dalsgaard describes the people and the paths they tread in the Faroes, showing sympathy with the less fortunate members of society. The influence of Djurhuus is clearly seen in the widespread—and at times heavy—use of alliteration.

Dalsgaard's prose shows the same attention to detail as his poetry. His stories were republished separately and collected at a late stage, this time under the title of *Bøndur og fátæk fljóð* (1969; Farmers and Poor Folk). They reflect village life and evince a tender understanding of the Faroese psyche. Best among them is "Nelsons sista bragd" (Eng. tr. "Nelson's Last Stand," 1972), the story of a mentally deficient boy who loses his life while saving another.

Dalsgaard also published a two-act play entitled *Jákup Sibbi* (1926), as well as a translation of Davíð Stefánsson's drama *Gullna hliðid* (1941; The Golden Gate) from Icelandic. Like other Faroese writers, he helped develop a Faroese literary language by translation from established literatures, and his translations from Icelandic, especially his version of Stefánson's play, are considered among the best of their kind in Faroese.

INTO THE MODERN AGE

The writers previously discussed established Faroese literature as viable, dynamic, and comparable with the work of their contemporaries elsewhere in Scandinavia. The succeeding generation entered the arena after the transition had been made from nineteenth-century national romanticism to a more measured twentieth-century literature and did not look back to the same extent. The new writers learned from their predecesors but wrote with a fresh awareness of modern trends and were more consistent in their experimentation.

Karsten Hoydal (1912–90) was the first of them to make his mark. Born in Hoydal, near Tórshavn, he grew up on the grounds of the tuberculosis sanatorium where his father was employed. Consequently, he early developed an unusual awareness of illness and death, an experience that profoundly affected both his poetry and his prose. After attending school in the Faroes, Hoydal went to Denmark and was trained in agriculture and fisheries. He spent World War II in Denmark, returning home in 1946 and becoming head of the fisheries department in 1950. He remained in this post until his retirement, with the exception of a three-year assignment to the UN's Food and Agricultural Organization in Ecuador.

Hoydal's work denotes a struggle between pessimism and optimism, between dark and light. His childhood awareness of suffering and brutality was intensified both by the experience of World War II and by his stay in South America. The mood is established in one of the three early poems with which Hoydal introduces his collected poems, *Teinur og tal* (Conversations on the Road), from 1972: "Everything oppressed me as I went forth in the black, cheerless night—the darkness sought to suffocate, to strangle me and wrest all strength from me." It is the struggle against this darkness which Hoydal illustrates throughout his work.

This effort is already apparent in the first volume of poems, *Myrkrið reyða* (1946; The Red Darkness), for while the young poet's dark view of life is made clear, so, too, is his urge to overcome it and to find some kind of balance between the two poles of his experience. As a whole, the volume denotes a mass of conflicting moods, which only reluctantly give way to a more optimistic conclusion. The second volume, *Syngjandi grót* (1951; Singing Stones), continues the process, but its structure makes plain the movement toward a more hopeful view. The first poem is a memorial to the somber Janus Djurhuus, while the volume is rounded off with a memorial to his brother, the far more optimistic H. A. Djurhuus. The third volume, *Vatnið og ljósið* (1960; Water and Light), brings the process to its conclusion. Hoydal is unable to turn his back on death and suffering, but he is able to subsume it into a balanced philosophy of life, and the volume ends on a note of reconciliation.

Hoydal's sole volume of short stories, *Leikapettið* (1971; Potsherd), shows the same conflict as the poems. Hoydal is an outstanding portrayer of children, and after a rather lighthearted sketch of a child's ability to make up stories and convince others in "Summarkvøld við Rockall" (Summer Evening at Rockall) he moves into far more somber areas of a child's experience. Clearly based on his own childhood memories is "Lítlá gúla húsið" (The Little Yellow House), set in the sanatorium and showing children playing in the mortuary when it is not in use for other reasons. "Í kirkjutíð" (At Church Time) is a darker story that delves deeper into the psyche. While the rest of the family is at church, Páll seeks to still his bad conscience for not going with them by climbing to a cave nearby and communing with the powers of nature. There he is filled with all manner of superstitious fears, culminating in his conviction that the black duckling in a family of ducks outside the cave is the devil himself. He kills it and throws it to the back of the cave. The episode seems to be an effort to find forgiveness for an imagined sin on a pagan foundation, and it both explores the depths of the psyche and betokens the writer's attempt to come to terms with the evil in life. The other stories, some of which are more like essays, show the same tendency: the child's sorrow at the fate of familiar horses is paralleled by the young student's unwillingness to take the blood of terrified horses for experimental purposes; the shoemaker's apprentice cannot bring himself to make shoes from the hides of calves he has known. "Vaktmaðurin" (The Security Guard) shows the uncomprehending wonder of the Scandinavian in South America at the corruption and brutality he witnesses. He wonders at it but has to accept. Acceptance is indeed one of the watchwords of this volume, as it is of Hoydal's work as a whole.

As a poet Hoydal builds partly on the work of Janus Djurhuus and Christian Matras, not least in the cosmic perspective of his nature descriptions. At the same time, he is by far the most cosmopolitan writer of his generation. He is familiar with a great deal of modern English and American poetry and translated both Walt Whitman and Edgar Lee Masters into Faroese. His translations also introduce poems by names new to Faroese letters, such as García Lorca and Pablo Neruda. He manages to combine his Faroese roots with influences from these poets in such a way that his work becomes uncompromisingly *modern*, at times even modernist. He experiments with new and sometimes difficult terminology, with daring rhythms, blank verse, lines of radically varying length. In the problems, too, that he reflects—not least the fear caused by the atomic bomb—he goes further than any of the earlier poets, encompassing both Faroese and international perspectives.

The other outstanding poet of the same generation is Regin Dahl (1918–). He was born in the manse of Sandagerði, the son of the hymn-writer and dean Jákup Dahl (1878–1944) and thus a member of an already established cultural family. He went to school in Tórshavn and then to Sorø Academy in Denmark. After studying literature at the University of Copenhagen, he entered the publishing house of Wivel, moving later to Gyldendal as a publisher's reader and consultant.

Different as they are, it is natural to juxtapose Regin Dahl and Karsten Hoydal, both of whom represent the transition from the classical tradition as represented by the brothers Djurhuus to the modern poetry of Europe at large. But whereas Hoydal's writing is clearly related to the older tradition, though no longer forming part of it, Dahl moves away from it more quickly and more radically.

Apart from a few prose pieces printed in *Varðin*, Dahl first went into print in 1937 with the collection of poems entitled *Í útlegd* (In Exile), reflecting the voluntary exile's longing for his native land. Even these poems by an eighteen-year-old show signs of a new treatment of poetic language, with their indifference to rhyme and scansion. So, too, do the poems in *Tok-kaljóð* (1944; Love Poems) with their optimistic tone, despite the ravages of war, of which Dahl was well aware. Nevertheless, the song is characteristic of Dahl's early work, showing a direct inheritance from H. A. Djurhuus.

In his early poems Dahl is optimistic, seeing the world in light colors, seeking to avoid the angst and the pessimism with which he is surrounded, looking for solace in love:

A wonder in my hands:
middle and thigh
marigold-smooth—
and close to my ear
your voice buxomly
ecstatically muttering.

Eyes shut,
nostrils quivering
and mouth open
until I close it
until we close
again in a hard grip.

A wonder in my hands:
trunk and turned hip—
and sea scent
and roar
unceasing, unceasing.
(Tr. George Johnston)

Nevertheless, he quickly assumes darker overtones under the influence of world events, and these change the nature of his otherwise optimistic poetry, to the extent that the term *demonization* has been used to describe his visions. By 1966 his idyllic pictures are couched in threatening terms: increasingly the idyll becomes a nonidyll in its hopelessness:

Where shall I hide you,
my child?
Air and water,
earth and maggots:
filled with poison,
my child.
("Orðakumlar" [Word Cairns], 1978)

Whereas Hoydal expresses his concerns regarding the dangers facing humankind indirectly, Dahl puts his fears in much more direct, even drastic, language. He is nevertheless not a political writer, properly speaking, but he is aware of suffering and the threats hanging over the modern world, and these are reflected in his visions and metaphors.

If the contents of Dahl's poems can be said to betoken a break with a more solemn past, so, too, does his use of language. He experiments with new rhythms, ignores established conceptions of syntax and line length, introduces drastic new terms, and uses new compounds and word combinations. He experiments, too, with an associative technique hitherto virtually unknown in Faroese. One result is poems of great concentration, lines pregnant with meaning despite their shortness, lines that have been compared with the poetry of the ancient North, and yet poems far removed from the modern, national-romantic tradition that had established itself in the Faroe Islands. That Dahl has learnt from Old Icelandic poetry can scarcely be doubted, any more than it can be doubted that he has roots in his Faroese predecessors. By dint of his work as a publisher's reader, however, he has throughout been aware of, and doubtless influenced by, the mainstream of modern Danish and European poetry and must stand as one whose contribution was to bring Faroese literature a step further into the modern age.

An interesting, though slightly anomalous, figure of the same generation as Karsten Hoydal and Regin Dahl is Valdemar Poulsen (1909–). Despite a brief period in Denmark after he had completed his schooling in Tórshavn, Poulsen is a Tórshavner through and through. He did not go on to take any form of secondary or tertiary education, and he spent his working life as a hairdresser in his home town. In this role he came into contact with a large proportion of the population and had ample opportunity to exploit his own powers of observation—of both character and social situation. It was not until the 1950s that Poulsen began writing, publishing some of his early efforts in *Varðin* under the name of Vilhelm S. Poulsen, and it was only in 1961 that he published his first book, *Meðan havaldan dúrar* (While the Wave Slumbers), a volume of stories and short essays.

That same year he also published a play, *Sat sapienti* (A Word to the Wise Is Enough), which had already been performed in the Tórshavn Theater in 1958. Provision for drama in the Faroe Islands has always been limited to amateur production, apart from the Tórshavn Sjónleikurhúsið (theater) with its mixture of amateur and professional actors. Consequently, relatively little drama has been written in Faroese, so Poulsen's play was something of an event. Carefully set outside the Faroe Islands, it is a gentle satire on artistic snobbery. It raises the problem of sincerity and falsity in modern art, and insofar as the main character, Jeremias, has shown signs of originality but has been turned out of the school of art because his ideas did not coincide with those taught there, it becomes an attack on narrow-mindedness and short-sightedness in general. One suspects that the portrait of the gifted but unrecognized outsider reflects Poulsen's own position in the literary world of the Faroes.

The misunderstood outsider is at the center of Poulsen's major prose work, the novel *Osvald* (1978). A sensitive if fairly traditional realist novel, it nevertheless bears certain resemblances to the Norwegian Tarjei Vesaas's *Fuglane* (1957; The Birds). Like Vesaas's Matthis, Poulsen's Osvald is mentally retarded, and like the Jeremias of the play, he is rejected by society. Yet like Matthis, he, too, is sensitive and poetical and filled with natural human instincts and urges. Although only dyslexic, he is treated at school as stupid; he remains ignored, unwanted, mocked for his true poetic fancy. He falls in love with Karin, a girl much younger than himself. She shows sympathy and understanding for him, and in his imagination he fancies a happy future together with her. It is an impossible situation, however, and he finally commits suicide.

By the time *Osvald* was published, a younger generation of writers, sometimes of a more experimental bent, had overtaken Poulsen. His novel has thus been overshadowed in the popular mind, but it must nevertheless stand as one of the most penetrating psychological studies by any Faroese writer of Poulsen's generation. It is his only novel, though he has written numerous short stories, some in a mildly satirical vein. A selection was published in 1979 under the title of *Ein tíðarmynd* (A Picture of an Age). Poulsen has also written other dramas. When a Faroese radio service was established in 1961, he was one of the first to realize the potential of this new cultural medium, embarking on a series of plays written especially for radio.

If Poulsen became an anomaly through a late start to writing, the much younger Tummas Napoleon Djurhuus (1928–71) also occupies an anomalous position in that he stands as the last representative of Faroese neoromanticism, writing in an age of modernism. He was born in Kollafjørður and attended school in Tórshavn; he started university studies in Copenhagen but gave them up and took a teacher-training course in Tórshavn, spending his career as a teacher in the Tórshavn school. Apart from the humorous *Tættir og vísur* (1961; Ballads and Songs), which gained him great popularity, he published three volumes of poems, *Ung løg* (1951; Young Melodies), *Greinar* (1955; Branches), and *Og dansurin gongur* (1958; And the Dance Goes On). A selection of these poems was published in 1978 under title of *Yrkingar* (Poems).

His early poems are the typical romantic products of a young man: love poems, pictures of spring, and expressions of longing. The intensely personal nature of this volume gives way to a more generalized and somber vision, sometimes accompanied by a sense of angst in the second volume. The pictures of the Faroe Islands and the awareness of their history and culture both here and in the final volume are reminiscent both of the earlier Djurhuus brothers and, at times, of Christian Matras, whose cosmic awareness is also echoed. The awareness of death, never far away in Faroese writing, emerges in the title poem of *Og dansurin gongur*, with its image of the drowned dancing a Faroese chain dance on the shore.

Djurhuus should not, however, be dismissed merely as an echo of an outdated fashion. His language was, at a late stage, of a different type, and he was not averse to introducing foreign terms or loanwords such as "request program" or "radio receiver" into his work, sometimes quite demonstratively. There are signs that toward the end of his life he was gradually moving out of the traditional mode of expression.

CONTEMPORARY LITERATURE

It was a younger generation again that took the definitive step into modernism. The 1960s saw the emergence of a completely new kind of poetry in Faroese.

The oldest of these modernists is Steinbjørn Jacobsen (1937–). He was born in Sandvík and followed what was a normal course in the Faroe Islands: local schooling, a period at sea, and further studies in Denmark. He qualified as a teacher in 1963, and after holding various teaching posts in Denmark, he returned to the Faroes, where he has worked both as a teacher and, for ten years, as the principal of the Faroese folk high school.

His first volume of poems, *Heimkoma* (1966; Homecoming), showed clearly the new line he was taking. The themes were in themselves well known—the Faroese landscape, its wildlife, the everyday lives of village people—but they were dressed in a different garb, devoid of every superfluous concept. Faroese nature was reduced to its essentials and projected, rather than described, in unrhymed, unscanned verse, often in incomplete sentences. Yet the well-known Faroese preoccupation with cosmic perspectives and with the insignificance of the human in the totality of the universe is also present. Jacobsen's metaphors are already often intangible, and his use of associative techniques, learned from European modernist poetry at large, is new to Faroese.

The move toward greater concentration and still less formal syntax was yet more pronounced in the next volume, with the characteristic single-word title *Fræ* (1968; Seeds), in which the Japanese haiku makes its presence felt in poems of the utmost conciseness. The lines often consist of one word only, with no verb, a series of single realistic and nonidealized observations, with an intense awareness of sound: birdsong, oars in the water, the dripping of water.

Wind
on
window
on
glass
and
eye
rain.
(Tr. George Johnston)

In the 1970s Jacobsen took a more political stance, writing poems critical of the EEC and of Nordic social democracy, praising instead the more radical views represented by Rosa Luxemburg. A more general criticism of modern civilization is seen in poems illustrative of alienation and dealing with subjects such as pollution and the environment. And as humanity and society in the later poems replace the early pictures of nature, so, too, the poems adopt a less concise form.

In *Lív* (1981; Life), subtitled "Ognað øllum ið missa" (To All Who Have Suffered Loss), Jacobsen departs from his previous pattern. These poems were inspired by the death of his child in an accident and are the direct expression of loss and the struggle to overcome it. They are straightforward and unadorned, expressive of dignified sorrow, and their value is in their simplicity.

As a dramatist Jacobsen excels in one-act social satires, often with a political edge to them. Some are little more than political and social discussions. The year 1975 saw the performance of the longer *Skipið* (The Ship), the first stage presentation of a trawlerman's life, arguing that insufficient attention is paid to trawlermen by a society ungrateful for their contribution to its well-being. The play was published in 1982, the same year as *Tey bæði í húsinum* (The Two at Home), whose subject is modern married life and the urge to earn money.

Four years younger than Jacobsen, and in her modernism a total contrast to him, is Guðrið Helmsdal Nielsen (1941–), the first woman in the Faroes to publish a volume of poetry (in 1961), one of the first to appear in the modernist vein. Born in Tórshavn, Helmsdal moved to Denmark at the age of twelve, not settling in the Faroes again until 1967 and consequently more Danicized than many other Faroese writers. She has written poems in Danish as well as Faroese, and there are hints of a cultural clash in her work. Showing her links with the neoromantic and symbolist poetry from the turn of the century, her main source of inspiration is the early Fenno-Swedish modernist Edith Södergran. In form the poems in her first collection, *lýtt lot* (1963; mild breeze), are heavy with symbolism, while those in the second volume, *Morgun í mars* (1971; Morning in March), are unassuming but sensitive, at times almost ethereal. Like others of her generation, she seeks to combine simplicity with expressiveness, and here, too, we find the compactness of the haiku:

> Morning
> in March
>
> my heart—
> an oystercatcher—
>
> flies
> to you

In her inspiration from Södergran, Helmsdal Nielsen reflects an early stage of the modernist movement in Scandinavia. Others, such as Arnbjørn Danielsen (1947–1980), Heðin Klein (1950–), and Alexandur Kristiansen (1950–), move into far more radical forms. Arnbjørn Danielsen was cosmopolitan in his outlook, leaving behind the Faroese landscape and concerning himself with impressions of urban life and with broader problems of the third world and the Vietnam War. Heðin Klein has published two volumes of concentrated allusive poetry, *Væmingar og vaggandi gjálv* (1969; Nausea and Rolling Sea) and *Strandvarp* (1983; Flotsam). Alexandur Kristiansen began as a disciple of Janus Djurhuus but later moved into an experimental stage at times reminiscent of the Danish "concrete poets," not least thanks to his play with typography and his highly developed associative technique. In this approach he is followed by the younger Carl Johan Jensen (1957–), who combines demanding metaphor with unusually concentrated allusions to classical literature.

The generation of the 1960s, with its anarchic rejection of established values, is most typically represented in the work of Rói Reynegard Patursson (1947–). Patursson's career resembles that of many of his colleagues: school in Tórshavn followed, at the age of sixteen, by a period at sea. He spent a year in Iceland and traveled around Europe before going to

Copenhagen to complete his schooling and to study philosophy at the university.

Although he published his first poem at the age of thirteen, it was 1969 before his first, untitled, volume of fifteen poems appeared. It has been suggested that the lack of title is intended to avoid forcing any interpretation of the poems on the reader, thus underlining the modernist stance of the poet. These poems introduce new themes and attitudes into Faroese poetry, some with erotic contents, some with social-political contents, and some with the desire to break out of established patterns. The presentation is new, too, even if perhaps "Býurin (og reklaman i glugganum)" (The City [and the Advertisement in the Window]) contains an echo of Christian Matras's "Hitt blinda liðið":

> I stopped,
> heard their walk this evening
> like yesterday
> and tomorrow.
> A thousand blind people
> from factories and offices
> weary and tired
> they pass the picture
> in the window
> that condemns and tempts.

Patursson's further progress into modernist poetry is clearly charted in his second volume, *Á alfarvegi* (1976; On the Highway). The first poems date from before the previous volume but are followed by others that are far more radical in their use of language and association and whose contents express increasingly left-wing political views. Patursson's anarchical opinions are echoed in an impious use of Faroese, completely disregarding the established usage of the purists:

> golgotha colgate goethe
> petrol stench & napalm god
> weekday
> get on
> love after work has finished
> but we are alive

The third volume, for which Patursson was awarded the Nordic Council's Prize for Literature, appeared in 1986 with the title *Líkasum* (As If). The anarchic language has been toned down, but the linguistic and associative complexity still exists, while the subtle effect is often achieved by means of contrast and juxtaposition. The overall implication is the need to reexperience and reinterpret accustomed things. The title of the first of the seven sections into which the book is divided, "Ein spegilsmynd af síni tíð" (A Mirror Image of the Age), is, in its own ambiguity, a fitting motto for the volume as a whole.

While the general development of European poetry in the mid-twentieth century is reflected in the work of some individual Faroese poets, the prose of a younger generation has since the 1950s been dominated by one figure, Jens Pauli Heinesen (1932–). Born in Sandavágur, Heinesen is the son of a farmer. He attended school in his own village, leaving at the age of fourteen to take an office job in Tórshavn. He returned to school, subsequently moving to Copenhagen, where he trained as a teacher. He returned to the Faroe Islands in 1957 but in 1968 gave up his career in teaching to devote himself to full-time activities as an author.

Heinesen was from an early age eager to write, but he found little encouragement in his immediate circle, either in Sandavágur or in Tórshavn. In Tórshavn he became a close friend of Tummas Napoleon Djurhuus and the journalist and founder of the Faroese Society of Authors, Ólavur Michelsen (1933–76), the three constituting as near a literary clique as is encountered in the Faroes. Heinesen began to publish sporadically in periodicals but attracted little attention. When in 1953 he collected his prose in a volume entitled *Degningsælið* (The Dawn Shower), that, too, met with virtually total silence, the only review being by Karsten Hoydal. In succeeding years he continued to be met by silence and distrust, for, much as he was indebted to earlier Faroese writers, his approach was a different one: his was neither the nostalgic, evocative picture of earlier times such as he found in Heðin Brú, nor William Heinesen's mixture of fantasy and satire. Instead, he was presenting in a drastically modern language a realistic picture of a country emerging from the romanticized idyll of the past into the far more dangerous world of the present. Certainly, both Hedin Brú and Martin Joensen portrayed the social changes of the 1930s, but such tensions and conflicts as they reflected were internal to the islands, and there is little in the way of international perspective. William Heinesen in *Den sorte Gryde* paints a picture of the Faroes under British occupation during World War II, but the emphasis is still on sectarian and social conflicts within the Faroese community. Jens Pauli Heinesen confronted the Faroe Islands with their own situation vis-à-vis the international community. He was the first to do so, and he was not understood.

In view of Heinesen's originally cool reception and the skepticism expressed toward his ambitions as a writer, it is not surprising that one of the problems to be confronted was, and still is, the role and position of the writer in society. This theme, together with the confrontational problem, is at the center of Heinesen's first novel, *Yrkjarin úr Selvík* (1958; The Poet from Selvík). There is a good deal of self-presentation in the portrait of Bjarni, the central figure in the novel. He is a poet whose work is well received but who cannot establish himself in his own society or come to terms with those around him. It is not just a treatment in the manner of Thomas Mann of the role of the artist in society, however, much as Heinesen admits his indebtedness to Mann. It also reflects the dichotomy between traditional Faroese values and those of the modern world in the juxtaposition of Bjarni's native village of Selvík, where life is lived in the traditional pattern, and Bernavágur, where life is increasingly modernized, commercialized, obsessed with material values, and, having lost the harmony on which its identity is based, prone to sectarianism.

Four years later, in 1962, Heinesen published the first part of the three-volume novel *Tú upphavsins heimur* (1962–66; World of Origin). Here, too, in a novel that combines the realist tradition with the humanist concerns of an Albert Camus, Heinesen seeks to confront the Faroes with the dangers implicit in moving from an idyllic but untenable way of life into a dynamic present. Baltasar Buch-Olesen returns from abroad to his native village, the unspoilt Leirun, and undertakes its rejuvenation. Superficially, he succeeds, though in doing so he alienates the villagers from their traditional culture and brings about a decline in their standards and an acceptance of fanaticism. Finally, the attempt to create what is in fact a fascist state within the state fails. Nevertheless, the concern of the author with the perspectives of fanaticism, brutality, and narrow dogmatism is clear and can scarcely have been lost on a society that in 1907 had given in to sectarian demands for the prohibition of alcohol in the Faroe Islands and where fanatical sectarianism was still rampant. The picture presented is that of the death of a harmonious culture and its replacement with a new society in which human and cultural values are trodden underfoot. It is a warning to the Faroese about the dangers of fascism.

So, too, is the next major novel, *Frænir eitur ormurin* (1973; Frænir Is the Serpent's Name). The overall title and the individual section titles all refer to the medieval ballad "Sjúrðar kvæði" (The Ballad of Sigurd), the Faroese version of Sigurd the Dragon Slayer, with the implied conflict between good and evil. It is not, however, a mere retelling of the ballad in modern garb. Just as in *Tú upphavsins heimur* Heinesen implanted a fascist regime within the Faroe Islands, so here he introduces a Tórshavn in the grip of a fascist organization, Frænir, led by one Tíðrikkur Tíðriksen.

Once more Heinesen has confronted the Faroes with the vision of dictatorship. Once more he speaks out in the cause of freedom, rejecting both the fascism of Tíðriksen and the communism with which the central character, Guðmundur, originally tries to oppose him. That Guðmundur has the author's sympathy is clear, and his ultimate defeat seems to signal concern that idealistic humanism is vulnerable in its own lack of ideology.

Frænir eitur ormurin has a Faroese setting, but the theme of the confrontation of extremes and the vulnerability of idealism has universal validity. Like William Heinesen before him, Jens Pauli Heinesen is here seeking to make the Faroe Islands a point of departure in a novel of wider significance. At the same time, there is an implied preoccupation with the Faroe Islands in their confrontation with the modern world, vulnerable to extremes of political view and, in their way, naively idealistic.

There is a clear affinity of theme in the two novels, and as if to underline this likeness, they are introduced in similar ways. *Tú upphavsins heimur* has as its first chapter a bold and violent description of a traditional Faroese whale hunt, with the sea running red with blood, while *Frænir eitur ormurin* introduces an equally brutal description of a Spanish bullfight at an early stage. Both are intended to represent the brutality of conflict and the vulnerability of the innocent.

Although the next major work, a novel cycle subtitled with the almost Proustian "Á ferð inn í eina oendaliga søgu" (1980–; On the Way Into an Unending Story), is different in kind, it, too, is introduced by an allegory pointing to the essential meaning of the book. The child Hugin, the central character, is carried into the mountains by a mythical woman wearing a white headscarf, the representative of the ideal, or of art, and is left there by her, to be found two days later by a worried village community. He has been both afraid and attracted by this figure with her constantly repeated "Come with me," and the combination of fear and attraction runs through his being throughout the novel cycle.

A modern version of the novel of development, the cycle traces the career of Hugin from his earliest days. We see his childhood and experience events through his eyes; we watch his growth from innocence to a sensitive maturity, and we watch him subjected to conflicting impulses, ever questioning, always seeking the answer to human personality and human actions. As in the earlier novels the innocent can be subjected to persecution, as when the musician Gøran settles in the village and is finally unjustly accused of having seduced the twelve-year-old Duruta, or when the sensitive Gutti becomes prey to Hans Kristian's jealousy and is finally driven to suicide when Hans Kristian sends a poison letter accusing him of homosexuality.

The first chapter of the sixth novel, *Í andgletti* (1988; Exposed to the Wind), is a prolonged consideration of how a human being becomes what he or she is, an examination of the significance of childhood experience. Like the soot hanging in the chimney in the psychological allegory by Christian Matras, "Sótrøll (Flakes of Soot), which has given the chapter its title, these experiences persist in their significance and cannot be removed. This seems to be the key to an understanding of the work as a whole so far. Other themes in the novel are well known from Heinesen's earlier work. Hugin is a poet, a writer, and must face the problem of a writer's role and position in society, not least when he is subjected to misunderstanding and mockery. One of his critics is the convinced Stalinist Hildibrandur, who ironically subsequently loses his faith and is unable to cope when robbed of his unquestioning acceptance of an ideology. And in its alternation between the Faroe Islands and Copenhagen, this work also reflects the dichotomy between Faroese tradition and the modern world.

In addition to these major novels Heinesen has written the shorter and less demanding *Rekamaðurin* (1977; The Beachcomber) and *Tey telgja sær gudar* (1979; They Carve Themselves Images) and is in addition a short-story writer of high standing. In his short stories he is able to explore the themes that he develops fully in the major novels. In particular he is a master in portraying children, both in their innocent play and in their confrontation with a grim reality. The volume *Tann gátufóri kærleikin* (1986; Mysterious Love) is, with its examination of different kinds of love, much closer to his novel cycle in its undogmatic examination of the mysteries of human nature.

Overall, Heinesen's work deals, on various levels, with the theme of the fall from innocence. He excels in depicting the child whose innocence is undermined. The innocence of the child is paralleled by that of the country faced by the modern world and, in its process of adaptation, prone to oppression and exploitation. There is no nostalgic longing for a lost paradise, fond as some of the portraits are, but a realistic presentation of the current situation. That the country most immediately concerned is the Faroe Islands should not obscure the wider significance of the problem and its treatment.

Stylistically, Heinesen betokens both a continuation and a renewal of the realistic novel technique. He is more radical in his linguistic usage than any other Faroese before him, spurning the efforts of the purists and happily employing a distinctly modern, international vocabulary. His descriptions of milieu and rural life are clearly in the tradition of Heðin Brú and Martin Joensen, but his Tórshavn is both Tórshavn and not Tórshavn, a slightly nightmarish presentation of a recognizable reality. His presentation of character owes much, on his own admission, to Thomas Mann and Sigrid Und-set, but here, too, he goes further and moves into the realm of *style indirecte libre* and Joycean stream of consciousness. Yet at the same time, he can also appear as the almost old-fashioned omniscient author, blithely presenting the thoughts of one character after another, alternating with swift changes of point of view. Above all, he creates his own myth with obvious implications far beyond the immediate action and surroundings.

There are no obvious successors to Jens Pauli Heinesen. Younger prose writers have put in an appearance, but none has embarked on a major novel. Gunnar Hoydal (1941–), the son of Karsten Hoydal, was born in Copenhagen and moved to the Faroe Islands after the war. With his parents he spent time in Ecuador and later became city architect in Tórshavn. As coeditor with Steinbjørn Jacobsen of *Varðin* from 1976 to 1981 and as chairman of the Faroese Society of Authors he played an important part in promoting Faroese literature in the 1970s and 1980s. In 1982 he himself published a collection of short stories (some of which had appeared individually before) under the title *Á longum leiðum* (On Far-Flung Paths). Written in a sensitive prose, they are part essay, part short story, accounts of meetings and experiences in many parts of the world and at many stages of life, from the first trip to Copenhagen as a child to adult journeys around the world. The first story's description of a Faroese child's visit to his grandmother in Copenhagen has something of Jens Pauli Heinesen's confrontation of two worlds about it. The final account of the author's school days in Denmark brings Gunnar Hoydal back to the childhood that was his point of departure.

Hanus Andreassen (1942–) has produced two volumes of short stories: *Dottir av Proteus* (1980; Daughter of Proteus) and *Við tenðradum lyktum* (1982; When the Lamps Are Lit). Both are concerned with human relations, the first predominantly with missed opportunities, the second with opportunities seized and the problems of conscience that sometimes result. They contain a strong erotic element, an unusual feature of Faroese literature, and some are sharply satirical.

Carl Johan Jensen, already referred to for his poetry, published a long novella entitled *Seinnapartur* (Afternoon) in 1979. It reflects the youth of the 1970s, to which he himself belongs, and is distinguished by its uninhibited use of modern linguistic expression.

The quality novel for children and young people enjoyed a period of intense interest in the 1970s and 1980s. Both Jens Pauli Heinesen and Steinbjørn Jacobsen have written in this genre. Others include Jens Pauli Heinesen's wife, Maud Heinesen (1936–), and Marianna Debes Dahl (1947–).

In the space of little more than a century Faroese literature has progressed from the well-intentioned but often unsophisticated efforts of amateurs to the highly professional writing found throughout Europe. The number of publications is small, but relative to the size of population—at present about forty-two thousand—one of the highest in the world. The size of the population, however, has created problems for those wishing to publish large-scale works, and the predominance of the poem and the short story is undoubtedly partly a result. Few Faroese authors have tried to live by their pens, and even the most successful have, for the most part, had writing as a hobby or sideline. The periodical *Varðin* has been of inestimable value as a vehicle for both original writing and literary criticism, a role that it maintains, together with the more recent *Brá* (Glance). The Christmas annuals, too, have provided outlets, as have many more ephemeral periodical publications and the daily newspapers. Those writers who have wished to publish their works in book form have had to finance the undertaking themselves (a very common practice) or turn to one of the small publishing ventures. There are now several small companies publishing Faroese literature, but without doubt the greatest contribution to the preservation of classical Faroese literature has been made by the Bókagarður publishing house under the leadership of Emil Thomsen. It is this company that has published modern editions of the collected works of Heðin Brú, Martin Joensen, and Christian Matras, as well as the works of some of the pioneers of early Faroese literature. Without its efforts much of the central core of Faroese literature would be available only in libraries.

The century spanned by modern Faroese literature has been a time of national awakening during which the Faroe Islands have developed from being a closed country (the monopoly was abandoned in 1856), through varying degrees of integration into Denmark (for a time as a county), to having a large measure of independence. It is not surprising, therefore, that national sentiment is one of the hallmarks of the literature: a romantic longing for an unspoiled country, felt especially by those who have been abroad, and a determination to assert the strength of the Faroese language, which for centuries played a subordinate role to Danish. Faroese literature has been intensely Faroese, aimed at a people who were zealous in expressing their Faroese character, and only a small number of its writers have looked beyond the borders of the islands. Nevertheless, some of the best have used the Faroe Islands as their focal point, but have given their work a perspective reaching far beyond the setting. They have succeeded in combining a Faroese character with an international outlook, parochialism with universality. It is in this combination that Faroese literature has reached its highest achievement.

Danish and Faroese Women Writers

Faith Ingwersen

9

Modern feminist study of Scandinavian literature has lasted for several de-cades—maybe it should be dated to the Red Stocking days of the late 1960s and early 1970s—and thus it may seem parochial to include a special chapter on women writers in a volume like this one. Why are the woman writers not integrated into the general discussion of Danish literature? They are, of course, represented in that study. It should be noted, however, that even if several feminist scholars were intricately involved in writing a Danish liter-ary history of the 1980s—the nine-volume *Dansk litteraturhistorie* (History of Danish Literature)—there is still an ongoing Nordic project called "Nor-disk Kvindelitteraturhistorie" (Nordic History of Women's Literature). It seems, then, that whether editors integrate the women authors or separate them, as Stig Dalager and Anne-Mari Mai have so ably managed in *Danske kvindelige forfattere* (1982; Danish Women Writers), the choice will call forth criticism. The decision to attempt both in the present work is not a wishy-washy compromise, but the effect of the desire to include women writers in the historical charting of Danish literature and simultaneously ad-mit that the creative conditions for women who wanted to write were differ-ent enough from those of male authors that a separate treatment of them is necessary.

Another reason for adding a separate chapter on women writers is that the feminist movement has achieved that pluralism (sometimes distinguish-ing between *feminist*, *feminine*, and *female*) that spurs disagreements among critics who have the same cause at heart. The ongoing debate as to whether or not it is possible to speak of a special female aesthetics cannot be resolved here. The very fact, however, that the issue is not resolved requires that special attention be given to the voices of women throughout Danish literary history.

THE ORAL TRADITIONS

It is necessary to consider the voices of women not only in written works but also from the age-old oral tradition; those voices echo from premedieval oral tradition through the nineteenth century, when the stories began to be recorded, to the early twentieth century. Earlier, folklorists did not concern themselves with the gender of either the storyteller or the listener, but it has recently been thought useful and necessary to operate with distinctions between so-called female and male narratives. Of course, the tales of old naturally cannot be divided into two rigid groups, for most tales may be related by both sexes with equal ease and delight.

The folktales, especially in the form of the "magic tale," often feature a female protagonist whose development from childhood through arduous trials, which constitute a rite of passage, brings her to maturity and "happiness ever after." In such magic tales as "Kong Hvidbjørn" (King Whitebear), "Den hvide and" (The White Duck), and "Den stumme dronning" (The Mute Queen) the woman is a decidedly active and resourceful protagonist. Initially, she may be passive, but she turns into a person who competently forges her own destiny. The materials collected from oral tradition in Jutland by Evald Tang Kristensen in the last third of the nineteenth century demonstrate that women were often eloquent storytellers who preserved, transmitted, and thereby altered the tales into variants that reflected their values and attitudes. Storytellers both transmit and cocreate their narratives, and those often ancient stories inevitably became vehicles for the female storytellers' experiences, hopes, and perhaps—in the spirit of their Old Nordic ancestresses—even their prophecies.

Although the folktale is difficult to date, the ballad—of which Denmark has one of Europe's richest and largest collections—is normally considered to be a late medieval genre, but one with a long afterlife, dealing predominantly with the lives of the aristocracy in feudal Denmark. The first collectors, and possible editors, were women of noble birth: Karen Brahe, Sofia Sandberg, and Ida Gjøe, who recorded the ballads in the late 1500s. Whether the ballad's voice is that of "woman" is impossible to resolve, but many a ballad features as one of its central characters a woman who is neither pliant nor passive, even if it is very clear that the feudal society of the time forced women into some quite well-defined roles. Marriages were often arranged to further alliances between nations or mighty families, and women were expected to live up to the roles prescribed for them. The hapless fiancée in "Ebbe Skammelsøn" may be seen as the victim of just such a rigid role, and young Dagmar in "Dronning Dagmar og Junker Strange" (Queen Dagmar and Sir Strange) must realize that the joys of youth are over and that she now must take up the repressibilities being bestowed on her as she is about to marry the king of Denmark—a union that has been negotiated between her parents and the Danish intermediary.

A few ballads express a female point of view. In the dramatic and bloody "Herr Ebbes Døtre" (Sir Ebbe's Daughters) two violated young women refuse to live with their shame or to commit suicide to wash away that shame but take revenge in kind: at church they slay with their own hands the two brothers who gleefully planned and carried out the rape. The last lines of the ballad record satisfaction that the blood of the slain brothers now runs down the aisle. It should be noted that although the father of the two women returns home from the Holy Land and with horror realizes what has happened, they, not he, take the revenge that the contemporary code of honor required.

In the humorous "Møens Morgendrømme" (The Maiden's Morning Dreams) and "Jomfruen paa Tinge" (The Maiden at the Assembly), women see their wishes come true. In the former a young woman dreams that she will marry the king of Wenden. In spite of her wrathful stepmother's attempts to prevent that glorious fate from coming about, her dream is fulfilled—with, in some variants, the added touch that her future husband, in appreciation of the power of her dream, readily permits her to sleep late every day. If this socially successful young woman may seem a passive recipient of a nicely preordained destiny, the protagonist of "Jomfruen paa Tinge" is decidedly a woman who has taken her future into her own hands. When the king is surprised to see a woman at the all-male judicial gathering, he requests an explanation, and the answer he gets is loaded with meaning: "She is here to review your men." The maiden has been forced to come up with a tricky plan, which, on request, she quite willingly reveals to the king: her father and mother have died, and she is being exploited by her kin. Thus, she wants to give her land to the king, with the expectation that he will return it to her as her fief and, in accordance with the custom of the feudal system, appoint an overseer who must marry her. She cleverly uses the system of the day to her own ends. The king quite willingly plays along and, as she expected, asks her which knight she wants. It seems that the maiden and the king understand each other very well, and both enjoy the game they are playing. That, however, is not true of the man she picks, who pleads to be allowed to continue his life as a carefree man of the world. He is admonished to change his ways, to start learning to work for a living, and—quite simply—to assume the responsibility of a husband. The conclusion of the ballad suggests that all is going well.

The comedy found in such ballads, in the otherwise often bleak ballad universe, offers relief from those many texts in which human beings seem to have little recourse against destiny. In many ballads, however, women react strongly against the lives that seem to be determined for them. They may take revenge; they may commit suicide in protest against their miserable fates, such as the woman who, in "Ridderens Runeslag" (The Knight's Casting of Runes), is made a pawn by two knights in a cruel game; and they may fight, valiantly if futilely, against the fate that would deny them happiness. The reaction on the part of the mother and the betrothed in "Germand Gladensvend" (Germand Gladenswain) suggests the strength of their determination. Germand's mother fights fate to the point of religious perjury, in denying her son's existence to the demon to whom, as an unborn babe, he was involuntarily promised; and his betrothed, as he prepares to leave for his final encounter with the demon, also readies herself for battle with the demon, whom in some variants she manages to kill, albeit too late, and in others, true to the bleak fatalism of the genre, she never finds.

Whether or not the women in the ballads succeed, they show their resentment over having the course of their lives determined without their consent, and they often attempt to take charge of their fates. Their possible success may not be the point to stress in this context—since the males in the ballads find themselves in the same predicament and since both sexes may find defeat to be more common than victory—but the female characters in the ballads do seem, more often than the male, to be granted the dignity of rebellion against unfair destinies.

The influence of Christian teachings on the ballads may seem scant (as is the case in most ancient folklore), but simultaneously with the ballads, a learned tradition of clerical poetry praising the Virgin Mary made its way to Denmark. The prominence of the cult surrounding that figure is difficult to determine, but its very existence suggests that there was a need for a maternal goddess who would show the charity that male deities seemed unwilling to grant. The austere Christianity of the late medieval period may have called for the importation of the merciful mother of Christ to Scandinavian regions. The Lutheran Reformation of the early 1500s, however, put a stop to any such worship of *Madonna Mater*.

The Reformation brought about the unity of monarchy and state church. Martin Luther's *Cathechismus* (1529) strongly enforced the idea of honoring authority figures, and within the family structure, given elevated, noble status in Lutheran theology, those were the males. Among the ordinary people living in rural areas, women were brought up within the family unit to perpetuate that attitude. They were "educated" to become wives, which meant many childbirths and much hard work, but contemporary sources indicate that such a life of chores and duties was nevertheless considered a sign of good luck. Whenever childbirth did not slow her down, the farmer's wife had to bake, brew, weave, sew, garden, and tend to the stables—to mention just a few of her chores. She was, however, not living in a "doll's house," and her partnership and work were essential and may well have therefore granted her not only a measure of respect but also some sense of equality. That sense is perhaps reflected in some of the folktales, but in those, too, it is apparent that the ideal is marriage, not single status. During the late medieval period and the following years—all the centuries leading up to our own—matrimony was considered the proper goal for human beings of both genders.

The educational system of the day was meant for the boys of the middle classes. So-called Latin schools—the high schools of the day—instructed their students in the classics. Those schools, which were promoted by the powerful new Lutheran state church, produced young men who would serve Crown and Church well as future ministers and, consequently, as moral judges of their parishioners. The Reformation sped up the king's effort to centralize feudal society, an undertaking that saw its final fruition in the establishment of the absolute monarchy in 1660. The centralization of all administration meant, in addition, a streamlining to the point of conformity of the ways people thought about anything of significance, including their gender roles.

In contrast to average women, the daughters of the aristocracy were not excluded from education, even if it was given to them under special conditions by female relatives and carefully chosen male tutors. An impressive number of those women engaged in cultural endeavors, not often as creative spirits, which at the time would hardly have been possible, but as translators (especially of religious texts), family historians, or editors. Some of the women were, or by their own efforts became, very learned and had achieved a consummate knowledge of the classical and present-day languages of Europe.

Karen Brahe (1657–1736) established an impressive library of Danish literature, which is still preserved. It was Mette Gjøe (1599–1664), a descendant of one of the recorders of the ballads, who in 1657 published an anthology of thirty ballads with a title that indicated her astute perception of the world view of the Danish ballad: *Tragica*. Birgitte Thott (1610–62) made her mark as an interloper among men, for she was proficient in six languages, including Hebrew. She was a highly competent translator of texts from antiquity, and her crowning accomplishment was her rendition of Seneca into a splendidly lucid Danish, in a text comprising more than nine hundred pages. In her preface to that work (publ. 1658), the major translation accomplishment of the seventeenth century, Thott voices a program that suggests—or rather demands—that women be given the same opportunities for education as men and not be held back by male prejudice. It might seem as if she were objecting to a male-oriented concept of what was manly or womanly (a concept that valued Latin above the mother tongue, sight above sound, thought or monologue above talk or dialogue, object above word, analysis above rhetoric, the pure above the erotic, and a clean, "manly" style above the decorative), one that would divide the sexes even more than hitherto had been the case. The division may not have seemed particularly threatening to those who resided at the very pinnacle of the strict, hierarchical world of the absolute monarchy, for they rarely shared in the beliefs of those below them on the social ladder.

Such a preeminent figure was Leonora Christina (1621–98), a daughter of King Christian IV who, because of her husband's condemnation for treason, spent twenty-two years in prison. Her journal, *Jammers Minde* (1869; Eng. tr. *Memoirs of Leonora Christina,* 1929), was written in a direct, narrative style that, oral in tone, was meant to be a record of the victimization of an innocent person. The memoirs reveal a woman who is determined not to allow others to shake her sense of selfhood. Although the work was not intended for publication, Leonora exhibits an author's sense of structure and of stylistic devices. Among her other writings only the first part of the ambitious *Hæltinders pryd* (publ. 1977; Heroines' Adornment) exists. It deals with women's contribution to history, demonstrating their natural equality with men with regard to common sense, the ability to learn, the wisdom to govern oneself, and the authority to rule.

Dorothe Engelbretsdatter (1634–1716), born in Norway, was the first published female poet. Her baroque hymns, published under the titles *Sielens Sangoffer* (1678; The Soul's Sacrifice in Song) and *Taare-Offer* (1685; Sacrifice of Tears), were enormously popular in the double realm of Denmark-Norway. With a sure grip on baroque rhetorical techniques she eloquently shows the soul in a state of penitence and dutiful acceptance of fate. In the baroque tradition also belongs Anna Margrethe Lasson (1659–1738), who wrote the first "original" novel in Danish, *Den beklædte Sandhed* (ca. 1715, publ. 1723; The Disguised Truth), in which a love story became the central element of the plot.

REASON AND SENTIMENT

With the rise of rationalistic thought, authority was more likely to be challenged than during times of dogmatic Lutheranism. That becomes obvious in the plays of Ludvig Holberg (1684–1754), in which ironic and savvy women mock and question male authority. Especially Holberg's servants, the many Henriks and Pernilles of a series of comedies, have a healthy lack of respect for the often foolish authority in the strict, quite feudally structured household and are allowed the delightful tasks of giving the fools their comeuppance and putting the world to rights for the sincere young lovers. With his *Heltinders sammenlignede Historier* (1745; Comparative Stories of Heroines) Holberg picked up where Leonora had left off and depicted resourceful women in European history, including Leonora Christina.

Among Holberg's successors, vying for the popularity that Holberg had enjoyed, were two women: Anna Catharina von Passow (1731–57) and Charlotte Dorothea Biehl (1731–88). The former, who was of noble birth, used a pseudonym and was an actress during her youthful years. After her marriage and abandonment of performing on stage, she turned playwright, and her *Elskov- eller Kierligheds-Feyl* (1757; Passion; or, The Problem with Love), a rococo play featuring shepherds and shepherdesses, brought emotional, "sensitive" taste to the Danish stage. The translation of Samuel Richardson's *Pamela* (1740) between 1743 and 1746 suggests that the rising bourgeoisie's concerns with the tender heart and female virtue were leaving early rationalism's common sense and wry irony behind.

That change is very obvious in the work of Charlotte Biehl, whose early popularity with *Den kierlige Mand* (1764; The Loving Husband) made some crown her as the possible successor to Holberg. The play shows how a virtuous and considerate husband manages to show his wife that she is taking an unnatural pleasure in the superficial party life of Copenhagen. Instead of asserting his authority and commanding her to stay home and take care of their child—as a gruff, old-fashioned friend tells him to do—he cleverly tricks her into seeing that she has been neglecting her true loves and duties. The fictional characters of the age, women and men, may be sensitive, loving people, but they are rarely very humorous. Thus, in Biehl's work elaborate emoting and stylized declarations of the heart took the place of the witty repartees of Holberg's comedies.

Biehl's sentimental plays—they were called comedies—may not be possible to put on stage outside their own period of popularity, but their emotionalism and pretentious view of human relationships reflect, in a revealing manner, the norms of the quickly rising bourgeoisie. *Den listige Optrækkerske* (1765; The Cunning Extortionist), in which there appears a new woman— a deceiver of men—aroused discussion, for the opposite of the virtuous woman was found to be unusually fascinating. In Biehl's five-volume *Moralske Fortællinger* (1781–82; Moral Stories) she objects to the unrestrained passion of Johann Wolfgang von Goethe's *Die Leiden des jungen Werthers* (1774; The Sorrows of Young Werther) and its imitations, and advocates self-discipline, thus suggesting boundaries for the newly released sentiments. Biehl's autobiography, *Mit ubetydelige Levnets Sløb* (1787; My Unimportant Course of Life), a title that would never have occurred to Leonora Christina, brings the reader much closer to the author than did Leonora's work.

The age of sentiment, as shown by the autobiography of Johannes Ewald (1743–81), *Levnet og Meeninger* (written 1773–77, publ. 1804–8; Life and Opinions), was much more confessional than the preceding ones, partly because the modern individualist—another result of the rise of the bourgeoisie—was emerging, one who found it legitimate to research "the soul." Biehl's autobiography touchingly describes her early battles not only to educate herself, against her father's adamant prohibition (he even had her books locked up when he once found her secretly reading), but also to create a life for herself within the narrow range her father would allow. In Biehl's works there is a yearning to allow the heart to speak freely, but that yearning is checked. In spite of the artifice and wordiness of the age, it seems as if two voices are echoing through her work, and they are not in harmony with each other; thus, Biehl foreshadows the women authors of the century to come.

ROMANTICISM

The nineteenth century, which turned from rationalism to romanticism and, in a quite dramatic reaction, finally to realism and naturalism, was typified by the dominance of the bourgeois family and, eventually, its crisis. The transition between rationalism and romanticism was a period marked by the rise of the "literary society" or, slightly later, the salon, in which women played major roles as advisers, confidantes, and sources of inspiration. In Denmark Karen Margarete (Kamma) Rahbek (1775–1829) and

Friederike Brun (1765–1835) were both highly influential "muses" of such societies. Rahbek's letters to male friends reflect her belief in intimate but platonic relationships, and thus she mirrors the sensitive morality of the preceding century. Brun's letters—and it should be noted that neither Rahbek nor Brun intended her letters to reach the public—give incisive observations of the famous figures of her day. Both these women may subtly indicate, privately, that their peers' perception of woman, as it was being shaped by the literature of the late eighteenth and early nineteenth centuries, was off the mark, but their protest, if it can be called that, is muffled.

As the consciousness of the bourgeoisie during the preceding century developed into quite fixed attitudes—into an ideology—the characteristics of the woman who embodies that ideology were emerging, and the image was solidified by male romantic authors. The ideal woman, as she is portrayed by romantic writers, is the wife who fulfills her family and herself (in that order, later critics would say, but that criticism would have made little sense at the time) within the sphere of the bourgeois home. The woman was idealized—patronized and desexualized—so that she achieved a status of redeemer in this life for poor erring males, unless, of course, she was a fallen woman, who would hardly be able to redeem others or be worthy of redemption herself. The ideal woman, nearly all soul, was close to God, whereas the fallible, sinning male, tempted by the flesh, might well fall prey to the devil. Consequently, there was little chance that the two sexes would meet on an equal footing. The woman was the holy virgin, the pure mother, or the saintly wife, or she was the dark, fallen woman, whose fate was unhappiness and damnation. The male adored and desired the pure and safe beauty but was adamant in viewing the desires of the sexual woman as sinfully dangerous; only rarely, however, was his lust for either honestly admitted. That both sexes, entrapped by myths about each other, would be quite lonely, is surely comprehendible, for neither had much chance of understanding, or of speaking the language of, the other. Consequently, the high-flown, elaborate rhetoric that was encountered during the end of the eighteenth century in, for example, Biehl's works, had a long afterlife, especially in the romantic novel, which tended to attempt fairly realistic portrayals of relationships.

That view of the fundamental difference between the sexes reflected the ideas of French writer Jean-Jacques Rousseau and his spiritual disciples, who polarized women and men and thus made old and new prejudices grow. One result of that ideological positioning was that whenever a woman was judged by her male peers (superiors), whatever characteristics were deemed feminine in her were considered positive—for a woman—whereas whatever qualities were deemed masculine, although usually positive, were in her considered undesirable. The distinction between what is feminine and what is not has haunted the perception and self-perception of women ever since and is a prominent theme in present-day feminist literature.

As suggested above in a work by the transitional author Charlotte Dorothea Biehl, the wayward woman, who has only scorn for the values of the ruling set, attracts the attention of both sexes; thus, romantic literature cautiously presents, more often than not as secondary characters, many destructively seductive women (forerunners of the femmes fatales of the fin de siècle) who offer men delight and devastation. From the very beginning of the rise of the bourgeoisie, its parlor walls were developing severe cracks.

The schism between the ruling mindset and female objections to that mindset can even be detected in the works of Thomasine Gyllembourg (1773–1856), mother of the famous playwright and critic Johan Ludvig Heiberg. She made her debut at age fifty-three, and her slightly romantic stories discuss problems of love and marriage in the homes of the bourgeoisie. *Ægtestand* (1835; Marriage) and "Maria" (1839) support the patriarchal ideal of woman but maintain a belief in women's right to an education, the freedom to choose a husband on the basis of love, and the economic independence of self-support.

Gyllembourg's daughter-in-law, Johanne Luise Heiberg (1812–90), was one of the age's most admired actresses (with 270 roles). Her four-volume work *Et Liv, gjenoplevet i Erindringen* (1891–92; A Life Relived in Reminiscence) was meant to honor her husband's contributions to the cultural life of his time. In various articles she declared that the male should be the female's disciplinarian and the family her school, and that female emancipation would violate the sexual/biological world order. She realized that, in spite of her colossal successes, she felt a lack in her life and interpreted her own longing and melancholy as proceeding from a religious instinct. Her memoir is a fascinating document of contradictory signals.

Some women writers, however, expressed more explicitly their sense of being trapped in a world that allowed them only roles and no sense of being themselves. Mathilde Fibiger (1830–72) lets her spunky, hopeful, yet anguished protagonist in *Clara Raphael. Tolv Breve* (1850; Clara Raphael: Twelve Letters) express her frustration in a letter to a close female friend: "Is it right that half of all human beings are exempted from any spiritual work? Or has the Lord really made us of lesser material than men?" The young governess thus summarizes the plight of the intellectually inclined woman, for whom no allowances were made by contemporary patriarchal society. It may have been such thoughts that inspired Thott's preface or Leonora Christina's commemoration of heroines, but the desperate outburst by Fibiger's protagonist could hardly have taken such a direct, blunt form until the nineteenth century.

Mathilde Fibiger and Pauline Worm (1825–83) recommended a brotherly-sisterly spiritual and intellectual relationship in marriage. Fibiger in *Clara Raphael* and Worm in *De Fornuftige* (1857; The Sensible) stressed the function of art in spiritual liberation as well as the many shortcomings of female education. Education also concerned Louise Bjørnsen (1824–99) in *Hvad er Livet?* (1850; What Is Life?). Elisabeth Haven (1811–96) with her *Tyroler Familien* (1840; The Tyrolean Family) and Athalia Schwartz (1821–71) with her *Livets Conflikter* (1853; Life's Conflicts) were a part of the group of writers who understood that, with the death of love, a woman could lose her position, status, and economic security as well. Schwartz participated in the controversy around "Clara Raphael," as Fibiger came to be called. (Fibiger's book influenced parliamentary debate that led to the 1857 law giving unmarried women the rights of adulthood.)

Mathilde Fibiger, her sister Ilia Marie Fibiger (1817–67), and Pauline Worm—all authors whose works were neglected until recently—voiced, both explicitly and implicitly, the trapped woman's problems, but at the same time it was difficult for them to find a language or literary form that would release their vision of woman. Women authors of the age who earnestly attempted to face their predicament felt that, since the female was being characterized only by negatives, they had to find ways to deal with themes, characters, narrative forms, images, and myths which would articulate their attempts to reach a truer vision of woman. Their quest is demonstrated by the Norwegian novelist Camilla Collett, whose *Amtmandens Døttre* (1854–55; The District Governor's Daughters) shows that various kinds of discourse were being tried to capture the experiences and self-perception of women who did not feel that their patriarchal society could offer them fulfilling destinies.

That sort of discontent on the part of women was shared, of course, by male writers who similarly were critical of the ideological hegemony of the age. For such authors it was difficult to write happy endings for their narratives that would be satisfactory, since those endings would seem to belie their criticisms in the works. That artistic problem surfaces in the novel *Phantasterne* (1857; The Fantasts) by Hans Egede Schack (1820–59) and Fibiger's *Clara Raphael*, for both promise their protagonists a happily-ever-after resolution that rings of compromise. Both works did, however, contain so much scorn of the bourgeoisie that they should have aroused a great deal of anger; it is telling, however, that Schack more or less got away with his radical insights and got away quite unscathed, whereas Fibiger was trounced in a nasty and scurrilous debate. Since Fibiger's novel was perceived to undermine what was considered the eternally ideal—patriarchal—form of the family, the work was deemed subversive and unacceptable.

REALISM WITH A DIFFERENCE

With the dramatic entry of the critic Georg Brandes (1842–1927) on the cultural stage the earlier reluctant and implicit challenge to the ruling order was replaced by a direct and blunt attack on the family as a harness that had unnaturally restricted the inherently free human being, woman as well as man. The transition from romanticism to the realism/naturalism of this Modern Breakthrough, a gradual process, was given dramatic intensity and showmanship in Denmark—and to some extent in Norway and Sweden—because Brandes, self-appointed advocate of the liberated individual, attracted the attention of anyone who was critically inclined toward the establishment. Brandes's translation into Danish of John Stuart Mill's *The Subjection of Women* (1869), as well as his public profession of the equal right of the sexes to enjoy their freedom as individuals, sent signals that drew women writers to his movement.

Brandes and the Norwegian Bjørnstjerne Bjørnson came to a parting of the ways in a debate on men's morals that became known as the "Gauntlet Controversy," named after a Bjørnson play called *En Hanske* (1883; A Gauntlet). Bjørnson's demand for sexual purity in men as well as women opened the eyes of many female writers to the erotic double standard that existed in "free love," just as in traditional marriage. The Dansk Kvindesamfund (Danish Women's Association), which was founded near the end of the century and represented the interests of the bourgeoisie, attempted to integrate women and their rights into the system. Since woman's traditional place in the family was under attack, the next objective for many was to obtain an identity for woman as someone with an independent position. The writers of the Modern Breakthrough no doubt shared the latter goal, but they made up a faction of their own.

It is startling, however, that most of the women writers who became part of the freedom-sponsoring Breakthrough tended to write pessimistically, not to say fatalistically, of women's lot. Their protagonists are apt to fail, to suffer breakdowns, to commit suicide, or to end in despair or despondency. At times and too close for comfort, life seemed to imitate art where women authors were concerned. It is difficult, if not impossible, to pick out one text by a woman author that jubilantly exhibits the blessings of her newly won freedom. The authors, with the eloquence gained from realistic aesthetics and point-of-view techniques, depict the empty and unfulfilled lives of both those who remain in the doll houses and those who break away from them. Despair on the part of the woman who gladly gave up one role and who found no new one is depicted in heartbreaking detail.

As could be expected, some women writers find a modus vivendi for their protagonists and thus grant them survival, but the smell of compromise is often rank. Those women writers who bluntly and brutally intended to capture the sham in their protagonists' bourgeois lives veered toward naturalistic techniques, a choice that was in itself sadly revealing, for naturalism tends to focus on the person who will inevitably be crushed. The fatalism or determinism of naturalism seems to have been an "objective correlative" for those women writers who partook in the Modern Breakthrough's high hopes of forming free individuals, yet who scarcely saw those hopes materialize and who thus found themselves depicting depression, desperation, and hopelessness.

Seemingly symbolic of that disappointment are the suicides of Adele Marie (Adda) Ravnkilde (1862–83) and the Swedish writer Victoria Benedictsson, and the Norwegian writer Amalie Skram's institutionalization of herself in a mental ward. Ravnkilde, Brandes's student, wrote three stories but saw only *Judith Fürste* (1884) published before she committed suicide. *En Pyrrhussejr* (A Pyrrhic Victory), which stressed equal rights for women, and *Tantaluskvaler* (Tantalus Torments), which was about the pain sought in passion, were published as *To Fortællinger* (1884; Two Stories). The protagonist was a sexually masochistic woman.

Ravnkilde, Benedictsson, and Skram, and especially the last two, who made Denmark their home, were rediscovered in the 1970s and 1980s as feminist authors and elevated to positions of mythical proportion. Until very recently, they served as figures that could symbolically spur on modern feminist writing. Whatever the restrictions, artistic and personal, that the age imposed on them, their courage in the face of adversity has been recognized, and thus they have become both martyrs and models for a generation of writers that has hoped not to become entangled in similar psychological snares. It is to the credit of Pil Dahlerup that, meticulously and scrupulously, she has brought the presence of so many other women authors from the same period to light and that she has made the entire picture much more varied and complex. With such writers as Emma Gad (1852–1921) and Erna Juel-Hansen (1845–1922), enlightened women seem, however, to rise above the crisis foisted on them by the men of the Modern Breakthrough: they resisted and survived the pressures under which they were put.

The call for total freedom for both sexes might have seemed tantalizing to all in theory, but the man's abandonment of family responsibility created traumatic situations for the woman. It might have been wonderful to share in the male's glorious/glorified sexual freedom, but such harsh realities as pregnancy, poverty, and loneliness—the three hang together as a causal chain—made the envisioned freedom a jaundiced dream. That dream destroyed some, made others bitter and disillusioned, and made of yet others clever compromisers who attempted to realize whatever degree of freedom was feasible within the strictures of the times and who still held onto their hopes for a world that would be freer for women—but not so merely on the premises of the men of the Modern Breakthrough.

It should be noted that the women who wrote during the 1890s did not often partake in the reaction against the reformist, analytical, extroverted literature of the 1880s, which characterized the male authors of the fin de siècle—in Scandinavia as elsewhere in western Europe—but continued to use realism and naturalism as methods of charting and exploring the role of women in society. Denmark has no Dagny Juel Przybyszewska, a Norwegian author who, in an extraordinarily perceptive way, captured the symbolist language of the 1890s. Amalie Skram and most of the women who made their debut in the 1880s continued that analytical probing of social and psychological issues which was the hallmark of the decade. In that "conservatism" one might detect some hope, for although the male writers of the 1890s in many ways gave up any struggle for meaning, most women authors refused to join in their defeatist attitude.

THE TWENTIETH CENTURY

Among authors who continued the struggle—and who often did so by combining a wish for the ideal with a depiction of the real—one may count such early twentieth-century women writers as Marie Bregendahl, Thit Jensen, and Agnes Henningsen.

Marie Bregendahl (1867–1940), a writer who debuted in 1904, wrote sketches and novels with psychological realism but with an ironic distance to the tragedies she described. In her works the young farm women who seek love, creativity, and a new life in the city find themselves exploited and doomed. Included in her cast of characters, however, is the powerful but all-giving mother figure, one seemingly advocated by the Swede Ellen Key's then-current stress on the ideals of motherhood and nurturing as nature's predetermined sphere for female activity. The farming culture provided literature a better arena for the exercise of female strength than did the new, urban industrial centers, where the wage earner became a mere face in the crowd. In *Sødalsfolkene* (1914–23; The People of Sødal) Bregendahl depicted everyday life within that particular farming region from 1864 through 1885.

Thit Jensen (1876–1957), however, felt that women had to choose love or work and that love was bound to the motherly, which represented the world's creative energy. She debuted with the novel *To Søstre* (1903; Two Sisters) and by 1928 had written twenty-five books. She was also a zealous promoter of birth control.

Agnes Henningsen (1868–1962) made her own life a work of art based on sexuality, the source of creativity—and whose symbol was dance—but she thought the Modern Breakthrough's "free love" degrading to women. From 1927 to 1930 she wrote a three-volume autobiographical novel, *Kærlighedens Aarstider* (Love's Seasons), and from 1941 to 1955 she published an eight-volume memoir, which began with *Let Gang paa Jorden* (Stepping Lightly through Life).

Karin Michaëlis (1872–1950) wrote seventy books, the best-known of which were translated into twenty languages. The book arousing greatest notice was *Den farlige Alder* (1910; Eng. tr. *The Dangerous Age*, 1912), in which a woman tries to escape society's decree that sexual desire is unsuitable for a woman of middle age.

Karen Blixen, who wrote in English as Isak Dinesen (1885–1962), first published *Seven Gothic Tales* (1934; *Syv fantastiske Fortællinger*, 1935) in the United States. Though raised in Denmark's upper bourgeoisie, she lived in Africa for many years. *Out of Africa* (1937; *Den afrikanske Farm,* 1937) was an autobiographical work describing her love and loss of that life. In 1931 Blixen resumed life in Denmark and wrote with fantasy and aristocratic understanding of other places and other ages. Believing in destiny, she rejected woman's (often uninspired and uninspiring) role in bourgeois life. In her writing, which combines Gestalt and Jungian psychology, her characters seem to be living through the mythic and representing the archetypal.

In contrast in nearly every way to Blixen's work were the writings of Tove Ditlevsen and Elsa Gress. Tove Ditlevsen (1917–76) was a poet, novelist, memoirist, and short-story writer who made her debut in 1939. Although a child of the working class who dreamed of the security and tenderness of a middle-class marriage, she was nevertheless a realist. Her lyric writing was reflective of her painful life, from her four marriages (in *Gift* [1971; Poison/ Married]), through psychic breakdown (*Ansigterne* [1968; Eng. tr. *The Faces,* 1991]), to a prophecy of suicide (*Vilhelms værelse* [1975; Vilhelm's Room]).

Elsa Gress (1919–88), one of the few female members of the Danish Academy (since 1975), made her writing debut in 1945. She wrote short stories, novels, memoirs, poetry, plays, and filmscripts. Her home, called the "Decenter," was a gathering place for artists and the scene of short-lived "happenings" and trial runs for plays, most of which were first written in English. The novel *Salamander* (1977) treats the demonic, erotic, flamboyant world of art: the theater. Gress viewed the unstereotyped individual—the androgynous—as capable of achieving the independence that *Bildung* demanded, that is, the understanding of cultural expectations so that the individual might defy the fate they held in store.

Two popular and prolific authors of whom some note should be taken were Ditlevsen's contemporaries but made their debuts much later. The first, a writer of novels, travel letters, and short stories, Anna Ladegaard (1913–), began in 1966 with *Opbrud i oktober* (Leave-Taking in October). Her psychologically realistic novels are often set in a time and place of greatly significant events, and her characters seek self-realization by freeing themselves from narrow milieus and restrictive or domineering relationships through art and/or a great love. The second author, a novelist and short-story writer, is Martha Christensen (1926–). A social realist, she writes about the handicapped, the lonely, the weak, and the put-upon. She has received numerous prizes, not for innovations in style, but for the humanity of her work. Among her many novels are the debut work *Vær god ved Remond* (1962; Be Good to Remond), *Vores egen Irene* (1976; Our Own Irene), and *En fridag til fru Larsen* (1977; A Day Off for Mrs. Larsen).

TOWARD A NEW CONSCIOUSNESS

During the decades after World War II a number of women poets gained prominence: Birthe Arnbak (1923–), Lise Sørensen (1926–), and Grethe Risbjerg Thomsen (1925–). But the shake-up that may have changed the scene forever did not occur until those dramatic months of 1968 during which the consciousness of intellectual Scandinavia seemed abruptly to take a sharp turn, not only to the left but to a more lasting, less repressive or oppressive attitude toward a recognition of the female voice in literature. It has been said that the women's movement of the 1970s sprang from women's disappointment in the unfulfilled promises of equality—in work, wages, and acceptance in the educational, scientific, and political fields. The middle class managed to achieve political cooperation with a part of the working class on the two issues of free abortion and equal pay. The former was achieved in 1973, and the latter by law in 1976. In the course of the 1970s female members of parliament increased from 10 to 25 percent, and women's circumstances became a part of the political agenda: no political organization could ignore them.

Those turbulent times—turbulent because the leftist assault on the academic establishments was forceful and resulted in a restructuring of academia: one voice, one vote—replaced a very patriarchal hierarchy that for ages had favored the appointed full professors. Very few women had assumed that rank, but the democratization of Danish academia, an event that was quite sudden, gave women critics a louder and more self-confident voice. There can be little doubt that the feminists' publications, as well as their reviews in the dailies and the journals, encouraged more women to write and to explore problems that earlier would have prohibited their works from seeing the light of day.

During the late 1960s and the early 1970s women writers, in a numerical sense, finally gained that equality so long denied them. Traditional publishing houses relinquished some of their biases and attempted to give female and male voices equal time, and new publishing houses were springing up.

To identify current trends would be a risky task, and it would be a futile effort to second-guess future literary histories. In the main body of this particular literary history a good many names of modern women writers are brought up; thus, the following is a supplement that is meant to serve as a reminder of the now indisputable fact that there are in Denmark numerous women writers of exquisite talent.

Cecil Bødker, Inger Christensen, Ulla Ryum, and Jytte Borberg all belong among the post–World War II modernists. Cecil Bødker (1927–), who has written several collections of poetry—such as *I vædderens tegn* (1968; Under the Sign of the Ram)—short stories, experimental radio plays, and children's books, received the Critics' Prize for the best prose writer in 1984. Her novels include *Tænk på Jolande* (1981; Remember Jolande).

Inger Christensen (1935–) is most famous for her poetry collection *Det* (1969; It). *Det* is the story of creation, which begins with "the word," but words begin to obscure the reality they would describe; new words must be found for a new beginning.

Ulla Ryum (1937–) is a novelist, dramatist, and short-story writer. Her novels, such as *Natsangersken* (1963; Night Singer) and *Latterfuglen* (1965; The Laughing Jackass), stress psychoanalytic symbolism and absurdist techniques in tales of sexual cruelty.

Short-story writer and novelist Jytte Borberg (1917–), who belongs to the same generation as Ditlevsen and Gress, made her debut in 1968. In her often humorous, stylized, and abstract modernism she shows the absurdity inherent in the repressive techniques used by those with power to maintain the present status and in the suppressed attempts of others to experience freedom. The novel *Orange* (1972) treats the superficiality of a young woman who is trying to test her new-found freedom. For Borberg the suppression of women leaves them in a childlike state in which they have not yet obtained a true identity.

There was a burst of increased publishing in the activists' decade of the 1970s. Among the newer authors are Kirsten Thorup (1942–) and Dorrit Willumsen (1940–). Kirsten Thorup's English-titled poetry collection *Love from Trieste* (1969; Eng. tr. 1980) and novel *Baby* (1973; Eng. tr. 1980) attempt to combine modernism with social realism, both of which tend to "object"-ify the individual. In Dorrit Willumsen's universe, as in Borberg's, the women are childish in their dependence, and they seem unable to develop as human beings. Two of her works are the short-story collection *Hvis det virkelig var en film* (1978; Eng. tr. *If It Really Were a Film*, 1982) and the novel *Manden som påskud* (1980; The Man as Pretext).

Artist and socialist Dea Trier Mørch (1941–), most famous for *Vinterbørn* (1976; Eng. tr. *Winter's Child*, 1986), pictures without mythification, in woodcuts as well as in text, birth and the sisterhood of the maternity ward. Perhaps one of Mørch's most charming works is *Kastaniealleen* (1978; The Chestnut Lane), which depicts a delightful and wonder-filled stay with grandparents: the dependable and responsible grandfather and the unpredictable, spontaneous, artistic, and humorous grandmother.

Hanne Marie Svendsen (1933–) writes of women who are successful—like Ellen in *Dans under frostmånen* (1979; Dance Beneath the Frost Moon)—but who have suppressed certain aspects of their characters to be so. Inge Eriksen (1935–) in *Fugletræet* (1980; The Bird Tree) warns against a woman's using her new freedom simply to escape.

Vita Andersen (1944–), in her poetry collection *Tryghedsnarkomaner* (1977; Security Junkies) or short stories *Hold kæft og vær smuk* (1978; Shut Up and Be Beautiful), reveals women's lives as consisting of superficiality and brutal sexual encounters. Suzanne Brøgger (1944–) would transform their limited lives into ideally erotic relationships encompassing mind and body. Brøgger debates modern morals in *Fri os fra kærligheden* (1973; Eng. tr. *Deliver Us from Love,* 1976) and describes her effort to live "erotically" in *Crème Fraîche* (1978; Sour Cream). The poet Marianne Larsen (1951–), in a collection such as *Fællessprog* (1975; Common Language), has contrasted in striking imagery the present alienation with a future reconciliation between the individual and the natural world. Affection, wonder, joy, and self-confidence compose life's essential truth. An intoxication with language will lend strength, in clarion calls to a new beginning, to that utopian reality.

Women writers have tried to describe the self as well as to achieve both a communality and a "general fellowship." To that end they have not primarily sought integration into men's histories but have first demanded a recognition of their own history and that of their international sisterhood. There are, in addition to a burgeoning generation of critics, a number of recent artists. Among the new prose writers are Charlotte Strandgaard (1943–), Vibeke Grønfeldt (1948–), Iris Garnov (1939–), Vibeke Vasbo (1944–), Suzanne Giese (1946–), Anne Marie Løn (1947–), Anne Marie Bjerg (1937–), and Jette Drewsen (1943–); and among the poets are Juliane Preisler (1959–), Merete Torp (1956–), Pia Tafdrup (1952–), and Maria Damsholt (1945–).

THE FAROES

The Faroes have had a somewhat separate history from the rest of Denmark, and among the critics dealing with the region is Malan Marnsdóttir Simonsen, a contributor to the fourth volume of the projected work "Nordisk Kvindelitteraturhistorie." She has provided an overview of Faroese women's literature from which most of the following information has been drawn.

Faroese resembles the ancient common language of Old Norse much more than most other Scandinavian languages do. Although the modern Faroese literary language was worked out by the mid-nineteenth century and the school system was organized by the end of that century, Danish was used for instruction in the grade schools until 1937. In the meantime, it was possible to take a *realeksamen* (junior high school diploma) on the Faroes, but training for work as anything other than a grade-school teacher had to be taken in Denmark. Besides seeking schooling there, one might also find work. Women, who after the introduction of fishing ships to the men of the islands in the 1870s became the heads of households, running farms and working to produce dried fish for export, were not as schooled as the men and were, therefore, the last to learn to write Faroese.

The Faroese national movement, which was started by students in Copenhagen in 1876, was instituted in the Faroes in 1889. The movement did not, however, allow women to attend meetings for many years.

One of the first of the women writers was Súsanna Helena Patursson (1864–1916). A women's-rights advocate, she was present in Copenhagen when the first Danish women's society was started, and she encouraged the founding there of a Faroese women's society in 1896. From 1905 to 1908 she edited and published *Oyggjarnar* (The Islands), the first journal in the Faroes for women. She published not only a cookbook (1907) and a book on housekeeping (1912)—both of which served the "national" good—but also a poem, "Far væl" (Farewell), signed "-e. -s."; it is a good-bye to love as one goes out into the world to find independence. In 1889 Patursson had also written one of the first two Faroese plays performed in the islands, *Veðurføst* (Layover Because of Bad Weather). The play, most of which is now lost, treated such topics as nationalism, the misuse of alcohol, and the young female characters' determination to learn to write Faroese.

Two Faroese anthologies were published in Copenhagen as a result of the nationalist movement there. Both works, *Føriskar vysur* (1892; Faroese Songs) and *Sálmar og sanger* (1898; Psalms and Songs), included poems and songs by Billa Hansen (1864–1951). She wrote in all just eight poems, some of which appeared in *Várskot* (1898–99; Spring Sprouting), the Faroese journal published in Copenhagen. In free verse and prose poems she writes without a longing for her island homeland ("Ain skægvarfer" [1892; A Picnic]) or a home of her own ("Í tonkum" [1899; In Thoughts]). There are often no dreams of sexual fulfillment, but rather the recognition of life as a boat trip through stormy waters ("Midnátt" [1899; Midnight]), whose goal is a longed-for death ("Heimleys" [1898; Homeless]). Writing of the loneliness of a modern woman, she did not fit in with an optimistic nationalism, and her works are not officially represented.

Andrea Reinert (1897–1941) went to Copenhagen in the 1920s. In the poem "Fráfaring" (1932; Departure), the narrator leaves the Faroes, for intellectual as well as social freedom. She sets out to seek not the love of her life but her love of life. Malan Simonsen has pointed out that though there is longing in women's poems, it rarely takes the form of pure homesickness that it does in men's poems. The work of some poets seems, however, somewhat ambiguous on that point.

Maria Mikkelsen (1877–1956), who spent most of her life in Copenhagen, wrote one poem and a novel fragment, the novella "Fyri fyrst" (1945; So Far). In the former, "Tjaldursunga beýð hin lagna harða" (The Hard Fate Bade the Young Oyster Catcher to Leave), from *Songbok Føroya Folks* (1913; Songbook of the Faroese People), she describes her life as that of a migratory bird, a symbol of the Faroes. In the latter work she describes the inhibiting effect on a young man of the female community's fear of sex.

Before 1963 most of the works by women were anthologized or published singly in newspapers or journals; from 1963 to 1990, however, five poets had books published. During the 1960s Faroese poetry concerned itself mainly with a criticism of society and environment, but there was a representative of another type of poetry as well, a poetry demanding a special consciousness of language. Guðrið Helmsdal Nielsen (1941–) was the first Faroese modernist and the first Faroese woman to have a collection of her poetry published, *lýtt lot* (1963; mild breeze). Her imagery is taken from nature, as are the titles of some of her poems: "Storm" and "Mjørki" (Mist) from *Morgun í mars* (1971; Morning in March), and "Náttargrátur" (Night Weeping) from *lýtt lot*. Her disciplined poems describe a state of modern existential crisis.

Astrid Joensen (1949–), who was given for her work *Morgunin drakk av flógvari toku* (1987; The Morning Drank of Lukewarm Mist) the only existing Faroese literary prize, by Tórshavn municipality, was not particularly well received by critics. The tradition of nature lyricism had prevailed throughout the 1920s and 1930s, but in Joensen's work nature symbols, which usually designate life, seem to bode ill: for the poet, the perfect place is where one knows nothing and is found only through death or in heaven. For the feminist and poet Malan Poulsen (1956–), in the anthology *Lát* (1988; Sing), the woman artist must use art to create her own portrait, to give birth to herself. Poulsen describes the poet with concrete symbols and draws on the female figures of Faroese legend.

Of the approximately twenty works in Faroese belles lettres appearing each year, few are by women, who still publish mainly in journals and newspapers.

Ebba Hentze (1930–) is, however, a short-story writer, children's novelist, and a poet. The poem "Kata, ein seinkaður monologur" (1984; Kata, A Delayed Monologue) stresses the need of a young woman to leave customary family demands behind, to create an independent life for herself. Another of the most productive of the women authors is Marianne Debes Dahl (1947–), who has also written some books for children and young adults. She made her debut in 1975 and, starting in 1984, wrote a novel every second year: *Lokkalogi* (i.e., first flame of a newly started fire), *Onglalag* (1986; i.e., tool for straightening a fishhook), and *Faldalín* (1988; i.e., ballad expression for a woman, such as Lady Fair), the first Faroese women's novel. Dahl treats a woman's development into an independent person.

In 1983 the prize-winning novel *Lívsins summar* (1982; Life's Summer) by Oddvør Johansen (1941–) analyzed the importance of longing to the achievement of a dream and dealt with the postwar period of strikes, the closing of a bank and the ensuing crisis of the 1950s, and a renewed nationalism.

Ingrid Hestoy (1949–) has written two collections of short stories, *Piprandi hjarta* (1983; Trembling Hearts) and *Bládýpi* (1986; The Blue

Depth), about women whose psychological illnesses are brought on by their marriages. A prose piece by Dagny Joensen (1944–) called "Byrgingin" (1981; The Dam) symbolically deals with a woman's desire for change and her fear of disappointment. Radio competitions in the 1970s and 1980s encouraged several authors to write radio plays. Joensen's debut work, *Gerandislagnur* (1981; Everyday Fates), describes the destructive effect of marriage on three women who represent the lower, middle, and upper classes, respectively; only the upper-class woman remains in a subject status.

The Tórshavns Kvindeforening (Tórshavn's Women's Society) started a short-story competition in conjunction with International Women's Day in 1986. In 1987 some of the texts were published, and the winning story, which belongs in the genre of the fantastic, helped give the collection its title, *Frostrósan og aðrar søgur* (Frost Flowers and Other Stories). Most of the texts deal realistically with women's problems in relationship to men and marriage, but Lydia Didriksen (1957–), the writer of the winning story, treats existential conflicts using motifs from legend (such as masses held by the dead) to describe emotional and spiritual fears and desires.

In Malan Poulsen's *Lát* feminist literary theory—or the part of it that refuses to grant that the art of writing belongs exclusively among men's rightful powers—is related to the strong women of legend. The critic Malan Simonsen sees Poulsen's description of the Faroese woman artist as a hopeful sign for future poetry.

Children's Literature

Flemming Mouritsen

10

EIGHTEENTH-CENTURY MORAL AND DIDACTIC LITERATURE

Danish children's literature has its origin in the eighteenth century as an off-shoot of an international phenomenon related to the newly established middle class. Children's literature is part of the bourgeois family institution and of its structuring of childhood and upbringing. The family with its children was segregated from the workplace and from some other social contexts. Because of this privatization of the family, children and their upbringing became a problem. In other family structures the children participated in most aspects and activities in life, learning almost as a matter of course what they would need when they grew up. Within the framework of the middle class, however, they were excluded from this experience.

Children (especially boys) did not automatically become qualified enough to manage their occupational and social functions as adults. Child-rearing therefore had to be engineered. These circumstances were the background for the development of pedagogic thought and practice as an important field of study and for the establishment of educational systems. Whereas school places major emphasis on the acquiring of professional and technical skills, children's literature has its primary function in psychic, emotional, and moral formation. Children's literature is directed at leisure time and the family.

The period's plan of rational enlightenment manifested itself in its view of children, in their upbringing, and in their literature. Danish children's literature at the close of the eighteenth century was an offshoot of its European counterparts, consisting by and large of translations, promoted in books or in magazines for children. A dominant type was the didactic tale, a factual piece of information incorporated within a meager fictional frame.

The period's other principal type was the moral tale, expressing a philosophy of admonition in its ingrained struggle against childish shortcomings and desires. Obedience, authority, duty, industry, fear of father and of God were its alpha and omega. If you do not behave, you will be punished, say these stories, and in many of them the least disobedience stands to get a kind of death penalty, with disease, for instance, as the executioner. Their chief concern was in restraining instincts, gaining self-control, and deferring needs. In some, reason and conviction were the means of internalizing middle-class virtues; in many others it was admonition. Another aspect of this trend was the struggle against play and imagination, which were perceived as expressions of the immediate satisfaction of needs. Along the same lines, popular and oral culture, such as fairy tales, were rejected. This culture is ostensibly dangerous to the ideology of the Enlightenment and the development of a rational approach to reality among children, as it is full of superstition and mysticism. The fairy tales form part of a vigorous physical cultural connection that threatens the way of life and character formation of the middle class.

Play was also considered profoundly problematic, and one attempted to tame it by developing it as a learning tool, as pedagogic play. This more subtle relationship is still of current interest, and it also proved functional when around 1800 it came into use in connection with fairy tales and fantasy.

There was a problem with the "proper" stories, however, caused by the children themselves. Children are like horses: you can take them to the water, but you cannot make them drink. The moral and didactic stories are boring; it is compulsory material. Children closed their ears to them, while lapping up thrilling yarns and listening to the racy or sad tales of the domestics in kitchens and stables.

This circumstance was one of the reasons for beginning to use fiction as a vehicle for upbringing. Fiction is used as a sugar coating that will help get the moral pill down. Even in the eighteenth century Madame Leprince de Beaumont began to employ the fairy tale, transforming it into a lesson. The German pedagogue Joachim Heinrich Campe's adaptation of Daniel Defoe's *Robinson Crusoe* from 1779–80 is another example. It is a study in how the principle of deferred needs, moralism, and Enlightenment interests are elaborated as aesthetic practice.

Children's literature of the eighteenth century was eventually overrun by the genre it had opposed so vehemently. With the romantic's view of imagination and children of the next century, fantastic tales swept away the barriers of bigotry, but only seemingly. For another side of this development was the taming of imagination and the fairy tale, and thereby the gaining of a more subtle control over children, storytelling, fiction, and upbringing.

A split took place in children's literature, between a reality-oriented moral and didactic trend and a literature oriented toward fantasy, suspense, and entertainment. This development provoked vehement debates, which have not abated even today. In recent times these debates have been prompted by conditions posed by new media: in the 1950s by comic strips and in the 1980s by television and video entertainment for children. In all instances educational interests have collided with the commercial market.

The fundamental structures determining the life of children, their upbringing, and their literature were developed in the bourgeois world of the eighteenth century. Thus the moral and didactic stories of the Enlightenment continued as a dominant type up through the nineteenth century. In Denmark they were still a vigorous undercurrent in children's magazines of the 1950s. Through the years they have been transformed to other types: books for girls, for instance, are their heirs, as are today's realistic problem novels for adolescents. The numerous fictional books for small children are likewise their descendants, both the so-called factual books that treat one isolated aspect of everyday life (e.g., the production of food from cow to milk) and the problem books treating a single social problem (e.g., illness or divorce); these still have either a didactic or a—nowadays indirect—moral intention.

Children's literature from about 1800 comes in two principal categories: a realistic and didactic orientation toward education and an imaginative orientation toward aesthetics or entertainment. Both types have a common fundamental function: the socialization of children as an element in taming both these little "savages" and the aesthetic savagery of these fictions.

THE NINETEENTH-CENTURY FAIRY-TALE BOOM

The transition to fairy tales and exotic adventure tales, which were the chief concern of nineteenth-century children's literature, was readied during the previous century. But what had been a subordinate necessary instrument now became the primary issue. Two central conditions came into play: romanticism with its basic aesthetic and philosophical view, and the commercial market. Romanticism represented a showdown with rationalism's aesthetics, view of society, and view of human nature. Nature, imagination, and the childlike became key values in its ideology. The opinion of folk poetry did an about-face from rejection to glorification, just as this poetry became a crucial source of inspiration, with regard to both material and aesthetic execution. That also meant that children's literature became part of mainstream literature. The influence of the fairy tales of the brothers Grimm, for instance, was by no means restricted to children's literature.

The fairy tales of Hans Christian Andersen (1805–75) are another example. Andersen's influence on Danish and Scandinavian literature, and not least of all on written Danish, cannot be overestimated. There is almost a before-Andersen and an after-Andersen. Like the fairy tales of the Grimms from 1812–15, Andersen's have also become part of world literature.

Andersen is the Danish writer who has reached the greatest dissemination of all. In this and in other ways he breaks out of the framework of children's literature and belongs to the general history of literature. And even in the history of Danish children's literature he is usually placed in a special bracket. He is too great, a monolith that the development of children's literature steals softly around. It is only in recent times that his direct influence on children's literature has become noticeable, for instance in the books of Egon Mathiesen, Ib Spang Olsen, and Ole Lund Kierkegaard. Some critics have claimed with some justification that Andersen's works even retarded the development of Danish children's literature in the nineteenth century. Indeed, a genuine Danish children's literature did not find its independence until the twentieth century. In the preceding century, as children's literature was establishing itself and reaching greater diffusion in Denmark, most works were translations.

Nevertheless, Andersen's fairy tales belong to children's literature and its history. They do so, moreover, in exemplary sense, precisely by transcending the traditional framework of both "children's literature" and "upbringing" in the same way as Lewis Carroll's works, for instance. Both Andersen and Carroll are "modern" authors, anticipating both modernism and postmodernism, and doing so precisely by virtue of writing for children. That is the background for the liberation of their narrative from established meaning structures without renouncing such "adult" experience as the divided state of mind. Both are great deconstructionists. They could have found inspiration for their deconstruction of narration, aesthetics, and reality from children, in whose oral culture such aesthetic methods and relationships flourish, in contrast to what was the case for contemporary children's literature from the adult establishment.

The way was prepared for Andersen's fairy tales through the period's preoccupation with folk poetry and fairy tales. Some of the fairy tales by the brothers Grimm were translated into Danish as early as 1814 and were followed by collections of Danish folktales. With the Grimms the fairy tales became linked with children and from then on are children's literature par excellence. Grimm's fairy tales are literary tales, complete literary adaptations of their original source material. Actually, they transform the folktale into middle-class reading for children. At the same time that they break open the narrower didactic and moral discourse of children's literature and develop an admirably simple and lucid narrative form, they subject the explosive aesthetic and textual force of oral narrative to a process of domestication. They psychologize and sentimentalize the tale and develop a more refined form for pedagogic literature. "Little Red Riding Hood" is a typical example. Here the psychic space of upbringing, childhood experiences, and educational conflicts of the middle class are thematicized in a mythic structure—the myth, par excellence, of the control of one's instincts.

This model formed a thematic and aesthetic-structural pattern for later children's literature. The "Little Red Riding Hood" structure can be found in numerous variants and also in modern realistic novels for young people. Similar configurations occurred in much contemporary literature, for instance in James Fennimore Cooper's *The Pathfinder* (1840). The message and aesthetic practice in "Little Red Riding Hood" are turned upside down relative to the folktale. Where the folktale says: Go out into the wide world, "Little Red Riding Hood" enjoins: Stay at home with your mother and behave yourself.

Hans Christian Andersen's transformation of the folktale and other types of narration is more complex. With him the social and aesthetic potentials for protest and dissent are realized. He reshapes linguistic orality into a literary expression that breaks written norms. His fairy tales, especially his highly original development of the tales in which animals and objects are the protagonists, become a medium for sparkling, ironically imaginative criticism of constrictive bourgeois lifestyles, such as in "Den grimme Ælling" (1844; The Ugly Duckling) and "Hyrdinden og Skorsteensfeieren" (1845; The Shepherdess and the Chimney Sweep). Here as in so many other of his tales Andersen demonstrates how personal experience and criticism could be expressed in the guise of fairy tales and childishness.

Andersen's fairy tales do not serve the cause of socialization. They critically and humorously penetrate the process of socialization, which is thereby deconstructed. The plot structure, if anything, consists of chance and "luck"—in itself a break with the bourgeois view of life and akin to the folktale. Especially in Andersen's fantastic tales, such as "Den lille Idas Blomster" (1835; Little Ida's Flowers), childhood experience is thematicized. These tales are further developments of E. T. A. Hoffmann's fantastic tales, and they have played a crucial role for the later development of the fantastic tale, both as adult literature (a central modernist genre) and as children's literature, for instance in the books of the Swedish writer Astrid Lindgren.

While the fairy tales of the brothers Grimm entered the mainstream of children's literature and became decisive for it, the impact of those features by which Andersen transcends the limits of children's literature remained somewhat marginal. This does not mean that his fairy tales were not read. They have been initial reading material for generations of Danish children. One of the exceptional features in Andersen's tales for children is that he combines an "adult" experience with a childish perspective on the world, where others apply an educator's perspective. Only in the children's literature of the most recent years has this attitude become common, although often as a disguise for other interests.

BIEDERMEIER AND NATIONAL ROMANTICISM

Beside Andersen's works, Danish children's literature developed by continuing the trends from the eighteenth century. Thus, some other established authors continued to write for children. Children, their upbringing, and their literature demanded increasing interest. With rising prosperity, the breakthrough of industrialization after 1850, the spread of literacy, and the increasing intimacy of the middle-class family, there arose a growing need for reading material and with it a broader market for children's literature as well. The bifurcation of the products of culture into a "high culture" and a "mass culture" directed at entertainment became manifest. In other words, the control of children's reading material seriously began to slip from the hands of educational authorities. We have yet to see the end of this process.

Two fundamental principles of the ruling middle class collided here head-on: free market competition, supply and demand, versus upbringing for the control of one's instincts; entertainment versus education and socialization.

One of the recurrent genres in the first half of the nineteenth century was the picture sheet, the so-called Neuruppin Pictures (named after the Prussian city where they were printed), the primitive precursor of the picture book, often legitimized as a moral story. At the same time, the mass production of children's accessories such as toys, games, and songs was begun. The dominant family-centered and idyll-seeking Biedermeier culture became the realm in which children's culture had its first manifestation. Reading aloud for children and adults alike was a central activity and assumed an almost ritual character. Children's literature of the period was less suitable because of its narrow scope. Thus, children's literature and reading material for children became two different entities. Authors such as Walter Scott, James Fennimore Cooper, and later Alexandre Dumas, Charles Dickens, and Frederick Marryat quickly gained a large readership, partly because of their suitability as family reading, and they all have enjoyed an afterlife as children's classics. They form a central element of the children's literature that established itself across a wide spectrum in the latter part of the nineteenth century. Their adaptation became the basis for the development of the exotic and suspense-oriented book for boys.

At the same time, the realistic novels thematicizing the family, the life of women, and the socializing of girls became the basis for the book for girls. This differentiation took place toward the end of the century. With it was established a basic pattern of functionally determined main types which still shapes children's literature. It is formed out of categories of age and sex, or social standing, or is determined by the marketplace. It was differentiated and further developed by the turn of the century into a fine-meshed net of different genres and types based on pedagogic and commercial motives: children's books for every age, for every purpose.

Until the turn of the century Danish children's literature was essentially an import, even though others did write for children besides Hans Christian Andersen. The particularly intimate family culture that developed in Denmark found expression in an idyllizing but also realistic and child-oriented production of tales, songs, and fables for children. Two such examples are *Flugten til Amerika* (1835; Eng. tr. *The Flight to America,* 1976) by Christian Winther (1796–1876) and *Fabler for Børn* (1845; Fables for Children) by Hans Vilhelm Kaalund (1818–85), which are classics even today. Also still very popular is the picture book *Peters Jul* (1866; Eng. tr. *Peter's Christmas,* 1968) by Johan Krohn (1841–1925). It contains the idyllic family setting of the Biedermeier period as in a concentrate and enjoys an almost mythical status as compulsory Christmas reading.

The Danish artist Lorenz Frølich (1820–1908) was one of the pioneers in the European development of the picture book for small children around 1850. He had his breakthrough in France (where a picture book is called *Un Froelich*). His books were spread over the entire European market, several being published in England. Most are unpretentious, realistic, and idyllic portrayals of everyday and children's life, surprisingly modern in their essential outline. Today such books for small children are a major genre.

Walter Scott's historical novels served as models for numerous works with a distinctly national-romantic coloration which gained a wide readership and an afterlife as perennial classics for boys. Bernhard Severin Ingemann (1789–1862) chose the Middle Ages as the setting for his historical novels from about 1830 (of which several were translated into English in the 1840s), whereas the even more popular Carit Etlar (pseudonym for Carl Brosbøll, 1816–90) chose later historical periods for his works, such as the war between Denmark and Sweden in 1675–79 for *Gjøngehøvdingen* (1853; Eng. tr. *The Gynge Chief*, 1931).

Beside Hans Christian Andersen's, fairy tales of a more traditional tap became a main current in children's literature. Svend Grundtvig (1824–83) inaugurated both an extensive collection of folklore and its research, activities that can be viewed as a continuation of the cultural politics and popular works of his father, the pastor and poet N. F. S. Grundtvig. They also constitute a significant element in the political and cultural movements that characterized the second half of the nineteenth century, and that, among other things, propagated themselves by establishing alternative educational institutions—for instance, the private, so-called Free Schools and folk high schools. Simultaneously, various forums were established for promoting popular cultural activities: sports clubs, festivals, and magazines.

Svend Grundtvig's collections of folktales, such as *Danske Folkeæventyr* (1878; Eng. tr. *Danish Fairy Tales*, 1972), were followed by a long line of later adaptations of tales, a trend that is still vigorous. A contemporary example was the rendition of folk legends about pixies (*nisser*) by Vilhelm Bergsøe (1835–1911). His brilliant tale, *Nissen paa Thimsgaard* (1889; Eng. tr. *The Nisse from Thimsgaard*, 1972, with Ib Spang Olsen's superb illustrations), exemplifies another approach to adapting this oral material than Hans Christian Andersen's. Bergsøe transforms the raw strength of folk literature into a popular agrarian paradigm of character formation, which makes his tale a forerunner of the so-called schoolteacher's literature for children of the following period.

A third type of fairy tale was produced at the close of the century by Carl Ewald (1856–1908) and was popular around the world. Ewald's tales clearly reflect the author's position in the liberal, urban industrial middle class and are written from the point of view of a natural scientist. They are at once rationalistic myth criticism and scientific mythologization of nature and conditions in society. Ewald's collection *Fem nye Eventyr* (1894; Eng. tr. *The Old Post and Other Nature Stories*, 1922) forms a significant Danish counterpart to the international cultivation of fantasy at this time by Edith Nesbit, Kenneth Grahame, and James Matthew Barrie.

SCHOOLTEACHER'S LITERATURE AND CHARACTER FORMATION:
1900–1930

In the period before the turn of the century the social basis for children's literature became broader. The urban middle class was increasing in size, the importance of school and education grew for ever-broadening social classes, and child labor was finally restricted. In short, childhood gained ground—and children's literature with it. The trend was intensified after 1900. In this sense the twentieth century was justly heralded as the "century of the child," although the Swedish writer Ellen Key's designation can seem absurd from other points of view.

An ample supply of reading material now came within reach of still more girls and boys, partly in books that to a greater extent were written by Danish authors, partly in magazines that gained large circulation. Concurrent with the spread of literacy, leisure, and spending power, the consumption of popular literature increased, including the first wave of American cultural products, detective stories, and westerns.

The introduction of new printing techniques made greater circulation of picture books and illustrated publications possible, an expansion that followed the main international trend. But from the turn of the century a specifically Danish development set in relative to children, schooling, and children's literature. It was rooted in the general political, social, and cultural movements that characterized the development of Danish society in the last half of the nineteenth century, leading to the introduction of parliamentarianism in 1901 when the Moderate Liberal party formed its first ministry. This change also brought about innovations in educational institutions and in children's literature. By 1903 a sweeping educational reform had been implemented. The Grundtvigian and liberal view of society and education which lies behind it was the ideological and practical basis for the Danish school system right up to the new reform in 1958. The essence of this educational ideology was clearly that of character formation.

As part of the agrarian movement a regional literature emerged, the "schoolteacher's literature," which had its heyday especially in the decades before 1900, that is, contemporary with and partially in opposition to the Modern Breakthrough of Georg Brandes and Copenhagen radicalism. After the turn of the century this literature began to address children—farmer's children now also had childhood thrust on them—and it remained a dominant genre right up to ca. 1960. The schoolteacher's literature for children was developed as a deliberate defensive move on two fronts. On one front it stood against popular literature and what was thought to be its "corrupting and destructive influence on character," and on the other, against the aesthetically oriented children's literature of the middle class, which was inspired by the German books-for-youth movement (*Jugendschriftbewegung*), among others, and was regarded as amoral.

Against both forces the formative and moral function of children's literature was upheld. Children's books should promote "healthy" values. In some respects it is a question of a revival of the traditional educational ideas of the middle class. The children's literature that came out of this re-action was nevertheless very different from eighteenth-century moral tales. The scene of action and gallery of characters were drawn from the Danish countryside, and the moral is wrapped up in an action-packed fic-tion. Its two main genres are the historical and the modern realistic novel, in which the protagonist (usually a boy) is a model for the reader. Both are structured on a pattern drawn from the classical bildungsroman. The theme of these books is the protagonist's character development, per-ceived as a battle. Outwardly, the medium of character formation is work, that is, the battle against nature; inwardly, self-discipline, that is, com-bating inner nature, sensuality. Work is both means and end for the battle for character formation.

These theories were formulated by the central writer and ideologue of schoolteacher's literature, Niels Knud Kristensen (1859–1924), who greatly influenced the development of Danish children's literature. His chil-dren's books became models for later authors such as Marius Dahlsgaard (1879–1941) and A. Christian Westergaard (1888–1951), whose novel *Klit-Per* (1923; Per from the Dunes) became a true classic with its unretouched descriptions of the life of fishermen. Kristensen's viewpoints were the basis for the evaluative criteria that had a dominant influence on the choice of books in libraries and collections for the next fifty years.

Schoolteacher's literature gained quite a large circulation by direct mar-keting to children and by setting up libraries in the schools. This practice be-came one of the starting points for the exceptional library system that has been established in Denmark, which continues to be of decisive importance for children's literature and its development.

Alongside schoolteacher's literature, Danish counterparts to the main in-ternational types were developed with their base in the growing urban mid-dle class. The picture book gained an impressive Danish representative with Louis Moe (1857–1945). His books were oriented toward aesthetic and imaginative qualities. They are connected both to the grotesque fairy tale and the force of imagination in folk culture and to the refined art nouveau style then current. Moe's illustrations are at once aesthetically ornamental and physically sensual. He gained a wide readership, and some of his picture books have been published in English—*Peter Kvæk* (1921; Eng. tr. *Peter Croak*, 1932) and *Brumle-Brumle* (1921; Eng. tr. *Little Bear Cub*, 1930), al-though his works (unlike those of the contemporary Swedish writer Elsa Beskow) are largely forgotten today.

Girls' books gained with Bertha Holst (1881–1929), a vigorous Danish offshoot. Her models were the works of Louisa May Alcott. Although Holst advocates the traditional woman's role, conflicts abound in her books, and her use of "tomboys" as protagonists is a clear indication of new directions. Girls' books, in general, can accordingly be seen as symptoms that the role of women is no longer a foregone conclusion.

Where girls' books are respectable and realistic, boys' books are wild and exotic. But in their own way they are an expression of the identical outlook regarding boys and their relationship to the male role. It is a long way from the many-colored and potent male figures roaming the world's wilderness in these books to those fathers who look more like faint-hearted office workers, to say nothing of the tame and wan schoolboys reading the books. Although teachers opposed this type of reading for boys, its production continued to increase.

From about 1920 Danish literature for boys became connected with the scout movement, which was an important factor in the period. This development is also related to a gradual shift in readership from rural environment to city, from farmers to the middle class. It is precisely in these environments that the scout movement had its foundation. The life of children gradually changed character, for more and more children in rural areas as well, in part because of increased school attendance. The most important author in this connection is Torry Gredsted (1885–1945), a teacher and scout leader himself with a past as an officer and adventurer. His first book, *Paw* (1918), is about a "wild" American Indian boy who is transplanted to the Danish countryside. He embodies everything in the life of children that is in opposition to the authoritarian and compulsory necessities of life, an explosive mixture indeed.

In Gredsted's books the opposition between constraints and freedom is so harsh that harmonization is hardly feasible. Only one solution is possible: exile to the exotic fringe of civilization, where an authentic life can be lived and where most of Gredsted's books take place. In many ways they reflect the cultural crisis and educational debate manifested in the cultural and literary landscape of the time, just as Gredsted's expository style is in some places colored by the expressionism prevalent in adult literature.

Gredsted's works in the 1920s and 1930s constitute a transformation of the tradition of schoolteacher's literature, a modernization, but from an almost atavistic and conservative position: there is no room for the strong loner within civilization with its constraints and indulgence. Gredsted became one of the first children's authors, for instance, who broke with the imperialistic point of view toward primitive people.

Whereas Gredsted pursued the ideal of character formation to the point of a breakdown, the tradition was reshaped and modernized with greater sensitivity by other authors such as Gunnar Jørgensen (1896–1963) in his realistic ten-volume series about *Flemming* (1918–29); these books, too, involve a criticism of authoritarian schooling.

In general, most children's literature was dominated by the traditions of schoolteacher's literature. The number of publications in this period rose drastically, from 31 titles in 1900, to 100 in 1911, to about 150 in the 1920s, up to 200 in 1942, of which a third are translations. These were, however, relatively fewer than in earlier and later periods.

THE CHILDREN'S BOOK OF THE CULTURAL LEFT: 1930–1960

The crisis in the tradition of schoolteacher's literature had its background in the 1920s, a period of new directions: on the social and economic level the population migrated from the country to the city. On a political level the Social Democratic party came to power in an alliance with urban radicalism, becoming the dominant political factor of the 1930s, and on the cultural level the rise of the intellectual left, the so-called cultural radicalism (*kultur-radikalisme*), became a significant movement with its criticism of prevailing pedagogic views and of the school system. Children's education was in the 1930s considered one of the battlefields of the antifascist cultural struggle. The social background for the new view of children and their upbringing was the change in living conditions of families and children, brought about by urban industrialized societies, which now manifested itself. Childhood tended to be prolonged as more children from more social strata spent more time in school. Both parents now held jobs, and authorities outside the family attended to larger areas of childrearing.

The critical pedagogic movement was crystallized in the organization called the Free School (the Danish offshoot of New Educational Fellowship), a federation of reform-minded teachers. This movement became exceptionally strong in Denmark and in the postwar period came to influence especially the development of nursery schools, but also the school system and the view of children, childhood, and childrearing as a whole. From about 1960 the Free School movement assumed the role of schoolteacher's literature as the principal foundation for school and pedagogy as well as for children's culture and literature. At first these currents had particular influence on small children. Thus it became the basis for a vigorous picture-book tradition.

The new development occurred in the 1930s and 1940s. Quantitatively, it was a matter of relatively few books. But these works gained crucial importance for children's literature as a whole in the postwar period and up to the present. They became the germ of the second main tradition in Danish children's literature: the children's book of cultural radicalism.

These books were written on the basis of general critical, social, and democratic values and signified a breach with the past in several ways. They took their starting point in children's needs and living conditions and portrayed the life of children and contemporary reality. A simple kind of language that children can immediately understand was developed. The traditional educational structure was converted into a structure for solving social problems. Through impulses from modern art, poster art, and children's drawings, pictorial expression was transformed into a simple, functional, and brightly colored expression.

Imagination, spontaneity, and sensuousness became central qualities in both theory and practice. The aim was to liberate and stimulate children's own creative abilities, as well as their social and individual development. There are two main genres. The first is a realistic picture book oriented toward useful knowledge. In the 1970s this type had a large-scale breakthrough in Scandinavia as a didactic and often tedious production of factual books. The second genre has an imaginative and artistic orientation and includes the best picture books produced in Denmark. This increase in artistic quality is due to the fact that after 1930 a large number of illustrators and authors turned to the picture book as their medium.

A modern classic, in Denmark and internationally, is *Palle alene i Verden* (1942; Eng. tr. *Paul Alone in the World,* 1942) by Jens Sigsgaard (1910–91). It has the form of a fantastic tale in everyday surroundings based on a child's wishful thinking. The book is about the conflict between asocial desire—everything you could do if you had the world for yourself—and social need. It is an indirect showdown with the bourgeois "struggler" morality. Its moral is implicit and is demonstrated through the action. In *Palle* the modern child's predicament finds expression. Loneliness, powerlessness, and consumption as a means of escape become characteristic of childhood and are not only part of Palle's dreams. The illustrations of Arne Ungermann (1902–81) depict this with icy precision. The drawings of the original edition are an exceptional application of the aesthetics of modern art to children's illustrations that activate the reader's creative imagination. Sigsgaard's books and his entire pedagogic activity radiate an unusually natural respect for children and their life.

The work of Egon Mathiesen (1907–76) is the most substantial among Danish picture books. Many of his books are classics on a par with *Palle*: Frederik med Bilen (1944; Frederik with the Car), *Drengen i Grøften* (1945;

Boy in a Ditch; Eng. tr. *A Jungle in that Wheat Field*, 1960), *Aben Osvald* (1947; Eng. tr. *Oswald the Monkey*, 1960), and *Mis med de blå øjne* (1949; Eng. tr. *The Blue-Eyed Pussy*, 1951). Mathiesen's works are based on a fertile imagination in both picture and text. They are distinguished formally by a naive simplicity associated with a highly developed stylization. They glow with a spontaneous colorful sensuality, and illustration and text combine in a single expression. Their point of departure in the child and his or her needs is not simply programmatically posited but is realized as aesthetic manifestation. Both picture and text have received impulses from children's own forms of expression. Thus, the texts have a background in children's jingles, in their puns, and in their rhythmic use of the spoken language. They spontaneously involve the reader creatively through their form of address. Their linguistic style, like their picture style, is a definite innovation.

Mis med de blå øjne is a masterpiece that ranks as one of the world's finest picture books. At the same time as the work experiments radically with especially its picture style, with regard to expressiveness and communicative effect it is of exceptional directness, and it is easy for small children to grasp. It is one of the few books that transcends its own status as text. It activates not only the readers' senses and consciousness, but also their bodies and togetherness both on the paper and in the readers' physical reactions, for instance in a fantastic sequence that visually goes uphill and downhill over many pages. With the works by Sigsgaard and Mathiesen the picture book of cultural radicalism was established as a solid foundation for later development.

In the area of girls' books a fundamental renewal occurred with the *Bibi* books (1929–39; Eng. tr. 1938) by Karin Michaëlis (1872–1950), which gained large international circulation in the interwar period. They are likewise written from a culturally radical viewpoint and caused something of an upheaval in relation to ordinary girls' books. The traditional role of girls and women is under liquidation in them. The protagonist, Bibi, is an independent, extroverted, curious, and active person who sets out on adventures in the wide world. These books thus express the beginning breakup in the socialization of girls. They have a distinct child's viewpoint and experiment with a "childish" style.

Quantitatively of greater importance than the types mentioned here was the mass literature for children introduced after World War II. Translated series like *Tarzan* and *Biggles* were marketed, and the series trend began to manifest itself with huge success in Danish book production as well. The campaign led by the schoolteachers turned out to be of little effect against the free play of market forces.

In the 1950s this literary type broke through with full strength and provoked one of the most vehement debates in the history of children's literature. It was a symptom that more profound changes were about to be effected in the living conditions of children and in the school system. The vehemence of these changes was due to the fact that upbringing was about to slip out of control, whereby the traditional middle-class childhood was further undermined.

THE POSTWAR PERIOD AND PROSPERITY OF
THE 1950S AND 1960S

In the 1950s and especially with the prosperity of the 1960s a violent economic and social process set in, which in the course of the next twenty years involved a revolution in lifestyles and thus in the life of children. The modern family structure manifested itself. The majority of mothers began to work outside the home, a development reaching 80 to 90 percent by the 1980s. This was the background for a large-scale establishment of nursery schools. Pedagogic theories and the school system were consequently changed and adjusted to these new conditions. The 1960s were characterized by a veritable educational explosion, the school reform of 1958 being the turning point.

Children's literature changed drastically as well. The international "pulp" debate in the mid-1950s inspired by the American Frederick Wertham was a signal. The debate was provoked by mass production in the cultural media, which also led to the Americanization of Danish mass culture. Comic books and series literature were first and foremost attacked because they were in opposition to both the pedagogic ideals of cultural radicalism and the ideals of moral character formation.

In the following years this cultural industry became a decisive factor in the lives of children—and of adults. This condition remained a recurrent element in the cultural debate up through the 1960s and was superseded in the following decade by a persistent ideology critique. The media industries expanded enormously, and new media, such as television, made their entry.

One of the counteractions taken was the support of serious children's books especially through the libraries, which at this time gained their exceptional place in the Danish cultural landscape. This development served as the background for the drastic expansion of Danish children's literature, both quantitatively and qualitatively, in the 1960s and 1970s; in 1970 about five hundred titles were published; in 1980 about one thousand (including translations and reprints). The cause of this expansion were sweeping economic and social changes that also meant upheavals in children's lives. The formation of character and the moral of renunciation from bygone days proved inadequate. They were a drag on solving emergent social and pedagogic problems and the necessary development of children.

These forces bowled over the traditional rearing of children with its suppression of needs and authoritarian practices. The outcome was pedagogic reform, which provided a basis for the development of a new pragmatic social education; the schools also adjusted to these new conditions. For children's literature the changes came a little later. In the early 1960s a debate on qualitative criteria developed into a final showdown with moralistic children's literature. In its place the fundamental qualitative criterion became an artistic one. Qualities like imagination, creativity, play, and childishness became central in the children's literature of the welfare society. The middle class and its values became the foundation for both children's literature and schooling. But this medal also had its reverse side. Children were separated into a special child's world; they were made superfluous. The life of children was ghettoized and despite freer conditions became more static through the frameworks into which everyday life was programmed. Powerlessness, conflicts, protests, and lack of motivation caused the process of childrearing to function anything but smoothly. This trend was particularly obvious in relation to adolescence.

Youth became a key concept in the 1950s, especially in the Americanized version as teenagers; members of this age group had problems of their own as they, like younger children before them, became isolated as a special group. An uncontrolled commercial youth culture was met with strong opposition. Means to a solution were changes in the schools and types of recreational organizations and the development of a teenage literature. This decade established conditions for teenagers that later were to cause considerable trouble for educational authorities with regard to the integration of young people into society.

Teenage books are realistic as they treat teenage problems: crime, sexuality, and relationships with parents and friends. This genre of youth literature, strongly influenced by Swedish and American teenage books, became predominant in the 1960s and 1970s. With their topics these books have broken quite a number of taboos in children's literature and have provoked several debates. Some of the writers whose works evolved in the two decades are representative for various aspects of these developments and at the same time mark high points in Danish children's literature. They continue, with respect to both their quality and their attitude, the trend from cultural radicalism.

Thøger Birkeland (1922–) published his first book in 1958, the year of the school reform; all his works share its ideological outlook. His books, such as *Når hanen galer* (1960; Eng. tr. *When the Cock Crows*, 1968), are realistic and usually humorous, characterized by linguistic vitality and creativity that are stimulated in part by children's own usage. Birkeland focuses on children and family life seen from a child's perspective, upholding their individual development against constrictive norms, fear, and authority. Play, imagination, social togetherness, and activity have replaced struggle and work as themes of formation—developmental psychology has replaced morality. The reverse side of the life of children manifests itself in hilarious humor with the devil's splinter in the eye, for instance, in *Saftevandsmordet* (1968; Eng. tr. *The Lemonade Murder*, 1971). In the 1970s Birkeland increasingly concentrated on treating the problematic aspects in the life of children. His humorous realism turned into a realistic problem discussion interwoven with social criticism, as in *Lasse Pedersen* (1972).

Ib Spang Olsen (1921–) is an illustrator, and his contribution to children's literature consists partly of illustrations, partly of picture books. These works mark a direct continuation of the tradition of cultural radicalism. Although both line and coloring are quite different from those of Egon Mathiesen, they share an experimental relation to the expression of illustration and text and a prioritizing of imagination and aesthetic practice. The protagonist of *Det lille lokomotiv* (1963; Eng. tr. *Little Locomotive*, 1976), the locomotive, becomes a catalyst for the breakup of solidified life and norms. It realizes a child's wishful thinking in a fertile imaginative and explorative flow.

Spang Olsen's books, even when they are more purely cultivated fantasy such as *Drengen i månen* (1962; Eng. tr. *The Boy in the Moon*, 1977) or idylls such as *Kattehuset* (1968; Eng. tr. *Cat Alley*, 1971), often depict alternatives to the alienated life of modern children. This alternative is put into aesthetic practice as a special imaginative world in line with much of children's literature of the 1960s. Both illustrations and story have in their narrative method a solidarity with the way children have of expressing themselves.

Spang Olsen has illustrated *Tosserier* (1951–57; Tomfooleries; Eng. tr. *Halfdane's Nonsense and Nursery Rhymes*, 1973; *Hundreds of Hens and Other Poems for Children*, 1983) by Halfdan Rasmussen (1915–), which continues a Danish tradition of nonsense poetry for children. This work, too, is stimulated by children's jingles and their games with words and sounds. With Rasmussen and Spang Olsen it is a matter not only of employing a style oriented toward children but also of drawing inspiration from children's own style. Spang Olsen received the international Hans Christian Andersen Prize in 1972.

In 1976 Svend Otto S.(ørensen) (1916–) received the same prize for his outstanding illustrations and picture books; one of his high points is *Mads og Milalik* (1979; Eng. tr. *Inuk and His Sledge-Dog*, 1979). His illustrations of fairy tales by the brothers Grimm and Hans Christian Andersen, in which he develops a special kind of fantastic realism, have earned him international recognition. Together with Spang Olsen, Egon Mathiesen, and Arne Ungermann, Svend Otto S. represents a high-water mark in the production of Danish picture books.

This genre is a counterpart in the area of children's literature to the preoccupation with the development and environment of small children which is characteristic for Denmark, manifesting itself both in the politics of the family and in an investment in nursery schools. This picture-book tradition is still very much alive, but signs of a crisis are obvious: costs are high, the country is small, the economy is poor, the library system is stagnant, and the import of international standard products and joint publications are taking over.

A younger writer who continues the tradition of cultural radicalism and sustains a high artistic level with a character all his own is Flemming Quist Møller (1942–). In his works the problematical aspects of children's lives and their relationship to imagination are more powerfully expressed than ever before in Danish children's literature. His first picture book, *Cykelmyggen Egon* (1967; Egon the Mosquito Biker), is an unreserved trip through the luscious landscapes of the imagination. It is in many ways an expression of the so-called youth rebellion at the end of the 1960s, flower power in psychedelic colors. Imagination, art, and artistic display are its dominant values. With different techniques but in the same manner as Mathiesen's *Mis med de blå øjne,* the reader is activated through the book's dynamically formed illustrations.

In *Bennys badekar* (1969; Benny's Bathtub) the contrasts are harsher. In stark colors the book depicts the contrast between a child's development and a constrictive environment created by his mother. Imagination and childishness are separated out in an absolute contrast to external reality. Quist Møller's *Snuden* books (1980–82; The Snout) are also fantastic stories. But fantasy here becomes a tool rather than the solution. These books represent an ecological trend found in children's literature of the 1980s.

Bennys badekar is an expression of those changes in Danish children's literature that set in at the end of the 1960s. It is not isolated in its openly critical profile but resembles some other children's books from this period, especially those by Ole Lund Kierkegaard and Cecil Bødker. In their works, too, primarily aimed at older children, the contrasts emerge more starkly: children versus adults, individual versus society, dream versus reality. Both

Lund Kierkegaard and Bødker have taken their point of departure in the life of children and in "childish" values with regard to development, imagination, and fellowship. Their works are based on a strong sense of solidarity with children against a cold, power-determined, and alienated social reality. With the books by these authors Danish literature for older children reached a height corresponding to that previously represented, for instance, by Egon Mathiesen.

Like Quist Møller, who clearly identified with the youth rebellion of the 1960s and its impact on pedagogy, Ole Lund Kierkegaard (1940–79) portrayed the relation between adults and children, between coercive authorities and the developmental needs of the individual child. Kierkegaard chose an imaginative, kindly grotesque, and farcical form, and the plots of his books often culminate in a child's development that leads to a collapse of the prevailing order. They take place in an imaginary locality that resembles, with respect to background, scenery, and character types, a stylized farcical version of a provincial Danish idyll. In *Otto er et næsehorn* (1972; Eng. tr. *Otto Is a Rhino*, 1975) the anarchistic bomb within a child's life ticks away beneath the established order. Fantasy and disorder are isolated into a special world in the same manner as in *Bennys badekar*. The protagonist has taught himself to live a double life, a situation characteristic of the existence of the modern child. Children are like Hamlet, only in reverse order. Hamlet had to pretend to be insane in order to survive; children today must pretend to be "normal"—for the same reason.

The widely translated ten-volume series about Silas (1967–88), opening with *Silas og den sorte hoppe* (Eng. tr. *Silas and the Black Mare*, 1978), by Cecil Bødker (1927–) is one of the most convincing achievements in Danish children's literature, for which the author received the Hans Christian Andersen Prize in 1976. The protagonist Silas embodies in many ways the explosive principal themes of the time, which break out openly in Bødker's writing as heavy-handed coercion and vigorous revolt. Where Lund Kierkegaard's works operate in a kindly idyll, the action in the *Silas* books is laid in a harsh, weather-beaten social environment, where the clash of the positive qualities of a child's life with the circumstances of social coercion is starkly and directly described. When they came out, these books broke many of the barriers of moderation then circumscribing children's literature. Their form has been labeled fantastic realism, their scene being a fictional, even mythical, nowhere land, but within this framework the portrayal is extremely realistic. The fundamental features of Bødker's universe are not essentially different from those of today, although their presentation is quite different. Indeed, every drama from the life of today's child is transposed in condensed form to the scene, action, and characters of the *Silas* series.

In addition to the works of these artistically oriented writers children's literature of the period was characterized quantitatively by an expanding popular literature for both younger and older children and by what one could label pedagogic literature for everyday use. The schoolteacher's literature was thus superseded by a functional literature for reading training, the so-called easy-reading books. In the last decade an entire special genre has sprung up. Some Danish writers, such as Robert Fisker (1913–), have made a pioneer effort in this field. The trend toward producing specialized functional literature is international, whether as thrilling entertainment or as informative and pedagogic fiction. In the last decade picture books have been dominated by such productions.

FROM SOCIAL CRITICISM TO A WAVE OF FANTASY: 1970–1990

At the close of the 1960s criticism and debate intensified with regard to the process of growing up, children's culture, and children's literature. These trends culminated in the beginning of the next decade with a general discussion in connection with the appearance of a thoroughly social-critical children's literature in which the front lines were firmly drawn.

This critical attitude had its background in the youth rebellion and in the movements originating in it, whether of political or feminist orientation. Criticism of bourgeois children's literature and the development of an alternative based on a socialist view of society were elements of a broader showdown with the institutions and media for children's culture and education. This confrontation was directly associated with the radical currents that characterized "adult" culture as well as the political arena in general.

This socialist orientation manifested itself in the early 1970s as a joint campaign in Scandinavia, and although the production of books reflecting this approach was rather sporadic initially, it was this trend that came to define the debate and to some degree the development of children's literature throughout the decade. It also played a role in the sweeping changes that occurred in the 1970s both in literature and in the school system.

The period's so-called socialist children's literature and criticism formed in many ways a parallel to the cultural radicalism of the interwar period. It also shared its fate in several respects as it partly came to function both as a battering ram and as product development for remodeling mainstream children's literature. Its critical claws were gradually trimmed, and thus methods and contents developed that could be converted into pragmatic and specialized texts. Schools and kindergartens and their pedagogic methods, together with the economic calculations of publishers, determined to a great extent the development of children's literature. It took on a practical character corresponding to the socially and technologically oriented socialization that characterizes the school system.

During the early 1970s both criticism and book production were ideologically determined, and the texts were frequently formulated as paradigmatic or didactic stories. Consciousness raising was the catchword. These books have the character of critical alternatives to traditional texts. In other instances traditional taboos were exploded and new sorts of material were made available for treatment: geographic, historical, political, and environmental. The period was clearly experimental with regard to form, genre, and material. Formal experimentation characterizes the first book by Hans Ovesen (1943–), *Krigerdrengen Nelo* (1972; The Warrior Boy Nelo), which in content is akin to the critical children's books from the end of the 1960s. The second phase from about 1975 was marked by an orientation toward children's life and experiences. The principal genre was the realistic story, again with a work by Ovesen as one of its most significant examples: *Skal vi slås?* (1976; How 'Bout a Fight?).

Realistic novels about the problems of teenagers were a major genre of the 1970s. The title of a widely distributed series, *Ung i dag* (Young Today), is characteristic of their content. Various youth problems, especially those related to sex, drugs, crime, friends, and school, are treated in volume after volume. Many of these works are solid and sympathetic and boring, as expressed in a review by a fifteen-year-old boy who called one "a book of solace for awkward boys."

Leif Esper Andersen (1940–79) wrote some of the most substantial works of this type. His books go strongly against the mainstream, also when, as in *Heksefeber* (1973; Eng. tr. *Witch Fever*, 1976), they have a historical setting. All of Esper Andersen's books have a psychological focus, treating the clash between the individual and society as an insoluble present-day conflict. In *Katamaranen* (1976; The Catamaran) by Bent Haller (1946–) these realistic portrayals of contemporary problems are pushed to their extreme. Here the social and psychological pressure cooker is subject to so much overheating that it explodes. The book's appearance had a provocative effect and started a fierce debate. After *Katamaranen* Haller wrote some fantastic tales such as animal stories for small children, among which is the ecological fable *Kaskelotternes sang* (1981; Song of the Sperm Whales). This orientation toward fantasy put Haller's works in line with a trend that became noticeable in the 1980s. During this decade the dominance of realistic problem debate weakened in favor of a resumption of a literature of imagination and suspense.

Bjarne B. Reuter (1950–) is an exponent for these trends, which are merged in his books about the boy Buster, such as *Busters verden* (1979; Eng. tr. *Buster's World*, 1988). Reuter's works are planned as farces, as picaresque tales, and are related to Ole Lund Kierkegaard's works. But the setting is no idyll and has an underlying desperation in its overwrought comedy, which is allowed to result in drastic confrontations and grotesquely fantastic consequences.

The picture book that dominated in the 1970s, despite formal experimentation and new critical approaches, was factual or problem-oriented, the first type being a modern kind of didactic and moral literature and the second being psychological literature. A few go beyond this thoroughly pragmatic tendency, such as the works of Bodil Bredsdorff (1952–). Her picture books, illustrated by Lilian Brøgger (1950–), do not atomize life into separate problems but depict a totality through a concrete everyday story. They demonstrate that the women's movement of the 1970s, so powerfully evident in Danish culture in general, also found expression in children's literature. That occurred indirectly as an undercurrent in the mainstream of the 1970s and 1980s, and directly in historical or realistic problem novels about the life of girls, and in fairy tale collections with alternative images of women. Books for girls, which had by and large disappeared in the 1960s, experienced a revival on totally new premises—for example, in the writings of Tine Bryld (1939–).

Moreover, children's literature of the 1980s was characterized by a recultivation of the imaginative genre, both in the form of fairy tales, newly written as well as reedited, and in the form of fantastic tales. This trend was international and spread over all the media. One element was a prioritizing of aesthetic quality, of which the works and criticism of Peter Mouritzen (1946–) are an example. Among other writers a social, critical, and ecological dimension was maintained in imaginative writing, as in the works of Torben Weinreich (1946–) and Louis Jensen (1943–). For several authors, such as Eske K. Mathiesen (1941–), the story itself became the main concern, as in Mathiesen's yarn *Heinrich Hundekok* (1983; Heinrich the Dog Cook), as an alternative to psychological problem debate and fantasy.

Another aspect of this wave of fantasy was its watering down as mass production. A flood of abridged, adapted, pedagogic, and trivial fantasy texts were published. They form part of the massive multimedia production of cultural fast food. This trend contributed to children's literature's becoming, like other artistic activities, diffuse in the 1980s, without real direction beyond the ever-faster turnover. The number of titles continues to increase, while the economy of the trade worsens. Economical belt tightening within the Danish library system has hastened this development. The signs of crisis for Danish children's literature are clear, while international standardization in all areas of cultural life is on the rise.

So as not to end in a curmudgeonly wail of woe, it should be stressed that Danish children's literature and culture has great breadth. Children's books are published as never before, and according to statistics, Danish children read more than most other children in the world. Even though the library system has suffered budgetary cuts, it has remained an integral part of the lives of most Danish children, and it forms, especially because of the small language area, the indispensable foundation for the further development of Danish children's literature.

In the last decades Danish children's literature has had qualitative strength, and there are clear indications that the more outstanding authors and titles, of which only a few have been translated, are being increasingly accepted as part of the overall cultural production. An essential element in the cultural picture of the 1980s is the prioritizing of children's own cultural productivity. This trend is also present in other countries but has in Denmark released a bustling cultural activity, in particular on the local level. The strength of this current probably derives from the democratization of cultural life prompted by the nineteenth-century popular movements, which was later augmented by the tradition of cultural radicalism. Here there is not only a countercurrent to "fast food" culture—here its media are made to serve as means of expression.

Finally, a tenacious tradition exists that is often overlooked. Behind the media boom, children's literature, and other cultural forms produced by adults for children, there is another and at least just as essential cultural sphere around children: their play culture. It, too, is worn down in the mill of modern life, but it is nonetheless robust, and children here produce a prolific oral poetry with great linguistic vitality—with manifold forms of expression: games, tales, jingles, songs, yarns—which has inspired and, it is hoped, will continue to inspire writers of children's literature.

Bibliography

The history of Danish literature, from the runes to contemporary authors, has been the object of numerous treatments since the eighteenth century. After focusing initially on bibliography, these works came to reflect the various critical and methodological trends of the period in which they were written: philosophy and formalism (J. L. Heiberg), comparative literature (Julius Paludan), and the biographical-psychological approaches of the nineteenth century (P. L. Møller, Georg Brandes). Around the turn of the century and later these methods were applied either separately or in combination, often with superb results (Valdemar Vedel, Vilhelm Andersen). The twentieth century, in addition, has seen the development of genre studies (Paul V. Rubow) and close-reading techniques (Hans Brix). Brix anticipated the school of New Criticism of the 1960s, which was succeeded by Marxist ideological criticism (Johan Fjord Jensen), feminist criticism (Pil Dahlerup), and a multitude of structuralist and deconstructionist approaches.

   This array of trends is less evident in the various foreign-language introductions to Danish literature. Here the foremost mandate obviously has been to present to an uninitiated foreign audience trends, authors, and works in a manner as factual and pedagogically accessible as possible. Such presentations were initially guided not only by the attempt to provide reliable information but also with a promotional intent. Agencies such as Det danske Selskab (The Danish Cultural Institute) or the Ministry of Foreign Affairs were the publishers. Mostly, their publications emphasized periods before 1900 and major literary figures such as Hans Christian Andersen and Søren Kierkegaard. *Contemporary Danish Authors* (1952) by Jørgen Claudi was unique in portraying some twentieth-century writers, most of whom were not known abroad. In contrast to Claudi, the German *Geschichte der dänischen Literatur* (1964; History of Danish Literature) by Hanne Marie and Werner Svendsen devotes only one-fifth of its content to the twentieth century. Much more chronologically balanced is the first major, comprehensive treatment of Danish literature in English, *A History of Danish Literature* (1957) by P. M. Mitchell—a pioneering work indeed. It is, however, like Claudi's study, almost forty years old, hardly going beyond World War II, and it is very selective in its choice of writers. Even more selective, or rather extremely subjective, is Poul Borum's essayistic *Danish Literature* (1979), treating Danish literature from the Renaissance to romanticism in fewer than fifteen pages, indiscriminately favoring lyrical poets over prose writers.

A presentation of Danish literature in a foreign language is usually part of a larger treatment of Nordic or Scandinavian literature. In most such treatments the various national literatures are discussed separately. That has been the case right from the first such attempt, Fr. Winkel Horn's *History of the Literature of the Scandinavian North* (1855), to the *Introduction to Scandinavian Literature* (1951), written by the Cambridge team of Elias Bredsdorff, Brita Mortensen, and Ronald Popperwell. A synthetic approach, attempting to integrate the national literatures, was undertaken in Sven H. Rossel's *A History of Scandinavian Literature, 1870–1980* (1982), focusing on the modern period. As one of the few such Scandinavian surveys the volume also includes the literatures of Iceland, Finland, and the Faroe Islands.

This bibliography, organized chapter by chapter, is selective and focuses primarily on works in English that provide further bibliographical references. It opens with general references. Each following chapter bibliography begins with general survey works and anthologies in English covering the period of the chapter in question. Some writers might also be covered in preceding chapter bibliographies.

For major writers one translation in English of selected or collected works is added if available.

Abbreviations

ASR   *American-Scandinavian Review*; since 1975 *Scandinavian Review*
SC   *Scandinavica*

SR   *Scandinavian Review*
SS   *Scandinavian Studies*
WLT   *World Literature Today*; until 1977 *Books Abroad*

General References

BIBLIOGRAPHIES

Bredsdorff, Elias. *Danish Literature in English*. Westport, Conn.: Greenwood Press, 1973; repr. of 1950.

Dania Polyglotta: Literature on Denmark in Languages Other Than Danish. Copenhagen: Royal Library, 1946–.

Dansk bogfortegnelse 1841ff. Copenhagen: Gad, 1861–.

Drastrup, Jette, ed. *Bibliografi over kvindelige forfatteres Lyrik, romaner og dramatik*. KVINFO 1. Gadstrup; Emmeline, 1983.

Jørgensen, Aage. *Dansk litteraturhistorisk bibliografi 1967–1986*. Copenhagen: Dansklærerforeningen, 1989.

Mitchell, P. M. *A Bibliographical Guide to Danish Literature*. Copenhagen: Munksgaard, 1951.

Schroeder, Carol L. *A Bibliography of Danish Literature in English Translation 1950–1980*. Copenhagen: Det danske Selskab, 1982.

GENERAL ANTHOLOGIES IN ENGLISH

Balslev-Clausen, Peter. *Songs from Denmark*. Copenhagen: Danish Cultural Institute, 1988.

Friis, Oluf. *A Book of Danish Verse*. New York: American-Scandinavian Foundation, 1922.

Gosse, Edmund, and W. A. Craigie. *The Oxford Book of Scandinavian Verse, Seventeenth Century–Twentieth Century*. Oxford: Clarendon Press, 1925.

Hallmundsson, Hallberg. *An Anthology of Scandinavian Literature from the Viking Period to the Twentieth Century*. New York: Collier, 1965.

Jansen, F. J. Billeskov, and P. M. Mitchell. *Anthology of Danish Literature*. 2 vols. Carbondale: Southern Illinois University Press, 1971.

Keigwin, Richard P. *The Jutland Wind and Other Verse from the Danish Peninsula*. Oxford: Blackwell, 1944.

Larsen, Hanna Astrup. *Denmark's Best Stories*. New York: American-Scandinavian Foundation/Norton, 1928.

Mitchell, P. M., and Kenneth H. Ober. *The Royal Guest and Other Classical Danish Narrative*. Chicago: University of Chicago Press, 1977.

Rodholm, S. D. *A Harvest of Song: Translations and Original Lyrics*. Des Moines, Iowa: American Evangelical Lutheran Church, 1953.

Stork, Charles W. *A Second Book of Danish Verse*. Freeport, N.Y.: Books for Libraries Press, 1968; repr. of 1947.

LITERARY HISTORY

Borum, Poul. *Danish Literature*. Copenhagen: Det danske Selskab, 1979.

Brøndsted, Mogens, ed. *Nordens litteratur*. 2 vols. Copenhagen: Gyldendal, 1972.

Jensen, Johan Fjord, ed. *Dansk litteraturhistorie*. 9 vols. Copenhagen: Gyldendal, 1983–85.

Marker, Frederick J., and Lise-Lone Marker. *The Scandinavian Theatre*. Oxford: Blackwell, 1975.

Mitchell, P. M. *A History of Danish Literature*. 2d rev. ed. New York: Kraus-Thomson, 1971.

Rossel, Sven H. *A History of Scandinavian Literature, 1870–1980*. Minneapolis: University of Minnesota Press, 1982.

Traustedt, P. H., ed. *Dansk litteraturhistorie*. 6 vols. 2d rev. ed. Copenhagen: Politiken, 1976–77.

Zuck, Virpi, Niels Ingwersen, and Harald S. Naess, eds. *Dictionary of Scandinavian Literature*. Westport, Conn.: Greenwood Press, 1990.

HISTORY AND CIVILIZATION

Jones, W. Glyn. *Denmark*. New York: Praeger; London: Benn, 1970.

Oakley, Stewart. *The Story of Denmark*. London: Faber and Faber, 1972.

Chapter Bibliographies

CHAPTER 1: THE MIDDLE AGES

LITERARY HISTORY

Andersen, Lise Præstgaard. "The Development of the Genres: The Danish Ballad." *Sumlen* (1981), 25–35.

Colbert, David W. *The Birth of the Ballad: The Scandinavian Medieval Genre*. Stockholm: Svensk Visarkiv, 1989.

Haugen, Einar. *The Scandinavian Languages: An Introduction to Their History*. Cambridge, Mass.: Harvard University Press, 1976.

Kulturhistorisk leksikon for nordisk middelalder. 22 vols. Copenhagen: Rosenkilde og Bagger, 1956–78.

Olrik, Axel. *The Heroic Legends of Denmark*. New York: American-Scandinavian Foundation, 1919.

Steenstrup, Johannes C. H. R. *The Medieval Popular Ballad*. Seattle: University of Washington Press, 1968.

ANTHOLOGIES

Dal, Erik, ed. *Danish Ballads and Folk Songs*. New York: American-Scandinavian Foundation, 1967.

Olrik, Axel, ed. *A Book of Danish Ballads*. Princeton: Princeton University Press, 1939.

Prior, R. C. A., trans. *Ancient Danish Ballads*. 3 vols. London and Edinburgh: Williams and Norgate, 1860.

Rossel, Sven H., ed. *Scandinavian Ballads*. Madison: University of Wisconsin, Department of Scandinavian Studies, 1982.

ANTHOLOGIZED SOURCES

This listing includes works mentioned in the text but not published separately. An asterisk in the text after the date of publication refers to the source in which the text is printed.

Brandt, C. J., ed. *Romantisk Digtning fra Middelalderen*. 3 vols. Copenhagen: Thiele, 1869–77.

Brøndum-Nielsen, Johannes, and Poul Johs. Jørgensen, eds. *Danmarks gamle Landskabslove med Kirkelovene*. 8 vols. Copenhagen: Gyldendal, 1933–61.

Diderichsen, Paul, ed. *Fragmenter af gammeldanske Haandskrifter*. Copenhagen: Schultz, 1931–37.

Gertz, M. Cl., ed. *Scriptores minores historiae Danicae medii aevi*. 2 vols. Copenhagen: Gad, 1917–22.

———. *Vitae sanctorum Danorum*. Copenhagen: Gad, 1908–12.

Grundtvig, Svend, Axel Olrik, H. Grüner-Nielsen, Karl-Ivar Hildeman, Erik Dal, and Iørn Piø, eds. *Danmarks gamle Folkeviser*. 12 vols. Copenhagen: Universitets-Jubilæets danske Samfund, 1853–1976.

Grüner-Nielsen, Hakon. *Danske Skæmteviser*. Copenhagen: Bianco Luno, 1927–28.

Jacobsen, Lis, and Erik Moltke, eds. *Danmarks Runeindskrifter*. 3 vols. Copenhagen: Munksgaard, 1941–42.

Kristensen, Marius, ed. *Harpestræng. Gamle danske Vrtebøger, Stenbøger og Kogebøger*. Copenhagen: Universitets-Jubilæets danske Samfund, 1908–20.

———. *En Klosterbog fra Middelalderens Slutning*. Copenhagen: J. Jørgensen, 1933.

Kroman, Erik, ed. *Danmarks middelalderlige annaler*. Copenhagen: Rosenkilde og Bagger, 1980.

Lorenzen, M., ed. *Gammeldanske Krøniker*. Copenhagen: S. L. Møller, 1887–1913.

Nielsen, Karl Martin, ed. *Middelalderens danske Bønnebøger*. 5 vols. Copenhagen: Gyldendal, 1946–82.

Smith, Sophus Birket, ed. *De tre ældste danske Skuespil*. Copenhagen: L. Klein, 1874.

Friis-Jensen, Karsten, ed. *Saxo Grammaticus: A Medieval Author between Norse and Latin Culture.* Copenhagen: Tusculanum, 1981.

Skovgaard-Petersen, Inge. "Saxo, Historian of the Patria." *Mediaeval Scandinavia* 2 (1969), 54–77.

Sunesen, Anders

Mortensen, Lars Boje. "The Sources of Andrew Sunesen's Hexaëmeron." *Cahiers de l'Institut de moyen-âge grec et latin* 50 (1985), 113–216.

CHAPTER 2: FROM THE REFORMATION TO THE BAROQUE

LITERARY HISTORY

Carlson, Marvin. "Renaissance Theatre in Scandinavia." *Theatre Survey: The American Journal of Theatre History* 14(1) (1973), 22–54.

———. "Scandinavia's International Baroque Theatre." *Educational Theatre Journal* 28 (1976), 5–34.

Dal, Erik. "Proverbs in Danish Prosodies and Grammars before 1700." *Proverbium* 15 (1970), 436–38.

Schepelern, H. D. "Latin Poetry in Denmark in the Seventeenth Century." *Acta Conventus Neo-Latini Amstelodamensis: Proceedings* (1979), 898–908.

MONOGRAPHS AND ARTICLES

Arrebo, Anders

Simonsen, Vagn Lundgaard. *Kildehistoriske Studier i Anders Arrebos Forfatterskab.* Copenhagen: Munksgaard, 1955.

Brahe, Tycho

Dreyer, J. L. E. *Tycho Brahe: A Picture of Scientific Life and Work in the Sixteenth Century.* New York: Dover, 1963; repr. of 1890.

Hegelund, Peder

Jørgensen, Aage. "Peder Hegelund and Danish School Drama." In *Idyll and Abyss: Essays on Danish Literature and Theater.* Arhus: CUK; Seattle: Mermaid Press, 1992, pp. 81–107.

Helgesen, Poul

Hansen, Paul-Erik. *Poul Helgesens historiske Forfatterskab.* Copenhagen: Munksgaard, 1943.

Kingo, Thomas

Simonsen, Johannes. *Thomas Kingo. Hofpoet og salmedigter.* Copenhagen: Frimodt, 1970.

Leonora Christina
Smith, S. Birket. *Leonora Christina grevinde Ulfeldts historie*. Copenhagen: Gylden-dal, 1879–81.

Palladius, Peder
Jørgensen, Gothard. *Peder Palladius*. Copenhagen: Gad, 1922.

Pedersen, Christian
Petersen, Erik. "Humanism and the Medieval Past: Christiernus Petri as a Humanist Scholar." *Acta Conventus Neo-Latini Bononiensis: Proceedings* (1985), 172–76.

Ranch, Hieronymus Justesen
Rahelt, Poul T. B. "Justesen Ranch og Holberg." *Litteratur & Samfund* 3 (1974), 4–21.

Stensen, Niels
Poulsen, Jacob E., and E. Snorrason, eds. *Nicolaus Steno: A Reconsideration by Danish Scientists*. Copenhagen: Nordisk Insulinlaboratorium, 1986.
Scherz, Gustav. *Niels Steensen*. Copenhagen: Ministry of Foreign Affairs, 1988.

Sthen, Hans Christensen
Frandsen, Ernst. *Hans Christensen Sthen*. Copenhagen: C. A. Reitzel, 1932.

CHAPTER 3: THE AGE OF ENLIGHTENMENT

LITERARY HISTORY
Eaton, J. W. *The German Influence in Danish Literature in the Eighteenth Century*. Cambridge: Cambridge University Press, 1929.

SELECTED WORKS IN ENGLISH
Holberg, Ludvig
Argetsinger, Gerald S., and Sven H. Rossel, trans. *Jeppe of the Hill and Other Comedies*. Carbondale: Southern Illinois University Press, 1990.
Mitchell, P. M., ed. *Ludvig Holberg: Moral Reflections and Epistles*. Norwich, England: Norvik Press, 1991.
———. *Selected Essays of Ludvig Holberg*. Westport, Conn.: Greenwood Press, 1976; repr. of 1955.

MONOGRAPHS AND ARTICLES
Baggesen, Jens
Albertsen, Leif L. "Trusting in the Antipodes: A Danish Poet's Epic Poem on James Cook." In *Captain James Cook: Image and Impact*, edited by Walter Veit. Melbourne: Hawthorn Press, 1972, pp. 173–89.
Bredsdorff, Thomas. "The Fox at Ploen." *Orbis Litterarum* 22 (1967), 241–51.
Henriksen, Aage. "Baggesen—The European." *Danish Foreign Office Journal* 48 (1964), 17–20.

Brorson, H. A.
Koch, L. J. *Salmedigteren Brorson*. Copenhagen: Lohse, 1931.

Ewald, Johannes
Greenway, John L. "The Two Worlds of Johannes Ewald." *SS* 42 (1970), 394–409.
Zeruneith, Keld. *Soldigteren. En biografi om Johannes Ewald*. Copenhagen: Gyldendal, 1985.

Holberg, Ludvig
Argetsinger, Gerald S. *Ludvig Holberg's Comedies*. Carbondale: Southern Illinois University Press, 1983.
Billeskov Jansen, F. J. *Ludvig Holberg*. New York: Twayne, 1974.
Campbell, Oscar J. *The Comedies of Holberg*. New York and London: B. Blom, 1968; repr. of 1914.

Rahbek, Knud Lyne
Jensen, Anne E. *Rahbek og de danske digtere*. Copenhagen: Bakkehusmuseet, 1960.

Rosenstand-Goiske, Peder
Carlson, Marvin. "Rosenstand-Goiske and 'Den dramatiske Journal.'" *SS* 47 (1975), 18–35.

Stub, Ambrosius
Brix, Hans. *Ambrosius Stub*. Copenhagen: Gyldendal, 1960.

Suhm, Peter Frederik
Mitchell, P. M. "The Author Loses his Public—in Eighteenth-century Denmark." In *Expression, Communication and Experience in Literature and Language. Proceedings of the Twelfth Congress of the International Federation for Modern Languages and Literatures* (1973), 198–200.

Wessel, Johan Herman
Langberg, Harald. *Den store satire*. Copenhagen: Gyldendal, 1973.

CHAPTER 4: FROM ROMANTICISM TO REALISM

LITERARY HISTORY
Albertsen, Leif L. *On the Threshold of a Golden Age: Denmark around 1800*. Copenhagen: Ministry of Foreign Affairs, 1979.
Bernd, Clifford A. "The Anticipation of German Poetic Realism in Danish 'Poetisk Realisme.'" *Modern Language Notes* 97 (1982), 573–89.
Gosse, Edmund W. *Studies in the Literature of Northern Europe*. London: C. K. Paul, 1883.
Greene-Gantzberg, Vivian Y. "Approaching the Concept of Family in Nineteenth-Century Danish Narrative." *SC* 18 (1979), 141–48.

Jørgensen, Aage. "Hidden Sexuality and Suppressed Passion: A Theme in Danish Golden Age Literature." In *Idyll and Abyss: essays on Danish Literature and Theater*. Århus: CUK; Seattle: Mermaid Press, 1992, pp. 35–56.

Kuhn, Hans. "Romantic Myths, Student Agitation and International Politics: The Danish Intellectuals and Slesvig-Holsten." *SC* 27 (1988), 5–19.

Kuhn, Hans. *Defining a Nation in Song: Danish Patriotic Songs*. Copenhagen: C. A. Reitzel, 1990.

Nielsen, Jørgen Erik. "Myth and Reality in Early Danish Byron Criticism." In *The Romantic Heritage*, edited by Karsten Engelberg. Copenhagen: University of Copenhagen, 1984, pp. 173–84.

SELECTED WORKS IN ENGLISH

Andersen, Hans Christian

Conroy, Patricia L., and Sven H. Rossel, eds. *The Diaries of Hans Christian Andersen*. Seattle and London: University of Washington Press, 1990.

———. *Tales and Stories*. Seattle and London: University of Washington Press, 1980.

Rossel, Sven H., ed. *Brothers, Very Far Away and Other Poems*. Seattle: Mermaid Press, 1991.

Blicher, St. St.

Larsen, Hanna Astrup, ed. *Twelve Stories*. New York: Kraus, 1972; repr. of 1945.

Grundtvig, N. F. S.

Jensen, Niels Lyhne, ed. *A Grundtvig Anthology*. Cambridge: James Clarke; Viby, Denmark: Centrum, 1984.

Knudsen, Johannes, ed. *Selected Writings*. Philadelphia: Fortress Press, 1976.

MONOGRAPHS AND ARTICLES

Aarestrup, Emil

Zeruneith, Kjeld. *Den frigjorte*. Copenhagen: Gyldendal, 1981.

Andersen, Hans Christian

Bredsdorff, Elias. *Hans Christian Andersen: The Story of His Life and Work, 1805–75*. New York: Scribner's, 1975.

Grønbech, Bo. *Hans Christian Andersen*. Boston: Twayne, 1980.

Marker, Frederick J. *Hans Christian Andersen and the Romantic Theatre*. Toronto: University of Toronto Press, 1971.

Bagger, Carl

Schwanenflügel, H. *Carl Bagger*. Copenhagen: Schubothske Forlag, 1909.

Blicher, St. St.

Baggesen, Søren. *Den blicherske novelle*. Copenhagen: Gyldendal, 1965.

Watson, Harry D. "Steen Steensen Blicher and Macpherson's Ossian." *Northern Studies* 17 (1981), 27–35.

Goldschmidt, Meïr Aron

Ober, Kenneth H. *Meïr Goldschmidt*. Boston: Twayne, 1976.

Grundtvig, N. F. S.

Koch, Hal. *Grundtvig*. Antioch, Ohio: Antioch Press, 1952.

Nielsen, Ernest D. *N. F. S. Grundtvig: An American Study*. Rock Island, Ill.: Augustana Press, 1955.

Grundtvig's Ideas in North America: Influences and Parallels. Copenhagen: Det danske Selskab, 1983.

Gyllembourg, Thomasine

Larsen, Lis Helmer, and Jannie Roed. "The Art of Womanhood and Wedlock: Thomasine Gyllembourg: A Writer in Spite of Herself." *New Comparison* 4 (1987), 92–105.

Mortensen, Klaus P. *Thomasines oprør*. Copenhagen: Gad, 1988.

Hauch, Carsten

Galster, Kjeld. *Carsten Hauch*. 2 vols. Kolding: Konrad Jørgensen, 1930–35.

Heiberg, J. L.

Fenger, Henning. *The Heibergs*. Boston: Twayne, 1971.

Hertz, Henrik

Brøndsted, Mogens. *Henrik Hertzes Teater*. Copenhagen: Munksgaard, 1946.

Hostrup, J. Chr.

Brandes, Georg. "C. Hostrup." In *Samlede Skrifter*, vol. 2. 2d ed. Copenhagen: Gyldendal, 1919, pp. 216–34.

Ingemann, B. S.

Rossel, Sven H. "Midnight Songs and Churchyard Ballads: The Other Ingemann." In *Vänbok. Festgabe für Otto Gschwantler*, edited by Imbi Sooman. Vienna: VWGÖ, 1990, pp. 237–64.

Kierkegaard, Søren

Gill, Jerry H., ed. *Essays on Kierkegaard*. Minneapolis: Burgess, 1969.

Hohlenberg, Johannes. *Søren Kierkegaard*. New York: Pantheon, 1953.

Kirmmse, Bruce H. *Kierkegaard in Golden Age Denmark*. Bloomington: Indiana University Press, 1990.

Stendahl, Britta. *Søren Kierkegaard*. Boston: Twayne, 1976.

Thulstrup, Niels, and Marie M. Thulstrup, eds. *Bibliotheca Kierkegaardiana*. 16 vols. Copenhagen: C. A. Reitzel, 1978–88.

Møller, Poul M.

Jones, W. Glyn. "Søren Kierkegaard and Poul Martin Møller." *Modern Language Review* 60 (1965), 73–82.

Thielst, Peter. "Poul Martin Møller (1794–1838)." *Danish Journal of Philosophy* 13 (1976), 66–83.

Oehlenschläger, Adam

Andersen, Vilhelm. *Adam Oehlenschläger*. 3 vols. Copenhagen: Det nordiske Forlag, 1899–1900.

Hanson, Kathryn S. "Adam Oehlenschläger's Romanticism." *Scandinavian-Canadian Studies/Études Scandinaves au Canada* 2 (1986), 39–50.

Jørgensen, Aage. "Oehlenschläger and Homeric Poetry." In *Idyll and Abyss: Essays on Danish Literature and Theater*. Århus: CUK; Seattle: Mermaid Press, 1992, 73–80.

Ørsted, H. C.

Billeskov Jansen, F. J. "Copenhagen—City of the Muses." *Danish Journal*, special issue: *H. C. Ørsted* (1977), 14–23.

Paludan-Müller, Fr.

Brandes, Georg. "Frederik Paludan-Müller. In *Creative Spirits of the Nineteenth Century*. New York: Thomas Y. Crowell, 1923, pp. 267–305.

Kühle, Sejer. *Frederik Paludan-Müller*. 2 vols. Copenhagen: Aschehoug, 1941–42.

Schack, Hans E.

Jørgensen, Aage. "On 'Phantasterne,' the Novel by Hans Egede Schack." *SC* 5 (1966), 50–53.

Madsen, Børge Gedsø. "Hans Egede Schack's 'Phantasterne.'" *SS* 35 (1966), 51–58.

Schack von Staffeldt, A. W.

Stangerup, Hakon. *Schack Staffeldt*. Copenhagen: Gyldendal, 1940.

Steffens, Henrich

Jørgensen, Aage, ed. *Henrich Steffens—en mosaik*. Copenhagen: Akademisk Forlag, 1977.

Winther, Christian

Bøgh, Nicolai. *Christian Winther*. 3 vols. Copenhagen: Gad, 1893–1901.

Larsen, Svend Erik. "The Speech of Silence and the Silence of Speech: Christian Winther's 'Til Een'." *SC* 15 (2) (1976), 101–35.

CHAPTER 5: THE MODERN BREAKTHROUGH

LITERARY HISTORY

Bredsdorff, Elias. "Moralists *versus* Immoralists: The Great Battle in Scandinavian Literature in the 1880s." *SC* 8 (1969), 91–111.

Egebak, Jørgen. "Changes in the Concept of Truth in Danish Literature during the Last Part of the Nineteenth Century." *SC* 24 (1985), 5–15.

———. "The Early Discussion of Nietzsche in Denmark." *SC* 24 (1985), 143–59.

Ingwersen, Niels. "A Danish Literary Debate: 1888–89." *Facets of Scandinavian Literature: Germanistische Forschungsketten* 2 (1974), 40–52.

Jones, W. Glyn. "France and the Danish Symbolists." *Rencontre et courants literaires franco-scandinaves. Actes du 7e Congrès International* (1972), 165–74.

Mickelsen, David J. "Beating Frenchmen into Swords: Symbolism in Denmark." *Comparative Literature Studies* 14 (1977), 328–45.

Nolin, Bertil, and Peter Forsgren, eds. *The Modern Breakthrough in Scandinavian Literature: Proceedings of the Sixteenth Study Conference of the International Association for Scandinavian Studies.* Gothenburg: University of Gothenburg, 1988.

ANTHOLOGIES

Allwood, Martin, ed. *Modern Scandinavian Poetry: 1900–1980.* 2d ed. N.p.: Persona Press, 1986.

SELECTED WORKS IN ENGLISH

Brandes, Georg

Jones, W. Glyn, ed. *Georg Brandes: Selected Letters.* Norwich, England: Norvik Press, 1991.

Moritzen, Julius, ed. *Georg Brandes in Life and Letters.* Newark, N.J.: D. S. Colyer, 1922.

Jensen, Johannes V.

Bodelsen, C. A., ed. *The Waving Rye.* Copenhagen: Gyldendal, 1958.

MONOGRAPHS AND ARTICLES

Aakjær, Jeppe

Westergaard, W. "Jeppe Aakjær." *ASR* 12 (1924), 665–69.

Bang, Herman

Bjørby, Pål. "The Prison House of Sexuality." *SS* 58 (1986), 223–55.

Driver, Beverly R. "Herman Bang and Arthur Schnitzler: Modes of the Impressionist Narrative." Ph.D. diss., Indiana University, 1970.

Nilsson, Thorbjörn. *Impressionisten Herman Bang.* Stockholm: Norstedt, 1965.

Simonsen, Sofus E. "Herman Bang: Life and Theme." *Germanic Notes* 3(5) (1972), 34–37.

Brandes, Edvard

Marker, Frederick J. "Negation in the Blond Kingdom: The Theatre Criticism of Edvard Brandes." *Educational Theatre Journal* 20 (1969), 506–15.

Brandes, Georg

Asmundsson, Doris A. *Georg Brandes: Aristocratic Radical.* New York: New York University Press, 1981.

Guillén, Claudio. *Literature as System: Essays toward the Theory of Literary History.* Princeton: Princeton University Press, 1971, pp. 420–69.

Hertel, Hans, and Sven Møller Kristensen, eds. *The Activist Critic: A Symposium on the Political Ideas, Literary Methods, and International Reception of Georg Brandes. Orbis Litterarum* (special Supplement 5). Copenhagen, 1980.

Nolin, Bertil. *Georg Brandes*. Boston: Twayne, 1976.

Claussen, Sophus

Frandsen, Ernst. *Sophus Claussen*. 2 vols. Copenhagen: Gyldendal, 1950.

Dinesen, Wilhelm

Vowles, Richard B. "Boganis, Father of Osceola; or Wilhelm Dinesen in America, 1872–1874." *SS* 48 (1976), 369–83.

Drachmann, Holger

Eddy, Beverley D. "The Use of Myth in Holger Drachmann's *Forskrevet.*" *SS* 61 (1989), 41–54.

Rubow, Paul V. *Holger Drachmann*. 3 vols. Copenhagen: Munksgaard, 1940–50.

Gjellerup, Karl

Zberae, Nicolae. "Karl Gjellerup: A Master of Expression of Indian Thought." *The Indo-Asian Culture* 19(1) (1970), 30–33.

Holstein, Ludvig

Frandsen, Ernst. *Ludvig Holstein*. Århus: Stiftsbogtrykkeriet, 1931.

Jacobsen, Jens Peter

Ingwersen, Niels. "Problematic Protagonists: Marie Grubbe and Niels Lyhne." In *The Hero in Scandinavian Literature*, edited by John M. Weinstock and Robert T. Rovinski. Austin and London: University of Texas Press, 1975, pp. 39–61.

Jensen, Niels Lyhne. *Jens Peter Jacobsen*. Boston: Twayne, 1980.

Jensen, Johannes V.

Rossel, Sven H. *Johannes V. Jensen*. Boston: Twayne, 1984.

Jørgensen, Johannes

Jones, W. Glyn. *Johannes Jørgensen*. New York: Twayne, 1969.

Kidde, Harald

Sørensen, Villy. "Erindringens digter: Harald Kidde." In *Digtere og dæmoner*. 2d ed. Copenhagen: Gyldendal, 1973, pp. 46–96.

Knudsen, Jakob

Roos, Carl. *Jacob Knudsen*. Copenhagen: Gyldendal, 1954.

Nansen, Peter

Eddy, Beverley D. "Peter Nansen's Epistolary Fiction." *SS* 58 (1986), 10–24.

Nexø, Martin Andersen

Ingwersen, Faith, and Niels Ingwersen. *Quests for a Promised Land*. Westport, Conn. and London: Greenwood Press, 1984.

"Martin Andersen Nexø: A Symposium." *SC* 8 (1969), 121–35.

Pontoppidan, Henrik
Mitchell, P. M. *Henrik Pontoppidan*. Boston: Twayne, 1979.

Rode, Helge
Hansen, Henrik Juul. *Dramatikeren Helge Rode*. Copenhagen: Gyldendal, 1948.

Stuckenberg, Viggo
Andersen, Jørgen. *Viggo Stuckenberg og hans Samtid*. 2 vols. Copenhagen: Gyldendal, 1944.

Wied, Gustav
Watkins, John B. C. "The Life and Works of Gustav Wied." Ithaca, N.Y.: Cornell University Abstracts of Theses, 1944, pp. 29–32.

CHAPTER 6: BETWEEN THE WORLD WARS

LITERARY HISTORY

Byram, Michael. "From 'l'art pour l'art' to 'Tendens': Art and Society in Denmark of the 1920s." *SC* 19 (1980), 151–63.
Claudi, Jørgen. *Contemporary Danish Authors*. Copenhagen: Det danske Selskab, 1952.
Francesco, Scott Edgar de. "Scandinavian Cultural Radicalism: Literary Commitment and the Collective Novel in the 1930s." Ph.D. diss., New York University, 1983.
Höskuldsson, Sveinn Skorri, ed. *Ideas and Ideologies in Scandinavian Literature since the First World War: Proceedings from the Tenth Study Conference of the International Association for Scandinavian Studies*. Reykjavik: University of Iceland, 1975.
Jensen, Rudolf Jay. "Danish Novels of the Nineteen-Twenties: A Study of Structure and Theme." Ph.D. diss., University of Wisconsin, 1978.
Mawby, Janet. *Writers and Politics in Modern Scandinavia*. London: Hodder and Stoughton, 1978.
Petersen, Teddy. "The Many Masks of Censorship: Literary-Sociological Notes on Danish Literature around the First World War." *SC* 21 (1982), 25–73.

ANTHOLOGIES

Bredsdorff, Elias, ed. *Contemporary Danish Plays*. Freeport, N.Y.: Books for Library Press, 1970; repr. of 1955.
———. *Contemporary Danish Prose*. Westport, Conn.: Greenwood Press, 1974; repr. of 1958.
Heepe, Evelyn, and Niels Heltberg, eds. *Modern Danish Authors*. Folcroft, Pa.: Folcroft Library Editions, 1974; repr. of 1946.
Holm, Sven, ed. *The Devil's Instrument and Other Danish Stories*. London: Owen, 1971.

Jensen, Line, Erik Vagn Jensen, Knud Mogensen, and Alexander D. Taylor, eds. *Contemporary Danish Poetry*. Boston: Twayne, 1977.

Koefoed, H. A., ed. *Modern Danish Prose*. Copenhagen: Høst, 1955.

Mogensen, Knud K., ed. *Modern Danish Poems*. New York: Bonniers, 1949.

SELECTED WORKS IN ENGLISH
Hansen, Martin A.

Schow, H. Wayne, trans. *Against the Wind: Stories*. New York: F. Ungar, 1979.

MONOGRAPHS AND ARTICLES
Abell, Kjeld

Hye, Allen E. "Fantasy + Involvement → Thought: Kjeld Abell's Conception of Theater." *SS* 63 (1991), 30–49.

Marker, Frederick J. *Kjeld Abell*. Boston: Twayne, 1976.

Becker, Knuth

Birket-Smith, Kjeld. "Knuth Becker." *ASR* 62 (1974), 285–90.

Blixen, Karen

Henriksen, Aage. *Isak Dinesen/Karen Blixen: The Work and Life*. New York: St. Martin's Press, 1988.

Johannesson, Eric O. *The World of Isak Dinesen*. Seattle: University of Washington Press, 1961.

Langbaum, Robert. *Isak Dinesen's Art: The Gayety of Vision*. 2nd ed. Chicago: University of Chicago Press, 1975.

Thurman, Judith. *Isak Dinesen: The Life of a Storyteller*. New York: St. Martin's Press, 1982.

Branner, H. C.

Markey, Thomas L. *Hans Christian Branner*. New York: Twayne, 1973.

Dinesen, Isak; see Blixen, Karen

Gelsted, Otto

Nordin, Lene. *Otto Gelsteds standpunkt*. Copenhagen: Tusculanum, 1983.

Grønbech, Vilhelm

Mitchell, P. M. *Vilhelm Grønbech*. Boston: Twayne, 1978.

Hansen, Martin A.

Ingwersen, Faith, and Niels Ingwersen. *Martin A. Hansen*. Boston: Twayne, 1976.

Kirk, Hans

Højlund, Inger. *En udviklingslinie i Hans Kirks forfatterskab*. Copenhagen: Samleren, 1978.

Kristensen, Tom

Byram, Michael. *Tom Kristensen*. Boston: Twayne, 1982.

la Cour, Paul
Schmidt, Poul. *Paul la Cour*. Copenhagen: Munksgaard, 1971.

Munch-Petersen, Gustaf
Mitchell, P. M. "The English Poetry of Gustaf Munch-Petersen." *Orbis Litterarum* 22 (1967), 352–62.

Munk, Kaj
Arestad, Sverre. "Kaj Munk as a Dramatist." *SS* 26 (1954), 151–76.
Harcourt, Melville. "Kaj Munk." In *Portraits of Destiny*. New York: Sheed and Ward, 1966, pp. 1–47.

Nielsen, Jørgen
Madsen, Børge G. "*Lavt Land* and Its Debt to *Himmerlandshistorier*." *SS* 31 (1959), 121–28.

Paludan, Jacob
Heltberg, Niels. "Jacob Paludan." *ASR* 40 (1952), 142–45.
Oldenburg, Henrik. *Janus fra Thisted. Jacob Paludan som romanforfatter*. Copenhagen: Gyldendal, 1988.

Petersen, Nis
Nielsen, Frederik. *Nis Petersen*. Copenhagen: Gyldendal, 1970.

Schade, Jens August
Larsen, Finn Stein. *Jens August Schade*. Copenhagen: Munksgaard, 1973.

Scherfig, Hans
Kristensen, Sven Møller. "How To Castigate Your Public—and Write Best Sellers." *Danish Journal* 76 (1973), 26–29.
Riegel, Dieter K. H. "Society and Crime in the Novels of Hans Scherfig." *Scandinavian-Canadian Studies/Études Scandinaves au Canada* 1 (1983), 109–14.

Soya, C. E.
Wamberg, Niels Birger. *Soya*. Copenhagen: Borgen, 1966.

Sønderby, Knud
Bager, Poul. *Fylde og tomhed. Om Knud Sønderbys forfatterskab*. Copenhagen: Gyldendal, 1984.

CHAPTER 7: DANISH LITERATURE, 1940–1990

LITERARY HISTORY
Brostrøm, Torben, ed. *Denmarkings: Danish Literature Today*. Copenhagen: Ministry of Foreign Affairs, 1982.
Marx, Leonie. "Literary Experimentation in a Time of Transition: The Danish Short Story after 1945." *SS* 49 (1977), 131–54.

Roger-Henrichsen, Gudmund. *A Decade of Danish Literature, 1960–70.* Copenhagen: Ministry of Foreign Affairs, 1972.

Schoolfield, George. "Recent Nordic Lyrics." *WLT* 59 (1985), 212–19.

Steen, Vagn. "Concretism?" *SC* (supplement) (1973), 23–39.

Wamberg, Bodil, ed. *Out of Denmark: Isak Dinesen/Karen Blixen 1885–1985 and Danish Women Writers Today.* Copenhagen: Danish Cultural Institute, 1985.

ANTHOLOGIES

Friis, Erik, ed. *Modern Nordic Plays: Denmark.* New York: Twayne, 1974.

Ingwersen, Niels, ed. *Seventeen Danish Poets.* Lincoln, Neb.: Windflower Press, 1981.

SELECTED WORKS IN ENGLISH

Andersen, Benny

Marx, Leonie, ed. *Selected Stories.* Willimantic, Conn.: Curbstone, 1983.

Taylor, Alexander, trans. *Selected Poems.* Willimantic, Conn. and Princeton: Curbstone, 1975.

Brandt, Jørgen Gustava

Brandt, Jørgen Gustava, and Alexander Taylor, trans. *Tête à Tête.* Willimantic, Conn.: Curbstone, 1978.

Taylor, Alexander, trans. *Selected Longer Poems.* Willimantic, Conn.: Curbstone, 1983.

Harder, Uffe

Harder, Uffe, and Alexander Taylor, trans. *Paper Houses.* Willimantic, Conn.: Curbstone, 1982.

Larsen, Marianne

Christensen, Nadia, trans. *Selected Poems.* Willimantic, Conn.: Curbstone, 1982.

Malinowski, Ivan

Critique of Silence: Selected Poems. Copenhagen: Gyldendal, 1977.

Nordbrandt, Henrik

Christensen, Nadia, and Alexander Taylor, trans. *Selected Poems.* Willimantic, Conn.: Curbstone, 1978

Rifbjerg, Klaus

Christensen, Nadia, and Alexander Taylor, trans. *Selected Poems.* Willimantic, Conn.: Curbstone, 1976.

Sarvig, Ole

Taylor, Alexander, trans. *Late Day.* Willimantic, Conn.: Curbstone, 1976.

Sonne, Jørgen

Sonne, Jørgen, and Alexander Taylor, trans. *Flights.* Willimantic, Conn.: Curbstone, 1982.

MONOGRAPHS AND ARTICLES

Andersen, Benny

Marx, Leonie. *Benny Andersen: A Critical Study*. Westport, Conn. and London: Greenwood Press, 1983.

Bjørnvig, Thorkild

Dahl, Per. *Thorkild Bjørnvigs tænkning*. Copenhagen: Gyldendal, 1976.

Bodelsen, Anders

Hugus, Frank. "Three Danish Authors Examine the Danish Welfare State: Finn Søeborg, Leif Panduro, and Anders Bodelsen." *SS* 62 (1990), 189–213.
Nielsen, Geert A. *Anders Bodelsens realisme*. Copenhagen: Vinten, 1978.

Bødker, Cecil

Malmström, Sten, and Mogens Poulsen. *Litteraturoplevelse. Nogle metodestudier*. Copenhagen: Akademisk Forlag, 1979.

Brandt, Jørgen Gustava

Holk, Iben, ed. *Livstegn. En bog om Jørgen Gustava Brandts forfatterskab*. Copenhagen: Schultz, 1979.

Christensen, Inger

Holk, Iben, ed. *Tegnverden. En bog om Inger Christensens forfatterskab*. Viby J.: Centrum, 1983.
Nied, Susanna. "Letting Things Be: Inger Christensen's 'Alphabet.'" *SR* 70(4) (1982), 24–26.

Dam, Albert

Lundbye, Vagn, and Poul Vad, eds. *Den lodrette bestäen. En bog om Albert Dam og hans forfatterskab*. Copenhagen: Gyldendal, 1980.

Hansen, Thorkild

Houe, Poul. "Documentarism and Moralism: A Case of Self-Conceited Humanism." *Paradigm Exchange* 2 (1979) (Minneapolis Center for Humanistic Studies).
Stecher-Hansen, Marianne. "Thorkild Hansen and Historical Narrative: A Study of Narrative Technique in 'Det lykkelige Arabien' and 'Jens Munk.'" Ph.D. diss., University of California, 1990.

Højholt, Per

Holk, Iben, ed. *Natur/Retur. En bog om Per Højholts forfatterskab*. Viby J.: Centrum, 1984.

Jæger, Frank

Harvig, Steen, ed. *Om Frank Jæger*. Herning: Systime, 1986.
Hugus, Frank. "Frank Jæger's Defeated Protagonists." *SS* 54 (1982), 148–59.

Kampmann, Christian
Syberg, Karen. "Virkeligheden der voksede over hovedet. Om Christian Kamp-
manns forfatterskab." *Poetik* 27 (1976), 1–73.

Knudsen, Erik
Hansen, Bente. *Forfattere i/mod kapitalismen. Omkring Erik Knudsen og Ivan Malinovski.* Copenhagen: H. Reitzel, 1975.

Larsen, Marianne
Barlby, Finn. *Og verden kan ikke erobres bagfra. En arbejdsbog om Marianne Larsen og
hendes forfatterskab.* Copenhagen: Dan-bog, 1982.

Laugesen, Peter
Krarup, Helge. *Sanserne bedrager ikke, bedraget ligger i normen. Peter Laugesens
kunstneriske strategi.* Århus: Jorinde og Joringel, 1983.

Linnemann, Willy-August
Frederiksen, Emil. *Willy-August Linnemann.* Copenhagen: Gyldendal, 1969.

Madsen, Svend Åge
Edal, Renny, and Ole Nielsen. *Identitet og virkelighed. En tematisk læsning i Svend Åge
Madsens forfatterskab.* Odense: Centerboghandelen, 1980.

Malinowski, Ivan (until 1980: Malinovski)
Hansen, Bente. *Forfattere i/mod kapitalismen. Omkring Erik Knudsen og Ivan Malinovski.* Copenhagen: H. Reitzel, 1975.
Kjeldsen, Birgitte Due. *Ivan Malinovski. Ledende motiver i Ivan Malinovskis forfatterskab.* Århus: GMT, 1971.

Nielsen, Hans-Jørgen
Kyndrup, Morten. *Æstetik og litteratur. "Fodboldenglen"—dens modtagelse og æstetik.*
Århus: Arkona, 1982.

Nordbrandt, Henrik
Holk, Iben, ed. *Ø. En bog om Henrik Nordbrandt.* Odense: Odense Universitetsforlag, 1989.

Panduro, Leif
Hugus, Frank. "Three Danish Authors Examine the Danish Welfare State: Finn
Søeborg, Leif Panduro, and Anders Bodelsen." *SS* 62 (1990), 189–213.
Jørgensen, John Chr. *Leif Panduro: En biografi.* Copenhagen: Gyldendal, 1987.

Reich, Ebbe
Pedersen, Ole. *Den historiske fortælling. Dannelsen i Ebbe Kløvedal Reichs forfatterskab.*
Copenhagen: Dansklærerforeningen, 1985.

Rifbjerg, Klaus

Gray, Charlotte Schiander. *Klaus Rifbjerg*. New York, Westport, Conn. and London: Greenwood Press, 1986.

Ryum, Ulla

Sokoll, Gabriele and Heike Witte. "Ulla Ryum's Novel Jeg er den I tror: A philosophical Reading." *SC* 29 (1990), 85–97.

Sarvig, Ole

Holk, Iben, ed. *Tidstegn: En bog om Ole Sarvigs forfatterskab*. Viby J.: Centrum, 1982.
Rossel, Sven H. "Crisis and Redemption: An Introduction to Danish Writer Ole Sarvig." *WLT* 53 (1979), 606–9.

Seeberg, Peter

Holk, Iben, ed. *Mytesyn. En bog om Peter Seebergs forfatterskab*. Viby J.: Centrum, 1985.
Rossel, Sven H. "The Search for Reality: A Study in Peter Seeberg's Prose Writings." *Proceedings of the Pacific Northwest Council on Foreign Languages* 27(1) (1976), 126–29.

Skou-Hansen, Tage

Søholm, Ejgil. *Fra frihedskamp til lighedsdrøm. En læsning af Tage Skou-Hansens forfatterskab*. Copenhagen: Gyldendal, 1979.

Sonne, Jørgen

Pedersen, Orla. "Jørgen Sonne." In *Danske digtere i d. 20. århundrede*, vol. 4, edited by Torben Brostrøm and Mette Winge. Copenhagen: Gad, 1982, pp. 157–68.

Sørensen, Villy

Jensen, Johan Fjord. *Efter guldalderkonstruktionens sammenbrud*, vol. 3. Århus: Modtryk, 1981, pp. 82–161, 180–86.
Rossel, Sven H. "Villy Sørensen: Mythologist, Philosopher, Writer." *WLT* 65 (1991), 41–45.

Stangerup, Henrik

Bluestone, Barbara. "In the Shadow of Northern Lights." *Encounter* 63(2) (1984), 73–77.
Holk, Iben, ed. *Henrik Stangerup*. Odense: Odense University Press, 1986.
Monty, Ib. "An Unsentimental Dane." *Danish Journal* 72 (1972), 14–19.

Thorup, Kirsten

Gray, Charlotte S. "Identity and Narrative Structure in Kirsten Thorup's Novels." *SS* 63 (1991), 214–20.

Turèll, Dan

Højris, Renè. *Dan Turèll. Samtale og introduktion*. Copenhagen: Borgen, 1977.

Willumsen, Dorrit
Richard, Anne Birgitte. *På sporet af den tabte hverdag. Om Dorrit Willumsens forfat-terskab og den moderne virkelighed.* Copenhagen: Gyldendal, 1979.

Wivel, Ole
Hansen, Birgit Helene. *Omkring Heretica. Vilhelm Grønbechs forfatterskab som for-udsætning for Hereticas første årgange med særligt henblik på Ole Wivels produktion.* Århus: Akademisk Boghandel, 1972.

CHAPTER 8: FAROESE LITERATURE

LITERARY HISTORY
Allan, R. "Fiction and Fact in the Faroese Novel." *Bradford Occasional Papers* 6 (1984), 72–87.
Brønner, Hedin. "The Short Story in the Faroe Isles." *SS* 49 (1977), 155–79.
Conroy, Patricia L. "Oral Composition in Faroese Ballads." *Jahrbuch für Volkslied-forschung* 25 (1980), 34–50.
Dahl, Árni. *Bokmentasøga.* 3 vols. Klaksvík: Forlagid Fannir, 1980–83.
Jones, W. Glyn. *Faroe and Cosmos.* Newcastle upon Tyne: University of Newcastle upon Tyne, 1974
Nolsøe, Mortan. "Ballads and Their Cultural Setting in the Faroe Islands." *Arv* 38 (1982), 155–64.
———. "The Faroese Heroic Ballad and Its Relations to Other Genres." In *The Eu-ropean Medieval Ballad*, edited by Otto Holzapfel. Odense: Odense University Press, 1978, pp. 61–66.

HISTORY AND CIVILIZATION
West, John W. *Faroe: The Emergence of a Nation.* London: C. Hurst; New York: Eriksson, 1972.
Wylie, Jonathan. *The Faroe Islands: Interpretation of History.* Lexington: University of Kentucky Press, 1987.

ANTHOLOGIES IN ENGLISH
Brønner, Hedin. *Faroese Short Stories.* New York: Twayne, 1972.
Johnston, George, trans. *Rocky Shores: An Anthology of Faroese Poetry.* Paisley, Scot-land: Wilfion Books, 1981.
Smith-Dampier, E. M., trans. *Sigurd the Dragon-Slayer: A Faroese Ballad Cycle.* New York: Kraus, 1969; repr. of 1934.
West, John F. *Faroese Folktales and Legends.* Lerwick, Scotland: Shetland, 1980.

MONOGRAPHS AND ARTICLES
Brú, Heðin
Brønner, Hedin. *Three Faroese Novelists.* New York: Twayne, 1973, pp. 81–123.

Jones, W. Glyn. "Fate and Fortune in the Work of Heðin Brú and Martin Joensen." *Northern Studies* 20 (1983), 33–44.
———. "Types of Determinism in the Work of Heðin Brú and Martin Joensen." *Skandinavistik* 14 (1984), 21–35.

Heinesen, Jens Pauli
Allan, Robin. "The Novels of Jens Pauli Heinesen." *Proceedings of the Conference of Teachers of Scandinavian Studies in Great Britain and Northern Ireland* (1987), 24–41.

Heinesen, William
Brønner, Hedin. *Three Faroese Novelists*. New York: Twayne, 1973, pp. 38–80.
Jones, W. Glyn. "Toward Totality: The Poetry of William Heinesen." *WLT* 62 (1988), 79–82.
———. *William Heinesen*. New York: Twayne, 1974.

Jacobsen, Jørgen-Frantz
Brønner, Hedin. *Three Faroese Novelists*. New York: Twayne, 1973, pp. 21–37.
Jones, W. Glyn. "Duality and Dualism: Jørgen-Frantz Jacobsen (1900–1938) reassessed." *SC* 27 (1990), 133–51.

Joensen, Martin
Jones, W. Glyn. "Fate and Fortune in the Work of Heðin Brú and Martin Joensen." *Northern Studies* 20 (1983), 33–44.
———. "Types of Determinism in the Work of Heðin Brú and Martin Joensen." *Skandinavistik* 14 (1984), 21–35.

Matras, Christian
Jones, W. Glyn. "Nature and Man in Christian Matras' Poetry." *SC* 19(2) (1980), 181–97.

CHAPTER 9: DANISH AND FAROESE WOMEN WRITERS

Dahlerup, Pil. *Det moderne Gennembruds kvinder*. Copenhagen: Gyldendal, 1983.
Dalager, Stig, and Anne-Marie Mai. *Danske kvindelige forfattere*. 2 vols. Copenhagen: Gyldendal, 1982.
Heitmann, Annegret, ed. *No Man's Land: An Anthology of Modern Danish Women's Literature*. Norwich, England: Norvik Press, 1987.
Palmvig, Lis, ed. *Lysthuse. Kvindelitteratur historier*. Copenhagen: Dansklærer-foreningen/Rosinante, 1985.
Richard, Anne Birgitte. *Kvindelitteratur og kvindesituation. Socialisering, offentlighed og æstetik*. Copenhagen: Gyldendal, 1976.
Simonsen, Malan. *Kvinnurøddir*. Tórshavn: Mentunargrunnur Studentafelagsins, 1985.
Simonsen, Malan. *Konurák*. Tórshavn: Mentunargrunnur Studentafelagsins, 1989.

Wamberg, Bodil, ed. *Out of Denmark: Isak Dinesen/Karen Blixen 1885–1985 and Danish Women Writers Today*. Copenhagen: Danish Cultural Institute, 1985.

CHAPTER 10: CHILDREN'S LITERATURE

Eilstrup, Lena, and Kari Sønstehagen, eds. *Dansk børnelitteratur historie*. Copenhagen: Høst, 1992.

Mouritzen, Flemming, ed. *Analyser af dansk børnelitteratur*. Copenhagen: Borgen, 1976.

Simonsen, Inger. *Den danske børnebog i det 19. århundrede*. 2d ed. Copenhagen: Nyt Nordisk Forlag, 1966.

Winge, Mette. *Dansk børnelitteratur 1900–1945*. Copenhagen: Gyldendal, 1976.

The Contributors

F. J. Billeskov Jansen is Professor Emeritus of Danish Literature at the University of Copenhagen, Denmark. His books include *Sources vives de la Pensée de Montaigne* (1935), *Danmarks Digtekunst*, 3 vols. (1944–58), *Søren Kierkegaards litterære Kunst* (1951), *Ludvig Holberg* (1974), and numerous editions of Danish authors.

David W. Colbert has a doctorate in Scandinavian languages and literature from the University of Washington, Seattle. He is the author of *The Birth of the Ballad: The Scandinavian Medieval Genre* (1989) and the translator of *Christmas in Scandinavia* (forthcoming from the University of Nebraska Press).

Poul Houe is professor of Scandinavian languages and literature and director of the Center for Nordic Studies at the University of Minnesota, Minneapolis. The founding editor of *The Nordic Roundtable Papers*, he has published *Carl Th. Dreyer's Cinematic Humanism* (1992) for that series.

Faith Ingwersen has a doctorate from the University of Chicago and is the former coeditor of *Scandinavian Studies* (1986–90). She is the coauthor of *Martin A. Hansen* (1976) and *Quests for a Promised Land* (1984).

Niels Ingwersen is professor of Scandinavian studies at the University of Wisconsin–Madison. He is the coauthor of *Martin A. Hansen* (1976) and *Quests for a Promised Land* (1984).

W. Glyn Jones is professor of Scandinavian studies at the University of East Anglia, Norwich, England. His books include *Johannes Jørgensens modne år* (1964), *William Heinesen* (1974), *Færø og kosmos* (1974), and *Vägen från Mumindalen* (1981).

P. M. Mitchell has taught at the universities of Cornell, Harvard, Kansas, Illinois, Wisconsin, Århus (Denmark), and Göttingen (Germany). He is curator of the

Fiske Icelandic Collection, Cornell University and author of numerous works on Danish, German, and Icelandic literature and bibliography.

Flemming Mouritsen is associate professor at the University of Århus, Denmark. An expert on children's literature and child culture, he has contributed to several publications, such as *Analyser af dansk børnelitteratur* (1976) and *Danske Digtere i det 20. århundrede* (1982).

Sven Hakon Rossel is professor of comparative and Scandinavian literature at the University of Washington, Seattle. His books include *Den litterære vise i folketraditionen* (1971), *A History of Scandinavian Literature, 1870–1980* (1982), *Johannes V. Jensen* (1984), and translations of Ludvig Holberg and Hans Christian Andersen.

Index

Note: Major discussions of an author and/or particular works appear in boldface. Foreign-language works beginning with an article (*Den, Der, Det, En, Et,* etc.) are indexed by the article. English titles are indexed in inverted order (e.g., *Doll's House, A*).

Index

Index

DATE DUE

#47-0108 Peel Off Pressure Sensitive